CICERO, CATULL
AND THE LANG
SOCIAL PER

ℭ

Brian A. Krostenko

# CICERO, CATULLUS,

## AND THE LANGUAGE OF

## SOCIAL PERFORMANCE

℃

THE UNIVERSITY OF CHICAGO PRESS

*Chicago & London*

BRIAN A. KROSTENKO is assistant professor of classics at the University of Chicago.

The University of Chicago Press, Chicago 60637
The University of Chicago Press, Ltd., London

© 2001 by The University of Chicago
All rights reserved. Published 2001
Printed in the United States of America

10  09 08 07 06 05 04 03 02 01 5 4 3 2 1
ISBN (cloth): 0-226-45443-6
ISBN (paper): 0-226-45444-4

Library of Congress Cataloging-in-Publication Data

Krostenko, Brian A.
    Cicero, Catullus, and the language of social performance / Brian A. Krostenko.
        p.      cm.
    Includes bibliographical references (p.    ) and indexes.
    ISBN 0-226-45443-6 (alk. paper) — ISBN 0-226-45444-4 (pbk. : alk. paper)
    1. Cicero, Marcus Tullius—Language. 2. Latin literature—History and criticism.
3. Catullus, Gaius Valerius—Language. 4. Speech and social status—Rome. 5. Latin
language—Social aspects. 6. Rome—Social life and customs. 7. Language and
culture—Rome. 8. Latin language—Semantics. 9. Social values in literature.
10. Rhetoric, Ancient.  I. Title.
PA6350 .K76   2001
875'.0109—dc21

                                                                00-030215

♾ The paper used in this publication meets the minimum requirements of the American
National Standard for Information Sciences—Permanence of Paper for Printed Library
Materials, ANSI Z39.48-1992.

To my father
and to the memory of
my mother

# CONTENTS

# PREFACE AND ACKNOWLEDGMENTS

rzeka, która cierpi, bo odbicia obłoków i drzew nie są obłokami i drzewami

A river that suffers because reflections of clouds and trees are not clouds and trees.

Czesław Miłosz, "Esse"

This book is an attempt to contribute to the history of Roman culture, not by analyzing texts, but by examining language itself, and that not as a set of stable signifiers, reliable witnesses to past moments, but as a mutable, and manipulable, cultural artifact. In the Roman Republic much of the weight of the perennial clash of style and substance, politics and performance, form and content, fell on a set of approbative terms meaning "elegant," "witty," "charming," and the like: *bellus, elegans, facetus, festiuus, lepidus,* and *uenustus,* which, for reasons made clear below, I have called the language of social performance. That language articulated not what was, but what was thought to be; or to put it more precisely, those words, like much approbative idiom, assigned actions and behaviors to ideological categories based on ideological needs. To describe the relationship between those lexemes and the categories they expressed is the object of this study. That description lends itself to the form of a narrative (as I hope, a narrative *non infestiuus,* p. 123) that moves from lexical observations to closer readings: from their several origins (ch. 1), the lexemes of the language of social performance coalesce in the second century in response to the creation of a new aspect of Roman cultural ideology (chs. 1, 2), whose successive growth they track from its glimmerings in early first-century rhetorical theory (chs. 3, 4) to its flashes in Cicero's speeches (ch. 5), its modulated glow in his *de Oratore* (ch. 6), and its sirenical gleam in the poetry of Cicero's younger contemporary Catullus (ch. 7). Each work configures the strain between style and substance in different ways, and collectively, through the passages where the language of social performance occurs, they suggestively illuminate an important aspect of the Roman conception of the social world.

The object of study has dictated the method and form of the work. In method it is partly philological, collecting and describing patterns of verbal expression, and partly conjectural, postulating underlying economies of literary response or cultural structure. The methods vary in proportion according to the needs of the analysand: chapter 1 has the most philology, chapter 5 the most cultural analysis, chapter 7 the most literary criticism. But while the argument therefore lends itself to being read in bits, I conceive of it as a single thing: the transcription of a dance between language and culture in which the movements of one partner or the other simply happen to provide more evidence, or require more attention, at different moments. When I am describing the movements of language, I have quoted many and large passages of text and many supporting parallels. I have preferred to err on the side of excess in this matter, especially in chapters 1 and 3, not least because this project has made me acutely aware of the danger of the ill-chosen subset of examples; but more important, the subtleties of Roman social ideology are made manifest in the subtleties of the language of social performance, and these cannot be tidily exampled in brief scope. If a language is taking small and measured steps, that is no proof the culture is playing a minuet; but if one wishes to make such a claim, one had damned well better prove her steps are measured. On the other hand, not every step, jump, or slide that I claim to have happened can have happened in just the way I say; semantico-cultural reconstruction is a tricky business. In those cases (which will be obvious, because by including many examples I have presumably provided counterexamples to myself . . . which should count for something) I hope my readers will remember that it is, in the end, the overall rhythm of a dance—the *lepos* (p. 70) of a collective social performance—that I am trying to describe. The translations of all passages are my own unless otherwise noted.

The germ of this book was my 1993 dissertation. The present volume is intended as repayment for the patience and encouragement of my advisors, Richard Tarrant, Richard Thomas, Cynthia Damon, and Mark Hale, who saw past the *inelegantia* (p. 117) of the earlier work. I have since accumulated more debts, which I gratefully record here. Harold Attridge, my former dean, permitted me to rearrange my course load in order to advance my research. In the *suauitas et grauitas* (p. 145ff.) of my fellow classicists I have found inspiration and guidance. The manuscript at various stages was read, in whole or part, by Shadi Bartsch, Tony Corbeill, Cynthia Damon, William Fitzgerald, Kirk Freudenberg, Erich Gruen, John Kirby, Christina Kraus, Alan Nussbaum, Catherine Schlegel, Dan Sheerin, Jeffrey Wills, and David Wray, who all were generous with their advice and improved the manuscript in many ways. The anonymous readers of the University of Chicago Press read with sympathy and commented with an acuity that was exceptionally helpful. I also benefited from discussions with Martin Bloomer, Leslie Kurke, Matthew Roller, Alexander Sens, Sarah Stroup, and Bob Vacca. I presented various portions of this argument to *belli homines* (p. 58) at Harvard, Berkeley, Georgetown, Johns Hopkins, the University of Michigan, the University of Chicago, and at a meeting of the American Philological Association; I gratefully acknowledge the stimulating receptions I received. I also owe debts to the assistance of Nicholas Catanese, Bill Darden, Helma Dik, John Fine, Liangyan Ge, Barbara Need, and Tatiana Senkewitz. My mother-in-law, Jean Bennett Downs of San Francisco, generously provided a subvention that permitted me to have translated from the Russian two of the articles of N. Fyëderov. Lou Jordan and Bożena Karol granted me access to the Anastos collection before materials that I needed had been catalogued. Prof. Sharon Herbert of the Classics Department at the University of Michigan kindly accommodated me during a leave by providing me with the most precious thing a visiting classicist in Ann Arbor can have (other than an expense account at Shaman Drum): a key to the study room in Angell. This book would not have come to light without the interest of Geoffrey Huck and the attentive management of Claudia Rex at the University of Chicago Press. The unwieldy manuscript was edited with *subtilitas* (218n.53) by Marta Steele and the book was designed with *uenustas* (p. 45) by Robert Williams. I am grateful to Edward Dandrow for his help with the indexes. Without the compact discs of the *Thesaurus Linguae Graecae* and the Packard Humanities Institute this undertaking would have been nearly impossible.

Never mind "modulated glows" or "the dance between language and culture" (really!): trying to tell the story of a set of lexemes and their mercurial relationship to fluid cultural idea(l)s was like trying to herd a bunch of frogs. I depended on the encouragement of Joaquín Font, Stephen Kaschke, Levi, Adam List, Daniel L. Minor Jr., Carlos E. Padilla, and Vain Warrior: I was sustained by the desire to do honor to Dennis Czerny, who gave me my love of Latin. If this project succeeds in any measure, I owe it above all to the unstinting love and support of my wife, Joan Marguerite Downs, which the many vexations of writing made yet more precious; and if I have succeeded in any measure, I owe it to my very first teachers, who always provided me with love and with books, and to whom, as small recompense, I dedicate this book with love.

*Chicago*
*28 June 2000*

# ABBREVIATIONS AND KEY WORDS

The following works are referred to by abbreviation only.

CGL     Lindemann, Friedrich. 1831–40. *Corpus Grammaticorum Latinorum*. Leipzig: Teubner.

CIL     1862–. *Corpus Inscriptionum Latinarum*. Berlin: G. Reimer.

CLE     Buechler, Franciscus (Franz). 1897. *Carmina Latina Epigraphica*. Leipzig: Teubner.

E-M     Ernout, Alfred, and Antoine Meillet. 1959. *Dictionnaire étymologique de la langue latine*. 4th ed. Paris: Klincksieck.

Ernest     Ernest, J. C. G. 1983 [1795]. *Lexicon Technologiae Graecorum Rhetoricae*. Leipzig. Rpt. Hildesheim: Georg Olms Verlag, 1983.

————. 1962 [1797]. *Lexicon Technologiae Latinorum Rhetoricae*. Leipzig. Rpt. Hildesheim: Georg Olms Verlag.

K-S     Kühner, Raphael, and Friedrich Holzweissig. 1966. *Ausführliche Grammatik der Lateinischen Sprache*. 4th ed., with additions and corrections. 2 vols. in 3 (vol. 2 by Raphael Kühner and Karl Stegmann). Hannover: Hahn.

LHS I     Leumann, Manu. 1963. *Lateinische Laut- und Formenlehre*. Vol. 1 of Manu Leumann, J. B. Hofmann, and Anton Szantyr, *Lateinische Grammatik*. Munich: Beck.

LHS II     Hofmann, J. B., and Anton Szantyr. 1965. *Lateinische Syntax und Stilistik*. Vol. 2 of Manu Leumann, J. B. Hofmann, and Anton Szantyr, *Lateinische Grammatik*. Munich: Beck.

LP     Leeman, Anton Daniël, and Harm Pinkster. 1981. *M. Tullius Cicero, "De Oratore" Libri III*. Vol. 1: I, 1–165. Heidelberg: C. Winter.

LPN     Leeman, Anton Daniël, Harm Pinkster, and Hein L. W. Nelson. 1985. *M. Tullius Cicero, "De Oratore" Libri III*. Vol. 2: I, 166–II, 98. Heidelberg: C. Winter.

LPR     Leeman, Anton Daniël, Harm Pinkster, and Edwin Rabbie. 1989. *M. Tullius Cicero, "De Oratore" Libri III*. Vol. 3: II, 99–290. Heidelberg: C. Winter.

LPW     Leeman, Anton Daniël, Harm Pinkster, and Jakob Wisse. 1996. *M. Tullius Cicero, "De Oratore" Libri III*. Vol. 4: II, 291–III, 99. Heidelberg: C. Winter.

OED     *The Oxford English Dictionary*. 2nd ed.

OLD     *Oxford Latin Dictionary*.

ORF     Malcovati, Enrica. 1976. *Oratorum Romanorum Fragmenta Liberae Rei Publicae*. 4th ed. Torino: Paravia.

Pok.     Pokorny, Julius. 1949–69. *Indogermanisches Etymologisches Wörterbuch*. 2 vols. Bern: Francke.

RE     Pauly, August Friedrich von. 1980. *Paulys Realencyclopädie der classischen*

|        | *Altertumswissenschaft.* 2d ed., ed. Georg Wissowa, Wilhelm Kroll, and Karl Mittelhaus. Munich: Alfred Druckenmüller. |
|--------|---|
| SB     | Shackleton Bailey, David Roy. 1965 –. *Cicero's Letters to Atticus.* 7 vols. Cambridge: Cambridge University Press. |
|        | ———. 1977. *Cicero: "Epistulae ad Familiares."* 2 vols. Cambridge: Cambridge University Press. |
| TLL    | 1904 –. *Thesaurus Linguae Latinae.* Leipzig: Teubner. |
| T-P    | Tyrrell, Robert Yelverton, and Louis Claude Purser. 1885–1901. *The Correspondence of M. Tullius Cicero.* 6 vols. Vol. 1, 3d ed., 1904; vol. 2, 2d ed., 1906; vol. 3, 2d ed., 1914; vol. 4, 2d ed., 1918; vol. 5, 2d ed., 1915; vol. 6, 1899. Dublin: Hodges, Foster and Figgis. |
| W-H    | Walde, Alois. 1938, 1954. *Lateinisches etymologisches Wörterbuch.* 3d ed. 2 vols. (vol. 1 A–L 1938, vol. 2 M–Z 1954). Revised by Johann Baptist Hofmann. Heidelberg: C. Winter. |
| Wilkins | Wilkins, Augustus S. 1979 [1890–95]. *M. Tulli Ciceronis "De oratore."* 3 vols. Oxford: Rpt. (3 vols. in 1), New York: Arno Press. |

Other abbreviations of primary source authors and works occur as listed in the *Oxford Latin Dictionary* and Liddell and Scott, *Greek-English Lexicon.*

# INTRODUCTION

# On the Language of
# Social Performance

Until a few years ago—within the memory of men still living—very little use
had been made of language itself, that is to say, of the historical forms and meanings of words as interpreters both of the past and of the workings of men's minds.
It has only just begun to dawn on us that in our own language alone, not to speak
of its many companions, the past history of humanity is spread out in an imper-
ishable map, just as the history of the mineral earth lies embedded in the layers
of its outer crust.

Owen Barfield, *History in English Words*

The principal difficulty of the undertaking therefore lies at the outset. The pursuit of poetry must begin more or less where it hopes to end—with a report of
the quarry. And the danger is precisely there. For if you start with the wrong report you will end up with the wrong phoenix or the wrong unicorn—or whatever the fabulous creature turns out to be.

Archibald Macleish, *Poetry and Experience*

The social performance of identity through aesthetic means was of extraor-
dinary importance to elite Roman culture. The display of cultivated abilities, exquisite artwork, or refined manners that indicated social status and
political identity was a regular feature of elite culture under many guises,
from elegant parties to the gracefulness of one's sense of humor, from the
decoration of private residences to the careful diction and choice figures of
speech used by orators. The importance of such displays to Roman culture
can be gauged, on the one hand, by the continual additions made to the
repertoire of display, often from the practices of Greek culture, and on the
other, by the continual recurrence of efforts to control who performed such
displays or how. The dinner party, or *convivium,* which permitted the host
to act the part of patron, to put his own wealth on display, and to create a
microcosm of the social order, became in the second century more elegant,
even extravagant, under the influence of Hellenistic *symposia,* and attracted
restrictive attention from 181 forward, with limits imposed on the number

1

of guests and the price of the meal.[1] Transplanted Greek rhetorical practices flourished—the Romans had, in Cicero's phrase, "caught fire with a virtually boundless desire" to study rhetoric[2]—and speechmaking acquired attractions that Cato the Elder, for one, tried to counterbalance with Stoic views of rhetoric, which stressed parsimony and truthfulness in speech.[3] Under the censorship of the famously witty and accomplished orator L. Crassus, the *rhetores* who taught public speaking in Latin were expelled from Rome.[4] Private residences began to be built and decorated in the Greek style and became targets of opprobrium when this styling evidenced needless expenditure or violations of the old distinction between sacred and profane loot.[5]

The purpose of this study is to illuminate the place of such "performances" in the Roman construction of the social world by tracking the origins, development, and use in Latin literature of a vocabulary associated with them. There is, to be sure, no Latin word for "aestheticism" or for "Hellenism," let alone for "identity" or "social performance." But it is a gross mistake to think the absence of a word must mean the absence of the concept. Neither Horace nor Milton had a word for the "originality" so obviously important to their poetic; no teenager needs the word "conformity" to possess, and wield, a finely calibrated instantiation of that notion. There are, rather, at least two reasons why a word for a central cultural concept may be absent. To be a member of a society is often to know intuitively, almost unconsciously, but not to be able to explain, the rules by which a society operates. One consequence thereof may be the absence of a word for a concept that all members of a society nonetheless grasp. Furthermore the absence may only be apparent; it may be that a given concept reveals itself not by taking the form of a single lexeme, but by partially appropriating several lexemes. Using lexemes in this way may be wholly sufficient for members of a culture to delineate a concept; the subtleties of a paratheoretical, rather than theoretical, and an evaluative, rather than a cognitive, idiom, however inconvenient for outside analysts, may certainly be more than adequate for the members of a culture.

1. The so-called *leges sumptuariae;* see below, I.2 n. 31.

2. *incredibili quodam nostri homines discendi studio flagrauerunt (de Orat.* 1.14).

3. See below, IV.4.

4. For an appreciation of this ostensible paradox, cf. Gruen 1992: 264–66, Gruen 1990: 179–92. Rhetoric was typically learned abroad or from Greek tutors kept in one's own household, which restricted access to the wealthier.

5. On the construction and decoration of private residences in the Greek style, cf. Clarke 1991: 12–19. For attacks on sumptuous residences as evidence of needless expenditure, cf. Cato *ORF* 8.133, 174, 185. For violations of the distinction between sacred and profane loot, cf. Cato *ORF* 8.98; Gruen 1992: 111.

The claim of this study is that the "social performance of identity by aesthetic means" was a concept that the Romans expressed, in a way just described, mainly through the partial appropriation of several approbative lexemes and their opposites: *bell(us)* 'nice, fine, pretty,' *lep(idus)* 'delightful, charming,' *festiu(us)* 'entertaining, witty,' *facet(us)* 'clever, funny, witty,' *uenust(us)* 'graceful, charming, attractive, deft,' and *elegan(s)* 'elegant, discriminating.'[6] Hereinafter I refer to this set as "the language of social performance." These lexemes were not simply occasionally used of social performances but were, as I argue, the primary lexical expression of a conceptual category in which aestheticism, formerly opposed to "real" social worth in Roman culture, was now constructed as its complement. The lexemes became, in effect, a kind of political speech, serving not only a semantic but also an ideological function. The history of the conceptual category can thus be tracked, in part, through the history of the lexemes. All of the lexemes undergo major semantic shifts in the late third or second centuries B.C., which marks the point of origin of the conceptual category in the very period when Rome saw a flowering of Hellenizing social practices.[7] The complementarity between aestheticism or Hellenism and social worth remained contentious, and shifting attitudes can be tracked, diachronically and synchronically, by analysis of passages where the language of social performance occurs. The heart of this study consists of six chapters that provide such analyses, covering the genesis of the theoretical language of rhetoric, Cicero in his speeches and rhetorica, and Catullus, with a brief treatment of later Latin. My object, in short, has been to measure the literary embodiments of semantic shifts precipitated by social change, and this has required shuttling between "straight" literary criticism, "straight" historical semantics, and "straight" social history. I might be prepared to call the agglomerative result a "literary semantic history," were I not afraid of recalling Voltaire's assessment of the Holy Roman Empire as neither holy, nor Roman, nor an empire.

In any case a thick description of the occurrences of *bellus, lepidus, uenustus,* and the rest, which have never been examined for their ideological functions,[8] promises to be fruitful. Those lexemes continually figure in passages

6. A fuller demonstration of the connection of these lexemes to social performance is made in chapter 1. By notations such as *lep(idus)*, I mean all morphological expressions of the lexeme *lep-*, viz., the abstract *(lepos, lepor);* the adjective and adverb in all degrees *(lepidus/ lepide, lepidior/ lepidius, lepidissimus/ lepidissime)* and in any compounds *(perlepide, illepidus,* etc.).

7. See I.11.

8. The semantic ranges of *uenust(us), lep(idus), elegan(s),* and *bell(us)* have been surveyed by Monteil 1964, who makes many valuable observations. However, our lexical methods are ultimately incompatible: Monteil's basic method is to collate referents, look for commonali-

of central import for understanding the theory and the practice of social performances in elite culture in the mid- to late Roman republic. The tension between the desire to perform and the desire to restrict performance, for example, seems to be reflected in passages where the language of social performance has both an approbative and disapprobative tone. Lucilius, the writer of satires (m. ca. 101 B.C.), was an intimate of the influential P. Cornelius Scipio Aemilianus (185/4–129 B.C.), who was not only a military hero, conqueror of Numantia, but also a learned philhellene, connected to the historian Polybius, the playwright Terence, and the philosopher Panaetius, as well as to Lucilius himself.[9] When Lucilius teases his powerful friend for his hypercorrect speech, probably produced under the influence of Greek linguistic theory, he turns to *facet(us)*:

> So you can look wittier *(facetior),* seem to
> know more than everyone else,
> [it is your habit] to say "the man is wearied,"
> with *pertisum* instead of *pertaesum.*
>
> (963–64M, 983–84W, 971–72K)[10]

The tensions associated with social performance are embodied in the single word *facetior:* an approbative, apparently, in Aemilianus's own self-representation, but pushed by Lucilius in the direction of disapprobation. The same peculiar tension about social performance is to be seen in M. Terentius Varro (116–27 B.C.), who uses *bellus* and *festiuus* to draw a contrast between real character and the self-congratulatory social performances of (probably) the participants in a *convivium:*

> We are jolly *(belli)* and jovial *(festiui),*
> so we think.
> Though in fact
> we stink,
> like fetid fish.
>
> (*Men.* 312)[11]

My "fetid fish" represents *saperdae . . .* σαπροί, 'rotten *saperdae*,' the *saperda* being a particularly cheap and nasty fish, and suggesting not only meanness but also, in the presence of a Greek adjective, the decadent Greek east. In

---

ties among them, and assign sets of meanings to a lexeme. My own method sees meaning as the result of a two-step process: a semantic "core" passes through cultural "filters" to yield the observable pairings of referents to lexemes. See further below.

9. For the connection between Scipio Aemilianus and Lucilius, cf. Gruen 1992: 280–83.

10. For further analysis of this passage, cf. I.8. Lucilius will be cited with reference to the editions of Marx 1904, 1905, Warmington 1938, and Krenkel 1970.

11. This passage is discussed further below, I.7.

both these passages the tensions between Greek and Roman, approbation and disapprobation, are palpable.

In other passages approbation and disapprobation are not both present at once, but one or the other seems to predominate. M. Tullius Cicero (106–43 B.C.), the prolific writer and orator, in whom the language of social performance is most frequently attested and in whom it is most ideologically revealing, uses the language both to blame and to praise, according to the position he wishes to take on the attractions of those performances. Speaking of the libertine aristocratic youth flirting with the revolutionary designs of L. Sergius Catilina (m. 62), Cicero styles social performance as proper to the *convivium* and not to politics:

> In that crowd you'll find every gambler, everyone who cheats on his wife, everyone shameless and unchaste. These fine *(lepidus)* pretty *(delicatus)* boys have learned much: not only how to love—and be loved—and how to dance and sing, but also how to brandish a knife and spike things with poison. Know this: if they do not go away, if they are not done away with, even if Catiline is, this state will be nothing but a breeding ground for more Catilines.
>
> (*Catil.* 2.23)

But another speech, referring sarcastically to Gaul, where Julius Caesar was detained at the time, styles *lepos* the common possession of cultured men, as against the barbarian Celts:

> What other reason keeps Caesar in the province except wanting to hand over to the state fully completed the tasks that he has largely finished already? What else could keep him there? The loveliness of the place and the beauty of its cities? The culture *(humanitas)* and charm *(lepos)* of those people and nations? The desire for victory and furthering the bounds of empire?
>
> (*Prov.* 29)

The language of social performance in its approbative guise figures importantly in the Latin rhetorical tradition. For example, it provides the programmatic terms for Cicero's discussion of humor, as in the following passage, part of the catalog of the requirements for being an orator pronounced by Crassus at the beginning of *de Oratore:*

> The orator also needs to have a certain charming wit *(lepos)* and sense of humor *( facetiae),* learning that befits a free man, as well as the ability to reply and attack quickly and curtly, with measured deftness *(subtilis uenustas)* and wittiness *(urbanitas).*[12]
>
> (*de Orat.* 1.17)

12. Treated in III.4.2, VI.2.

Such purely approbative uses are not confined to Cicero. The tombstone of a noble woman from the *gens Claudia,* for example, dating to the time of the Gracchi, recalls not only her traditional maternal duties but also her social graces, using *lepidus:*

> Her speech was charming *(lepidus),*
> her gait attractive *(commodus).*
> She kept the house,
> she wove the wool.[13]
>
> $$(CIL\,1^2\;1211.7-8 = CIL\;6.15346.7-8)$$

All of these passages use the language of social performance to describe qualities of great importance to elite culture: convivial gaiety, distinctive speech, and performative attraction. A close examination of the native semantics of the words and the place they played in social ideologies, by illuminating such passages, may hope to illuminate the Roman constructions of social performance. What in the Roman cultural map of social performance permitted its characteristic language to be both positive and negative? Who styled it which way, in what contexts, and why? What was the place of performative attraction in models of social and political selves? These are the sorts of questions to which a thick description of the language of social performance can provide answers.

A study that would explore the intersections between semantics and cultural history must meet two requirements. Since such a study depends centrally on lexical data, it must first include a treatment of semantics, in order to have a principled way of describing semantic structure and understanding semantic change. A study that depends on what lexemes mean cannot afford to neglect the question of how they mean. The approach that I have found most useful, and whose theoretical particulars cannot be illustrated here in detail, may be illustrated by a metaphor that (tendentiously) compares human cultural structures to the patterns of the natural world. Suppose that one habitually observed a particular flock of urban crows, with an interest in the crows' practice of stationing sentries around the perimeter of the flock's feeding area.[14] A log of the places where the sentries perched might include entries like "maple tree," "oak tree," "gable of clapboard house on the corner," "telephone pole," and "fire hydrant." The problem of analyzing the relationship between a crow and these perches is like the problem of analyzing the relationship between a lexeme and its referents. The attraction of a lexeme to its referents is based on the possession by the

---

13. Treated in more detail below, I.9.

14. The crow is indeed proverbially wary, as in the Latin *cornicum oculos configere* 'to fix shut the eyes of the crow,' something like 'to sneak past the watchdog' (cf. Cic. *Mur.* 25).

latter of a feature or features described by the former, and the task of analysis is the task of distinguishing which are the relevant features. Although most of the "referents" in this example are wooden, the perching sentry crow is probably indifferent to construction material. Long or astute observation will reveal that from the crow's point of view two things matter about the perch: it must have a view of the crows feeding on the ground, and it must have a view of the quadrants from which danger may come. Practically this means that the perch will also be "high"; but the "highness" of a perch is really a secondary effect of the real requirement, the "clear views," as is demonstrated by the "fire hydrant."

In analyzing a lexeme it is therefore not sufficient to gather and group its referents. There are two points to bear in mind. First, the set of referents must be examined not for commonalities as such, but for *commonalities that are a function of the lexeme*.[15] To take our crow example, the fact that the "referents" are mostly "wooden" is not relevant. If a perch were high enough, *ceteris paribus* a crow wouldn't care if it was wood, or metal, or concrete. Chapter 1 examines *bell(us), uenust(us), lep(idus), facet(us), festiu(us),* and *elegan(s)* for such "lexemic commonalities." This may mean working back from odd or marginal patterns of occurrence—the "fire hydrants" of the set.[16] Second, the enumerable features of a lexeme's semantic core may display hierarchical relationships. The features of a semantic core do not supply the necessary and sufficient conditions for the application of a lexeme to a referent; rather they describe prototypical characteristics, from which a given referent may depart in greater or lesser degree. Probably most sentry crows, in looking for a perch, do look for "high" spots, so that "high" is practically speaking a part of the "meaning," as it were, of their eventual choice of a perch. But the most important aspect is the "clear views." One can even imagine how in particular circumstances those "clear views" may themselves be hierarchically arranged. A seasoned old crow may know, for example, that foxes lurk in a certain thicket, so that keeping an eye on that thicket becomes more important than actually being able to see his fellows. The crow metaphor does not illustrate that in a given case a lexeme may be only "partially" present, that is, with only a subset of its significative features in play in a given case.[17]

15. The failure to distinguish between the two kinds of commonalities, and sometimes between historical stages, is common in Monteil 1964, which nonetheless remains valuable as a collection of data.

16. For examples of this process, cf. the treatments below of *belle* vs. *bene habere* (I.7), the probable connection of *lep(idus)* to 'soft' (I.9), and that of *uenust(us)* to gardens (I.6).

17. Cf. on the loss of an erotic element in *uenust(us)* (I.6). This aspect of the flexibility of a lexeme, indeed any cognitive category, is conveniently summed up by Lakoff 1987: 83–

The second requirement for a study such as this is a treatment of the interaction of semantics with the social world. Isolating the features of a lexeme's semantic core, as just described, is the key to such a treatment. A given semantic feature can react with a prevailing set of ideas, be they ideologies shared by the whole culture or conceptions put forward by a particular author, text, or passage, and so cause a word to behave differently in different contexts. Thus not only must a semantic survey distinguish the commonalities between referents that are a function of the lexeme, and not coincidental, but it must also be aware that different sorts of referents will be selected for a lexeme under different ideological conditions. At this point the metaphor of the crows breaks down, but perhaps I may extract one last image from it. Suppose that the flock is more threatened by bobcats in fall and by hawks in summer. The shrewd sentry crow will of course still want perches with a "view of dangerous quadrants," but the perches will differ accordingly: all still "high" perhaps, but in autumn perches with a better view of the ground, and in summer perches with a clear view of the sky overhead. The "seasonal conditions" are, in this comparison, like the ideological environment in which a word is deployed. The semantic core need not be affected, but the referents to which it is deemed appropriate are different.

Accordingly different speakers, with different ideals, can apply a lexeme to different sets of referents. To take one example, *bellus* 'pretty, fine, nice' has as one of its semantic features a "reference to evaluator": that is, *bellus* delivers a positive evaluation not as absolute but as a relative or subjective claim (something rather like AmE "nice," as opposed to "good").[18] The primary diachronic difference in patterns of the usage of *bellus* is in the composition of the evaluating party. In Plautus the evaluating party is generally composed of a single person, who uses *bellus* to describe what accords with his own preferences. When Chrysalus finds a courtesan's house to his satisfaction, he says *euax, nimi' bellus atque ut esse maxume optabam locus* "Wow! lovely place, just the way I wanted it" (Pl. *Bac.* 724–25). That same use continues into later Latin, but by the first century another use has arisen, in which the evaluating party clearly comprises a smallish number of like-minded persons. So Varro's *omnes uidemur nobis esse belli festiui* "we are jolly

---

84, 91–92 et passim in the name "radially structured category"—as though each of the features were a spoke that points off more or less in its own direction. For example, sentences like "Osna was a mother to me" or "Barb's not my real mother" reveal first that the internal semantic structure of the word "mother" contains a number of features, in the case of these examples "primary female care-giver" and "woman who gave birth to a child"; and furthermore that the term "mother" can be applied by a kind of synecdoche to a person who possesses any of the features.

18. This argument is made in more detail below, I.7.

and jovial, so we think," which seems to refer to mutually attractive convivial behavior. Elsewhere in Varro "stylish men"—men aware of their own
stylishness, and putting it on display for other *cognoscenti*—are *belli homines*
or *homunculi* (*Men.* 312, 335, below I.7). Synchronic differences in the use
of *bellus* are produced when speakers define members of the small evaluating party according to their own ideological needs and designs. In Cicero's
*de Oratore,* for example, *bellus* is used to describe certain kinds of witticism
which are implicitly referred to the standards of an idealized social elite
(VI.3). In speeches, however, *bellus* is used to refer to 'stylish,' 'flashy,' or
'clever' speech in which the small evaluating party is constructed not as a
social ideal but as a threat to the integrity of public speech.[19] Consistent sets
of such choices across words permit the speculation that the words, or more
properly certain features of their grids, are being marshaled by some governing idea. For example, Cicero's pejorative handling of *bellus* in speeches
is paralleled there by other such uses of the language of social performance,
all of which illuminate one social construction of attractive performance.
And to the extent that different strata of the social world have different vi-
sions, such sets may reveal the social ideology of those strata.

Our task in analyzing the set of a word's referents, in short, is not trying
to find what all the referents share, a practice that may elide synchronic and
diachronic distinctions, but instead trying to isolate the semantic features of
the grid, and then to determine how the grid interacts with prevailing ideologies. In this way one may hope to trace a concept for which there never
really was a single word, something like "the social performance of Hellenism or aestheticism as a means to individualize oneself." As a rough parallel to the project of this study, one may imagine that no word "creativity"
existed and that one tracked the history of the concept by examining the deployment of words like "clever," "inventive," "original," and "traditional."
In fact the issue is more complicated than that, because a word itself, as we
have seen, cannot provide the minimal unit for such analysis. Consider as
another example a putative history of American political language in the
late twentieth century. The word "family" would be of interest in formulations like "Focus on the Family," "family values," and "Faith, Family, and
Freedom" (the theme of Senate majority leader Trent Lott's response to the
1998 State of the Union Address). One would even be interested in the
seminal sitcom "All in the Family," with Archie as Demea to Edith's Micio. However, one would exclude "the fine family of Wisconsin Pure dairy
products," "My wife's whole family brays like a bunch of mules," and "Baboons live in extended families." Instances of "family" in both sets share se-

19. Cf. *Ver.* 2.2.145 (V.3), *Flac.* 9 (V.4).

mantic characteristics, but (in normal circumstances) only the former set is "loaded" political speech. One may say that the lexeme "family" contains a semantic core, something like "a group of items or creatures connected by a specifiable relationship." That semantic core becomes political speech when plugged into a map of the world[20] that assigns certain kinds of ideological value to those characteristics. Though this study focuses on words, *the word is not the minimal unit of analysis.* By the "language of social performance," I mean *our set of lexemes in their connection to a particular cultural model.* Instances of the lexemes outside the model sometimes prove useful, but they are not closely analyzed unless they track the set of ideological issues that interest me. I am interested, to continue the image, much more in the "family" of Archie Bunker and Trent Lott than in the "family" of baboons, and in the latter only to the extent that it reveals semantic characteristics that illuminate the ideological deployment of the former. It will not be my purpose to give an account of all aspects of the relationship between Archie Bunker, Trent Lott, and baboons.

This approach to the language of social performance, beginning from texts in which the language has for the most part not been studied, illustrates the deficiencies of the scattering of approaches to those lexemes in Cicero's younger contemporary, Catullus. The prominence of the lexemes of the language of social performance in this relatively small collection of avant-garde poetry has earned them more attention than they have received elsewhere. Let us first review some typical appearances of the language. The bon vivant Suffenus is *uenustus:*

> *Suffenus iste, Vare, quem probe nosti,*
>> The Suffenus whom you know so well, Varus,
> *homo est uenustus et dicax et urbanus,*
>> Is a lovely and witty and civilized man,
> *idemque longos plurimos facit uersus.*
>> and unfortunately also writes poems without end.
>> (22.1–3)[21]

He is also *bellus* (22.9) and, because of his bad poetry, *infacetus* (22.14). In c. 16 a poetic creed is expressed in part by *lepos:* a poet's verses "have wit and charm" (*tum denique habent salem ac leporem,* 16.7) only if they are soft and sassy and titillating (cf. below VII.7). Licinius Calvus's charms, social and poetic, are *lepos* and *facetiae* (50.7–8, VII.4). The theft of a napkin with sentimental value is described in c. 12 by *non belle,* as a *res inuenusta* and is re-

---

20. = a cultural model; cf. II.1.
21. Analyzed in detail below, VII.6.

ferred to the judgment of a "boy expert in *lepores* and *facetiae*" (VII.4). The physically attractive Quintia lacks a "wit" expressed by *uenustas* (VII.2):

> *Quintia formosa est multis. mihi candida, longa,*
>> Quintia is beautiful,
>> so they say:
>> I would say, tall and fair-complected,
>
> *recta est: haec ego sic singula confiteor.*
>> perfect posture,
>> would grant
>> the single points, deny
>
> *totum illud formosa nego. nam nulla uenustas,*
>> they all add up to beauty.
>> So grand a body!
>
> *nulla in tam magno est corpore mica salis.*
>> But without attraction *(uenustas)*,
>> without a single grain of salt.

$$(86.1-4)$$

It is plain, in light of the other examples discussed above, that Catullus's poetry is drawing on the language of social performance. Verbal distinction and social style, and even eroticism (cf. Cicero's "fine *[lepidi]* pretty boys"), are the very sorts of things that the language of social performance elsewhere describes.

The connection of our lexemes to spheres of life that are self-evidently important to Catullus and his social circle—poetry, eroticism, and social style—has led to the obvious conclusion that these words are the catchwords of Catullus's circle.[22] Supporting this conclusion is the generic distinctiveness of the language. Catullus's poetry is conventionally sorted into three types on the basis of meter, language, length, and subject matter: the poly-

22. So Fordyce 1961 ad 43.8, Syndikus 1984: 128. Ross 1969 says that "certain words obviously belong in a discussion of the vocabulary of urbane Rome" and includes *delicatus, dicax, elegans, facetiae, ineptiae, lepos, sal, urbanus,* and *uenustus,* "with their other forms and opposites" (105–6); he adds, "As has often been recognized, in every case [these words are] used of Catullus's friends and society in a way that makes their association with this society certain" (pp. 106–7). Quinn 1973: xxx says of *bellus, dicax, delicatus, doctus, facetus, formosus, iucundus, lepidus, miser, urbanus,* and *uenustus* that they "embody the key concepts of the smart set to which [Catullus] belonged"; cf. Quinn 1972: 216. *Iucundus* and *formosus* do not belong in this list. *Formosus* in c. 86 is foil (v. infra, VII.2); *iucundus* in Catullus is faux elegant, as is clear enough from *iucundissime Calue* (14a.2), which is plainly meant to ape, not exemplify, a certain idiom. No "hot" word of Catullus's circle is used in the superlative, but cf. *mi iucundissime Cicero* (*Fam.* 9.9.3, Dolabella); Cicero is inclined to assign *iucundissimus* to letters (e.g., *Fam.* 10.26.1, 11.15.1, 16.21.1, *Q. fr.* 2.7.1, *Att.* 5.20.8, 7.1.7, 16.16.1). See also 286 n. 126.

metrics, the elegiacs, and the "long poems."[23] The language of social performance, rare in the second type of poetry, and never in the third, is concentrated in the first type, the polymetrics, among which are the poems wherein the "social aesthetics" of Catullus's circle are of central concern.[24] It is this evident importance of the language of social performance that has prevented scholars from looking for wider, systematic connections; two, not mutually exclusive, and, as I will argue, erroneous, ways of treating the language have resulted. To some scholars the connection of our lexemes to a small stylish social group prevents readers from attaining anything more than a distant appreciation; as Fordyce 1961: 197 puts it,

> *Facetus* and *infacetus*, *salsus* and *insulsus*, *uenustus* and *inuenustus*, *elegans* and *inelegans*, *urbanus* and *rusticus* are the clichés which, though their nuances must elude us, reflect the attitudes and values of Catullus's society, a society which puts a premium on attractiveness *(uenustas)*, discrimination *(elegantia)*, piquancy *(sal)*, metropolitanism *(urbanitas)*, and has only scorn for the dull, the insensitive, the clumsy and the provincial.

Fordyce isolates the semantic spheres from which the "clichés" issue, a springboard from which further analysis might have begun; for "attractiveness," "piquancy" and the rest were not only the values of "Catullans" but were important to Roman society as a whole. In Cicero's treatment of humor in *de Oratore* (2.216–90), *facet(us)*, *sal(sus)*, *uenust(us)*, and *elegan(s)*, as well as *lep(idus)*, which belongs in Fordyce's list, figure prominently; but they are not brought to bear here. Ultimately Fordyce—who, to be fair, was writing a commentary, and not an extended treatment—seems to take Catullus's language as a kind of "jive talk," a piquant subcultural speech register that happens to be preserved to us in his poetry but is really unknowable to us because we are not "flappers" or "sheiks," much less the "hepcats" themselves.[25] I hope, by contrast, to illustrate what is perhaps already clear,

23. See ch. 7 n.2.
24. Cf. Ross 1969: 109. It is necessary to distinguish between kinds of elegiacs, the experimental "neoteric" elegiacs and the "epigrams"; cf. below, ch. 7 n.2.
25. I may define these terms for readers unfamiliar with the history of American English. In the 1920s and 1930s, the vernacular of black jazz musicians (the "jive talk" of the "hepcats"), ultimately based on Southern Black speech, found its way into the language of the stylish white clientele ("flappers" [f.] and "sheiks" [m.]) who frequented the jazz clubs in Harlem, such as the famous Cotton Club. The radio show *Amos and Andy* introduced much "jive talk" to a wider audience. "Jive talk" was also the source of much of the slang of "hippies" in the 1960s (e.g., "groovy," "hip," "cool").

that Catullus meant to appropriate, and subvert, a generally understood idiom. His is not "jive talk" but the lingua franca, subjected to a poet's scrutiny and, as we see below, forced to confront its own contradictions.

The idea of the vocabulary of a closed circle has led other scholars to a different approach, also deficient, and I hope this study may go some way toward correcting it. The prominence of a lexeme in a poem where a particular idea also prevails suggests that the lexeme is the *vox propria* for that idea. The characteristic "closed" method of New Criticism, where the unity of the poem is all and poems are sufficient to explain themselves, is here trajected onto the level of semantics. As the poem's source of meaning is said to be internal coherence, so the meanings assigned to a lexeme are those which seem to meet the needs of the poem. For example, Singleton has it, "What, then, does *lepidus* mean? Strictly speaking, as little or as much as our 'charming.' Its meaning, that is, depends almost entirely on the context; what constitutes the *lepos,* therefore, of Catullus' little book we shall have to discover when we know more about the context" (1972: 192).[26] To be sure, the context is important, but it is much more important that *lep(idus)* was commonly used for the performative attractiveness of games, rhetorical presentations, figures of speech, and charming humor, semantic spheres patently important for understanding the precious and highly self-conscious polymetric poems. An otherwise valuable article of F. O. Copley follows a similar path: in treating the phrase *lepidus nouus libellus,* "a nice new book," which appears in the first poem of Catullus to describe his collection, Copley asserts that "the adjective *lepidus* refers primarily to qualities of character and personality, and to external appearances only insofar as these reflect character" (1951: 203). That is by no means true historically: external appearance is exactly what *lepidus* describes in any number of instances from Plautus, for example *nimi' lepide exconcinnauit hasce aedis* "He's set this house up really nicely" (*Cist.* 312).[27] Copley's definition of *lepidus* begins from his own interpretation of the meaning of the phrase *lepidus nouus libellus* in the context of the poem: the collection of poetry is, on his reading, "agreeing, amusing, amiable, and charming," and thus he defines *lepidus* as being primarily a quality of "personality." There is much of value in

---

26. Comparable are the slight comments of Seager 1974. Even vagaries like "charming" are driven by culture-specific models of situations: cf. D. Holland and D. Skinner, "Prestige and Intimacy: The Cultural Models behind Americans' Talk about Gender Types," in Holland and Quinn 1987: 79–111, where it is demonstrated that such ordinary words as "man," "boy," "guy," "jerk" have distinct values in the appraisal of men by women.

27. See I.9 below.

Copley's observations, but such a "closed" semantic procedure leads him to distort the evidence outright.[28]

The most productive treatments of the lexemes of the language of social performance in Catullus have come from those scholars who, eschewing both judicious *aporia* and "New Critical semantics," have looked to make broader connections to the contemporary language and its ideological resonances. Vinzenz Buchheit, for example, speaking of *tener* 'soft' (Catul. 35.1), makes an incidental, but exact, admonition: "As so often in Catullus, a look into the rest of the literary-critical, in particular the rhetorical, tradition of his time is helpful" (1976b: 49).[29] There has been no systematic attempt to follow Buchheit's suggestion, not least because applicable studies of the rhetorical tradition are wanting. The comparandum of Cicero's rhetorica (ch. 6) is particularly fruitful for reading Catullus, as I argue below (ch. 7). Much of the programmatic language of Catullus, as I have already suggested, is prominent in Cicero's rhetorica and illuminated by its appearances there. *Lepos,* for example, is used in *de Oratore* to mean "humor," thus Caesar's description of Crassus as *in utroque genere leporis excellens* (*de Orat.* 2.220) "outstanding in both kinds of humor," refers to the just-made distinction between *cauillatio,* extended or narrative humor, and *dicacitas,* the humor of biting one-liners. It is also used for the "figures" permitted to a type of "middle" style, which are called *uerborum [et] sententiarum lepores* "beauties of diction and thought" (*Or.* 96). It is reasonable to see some connection between this *lepos* of verbal flourish and Catullan *lep(idus),* which, as we have seen, may serve as a programmatic term for poetry.

But the slipperiness of certain lexical items makes it difficult to carry out Buchheit's suggestion in detail. *Venustas,* as we have seen, is the quality that Lesbia possesses and Quintia lacks; *uenustas* is also important to Cicero's rhetorica, but it is difficult to build a bridge between him and Catullus. There are at least three kinds of *uenust(us)* in Cicero's rhetorica.[30] One describes

28. For example, Copley 201 cites Ter. *Andr.* 948 *o lepidum patrem* as a prototypical example of the adjective, without considering that most, if not all, instances of *lepidus* in Terence are ironic (cf. IV.5, with n. 35) or that there are only twelve instances in Terence against some 190 in Plautus. He also notes (ibid.) that the "relative rarity [of *lepidus*] in 'high' or 'classical' Latin is an indication of the fact that the writers of that dialect considered the ordinary and everyday unsuitable for their purposes and antipathetic to their literary aims and ideals (When Cicero, for example, uses the term, it is with a sneer: *hi pueri tam lepidi ac delicati, Cat.* 2.10.23)." On the contrary, instances of *lepos* and *lepidus* in the speeches have clear motivations (cf. ch. 5); and Copley completely ignores *lepos* in the rhetorica, where it is not rare.

29. "Wie so oft bei Catull, hilft ein Blick auf die sonstige literarkritische, speziell auf die rhetorische Tradition seiner Zeit."

30. See below, III.4.

graceful stage gestures (*gestusque natura . . . uenustus,* "natural grace of movement" *Brut.* 272), one the "plain grace" of simple narration (*nudi . . . recti et
uenusti* "bare, erect, and graceful," of Caesar's commentaries on the Gallic
War, *Brut.* 262), and a third the cleverly humorous comment, especially in
reply (cf. *subtilis uenustas* in Cicero *de Orat.* 1.17 above). At first appearances
the most appropriate of them to Lesbia may be the *uenustas* of the humor
of reply, which implies something "interactive" or "responsive," unlike
Quintia's statuesque stolidity. But surely Lesbia's attraction is erotic? We
might take the application of *uenust(us)* to Suffenus to be erotic, too, a plausible enough assumption for Catullus's circle. But then what has become of
the eroticism in Cicero's use of the word? Furthermore Cicero himself used
*uenust(us)* in senses that seem to be erotic; for example, the retinue of stylish young men who frequent the house of Clodia Metelli, depicted by Cicero in his speech *pro M. Caelio* as a brazen hussy, are told to "flourish in their
*uenustas*" (*Cael.* 67, V.6). Such complications reinforce the notion that Catullus's poetry is in itself and for itself—"jive talk." A model of semantics,
and of the interaction between semantics and the social world, will, as I
hope, ultimately permit the resolution of such impasses.

   A summary of the argument follows. Chapter 1, "*Libertino Patre Natus:*
The Birth of the Language of Social Performance," analyzes hitherto largely
undocumented semantic shifts in *elegan(s), uenust(us), bellus, facet(us), lep(idus),*
and *festiu(us)*. Following the principles described above, I attempt to describe
the main elements of the semantic core of the adjectives. That, in turn, sheds
light on their differentiation over time: all of them shift consistently with
their adaptation to describe the Hellenizing and aesthetic social practices
that flowered in Rome in the second century B.C. I suggest that the shifts
are not piecemeal, but signs of a large-scale attempt to create a new cultural
category in which certain kinds of aestheticism could be understood as the
complement of social worth.

   The complementarity of aestheticism and social worth, as I have suggested above, remained contentious. Chapter 2, "*Grauitate Mixtus Lepos:*
The Ideologies of the Language of Social Performance," offers a scheme for
modeling the complementarity. In particular, it is suggested that "aestheticism" could be mapped onto "social worth" only partially, with the paradoxical result that the language of social performance, ultimately an aesthetic
idiom, could imply both the presence and absence of social worth. The language of social performance is therefore a fine instrument for tracking an
author's attitudes toward the complementarity of social worth and aestheticism. This chapter suggests further that "aestheticism" was of a piece with
"Hellenism" and "individualism" as a means for forging social identity, and

that the language of social performance can be used to track attitudes to these qualities as well.

The next two chapters describe the role of the language of social performance in the creation of rhetorical technical language in Latin. Chapter 3, "DE · SVO · FECERVNT: The Language of Social Performance in the Latin Rhetorical Tradition," surveys the place of the language of social performance in extant rhetorical treatises and similar texts. Observing that no member of the language of social performance consistently translates any term from the Greek, I demonstrate that the senses of the lexemes in rhetorical contexts are borrowed wholesale from their (putatively) earlier, non-rhetorical, especially convivial, uses. The language of social performance is a uniquely Roman contribution to the critical language of rhetoric. This contribution is analyzed in chapter 4, "*Suauis Grauis:* The Birth of the Language of Rhetoric." This chapter argues that the language of social performance in the Latin rhetorical tradition is the result of an act of cultural translation dating to the second century. The language of social performance first arose to describe the pleasant, inessential aspects of semiotically significant social practices. Romans who wished to defend certain "flashy" aspects of Greek rhetorical practice described them with the language of social performance in order to imply that, in the same way as, for example, witty banter in the *convivium* supported the task of reinforcing social order, so rhetorical effects, though "merely" pleasant, could be construed as supporting a serious task, namely speechmaking. Such a view was not shared by those sympathetic to Stoic rhetorical theory, including Terence, who always uses the language of social performance sarcastically in descriptions of rhetorical flourish.

The next three chapters use the language of social performance as a means of exploring the ideology of performance in Cicero and Catullus. Chapter 5, "*Non ut Vincula Virorum:* The Language of Social Performance in Cicero's Speeches," is a contribution to understanding the creation of Ciceronian *ethos*. Nowhere is it clearer than in Cicero's speeches how the use of the language of social performance tracks ideological stances. Cicero uses the language of social performance in speeches in two ways, one "older" and one more ideologically revealing. He may use the language to rebuke or patronize the aestheticism of social lessers. But he also uses the language of social performance in contexts where he depicts himself as an outsider, where he attempts to countermand the qualities that the language of social performance describes altogether by extravagant reference to traditional Roman social values, and where he seems to be trying to wrest the language away from certain of its adherents. I suggest that this latter ideological contextualizing signifies a shift in the "balance of power" between style and substance, so that they were now taken to be coextensive, rather than complementary. Aestheticism had become a dominant paradigm for social interaction in the late Republic, and Cicero's hostile or deprecatory treatment is an atavistic attempt to decouple aestheticism from social worth.

Chapter 6, "*Sermo Facetus et in Nulla Re Rudis,*" describes Cicero's use of the language of social performance in his rhetorica, a use that sheds light in particular on the project of *de Oratore*. The *de Oratore* features a specially adapted version of the language of social performance to describe not rhetorical effect generally but only wit and humor. This treatment of the language of social performance by Cicero has two ideological motivations. On the one hand, as a notorious wit himself, Cicero was interested in justifying his own propensities, which were taken by some social conservatives as incompatible with *gravitas*.[31] Cicero's treatment of humor in the rhetorica is an attempt to justify it to such critics. He carefully tailors the kind of humor the orator is to have so that it suits, indeed seems required of, aristocrats. On the other hand Cicero's use of contemporarily piquant idiom to describe primarily wit and humor, or other effects only in passing, is also a refusal to enshrine the qualities that that language described as the overall ideal of oratory. To have done so would have opened his ideal orator up to the charge of preening that he himself lays against opponents. He thus gives "sparkle" and "charm" only a narrower place.[32] Cicero's clear attempts to control "sparkle" suggest incidentally that "stylish self-presentation" had become a dominant paradigm, required of all social performers.

Chapter 7, "*Leporum Disertus Puer:* The Language of Social Performance in Catullus," describes Catullus's double handling of the language of social performance, which throws light on the project of the polymetrics in particular. In the polymetrics (or experimental elegiacs) Catullus takes a language associated with public displays and political power and cuts it away from both, using it for "private" displays of stylishness and suavité. Somewhat as the language of political alliance (*foedus amicitiae* etc.) is made to serve for the "language of true love," so the language of social performance is made to serve for "the language of poetry," of "erotics," and of "social style." The elevated associations of the language of social performance, which described

31. For example, Cicero's comic tactics in the *pro Murena* led Cato (the prosecutor) to exclaim, "What a funny consul we have, gentlemen!" (ὡς γελοῖον, ὦ ἄνδρες, ἔχομεν ὕπατον, *Comp. Dem. et Cic.* 1.5, cf. VI.5).

32. Cf. Crassus's point *qua re "bene et praeclare" quamuis nobis saepe dicatur; "belle et festiue" nimium saepe nolo* "I want to hear 'well done! splendid!' as often as possible, 'nicely done! delightful!' not too often" (*de Orat.* 3.101). Cf. below, VI.6.

semiotic practices of central cultural import, provide Catullus with a way of suggesting that poetry and erotics are also of import.

Another notable aspect of Catullus's use of the language of social performance is his propensity to exploit several possible aspects of a word's meaning. This propensity has the deliberate effect of destabilizing language, distinct from the elite ideal of controlled speech. The paradox of the language of social performance in Catullus's poetry is therefore that a political idiom is made to undercut a political ideal. In the elegiacs (and in some polymetrics) Catullus also performs the neat trick of hearing his own circle's argot as if from the outside, using the language of social performance pejoratively, which acts to destabilize language further. The effect of this destabilizing, accompanied by the elevation described above, is to issue a kind of critique of Roman society by pushing its semiotic categories to their limits. When the language of social action can be converted into the language of private indulgences, the weakness of the old models of social action, to which private indulgence was anathema, is demonstrated.

Chapter 8, "*O Omnia!*" explores more briefly the subsequent history of the language of social performance. It is suggested that the disappearance of the language of social performance from Augustan poetry had to do with its ideological inappropriateness to a time when more serene images, taken from a fifth-century Greece constructed as an ideal of political calmness, were the acceptable, indeed the "official," symbolic currency. Possibly the language of social performance was discredited specifically by its associations with Antonian propaganda. Marc Antony, at any rate, is put forward as the culmination of the trend, observed in chapter 5 in Verres, and here traced through Julius Caesar, to use aestheticism as a model for political life. In response the "grammar" of Octavian's propaganda shifted to stabler images. With the gradual consolidation of power in the hands of an emperor, the creation of a new kind of social elite, who practiced aestheticism as a private pursuit in a time of political reorientation, precipitates the conversion of the language of social performance into simply a technical language of literary criticism, divorced from broader public issues. The language of social performance, once in the vanguard of the cultural struggles of the Republic, ends up as the critical pratings of *honestiores* ringing a *stibadium*.

If a critical language is only the metalanguage of a given text, an approach that seeks subtle semantic differentiations keyed to context is well suited to the study of late Republican culture. Roman culture, as a whole, was intensely aware of what might be called broadly semiotic distinctions. Who dressed how, who sat where in the theater, who got a triumph, who appeared how on coins: all these questions were intensely important. Presenting themselves was what most elite Romans were doing most of the time, in the forum as well as on the villa. In suggesting that the distinctions I detect, sometimes minute, were important to Roman culture, and especially to Cicero and Catullus, I am no more than suggesting that language was one place where such semiotic distinctions were being made, and that Romans paid as much attention to the talk about performance as they did to performances themselves. It seems like an obvious point, but treating it in its particulars is difficult because of the long and broad shadow of Cicero, who blinds us to how varied and complex linguistic behavior must have been in the late Republic, and how particular his idiolect.[33] The perennial attractiveness of Catullus is equally unhelpful, since it is usually treated as having sprung full-grown from his head, or from his circle, with scant reference to the resources of the contemporary language. If social performance is important to a culture, we may expect the language it uses to assess performance to be subtle; and if social performance is important, the use of the language of social performance will itself have been a performance, calibrated as carefully as any other.

33. On syntactic issues, for example, cf. Lebreton 1901.

# CHAPTER I

# *Libertino Patre Natus*
# The Birth of the Language
# of Social Performance

We do not prove the existence of the poem
It is something seen and known in lesser poems
It is the huge, high harmony that sounds
A little and a little, suddenly,
By means of a separate sense. It is and it
Is not and, therefore, is. In the instant of speech,
The breath of an accelerando moves,
Captives the being, widens,—and was there.

Wallace Stevens, "A Primitive Like an Orb," II

Vocabulary is a very sensitive index of the culture of a people.

Edward Sapir

## I.1. Introduction

*Bell(us), uenust(us), lep(idus), facet(us),* and a few other words as a body supply the argot of Catullus's circle for describing stylish behavior, as has been noted above. When Marrucinus Asinius thieves a napkin, the action is done *non belle* (Catul. 12.2) and is a *res inuenusta* (12.5). When Catullus meets Varus's girlfriend, she is *non sane illepidum neque inuenustum* (10.4); the same pairing occurs in c. 36 (*si non illepidum neque inuenustum est,* 17). Within Cicero, the same words also behave as a group, occurring in identical patterns. In programmatic passages of the rhetorica, *lepos, facet(us), uenust(us),* and *bell(us)* all assign positive connotations to humor. In speeches the words are generally used more broadly and with a curious combination of approval and disapproval. These same words, however, do not form a coherent set in Plautus. That is, they do not occur jointly applied to the same item, or severally applied to allied semantic spheres, except loosely.[1] Furthermore the denotation or connotation of several of the lexemes seems very different after Plautus. *Elegan(s)* for Plautus is 'fastidious,' even 'prissy' (below, I.5), for Cicero 'elegant, discriminating' (below, I.5, III.6). *Lep(idus)* in Plautus de-

---

1. *Lepidus* and *facetus* are a partial exception; see further I.10 fin.

scribes dinners and courtesans, whereas for Cicero *lepos* is a distinctly aristocratic brand of wit and humor (below, VI.3).

The difference between Plautine and later Latin suggests two, not wholly
exclusive, possibilities: either something happened after Plautus that forged
the language of social performance into a coherent set; or circumstances
changed sufficiently to allow the appearance of a set that was already coherent, perhaps only partly or incipiently so. The state of the evidence does
not permit more exact detail or precise chronology, but it does permit a
more important claim: that the development, or emergence, of the language
of social performance as a coherent set should be attributed to the social
climate of the late third and second centuries. I myself prefer the hypothesis of development, for reasons discussed below (I.11), but I have tried to
present the evidence in sections I.5 through I.10 without unnecessarily
privileging that hypothesis. What is certain, and most important, is that the
words became connected to an aestheticism that, unlike the aestheticism of
a Plautine *meretrix*, was considered politically and socially worthwhile. It
became possible, in Sallust's phrase, *conuiuiis gratiam quaerere* "to seek political influence by entertaining" (*Jug.* 4.3). This emergent aestheticism required a new approbative language, which was provided by the previously
unconnected words just surveyed. Once an idiom particularly suited to the
aesthetic ideals of comic characters, the lexemes would acquire a certain,
though still volatile, respectability; they were, so to speak, "born of a freedman father" (Hor. *Serm.* 1.6.6), having achieved a new status, but not so as
to lose the stigma of their origins.[2] Somewhat as attitudes toward freedmen
might be a litmus test for a Roman's attitudes toward social mobility, so the
history of attitudes toward aestheticism, as we see below, can be ascertained
by attention to occurrences of *lep(idus), bell(us), uenust(us),* and their like.

## I.2. The Growth of Elite Aestheticism

It is a mistake to think that Roman interest in the cultural products of the
Greek world is an artefact of the second century, as later historians, in their
search for an ἀρχὴ κακῶν, would have us believe.[3] Rather the Romans al-

2. Some of the best evidence for this shift, treated in chapters 3 and 4, is the technical
language of rhetoric, which, as I argue, used this newly minted idiom to assimilate rhetoric
implicitly to other aesthetic practices. The passages discussed in those chapters support the
claims that are sometimes only tentative here.

3. Livy 25.40.1–3, for example, while admitting that the booty taken by Marcellus from
the sack of Syracuse was legitimate war spoils *(hostium quidem illa spolia et parta belli iure)*, sees
in the event "the beginning of the fascination with Greek artistic productions and of the un-
inhibited practice of looting everything, sacred and profane, without discrimination" *(cete-
rum inde primum initium mirandi Graecarum artium opera licentiaeque hinc sacra profanaque omnia*

ways seem to have been interested in the artistic productions of foreign cultures, and usually out of more than a churlish greed for war booty. Foreign artwork served important religious, political, and social purposes. Captured cult statues would be rededicated at new sites in Rome itself, as a symbol of the integration of the defeated enemy's cults into the state religion.[4] War trophies were established in the Forum as a reminder of the achievements of returning generals and the glory of the state.[5] The erection of statues or other monuments to commemorate important successes was an established practice by the third century.[6]

When, with the conclusion of the eastern wars in the second century, the treasures of the Greek world began to flow into Rome at a greater pace, the use of artwork to express social and political ideals was therefore already well established. The late third and second centuries saw not only an increased use of established forms, but also the introduction of new forms, and furthermore a new application for both of these. In this period a Roman social elite that was more diverse and at the same time more distinctive began to coalesce. The old senatorial class, who had successfully conducted the Punic and eastern wars, earned thereby not only wide respect but more clients and more wealth. The bankers, traders, and merchants among the equestrian class had benefited both from the need to equip armies and from the opening up of new territories, and the equestrians began to emerge as an increasingly distinct group. Both senatorials and equestrians benefited from the depletion of Italian peasantry and a deep pool of slave labor, which enabled them to acquire and man lucrative plantations.

The artistic symbols already in use for expressing generally shared civic ideals were appropriated and expanded by this newly coalescing and newly self-conscious elite in order to express not a civic but a class-specific identity. Individuals began to collect Greek art and employ Greek architectural and decorative forms at an increasing rate. Cato records the setting up of

---

*uolgo spoliandi)*. Plutarch says that before the sack of Syracuse the Romans had no taste (*Marc.* 21.1). Pliny blames the lavish triumph of Scipio Asiagenus in 189 for introducing luxury into Italy (*Nat.* 33.148). For a convincing refutation of the historical validity of this literary trope, see Gruen 1992: 84–130.

4. One of the earliest events is the transport of Veientane Juno by M. Furius Camillus in 396; cf. Livy 5.21.3, Gruen 1992: 86–88.

5. The Rostra gets its name from such a trophy, the prows or *rostra* of the Antiate ships surrendered to C. Maenius in 338; Livy 8.14.12.

6. For example, C. Duilius's naval victory over the Carthaginians in 260 was commemorated by a column; cf. Plin. *Nat.* 34.20, Quint. *Inst.* 1.7.12, Silvius 6.633ff., Serv. ad G. 3.29. An inscription (*CIL* 1²25 = 6.1300 = Degrassi 319) whose stone and lettering are imperial (cf. Degrassi 189 n.) may nonetheless preserve the original text.

statues in private homes.[7] He also attests to the practice of "finishing off" domestic surfaces with citron wood, ivory, and marble, referring to revetments.[8] Private houses now included a *peristylium,* a garden enclosed by a colonnade, after the Greek fashion. Many of the Greek artistic forms were used to enhance the increasingly Hellenized "feasts" *(epulae)* and "parties" *(convivia).*[9] The gold and silver tableware that M'. Acilius Glabrio (consul in 191) diverted to private use presumably went to adorn his table.[10] When Cato complains that smoked fish and pretty boys were now worth more than farms and farmhands, he is referring to convivial practices.[11] C. Sempronius Gracchus also alludes to the practice of having "pretty boys" stationed about a convivial room.[12] While theatrical performances have an older pedigree, the increasingly Hellenized *convivium* now also included performances. According to Livy, it was the soldiers of Cn. Manlius Vulso returning from Galatia in 187 who

> were the first to import to Rome bronze couches, expensive bedding, coverlets, and other textiles, as well as one-legged tables (*monopodia* =

7. *miror audere atque religionem non tenere, statuas deorum, exempla earum facierum, signa domi pro supellectile statuere* "I am surprised at their audacity and sacrilege: they take statues of the gods, their very images, and set them up as artwork at home, as if they were furniture" (*ORF* 8.98 = Prisc. in *G.L.* 2 p. 3667.14). The speech was entitled *uti praeda in publicum referatur* "That booty should be turned over to the treasury," referring to the established practice of distinguishing between sacred and profane booty; cf. Polyb. 9.10.13 ταῖς μὲν ἰδιωτικαῖς κατασκευαῖς τοὺς αὐτῶν ἐκόσμησαν βίους, ταῖς δὲ δημοσίαις τὰ κοινὰ τῆς πόλεως with reference to booty from the sack of Syracuse by Marcellus.

8. *dicere possum, quibus uillae atque aedes aedificatae atque expolitae maximo opere citro atque ebore atque pauimentis Poenicis sient* (Cato *ORF* 8.185 = Paul. Fest. p. 282 Lindsay). By "Punic pavements" Cato means "Numidian marble" (cf. *ORF* n. ad loc.).

9. For collection and analysis of the sparse material concerning Roman communal dining before the Hellenized *luxus mensae,* cf. Landolfi 1990.

10. *is* [sc. *Cato*] *testis, quae uasa aurea atque argentea castris captis inter aliam praedam regiam uidisset, ea se in triumpho negabat uidisse* "Cato testified that he had not seen in the triumph those gold and silver vases that he had seen among the other royal booty in the captured camps" (Livy 37.57.14). Cf. Cato *ORF* 8.224 *fures priuatorum furtorum in neruo atque in compedibus aetatem agunt, fures publici in auro atque purpura* "Steal from a private citizen, and you spend your life in fetters and bonds; steal from the treasury, and you spend your life in gold and purple."

11. ἐφ' οἷς καὶ Μάρκος (ἀγανακτῶν) εἶπέ ποτε πρὸς τὸν δῆμον ὅτι μάλιστ' ἂν κατίδοιεν τὴν ἐπὶ (τὸ) χεῖρον προκοπὴν τῆς πολιτείας ἐκ τούτων, ὅταν πωλούμενοι πλεῖον εὑρίσκωσιν οἱ μὲν εὐπρεπεῖς παῖδες τῶν ἀγρῶν, τὰ δὲ κεράμια τοῦ ταρίχου τῶν ζευγηλατῶν, Polyb. 31.25.5a.

12. *nulla apud me fuit popina neque pueri eximia facie stabant et in conuiuio liberi uestri modestius erant quam apud principia* "I did not run an eating house nor have in attendance boys of excellent appearance; at my dinners your children behaved more properly than at military headquarters" (*ORF* 48.26 = Gel. 15.12.2; cf. *ORF* 52.1 = Gel. 15.8).

μονοπόδια) and sideboards (abaci = ἄβακες), which at the time were extravagant furniture. It was at this time that psaltriae (ψάλτριαι) and sambucistriae (σαμβυκίστριαι), as well as other pleasant convivial relaxations, began to be featured at banquets (epulae). The dinners themselves also began to be prepared with greater attention and expense.[13]

The new convivial practices formed a complex Sallust's Marius would scorn: "They call me vulgar and unpolished, because I do not know how to put on an elegant dinner and do not have actors at my table or keep a cook who has cost me more than my farm overseer."[14]

Not only were the elite observing new types of performance, probably often in convivial contexts, but they themselves engaged in some of them. In 184/83 Cato decried an opponent's taste for such performance: "And besides he sings, when it strikes his fancy, occasionally he performs Greek verses, he tells jokes, he changes voices, strikes his little poses."[15] The telling of jokes and performing verses were typical Hellenic ἀκροάματα or verbal diversions practiced at συμπόσια,[16] although Cato may here be referring

13. ii primum lectos aeratos, uestem stragulam pretiosam, plagulas et alia textilia, et quae tum magnificae supellectilis habebantur, monopodia et abacos Romam aduexerunt, tunc psaltriae sambucistriaeque et conuiualia alia ludorum oblectamenta addita epulis; epulae quoque ipsae et cura et sumptu maiore apparari coeptae (39.6.7−9), cf. Plin. Nat. 18.108, 33.148, 34.14. Psaltriae and sambucistriae are female players of stringed instruments and (probably) a kind of small Asiatic harp, respectively. See the introductions in Walsh 1993 and 1994 and commentary ad loc.

The reading and sense of the phrase conuiualia alia ludorum oblectamenta is somewhat problematic. One branch reads conuiualia alia, accepted by modern editors; other manuscripts read only conuiualia, others conuiuia alia with minor variations (cf. Briscoe 1991, Walsh 1999 app. ad loc.). The phrase conuiualia alia ludorum oblectamenta is typically taken to mean something like the translation in Walsh 1993, "other festive entertainments of relaxation," taking ludorum as 'sport, play, fun.' As Weissenborn and Müller 1962 ad loc. observe, the phrase refers to the introduction of "Tänzer, Mimen, Gaukler, Possenreißer." Those were the sorts of entertainments associated with ludi in the narrower sense of 'games, festival,' so that the phrase should perhaps be punctuated conuiualia alia, ludorum oblectamenta and translated "and other convivial activities, pleasures proper to the games."

14. sordidum me et incultis moribus aiunt, quia parum scite conuiuium exorno neque histrionem ullum neque pluris preti coquom quam uilicum habeo (Jug. 85.39), tr. S. A. Handford (Baltimore: Penguin Books, 1963).

15. praeterea cantat, ubi collibuit, interdum Graecos uersus agit, iocos dicit, uoces demutat, staticulos dat (ORF 8.115 = Macr. 3.14.9). Probably from the speech si me M. Caelius tribunus plebis appellasset; cf., from the same speech, descendit de cantherio, inde staticulos dare, ridicula fundere "He gets off his gelding, strikes poses, pours out jokes" (ORF 8.114). The speech seems to date from Cato's censorship of 184/3; cf. Till 1953.

16. For the continued real presence of poetry, especially in the form of epigram, and witty banter at the Hellenistic symposia, by way of continuing archaic practice, cf. Cameron 1995: 71−103. The symposiastic setting of many Hellenistic poems is typically taken as an imaginary motif, as if the development from an oral to a written literary culture meant that

to Caelius's rhetorical style.[17] The αἴνιγμα or *captio* preserved in Lucilius (1284–86M, 1250–52W, 1301–3K, below III.8) should probably be imagined as being posed at a *convivium,* as were similar puzzles in Gellius (III.7). In a speech delivered in 129, Scipio Aemilianus described noble youths who went to dancing school and took lessons on the *sambuca* and *psalterium,* surely to perform at *convivia.*[18] In short, there is good evidence that all manner of aesthetic forms began to be used in the second century not to express Roman civic ideals, as seems to be true of the earlier period, but also to advertise the status of a particular social class.

These new social practices placed considerable, and as I argue a deforming, strain on Latin's approbative vocabulary. To understand these strains, it is important first to consider the function of aestheticism in the symbolic self-representation of the Roman elite. What aesthetic productions symbolized for the state as a whole they might also symbolize, mutatis mutandis, for the social elite. For example, the acquisition by the Roman treasury of art treasures advertised the depth of its own coffers. The construction of a new type of house, its decoration in the latest fashion, and the hosting of elegant parties served a comparable function for the social elite. In planning a dinner, Plautus's Ballio asserts *magnufice uolo me uiros summos accipere, ut mihi rem esse reantur* "I want to welcome the upstanding men splendidly, so they think that I am well off" (*Ps.* 167). Even practices like dancing or playing the *sambuca* were a form of the display of wealth: the possession of such a skill, rather like riding dressage nowadays, speaks to the time and money of the practitioner. The acquisition, use, and patronage of artistic productions also advertised Rome's status as an important power: she, too, would exercise the artistic prerogatives of a world-class state. The social elite followed suit in their own sphere, cultivating cosmopolitan artistic interests. In the second century the Roman state also seems to have become more interested in providing entertaining spectacles for the populace. The charge of the games to the aediles and the formalizing of positions for prominent citizens nearest the stage had not to do with political self-advertisement but with a policy of state sponsorship of the arts, as Gruen has argued.[19] The social elite as-

---

the symposium, where oral poetry was disseminated, could not serve the same function for written poetry; cf. ibid.: 74.

17. Cf. Cato *ORF* 8.111 (IV.4).

18. *ORF* 21.30 = Macr. 3.14.6, in full below (II.2). Corbeill 1996: 135–39 points out that in Latin literature invective associated with dancing is always connected to feasting. Cf. Cic. *Catil.* 2.23 (below, V.6), Hor. *Carm.* 3.6.21–26 (below, VIII.3).

19. Gruen 1992: 183–222. The *ludi* or 'public games' were a native Roman institution that changed significantly during this period. By the second century the funding structure

sumed their own brand of sponsorships, hosting Greek artisans and literary figures, and putting on shows at their dinner parties. One could say that as *ludi* were to the state, so were *convivia* to the social elite.

In these ways the social elite—who were after all behind the policies of the state—adopted versions of the aestheticism practiced by the state to define their own status. One more example concerns not the "privatization" of civic aestheticism but the instantiation of a civic cultural propensity. The Romans had a strong taste for the imposition of orderly form, be it on a battleline or in a centuriated field. The practical effectiveness of such arrangements only reinforced the moral propensity that created and promulgated them. The new aesthetic forms embraced by the social elite also afforded an opportunity for creating order. The neat design of a *peristylium* indicated a man of grace, harmony, precision—and control. The *convivium*, too, afforded an opportunity for creating order. Plutarch's Aemilius Paullus thought that much as an orderly battle-line increased the enemy's fear, so an orderly banquet increased a guest's pleasure.[20] The *exstructus* commonly associated with dinner tables, first attested in Lucilius, is perhaps to be taken not as 'heaped up' (*OLD* 1a) but as 'arranged' (*OLD* 2b), expressing not only quantity but also orderly display.[21]

Other aspects of the aesthetic articulation of their status by the social elite have to do with expressing in different ways symbolic privileges already accorded specifically to them. The Romans had a propensity for articulating political status in physical space. When a dozen lictors preceded a magistrate, he literally took up as much space as thirteen men. When, because of Cicero's intellectual superiority, his schoolmates yielded him the center space as they walked along (Plut. *Cic.* 2.1), they were modeling themselves

---

of such games had changed. From 200 on the Senate stopped specifying beforehand the sum to be spent and thereafter the games became more lavish. There was a *senatus consultum* passed in 182 to combat the practice, but it had little effect.

20. καὶ πρὸς τοὺς θαυμάζοντας τὴν ἐπιμέλειαν ἔλεγε, τῆς αὐτῆς εἶναι ψυχῆς παρατάξεώς τε προστῆναι καλῶς καὶ συμποσίου, τῆς μὲν ὅπως φοβερωτάτη τοῖς πολεμίοις, τοῦ δ' ὡς εὐχαριστότατον ᾖ τοῖς συνοῦσιν (28.9). Cf. *uulgo dictum ipsius ferebant et conuiuium instruere et ludos parare eiusdem esse, qui uincere bello sciret* "A saying of his was in circulation that setting a table and organizing games were part and parcel of being the sort of person who knew how to secure military victory" (Livy 45.32.11).

21. Lucilius has *nam sumptibus magnis | extructam ampliter atque <apte> cum accumbimus mensam* "When we reclined at a table arranged amply and <fittingly> at great expense" (442–43M, 470–71W, 451–52K). Cf. *mensae conquisitissimis epulis exstruebantur,* Cic. *Tusc.* 5.62; *caret epulis extructisque mensis,* Cic. *Sen.* 44; *mensas posuere ministri extructas dapibus,* Ov. *Met.* 11.120; and Cic. *Pis.* 67, 195–96.

into the *comitatus* of a great man.[22] The *convivium* provided opportunities for the same kind of articulation, with the added boon that that host himself had considerable control. At the dinners (δεῖπνα) that Aemilius Paullus hosted in Greece, he was careful to create a sense of social rank by arrangement (Plut. *Aem. Paul.* 28.7–8).[23] The structure of the Roman house, with the *dominus* framed by the *peristylium* behind him, served to highlight his rank and status in somewhat the same way as did sitting on the dais perched on the *sella curulis.*[24]

The new aesthetic practices also permitted the sponsor to strike a pose analogous to one that was already established in Roman society, that of the *patronus* 'patron.' In the early Republic *patroni* were members of wealthy families who, in return for financial and legal assistance, received political and even military services from poorer citizens, referred to in the reciprocal relationship as *clientes* 'clients.'[25] This arrangement provided a template for mapping other social relationships well into the Empire: emancipated slaves bore the relationship of *clientela* to their emancipators; generals acted as *patroni* of territories they had conquered; and local municipalities had their *patroni* at Rome to defend their interests.[26] The social arrangement of patron and client reflects a basic tenet of Roman culture, that giving placed recipients under obligation to the giver.[27] Lavish entertainment, whether of a few

22. The gods provide Jupiter the same courtesy: *solio tum Iuppiter aureo | surgit, caelicolae medium quem ad limina ducunt* (Verg. *Aen.* 10.116–17).

23. τάξιν δὲ καὶ κόσμον καὶ κατακλίσεις καὶ δεξιώσεις καὶ τὴν πρὸς ἕκαστον αὐτοῦ τῆς κατ' ἀξίαν τιμῆς καὶ φιλοφροσύνης αἴσθησιν οὕτως ἀκριβῆ καὶ πεφροντισμένην ἐνδεικνύμενος, ὥστε θαυμάζειν τοὺς Ἕλληνας, εἰ μηδὲ τὴν παιδιὰν ἄμοιρον ἀπολείπει σπουδῆς, ἀλλὰ τηλικαῦτα πράττων ἀνὴρ πράγματα καὶ τοῖς μικροῖς τὸ πρέπον ἀποδίδωσιν " . . . demonstrating such minute and thoughtful feeling for the arrangement, order, seating, and welcoming [of guests] and for paying to each one his due measure of honor and kindliness, that the Greeks were amazed that he devoted his energy even to recreation and that, though performing important tasks, he gave proper attention even to minor matters."

24. Cf. Wallace-Hadrill 1988, Edwards 1993: 150–53.

25. Cf. Wallace-Hadrill 1989, Drummond 1989.

26. On generals, cf. Badian 1958, Rich 1989. An example of the patron of a municipality is Q. Fabius Sanga, who provided *patrocinium* to the Allobroges, the Gallic tribe solicited by the Catilinarian conspiracy (Sal. *Cat.* 41.4). Sanga had probably inherited the *patrocinium* from Q. Fabius Maximus Allobrogicus, who, with Cn. Domitius, had annexed the tribe in 121. In the Empire this kind of patronage becomes something of an institution; cf. the *tabula patronorum* (*ILS* 6121) and Saller 1982.

27. This idea is captured by the well-known Roman religious attitude *do ut des* "I give (to you, god), that you may give (to me)," expressed, for example, in Iarbas's outburst when he discovers Dido has taken up with Aeneas: *et nunc ille Paris cum semiuiro comitatu | Maeonia mentum mitra crinemque madentem | subnexus rapto potitur: nos munera templis | quippe tuis ferimus famamque fouemus inanem* "And now that Paris, surrounded by men that are no men,

fellow potentates or middle-rung arrivistes, permitted the host to act as a kind of *patronus* and made his guests into *clientes* of a kind, under obligation to their host. This is not far from outright bribery, and in fact in the second century virtual bribery was rife, under the names *ambitus* 'canvasing' and *munificentia* 'munificence.'[28] Furthermore, the Roman nobleman was used to being on display. Clad distinctively and escorted by a retinue, he was described as *nobilis,* once literally 'knowable, notable, easy to know' or *clarus* 'bright' and so 'easy to see,' terms that, so to speak, picked him out of the crowd.[29] The *convivium* permitted analogous postures. Aemilius Paullus considered himself to be as much a part of the display as the dinner itself.[30] The *convivium* has thus appeared several times as the locus for the practice and dissemination of elite aestheticism. Its centrality should not be doubted, since it attracted attempts to restrict it. The *leges sumptuariae* that regulated the details of convivial practice do no more than extend to a new sphere of display the restrictions the Romans continually imposed on symbolic capital, from emblems of office to triumphs.[31]

Reciting Greek poetry or witty banter must also have served an important social function. Roman society was acutely hierarchical and carefully discriminated among its tiers with every semiotic means available to itself— modes of dress, personal retinues, death rituals, and so forth. Displays of lit-

bound around the chin with a Maeonian mitre, perfume dripping from his hair, took what he wants and keeps it: and what do I do? Bring gifts to your temples, foster belief that does no good" (Verg. *Aen.* 4.215–18).

28. Cf. Cato *ORF* 8.173; Lucilius 1220M, 1193W, 1244K *nequam aurum est; auris quouis uehementius ambit* "Gold is wicked, it goes about *(ambit)* our ears with more energy than anything else," with a pun on *aurum* 'gold' and *auris* 'ears,' and a reference to 'canvasing' *(ambitus);* Lucilius 1119–20M, 1194–95W, 1127–28K, *aurum atque ambitio specimen uirtutis uirique est | tantum habeas, tantum ipse sies, tantique habearis* "Gold and canvasing are the image of a man and his quality *(uirtus);* that's how much you can have, that's how much you can be, that's the maximum value you can have." The readings of the last verse are somewhat problematic; cf. Krenkel 1970 ad loc.

29. For the political implications of these terms, see Hellegouarc'h 1963: 224–29, 430–39.

30. ὁ δὲ καὶ τούτοις ἔχαιρε, <καὶ> ὅτι πολλῶν παρεσκευασμένων καὶ λαμπρῶν τὸ ἥδιστον αὐτὸς ἦν ἀπόλαυσμα καὶ θέαμα τοῖς παροῦσι "He was delighted by the fact that of all the splendid preparations the guests took the most enjoyment in the spectacle of Paullus himself" (Plut. *Aem. Paul.* 28.9).

31. From *sumptus* 'expense.' The first piece of such legislation was the *lex Orchia* of 181, which restricted the number of guests at dinner. In 161 the *lex Fannia* forbade ordinary dinners from costing more than ten *asses* and dinners on feast days from costing no more than one hundred. Hence Lucilius's jibe *Fanni centussis misellus* "Fannius's pathetic hundred" (1172M, 1241W, 1192K). The *lex Fannia* was replaced after 143 B.C. by the *lex Licinia,* whose strictures are not clear. Cf. Landolfi 1990: 52–67 ("Le legge suntuarie e la polemica sul dispendio simposiale"), Sauerwein 1970.

eracy and wittiness also served to hierarchize: among peers in an increasingly self-aware social class, they could foster new kinds of camaraderie that
distinguished that class from subordinate ones. Cato the Elder, as we saw,
disparages an opponent M. Caelius for such practices: he "occasionally re-
cited Greek verse" and "told jokes." [32] But Caelius and others like him can
hardly have thought they were taking up a low social role like that of the
*scurrae* or *mimi;* that (at this point in Roman history) would have been to
throw away their political capital altogether. Their sauciness, paradoxically,
must have been an attempt to define a new kind of propriety, a learned and
literate "us." In reciting Greek verse, Romans like Caelius may even have
been substituting something chic and new for an old practice. The custom
of reciting noble deeds at dinners had perhaps not survived to the second
century,[33] but some other practice may have developed in the meantime
that, whatever it was, looked old-fashioned by comparison to suave Greek
poetry or delicate dances, much as Pheidippides thought that, compared
to reciting Euripides, singing to the lyre was old-fashioned (Aristophanes
*Nubes* 1354ff.).[34] As for wittiness, Cicero's Antonius would be able to aver
that "there is no situation ('time of life') in which civilized humor *(lepos hu-
manitasque)* is inappropriate" *(de Orat.* 2.271).[35] A probable inference is that
humor had long since become a tool of social solidarity and exclusion.[36] But
within the social group so demarcated, displays of literacy and wittiness

32. Cf. n. 15.

33. According to Cicero, Cato mentioned in his *Origines* that his ancestors used to practice "singing to horn-music the praises and virtues of famous men" *(canere[nt] ad tibiam claro-
rum uirorum laudes atque uirtutes, Tusc.* 4.3). Cf. also *in conuiuiis pueri modesti ut cantarent carmina
antiqua, in quibus laudes erant maiorum et assa uoce et cum tibicine* (Varro *Vit. p. R.* 84 ap. Non.
Marc. p. 77M = 107L), *maiores natu in conuiuiis ad tibias egregia superiorum opera carmine con-
prehensa † pangebant, quo ad ea imitanda iuuentutem alacriorem redderent* (V. Max. 2.1.10). Cicero
quotes Cato as dating the practice to "many generations before his [= Cato's] time" *(multis
saeculis ante suam aetatem, Brut.* 75). See Landolfi 1990: 32–36, Momigliano 1960: 69–87.
On Latin sympotic poetry, cf. Gellius 19.9, Zorzetti 1990, Murray 1993.

34. Cf. Zorzetti 1990: 304–5: "We can easily explain the disappearance of the *carmina
convivalia.* Traditional music would have quickly been replaced by Hellenistic music after the
'theatralization': when a virtuoso arrives and starts exhibiting his professional repertoire, the
amateur rapidly loses his enthusiasm for the modest performances given at home among
friends." On Aristophanes, cf. the commentary of Dover ad loc., and Cameron 1995: 72.

35. *nam sicut quod apud Catonem est—qui multa rettulit, ex quibus a me exempli causa non
nulla ponuntur—per mihi scitum uidetur, C. Publicium solitum dicere "P. Mummium cuiusuis temporis hominem esse," sic profecto se res habet, nullum ut sit uitae tempus, in quo non deceat leporem
humanitatemque uersari (de Orat.* 2.271). On *lepos* as 'humor' (the subject of this part of *de Oratore),* cf. below, VI.3.

36. Cf. Corbeill 1996, David 1983: 316–21.

could also serve as a vehicle of competition. Lucilius parodied Scipio Ae-milianus's attempts to seem "more clever than everyone else" by using certain grammatical forms.[37] Wit and humor, in effect, are proxy politics: in both, the elite distinguished themselves from the less privileged even as they competed fiercely with each other.

## I.3. The Paradoxical Semiotics of Elite Aestheticism

In short, in the second century the social elite adopted and augmented, as a way of defining its own position in society, aesthetic practices that had been, in general, originated by the state as a means of displaying civic ideals. That expansion of the symbolic grammar produced a keen paradox. On the one hand, the new practices sent social and political messages entirely in accord with those the elite were already sending. On the other hand, the new practices were patently different. It might take the same sort of mind to set a table and win a war, but setting a table, after all, is not winning a war. Witty banter and reciting poetry might build social solidarity, but they were hardly the marriages, financial arrangements, or shared political interests that really did produce such unity as the social elite ever attained. Banter and poetry might serve as proxy politics, but a *diadema* won at table was no quaestorship. This much is obvious, but it has important consequences. If by "aestheticism" we mean an interest in the articulation of personal status by aesthetic means, it is probably safe to say that before the second century "aestheticism" standardly implied "social valuelessness." In Plautus, at least, aestheticism is the province of courtesans and lovesick youth (cf. I.5, I.9); it would be strained to read the language of social performance in Plautine comedy as ironic inversion of an established elite evaluative language.[38] "Social worth," on the other hand, was ideologically coextensive with a variety of ideas, such as "manliness," "glory," and "wealth," on which social distinction largely depended. With the widespread adoption of aestheticizing practices as a means of elite social distinction, Roman culture had created a new conceptual category that, paradoxically, paired pragmatic opposites as semiotic parifunctionals. That is, "aestheticism" and (say) "military glory," one of which was based on mere accumulation and the other on real accomplishment, now both were symbols of social value. We might represent this diagrammatically. Formerly "aestheticism" was wholly contained by "social valuelessness" (fig. 1):

37. Treated below, III.2.
38. Terence is a different matter: his use of the language of social performance reflects both the "aestheticizing" of the language (cf. IV.5) and its stereotyped use by Plautus (cf. IV.5 n. 35).

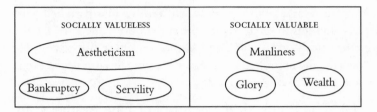

In the second century a new possibility was created by the intrusion of "aestheticism" into "social value" (fig. 2):

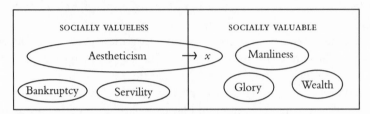

## I.4. Elite Aestheticism and the Crisis of Vocabulary

This rearrangement created a crisis of vocabulary. The problem is illustrated by the suppleness of Plutarch's formulation παρατάξεώς τε προστῆναι καλῶς καὶ συμποσίου "to preside over both battle-line and symposium beautifully" (above, n. 20), in which καλῶς effortlessly bridges the military and the aesthetic. The Roman vocabulary did not tend to traject the "aesthetic" with "manliness," "glory," or "wealth." Livy uses no adverb in representing the same idea (45.32.11, n. 20 above).

To solve the problem, the Romans drew from two sources. Aemilius Paullus's attempt to rationalize his convivial practices in terms of military prowess was probably matched by attempts to stretch "down" over such practices approbative vocabulary associated with the other, weightier semiotic practices. *Ornare*, for example, originally 'arrange, put in order, equip' *(*ordnare)*, was used of the "decoration" of temples or festal places by the aediles, or of correlative practices, as in Lucilius's *Romanis ludis forus olim ornatus lucernis* "the forum betimes arrayed with light during the Roman games" (146M, 148WK).[39] This use continues to the late Republic (*ludis ipsis Romanis foro ornato*, Cic. *Ver.* 2.1.141), but by then *ornare* has expanded to include the decoration of private spaces with artwork (*uillas ornaturus*, Cic. *Ver.* 2.2.183; *in uillam Luculli . . . omni apparatu uenustatis ornatam*, Cic. *Hort.* fr. 2). This latter use, I suggest, should be dated to the second century. *Honestus*, originally 'honorable,' shaded not only into 'wealthy' (cf. *TLL* s.v. 1B) but into 'attractive,' applied not only to persons who were attrac-

39. Cf. *initium . . . fori ornandi* (Livy 9.40.16).

tive by virtue of being wealthy (and were therefore 'honorable'), but to attractive items that were the prerogative of the wealthy (*Sicyonia . . . honesta* "fine Sicyonian shoes," Lucil. 1161M, 1157W, 1181K).[40] *Decus,* etymologically 'what is befitting' and then 'esteem, glory' (*OLD* 1), came to describe other 'marks of distinction,' such as material objects, that redounded to the 'glory' of their owner (*OLD* 4; cf. *arma non supellectilem decori esse* "the true ornament is a weapon, not furniture," Sal. *Jug.* 85.40). The *convivium* lent itself to being described as a display of wealth, which explains Lucilius's *ampliter* above. In Lucilius's formulation *pulchre inuitati acceptique benigne* "hosted beautifully, welcomed generously" (1269M, 595W, 1287K), a dinner is perhaps represented in the terms appropriate to a patron, viz., *benignus* 'liberal, generous.'[41] Cicero has *ornare magnifice . . . conuiuium* (*Quinct.* 93, below V.4), combining images of wealth *(magnifice)* and order *(ornare).*

These "downward" extensions often have apparent precedents in the language of Roman comedy,[42] and to examine them in further detail here would lead to the question whether those comic uses are nonce innovations based on the language of Greek New Comedy and not anchored in social change.[43] What is important, by the late Republic the language of "wealth" and "honor" has expanded to include private refinements, and that pattern probably resulted from the conceptual rearrangement of the second century. This stretching of language "down" into new territory is matched by another stretch "up" into the same territory—a stretch whose ideological reverberations are the focus of this book. While certain aspects of the new aestheticism might have lent themselves to description in the language of "wealth" or "order," other aspects of those new semiotic practices—witty banter, delicate gesture, jovial spirits—did not. To describe these aspects, pre-existing aesthetic language was stretched "up." Lexemes such as *bell(us), uenust(us), lep(idus),* and *facet(us),* which could serve as *voces propriae* for the aesthetic standards of comic characters, come to describe semiotic acts of social and political consequence. The lexemes were, so to speak, emancipated from their original status. Unlike the language of "wealth," "order,"

---

40. *et pedibus laeua Sicyonia demit honesta.* Possibly *honesta* refers to *laeua* 'left [hand].'

41. The sense of *inuitati* here is 'provided with hospitality' (*OLD* 2, Nonius p. 321.10). The only time *benigne* appears in connection with a dinner in Plautus (*Mil.* 739) is in the course of a polite and gentlemanly discussion where the dinner is treated as a function of ξενία.

42. For example, Plautus has *prandium ornari* "for breakfast to be set out" (*Rud.* 141) and Terence *eunuchus honestust* "he's a beautiful eunuch" (*Eu.* 474; in his commentary Donatus glosses *honestus* as *pulcher*).

43. For example, with Plautus's *prandium ornare,* cf. τοὔψον . . . σκευάζετ' (Alex. 49.1–2, cf. 141.10–11, 149.6–7, Dionys. Com. 2.6–8, Nicom. Com. 1.9–11), τὸ δεῖπνον . . . συσκεύαζε (Ar. *Vesp.* 1251, cf. *Eccl.* 1147), σκεύαζε . . . τοὐψάριον (Anaxil. 28–29.2).

etc., whose shifts are harder to trace, these lexemes seem to have been sufficiently deformed by the effort to unite aestheticism with social value that
by the late Republic they had all acquired distinctly new connotations and
sometimes new meanings altogether. Since this language describes acts of social consequence, at the same time often implying that those acts are not as
"real" as others, I refer to it as "the language of social performance,"[44] since
"performance" has the same ambiguities in English. I examine the lexemes
severally in the following sections, describing their semantic structure and
the changes they seem to have undergone in response to the social changes
of the second century B.C.

## I.5. *Elegan(s)* and the Display of Status

A clear example of "upward stretch" is *elegan(s)*.[45] *Elegans* is formed as if it
were the participle of *\*ēlegāre,* a verb related to *eligere* 'extract, select,' *legere*
'choose, gather.'[46] In the absence of attestations, the semantics of *\*ēlegāre*
may be surmised by examining parallel formations. The addition of the suffix *-āre* to a root, often in combination with a preverb, may modify the semantics of a root by adding an element of duration, resultativity, or thor-
oughness, as the following table suggests:[47]

| Root | Primary | Compound in *-āre* | Semantics of Compound as Derived from Primary |
|---|---|---|---|
| **\*kub–** | *accumbere* 'lie down' | *accubāre* 'lie' | 'stay lying down' |
| **\*kap–** | *capere* 'take' | | |
| | *occipere* 'begin' | *occupāre* 'seize, appropriate' | 'take permanently, thoroughly' |
| **\*deuk–** | *dūcere* 'lead' | | |
| | *ēdūcere* 'lead out' | *ēducāre* 'tend, nurture' | 'continue to lead out with an eye to result' |

44. By the language of social performance, I mean a set of lexemes as manifestations of
a particular cultural model; cf. Intro. p. 10 and II.1, II.3.

45. For this notation, cf. Intro. n. 6. For another survey of the spheres of reference of
*elegan(s),* cf. Monteil 1964: 193–220.

46. Cf. W-H, E-M s.v.

47. For a list of such derivatives, see LHS I §225c.

| **\*bhlīg-** | *-flīgere* | *prōflīgāre* | |
| | 'knock' | 'defeat' | 'knock down completely' |
| **\*lab-** | *labī* | *labāre* | |
| | 'slip' | 'totter' | 'continue to slip' |

*\*Ēlegāre* ought therefore to have meant something like 'carefully choose,' 'choose with a careful eye to result,' or even 'constantly make discriminations.' The derivative *elegans* would not be far in sense from English "choosy." Indeed *elegan(s)* is several times explicitly associated with "economy" or "discrimination."[48] We can add one more element to the mix. For its whole life, and certainly in its earliest attestations, *elegan(s)* is especially connected to aesthetic choices, such as personal comportment or artwork, so that for our purposes we may consider that, too, part of the lexeme's meaning. We may model the lexeme as follows (fig. 3):

**The Semantic Structure of *Elegan(s)***

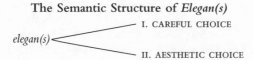

The history of *elegan(s)* is the history of the social construction of "careful aesthetic choice." *Elegan(s)* in Plautus always has to do with personal comportment and is always pejorative. "Love," says Charinus in the *Mercator*, "brings on every vice, worry, sickness, and too much prissiness *(nimiaque elegantia)*."[49] *Elegans* appears in a vituperative litany applied to a lover:

> *blandiloquentulus, harpago, mendax,*
> *cuppes, auarus, elegans, despoliator,*
> *latebricolarum hominum corruptor*

> smooth-talker, grabber, liar,
> gluttonous, greedy, persnickety, plunderer,
> ruiner of men into back-alley lurkers

> (*Trin.* 239a–240a)

---

48. *Crassus erat elegantium parcissimus, Scaeuola parcorum elegantissimus,* Cic. *Brut.* 148 (of personal, not rhetorical, style); *nam sic ut in epularum apparatu a magnificentia recedens non se parcum solum sed etiam elegantem uideri uolet, et eliget quibus utatur,* Cic. *Or.* 83; *modicoque et eleganti imperio percarus fuit,* Sal. *Hist.* 1.94; *elegans, non magnificus, splendidus, non sumptuosus,* Nepos *Att.* 13.5. Cf. below, III.6.

49. *nam amorem haec cuncta uitia sectari solent,* | *cura, aegritudo nimiaque elegantia* (Pl. *Mer.* 18–19).

Other examples in Plautus also refer to similar "prissiness" or even "fastid-
iousness."[50] Cato in his *carmen de moribus* grouped the *elegan(s)* person with
other socially useless persons: *auaritiam omnia uitia habere putabant: sumptuosus
cupidus elegans uitiosus inritus qui habebatur, is laudabatur* "[Our elders] thought
stinginess was the root of all vices. By that they meant the extravagant,
lustful, fussy *(elegans)*, depraved, or useless person" (*Carm. mor.* fr. 1 = Gel.
11.2.2).[51] Nor is *elegan(s)* entirely complimentary in Terence. Parmeno uses
it for the enthrallment of callow youth, who are convinced that there is
nothing "more elegant" than dinner with courtesans.[52] Chremes rebukes his
too-fastidious son by saying *heia ut elegans est!* "My, my, what fine tastes he
has!" (*Hau.* 1063).[53] Gnatho, a parasite, uses *elegan(s)* to flatter the *miles gloriosus* Thraso by attributing the quality to the king who selected Thraso as a
dinner partner.[54]

By the late Republic, however, *elegan(s)* is distinctly ameliorative, as Gel-

50. *nec pol profecto quisquam sine grandi malo | praequam res patitur studuit elegantiae* "And, I
tell you, no one has ever spent beyond his means in order to be *chic* without great ill com-
ing of it," *Mer.* 22–23); *ergo iste metus me macerat, quod ille fastidiosust, | ne oculi eiius senten-
tiam mutent, ubi uiderit me, | atque eiius elegantia meam extemplo speciem spernat* "And so because
he's persnickety, I'm consumed with fear that when he sees me, his eyes will change his mind,
and his precious taste will immediately reject the sight of me," *Mil.* 1233–35, spoken by
Acroteleutium of the discriminating taste of Pyrgopolynices; cf. *fastidiosus*. The line *numquam unius me comparaui seruire elegantiam* "I have never set myself up as the servant of one
man's taste" (Sex. Turpilius *pall.* 100), as Ribbeck (*CRF*[3] p. 111) imagines, is probably spoken by a *meretrix;* on the sense of *comparare* here, cf. Nonius 256.9.
  51. For the puzzling *is laudabatur* of the text, Baehrens read *is audiebat auarus* "He was
said to be greedy"; others interpret "was praiseworthy [by comparison]." Baehren's instinct,
to see *auarus* as subsuming the following list of vices, was correct but does not require emendation. *Laudare* simply has here its antique meaning 'call': cf. *'laudare' significat prisca lingua
nominare appellareque. sic in actionibus ciuilibus auctor 'laudari' dicitur, quod est nominari* "In the
ancient language *laudare* means 'name' and 'call,' as in civil actions, where *laudare* is said of
bail-givers, meaning they are 'named'," Gel. 2.6.16.
  52. *nil uidetur mundius, | nec magis compositum quicquam nec magis elegans | quam cum ama-
tore cenam quom ligurriunt* "Nothing seems cleaner, better put together, or more elegant [to
youths] than when [courtesans] nibble a dinner with a lover" (*Eu.* 934–36).
  53. Cf. Chaerea's keen eye for girls: *quom ipsus me noris quam elegans formarum spectator siem*
(*Eu.* 566).
  54. Thraso represents himself as the king's confidant, to which Gnatho replies *hui | regem
elegantem narras* "You're talking one tasteful king!" (*Eu.* 407–8). Gnatho also ironically attributes *elegantia* to Thraso at the play's end: when Thraso says, "I've never yet been the sort
of person that everyone didn't love dearly" *(numquam etiam fui usquam quin me amarent omnes
plurimum)*, Gnatho asserts, "Didn't I tell you he has the good taste of Attica?" (*dixin ego in hoc
esse uobis Atticam elegantiam?* 1093). Terence often uses the language of social performance as
cloying flattery; cf. below, IV.5.

lius noticed (11.2.3),[55] and the range of referents is different.[56] When Cicero mocks Piso's cultural crudeness, he says *nihil apud hunc lautum, nihil
elegans, nihil exquisitum* "At Piso's there is nothing fine, nothing elegant,
nothing choice" (*Pis.* 67), where the qualities at issue are plainly represented
as the proper possession of aristocrats.[57] *Elegantia* was de rigueur at the elite
table: *delectant etiam magnifici apparatus uitaeque cultus cum elegantia et copia*
"People enjoy grand displays and a high life of discrimination and abundance" (Cic. *Off.* 1.25). So in Cicero's description of a dinner, "I received
my refined guests *(lautiores)* tastefully *(eleganter)*."[58] Paetus is banteringly assured that Cicero would make a better dinner companion than Balbus, since
Cicero can offer "a pair of ears just as discriminating" (*auris ad te adferam non
minus elegantis, Fam.* 9.19.2). *Elegan(s)* can be applied to the collection and
display of artwork, or to the artwork itself. The position of *elegan(s)* as nearly
a *vox propria* in that connection is assured by Cicero's use of it as a compliment to Gallus, with whose taste in a specific instance he has some disagreement.[59] All of these referents described by *elegan(s)* involve "careful
aesthetic choices" made specifically by members of the elite in aestheticiz-

55. *ex quibus uerbis apparet "elegantem" dictum antiquitus non ab ingenii elegantia, sed qui nimis
lecto amoenoque cultu uictuque esset.*

56. *Elegan(s)* has by this time also acquired a "passive" sense, describing not those who
exercise careful aesthetic choice but the products that exhibit it. The shift can be compared
to that of *honestus,* which passed from 'honorable' to 'characteristic of the honorable person,'
and hence 'attractive' (cf. I.4): *elegan(s),* first 'a person who exercises careful aesthetic choice,'
came to describe 'what is characteristic of persons who exercise careful aesthetic choice.'

57. For the association of *lautus* with wealth, and therefore the social elite, cf. *prope diem
uideo bonorum, id est lautorum et locupletum, urbem refertam fore* (Cic. *Att.* 8.1.3), *lauta et copiosa
patrimonia* (Cic. *Rab. Post.* 38). *Lautus* could mean 'respectable' without reference to cash:
helping out the needy by *opera* 'work' as opposed to *pecunia* 'cash' is *lautior ac splendidior et
uiro forti claroque dignior* (*Off.* 2.52); of L. Quinctius, Cicero says, *quis eum umquam non modo
in patroni sed in lautioris aduocati loco uiderat?* "Who ever saw him in the role of a reasonably
respectable advocate—to say nothing of a patron?" (*Clu.* 110).

58. *nam lautiores eleganter accepi, quid multa? homines uisi sumus (Att.* 13.52.2); the *lautiores*
are the better freedmen among Caesar's retinue. (*Homines uisi sumus,* lit. "We seemed men,"
probably means "I looked like a man of the world" T-P = "I showed I knew how to live"
SB; T-P also suggest the possibility "Caesar and I acted on good terms.") In another example
Cicero was getting good enough at giving dinner parties that he dared to invite Verrius and
Camillus, men of 'refinement' *(munditia)* and 'taste' *(elegantia, Fam.* 9.20.2, tr. T-P).

59. *plane enim intellego te non modo studio sed etiam amore usum quae te delectarint, hominem,
ut ego semper iudicaui, in omni iudicio elegantissimum, quae me digna putaris, coemisse* (*Fam.* 7.23.1),
cf. *Att.* 1.8.2 (of Atticus's taste in decorating Cicero's villa), *Q. fr.* 3.7.7 (of Quintus's estate
at Arcanum), *Ver.* 2.2.83 (of bronze furniture). On the import of decorative schemes and
Cicero's appreciation thereof, cf. Leen 1991, Bartman 1994.

ing practices that displayed their social identity. The pleasant and cultured conversation Cicero and Paetus could have had is certainly to be included among such practices: conversation was an important means of sustaining *amicitia*.[60]

I suggest that the changes in *elegan(s)* over time be attributed to the social changes of the second century. With aestheticism on the rise as a means of expressing social identity, the social construction of "careful aesthetic choice" changed, and this shift in ideological terrain took *elegan(s)* with it, altering its tone and applying it to the set of the referents with which it continued to be associated in the late Republic.[61] In short, in the presence of a social model that took a dim view of careful aesthetic choice, *elegan(s)* had pejorative connotations, and vice-versa, for a model that approved of careful aesthetic choice. Here, then, is an instance of the principle I sketched out in the introduction, that the observed distribution of the lexeme is a function not only of its native semantics but of the interaction of those semantics with prevailing cultural models. Those models acted as a kind of filter that determines the referents of a lexeme (fig. 4):

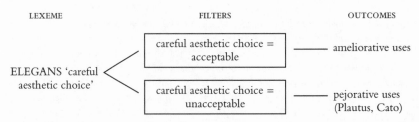

The English *nice* presents a comparable case: from the Old French *nice, nisce,* deriving ultimately from Latin *nescius* 'ignorant,' in its earliest attestations it meant 'foolish' (*OED* 1) and probably acquired its current meanings through the sense of 'foppish, delicate' (*OED* 7a, cf. 4d), which was once considered as a species of 'foolish.'[62]

---

60. Cf. *accedat huc suauitas quaedam oportet sermonum atque morum, haudquaquam mediocre condimentum amicitiae* "[Friendship] must also have a kind of sweetness expressed in conversations and conduct, which is no small condiment in friendships" (*Amic.* 66). Cf. also *Fam.* 9.24.3, with Dyck 1996: 309–10.

61. Cf. Monteil 1964: 199, "Que l'hellénisme ait finalement réussi à triompher à Rome est un fait. Si l'histoire de *ēlegans* est liée, au moins en partie, au destin de l'hellénisme, le triomphe de ce dernier devait entraîner le triomphe de l'acception laudative de *ēlegans, ēlegantia.*"

62. Cf. *OED* s.v. "They seiden he was a fool . . . and that they sien neuere so nice a man" (Lovelich *Grail* 42.73); "All the Roman Youth that had . . . grown effeminate with nice living, joined and favoured Catiline" (Ozell *Vertot's Rom. Rep.* 2.12.221).

This shift in *elegan(s)* might be connected either with the broadening civic aestheticism of the second century or with the elite version thereof. But one later application has specifically to do with elite self-definition. Cicero often uses *elegan(s)* in connection to systematic knowledge. *Elegantia doctrinae* (*de Orat.* 1.5) are the higher intellectual arts, from which Quintus thinks oratory, a mere "knack," is disjunct (cf. VI.1). There was a time philosophy had only substance and rhetoric had only style: "The learned could not present their ideas to the people, whereas orators lacked intellectual sophistication *(elegans doctrina)*."[63] The connection of systematic knowledge to social class is made clear by a description of C. Sulpicius Gallus, an accomplished astronomer, who was "a man of distinction and taste in other fields (than oratory)" (*reliquis rebus ornatus atque elegans, Brut.* 78, tr. Douglas). In the second century also, intellectual accomplishment probably began to serve as a mark of elite distinction,[64] and the origins of this use of *elegan(s)* should perhaps also be traced to that period. In any case the associations of *elegan(s)* with elite behavior were such that by the late Republic it could be applied to careful choices of action, "neat" solutions to a difficulty, in virtually an ethical sense.[65]

63. *ita et doctis eloquentia popularis et disertis elegans doctrina defuit* (*Or.* 13).

64. On the status of intellectual life in the late Republic, cf. Rawson 1985.

65. Cicero writes to Appius Claudius Pulcher of a difficult situation, *nam quod ad legatos attinet, quid a me fieri potuit aut elegantius aut iustius quam ut sumptus egentissimarum ciuitatum minuerem sine ulla imminutione dignitatis tuae, praesertim ipsis ciuitatibus postulantibus?* "As far as the legates, what could I have done more properly *(elegantius)* or more justly *(iustius)* than to reduce the tax burden of the neediest municipalities without damaging your stature, particularly when the request came from the municipalities themselves?" (*Fam.* 3.8.2). Cicero, as governor of Cilicia, had rescinded a deputation to the senate which was intended to praise Claudius's just-ended administration; Cicero "had given notice that he would not permit excessive expense grants" (SB ad *Fam.* 3.10.6). Cf. also *Ver.* 2.3.140 (ironic), *Caec.* 57, *Phil.* 13.38–39, ad *Brut.* 23.1, perhaps *uitaeque elegantissimae uerissimis laudibus, Brut.* 295; also Livy 37.1.7. *Elegan(s)* in this "moral" capacity could refer not only to courses of action deliberately taken but also to those deliberately avoided. It was applied to those who were "careful" in their choice of contacts: in the complex web of shifting alliances that was late Republican politics, the *elegans* person had managed to emerge with his hands clean. Cicero lauds the jurors in the *pro Sulla* for their "discrimination and carefulness" *(elegantia et integritas)*, meaning they had not become involved with any Catilinarian conspirators (*Sul.* 79). Plancius had managed to keep his hands clean: *O adulescentiam traductam eleganter, cui quidem cum quod licuerit obiciatur, tamen id ipsum falsum reperiatur!* "It is youth conducted very properly *(eleganter)* indeed in which accusations of actions that were permissible turn out to be groundless!" (*Planc.* 31; "eleganter = honeste, wie unser sauber = sittlich," Köpke 1873 ad loc.); cf. *Scaur.* 15, Livy 35.31.14, *magnae auctoritatis ob uitam eleganter actam,* Holden 1881 ad *Planc.* 31. Both senses, avoidance of trouble and praiseworthy choice, perhaps figure in Cicero's application of *elegantia* to the conduct of his governorship, when he calls Atticus

## I.6. *Venust(us)* and the Erotics of Artfulness

The meaning of *venust(us)* also changed in the second century as a result of social shifts. To appreciate these shifts rather more detail about the early semantic history of the lexeme is required than was of *elegan(s)*. *Venust(us)* derives from \*wenH-, an old Indo-European root for 'desire.'[66] The noun \*wenos 'desire' (later the goddess *Venus*)[67] yielded an adjective \*wenosto- that must have originally meant 'desirous' or 'desirable,' that is, describing "celui ou celle qui est doué de, qui possède ou inspire la *uenus*."[68] This is quite in accord with the semantics of the \*-to- suffix, which express "l'accomplissement de la notion dans l'object."[69] The noun and adjective functioned as a part of the large family of derivatives of \*wenH-, which in-

---

"praiser of my care and discrimination" (*laudator integritatis et elegantiae nostrae, Att.* 6.2.8), cf. *Att.* 5.20.6. Cf. also *est etiam quiete et pure atque eleganter actae aetatis placida ac lenis senectus* "A life led serenely, cleanly, and tastefully makes for a peaceful and mild old age" (*Sen.* 13), in reference to the scholarly withdrawal of Plato and Isocrates, contrasted with public lives like Scipio's.

66. \*wenH- > Skt. **vánati** 'he desires,' **vánaḥ** 'desire,' suffixed zero-grade \*wn̥H-sko- in OHG **wunscen**, NE **wish**, cf. Pok. 1. *u̯en-* 1146, W-H, E-M s.v. R. Schilling 1954: 30–59 sees in *uenus* a specifically Roman (i.e., not IE) sense 'charme religieux' and the derivational family as reflecting magic in different ways. It is, however, not necessary to assume such a meaning to explain the oldest instances, for which postulating a simple 'desire' is more economical; to say the root semantics need specifically reflect the religious applications of a word is to confound *Sinn* with *Bedeutung* (cf. Ernout 1957: 89). *Venerari* 'adore' (cf. n. 70), which is important to establishing Schilling's claims, is not proof of a special "magical sense" in the root. Rather, unlike other derivates of *uenus* (cf. n. 70), it resisted being "secularized" not because it retained special "magical" meaning but because it was not felt to correspond to some "secular" activity, as were *uenia* and other originally (?) religious terms like *respondere* ('repeat a solemn assertion [in oath-taking]' > 'answer, respond'; cf. Ulp. *dig.* 45.1.1.1, on the *sponsio*), *contemplor* ('observe the ritually demarcated space' > 'contemplate'), *considerare* ('observe the stars' > 'consider'), or *credere* ('give magical power to' > 'believe'; for these connections of *credere*, cf. W-H s.v. with bibliography). Curiously Schilling's treatment does not take account of *uenustus*, which is the best-attested member of the family outside of the goddess's name.

67. Whether under the influence of Ἀφροδίτη specifically or that of other divinized feminine abstracts (*Fides, Spes, Salus, Ops*, etc.), the personification of *uenus* typically led to the feminizing of the noun (not always: *Venerem igitur almum adorans | siue femina siue mas est,* Laev. *poet.* 26; Macr. 3.8.3); see Monteil 1964, Schilling 1954: 59–64. Nouns in *-us/-er-* < \*-os/-es- are otherwise always neuter, cf. *onus, genus*. *Cupido*, though it appears also as a feminine, was apparently masculinized in a comparable way, perhaps under the influence of Eros or Priapus; nouns in *-ido/-idinis* are otherwise feminine: cf. *crepido, cupido, formido, grauido* (alt. of *grauedo*), *libido*.

68. Ernout 1957: 106.

69. M. E. Benveniste apud Monteil 1964: 112.

cluded *uēnārī* 'hunt,' *uenia* 'indulgence,' *uenēnum* 'poison,' and *uenerārī* 'do reverence,' and probably a verb **\*\*uenere* 'desire.'[70] This coherent family was disrupted probably by the ouster of that verb by a new word for 'desire,' *cupere.*[71] With the death of **\*\*uenere*, the derivatives of *\*wen-* became a less

70. *Vēnārī* 'hunt' may be from a lengthened grade *\*wēnH-* (viz., 'to continue to desire,' cf. *cēlāre* 'keep hidden' vs. *\*kĕl-* in *occultus*).

*Venia* 'indulgence, forgiveness' is *\*wen-yā*, originally the '(good) will' of a superior party, especially of the gods. Cf. *facilius si qui pius est a dis supplicans, | quam qui scelestust, inueniet ueniam sibi* (Pl. *Rud.* 26–27), *ueniam irarum caelestium finemque pesti exposcunt* (Livy 3.7.8). The rare *heries*, preserved in *heriem Iunonis* (Gel. 13.23.2) and *her<i>em Martiam* (Paul. Fest. 89 Lindsay), is the equivalent formation with the root *\*her-*, which provides the verb 'desire' in Oscan and Umbrian, e.g., O. **herest** 'uolet,' Umbr. **heri** 'uult.' A similar formation is attested in Oscan: *heriam suvam* in a curse tablet = 'arbitrium suum, uim suam' (Buck 1974 no. 19.1). This same root provides Italic equivalents for *Venus*, i.e., **Herentateí Herukinaí,** Buck (1928) 41 = *Veneri Erycinae* whose Capitoline temple was dedicated in 217. Paelignian has a nom. **Herentas** (*CLE* 17.7). On the further connections of *\*her-* in Italic, v. Nussbaum 1976.

*Venēnum* is from an original *\*wen-es-nom,* perhaps 'love potion.'

The exact morphological parallels to *uenerārī* (sometimes *uenerāre* in Plautus), from neuter *s*-stems, fall into two groups, (a.) those that mean 'cause to have' (e.g., *funerāre* 'cause [one] to have [one's] funeral rites,' *onerāre* 'cause to have a burden,' *munerārī* 'cause to have a gift,' c. acc. pers.) and (b.) those that mean 'cause to be' (e.g., *faenerārī* 'cause to be interest-bearing [*faenus*], lend out at interest,' *munerārī* 'cause to be a gift to,' c. dat. pers., *ponderāre* 'cause to have a fixed weight [*pondus*]'). *Venerārī* belongs to the former group, 'cause [a god] to have a desire.' In Republican Latin the object is always a god (cf. Schilling 1954: 33–38) and frequently has a complementary clause, e.g., *deos deasque ueneror, qui hanc urbem colunt, | ut quod de mea re huc ueni rite uenerim* (Pl. *Poen.* 950–51), cf. Pl. *Rud.* 257, *Trin.* 40–42, Cic. *Catil.* 2.29, Livy 8.9.7. Having come to be identified with the ritual actions that accompanied requests for divine favor (cf. *date mi huc stactam atque ignem in aram, ut uenerem Lucinam meam,* Pl. *Truc.* 476), the verb acquired the meaning 'adore, reverence.' For an equivalent development, cf. *\*gʷhedh-* 'ask, pray,' source of Germanic *bitten,* Eng. *bid;* Mid. Eng. *bede* 'prayer' was transferred to the item that symbolized the prayer, viz., the *bead* of a rosary. The derivatives of *\*wen-* are also treated by Schilling 1954: 30–59.

**\*\*Venere* is a putative form (the double asterisk indicates a reconstruction arrived at not by the comparative method proper, but by other methods of inference; see Sihler 1995: 34). The death of **\*\*uenere* will have been abetted by *\*gʷem-* 'come,' which yielded the Latin *uenīre,* putatively homophonous with *\*uenere* in the subjunctive: cf. such forms as *aduenat* (Pl. *Ps.* 1030), *euenat* (Enn. *scen.* 183 Jocelyn *et alias*), *peruenat* (Pl. *Rud.* 626, cf. *Trin.* 93); cf. Meillet-Vendreyes 1948 §431 "En latin archaïque, les subjunctifs *aduenat* (etc.) . . . représentent une formation indépendante des présents." For a parallel cf. the loss of *horior* (ἅπαξ in Enn. *Ann.* 16.424 Skutsch) to the frequentative *hortor,* possibly, as E-M observe, because of *orior.* The similarity of *Venus* and *uenire* was felt by the ancients, as revealed in their incorrect etymologizing: *quae autem dea ad res omnes ueniret, Venerem nostri nominauerunt,* Cic. *N.D.* 1.69, cf. 3.62, Arnobius 3.33.

71. Related to L. *cuppēs (cūpēs)* 'fond of delicacies,' Sabine *cuprum* (Var. *L.L.* 5.159, cf. W-H s.v. *cupiō*), OIr. **accobor** (< *\*kŭpro-*) 'a wish,' Skt. **kúpya-** 'is excited.' For another

transparently related family and drifted off in their own directions. *we-nosto- seems to have drifted, by way of 'desirable,'[72] into 'attractive,' since the referents of 'desirable' and 'attractive' are, for obvious reasons, largely coextensive. This drift of *wenosto- away from even *wenos is suggested by the existence of the abstract *uenustas*. *Venustas* was probably formed when some semantic distance had developed between the adjective and its original noun *uenus*, much as *honestas* was formed when some semantic distance had developed between *honestus* and *honos*.[73]

In the oldest instances of *uenust(us)*, in Plautine comedy, it is not always possible to say if the heart of the lexeme is 'attractive' or 'desirable.'[74] Whatever the quality was exactly, it is virtually always erotic and generally applied to women. The comment *ut uenusta es* "How attractive [or 'desirable'] you are!" (Pl. *Mos.* 182) is addressed to a courtesan who is trying on a new dress. Another courtesan declares that unless women spend considerable money on themselves, they are *insulsus* 'saltless; dull, boring' and *inuenustus* 'unattractive' or 'undesirable' (Pl. *Poen.* 246). When a *senex lepidus* promises that he can provide much *uenustas* (Pl. *Mil.* 651), he means "attractive behavior that secures the right atmosphere for love": he never hacks up phlegm balls, or flirts with the escorts of other guests, or gets involved in quarrels at the table, instead "devot[ing himself] at table to desire, and love, and charm" (*Venerem, amorem, amoenitatemque accubans exerceo, Mil.* 656). A rendering as 'charming' or 'attractive' *(OLD)* is not out of place, but sexuality is always overt, as not in such translations, and is easily reinvigorated by punning off

---

treatment of *uenus* and *cupido*, see Ernout 1957: 87–111 = *Revue de Philologie* 3. ser. 30 (1956): 7–27.

72. More expansively, the transitivity of *cupere* seems to have been imputed to its derivatives (hence *cupido* 'desire,' not 'desirability'), whereas the loss of a verb in the *wenH-group and the voice ambiguity of its verbal abstract *wenH-o/es- allowed the derivatives of the group to become "passive," i.e., 'desirable.' (I am indebted to Alan Nussbaum for formulating the matter this way for me.)

73. The original noun-adjective pair was *honos ~ honestus*. The formation of a new abstract *honestas* from the adjective was encouraged by the fact that either *honor* or *honestus* or both had acquired sufficiently idiomatic meanings. *Honor* became associated with particular conditions or offices, that is to say, instantiations of *honor* (cf. *cursus honorum*), depriving *honestus* of an abstract. *Honestus* may also have acquired a sense not in *honor*: *honestus* was associated with wealth and social station (cf. supra, I.4), and further with the moral ideas appropriate to the upper classes (so *honestas* as 'moral rectitude,' sometimes used by Cicero to render τὸ καλόν, cf. below, III.4.2). The acquired sense of *honestus* could have increased the pressure to form a new abstract. As with *uenustus*, it was formed with the productive *-tas, -tatis* suffix.

74. For a survey of the range of application of *uenustus*, see Monteil 1964: 117–33, Fyëdorov 1990.

the goddess's name.[75] *Venust(us)* maintains its connections to erotic attractiveness, particularly that of women, throughout the history of Latin (see below, VII.2).

This prevalence of erotic applications of *uenust(us)* in early attestations is
in part a trick of the sources, which are New Comedies where love is a central concern. There must have been another application, suggested by an obscure domain of the goddess Venus. Venus was a goddess not only of love but
also of gardens, a connection attested in Varro, Pliny the Elder, Festus, and
a Pompeian inscription.[76] The antiquity of the connection is vouched for
by a triple metonymy in Naevius (fl. ca. 230–200) which means "cooked
vegetables and wine":

> *cocus edit Neptunum Cererem*
> *et Venerem expertam Volcanom, Liberumque obsorbuit*
> *pariter*
>
> The cook ate Neptune [and] Ceres . . .
> and Venus that had known Vulcan, and consumed Liber
> along with them.[77]
>
> (*pall.* fr. 121a–c)

This connection of Venus with gardens may be the result of the original application of *uenus* as 'desired stuff' or 'desirable stuff' to the products of the

---

75. Cf. *O Venus uenusta*, Pl. *Mos.* 161; *diem pulchrum et celebrem et uenustatis plenum,* |
*dignum Venere pol, quoi sunt Aphrodisia hodie* "O beautiful day, o famous day, o day replete with
delight *(uenustatis)* | worthy indeed of Venus *(Venus)*, whose festival is today" (Pl. *Poen.* 255,
cf. 1177, *Bac.* 115).

76. Varro *R.* 1.1.6; Paul. Fest. pp. 322, 366 Lindsay; Plin. *Nat.* 16.50; *CGL* 521.5,
5.565.6; *CIL* 4.2776 *presta mi sinceru, sic te amet que custodit ortu Venus* (= *praesta mi sincerum,
sic te amet quae custodit hortum Venus*). Possibly *Caelicolae Veneris sacra semina* "holy seeds of
sky-dwelling Venus" (Anon. Ep. et Lyr., ser. aet. vers. 56.1 Morel) is to be referred to the
same function of Venus. Some nexus between "erotic love" and "gardens," via the notion
of "fertility," is thinkable. The purported hatred of Venus for pigs is perhaps the result of this
association with gardens, to which pigs pose considerable danger: *suillum genus Veneri inuisum
prodiderunt poetae*, "The poets pass on the idea that Venus despises pigs" (Paul. Fest. p. 408
Lindsay); cf. *et prima putatur* | *hostia sus meruisse mori, quia semina pando* | *eruerit rostro spemque
interceperit anni* (Ov. *Met.* 15.111–13); ὗς διὰ ῥόδων (Crates *Com.* fr. 4) = "a bull in a china
shop." A remoter, but still literal, possibility has to do with the quality of pigs' manure for
fertilizing: according to Columella, manure from barnyard quadrupeds is the least desirable
kind, after avian and human; of manure from quadrupeds the least desirable is porcine: *de-
terrimum ex omnibus suillum habetur* (Col. 2.14.4). Paul. Fest. cites as reasons for the origin of
the enmity the death of Adonis, killed by a boar, or their shameful promiscuity (?).

77. The line may possibly be nonce metonymizing (so Schilling 1954: 17–18, following Wackernagel 1928: 63), but even a comic exaggeration requires the connection of Venus

garden.[78] *Venus* in the meaning 'desired stuff' (not in connection to a garden) is preserved in a passage of Plautus.[79] The productive garden was therefore *uenustus* 'endowed with the desirable stuff' (cf. *onus* 'burden': *onustus* 'burdened,' *robur* 'strength': *robustus* 'strong, endowed with strength'). *Venustus* may also have been applied to gardens simply in view of its nascent meaning 'attractive,' abetted by, or causing, the association of Venus with gardens.

The connection with gardens may well be partly responsible for the acquisition by *uenust(us)* of the sense 'well-arranged,' which is frequently a characteristic of its referents. When words occur repeatedly or exclusively in the same context, their original senses can be lost or modified and new ones generated. "Prodigal," for example, which meant 'wasteful,' has come to mean 'wandering' under the pressure of the parable of the Prodigal Son (Luke 15: 11–32), an heir wasteful of his inheritance who, in the parable, also wanders abroad.[80] Since gardens, when 'attractive' or 'productive of the desirable stuff,' are also 'well-arranged' (as Vergil observed of vineyards),[81] *uenust(us)* might have acquired the last sense by an old association with gar-

---

with garden products to be recognizable. The interpretation of *Venerem* as 'vegetables' is assured by Paul. Fest. p. 51 Lindsay, who remarks *cocum et pistorem apud antiquos eundem fuisse accepimus. Naeuius: cocus, inquit, edit Neptunum, Venerem, Cererem. significat per Cererem panem, per Neptunum pisces, per Venerem holera* "We know that the ancients meant the same thing by *cocus* 'cook' and *pistor* 'baker,' as in the line of Naevius: 'The cook eats Neptune, Venus, Ceres.' By Ceres he means bread, by Neptune fish, and by Venus vegetables." For the possible Campanian origins of Venus as goddess of gardens, v. Schilling 13–30. Venus was worshiped in some places with Ceres (v. Schilling 20).

78. The products of the garden are described by a noun of the same stem class, viz., *holus holeris*, from *\*ĝhel-* 'green' (> Gr. χολή, OCS **zelenŭ**, Pol. **zielony**), i.e., 'the green stuff' (Pok. 1. *ĝhel-* 429).

79. At Plautus *St.* 274–79 Pinacium is delighted to be the bearer of good news: he "bring[s] the pleasantries of every desire and delightfulness" (*amoenitates omnium uenerum et uenustatum adfero* 275). *Veneres* and *uenustates* here probably have the old sense 'desire' and describe the '[objective] desirability' of the news Pinacium is bringing. Note that the implicit metaphors of the passage differentiate external and internal. Pinacium brings good news (*adfero*), but his subjective experience of joy is described as *laetitia* and is constructed internally: he "carries a heart filled with happiness and pleasure" (*onustum pectus porto laetitia lubentiaque*, 276) and his "heart runneth over its banks in waves of joy" (*ripisque superat mi atque abundat pectus laetitia meum*, 279).

80. The word was so used, for example, in the *NYT,* 15 April 1997, p. B1: "The Return of a Haitian Prodigal," referring to the Fugees, a band with Haitian roots that had returned to the island. The Fugees had not been particularly wasteful of resources in their time abroad, at least not according to the reporter.

81. *omnia sint paribus numeris dimensa uiarum* | *non animum modo uti pascat prospectus inanem,* | *sed quia non aliter uiris dabit omnibus aequas* | *terra, neque in uacuum poterunt se extendere rami* (Verg. *G.* 2.284–87).

dens. The transitional context seems to be preserved in Varro, for example: "As far as the cultivation of form, the result of arranging crops with more visual attractiveness *(specie uenustiora)* is to increase their yield" (R. 1.7.2).[82]

Whether gardens provided a transitional context or not, nonerotic instances of *uenust(us)* in the late Republic and after often have to do with the attractiveness induced by neat arrangement. Cicero was delighted with some new bookshelves:

> Now that Tyrannio has set up *(disposuit)*[83] my books for me, my house seems to have been put in order. Your Dionysius and Menophilus were fantastic on that job. There is nothing more delightful *(uenustius)* than the bookshelves you sent me, once I had the labels affixed to the books.[84]

> (*Att.* 4.8.2)

82. *subicit Scrofa, de formae cultura hoc dico, quae specie fiant uenustiora, sequi ut maiore quoque fructu sint, ut qui habent arbusta, si sata sunt in quincuncem, propter ordines atque interualla modica, itaque maiores nostri ex aruo aeque magno[s] male consito et minus multum et minus bonum faciebant uinum et frumentum, quod quae[que] suo quicque loco sunt posita, ea minus loci occupant, et minus officit aliud alii ab sole ac luna et uento* "Scrofa added, 'As far as the cultivation of form, the result of arranging crops with more visual attractiveness *(specie uenustiora)* is to increase their yield (as for example when orchards are planted like the five on a die [i.e., in an arrangement that resembles the five on a die (∷); cf. Thomas 1988 ad 2.277–78]), which happens on account of the orderly rows and moderate spaces between the plants. This is why our forefathers produced less wine and grain and of lower quality, since their plowland, though the same size as ours, was poorly arranged *(male consitus);* when things are arranged *(positus)* in their proper place, they take up less space, and each plant deprives the next less of the sun, moon, and wind' " (Var. R. 1.7.2). Varro also applies *venustus* to the attractiveness of fruit-storage rooms: *etenim in quibus luxuria concesserit ut in pinacothece faciant, quod spectaculum datur ab arte, cur non quod natura datum utantur in uenustate disposita pomorum?* (R. 1.59.2). Columella also preserves the transitional context: *sed ut densum arbustum commendabili fructu et decore est, sic, ubi uetustate rarescit, pariter et inutile et inuenustum est* (R 5.6.37). Probably this is also the sense of *cum uenustis hortulis* "with the lovely gardens" in Phaedrus (4.5.34), surely 'well-tended.'

83. *Dis-* emphasizes the assignation of parts in their places to form an orderly whole. Cf. *disposita* in Varro R. 1.59.2 (note 82, above). In another letter Cicero also describes Tyrannio's handiwork with a compound in *dis-*, calling it "Tyrannio's wonderful arrangement of my books" (*dissignatio Tyrannionis mirifica librorum meorum, Att.* 4.4a.1). The official who assigned seats in the theater was called a *dissignator* (e.g., Pl. *Poen.* 17).

84. *postea uero quam Tyrannio mihi libros disposuit, mens addita uidetur meis aedibus* (lit. "a mind seems to have been added to my house"; T-P suggest Cicero had in mind the Anaxagorean νοῦς, or principle of order; SB renders "my house seems to have woken to life"). *qua quidem in re mirifica opera Dionysi et Menophili tui fuit. nihil uenustius quam illa tua pegmata postquam sittybae libros inlustrarunt* (lit. "once the labels illuminated the books for me"). On *sittybae*, small labels of leather, v. T-P 107.1 (= *Att.* 4.4b) and Hesychius s.v. σιττύβαι;

*Venust(us)* seems to have this value in two passages where Cicero discusses the human ability to perceive the beauty of organized shapes. Only humans perceive the "beauty *(pulchritudo)*, loveliness *(uenustas)*, and coherence of parts of visible objects," an aspect of human perception that serves as an analogue for virtue (*Off.* 1.14), where the context requires *uenustas* to refer to proportionality.[85] Similarly, the human eye assesses *colorum etiam et figurarum †tum uenustatem atque ordinem et ut ita dicam decentiam* "the beauty *(uenustas)*, order, and so to speak propriety of colors and shapes" (*N.D.* 2.145).[86] In a discussion of the relationship of utility and beauty in *de Oratore* (3.178 ff.), trees and ships are cited as examples where each part is individually beautiful and has a function in the whole: *uenust(us)* is used for that sort of "componential" beauty, in distinction to the august gables of a temple, which

---

*sillybis;* (< σίλλυβος, σίλλυβον) is also read. Dionysius and Menophilus are library-slaves sent to Cicero by Atticus (v. *Att.* 4.4a).

85. *itaque eorum ipsorum, quae aspectu sentiuntur, nullum aliud animal pulchritudinem, uenustatem, conuenientiam partium sentit.* Beginning from these three kinds of physical beauty, the "natural operation of reason" *(natura ratioque)* discerns three kinds of "mental" beauty that ought to be observed in the conduct of one's life, namely *pulchritudo, constantia,* and *ordo.* Since the two sets of beauties correspond *(pulchritudo: pulchritudo; uenustas: constantia; conuenientia partium: ordo),* there must be some common ground between *uenustas* and *constantia.* *Constantia* in *de Officiis* ranges from a 'consistency' that takes in even emotional states (1.69, 1.102, 1.131) and fidelity to one's word (1.23) to a 'proportionality' governing the apportionment of goodwill to friendly parties (1.47) and choices of action corresponding to one's place in life. Examples of the last kind are *ita fere officia reperientur, cum quaereretur quid deceat et quid aptum sit personis temporibus aetatibus; nihil est autem quod tam deceat quam in omni re gerenda consilioque capiendo seruare constantiam* "As a rule one's duty can be determined by asking what is fitting and what is appropriate to status, situation, and age; but there is nothing that so befits action and choice as maintaining *constantia*" (1.125); *qui igitur ad naturae suae non uitiosae genus consilium uiuendi omne contulerit, is constantiam teneat, id enim maxime decet, nisi forte se intellexerit errasse in deligendo genere uitae* "Thus the person who has referred his choice of a manner of life to his own nature (provided it is not flawed) should maintain *constantia*, for that is what is most fitting—unless he determines that he erred in choosing a way of life" (1.120). Cf. also *in oratione constanti* 1.144. The link between *constantia* and *uenustas,* then, is that both have do to with neat arrangements, the latter typically in the physical world, the former in the moral world, which in *de Officiis* is largely a world of balance and propriety.

The application of *uenustas,* elsewhere in *de Officiis,* to distinctly feminine beauty *(cum autem pulchritudinis duo genera sint, quorum in altero uenustas sit, in altero dignitas, uenustatem muliebrem ducere debemus, dignitatem uirilem* "Since there are two kinds of beauty *(pulchritudo)*, the one comprising handsomeness *(dignitas)* and the other attractiveness *(uenustas)*, we should consider the latter feminine and the former masculine," 1.130) derives from a different branch of the word; the 'feminine' and 'well-arranged' branches generally worked independently (but see VII.2).

86. *Decentia,* a coinage of Cicero for τὸ πρέπον or εὐπρέπεια, also appears in *de Orat.* 3.200 (cf. III.4.2 n.46).

have *dignitas,* and the perfect shape of the heavens, which has *pulchritudo.*[87] In Vitruvius *uenustus* commonly refers to the beauty of proportionality.[88] Such instances are consistent enough across authors to suggest that 'well-arranged' was part of the semantic core of *uenust(us)* itself and not merely occasionally present in its referents.[89]

87. In trees "every element—the trunk, the branches, the leaves—is designed to maintain and preserve its nature, but nowhere is there any part that is not attractive *(uenustus)"* *(quid in eis arboribus? in quibus non truncus, non rami, non folia sunt denique nisi ad suam retinendam conseruandamque naturam, nusquam tamen est ulla pars nisi uenusta).* As for ships, their "attractiveness *(uenustas)* of appearance is such that they seem to have been devised not merely for the sake of function (lit. 'safety') but for the sake of form (lit. 'pleasure')" *(hanc habent in specie uenustatem, ut non solum salutis, sed etiam uoluptatis causa inuenta esse uideantur).* Cf. *quam sint omnia in hominis figura non modo ad usum uerum etiam ad uenustatem apta* "How every feature of the human form is designed *(apta)* not only for use but also for beauty" *(N.D.* 1.48). A *fastigium,* by contrast, has *dignitas (utilitatem templi fastigi dignitas consecuta est),* whereas the heavens have *pulchritudo:* The nature of the heavens is "such that they cannot remain integrated *(cohaerere)* with even the slightest change and their beauty such that a more exquisite *(ornatior)* shape cannot even be imagined" *(haec tantam habent uim, paulum ut immutata cohaerere non possint, tantam pulchritudinem, ut nulla species ne cogitari quidem possit ornatior).* For a different function of *uenust(us)* in discussions about beauty and utility, cf. III.4.2.

88. Describing gross architectural effects, *uenust(us)* refers to proportionality: *eurythmia est uenusta species commodusque in compositionibus membrorum aspectus* "Proportion implies a graceful semblance and the suitable display of details in their context" (1.2.3, tr. F. Granger), *uenustatis [sc., erit habita ratio] cum fuerit operis species grata et elegans membrorumque commensus iustas habeat symmetriarum ratiocinationes* "[Account will be taken] of *grace,* when the appearance of the work shall be pleasing and elegant, and the scale of the constituent parts is justly calculated for symmetry" (1.3.2, tr. F. Granger), *uenustates enim persequitur uisus, cuius si non blandimur uoluptati proportione et modulorum adiectionibus, uti quod fallitur temperatione adaugeatur, uastus et inuenustus conspicientibus remittetur aspectus* "For sight follows gracious contours; and an uncouth and ungracious aspect will be presented to spectators unless we indulge the pleasure of sight by proportionate additions to the modules, to increase by adjustment what appears to be missing" (3.3.13, tr. based on Granger). Vitruvius also observes that *opus reticulatum,* stonework built in a "netlike" pattern, is "more *uenustus"* than *opus incertum,* stonework built of irregular stones (2.8.1). *Venust(us)* thus forms a contrast to *elegan(s),* which Vitruvius typically uses to refer not to proportionality but to overall finished effect, e.g., *operum . . . ingressus qui manu aut tractationibus ad elegantiam perducuntur* "The taking up of work which is finely executed by hand, or by technical methods" (1.1.16, tr. F. Granger); *elegantes prospectus* "tasteful appearance," of a well-appointed house (1.2.6); *acanthos eleganter sculptos* "carefully carved acanthus flowers" (2.7.4). Vitruvius uses *uenust(us)* without reference to proportionality only in connection to color or surface *(atramentum . . . non inuenustum,* 7.10.3; *inuenusto uarioque colore,* 7.9.2; *subtili facie uenustatis,* 2.8.8, of facing on soft rubble; *species . . . inuenusta,* 4.2.2, of the appearance of cut roof-beams before the ends were capped and painted blue).

89. The occasional use of *uenustus* of places in Cicero seems to have to do with their neat arrangement. The villa at Astura is tidy, a ῥωπογραφία: *narro tibi, haec loca uenusta sunt, abdita certe et, si quid scribere uelis, ab arbitris libera. sed nescio quo modo* οἶκος ὃς φίλος. *itaque me refe-*

In short, *uenust(us)* developed in such a way as to have three nodes of meaning: 'attractive,' 'erotic,' and 'well-arranged' (fig. 5).

**The Semantic Structure of *Venust(us)***

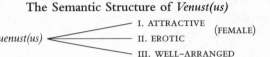

The social changes of the late third and early second century created expressive needs a word of that structure was perfectly suited to fill. One such need was created by the increasing popularity of theatrical performance and dancing in the second century. *Venust(us)* must have become the word for the gestures employed by actors and dancers. The use of *uenust(us)* for gesture is preserved only in later rhetorical treatises, often referring to oratorical gesture. But the use clearly belonged properly to the stage, as in the *Rhetorica ad Herennium:*

> One's expression should be modest and intense; in one's gesture there should be neither charm *(uenustas)* nor coarseness, to avoid the appearance, respectively, of actors or workmen.[90]

(3.26)

In a passage that pairs opposites, Cicero sets *[res] forensis* against *scaenica uenustas*.[91] Sulpicius exhibited "a gesture and bodily motion [that] although graceful *(uenustus)* seemed designed not for the stage but for the forum" (*Brut.* 203).[92] Cicero twice applies *uenustas* to the famous actor Q. Roscius.[93] Gellius records that Roscius was *histrio summa uenustate* "an actor of supreme grace" (5.8.4) and that the actor Polus was *gestus et uocis claritudine et uenustate* (6.5.2) "clear and graceful in gesture and voice." *Venust(us)* was an ex-

---

runt pedes in Tusculanum. et tamen haec ῥωπογραφία ripulae uidetur habitura celerem satietatem, *Att.* 15.16a.1; ῥωπογραφία = 'artificial prettiness,' from ῥῶπος 'petty wares,' the subject of still lifes, hence any 'pretty painting'; v. SB ad loc. *Att.* 9.9.4, which refers to a villa, should be read in this light: *sed eiusdem Antias caue contemnas; ualde est uenustum.* Lucullus's villa was fully, presumably neatly, equipped: *cum in uillam Luculli uentum esset, omni apparatu uenustatis ornatam* (*Hortensius* fr. 2).

90. *conuenit igitur in uultu pudorem et acrimoniam esse, in gestu nec uenustatem conspiciendam nec turpitudinem esse, ne aut histriones aut operarii uideamur esse.*

91. *quis umquam res praeter hunc tragicas paene comice, tristis remisse, seueras hilare, forensis scaenica prope uenustate tractauit atque ita, ut neque iocus magnitudine rerum excluderetur nec grauitas facetiis minueretur?* (*de Orat.* 3.30, of C. Caesar L. f.).

92. *gestus et motus corporis ita uenustus, ut tamen ad forum, non ad scaenam institutus uideretur.*

93. *uidetisne quam nihil ab eo nisi perfecte, nihil nisi cum summa uenustate fiat* (*de Orat.* 1.130); for *Arch.* 17, cf. below, V.2. Cf. also *Quinct.* 77 (below, V.4), of Hortensius.

cellent word to describe such gesture. Artful gesture is of course meant to be 'attractive.' The element of 'well-arranged' was especially well suited to describe disciplined motions of body or hand, which circumscribe or create well-formed shapes in space. That was the ideal of stage actors, which Plautus expresses by the borrowing *euscheme* (from εὔσχημος), lit., 'in a way that exhibits fine shape.' [94]

The origins of two other uses of *uenust(us)* found later probably also date to the late third or early second centuries. *Venust(us)* occasionally appears as an art-critical term for the 'charm' of artworks, which, as we have seen, began to be imported with greater frequency in the second century. In one instance Cicero is describing a copy of Polyclitus's *Canephoroe:* "There were besides two bronze statues of young girls, whose charm *(uenustas)* was not merely great but truly outstanding." [95] *Venust(us)* also began to be applied to various sorts of artful speech. The earliest instance is in Terence, where *quam uenuste! (Eu.* 457) is used (sarcastically) as a rhetorical approbative (IV.5). The other applications of *uenust(us)* to artful speech, comprising the 'charm' of narrative, the 'attractiveness' of certain figures of speech, and the 'neatness' of a particular sort of humor are further described below (III.4). The elements of 'attractive' and 'well-arranged' are obviously appropriate to well-fashioned objets d'art and careful or clever speech.

In instances of *uenust(us)* applied to gesture, artwork, or artful speech, the 'erotic' element of the lexeme does not make itself felt. [96] But it is possible that it figured in the original application of *uenust(us)* to dancing and artwork. Dancing was considered effeminate, to the extent that *cinaedus* (from κίναιδος) meant both 'dancer' [97] and the passive partner in a male homosexual relationship. [98] The pejoratively erotic quality of *cinaedus* can be felt in Scipio Aemilianus's complaint about young nobles who went to dancing

94. *euscheme astitit et dulice et comoedice* "How graceful a pose he has struck, just like a slave in comedy" (Pl. *Mil.* 213).

95. *Ver.* 2.4.5. Cicero also applies *uenustas* to the several images *(singulorum operum)* to be found on the shield crafted by Phidias for the cult statue of Athena Parthenos (*Or.* 234, where see Sandys's note).

96. It belongs to Catullus's art that he resurrected it in some of these connections; cf. ch. 7.

97. The word typically denotes simply 'dancer' in Plautus. By *lepida et suauis cantio . . . cinaedica (St.* 760), Plautus means "a nice sweet song we can dance to," which is exactly what the characters proceed to do. Cf. *qui Ionicus aut cinaedicust, qui hoc tale facere possiet?* "What Ionian or bawdy dancer (tr. Nixon) can do a move like this?" (ibid., 769), *omnis uoco cinaedos contra* "I call out all the bawdy dancers" (772).

98. See Colin 1952–53: 329–35, Corbeill 1996: 136–37, W. Kroll "Kinaidos," *RE* 11.1.459ff.

schools (*ORF* 21.30 = Macr. 3.14.6; below, II.2) and may be imagined for Lucilius's comment *stulte saltatum te inter uenisse cinaedos* "that you foolishly went to dance among the *cinaedi*."[99] The association of dancing with eroticism remains throughout the history of Roman culture.[100] Acting, too, was considered less than manly. Cicero claims that in olden times actors could not even be citizens (*Rep.* 4.10.fr).[101] In the *Commentariolum Petitionis* formerly attributed to Q. Cicero, actors are associated with sexual activity.[102] Actors' gestures might themselves have been seen as "erotic." As for artwork, it is easy to imagine that many Greek statuary types, when they began to be introduced with greater frequency in the second century, might have seemed to some Roman eyes not only "attractive" and "well-arranged" but also very "erotic." Statues of nudes or figures clothed in the "wet drapery" style, whatever their original symbolic intent, may well have seemed sexual to a Roman audience. To the extent that "erotic" in the Roman context shaded into "delicate" or "indulgent," even statue types that were not erotic in the strict sense, for example small delicate bronzes, might have merited the description *uenustus*.

The absence of a note of eroticism in later instances is to be attributed to new patterns of use. There is an illustrative parallel in the English word "queer" as a term for homosexuals: once a term of rebuke ('odd,' 'strange'), by steady application to the same group of referents by friendly parties with a different view of sexuality, "queer" has become neutral or even (aggressively?) ameliorative (hence "queer theory," "Queer Nation"). As theatricality and displays of artwork came to be viewed more and more positively, the *uenust(us)* applied to them will have concomitantly come to seem less and less erotic. *Venust(us)* could, in short, be reinterpreted as a kind of technical term in these applications. (The loss of the element of 'eroticism' is easily explained by the concept of a radially structured category, Intro. n. 17). The result is that in all those applications where *uenust(us)* had to do with practices of elite self-definition, it has been de-eroticized by the late Republic. We may represent this as follows (fig. 6):

99. 32M, 33W, 30K. This line occasioned Nonius's remark *'cinaedi' dicti sunt apud ueteres saltatores uel pantomimi* "Dancers or pantomimes used to be called *cinaedi*" (p. 5 [Mercer])—a remark necessitated by the restriction of *cinaedus* to the meaning 'passive homosexual.'

100. Cf. Corbeill, n. 18 above.

101. Cf., however, Livy 7.2.12 for the special exception of actors of the Atellan farces.

102. *qui postea cum histrionibus et cum gladiatoribus ita uixit ut alteros libidinis, alteros facinoris adiutores haberet* "[Catiline,] who lived with actors and gladiators, so as to have in the former partners ('helpers') in sex *(libido)* and in the latter partners in crime" ([Q. Cic.] *Pet.* 10).

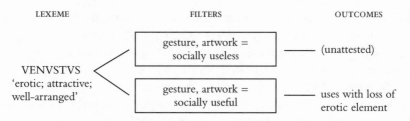

It is possible that the influence of Greek is to be detected here. If smart second-century Romans used *uenust(us)* as a kind of calque for χάρις, which though also erotic is less so than aboriginal *uenust(us)*, that might have contributed to diminishing the eroticism of *uenust(us)*.[103]

## I.7. *Bellus* and the Expansion of the Evaluating Pool

*Bell(us)* is in origin the diminutive of *bonus* 'good,' viz. \***dwen-olo-**.[104] The semantics of *bell(us)* are suggested by its contrast with *bon(us)* in two constructions. *Bene (se) habere,* apparently only twice in Cicero, is used to mean 'to be well situated,' of political or rhetorical position. If the youth are disgruntled with the triumvirate, writes Cicero to Atticus in 59, then *bene habemus nos* "we're in a good position" (ironic, *Att.* 2.8.1). At the outset of the *pro Murena*, Cicero avers *bene habet, iacta sunt fundamenta defensionis* "Good, then, the basis of my defense is laid" (*Mur.* 14).[105] *Belle (se) habere,* by contrast, refers exclusively to physical or emotional health.[106] In one instance Cicero writes to express concern about Tiro's health, even though Aegypta had told him the fever had broken and Tiro was "feeling fine" *(belle habere)*.[107] Dolabella informs Cicero that *Terentia minus belle habuit, sed certum scio iam conualuisse eam* "Terentia did not feel very good, but I'm certain she

103. On the connection of *uenustus* and χάρις, see III.4. ad fin.

104. *Bellus* is treated by Monteil 1964: 221–40. It is hoped that this account goes some way to satisfying the wish of Hanssen 1951: 175–76: "I cannot here give the story, or something like the story, of 'bellus,' that would require a monograph; but it is a story that ought to be written, for it would be both interesting and instructive."

105. Quintilian notices the expression (*Inst.* 9.2.26). With or without a reflexive, it is occasional in the language of comedy, e.g., Pl. *Aul.* 372, *Epid.* 696, *Mer.* 549, *Mil.* 717, 724, Ter. *Ph.* 429, and elsewhere.

106. *Bene habere* is occasionally attested in this function (*qui autem non bene se habent et fastidium patiuntur et pultes recusant,* Phil. *med.* Lat. 2.123), but not exclusively so, and indeed *bene habet* seems to have a special place in political contexts (e.g., Livy *bene habet; di pium mouere bellum* 8.6.5, *'atqui bene habet' inquit Decius, 'si ab collega litatum est'* 8.9.1, cf. 6.35.8, 8.35.4).

107. . . . *etsi mihi nuntiauit te plane febri carere et belle habere* (*Fam.* 16.15.1).

has now recovered" (*Fam.* 9.9.1).[108] *Bell(us)* is indeed common when comfort is at issue. Cicero and Atticus's sons would find Deiotarus's court "very agreeable" *(bellissimum);*[109] Tullia and Terentia would find it "very comfortable" *(bellissime)* at Cicero's country houses.[110]

*Bell(us)* and *bon(us)* also bring quite different nuances to *facere. Bene facere* is 'do [someone else] a favor, perform a service [for someone].' "You are very kind," writes Cicero to Atticus, "to have no doubts about my attitude toward the government" (*de animo autem meo erga rem publicam bene facis quod non dubitas, Att.* 7.3.3). *Bene facis . . . quod me adiuuas (Fin.* 3.16) is "It's very kind of you to help me."[111] *Bene facere,* indeed, is something of a technical term for social services rendered (cf. *benefactum). Belle facere,* by contrast, which occurs once in Cicero, seems to mean 'do *oneself* a favor.' When Cicero is eager to have Atticus see his remodeled library, he writes *perbelle feceris si ad nos ueneris* "You'll do yourself quite a favor if you come to visit me" (*Att.* 4.41.1; probably not "It will be delightful of you" SB sense).

The contrast between *bon(us)* and *bell(us)* in these constructions suggests the character of *bell(us):* it offers a positive evaluation that specifically highlights the subjective interest or aptitude of the evaluating party. In distinction to political position or social favors, which outside parties can also judge, health and comfort are personal issues that can only be judged by the principal. Such subjectivity is entirely in accord with the origin of *bell(us)* as a diminutive[112] and very often quite clear when the adjective is used.

---

108. Cf. *fac bellus reuertare* "Come back healthy" (*Fam.* 16.18.1, to Tiro in a letter about his health); cf. also *Att.* 12.37.1 *(belle se habere), Att.* 14.16.4 *(belle fuisse), B. Hisp.* 32.7 *(eum minus belle habere). Att.* 5.11.7, *cum ego me non belle haberem,* is used of emotional health.

109. *dum in aestiuis nos essemus, illum pueris locum esse bellissimum duximus (Att.* 5.17.3); cf. *ego puto te bellissime, si recte erit, cum quaestore Mescinio decursurum (Fam.* 16.4.3).

110. *bellissime uel mecum uel in nostris praediis esse poteritis (Fam.* 14.14.1). Cf. *oblecta te cum Cicerone nostro quam bellissime (Q. fr.* 2.12[11].4), *cum, ut spero, se Cicero meus belle habebit (Q. fr.* 3.6.2). This is the sense of *bellus* that underlies Varro *Men.* 541 (Bücheler, Cèbe) *uenio nunc ad alterum genus testamenti quod dicitur* φυσικόν; *in quo Graeci belliores quam Romani nostri* "I come now to another type of will, the so-called 'natural' will, in which the Greeks are nicer than our Romans." As Cèbe 1998: 2023 points out, Varro's reference is to the law of Solon which forbade wills if there were natural heirs; at Rome sons could be disinherited. The Greeks are *belliores* 'nicer' to their kin in that respect. In the absence of context, it is hard to tell whether the comparative of *bellus,* not otherwise attested and censured by the grammarians (cf. refs. in Cèbe), is supposed to be jolly, wry, or sarcastic.

111. Cf. also *bene sane facis (Ac.* 1.25, "You are kind to do so," of Atticus's acquiescence in Varro's use of Greek), *bene hercle faciunt (Leg.* 3.1), of those who acquiesce in Atticus's admiration for Plato.

112. Monteil 1964: 224 labels one of his categories of *bellus* and *belle* "diminutifs de modestie."

*Bell(us)* is well suited to highlight affective bonds and so appears in saluta-tions.[113] Cicero twice uses *bell(us)* of weather conditions that favored his travel plans.[114] In Crassus's dictum, "Even without knowing the law, we can understand how nice *(bellum)* it is to avoid troubles" (*de Orat.* 1.247), the nuance of *bell(us)* is to highlight the personal satisfaction of someone who has escaped difficulty.[115] What is "nice for one" can take on a wide variety of tones, from wistful to self-congratulatory to amused,[116] but the personal

113. E.g., *Cicero bellissimus tibi salutem plurimam dicit* "Your darling Cicero sends you hearty greetings" (*Fam.* 14.7.3), *Piliae et puellae Caeciliae bellissimae salutem dices* "Please say hello to Pilia and my dear little Caecilia" (*Att.* 6.4.3, probably not "pretty little," SB).

114. *Inde a. d. V Id. Corcyram bellissime nauigauimus* "From there we had a very nice *(bel-lissime)* trip to Corcya on 9 Nov." (*Fam.* 16.9.1); *Brundisium uenimus VII Kal. Dec. usi tua fe-licitate nauigandi; ita belle nobis 'flauit ab Epiro lenissimus Onchesmites' (hunc* σπονδειάζοντα *si cui uoles* τῶν νεωτέρων *pro tuo uendito)* "We arrived in Brindisi on Nov. 25, enjoying your good luck in sailing; so nicely *(belle)* 'did blow Onchesmites very gentle from Epirus' for us (you can sell this *spondeiazon* to any of the New Poets you like; keep the profits!)" (*Att.* 7.2.1).

115. *nam ipsum quidem illud etiam sine cognitione iuris, quam sit bellum cauere malum, scire pos-sumus.* For a similar use of *bellus,* cf. *bella est autem huius iuris quinquenni licentia* "The freedom of this five-year commission is really nice" (*Att.* 15.11.4). *Att.* 13.49.2 can be classed here: *est bellum aliquem libenter odisse et quem ad modum <non omnibus dormire, ita> non omnibus seruire* "It's nice to be able to hate someone openly, and not to serve everyone—just like not be-ing asleep for everyone." The expression "I'm not asleep for everyone" is in reference to a story about a Cipius who feigned sleep to avoid having to see his wife's peccadilloes; when a slave tried to thieve some wine while Cipius was putting on his act, Cipius said, "I am not asleep to everyone." Cicero uses the same expression in the letter written immediately be-fore this one, *Fam.* 7.24.1; cf. *Fest.* 174 Lindsay.

116. To Atticus of the acquittal of Gabinius on *maiestas* (Oct. 54), Cicero writes *dices 'tu ergo haec quo modo fers?' belle mehercule et in eo me ualde amo. amisimus, mi Pomponi, omnem non modo sucum ac sanguinem sed etiam colorem et speciem pristinam ciuitatis. nulla est res publica quae delectet, in qua acquiescam. 'idne igitur' inquies 'facile fers?' id ipsum. recordor enim quam bella pau-lisper nobis gubernantibus ciuitas fuerit, quae mihi gratia relata sit* "You will say, 'Well how are you taking it then?' Just fine, thank you *(belle mehercule),* and I'm happy with myself in the middle of it all. Ah, my Pomponius! We have lost not only the meat and marrow but even the old look and feel of a state. There is no government that pleases me, that I can accept. 'And you're taking it well?' you'll say. Quite so—for I remember how wonderful *(bella)* the state *(ciuitas)* was for the short time I was in office, I remember the gratitude I received" (*Att.* 4.18.2). Here the tone of *belle mehercule* (as I have translated) is much like "Just fine, thank you"; the self-reference is continued in the following sentence about self-love. The state that Cicero governed was "lovely"; the rememberer has blended with the remembered (vanity?), but the diminutive tells us he senses his own wistfulness (self-deprecation? bitterness?). In an-other example Cicero tells an amusing tale to Atticus which he closes thus: *haec te uolui* παριστορῆσαι; *sumus enim ambo belle curiosi* (*Att.* 6.1.25). *Ambo* comprises hearer and speaker grammatically; *belle* adds an amused, sympathetic note to the inclusion: "We're a fine pair of curious cats, after all." In a last example, Cicero speaks of one of his own letters: *Epistulam*

interest of some evaluator is typically quite clear. *Bonus,* by contrast, generally makes a claim presented as objective, and in its most serious moral register assumes, or even demands, the hearer's consent to the evaluation (hence, no doubt, its use as a political term for the optimates).[117]

A minimal semantic skeleton of *bell(us)* can be sketched as follows (fig. 7):

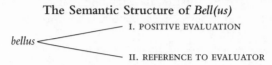

### The Semantic Structure of *Bell(us)*

I. POSITIVE EVALUATION

*bellus*

II. REFERENCE TO EVALUATOR

The social history of *bell(us)* is a function of how the "evaluator" is defined. We may conveniently describe different parties of "evaluators" by means of the grammatical persons. When Cicero calls Caecilia *bellissima* (*Att.* 6.4.3), we may speak of the "*bell(us)* of the first person singular," where Cicero, the speaker, is the evaluating party. When Cicero uses *bell(us)* to describe what he thinks Tullia and Terentia would feel (*Fam.* 14.14.1), we may speak of the "*bell(us)* of the second person plural," where the evaluating party is formed by Cicero's addressees. In the earliest attestations of *bell(us)*, the central place in the evaluating party is usually occupied by the first person singular. A young lover declares a door *bellissimus* because it never squeaks, facilitating his trysts (Pl. *Cur.* 20). A "lovely place, just the way I wanted it" is *nimi' bellus atque ut esse maxume optabam locus* (Pl. *Bac.* 724–25). Truculentus is taken in by "cheeks so prettily rouged" (*buccae tam belle purpurissatae* Pl. *Truc.* 290). Uses of *bell(us)* for 'pretty' in Plautus sometimes seem broader, viz., as "first person plural," expressing standards everyone accepts. There is also a sprinkling of "second person singular" uses of *bell(us)*, that is, those where a speaker sympathizes with the standards of an addressee. Thus *bellus blanditur tibi* "He's being nice to you" (*Men.* 626), said by Peniculus to the wife of Menaechmus I, of a comment made by Menaechmus.

It is not always possible to discriminate sharply between the "persons" of *bell(us)*, because its nuances often reflect the complexity of the discourse contexts in which it is embedded. The main point is that the "first person singular" evaluator is the standard one in older material, and that a new use appears from the second century forward. To characterize it in terms of the grammatical persons, we must use a non-Indo-European number and call it the "*bell(us)* of the first person paucal inclusive," referring to a small group

---

*Lucceio quam misi, qua meas res ut scribat rogo, fac ut ab eo sumas (ualde bella est)* (*Att.* 4.6.4). Here the tone of *ualde bella* is rather like "a good one, if I do say so myself."

117. V. Hellegouarc'h 1963: 484–95.

that includes the hearer and speaker.[118] This use of *bell(us)* suggests an awareness of the standards of some subgroup, of which the speaker and addressee are usually members. The standards are not those of (say) "the Quirites" but "one of us" in a narrower sense; this use belongs to the language of social performance proper. This sense of *bell(us)* appears very clearly in Cicero. In some examples the standards at issue concern the etiquette (not the morals) of a Roman gentleman. During his irksome governorship Cicero hoped he exhibited cheerful endurance because that was what was expected of men in his position: *etsi haec ipsa fero equidem etiam fronte, ut puto et uolo, bellissime, sed angor intimis sensibus (Att.* 5.10.3) "Even if I put up with these things with a cheerful expression *(fero . . . bellissime)*, as I think I do and try to do, still in my heart of hearts I am anguished."[119] Caecilius was displeased that Cicero refused to take his case against Satyrus: *durius accipere hoc mihi uisus est quam uellem et quam homines belli solent* "I thought he took it harder than I would have liked and harder than gentlemen *(belli homines)* usually do" *(Att.* 1.1.4). Refusals to grant favors must have been common in a society that depended so much on securing them, and *belli homines,* knowing that such refusals are not necessarily personal, must accept them to permit the system to function. This use of *bell(us)* is the origin of what may have been a set phrase *belle negare,* something like "respectfully decline," referring to a refusal that is sensitive not only to the feelings of the addressee but also to a more generally shared etiquette of refusal.[120]

The circle drawn by *bell(us)* may describe those of a certain intellectual

118. The "paucal" is a grammatical number used to refer to "a few" entities in certain languages, for example Fijian, Paamese, Yimas, and Meryam Mir. "Inclusive" refers to grammatical categories that include the speaker; so in Baka (a Ubangi language spoken in Niger and the Congo) 'we' = both *nganga* ('I and others but not you') and *ngangatini* ('I and you') and in Annatom (spoken in Melanesia) 'we two' = both *aijumrau* ('I and somebody other than you') and *akaijau* ('I and you').

119. *Belle* was conjectured by Sjögren for the *bellis* of the codd.; SB reads *bellis<sime>.* For an adverb in that position, cf. *Q. fr.* 3.5.5 *tenui me, ut puto, egregie.*

120. On *belli homines* in Cicero, see also Hanssen 1951: 217–18. Examples of *belle negare* are *pars benefici est quod petitur si belle neges* "Generosity includes polite *(belle)* refusal of requests" (Pub. *Sent.* P 20); *nam cum id petitur quod honeste aut sine detrimento nostro promittere non possumus, quo modo si qui roget ut contra amicum aliquam causam recipiamus, belle negandum est, ut ostendas necessitudinem, demonstres quam moleste feras, aliis te id rebus exsarturum esse persuadeas* "When a request involves what we cannot promise honorably or without harm to ourselves, as for example if someone requested that we plead a case against a friend, one must respectfully decline, pleading one's other connections, making clear how hard it is for one to refuse, convincing the person that one will make amends in other situations" [Q. Cic.] *Pet.* 45. On graceful refusals in aristocratic intercourse, cf. Hall 1996.

character or literary taste. The "fit readers but few" before whom Atticus gave a reading of Cicero's *pro Ligario* were a *bellum theatrum*.[121] They were "a nice bunch" or "a good group," as literary men like Cicero and Atticus would agree. An interesting example appears in the *de Divinatione,* where Quintus and Marcus Cicero debate whether divination is possible. Quintus in the first book appeals to such famous events as the gathering of bees on Plato's lips, which was taken to have presaged his expressive ability.[122] In the second book Marcus rejects such omens by characterizing them as *non tam mirabilia . . . quam coniecta belle* "not so much matters for wonderment as instances of clever interpretation" (*Div.* 2.66). *Belle* registers the judgment of the type of audience to be impressed by that sort of thing. In this instance one may perhaps speak of a "*bell(us)* of the second person plural" (or "paucal"?), if Marcus is disparaging the intellectual character of the proofs persuasive to Quintus and those like him. In most cases, however, speaker and addressee are themselves members of the groups whose standards are at issue. As in Plautus, such distinctions depend closely on discourse contexts and it is unwise to look for crisp lines. Still this sort of *bell(us)* is palpably different from those of comedy.

I suggest that the social changes of the second century caused, or abetted, the creation of the *bell(us)* of the "first person paucal inclusive." It is of course possible that the difference between Plautus and Cicero is a trick of the sources, and that elite speakers, in their own circles, were already using this sort of *bell(us)* in Plautus's time. However, the special association of this *bell(us)* with social practices that flowered in the second century suggests that it owes its dissemination, if not its birth, to them. The *convivium* certainly provided one context for this expansion of the evaluating pool. The *convivium* required a self-conscious participation in conviviality, behavior designed to be pleasant both to oneself and to the host and guests. It is exactly this sort of participation that *bell(us)* is used to describe in Varro's *Menippean Satires.* According to Varro these are the requirements for a good *convivium*:

> Four elements are required for the perfect *convivium:* a gathering of the right sort of participants *(belli homunculi),* the selection of a place, the choice of a time, and some attention to the furnishings.[123]
>
> (*Men.* fr. 335 Bücheler, Cèbe)

---

121. *theatrum quidem sane bellum habuisti* (*Att.* 13.20.2).

122. The attestations are gathered by Pease 1920: 229 ad 1.78.

123. *ipsum deinde conuiuium constat ex rebus quattuor et tum denique omnibus suis numeris absolutum est, si belli homunculi conlecti sunt, si electus locus, si tempus lectum, si apparatus non neglectus.*

The context makes clear that what is meant by *belli homunculi* is 'good dinner guests,' or as I have translated here, "the right sort of participants," persons ready to behave as appropriate. *Homunculi,* literally 'little men,' expresses the same sense of communal affection as the English "fellows"; [124] *belli* highlights their shared aesthetic and behavioral sense. The self-conscious or performative character of this *bell(us)* is suggested by another passage that contrasts festive spirit with real character:

> *omnes uidemur nobis esse belli festiui, saperdae cum | simus σαπροί*

> We are jolly and jovial,
> so we think.
> Though in fact
> we stink,
> like fetid fish.

(Men. 312 Bücheler, 311 Cèbe) [125]

There is one clear instance of this convivial use of *bell(us)* in Cicero. Here the character of Marcus Cicero in *de Finibus* attacks the Epicurean practice of celebrating their founder's birthday as a feast day:

> I can't deny that thinking someone has a birthday is perfectly appropriate for a civilized *(humanus)* and sociable *(bellus)* person, but it is wholly inappropriate for a philosopher, particularly a natural philosopher, which is what Epicurus claims to be.[126]

(Fin. 2.102)

*Bellus,* accompanied here by *humanus* 'civilized,' highlights the convive's willing participation in an occasion, whence my translation 'sociable.' Such occasions are viewed archly by Cicero in the context of a philosophical tract.

---

124. Cèbe 1141 observes that *homunculus* has a positive charge in this context ("braves gens" and not "pauvres petits hommes"). The other diminutive of *homo, homullus,* is pathetic in Varro, as in 92 Bücheler = 92 Cèbe ("ici dépréciatif et marqu[ant] le dédain ou la pitié" Cèbe).

125. *saperdae, cum:* Aldina et al. The punctuation here followed is that of Cèbe. Whether *saperdae* is to be joined with the first or the second clause is an issue that plainly hinges on whether the *saperda* (Gk. σαπέρδης) is a good fish or not, and it seems not to be (*saperda genus pessimi piscis,* Paul. Fest. 435 Lindsay; cf. Olson-Sens [2000] ad 39.3; 20.3). In favor of Cèbe's punctuation is also Varro's tendency to anchor his points with puns, viz., *SAPerdae . . .* ΣΑΠροί; cf. Woytek 1970: 34, 51, and compare the occurrence of *lect-* in fr. 335 above (*conLECTi . . . eLECTus . . . LECTum . . . negLECTus*).

126. *haec ego non possum dicere non esse hominis quamuis et belli et humani, sapientis uero nullo modo, physici praesertim, quem se ille esse uult, putare ullum esse cuiusquam diem natalem.*

*Bell(us)* also came to be applied to those who participated in exclusive literary culture, both of writers and of readers or hearers (cf. *bellum theatrum* above). As with convivial *bell(us),* there are no examples from the early second century, but it is easy to imagine that the burgeoning literary culture of that period produced the use of *bell(us)* preserved, again, in Varro:

> . . . that Diogenes knew enough of literature for everyday use, whereas this fellow knows enough for a public lecture in front of a fashionable audience *(belli homines).*[127]

> (*Men.* 517 Bücheler, Cèbe)

The public lecture, or ἀκρόασις, was a place, at least from the point of view of certain Romans, where the intellectual, and the intellectually foppish, displayed their talents. The *belli homines* are those who would expect certain intellectual, and rhetorical, flourishes. According to Varro they were indeed the sort to delight in verbal jousting:

> A fashionable man *(bellus homo)* more pleased by the wrestling of Stoic dialectic than of athletes[128]

> (*Men.* 519 Bücheler, Cèbe)

In short, in the late Republic we find that the evaluating party implicit in *bell(us)* has expanded to include the shared standards of social subgroups. This expansion should be seen as the result of the social changes of the second century, the kind of shift that created the language of social performance. Passages in Varro and Cicero permit the suggestion that the growth of literary culture and the *convivium,* which required certain behavior, provided the context for such an expansion. The development may be represented as follows (fig. 8):

---

127. *Diogenem litteras scisse, domusioni quod satis esset, hunc quod etiam acroasi bellorum hominum.* The reference in *hunc* (an emendation of Popma for the *tunc* of the codices) may be to Menippus, as contrasted to the practical (cf. *domusioni*) Diogenes. See discussion in Cèbe 1998: 1984–87.

128. The received text published by Bücheler, *in charteo stadio* ἐπιτάφιον ἀγῶνα *quo quis certasset animo, bellus homo magis delectatus Stoicorum pancratio quam athletarum,* has been the subject of various interpretive and textual disputes, which are summarized in Cèbe 1998: 1988–90. Cèbe, reading *quiuis* for *quis* (after Havet) and *certassit* for *certasset* (after Barthes), and taking *quo* in the sense "à la faveur duquel," renders " . . . dans le stade de papier [ . . . ] des jeux funèbres qui feront lutter avec cœur n'importe quel homme distingué qui goûte plus le pancrace des Stoïciens que celui des athlètes" (p. 1971, second ellipse mine). Astbury 1983: 151 is surely correct to see the ἐπιτάφιος ἀγών as the subject of the satire, a discussion "in a paper stadium" held by "fashionable men" in honor of Menippus (the book from which this fragment comes was called Ταφὴ Μενίππου).

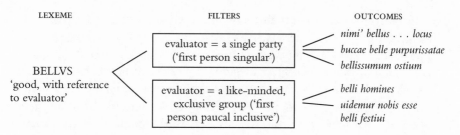

LEXEME                    FILTERS                        OUTCOMES

BELLVS
'good, with reference
to evaluator'

evaluator = a single party
('first person singular')

*nimi' bellus . . . locus*
*buccae belle purpurissatae*
*bellissumum ostium*

evaluator = a like-minded,
exclusive group ('first
person paucal inclusive')

*belli homines*
*uidemur nobis esse*
*belli festiui*

This *bell(us)*, as we see in chapter 3, provided the *bell(us)* of the language of rhetoric, which is used for certain rhetorical "moves" directed to a small circle of knowledgeable critics.

## I.8. *Facet(us)* and Verbal Flash

The etymology of *facetus* is not absolutely certain. It may have originally meant 'bright,' from an IE root $*ghweH_2k^w$- appearing in *fax* 'torch' ($*ghwH_2k^w$-s), Lithuanian **žvãkė** 'light, candle'[129] and the Hesychian glosses διαφάσσειν ($*-ghwH_2k^w$-yo)· διαφαίνειν 'show through' and φώψ ($*ghwoH_2k^w$-s)· φάος, φῶς 'light.' This *facetus* may have been built to *faces,* an archaic biform of *fax* (Paul. Fest. 77 Lindsay).[130] However, the phonetic similarity of *facetus* to *facere* 'do,' *factus* 'done' may have influenced its semantics and caused it to acquire a sense like 'polished' or 'finished,' a sense that certainly seems to fit the earliest attestations somewhat better. Indeed a genuine etymological connection to *facere* is not out of the question.[131]

129. Cf. ref. in Fraenkel 1965 s.v. **žvãkė**. The word formerly had a broader range of meaning that included 'torch,' as is shown by Širvydas 1620, a dictionary that glosses Polish with Latin and Lithuanian. The current Lithuanian words for 'torch' (**dervókšnė** < **darvė** 'pitch, resin,' **žiburỹs** < **žibė** 'lamp') do not appear in Š's dictionary, where **žwakie lieta** (**žvãkė lieta**) = *funale* 'wax torch,' s.v. Pol. **lana świecá** 'poured candle' (148); **žwakie** = *fax, teda, lampas*, s.v. **pochodnia** 'torch' (304); **žwakie dide ilga** = *cereus magnus longus*, s.v. **postawnik** (333). **Žvãkė** is also 'candle' (= *candela*, s.v. **świeca**, 429; **žwakie waskine** = *cereus, cerata taeda*, s.v. **świeca woskowa** 'wax candle,' 429). An old $*ghwH_2k^w$- would have fallen together with $*dhH_1k$-, both yielding *fac-;* the 'light' sense will have been driven out by the 'do, make' sense, much as $*wenH$- 'desire' was driven out by $*g^wm$- when they both became $*uen$- (cf. above, n. 70).

130. Cf. W-H s.v., who compare *prōlēs*: **prōlētus,** whence *prōlētārius*. *Facētus* could also have been built to a verb \*\**facēre* 'be bright, shine, flicker (?)' which has subsequently vanished.

131. Much as *iacĕre* 'throw' formed a stative-resultative *iacēre* 'to be in the state of having been thrown, to lie,' *facĕre* 'to do' might have yielded a similar formation \*\**facēre* 'to be in the state of having been done, to be finished off.' \*\**Facēre* in turn might have yielded a participle *facētus* 'finished off, finished up, done up' (rather as *acēre* 'to be sour' yields *acētum*

In Plautus, at any rate, the uses of *facetus,* whether 'flashy' or 'polished,' fall into three groups. There was the "flash" or "finish" of striking personal appearance. *Facet(us)* is appropriate to someone who is as "pretty as a picture": *satin ut facete, aeque atque ex pictura* (*St.* 271). When Leonida dresses himself up, he wants to make himself a *facetus atque magnificus uir* "a grand and striking *(facetus)* man" (*As.* 351). Toxilus exclaims to Paegnium, *hui, babae, basilice te intulisti et facete* "My my my! You've come in in royal splendor" (lit. "royally and splendidly," *Per.* 807). Another kind of "bright flash" or "smooth polish" was seen in the "brilliance" of apt or clever speech or the intelligence it suggests. *Facete dictum* (*Poen.* 637) "nicely put" is Lycus's sarcastic reply to a sententious aphorism. When Sagaristio eludes a command to go to Eretria by dubbing Toxilus's home "Eretria," so he can say he went where he was supposed to, Toxilus says *nimi' tu facete loquere* (*Per.* 323) "that's quite some clever talk." Anterastilis is surprised at her sister's untypical complaints:

> *miror equidem soror te istaec sic fabulari,*
> *quae tam callida et docta sis et faceta.*

> Sister, I'm surprised to hear such blather from you;
> you're usually so shrewd and smart and clever!
>
> (*Poen.* 233–34)

A third kind of "clever flash" or "smooth polish" described plans, tricks, ruses, and devices. The deceitful mind is full of *facetiae* "clevernesses, clever acts, wit." [132] "Clever ruses" are *facetae fabricae* (*Mil.* 147), beside "shrewd deceptions" *(docti doli).* To be "brilliantly duped," that is, "to suffer at the hands of a brilliant duper," is *ludificiarier . . . facete.*[133] "Having begun with brilliance and shrewdness" is *exorsus . . . facete et callide* (*Per.* 455). Plautus seems to have felt *facet(us)* particularly suitable for describing the wittiness of actions and words. If *facet(us)* retained any connection to its original sense, the witty act or word may well have seemed more like the "bright flash" of flame than the "gleam" described by *nitidus* or the "shine" described by *splendidus.*[134]

---

'the sour stuff' = vinegar). I owe this formulation to Alan Nussbaum. The phonological similarity of *facere* inspired the ancient etymologists: *facetus est qui facit uerbis quod uult* (Don. Ter. *Eun.* 427); *facetus, qui iocos et lusus gestis et factis commendat, a faciendo dictus* (Isid. *Orig.* 10, 95).

132. *ecquam tu potes reperire forma lepida mulierem | cui facetiarum cor pectusque sit plenum et doli* (*Mil.* 782–83).

133. *numquam edepol hominem quemquam ludificarier | magis facete uidi et magis miris modis* (*Mil.* 538–39) "I've never seen anyone tricked more cleverly or in more wondrous wise."

134. In Plautus *nit(idus)* describes the 'gleam' of a well-oiled head (*nitidiusculum caput Ps.* 220), the 'glow' of spring (*uer uide, | ut tota floret, ut olet, ut nitide nitet Truc.* 353–54), and

In any case the post-Plautine development of *facet(us)* is a matter of the narrowing of its range of reference. Its associations with personal comportment and with the wit of action (the ruse, scheme, or "practical joke") largely wither away, leaving *facet(us)* virtually always associated with verbal "flashes" of wit, humor, or intelligence.[135] There is further the sense that the "flash" or "polish" in question has the function of establishing social status. The earliest such use of *facetus* is preserved in Lucilius:

> *quo facetior uideare et scire plus quam ceteri*
> *"pertisum hominem" (non "pertaesum") dicere †ferum nam*
> *genus†*

> So you can look wittier (*facetior*), seem to
> know more than everyone else,
> [it is your habit] to say "the man is wearied,"
> with *pertisum* instead of *pertaesum*.

> (963–64M, 983–84W, 971–72K)

The issue in these lines is the establishment of social status through choice of linguistic forms. Medial vowels in Latin undergo a series of raisings known as "vowel weakening,"[136] whereby, for example, *-ae-* in the middle of words becomes *-ī-*, hence *caedō* 'cut' but *incīdō* from *\*inkaedō* 'cut in(to); incise.' This weakening is by no means without exceptions, partly because of compositions postdating the effective date of the raising,[137] and partly because

---

the 'gleam' of a clean house (*facite sultis, nitidae ut aedes meae sint, quom redeam domum*, St. 65). *Splend(idus)* describes the 'shine' of polished metal (*in splendorem dari bullas*, As. 426) or the 'shine' of celestial bodies (*caelum . . . splendore plenum*, Mer. 880); *splendens stella candida*, Rud. 3). Both spheres meet at *Mil.* 1–2: *curate ut splendor meo sit clupeo clarior | quam solis radii esse olim quom sudumst solent*.

135. An almost solitary nonverbal exception is from a fragment of a speech probably delivered about 104, which contrasts *facetiae* to *sumptus* and *fastidium*: *is nunc flos cenae habetur inter istos, quibus sumptus et fastidium pro facetiis procedit* "These days this is the very flower of a feast among those with whom extravagance and fastidiousness take the place of elegance" (*ORF* 52.1 = Gel. 15.8). The MSS of Gellius have the speaker as Favorinus, surely a mistake; cf. Malcovati's n. ad loc. 'Elegant' or 'stylish' is also the required sense in Hor. *Serm.* 1.2.25–26 *est qui | inguen ad obscenum subductis usque facetus* (sc. *tunicis*) "Another goes around, the height of fashion (*facetus*), with his tunic hiked so high you can practically see the organ you shouldn't." Some editors take this *facetus* with the following line, viz., *facetus | pastillos Rufillus olet, Gargonius hircum* "Elegant Rufillus reeks of lozenges, Gargonius of a goat." In either case, nonverbal social performance is at issue. On Horace, see VIII.3.

136. Cf. Sihler 1995: §§66–70, LHS I §§62–76.

137. E.g., *inaequalis* (not *iniqualis*), first attested under Augustus, vs. *iniquus* (< *\*inaequus*), already in Plautus.

of recompositions, where the constituent parts were still felt as separate.[138] There was thus the possibility of variation, which still existed among educated speakers in Cicero's time (cf. below III.6).

Lucilius in this passage refers to a speaker, said by Festus (334, 336 Lindsay) to be Scipio Aemilianus, who applied the weakening to *pertaesum* 'bored, vexed,' so yielding the uncommon variant *pertisum*.[139] *Per-* 'very much' was a weaker binder than other prefixes[140] and in the case of this verb did not normally induce the raising.[141] The motivation of such regularizing speakers can be traced to their familiarity with Greek linguistic and rhetorical theory.[142] The complexity of the inflectional systems of ancient Greek attracted the attention of philosophers, who fell into two camps. The Alexandrians favored systematizing inflected forms, under the principle of ἀναλογία 'proportion' (L. *ratio*), whereas Chrysippus stressed the importance of irregularity (ἀνωμαλία, L. *consuetudo*). *Pertisum* and such forms were, perhaps, like "attorneys general" or "I prefer never to eat meat," strictly correct but slightly pedantic. Furthermore in these verses Aemilianus may be quoting a New Comic aphorism. If we accept Mueller's emendation *humanum genus* for the *ferum nam genus* of the manuscripts, yielding for *pertisum*

138. E.g., *satisfacere* (not *satisficere*, like *reficere* etc.); LHS I §63. A parallel to recompositions in English can be found in names like *St. Clair*, which are pronounced both in a form generated by sound change (|sIn'clɛɪ|, whence *Sinclair*) and in a recomposed, etymological form (|seynt'cler| *Saint Clair*). American English often has recomposed forms where British English preserves the results of sound change, e.g., *waistcoat* (BrE | 'weskIt|, AmE | 'weystkowt|).

139. In the same passage Festus records that Aemilianus also said *rederguisse* for *redarguisse*, where *-r-* before consonant might have blocked the raising, hence the variants *ef-, infarcio : ef-, infercio; com-, reparco : com-, reperco*. The "lowering power" of *r* is in evidence in the *-ĕris* (not *-iris*) of the passive system, where the thematic vowel was otherwise weakened to *-i-*. On the lowering power of *r*, see LHS I: 51, 80f.

140. That *per-* 'very much' was a relatively weaker binder than most preverbs is clear because (a.) it can undergo tmesis and (b.) it can occur before caesura. For (a.) cf. *per mihi gratum* (Cic. *Att.* 1.4.3), *per mihi per inquam gratum* (Cic. *Att.* 1.20.7), *pergrata perque iucunda* (Cic. *de Orat.* 1.205), *per uidere uelim* (Cic. *Att.* 15.4.2). For (b.) cf. Hor. *Carm.* 1.18.16 *arcanique fides | prodiga per- | lucidior uitro* (Fifth Asclepiadean). On the gradedness of grammatical categories, see Lakoff 1987 passim, esp. the example of "nouniness" 63–64 after Ross 1981.

141. *Pertisum* at Pompon. *com.* 93 *(Quid? dedi nebuloni, quem pertisumst <esse> pauperem)* is Ribbeck's conjecture for the *pertesunt* of the MSS. Other examples of *per-* failing to induce raising are easily multiplied, cf. from Plautus *perfacilis, permadefacio, perplaceo* (contrast *displiceo*).

142. Cf. Puelma Piwonka 1949: 13. On the anomaly-analogy controversy, see with refs. Kennedy 1963: 296–97, Siebenborn 1976: 109–16, Ax 1991: 289–95.

*hominem humanum genus* the sense "The man is disgusted with men," we have an aphorism that could have come from the *Timonlegende*.[143] Indeed the phrase would then be a virtual translation of something like μισάνθρωπος ἄνθρωπος or Menander's ἀπάνθρωπός τις ἄνθρωπος (*Dysk.* 6), complete to the level of a *figura etymologica (hominem ~ humanum)*. To quote such a thing was not out of character for Aemilianus, a noted philhellene.

Many later instances of *facetus* are clearly related to such verbal "performances" that establish social status. For example, *facetus* is the word that Cicero uses to distinguish socially acceptable wit from mere humor (*non esse omnia ridicula faceta, de Orat.* 2.251). These and like instances from the rhetorical tradition are discussed further below (VI.3). We may note here a few instances of *facetus* from outside of the rhetorica which refer to the establishment of social status by verbal "flash" or "polish." Cicero here posits a difference between kinds of slander:

> An accusation requires a formal charge, which establishes the issue at hand, names a defendant, proves its point by evidence, and supports it with witnesses. Slander, on the other hand, has no other purpose than to injure. If slander is impudent, it's considered offensive, but if it's wittily done (*facetus*), it's considered urbane (*urban[us]*).[144]
>
> (*Cael.* 6)

The insult is permissible if done artfully, and *facetus* is the word that distinguishes art from garden-variety calumny. It is probably ultimately this sense of 'possessed of socially exclusive wit or cleverness expressed verbally' that is at the root of the occasional use of *facetus* for 'companionable." In the *de Inventione*, in a list of opposites, Cicero pairs *comis* 'companionable' with *infacetus* (*Inv.* 1.35). This use of 'companionable' is to be seen in Horace's *ita quemque facetus adopta* "agreeably adopt everyone into your family"—a bit of advice to a social climber, who is to ingratiate himself to well-connected people by adding *frater* 'brother' or *pater* 'father' when he addresses them (*Epist.* 1.6.55).

143. This interpretation of the line takes *pertisum* as personal and active (as in Suet. *Jul.* 7.1, *Aug.* 62, *Tib.* 67) with *hominem* as its subject and *humanum genus* as its object (not, as in many interpretations, the subject of *dicere* in the preceding line). The materials concerning Timon, the partly lengendary misanthrope, are gathered by F. Bertram, *Die Timonlegende* (diss. Heidelberg, 1906), a work not available to me at this writing. He appears first in Aristophanes (cf. *Lys.* 807–16); Lucian has a dialogue *Timon*.

144. *accusatio crimen desiderat, rem ut definiat, hominem notet, argumento probet, teste confirmet; maledictio autem nihil habet propositi praeter contumeliam; quae si petulantius iactatur, conuicium, si facetius, urbanitas nominatur.*

We could model the semantic core of *facet(us)* thus (fig. 9):[145]

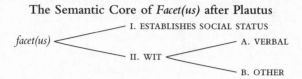

The Semantic Core of *Facet(us)* after Plautus

I. ESTABLISHES SOCIAL STATUS

*facet(us)*

A. VERBAL

II. WIT

B. OTHER

The shift in *facet(us),* I suggest, ultimately reflects the activities of the second-century elite. New habits of speech, such as witty banter of the kind purveyed by Cato's M. Caelius or the ἀκροάματα of Hellenizing *convivia,* required an approbative vocabulary, and *facet(us),* which described roughly comparable verbal flashes, was pressed into service. Its nuance shifted to imply a performance that established social status. Social shifts transformed a word describing the forte of a Plautine *servus callidus* into a word describing the social graces of a powerful elite. Though this diagram obscures the metaphorical fade that seems complete by the first century, for our purposes we may model the development thus (fig. 10):

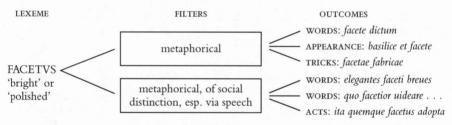

LEXEME                          FILTERS                          OUTCOMES

metaphorical

WORDS: *facete dictum*
APPEARANCE: *basilice et facete*
TRICKS: *facetae fabricae*

FACETVS
'bright' or
'polished'

metaphorical, of social
distinction, esp. via speech

WORDS: *elegantes faceti breues*
WORDS: *quo facetior uideare . . .*
ACTS: *ita quemque facetus adopta*

## I.9. *Lep(idus)* and Performativity

*Lep(idus)* was probably in origin an adjective meaning 'soft' or 'delicate,' derived from the *\*lep-* well-attested in Baltic and the root of Greek λέπειν 'peel.'[146] There are a few traces of a literal meaning left in Plautus. When

145. Feature I 'establishes social status' apparently survives, constructed negatively, in Mexican Spanish *faceto: faceto* is either 'cocksure, arrogant' or 'unsuccessfully humorous' (cf. the definition of Santamaria 1959 s.v. "chistoso, para afectado y sin gracia"; Ramos i Duarte 1895 has "patarato, amanerado, afectado, mono"). *Facetada* is a 'bad joke.' Cf. Hamel 1996.

146. So W-H s.v., cf. Pok. 2.429. Cf. also Ern. Fraenkel 1962, s.v. **lèpti.** The 'peel' of Greek λέπειν is probably the original sense. In Lithuanian the inherited *\*lep-* yielded *\*lopos* > **lapas** 'leaf' (cf. Greek λοπός, λόπος 'peel, shell, husk') and probably a *\*\*lepia-* 'peel, strip off,' hence 'refine, pamper,' which underlies the ingressive/stative **lèpti** 'become pampered, fastidious, delicate' and related forms, e.g., **lẽpnas** 'pampered, spoiled, fastidious, voluptuous, finicky,' **lepūnas** 'pampered person, sissy,' **lẽpinti** 'pamper, spoil, effeminate.' **Lẽpti** 'go slack' (with a lengthened grade) is probably a derivative of the same root. *\*Lep-* was also productive in Latvian, yielding, presumably by way of 'pampered, delicate,' **lẹpns**

saltfish are not soaked long enough, they lack *lepos* 'softness' and *suauitas* 'mildness' (*Poen.* 242), the opposite, respectively, of the 'dry' and 'briny' quality of the fish.[147] The literal meaning is the source of a metaphorical 'softness' that, I suggest, was the original impetus for the frequent application of *lep(idus)* to three semantic spheres. *(Lepide) accipere (lepido) uictu* "to receive in *lepidus* fashion with *lepidus* repast" is virtually a *vox propria* for lavish entertainment, for example *i hac mecum intro, ubi tibi sit lepide uictibu', uino atque unguentis (Bac.* 1181) "come on inside with me, there's a fine spread of food, wine, and perfume for you."[148] Plautus also frequently applies *lepidus* to exquisite accoutrements, particularly in erotic contexts, e.g., *in lecto lepide strato* "in a nicely covered bed" (*Poen.* 696, spoken by a courtesan) or *nimi' lepide exconcinnauit hasce aedis* "He's set this house up really nicely" (*Cist.* 312).[149] Last, Plautus frequently applies *lepidus* to the physical form of attractive women, often in conjunction with *liberalis*.[150] I suggest that

---

'splendid, lovely, proud, arrogant' (see further n. 151). The derivation of a sense 'soft' in Latin is not entirely straightforward: a **lepere* 'peel; soften' might have yielded a **lepēre* 'be in the state of having been peeled, be soft,' from which *lepos* and *lepidus* were in turn derived. I hope to treat these developments more fully elsewhere. I am grateful to Bill Darden for his assistance with the Balto-Slavic.

147. Lysidamus's opening *canticum* in the *Casina* (217a–27) is filled with double language applicable to food and personality: there is nothing that has "more salt or more mildness" *(quod plus sali' plusq' leporis . . . | habeat)* than love; love "makes honey out of bitter bile, and a soft *(lepidus)* and mild *(lenis)* man out of a sourpuss *(tristis = '*bitter,' cf. Enn. *Sat.* 12 *triste . . . sinapi* 'bitter mustard')." The thoroughgoing doubleness of language in the food passages makes it very likely that *lepos* and *lepidus* had a more specific meaning than simply, say, 'delight' and 'delightful.' It is notable that *unguenta*, which are quite literally 'soft,' are, except for adjectives of possession or quantity and *exotica* (*Mos.* 42), described in Plautus by no other word than *lepidus* (*Cas.* 226, *Ps.* 947; possibly *lepidissima munera meretricum, Poen.* 1177, which surely included scented oils).

148. Cf. *Cas.* 491–92, *Cas.* 746–48, *Cist.* 10–11, *Mil.* 739, *Mos.* 317–18, *Ps.* 946–47, *Ps.* 949, *Rud.* 408–10, *St.* 685. The other adverbs that appear with *accipere* in the sense of 'receive a guest' are a miscellany, some of which seem to have a roughly similar sense but do not appear more than once or twice, suggesting that *lep(idus)* is the *vox propria* in this connection.

149. Cf. also *uenerem meram haec aedes olent, quia amator expoliuit* "This house exudes pure love, because a lover has decorated it" (Pl. *Cist.* 314); *sed uestita aurata ornata ut lepide ut concinne ut noue* "Her dress and gold and finery—how nice, how neat, how novel!" (*Ep.* 222).

150. *eu edepol specie lepida mulierem!* "Dear Lord! What a good-looking woman!" (*Rud.* 415), *forma lepida mulierem | quoi facetiarum cor pectusque sit plenumque doli* "a woman of fine form, with heart and mind full of jest and deceit" (*Mil.* 782–83). With *liberalis: forma lepida et liberali captiuam adulescentulam* "a young little captive girl of a fine, free-born form" (*Ep.* 43), *quam ei mandaui mulierem | nimi' lepida forma ducit* (*Mil.* 870–71), *lepida et liberali formast* (*Mil.* 967), *quia forma lepida et liberali est* (*Per.* 130).

*Lepidus* is also occasionally applied to men's attractiveness in exceptional circumstances. When Menaechmus, who has made his entrance dressed in his wife's *palla,* fishes for a com-

*lep(idus)* has a special connection to these spheres because they originally attracted the lexeme when it meant 'soft,' both in its literal sense and in a putative metaphorical sense 'indulgent,' even 'decadent.'[151]

The semantic core of *lep(idus)* is difficult to model. The frequency of metaphorical uses dislodged *lep(idus)* from its literal center and evidently occasioned its reconstruction from its contexts as a broad ameliorative like 'delightful' or 'agreeable,' originally perhaps in erotic[152] but also in non-erotic[153] contexts. Since *lep(idus)* once meant 'soft,' which metaphorically

---

pliment from Peniculus, he says *dic hominem lepidissimum esse me* "Say that I'm a very *lepidus* man" (*Men.* 147). *Lepidus* is applied twice to Pyrgopolynices, the vain *miles gloriosus* of the play of that name. Once Milphidippa, a serving woman, feigns a soliloquy for him to overhear in which she inflates her praise of him (*quae amat hunc hominem nimium lepidum et nimia pulchritudine | militem Pyrgopolynicem* "who loves Pyrgopolynices, this too, too handsome man and a soldier of too much beauty" *Mil.* 998–99); and once the boy sent to lure him into the trap addresses him in flattering, and overstated, terms: *salue, uir lepidissume, | cumulate commoditate, praeter ceteros | duo di quem curant* "Hail, handsomest man, towering in timeliness, whom the two gods care for best of all" (*Mil.* 1382–84). The courtesan Bacchis uses *lepidus* in her attempts to entice Pistoclerus: PI. *ubi ego tum accumbam?* BA. *apud me, mi anime, ut lepidus cum lepida accubet* "Where shall I lie then?" "*Chez moi,* my love, that a lovely man may sleep with a lovely woman" (*Bac.* 81).

151. A comparable development took place in the Baltic derivatives: 'slack' or 'soft' was used as a metaphor for 'pampered,' and the other meanings were generated from associations with the pampered social classes. Thus in Latvian from such formulations as **lepnas dzīres** 'sumptuous feast,' **lepna iekārta** 'luxurious furniture,' **lepni ģērbies** 'splendidly dressed' came 'proud,' the usual sense of **lepns,** and 'be proud, be arrogant,' the usual sense of **lepuôt.** The development is easy to parallel: cf. Russian **nachal'nyj** 'impudent' (= Pol. **nachalny**) < 'pampered' ~ **cholit'** 'clean, fondle, pamper'; Moroccan Arabic *šiki* 'elegant' (of things) or 'arrogant' (of persons). In Lithuanian the sense of 'pampered, effete' was usual by the time of our earliest attestations. The trilingual dictionary of Konstantinas Širvydas (*Pirmasis Lietúvių Kalbos Žodynas,* first published in 1620, which glosses Polish with Latin and Lithuanian, provides excellent attestation for the range of the root at that time, e.g., Pol. **miękki** 'soft' = *indulgens, mollis (vitiose de homine)* = Lith. **lepus;** Pol. **rozkosznik** 'voluptuary' (obs.) = *voluptarius homo, delicatus* = Lith. **gierunas, lepunas.** For another classification of the semantic spheres to which *lep(idus)* is applied, cf. Monteil 1964: 138–62, Fyëdorov 1987.

152. When to Pistoclerus's *tuo' sum, tibi dedo operam* "All yours, at your service," Bacchis replies *lepidu's* "There's a good fellow" (*Bac.* 93), Pistoclerus has agreed to pose as her lover. Scapha's observations have to do with love (*lepidast Scapha, sapit scelesta multum* "Scapha's great, the naughty girl knows plenty" *Mos.* 170). Phaedromus, to his slave's ridicule, even applies this *lepidus* to the doorhinge of his lover's house (*Cur.* 94); agreeably, it never squeaks when he sneaks in or his lover sneaks out (cf. 15ff.). When Lysidamus says of his wife *lepidiorem uxorem nemo quisquam quam ego habeo hanc habet* "No one anywhere's got a wife as agreeable" (*Cas.* 1008), the reason is that he cannot believe she is not angry about his wandering eye. Hence also the name of *senex lepidus* for stock characters, like Periplectomenus of the *Miles Gloriosus,* who aid youths in pursuit of love (e.g., *Mil.* 135, 155, 649, 660, *Ps.* 435).

153. The use of *lepidus* described in the previous note goes beyond the erotic to include a general agreeability or the satisfaction of expectations. So for a successful performer of a

implied 'decadent,' and since even if the origins of *lep(idus)* were forgotten, it still had a special home in the bordello, where the bulk of its common referents—attractive women, exquisite accoutrements, and lavish entertainment—could be found, it may be that *lep(idus)* had, or came to have, an element like 'decadent,' 'indulgent,' or 'erotic' as a part of its semantic core. A further peculiarity is that the lexeme seems to have become partly reliteralized as a light term, of which there are clear instances later,[154] and which, if it was sensible to Plautus, may have induced him to use *lepidus* for the Greek New Comic λαμπρός, whose range is similar to that of Plautus's *lepidus*.[155]

---

task (*sumne probus, sum lepidus ciuis, qui Atticam hodie ciuitatem* | *maxumam maiorem feci atque auxi ciui femina?* "Am I not a good and proper citizen, who today has made the great Attica greater and increased it by a new citizen?" *Per.* 474). If an agreeable person is *lepidus,* so plausibly is news gladly heard (*Mercurius, Ioui' qui nuntius perhibetur, numquam aeque patri* | *suo nuntium lepidum attulit quam ego nunc meae erae nuntiabo, St.* 275) or what "sounds good on paper" (*uia istaec lepida sunt memoratui:* | *eadem in usu atque ubi periculum facias aculeata sunt etc., Bac.* 62–63). Probably derived from this sense is the frequent use of the adverb *lepide* in connection with successful outcomes (real or prospective), as in the examples later in this section, to which add *iam ego in uno saltu lepide apros capiam duos* "I'll quite nicely kill two birds with one stone" (lit. "catch two boars in one clearing," *Cas.* 476), *canes compellunt in plagas lepide lupum* "The hounds are driving the wolf smack into the net" (*Poen.* 648).

154. For example, *aurea pauonum ridenti imbuta lepore* | *saecla* "the golden race of peacocks steeped in laughing splendor" (Lucr. 2.502–3), *quae cum concreta uidebant,* | *posterius claro in terra splendere colore,* | *tollebant nitido capti leuique lepore* (5.1257–59), "Later, when they would see them congealed on the surface, glittering and bright, they would pick them up, enchanted by the smooth and shiny beauty *(lepore),*" cf. 4.83–85 (the *lepos* of light entering a theater), Cic. *Att.* 2.3.2 (of light entering windows). *Varios . . . lepores* "varied charms" (Lucr. 3.1006) and *uario distincta lepore* "marked out by varied charm" (Lucr. 5.1376) thus probably refer to the variegation of color produced by springtime and the flowering of trees, respectively. In *Or.* 96 (cf. III.3) Cicero may have been thinking of a chaplet of flowers. The development of *lep(idus)* into a 'light' word could have been eased because the morphological family from which it came, the *-idus* adjectives, comprised not only "hardness/softness" words, but also "color/light" words. "Hardness/softness" words are *callidus* 'hard, leathery,' unattested, but cf. *callēre* 'be hard, stiff'; 'clever' (first in Pl.), *flaccidus* 'drooping' (Col.), *fluidus* in the sense 'soft' (Livy), *fracidus* 'soft, pulpy' (Cato), *languidus* 'limp' (Prop.), *marcidus* 'drooping, withered, rotten' (V. Max.), *rigidus* 'rigid, set, stiff, stern' (Cic.), *solidus* 'solid, firm, unyielding' (Pl.), *stolidus* in a putative 'solid,' cogn. w. Gr. στόλος; attested as 'dull, brutish, inert' (Enn.). "Color/light" words are *albidus* 'white, whitish' (Vitr.), *candidus* 'bright, white, fair' (Pl.), *euanidus* 'disappearing' (Ov.), *fulgidus* 'brilliant, shining' (Lucr.), *limpidus* 'clear, transparent' (Catul.), *liquidus* in the sense 'limpid, clear' (Cato), *liuidus* 'greyish-blue, livid' (Catul.), *lucidus* 'bright, shining' (Lucr.), *nitidus* 'bright, radiant, gleaming' (Pl.), *pallidus* 'pale, colorless, dim' (Pl.), *rauidus* '(yellowish?)-grey' (Col.), *rubidus* 'flushed, reddish' (Pl.), *sordidus* 'dirty' (Caec.; orig. 'blackish'; *sordēre* from \***swṛd-ē-** seen also in Germanic \**swarta-,* source of OE *sweart* 'swarthy'), *splendidus* 'bright, dazzling' (Pl.), *squalidus* 'dirty' (Enn.). On the origins of adjectives in *-idus,* see Alan Nussbaum in the forthcoming Schindler Gedenkschrift.

155. OF FORTUNATE OUTCOME OR CIRCUMSTANCES: Ὡς εὐκόλως πίπτουσιν αἱ λαμπραὶ τύχαι (Menander *Mon.* 1.755); ἐκ Κύπρου λαμπρῶς πάνυ | πράττων· ἐκεῖ γὰρ ὑπό τιν'

This last development may be due partly to the influence of *facet(us)*, with which *lep(idus)* is especially associated (cf. III.3); *facet(us)*, which was applied to many of the same semantic spheres as *lep(idus)*, may have still been felt as a light term. The semantic structure of *lep(idus)* may be depicted tentatively as follows (fig. 11):

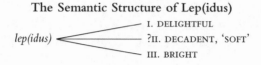

The Semantic Structure of Lep(idus)

lep(idus) &lt; I. DELIGHTFUL
?II. DECADENT, 'SOFT'
III. BRIGHT

As a broad ameliorative, *lep(idus)* described mainly the response of an observer to a stimulus, whether or not the stimulus was intended to elicit the observer's favorable response. That is, *lep(idus)* was used irrespective of whether the stimulus was performative or nonperformative. *Lep(idus)*, like *facet(us)*, could describe performed actions, for example, *edepol senem De-maenetum lepidum fuisse nobis* "Lordy! The old man Demaenetus did great for us!" (*As.* 580), or *loquere lepide et commode* "What you say is nice and fitting" (*Mil.* 615).[156] But unlike *facet(us)*, *lep(idus)* is usual when a stimulus is non-performative. A fisherman surprised to have fished a treasure chest out of the sea exclaims, *miroque modo atque incredibili hic piscatus mihi lepide euenit* "My day's fishing has come out delightfully *(lepide)*, in a wonderful, unbelievable way!" (Pl. *Rud.* 912). Such formulations as the following also describe an observer's response to fortuitous outcomes:

> *lepide hoc succedit sub manus negotium* (Pl. *Mil.* 873)
> Matters are falling nicely *(lepide)* into place

---

ἦν τῶν βασιλέων (Menander *Mis.* fr. 5); OF THE HIGH LIFE: Λεπτῶς γέ τοι ζῆν κρεῖσσον ἢ λαμπρῶς κακῶς (Menander *Mon.* 1.682); OF AGREEABILITY: λαμπρὸς εἶ (Menander *Her.* 44); OF VICTUALS OR ENTERTAINMENT: Στράτιε, φιλεῖς δήπου με. ΣΤΡ. μᾶλλον τοῦ πα-τρός· | ὁ μὲν γὰρ οὐ τρέφει με, σὺ δὲ λαμπρῶς τρέφεις (Alexis fr. 201–2 line 6 = *Pyr.* 1–2 l. 6); Κἂν ταῦτα ποιῇς ὥσπερ φράζω, | λαμπροῖς δείπνοις δεξόμεθ' ὑμᾶς (Anaxan-drides fr. 41.1–2); λαμπροὺς γενέσθαι βουλόμεσθα τοὺς γάμους (Euangelus *Anakalypto-mene* fr. 1.3). Of course *lep(idus)* need not have had any 'light' sense for Plautus to have used it as an equivalent for λαμπρός; he may have been offering a cultural, rather than a literal, translation. Indeed it is difficult to account for what I take to be preservations of an original sense 'soft' if 'bright' had come to be central in the lexeme's connotations at the time of Plautus.

156. Cf. *lepidam et suauem cantionem aliquam occupito cinaedicam* (*St.* 760) "Strike up some nice sweet song we can dance to." On *cinaedicam*, v. supra I.6 n. 97.

*uolup est, quod agas, si id procedit lepide atque ex sententia* (Pl. *Mil.* 947)

It's a joy when what you're doing goes nicely *(lepide)* and according to plan

*inest lepos in nuntio tuo magnus* (Pl. *Rud.* 352)

What delight *(lepos)* your message brings

The salient fact of the post-Plautine development of *lep(idus)* is that the latter type, so prominent and so natural-seeming in Plautus, vanishes. It is simply not found again. The difference between post-Plautine and Plautine *lep(idus)* is thus roughly that between American English "brilliant," which is used only of performed or performable actions or states ("brilliant move"; "brilliant idea") and British English "brilliant," which is used also of non-performed actions etc. ("brilliant weather"; "brilliant taste"; "me mum's brilliant" = "she's great, delightful, agreeable"). We might say that *lep(idus)* was "performativized," that is, it came to require that its referents (with the exception of natural light sources, I.9 n. 154) be performed actions. To produce this development, a linguistic and a social cause dovetailed. In linguistic terms the "performativizing" of *lep(idus)* may be the final outcome of its lost connection to 'softness.' If *lep(idus)* came to be construed as a light term, as described above, it may have fallen under the influence of *facet(us),* a native-born light term, so to speak, which perhaps imparted to metaphorical *lep(idus)* its own characteristic of only modifying performative referents. The two words were certainly associated, since by the late Republic *lepos et facetiae* appears as a set phrase attested in Cicero, Sallust, and Catullus (v. infra).

There is also a social cause for the performativizing of *lep(idus),* namely the increasing prominence of performances from the third century on. That such performances came to be described by *lep(idus)* at that time is suggested by later attestations.[157] Cicero complains that the games for the dedication of Pompey's theater "didn't even have the charm *(lepos)* of ordinary games."[158] About a dancer in Horace called *Lepos* (*Serm.* 2.6.72), Porphyrio

157. *Lep(idus),* as we saw, was associated with lavish entertainment, and this old connection of *lep(idus)* may perhaps have played a part in the development. With the changes to the *convivium,* such lavish entertainment was no longer the personal indulgence of visitors to bordellos, but was now a political and social tool. The *lep(idus)* items on display at a *convivium* were offered for the approval of other diners; the items were, so to say, "performed," that is, put on display and meant to elicit a favorable response. No such use of *lep(idus)* is attested, however. *Lepores* is used by Lucretius of the "delights" of a dinner party (4.1133), a Plautine use and not palpably performative in sense, and it seems better to look elsewhere for the source of the change.

158. *(ludi) ne id quidem leporis habuerunt quod solent mediocres ludi* (*Fam.* 7.1.2).

ad loc. guesses the obvious: "Lepos is the name of a chief mimic actor, who got his name because of his pleasing *(iucundus)* and delicate *(mollis)* dancing and speech" (enumerating two of the qualities postulated above in fig. 11).[159] Lucretius uses *lepores* for the creative arts generally, in distinction to *doctrinae* "science and philosophy."[160] Like *uenust(us)*, *lep(idus)* may have originally been applied to such performances because of their 'titillating' or 'soft' quality. With the increasing importance of performance, the 'soft' element, already weak, might well have faded away altogether.

The performance described by *lep(idus)* might be one of verbal dexterity or grace, a use probably generated or disseminated in the context of the *convivium*, with its ἀκροάματα. A fragment of Pomponius which refers to a *diadema*, or 'crown,' given for victories at table, uses *lepos* in this connection: *cuiusuis leporis Liber diademam dedit* "Lord Wine gave a prize for every possible kind of *lepos*" *(com.* 163). The pair *lepos et facetiae*, which has slightly different connotations in Cicero, Sallust, and Catullus, generally has to do with "performed" verbal wit.[161] Sallust, for example, uses it of Sempronia's abilities:

> *uerum ingenium eius haud absurdum: posse uersus facere, iocum mouere, sermone uti uel modesto uel molli uel procaci; prorsus multae facetiae multusque lepos inerat.*

> But Sempronia's intellect was not dull: she could compose poetry, raise a joke, choose to speak in a manner balanced or delicate or impudent; in short *(prorsus),* hers was much wittiness *( facetiae)* and much charm *(lepos).*[162]

*(Cat.* 25.5)

Sempronia's expertise, displayed in *convivia* no doubt, comprises the very practices for which Cato ridiculed his opponent M. Caelius (I.2 above):

| *Cato (ORF 8.115)* | *Sallust (Cat. 25.5)* |
| --- | --- |
| *iocos dicit* | *iocos mouere* |
|   cf. *ridicula fundere* (ORF 8.114) | |
| *Graecos uersus agit* | *uersus facere* |
| *uoces demutat* | *sermone uti uel modesto uel molli uel procaci* |

159. *Lepos nomen archimimi, qui eo, quod iucunde et molliter et saltaret et eloqueretur, sic appellatus est.*

160. *adde repertores doctrinarum atque leporum,* | *adde Heliconiadum comites,* 3.1036–37; cf. Bailey ad loc. and Verg. *Aen.* 6.662–63; Fyëdorov 1987: 217.

161. Cicero uses the pair to refer to humor (VI.3), and Catullus to refer to the interactive grace of the convivial table (VII.3) and to polymetric poetry (VII.4).

162. Cf. Plutarch's description of Cornelia: ἐνῆν δὲ τῇ κόρῃ πολλὰ φίλτρα δίχα τῶν ἀφ' ὥρας. καὶ γὰρ περὶ γράμματα καλῶς ἤσκητο καὶ περὶ λύραν καὶ γεωμετρίαν, καὶ

Sallust's use of *lepos* and *facetiae* here, I suggest, preserves an instance of the application to attractive verbal performance of the new senses of *lep(idus)* and *facet(us)* that were developing in the second century. The use of *prorsus,* which functions here, as elsewhere in Sallust,[163] to sum up a series of points, makes this passage effectively a definition of *lepos* and *facetiae:* they comprise various forms of attractive verbal performance, particularly those that display social status. That very sense of *lepid(us)* is found in the epitaph of Claudia, which dates to the time of the Gracchi and records both Claudia's matronly and maternal duties and her social attractiveness:

> *hospes quod deico paullum est: asta ac pellege.*
>> Stranger, what I have to say is brief:
>> Stand by and read it through.
> *heic est sepulcrum hau pulcrum pulcrai feminae.*
>> This is the uncomely catacomb[164]
>> of a comely woman.
> *nomen parentes nominarunt Claudiam.*
>> Her parents named her the name Claudia.
> *suom mareitum corde deilexit souo.*
>> Her husband with all her heart she loved.
> *gnatos duos creauit. horunc alterum*
>> She bore two sons. The one of them
> *in terra linquit, alium sub terra locat.*
>> she leaves on the earth,
>> the other lays beneath it.
> *sermone lepido, tum autem incessu commodo.*
>> Her speech was charming,
>> her gait attractive.
> *domum seruauit, lanam fecit. dixi. abei.*
>> She kept the house,
>> she wove the wool.
>> I have spoken. You may go.
>> (*CIL* 1² 1211 = *CIL* 6.15346)

---

λόγων φιλοσόφων εἴθιστο χρησίμως ἀκούειν. καὶ προσῆν τούτοις ἦθος ἀηδίας καὶ περι-
εργίας καθαρόν, ἃ δὴ νέαις προστρίβεται γυναιξὶ τὰ τοιαῦτα μαθήματα (*Pomp.* 55.1).

163. *OLD* 4; cf. *Cat.* 15.5, *Jug.* 76.4.

164. The inaccurate and bad paranomasia is intended to represent a *figura etymologica* in the Latin: *hau pulchrum* 'not beautiful' is an epithet of *sepulchrum* 'tomb' but also its etymology, reading *sepulchrum* as a compound of *pulchrum* 'beautiful' and *se* 'apart, not, lacking' (cf. *securus* 'carefree').

The seventh line describes Claudia's social performance: she knew how to speak and move in an attractive and charming way.[165] Notably the language of the epitaph is rife with figures of speech, some of which have older pedigrees but which, as I explain below, also exemplified the verbal ethic of the *convivium* (cf. III.7).[166] The entrance of "immoral" language into the approbative vocabulary of the social elite is clearly displayed in this text, which belongs to the relatively conservative genre of the tombstone.

Because of the complexities of its semantic history, *lep(idus)* is particularly difficult to diagram, but the development may perhaps be graphed as follows (fig. 12):

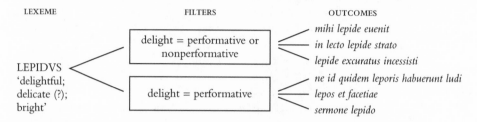

### I.10. *Festiu(us):* From *Dies Festi* to *Convivia*

The claim that the shift of *lep(idus)* and *facet(us)* should be attributed to the *convivium* is bolstered by the case of *festiu(us)*. Connected to *festus* 'festal,' *festiuus* originally meant 'pertaining to a festal celebration,' which is clear from older Latin. On festal days people assembled for games and shows, to which Plautus applies *festiuus:* an audience is described as sitting *in festiuo loco* "in a *festiuus* place" (*Mil.* 83); the games at Nemea and Olympia are *ludi festiui* "*festiuus* games" (*Cas.* 760). The home was specially decorated. An anonymous tragic fragment reads, "to decorate this festal day very festally" (*diem hunc decorare festum festiuissime,* Anon. Trag. 223). Novius refers to "a house

165. *Incessus* 'gait' often has overtones of 'gait as indicative of character,' inasmuch as bodily motion was taken as reflecting one's inner nature (cf. Corbeill 1996: 165–67). In *de Officiis,* Cicero advises that one's carriage be neither too delicate *(tarditates molliores)* nor too hasty *(nimiae celeritates),* the latter to be avoided because it causes panting and facial distortion, "which give considerable suggestion that the person is not collected" (*ex quibus magna significatio fit non adesse constantiam,* 1.131). For some examples of *incessus* in this function, cf. *uiden tu Phrugis incessum? quam est confidens! di istunc perduint* "Look at how that Phrygian walks! Boy is he cocky! I hope he drops dead" (Turpil. *pall.* 102); *quodsi uultum tibi, si incessum fingeres, quo grauior uiderere, non esses tui similis* "If you were affecting an expression and a gait to look more serious, you wouldn't look like yourself" (Cic. *Fin.* 2.77); *incessus psaltriae* "a walk like a lute girl's" (Cic. *in P. Clodium et Curionem,* fr. 22, V.6).

166. *Sepulchrum hau pulchrum = adnominatio commutandis litteris* (παρονομασία, *Rhet. Her.* 4.29); *suom . . . suou* = κύκλος (Eustath. ad Hom. *Il.* 10 p. 818); *in terra . . . sub terra* = πολύπτωτον (cf. *Rhet. Her.* 4.30, where, however, it is classed as a type of παρονομασία).

prepared festally for a beautiful family" (*domus parata pulchrae familiae festuiter, com.* 40). Hence in Plautus lodgings where the care is "softer than King Antiochus gets" are described as *festiuus* (*Poen.* 695). Special meals were also served.[167] The ideas of food and decoration combine in a line of Plautus: "we were welcomed festively *(festiue)* in a festive place *(in festiuo loco)* with carefully prepared food and elegances worthy of the gods" (*Ps.* 1254).[168]

*Festiu(us)* also referred to the jolly and agreeable frame of mind typical of celebrations. In an address to Jupiter (which imitates the heavy verbal play of authentic archaic prayers), Ergasilus lists among the blessings Jupiter gives him *laudem lucrum ludum iocum festiuitatem ferias* (Pl. *Capt.* 770) "glory and gain, fun and games, feasts and festivity." Plautus uses *festiuus* in this sense to refer to "jolly" or "fun" tricks *(facinus facere lepidum et festiuom, Poen.* 308; *festiuom facinus, Poen.* 1086, *festiuam . . . operam, Mil.* 591). This sense comes directly out of the connection to festal days, when the social order was inverted and pranks were the order of the day.[169] The laxity associated with festal days probably generated the sense 'agreeable,' the likely sense in Plautus's use of *festiu(us)* as a term of endearment (*Poen.* 839, *Cas.* 135, 577). The same use is known to Terence (*mei patris festiuitatem et facilitatem, Eu.* 1048; *festiuom caput, Ad.* 261; *o pater mi festiuissime, Ad.* 983; *facilem et festiuom, Ad.* 986).

By the classical period, however, the range of *festiu(us)* has changed considerably. There are some uses that resemble the old ones. The connection to 'jollity' or 'fun' remains. When Falcidius lies to his mother that he has lent a large sum to Flaccus, Cicero calls him a *festiuus filius* ( jolly lad) lying to his *matercula* (mother dear, *Flac.* 91), recalling social inversion, though ironically of course. In a letter to Torquatus, Cicero refers to his sons, whom Torquatus misses, as *(pueri) quibus nihil potest esse festiuius* "the boys than whom nothing can be more *festiuus*" (*Fam.* 6.4.3). Other instances of *festiu(us)*, however, seem to have to do with a more socially exclusive humor than that in Plautus. One may hazard that *festiu(us)* continued to mean 'connected to festal days,' but that by 'festal' was now meant not the traditional cult celebration, whether familial or civic, but the exclusive *convivium*.[170] *Festiuus* is used

167. Cf. *quae haec daps est? qui festus dies?* "What is this feast? What this festal day?" (*Andr. Od.* 8, translating Hom. *Od.* 9.225).

168. *ita uictu excurato, ita magnis munditiis <et> dis dignis | itaque in loco festiuo sumus festiue accepti.*

169. Cf. E. Segal 1987.

170. *Festiu(us)* was in any case evidently something of an elegant cotidianism for 'nice'; cf. *libris . . . quorum habeo Anti festiuam copiam* 'a jolly lot' = 'very many' (*Att.* 2.6.1); *festiue . . . et minore sonitu quam putaram* 'great . . . and without the crash I'd expected' (*Att.* 2.9.1); *soles enim tu haec festiue odorari* 'you're hilariously good at sniffing these things out' (*Att.* 4.14.2).

by Varro beside *bellus* as a word for the jolly convive (*Men.* fr. 312 Bücheler, above I.7). Cicero refers to Verres' practice of always leaving a party with something valuable of the host's as a *festiuum acroama* "delightful diversion" (*Ver.* 2.4.49), where the irony ensures the status of *festiu(us)* as a *vox propria* in this connection. Nothing will prove to be "more *festiuus*" than Verres' son (*Ver.* 2.3.162), who has grown up in a *luxuria* that features libertine *convivia* (cf. 160). Egilius, whom Cicero describes as *festiuus*, was also thought to be *mollis* (*de Orat.* 2.277; below, VI.3), which suggests that *festiuus* there may mean 'participating in a gay social life,' rather than simply 'witty.'

In any case, *festiu(us)*, like *lep(idus)* and *facet(us)*, narrows to describe primarily verbal humor. *Festiu(us)* is occasional in Cicero's rhetorica as a term for 'humor.' Extended narrative humor is *perpetua festiuitas* (*de Orat.* 2.219). There was no speech "more salted with charm and humor" *(neque lepore neque festiuitate conditior)* than the one Crassus gave against Cn. Domitius (*de Orat.* 2.227). The effects of the poetics of the *convivium* on the use of *festiu(us)* as a rhetorical critical term are especially notable and are discussed below (III.7). We may represent the development as follows (fig. 13):

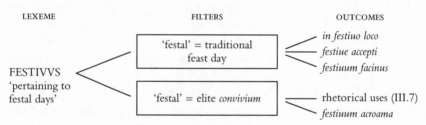

The development of *lep(idus)*, *facet(us)*, and *festiu(us)* may be represented as follows (fig. 14): [171]

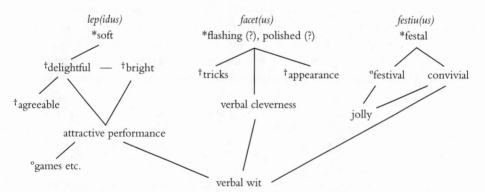

171. In this figure [*] indicates original meanings, [†] indicates semantic applications obsolete by the late Republic, and [°] indicates uses that are marginal or rare by the late Republic.

It is possible to view the narrowing of *lep(idus)*, *facet(us)*, and *festiu(us)* to describe verbal wit not as a function of real semantic development but as a trick of the sources: a more prominent role is played by "tricking" or "jollity" in comedy, the context for most of the earlier attestations, and by verbal wit in Cicero, source of most of the late Republican attestations. I suggest, however, that this narrowing was real, a function of the social elite's use of the words. Competition among the elite was largely verbal: they controlled their world with words: rallying the troops, swaying the populace, persuading their peers, needling their opponents, showing off or scoring points at *convivia*, producing bon mots worthy of circulation.[172] It is clear that some tradition, oral and written, of preserving witticisms extended back to the second century.[173] The narrowing of *lep(idus)*, *facet(us)*, and *festiu(us)*, especially beside the developments in *bellus* and *elegan(s)*, is better attributed to their appropriation by a particular social class.

## I.11. Conclusion

We have seen, then, that there is a set of lexemes, which I have been calling the language of social performance, whose semantics shifted, or whose range of application changed dramatically, in the period after Plautus. The character of the changes suggests that they occurred in response to the social practices that were growing rapidly in popularity in the second century. It is possible that some of these semantic developments had happened during, or even before, Plautus's lifetime and simply left no trace; that is, the appearance of change between Plautus and later Latin might be a function of genre. However, if the changes had happened, one might have expected them to be parodied in Plautus, who parodies so much else, such as legal language, tragedy, and prayer. I have been able to find no convincing example of the language of social performance used as a parody of elite aestheticism in Plautus. It might be possible to argue that the programmatic character of the language of social performance for comic characters, of whose core values it constitutes the central semantic field, signifies exactly that sort of parody, and that, in accord with the carnival atmosphere of Plautine plays, what was otherwise the language of noble self-creation was being turned on its head. However, in that same atmosphere, it is equally plausible that what was disreputable language might have been put to use as if it were not. The language of social performance appears in ways that might parody elite speech only in Terence (cf. IV.5 with n. 35)—whose writing coincides exactly with the period to which I have been attributing

172. For the political power of humor, cf. Corbeill 1996.
173. Some of the jokes in the *de Oratore* probably derive from oral tradition. Cf. LPR 200–204.

the shifts. In any case, even if the semantic developments detailed in I.5 to I.10 had begun before the adoption of Hellenizing practices as I have described, they could not have failed to be quickened by the adoption of more and more Greek-style aesthetic practices, with which the language of social performance is forever after closely associated (cf. II.3). Those practices may therefore fairly be regarded as the crucible responsible for the alteration of our lexemes. Indeed they are one small aspect of the linguistic change that accompanied an increasingly self-conscious social class that was learning Greek rhetoric and Greek linguistics, speaking more carefully, and pruning and refining its own language into a distinctive instrument of social control. Chapter 2 frames some of the ideological issues implicated in the language of social performance that concerns the rest of this study.

## CHAPTER II

# *Grauitate Mixtus Lepos*
# The Ideologies of the Language
# of Social Performance

Krzyczano na modnisiów, a brano z nich wzory,
Zmieniano wiarę, mowę, prawa i ubiory.

They cried against the dandies, adopted their ways nonetheless,
Changing their faith and their law, and their manner of speech and
dress.

Adam Mickiewicz, Pan Tadeusz, Book I

## II.1. Introduction

The intrusion of aestheticism into the terrain of social value in the second
century required an approbative vocabulary, which was formed from the
lexemes surveyed in chapter 1. As we saw, they underwent changes both semantic and tonal consistent with the cultural developments of the second
century. In this chapter I suggest that that set of lexemes, which I have called
the language of social performance, provides a sensitive instrument for tracking the attitudes of texts toward those cultural developments. *Grautitate mixtus lepos,* "charm combined with weight of character" (cf. Cic. *Rep.* 2.1), was
for some very few Romans an impossibility, for some an excuse, and for most
an ideal—but not unequivocally.

In this chapter I also introduce a diagram of a "cultural model" useful to
the rest of the book. By a cultural model I mean simply a mental grid that
represents in reduced, idealized form some aspect of cultural reality and is
used as a map to guide expectations and decisions in lived reality.[1] A cultural model is not unlike a legal principle, which represents an ideal, ab-
stracted model of some aspect of human action and provides a frame for understanding individual cases. In the second century the Romans created a
new cultural model with which the language of social performance was intimately associated. Section II.2 describes that model and its utility for our
analysis, and II.3 the relationship of the language of social performance to
that model.

---

1. For several case studies of cultural models, cf. Holland and Quinn 1987.

## II.2. The Ambiguities and Analogues of Aestheticism

We can understand the aestheticism of the social elite, described in chapter 1, in terms of a few conceptual equations. The widespread adoption of aestheticizing practices meant that for many the equation "aesthetic = socially valuable" was valid. But negate either term of this equation, and equations emerge that are equally valid: "aesthetic = socially valueless" and "inaesthetic = socially valuable." Both latter equations are implicit, for example, in Cato's occasional tendentious stance as a contrarian and in the disparagement by Sallust's Marius of the by-then entrenched social elite. The fact that all three of these equations retained some validity points toward a useful model for the conceptual development that created them. We may say that the polarity "aesthetic : inaesthetic" mapped over the polarity "socially valuable : socially valueless" incompletely (this much was implied in fig. 2 above). The only partial overlap of the two polarities created a new cultural model with three categories, which we may represent as follows (fig. 15):

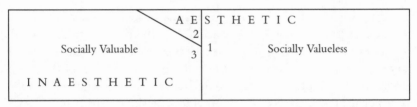

(1) = Socially Valueless: Aesthetic
(2) = Socially Valuable: Aesthetic
(3) = Socially Valuable: Inaesthetic

The imperfect melding of the two polarities permitted different responses. Some, evidently very few, Romans will have held that aestheticism was incompatible with social value—that aestheticism ought never to have "crossed the border" to create category (2). Such Romans, in effect, refused to allow their old cultural models to be updated. The sententious formulations of Sallust's populist Marius may owe something to a tradition of moralist rhetoric that took a dim view of the new developments. When Marius attributes to his father the lesson that *arma non supellectilem decori esse* (*Jug.* 85.40), that "the true ornament *(decus)* is a weapon, not furniture," Marius is attempting to restore *decus* to its original meaning, 'glory, honor,' and not the meaning 'decoration' that it had in the meantime developed (cf. *OLD* I.4).[2] Marius's phrase *conuiuiis gratiam quaerere* "to seek political influence by

2. Cf. Skinner 1980: 570–72 for the semantic effects caused by tendentious applications of evaluative language.

entertaining" (*Jug.* 4.3) is meant as a jarring paradox. Cicero sometimes takes this stance, but only to attack foreigners or social inferiors (V.3).

The social elite, as a whole, certainly did not agree that aestheticism was incompatible with social worth, as we saw in chapter 1. But the fact that the polarities mapped over each other imperfectly meant that, even with broad acceptance that category (2) was valuable, the border between (2) and (1) remained contentious. Those engaging in some particular brand of aestheticism doubtless represented and even understood it as belonging to category (2), the sort of aestheticism that had social worth. Aemilius Paullus, for example, in claiming that the same sort of mind was required to set a table and array a battle line, effectively asserts that the aestheticism of the *convivium* belongs to category (2) because of its structural similarities to war, which is resolutely a category (3) activity. Noble youths who were learning how to dance and play the *sambuca* no doubt believed the possession of those skills was something positive, for example an advertisement of their parents' wealth or patronage of the arts. Opponents of a particular practice, on the other hand, would try to link it not with category (3) but with category (1). Scipio Aemilianus attacked the practice of sending youth to dancing school by depicting dancing as a province of the socially inferior:

> They are taught unseemly posturings; they go to acting schools with catamites, sambuca and psalterium in hand; they learn to sing, which our elders considered reproachful in the freeborn. Freeborn girls and boys, I tell you, are going to dancing school among catamites. When someone told me this story, I could not convince myself that nobles were teaching their children these things; but when I was taken to a dancing school, I swear to you I saw there more than five hundred boys and girls, among them—and this caused me sadness for the state—a boy wearing his bulla, the son of a candidate for office, no less than twelve years old, dancing, with crotala in hand, a dance that a shameless slave boy could not decently dance.[3]
>
> (*ORF* 21.30 = Macr. 3.14.6)

Hosts of luxurious dinner parties no doubt believed the parties to be symbolic of order and wealth, and thus linked to category (3); but Cato's pun-

---

3. *docentur praestigias inhonestas; cum cinaedulis et sambuca psalterioque eunt in ludum histrionum; discunt cantare, quae maiores nostri ingenuis probro ducier uolerunt. eunt, inquam, in ludum saltatorium inter cinaedos uirgines puerique ingenui. haec cum mihi quisquam narrabat, non poteram animum inducere, ea liberos suos homines nobiles docere: sed cum ductus sum in ludum saltatorium, plus medius fidius in eo ludo uidi pueris uirginibusque quingentis, in his unum (quod me rei publicae maxime miseritum est) puerum bullatum, petitoris filium non minorem annis duodecim, cum crotalis saltare, quam saltationem impudicus seruulus honeste saltare non posset,* from the speech *Contra legem iudiciariam Ti. Gracchi*, delivered in 129. Cf. also Plato *Leg.* 2.669c.

gent formulation *magna . . . cura cibi, magna uirtutis incuria* "too much attention to food means too little attention to virtue"[4] takes such parties as
indicative of laxity, so linking them to category (1).[5] In short, the imperfect
melding of the two polarities sorted Romans into reactionaries, who have
left little trace, and aesthetes of various kinds. The latter group ranged from
those who used the partial acceptance of aestheticism to justify whatever
practices they themselves fancied, to those who carefully examined any aesthetic practice to ensure that it was not at odds with more traditional conceptions of social worth. These three positions survive to the late Republic,
providing, respectively, an occasional rhetorical stance for Cicero (*lepos* is
nothing before *grauitas*), a keynote of Catullan polymetric (*lepos* can substitute for *grauitas*), and the guiding principle for Cicero's *de Oratore* (*lepos* must
serve *grauitas*).

Another polarity can be fitted onto our diagram. All of the aestheticizing practices adopted in the second century were, as we have seen, Hellenic.
The literary lecture, the elegant dinner party, the lavish banquet, verse and
banter, were in whole or part distinctly Greek. Different polarities or com-
plementarities could be inscribed over the opposition between "Roman"
and "Greek." "Greek" could stand for "frivolous" and "Roman" for "serious," justifying attack on the "Greek." Cato can declare the Greeks an "entirely useless" *(nequissimus)* and "intransigent" *(indocilis)* race, and advises
"looking into" *(inspicere)* their literature but not "mastering" *(perdiscere)* it
(*Med.* fr. 1 = Plin. *Nat.* 29.14).[6] Cicero derisively describes L. Calpurnius
Piso as *crepidatus*, i.e., wearing Greek sandals or κρηπῖδες, which were "suitable for a phil-Hellene, unseemly for a proconsul."[7] In Horace the one "used
to Greek living" (*adsuetus graecari, Serm.* 2.2.11) is too feeble for the "real"
exercise of *Romana militia* "Roman military training." But the construction
of "Greek" as "other" paradoxically also permitted the "Greek" to stand for
"up-to-date," turning "Roman" into "staid." L. Scipio Asiagenus had erected
on the Capitol a statue of himself wearing a Greek cloak *(chlamys)* and

4. *ORF* 8.146 = Amm. Marc. 16.5.2.

5. It is important to add that Cato was no "pure" curmudgeon, opposed virulently to
all Hellenic art. His stance, which both embraced and rejected different aspects of Hellenism,
was entirely consistent throughout his life: before admitting any aesthetic practice into category (2), he applied rigorous tests to ensure that it was compatible with the demands of
category (3); cf. Gruen 1992.

6. For a persuasive interpretation of the *de Medicina* as deliberately tendentious and an-
tagonistic, rather than a true expression of Cato's feelings, see Gruen 1992: 75–80.

7. Nisbet 1975 ad 92, where see note; cf. *consularis homo soccos habuit et pallium* (*Rab. Post.*
10) and Heskel 1994.

κρηπῖδες (Cic. *Rab. Perd.* 27),—the very footwear Cicero mocks on Piso (*Pis.* 93, below V.6). The paradoxes of the variable polarities are captured by Lucilius:

> *porro "clinopodas" "lychnos" que ut diximus semnos*
> *ante, "pedes lecti" atque "lucernas"*

> When we solemnly said "*les pieds de divan*" and "*les lampes*"
> instead of just "couch legs" and "lamps"
>
> (15–16MW, 16–17K)[8]

*Clinopodes* and *lynchnoi* are convivial appurtenances, not belonging to the 'solemn' side of life, but their naming in Greek is styled as 'grave' or 'solemn' because it departs impressively from dull, ordinary practice. Another

8. This translation follows the clause division of Warmington, taking *ante* as a preposition ("in preference to," *OLD* 8), not an adverb, and *clinopodas lychnosque* as fronted around *ut*. Other scholars construe differently. Puelma Piwonka 1948: 30–31 takes *ut diximus semnos ante* as a parenthesis, referring to *clinopodas* and *lynchos;* supplies *dicere oportet* to fill out the second verse, making *pedes lecti* and *lucernas* into predications; and brings 17M = 14W = 18K *arutaenaeque inquit aquales* (sc. *significentur* ἀφελῶς) into close relation. Thus: "'<One should call>' "*clinopodes*" and "*lychnoi*," as we said before, "*pedes lecti*" and "*lucernae*" (instead) . . . and "*arutaenae*" (should be called simply) "*aquales*,'" he said." Krenkel 1970: 110–11 takes *clinopodas lynchosque* as a sentence fragment and *ut diximus* . . . "*lucernas*" as a single clause, thus: "sodann Klinopoden und Lüster, wo wir früher—<sogar> in gravitätischen Situationen—<nur> Füße vom Bettgestell und Lampen sagten." Krenkel's interpretation can be dismissed: the 'solemnity' in question is a less appropriate description of ordinary Latin words than of Greek words impressively trilled (and ironically so, since σεμνότης in Greek rhetorical theory typically concerns the discussion of important topics like virtue and religion, which convivial appurtenances are not). But neither must the interpretation of Puelma Piwonka be accepted entire to secure this sense.

Assigning the verses to a speaker has also occasioned some disagreement; Macrobius, who preserves the fragment (*Sat.* 6.4.18), does not specify a speaker. That book I featured a council of the gods, dealing with the death of a certain Lupus (L. Cornelius Lentulus Lupus; see Marx 1904: xxxviff.), is clear from Serv. *Aen.* 10.104ff. and has occasioned attempts to fit the fragment into the context of such a council. Marx 1905: 10 supports the idea that a god is the speaker by the parallel of Varro *L.L.* 9.22, which features a god complaining about changed names. Cichorius 1908: 227–28 and Terzaghi 1934: 274–75 assign the verses to Romulus as a god apt to have said *diximus ante:* "In seinem Munde ist aber auch '*diximus ante*' vollkommen verständlich, denn er kann allerdings sagen 'zu meiner Zeit, da haben wir so und so gesprochen'" (Cichorius 228). This explanation is rejected by Puelma Piwonka 1948: 30 n. 4 on the grounds that there is no evidence for Romulus's participation in the council; he takes *diximus* as simply a *pluralis majestatis,* referring to an earlier utterance by the god himself, and not to patterns of Roman speech. I see no way to decide the issue; a god may be quoting a Roman defender of convivial practice *in extenso* or the patron-god of the *luxus mensae* may be defending his practice.

passage, in the voice of Q. Mucius Scaevola, concerns the Hellenophilia of T. Albucius:

> *Graecum te, Albuci, quam Romanum atque Sabinum*
> *municipem Ponti, Tritani, centurionum*
> *praeclarorum hominum ac primorum signiferumque*
> *maluisti dici. Graece ergo praetor Athenis*
> *id quod maluisti te, cum ad me accedis, saluto:*
> *"chaere" inquam "Tite." Lictores, turma omnis chorusque:*
> *"chaere, Tite." Hinc hostis mi Albucius, hinc inimicus.*

> You'd rather be called a Greek, Albucius, than a Roman,
> a Sabine, a townsman of Pontius and Tritanus, centurions,
> famous, distinguished men, standard-bearers!
> And so in Athens, during my praetorship,
> when you approached me, I followed your wishes,
> greeted you in Greek: "χαῖρε, Titus!" Then my lictors
> and retinue chimed in "χαῖρε, Titus!" And ever since then
> Albucius has been my enemy and opponent.
>
> (88–94M, 87–93W, 89–95K)

Albucius doubtless thought his love of Greek was suave and distinguished; Scaevola explodes his pretense, not accidentally, by using his lictors: traditional symbols of power, solid bastions of (3). In short, for "aesthetic : inaesthetic" in fig. 15, the opposition "Greek : Roman" may be substituted, with the same skewed mapping (fig. 16):

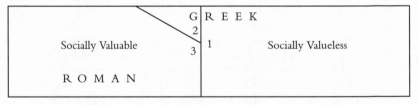

(1) = Socially Valueless: Greek
(2) = Socially Valuable: Greek
(3) = Socially Valuable: Roman

Scipio Asiagenus surely wanted to be considered as belonging to category (2), taking advantage of the Hellenism permissible to the upper classes. Cicero, on the other hand, is attempting to put Piso into category (1). Just like the polarity "aesthetic : inaesthetic," the polarity "Greek : Roman" mapped imperfectly over the opposition between social value and social valuelessness, producing the same struggles about the border between (1) and (2) as the first polarity did.

One more polarity may be inscribed over our diagram, and it is suggested by Asiagenus's statue. His Hellenic additions to the Roman visual vocabulary must have been felt as agonistic. The togate statue, the norm from which such statues depart, emphasized "a strictly ordered power structure with officials rotating every year."[9] A new formula must have been seen in part as stressing individuality. Statues did not need to be as Hellenic as Asiagenus's to serve the same function: the censors of 158 ordered the removal of all statues around the Forum which had not been positioned there by popular or senatorial decree.[10] As Gruen 1992: 121 puts it, "The distinction drawn by the censors enunciated an important principle: that statuary should memorialize national achievements and serve the collective interest rather than private ambitions." Statuary was not the only means whereby individuals could draw attention to themselves as outside of the civic system. The Hellenized *convivium,* whether it ever served as a practical means for currying political support or not, certainly drew attention to the host, putting him on display as master of ceremonies. Aemilius Paullus, as we saw, was an ἀπόλαυσμα and θέαμα at his own banquets.[11] The sorts of performance embraced by M. Caelius or Aemilianus's dancers also must have focused attention on them as performers. In short, much as the elite had adopted and augmented, for the expression of their own class identity, the aesthetic means they had introduced for the expression of civic ideals, so did individual members of the elite use some of the same means to draw attention to themselves alone. Aestheticism, embraced by the state to express collective identity, could paradoxically be used to express individualism.

The aestheticism of such parties could be attacked as antithetical to communal identity. Aemilianus's attack on noble children's dancing depends on reference to the *maiores,* who forbade dancing, and to the contemporary structure of society, which distinguished between tasks fit for slave and free; in short, to two paradigms for the construction of communal identity. The limiting of the number of guests at *convivia,* frequently stipulated by sumptuary legislation, can be seen as intended to preserve communal identity, hindering individuals (without notable success) from running a kind of cycle of private festivals. In short, the burgeoning elite aestheticism of the second century might serve to highlight individuals; while that highlight-

9. Zanker 1988: 5.

10. *statuas circa forum eorum qui magistratum gesserant sublatas omnes praeter eas quae populi aut senatus sententia statutae essent,* Plin. *Nat.* 34.30.

11. Plut. *Aem. Paul.* 28.9; above, I.2 n.20.

ing was obviously acceptable to some degree, it was also sometimes unacceptable or could be presented as unacceptable. Therefore another polarity might be inscribed over our diagram, contrasting "individualist" and "communalist" strains in the depiction of self (fig. 17):

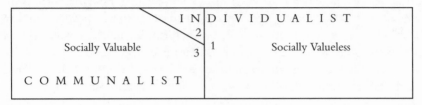

(1) = Socially Valueless: Individualist
(2) = Socially Valuable: Individualist
(3) = Socially Valuable: Communalist

## II.3. The Antagonism of the Language of Social Performance

The members of the language of social performance are intimately connected to the several terms of this new cultural model. That they formed an aesthetic language is obvious. *Lep(idus),* for example, referred to the attractiveness of performances (I.9), and *uenust(us)* to the grace of gesture (I.6). *Elegan(s)* could describe the collection of artwork (I.5), and *facet(us)* elements of linguistic distinction (I.8, cf. III.2 below). All of the lexemes become part of the critical language of rhetoric (ch. 3). But there also remained something "Greek" about the language of social performance up through the late Republic. The *facetus* that Lucilius applies to Scipio Aemilianus probably has to do with his knowledge of Greek linguistic theory (I.8). *Festiuus* in Cicero describes an epigram of Philodemus (*Pis.* 70, V.2) and an *acroama* (= ἀκρόαμα, *Ver.* 2.4.49, I.10). *Sermonis lepos* is a characteristic Cicero assigns to the Greeks besides their "clever minds" *(ingeniorum acumen)* and "ready tongues" *(dicendi copia, Flac.* 9, V.3). The *lepos* that is so essential to Cicero's understanding of the place of humor in the elite world probably aims to capture some of the sense of χάρις (VI.3). Falcidius, who is described as *festiuus,* frequented Greek parties (*Flac.* 91, cf. I.10, V.3 fin.). Catullan *uenust(us)* can serve as a term to indicate those who appreciate the tropes of Greek poetry (VII.5), and in Catullus *lepos* and *facetiae* are terms for Callimachean poetics (VII.4).

The language of social performance was also amenable to expressing ideals of individualism, inasmuch as the semantics of most of the words, after the second century, have to do with deliberate arrangements or presentations on the part of performers, that is to say, with "making oneself" rather than "being oneself." *Elegan(s)*, which has obviously to do with choice, is very clearly a "making word." *Venust(us)*, one of whose semantic nodes is 'well-arranged,' could thus be used as a "making" word, describing "made" arrangements. The person who acts *belle* is acting: assuming a role as if donning a sympote's wreath. *Facet(us)* already described performative actions, and *lep(idus)*, as we have seen, loses all nonperformative functions in the second century.

*Facet(us)* and *lep(idus)* raise a further question. As we have seen, *facet(us)* may have been a 'light' word (I.8) and *lep(idus)* partly followed suit (I.9). Latin has many other words for 'bright' or 'lighted' that were not coopted into the language of social performance, such as *splendidus, nitidus, lucidus,* and *clarus.* Why did they, too, not become words for verbal wit? The answer may lie in the kinds of light sources with which they are connected. Most of the latter words are connected mainly with natural light sources. When used metaphorically, these typically represent aristocratic achievement or status. *Clarus* is a word especially associated with the *nobiles.*[12] *Splend(or)* is the word "qui convient le mieux à marquer la 'dignité' équestre";[13] *illustris* is sometimes a rough equivalent.[14] *Lepidus* and *facetus,* by contrast, are the two words for 'bright' that had to do above all with brightness of human origins—not the glow of dawn or the bright light of day, but the gleam of elegant accoutrements or (originally, at any rate) the flashing light of a torch.[15] It is to these latter kinds of "willed" or "created" light that performances were likened. *Lepidus* and *facetus* described individual points of light and not suffuse gleam and were therefore suitable to the "flashes" of individuals and not the "gleam" of communal identity.

The language of social performance is therefore a kind of diagnostic for the attitudes of a speaker to aestheticism, Hellenism, and individualism. Speakers who take the stance of rejecting category (2) altogether use the language of social performance to derogate. Perhaps the harshest example is a bold synaesthesis in Lucretius that forms part of a diatribe against Heraclitus:[16]

12. Hellegouarc'h 1963: 227–29.
13. Ibid. 458; cf. 458–62.  14. Ibid. 461–62.
15. The only real exception is Lucretius, who does use *lepos* of natural light sources; cf. I.9 n.154.
16. As Bailey notes ad loc., it is "a very bold metaphor, probably in intentional imitation of Heraclitus's style, as *latitantia cernunt . . .* may be intended to reproduce his use of oxymoron." On the force of *belle,* cf. Brown 1988: "The colloquialism *belle* for *iucunde* points to the superficiality of the attitude of the *inanes.*" We can make Brown's observation more precise by saying that *belle* circumscribes the judgment of a small, in this case deluded, group;

*omnia enim stolidi magis admirantur amantque,*
*inuersis quae sub uerbis latitantia cernunt,*
*uera constituunt quae belle tangere possunt*
*auris et lepido quae sunt fucata sonore.*

Dullards delight the more in, have more love for,
what they see concealed under twisted words;
and what can touch the ear with pleasure *(belle),* that they
　　take for true,
or what is rouged with charming *(lepidus)* sound.

　　　　　　　　　　　　　　　　　　　　　　　(1.641–44)

The stance of this passage is that of the perceiver of truth, undistracted by
rhetorical preenings. Cicero, as we see below, sometimes takes this stance in
speeches, when it suits his purposes (V.3). For example, the *uenustas* and *facetiae* of the Pergamenes prevents them from making dedications with *fides*
(V.3). Most speakers most of the time take the stance that (2) in some form
is worthwhile, and their use of the language of social performance follows
accordingly. When Lucretius adopts the stance of the Hellenistic poet, *lepos*
becomes a programmatic term: *quo magis aeternum da dictis, diua, leporem*
(1.28). The depressing political discussion that begins the dramatic portion
of *de Oratore* gives way to a pleasant discussion of rhetoric because of Crassus's *lepos* (1.27). Chapters 5 through 7 focus entirely on the considerable
light that the language of social performance sheds on Cicero and Catullus's
views of aestheticism, Hellenism, and individualism.

　　More important, not only is the language of social performance diagnostic, but it is, in fact, an agonistic shibboleth. To use the language of social
performance in any one way was not to use it in other possible ways—ways
that the whole community, or the relevant part thereof, knew were possible. There is a loose parallel in the recent linguistic history of Greece. To
speak *katharevousa,* the educated, classicizing register, was, perforce, not to
speak the popular *demotikē,* and in the choice of one of the absence of the
other was felt.[17] To use the language of social performance in one way was
not to use it in other ways, and this refusal distinguishes a speaker (hence
"shibboleth") and his attitude toward other speakers (hence "agonistic").
The language of social performance often displays the tensions that result
from this situation. Part of Lucretius's rebuke of Scipio Aemilianus was that

---

cf. Cic. *Div.* 2.66 (above, I.7). For other examples of Lucretius's use of the language of social performance, see I.9 n.160, IV.5, VII.5 n.69.

　　17. Cf. Browning 1983: 100–118. To say, for example, ἧπαρ 'liver' or ἵσταμαι 'stand'
is not to say συκώτι and στέκομαι; to end a verb in -όμεθα is not to end it in -όμαστε.

he wanted to "look wittier" *(quo facetior uidea[tur])* than everybody else. That is, Aemilianus himself thinks his wit places him in quadrant (2), whereas Lucilius seems to be hinting that he belongs in quadrant (1). In the passage we saw above (I.7), Varro contrasts a self-congratulatory use of the language of social performance *(belli festiui)* by convives to the reality of their rottenness *(saperdae* σαπροί*).* To use the language of social performance was thus to venture onto the frontiers of social value on the one hand and on the other aestheticism, individualism, and Hellenism. The purpose of this book is to use the language of social performance to explore that terrain.

# CHAPTER III

# DE · SVO · FECERVNT
## The Language of Social Performance
## in the Latin Rhetorical Tradition

*quid si nos non interpretum fungimur munere, sed tuemur ea quae dicta sunt ab eis quos probamus, eisque nostrum iudicium et nostrum scribendi ordinem adiungimus?*

One may go beyond the simple task of translating; one may instead pay heed to what has been said by respectable writers, and add to it one's own judgment and order of presentation.

Cicero de Finibus 1.6

*non e verbum e verbo, sed sensum exprimere de sensu*

To translate not word for word, but sense for sense.

St. Jerome Epistola LVII.5 (ad Pammachium)

## III.1. Introduction

In the first chapter, I described the semantic shifts undergone by a vocabulary set I have called the language of social performance, connecting the shifts to the social changes of the second century. In chapter 2 I suggested that the language of social performance was associated with a new cognitive model created in the second century, and that the language can therefore serve as a diagnostic for a speaker's attitudes toward the terms of the cognitive model. The remaining chapters apply the language of social performance toward such diagnostics.

The object of this chapter and chapter 4 is to explore, by way of the language of social performance, the reception of Greek rhetorical theory at Rome in the second century B.C.—that very period when the flowers of Hellenistic rhetorical thought, of which almost none survive directly, were entering more widely into the consciousness of the Romans, almost none of whose reactions survive directly.[1] The language of social performance, I argue below, provides illuminating evidence for the reception of rhetoric in this thinly documented period. In order to use the language of social performance in this way, two steps are necessary, provided respectively by this chapter and chapter 4: a survey, and an analysis, of the place of the language

---

1. Cf. IV.2 n.2.

in the Latin rhetorical tradition. (Although by "rhetorical tradition" I mean primarily *rhetorica* proper, I also include works that are clearly using the critical language of rhetoric, e.g., certain passages in Cicero's letters or in the *Noctes Atticae* of Aulus Gellius). The survey of the appearances of the language of social performance in the Latin rhetorical tradition in this chapter establishes two related points: first, that the denotations of the language of social performance in its capacity as rhetorical critical language derive directly from the new meanings of the lexemes that developed in the second century and were described in chapter 1. The language of the *convivium,* so to speak, was directly adapted to become the language of the *corona.*

The second point concerns the relationship of the language of social performance to the Greek. Latin rhetorical writings of course depend heavily on their Greek predecessors. By the time the Romans encountered Greek rhetorical theory, its vocabulary, both technical and evaluative, was well developed. The technical vocabulary was very rarely borrowed outright, and that generally later (*prosopoeia,* Quint. *Inst.* 3.8.52; *tropus,* ibid. 8.6; *antonomasia,* ibid. 8.6.29); rather it was translated by adapting native Latin words. Μεταφορά 'metaphor' (a bringing over), for example, was rendered by *translatio* and *transferre* (Cic. *de Orat.* 3.38, Quint. *Inst.* 8.6), μερισμός 'division of subjects' by *distributio* (*Rhet. Her.* 1.10), and τάξις 'arrangement' by *dispositio* (*Rhet. Her.* 1.2). The evaluative vocabulary, on the other hand, naturally enough posed greater difficulty. Subtle and wide-ranging words like ἡδύς 'pleasant' and χάρις 'charm' are prominent in Greek rhetorical theory, and the Romans were sensitive that they could not be rendered mechanically by single Latin equivalents. Such evaluative terms are sometimes translated by members of the language of social performance, but the relationship is never one of simple equivalency. Individual lexemes of the language of social performance typically appear in rhetorical contexts in places where there was not a single corresponding Greek word, if indeed it is possible to find a corresponding word at all.

In short, this chapter demonstrates that the place of the language of social performance in rhetorical theory is not a matter of mechanical translation from the Greek, but a uniquely Roman contribution, which *de suo fecerunt* "they fashioned from their own resources," to adapt the familiar epigraphical phrase for those who paid for their own memorials (D·S·F = *de suo fecit*). Not only did the Romans draw upon "convivial" language, and very deliberately so, as I argue in chapter 4, but they used it only where they saw fit, without permitting the Greek to suborn the native semantics of the Latin words and turn the words into merely a kind of code for the Greek. These observations permit the subsequent arguments of chapter 4, namely that presence of the language of social performance in the Latin rhetorical tradition results from an act of cultural translation by "aesthetic moderates" (cf. II.2) assimilating rhetorical to convivial and other aesthetic practices, and thereby claiming for rhetoric the status of such practices.

## III.2. *Facet(us):* 'Flashes of Wit'

As we saw in section I.8, *facet(us)* described various 'clever flashes' or instances of 'smooth polish,' from ruses to verbal performances; after Plautus it narrowed to describe mostly verbal performances, especially wit, and particularly in regard to the establishment of social status. This sense was borrowed directly into the rhetorical tradition. *Facet(us)* occasionally refers to a larger quality of a composition, stressing not its humor per se, but its wit in a broader sense, "learning" or "intelligence," especially as indicative of social status. The earliest attestation of *facet(us)* in the rhetorical tradition is in this sense, in the *Rhetorica ad Herennium:*[2]

> *qui non possunt in illa facetissima uerborum attenuatione commode uersari, ue-niunt ad aridum et exangue genus orationis, quod non alienum est exile nomi-nari, cuiusmodi est hoc: "nam istic in balineis accessit ad hunc; postea dicit: 'hic tuus seruus me pulsauit.' postea dicit hic illi: 'considerabo.' post ille conuicium fecit et magis magisque praesente multis clamauit." friuolus hic quidem iam et inliberalis est sermo: non enim est adeptus id, quod habet attenuata figura, puris et electis uerbis conpositam orationem.*

Speakers who are incapable of remaining within the limits of the very intelligent *(facetissimus)* "plain style" end up speaking in a dry and bloodless way, a meager way, as it were; for example: "He went up to him in the baths. Then he said, 'Your slave here hit me.' The second man replied, 'I will look into it.' Then the first made a clamor and shouted with more and more people there." This style of speech is useless *(friuolus)* and undignified *(illiberalis);* for it has failed to achieve the characteristic diction of the plain style, with its properly chosen words.[3]

*(Rhet. Her. 4.16)*

Our passage is intended to give an example of a faulty style that aims to be, but falls short of, the "plain" style of speaking.[4] Ancient rhetorical theory

---

2. Hereinafter *Rhet. Her.* It is an anonymous rhetorical work of the early first century; see Calboli 1969: 1–17.

3. Lit. "composed with pure and well-chosen words," recalling the Theophrastean ἐκλογὴ τῶν ὀνομάτων, cf. Calboli 1969 ad loc.

4. In this the author follows the method of Demetrius's περὶ ἑρμηνείας *(On Style)*, which defines a "faulty" version of each of the four styles Demetrius recognizes. In the *de Oratore* Crassus observes that the ideal "plain" style is *tenuis non sine neruis ac uiribus* "slight,

typically recognized three "styles," or modes of speech, characterized by different patterns of word choice, sentence construction, and overall tone and purpose. These styles, the "grand," the "middle," and the "plain" (whose precise definitions vary over time), were used to classify both the overall impression speakers made and the character of individual passages. With the phrase *in illa facetissima uerborum attenuatione,* lit. "in that very *facetus* reduction of words," at the beginning of our passage, the author of *Rhet. Her.* is referring to the plain style; *attenuatio* recalls his definition of the "plain" style at 4.14 (*adtenuatum figurae genus,* lit. "the reduced type of style"). That our passage is meant to represent an unsophisticated speaker is obvious. The narrative structure is extremely simple, almost childlike: *postea . . . postea . . . post.* Several grammatical forms were probably out of date or déclassé (*istic* for *iste* 'that one,' *post* for *postea* 'afterward').[5] There is even one solecism (*praesente multis* for *praesentibus multis*).[6] Furthermore the author characterizes the passage in terms suggesting its lack of distinction: it is "meager" *(exilis),*[7] "useless" *(friuolus),* and above all "undignified" *(illiberalis,* lit. "unworthy of a free man"). *Facetissimus* in this passage plainly characterizes a verbal performance suggestive of social status, hence my translation "intelligent."

*Facetus* is several times connected to the "intelligence" or "wit" of the plain style. In the course of equating the elder Cato to Lysias as a proponent of the "plain style," Cicero describes Cato's speeches as *acuti . . . elegantes faceti breues* "keen, elegant, smart, and concise" (*Brut.* 63).[8] In another

---

but not so as to lack strength and vigor" (3.199). On the three (or more) kinds of style, see Kennedy 1963: 278–82.

5. The addition of the extra deictic particle *-c(e)* was standard in many case forms of *hic* 'this,' but its addition to other demonstrative pronouns such as *iste* 'that (by you),' *ille* 'that' characterized common speech; cf. Marouzeau 1946: 161–63, LHS I §200d. *Post* for 'afterward' (instead of *postea*) is commoner in ante-classical Latin; cf. Marouzeau 1946: 193.

6. The expression evidently had something of a chancellary flavor not inappropriate in our passage; cf. <*is*> *quidem apud forum praesente testibus mihi uendidit* "in the presence of witnesses" (Pomp. *com.* 168), *astante ciuibus* "in the presence of the citizens" (*CIL* 5.895). Other examples are *absente nobis* (Ter. *Eu.* 649), *te uolumus dono donare pulchro praesente omnibus* (Nov. *com.* 57); cf. Marouzeau 1946: 195, LHS II §238b.

7. *Exile* recalls ἰσχνός, a common term for the "plain" style.

8. On the sense of *facetus* here, cf. the note of Douglas 1966 ad loc. A "naive" or "purely Italic" style, one might say, sounded to Cicero like the Greek plain style; cf. *Brut.* 167, of the orations of C. Titius (fl. mid-second c., *RE* Titius 7): *eiusdem fere temporis fuit eques Romanus C. Titius, qui meo iudicio eo peruenisse uidetur quo potuit fere Latinus orator sine Graecis litteris et sine multo usu peruenire. huius orationes tantum argutiarum, tantum exemplorum, tantum urbanitatis habent, ut paene Attico stilo scriptae esse uideantur* "Of approximately the same date was the Roman *eques* C. Titius, who in my judgment achieved as much as a Latin speaker could without knowledge of Greek literature and without considerable practice. His speeches have

passage Cicero describes the plain style as *partite definite distincte facete dicere* "speaking with clear, careful, and intelligent discrimination" (*Or.* 99).[9] The sense of *facetus* is plainly more like 'intelligent' or 'witty' in a broader sense, rather than 'humorous.'[10] When Crassus at the beginning of *de Oratore* argues that speech is pleasant even with practical considerations set aside, the word he uses is *facetus:*

> Leaving aside the forum and the courts, the podium and the senate house, what can there be that is more pleasant or more proper to culture *(humanitas)* in one's free time than witty *(facetus)* speech *(sermo)* free of all vulgarity?[11]
>
> (*de Orat.* 1.32)

---

so much in the way of subtleties, illustrations, and urbanity, that they seem virtually to have been written with an Attic pen." Atticus attacks the equivalency of Cato and Lysias (*equidem in quibusdam risum uix tenebam, cum Attico Lysiae Catonem nostrum comparabas, Brut.* 293), and the judgment made no sense to Plutarch either: . . . οὐκ οἶδ' ὅτι πεπόνθασιν οἱ τῷ Λυσίου λόγῳ τὰ μάλιστα προσεοικέναι φάμενοι τὸν Κάτωνος "I don't know what's wrong with the people who say Cato's speech resembles most especially that of Lysias" (*Cat. Maj.* 7.2).

9. The passage describes speakers who can use only the grand style: *qui enim nihil potest tranquille nihil leniter nihil partite definite distincte facete dicere, praesertim cum causae partim totae sint eo modo partim aliqua ex parte tractandae, si is non praeparatis auribus inflammare rem coepit, furere apud sanos et quasi inter sobrios bacchari uinulentus uidetur* "If someone cannot speak in a calm and gentle manner [i.e., in the middle style], nor with clear, careful, and intelligent *(facete)* discrimination [i.e., in the plain style], especially since some cases need to be handled that way in their entirety, others to some extent—if such a speaker begins to give a rousing presentation to unprepared ears, he seems like a madmen among the sane, as it were a raving drunk among the sober" (*Or.* 99).

10. For another example of *facetus* connected to the plain style, cf. *Or.* 20, where some plain-style speakers are not deliberately rough but "more refined in their sparseness, that is to say witty, florid even, and lightly decorated" (*alii in eadem ieiunitate concinniores, id est faceti, florentes etiam et leuiter ornati;* on the reading, see Sandys 1885 ad loc.); perhaps also *Philippum tam suauem oratorem tam grauem tam facetum* (*Brut.* 186), where the three adjectives may recall, respectively, the middle, grand, and plain styles (for *suauis* of the middle style, cf. *Or.* 99 and *Part.* 21). For another example of *facet(us)* as 'intelligent, discriminating,' cf. *Brut.* 325, where two types of Asiatic style are described, one of which, the forte of Aeschylus of Cnidus and Aeschines of Miletus, is "characterized not so much by frequent epigrams as by swift and rushing words, nor by a river of speech only, but also by a cultivated and witty *(facetus)* type of vocabulary" (*genus . . . non tam sententiis frequentatum quam uerbis uolucre atque incitatum . . . nec flumine solum orationis sed etiam exornato et faceto genere uerborum);* cf. the comment of Jahn and Kroll 1962: "*faceto* müßte etwa = *eleganti* sein, gewählt (ἀστεῖος)." Perhaps also to be included in this latter type of *facet(us)* is *Brut.* 105, in which Carbo's delivery is described as *acer* and *uehemens,* and his style as *dulcis* and *perfacetus,* where *perfacetus* may refer to a general 'wit' or 'intelligence.'

11. *age uero, ne semper forum, subsellia, rostra curiamque mediterere, quid esse potest in otio aut iucundius aut magis proprium humanitatis, quam sermo facetus ac nulla in re rudis?*

*Facetus,* along with *nulla in re rudis,* marks speech as a token of social solidarity, a pleasurable diversion for the potentates freshly come from the senate. A sense 'intellectually distinctive, elegant' should be imagined for Columella's statement that the two volumes of Iulius Graecinus on vineyards were composed *facetius et eruditius* "more elegantly and learnedly" (1.1.14). When Horace declares that "the Camenae who delight in the countryside have granted Vergil the province of softness *(mollis)* and elegance *(facetus)*" (*Serm.* 1.10.43–44), the reference is to the *Eclogues,* with *mollis* recalling the gentle quality of the bucolic verse and *facetus* Vergil's polished (not 'funny'!) presentation, which represented an advance in the Latin hexameter.[12]

In Cicero these broader uses of *facet(us)* are not particularly common, and the lexeme usually refers more specifically to 'humor.' When Caesar Strabo says *loquar de facetiis* (*de Orat.* 2.233), he does not mean witty speech generally, but more specifically 'humor' (τὸ γελοῖον), the subject that the other participants in the conversation have just prevailed on him to discuss. When Crassus refers to "the principle of when to avoid jesting," it is *praeceptum praetermittendarum . . . facetiarum* (*de Orat.* 2.229). The implication of these uses, as I argue below (VI.3), is that the humor in question evinces superior social status.

No word in the Greek rhetorical tradition has quite this range or nuance. A lexeme that covers both 'attraction' and 'humor' puts one in mind of χάρις, but χάρις has much more effect on *uenust(us)* and (especially in Cicero's case, cf. VI.3) on *lep(idus)*. Cicero's association of *facet(us)* with clear division (*partite definite distincte facete, Or.* 99) and the attribution of *facet(us)* to the "plain" style by Cicero and the *Rhet. Her.* loosely suggest σαφής 'clear,' a distinct virtue of the plain style (cf. Demetr. *Eloc.* 191 μάλιστα δὲ σαφῆ χρὴ τὴν [sc. ἰσχνὴν] λέξιν εἶναι). The native semantics of *facet(us)* were not wholly inappropriate to such a function, if any element of literal 'brightness' continued to be felt, since in Latin 'bright' and 'clear' largely overlap *(clarus, lucidus)*. *Facetus* also has affinities to ἀστεῖος 'urban; urbane, witty'; the Greek word covers both a broader "sophistication" and humor

12. *molle atque facetum* | *Vergilio adnuerunt gaudentes rure Camenae.* Quintilian's speculation about this passage (*Inst.* 6.3.20), where he opines that *facetus* has not only to do with humor *(ridicula)* but may serve as the name for "beauty and a certain polished elegance" *(decoris . . . et excultae cuiusdam elegantiae appellationem),* is forced by the fact that the narrowing observed above (I.8, I.9 fin.) was complete by his time. In the same passage Quintilian quotes a similar phrase of Brutus from a (now otherwise lost) letter of Cicero: *ne illi sunt pedes faceti ac †deliciis ingredienti mollius†* "Really his meter is sophisticated and (?)." Modern Vergilian commentators have typically arrived at the conclusion that *facetum* here means 'elegant' or the like (e.g., Lejay 1966 ad loc.: "l'élégance brillante, mais de bon goût, le fini") by relying on Quintilian rather than the abundant evidence in Cicero.

specifically. (*Vrbanus*, the most obvious equivalent for ἀστεῖος, seems not to be put to that use until the first century.)[13] There is also some common territory between *facetus* and εὐτράπελος 'lively of wit, ready of reply.' In describing fondness for laughter among the young, Aristotle observes that "wit is educated insolence" (ἡ γὰρ εὐτραπελία πεπαιδευμένη ὕβρις, *Rh.* 1389b11 = 2.12.16 ad fin.), suggesting the element of "social distinction" to be found in *facetus*.[14] Similarly Aristotle defines εὐτραπελία as the middle ground between "rusticity" (ἀγροικία), which does not like humor, and "buffoonery" (βωμολοχία), which jokes constantly (*Magn. Mor.* 1193a11–19 = 1.30.2, cf. *Eth. Eud.* 1234a14 = 3.7.7–9, *Eth. Nic.* 1108a24 = 2.7.13). It is possible that some instances of *facetus* look to εὐφυής, basically 'well-formed,' but also 'naturally suited, naturally clever,' which jibes well with several of the senses of *facetus;* εὐφυής is not, however, common in Greek rhetoricians. But these parallels to *facetus* are more cases of convergent evolution than real equations, and it is best to regard *facet(us)* as a native Latin contribution, inspired perhaps by various Greek words but describing a native Latin conceptual category. *Facetus* in all these applications is a straightforward adaptation of the sense we saw the lexeme had developed to describe behavior, especially verbal, that marked elite status (I.8). Ἀστεισμός, εὐτραπελία, εὐφυία, and σαφήνεια were all elements that the social elite recognized, or coveted, in their own exclusive speech: wittiness, urbanity, organization, and clarity. Expositing clearly and elegantly was no less a linguistic mark of elite status than making apt comments, and in that respect both of them were suitable for description by *facetus*. This importation of the language of elite aestheticism into rhetoric is analyzed in chapter 4.

## III.3. *Lep(idus)*: 'Attractive Affectations'

In chapter 1 we saw that *lep(idus)* became associated with performances (I.9). The connection of *lep(idus)* to the attractive quality of a performance, broadly taken, is the direct ancestor of the *lep(idus)* of the rhetorical tradition. Cicero occasionally applies *lepos* to *actio* 'delivery' (ὑπόκρισις), the actual act of performing a speech. For example, according to Cicero, C. Macer's "voice, gesture, and entire delivery lacked *lepos*" (*uox gestus et omnis actio sine lepore, Brut.* 238).[15] Far and away the commonest use of *lep(idus)*, however,

13. Cf. E. Saint-Denis 1939, who contends that the nonliteral senses of *urban(us)* occasionally to be seen in Plautus and Terence (e.g., 'sophisticated' rather than simply 'living in the city') are an artefact of their New Comic models and not of Roman society as such.

14. Cf. οἱ δ' ἐμμελῶς παίζοντες εὐτράπελοι προσαγορεύονται, οἷον εὔτροποι (*Eth. Nic.* 1128a9–10).

15. Cf. *huius actio non satis commendabat orationem; in hac enim satis erat copiae, in illa autem leporis parum* "His delivery did not do enough to recommend his speeches; while the lat-

is to describe not delivery but the attractive character of artful speech, typically styled as an affectation aimed at the delight of an audience. *Lep(idus)* may describe the 'attractiveness' of particular verbal effects. The oldest instance is probably Terence's use of the phrase *facete laute lepide nil supra* (*Eu.* 427), mock praise for an instance of rhetorical stolidity, which I treat below (IV.5). The oldest independent instance (which may show reliteralizing as 'bright,' cf. I.9, p. 67) is in Lucilius. A part of "style" (λέξις) in Hellenistic rhetorical theory was the careful selection of words (ἐκλογή) and their arrangement into clauses (σύνθεσις). Albucius's scrupulous σύνθεσις, which avoided hiatus and ungainly consonant clusters, is described by Lucilius, in the voice of Q. Scaevola, with *lepide* (cf. Cic. *de Orat.* 3.171):

> *quam lepide* λέξεις *compostae! ut tesserulae omnes*
> *arte pauimento atque emblemate uermiculato.*

> How prettily *(lepide)* he sets a phrase!
> artfully, like mosaic stones
> in curving lines inlaid in pavement.

(84–85MW, 74–75K)

Cicero applies *lepos* to the same aspect of "style" when he says that M. Antonius "applied a thoroughgoing, veritably scientific scheme to the selection and arrangement of words and their rounding off into periods—and that less in the service of attractiveness than of gravity" (*in uerbis et eligendis, neque id ipsum tam leporis causa quam ponderis, et collocandis et comprehensione deuinciendis nihil non ad rationem et tamquam ad artem dirigebat, Brut.* 140).[16] The only figures of speech to which the author of *Rhet. Her.* and Cicero apply *lepos* feature repetition. Cicero finds *lepos* in *geminatio uerborum* or 'word-doubling': *nam et geminatio uerborum habet interdum uim, leporem alias* "Doubling words is occasionally forceful, otherwise attractive" (*de Orat.* 3.206).[17] The author

---

ter were sufficiently well developed, there was too little *lepos* in the former" (*Brut.* 240, of Q. Pompeius A. f. Bithynicus). Cf. also *de Orat.* 1.213 (below, VI.2 n.5). The sense of 'performative charm' is perhaps to be seen in *Off.* 1.98, which has to do with the presented aspect of a beautiful body: *ut enim pulchritudo corporis apta compositione membrorum mouet oculos et delectat hoc ipso, quod inter se omnes partes cum quodam lepore consentiunt, sic hoc decorum quod elucet in uita mouet approbationem eorum quibuscum uiuitur et constantia et moderatione dictorum omnium atque factorum* "For just as the beauty of a body attracts ('moves') the eyes by the proportional composition of its limbs and provides pleasure by the very fact that all the parts are in a certain graceful concord *(cum quodam lepore consentiunt)* . . ." etc. The emphasis in the context is on the active attraction exercised by 'propriety' *(decorum)*, and the image of performance precedes the passage, in the form of the propriety exercised by poets; see Dyck 1996. Cicero never otherwise uses *lepos* for beauty in this way; see also below, VI.3 n.35.

16. On Antonius and *lepos*, see further VI.2 n.5.

17. *Geminatio* represents the Greek ἀναδίπλωσις or, if more than one word is repeated, ἐπανάληψις; see Ernest s.v. ἀναδίπλωσις, Wilkin's note to the *de Oratore* passage, and Cal-

of *Rhet. Her.* finds *lepos* in the figure called *gradatio* 'climbing' (a translation of the Greek κλῖμαξ 'the ladder'), a figure that links clauses by repeated words.[18] Here is one of his several examples:

> *Africano uirtutem industria, uirtus gloriam, gloria aemulos comparauit.*

> Africanus's toil brought him strength, his strength brought him glory, and his glory brought him rivals.

As Aristotle noted, repetition is one of the most overtly performative of tropes, "lending itself to delivery" (ὑποκριτικός, in contrast to γραφικός).[19] Repetition as a verbal effect typical of convivial speech is explored below (III.7). Cicero also uses *lepos* as a word for the "figures" permitted to a type of "middle" style:

> There is really a brilliant and florid, bright and polished, style of oratory in which all the beauties *(lepores)* of diction and of thought are intertwined.

> (*Or.* 96)[20]

Quintilian's sole use of the lexeme *sua voce* describes the effect of subarguments cleverly articulated according to expected *topoi* (*Inst.* 11.1.53; below,

---

boli 1969: 362–64 n. 162. The author of *Rhet. Her.*, who calls the same figure *conduplicatio* (4.38), gives this among several examples: *tumultus, Gai Gracce, tumultus domesticos et intestinos conparas!* "You're causing chaos, Gaius Gracchus, domestic and internal chaos!"

18. *(gradatio) habet in se quendam leporem superioris cuiusque crebra repetitio uerbi, quae propria est huius exornationis* (4.35) "The insistent repetition of each successive preceding word, which is the characteristic of this figure, has a certain attractiveness *(lepos)*." Cf. Ernest s.v. κλῖμαξ, Lucilius 1133 (Marx), Cic. *de Orat.* 3.207, Quint. *Inst.* 9.3.54, Wills 1996: 329–36.

19. οἷον τά τε ἀσύνδετα καὶ τὸ πολλάκις τὸ αὐτὸ εἰπεῖν ἐν τῇ γραφικῇ ὀρθῶς ἀποδοκιμάζεται, ἐν δὲ ἀγωνιστικῇ οὔ, καὶ οἱ ῥήτορες χρῶνται· ἔστι γὰρ ὑποκριτικὴ (*Rh.* 3.12.2 = 1413b).

20. *est enim quoddam etiam insigne et florens orationis pictum et expolitum genus, in quo omnes uerborum, omnes sententiarum illigantur lepores,* tr. Sandys 1885. It is possible that Cicero was thinking of the "bright colors" of a chaplet of flowers here. That image, suggested by *florens* and *illigantur,* is improved, if, as Sandys 1885 notes, the epithets *pictum et expolitum,* already suspected by Jahn, are excised. Lucretius also uses *lepos* to describe the variegation of blooming plants (*uarios . . . lepores* 3.1006 and *uario distincta lepore* 5.1376, cf. I.9 n. 154). This use of *lepos* is probably an instance of Cicero's reinvigorating of technical or quasi-technical language by playing off another sense of the lexeme; cf. on *uenustus* (III.4.2). The use of *illigare* is certainly unique here. At *Or.* 215 and *de Orat.* 3.175, it has to do with prose rhythms, a use that is close to the συμπλέκειν of Greek rhetorical theory, e.g., Dion. Hal. *Comp. Verb.* 18 ἐάν τε ἀλλήλοις κατὰ τὰς ὁμοζυγίας συμπλέκωνται "or whether [certain rhythms] are woven together according to their mutual affinity" (tr. Roberts 1910). At *de Orat.* 2.61 *inligati* means 'entangled.'

IV.2).[21] In Gellius *lepidus* most commonly applies to clever etymologies or definitions or to delightful αἰνίγματα (something like verbal party games).[22] The "performative" character of such instances of *lep(idus)* is tolerably clear: its referents are instances of artful speech deliberately designed to be attractive to its hearers.

*Lep(idus)* may also describe a more diffuse quality, typically also in reference to artful speech directed to the delectation of an audience. Cicero uses *lepos* of Pericles to translate Πειθώ 'Persuasiveness.'[23] The quality of the speech of T. Pomponius Atticus, Cicero's friend, is described by Nepos as "a kind of natural, and not acquired, charm *(lepos)*," suggesting *e contrario* the association of *lepos* with learnable, performative artfulness.[24] The 'attractiveness' or 'charm' of the Greek language is described by Cicero (sarcastically) as *sermonis lepos* (*Flac.* 9, V.4), with the implication that Greek is naturally the sort of language that is attractive to hearers, unlike Latin, which requires careful manipulation to achieve the same attraction.[25] Apuleius uses *lep(idus)* for the 'delightful' quality of the "Milesian tales" that weave in and out of his story line, and Aulus Gellius may use *lep(idus)* to describe simply a well-composed literary work.[26]

In Cicero the verbal performance that *lep(idus)* describes is usually humor, a use treated in more detail below (VI.2). Here we may note that Cicero several times applies *lepos* to Socratic dialectic. Cicero follows Panaetius in holding in high regard what Dyck (1996 ad 1.108) calls the "civilized repartee of the Socratic dialogues," and it is *lepos* that Cicero felt especially suited to describe that way of speaking, which notably combines humor, diffuse charm, and individual instances of clever verbal manipulation—the very

21. *Lep(idus)* also appears in Quintilian in quotations from Domitius Marsus on humor (*Inst.* 6.3.102) and Cicero on *geminatio* (9.1.3).

22. On etymologies cf. VIII.4 pp. 309–10; on αἰνίγματα cf. VIII.4 n. 50.

23. With Cic. *de Orat.* 3.138 *in labris [Periclis] ueteres comici . . . leporem habitasse dixerunt* cf. Eupolis 94.5 Πειθώ τις ἐπεκαθίζεν ἐπὶ τοῖς χείλισιν. *Brut.* 59 attributes this quote to Eupolis by name but uses Ennius's *Suada* to translate Πειθώ.

24. *tanta autem suauitas erat sermonis Latini, ut appareret in eo natiuum quendam leporem esse, non ascitum* (*Att.* 4.1), "The pleasure afforded when he spoke was such that it seemed he had a kind of natural, and not acquired, charm."

25. The idea of the superior attractiveness of Greek, also expressed by a member of the language of social performance, is used in a different way by Antonius to compliment Catulus: *cui [= Catulo] non solum nos Latini sermonis, sed etiam Graeci ipsi solent suae linguae subtilitatem elegantiamque concedere* (*de Orat.* 2.28).

26. On Apuleius, cf. VIII.4 n. 48. Gellius has *lepide . . . et uenuste* (2.23.2) of Roman comedies, *lepide atque iucunde promonet* in reference to a fable of Aesop (2.29), and *lepide admodum et scite* (6.16.1) of certain of Varro's verses. Cf. also 9.9.5, 9.16.5, 10.19.2, 13.11.1, 17.12.2, 17.14.3, 19.9.5, 19.11.1, and VIII.4 below.

things, as we have seen, that *lep(idus)* describes. "What I mean by *sermo*," advises Cicero, in discussing *decorum*, "is the kind the Socratics excel in: gentle, with very little obstinacy, and possessed of charm *(lepos)*."[27] *Lepos* is associated in particular with Arcesila(u)s, who headed the Academy in the third century B.C.[28] When Epicurus is attacked for a signal lack of *lepos*, Cicero no doubt has in mind the crabbed and unpleasant style of Epicurean prose.[29] Epicurus did not put on a graceful verbal show.

There is no single Greek correspondent for these uses of *lep(idus)*. As I suggested above (I.9 n. 155), comic *lep(idus)* has some consanguinity with λαμπρ(ός). That cannot possibly be the source of rhetorical *lep(idus)*. In extant theory λαμπρ(ός) always connotes 'loftiness'; if there is any Latin equivalent to λαμπρ(ός), it is *splend(idus)*.[30] Comic *lep(idus)* may have commonalities with λαμπρ(ός), but rhetorical *lep(idus)* is a different animal, closely reflecting the character of the "performative" *lep(idus)* that arose in the second century. In that guise it has a few partial equivalents. The connection of *lepidus* to certain figures of speech recalls κομψός. Just as the *Rhet. Her.* contrasts *lepidus, concinnus,* and *festiuitas* to *amplitudo, dignitas,* and *pulchritudo* (4.32, v. IV.4), so Dionysius of Halicarnassus contrasts κομψός to σεμνός, for example, ὁ δὲ Ἰσοκρατικὸς κομψεύεται μέν, ἀλλὰ μετὰ σεμνότητος "Isocrates's style makes use of decoration, but not so as to diminish his solemnity" (Dion. Hal. *Imit.* fr. 31.5.2).[31] Cicero's normative use of *lepos* for

27. *sit ergo hic sermo, in quo Socratici maxime excellunt, lenis minimeque pertinax, insit in eo lepos* (*Off.* 1.134), cf. *leporem Socraticum subtilitatemque sermonis* (*Rep.* 1.16, of Plato). For a formulation of the same idea without *lepos*, but with two other members of the language of social performance, cf. *de Graecis autem dulcem et facetum festiuique sermonis atque in omni oratione simulatorem, quem* εἴρωνα *Graeci nominarunt, Socratem accepimus* (*Off.* 1.108).

28. *quem ferunt eximio quodam usum lepore dicendi* (*de Orat.* 3.67); *floruit cum acumine ingeni tum admirabili quodam lepore dicendi* (*Ac.* 2.16), and see refs. in LPW ad 3.67 *lepore dicendi*.

29. *nec uero hoc in te unum conuenit moribus domesticis ac nostrorum hominum urbanitate limatum, sed cum in reliquos uestros tum in eum maxime qui ista peperit, hominem sine arte sine litteris, insultantem in omnes, sine acumine ullo sine auctoritate sine lepore* (*N.D.* 2.74).

30. According to Dionysius of Halicarnassus, for example, the "austere" style is characterized by clauses that are εὐγενῆ καὶ λαμπρὰ καὶ ἐλεύθερα "noble, conspicuous, and free" (*Comp. Verb.* 22, tr. Usher 1985). For Hermogenes λαμπρότης 'brilliance' (p. 264ff. Rabe) is a part of μέγεθος 'grandeur,' which is in turn a part of δεινότης 'force.' Cf. Wooten 1987: xii. 'Brilliant' diction is produced by the same figures that produce 'solemn' (σεμνά) diction. These figures are not 'histrionic' but forceful and direct: 'blunt denials' (ἀναιρέσεις), 'fresh starts' (ἀποστάσεις), and 'lack of connective particles' (τὰ ἀσυνδέτως εἰσαγόμενα, p. 267 Rabe).

31. Cf. ἡ δὲ μετὰ ταύτην <ἡ> γλαφυρὰ καὶ θεατρικὴ καὶ τὸ κομψὸν αἱρουμένη πρὸ τοῦ σεμνοῦ τοιαύτη (Dion. Hal. *Dem.* 40).

'humor' has χάρις in mind (cf. VI.3), and the fixed pair *lepos et facetiae* (cf. I.9 n.161, VI.3) may possibly represent something like χάρι(s) καὶ εὐτράπε-λ(os).[32] However, the place of *lep(idus)* in Latin rhetorical theory has more to do with Roman cultural constructions than Greek vocabulary: all the instances of *lep(idus)* involve a kind of histrionic performative ability that draws attention to the attempt of a performer or performance to impress an audience. The clever figure, charming manner, and deft *actio* are all parts of stylish self-presentation. *Lep(idus)* entered the technical language of rhetoric in the guise it acquired in the second century.

## III.4. *Venust(us)*

*Venust(us)* has several distinct applications to rhetoric, which should be treated separately.

*Venust(us) (1): The 'Grace' of Gesture.* *Venust(us)* is applied to the gestures of the orator (cf. I.6, pp. 48–49), a use attested from the late Republic on. Cicero occasionally uses *uenust(us)* in this way: "Who would say an orator, in moving or posing as orators do, has no need of the charming gesticulation *(gestus et uenustas)* of Roscius?" *(de Orat.* 1.251). P. Lentulus Sura's bodily motion had "both artfulness and grace" *(et ars et uenustas, Brut.* 235).[33] C. Calpurnius Piso was endowed with considerable "natural grace of movement" *(gestusque natura . . . uenustus, Brut.* 272).[34] As we saw above (I.6), Sulpicius's "gesture and bodily movement was graceful, but without seeming it was meant for the stage and not the forum" *(gestus et motus corporis ita uenustus, ut tamen ad forum, non ad scaenam institutus uideatur, Brut.* 203).

The connection of *uenust(us)* with gesture accounts for its broader application to *actio* or *pronuntiatio,* 'delivery.' The *Rhet. Her.* describes *pronuntiatio* as "graceful modulation of voice, expression, and gesture" *(uocis uultus gestus moderatio cum uenustate,* 1.3). The author of *Rhet. Her.* and Cicero have similar formulas for the ideal delivery, which is to be done "with dignity

32. εὐτραπελίας τε καὶ χαριεντισμοῦ (Plat. *Resp.* 563a), ἡσθεὶς δ' ἐπὶ τῇ χάριτι καὶ τῇ εὐτραπελίᾳ τοῦ νεανίσκου (Jos. *Ant. Jud.* 12.173), ὑπὲρ τοῦ τὸ λεχθὲν δοκεῖν σὺν εὐτραπελίᾳ καὶ χάριτι εἰρῆσθαι (Phil. Jud. *Leg. Gai.* 361), μετ' εὐτραπελίας ζῶν καὶ χάριτος (Plut. *Mor.* 52E [*quomodo adulator ab amico internoscatur*]).

33. Virtually, by a kind of hendiadys, 'the attractiveness that comes from studied practice.' Contrast *C. Censorinus Graecis litteris satis doctus, quod proposuerat explicans expedite, non inuenustus actor sed iners et inimicus fori (Brut.* 237): Censorinus had the "attractiveness" but was "unpracticed."

34. *gestusque natura ita uenustus, ut ars etiam, quae non erat, et e disciplina motus quidam uideretur accedere.* For other applications of *uenust(us)* to bodily motion, cf. III.4 n.45; Fyëdorov 1990: 121.

and grace": *grauiter et uenuste* (4.69) and *agere cum dignitate ac uenustate* (*de Orat.* 1.142).[35] Suetonius reports that Caesar "spoke with a clear voice, used passionate movement and gesture, not without grace" (*pronuntiasse autem dicitur uoce acuta, ardenti motu gestuque, non sine uenustate, Jul.* 55.3).

The element of 'well-arranged' made *uenust(us)* an appropriate word for this function. Not only does apt gesture trace attractive forms in time and space, but gesture was to be in harmony with the tenor of a speech. Cicero praises M. Antonius for his "outstanding delivery" *(actio singularis),* which included excellent use of gesture:

> *gestus erat non uerba exprimens sed cum sententiis congruens: manus umeri latera supplosio pedis status incessus omnisque motus cum uerbis sententiisque consentiens.*

Antonius's gesture did not stress individual words but matched his sentiments.[36] He used his hands, shoulders, sides, stamped his foot, stood, walked, or moved only in a way that agreed with his words and ideas.

(*Brut.* 141)

The origins of this use of *uenust(us)* should be attributed to the critical language of theater, as I have suggested above (I.6). The evident loss of the word's 'erotic' nuance in these instances may suggest it had become something of a technical term in this capacity (cf. I.6 ad fin.).

*Venust(us) (2): The 'Neatness' of Humor. Venust(us)* was also applied to a certain kind of wit or humor: apposite comments, especially if they were 'neatly done' by way of rejoinder to someone else's word or deed, were

35. Cf. *Or.* 60 *uoltus uero qui secundum uocem plurimum potest quantam adferet tum dignitatem tum uenustatem* "Indeed facial expression, which is the next most powerful element [of delivery] after the voice, can bring dignity or charm" (or "beauty or prettiness").

36. Cf. Quint. *Inst.* 11.3.89 *abesse enim plurimum a saltatore debet orator, ut sit gestus ad sensus magis quam ad uerba accommodatus, quod etiam histrionibus paulo grauioribus facere moris fuit* "There ought to be considerable distance between an orator and a dancer; an orator's gesture must fit the meaning rather than the individual words, a practice followed even by actors with any sort of dignity." What Quintilian, and presumably Cicero, meant is explained in the following sections: to point to oneself, for example, when referring to oneself. For other examples of the harmony between gesture and speech, cf. *facit enim* [sc., *pronuntiatio*] *et dilucidam orationem et illustrem et probabilem et suauem non uerbis, sed uarietate uocum, motu corporis, uultu, quae plurimum ualebunt, si cum orationis genere consentient eiusque uim ac uarietatem subsequentur* (Cic. *Part.* 25), *haec igitur in uerbis* [sc., *perorationis facienda sunt*], *quibus actio uocis, uultus et gestus congruens et apta ad animos permouendos accommodanda est* (Cic. *Part.* 54), [*actio*] *quae motu corporis, quae gestu, quae uultu, quae uocis conformatione ac uarietate moderanda est* (*de Orat.* 1.18), and *de Orat.* 3.220. For Antonius's use of gesture, see Cic. *Ver.* 2.5.3, *de Orat.* 2.124, 2.194, 3.32, *Tusc.* 2.57.

*uenustus*. In the catalogue of the orator's attributes at the beginning of *de Oratore, uenustas* characterizes the ability to make such "comebacks":

> The orator also needs to have a certain charming wit *(lepos)* and sense of humor *(facetiae)*, learning that befits a free man, as well as the ability to reply and attack quickly and curtly, with measured deftness *(subtilis uenustas)* and wittiness *(urbanitas).*[37]

Cicero often uses *uenust(us)* in exactly this way; the examples are discussed further below (VI.4). This sense of *uenust(us)* survives later. Quintilian applies *uenust(us)* especially to the humor of reply. He observes that "everything is more charming *(uenustiora)* in a comeback than on the attack" *(sunt enim longe uenustiora omnia in respondendo quam in prouocando, Inst.* 6.3.13). Witnesses may get the better of an attorney by "making an amusingly deft reply" *(uenuste . . . respondent,* 5.7.31).[38] Both Senecas use *uenustus* in connection with *scurrae* 'wags' or 'wits.'[39] The elder Seneca uses *uenust(us)* commonly for the wit or humor of the apt comment *(Con.* 1.2.22, 9.3.14, 10.pr.2, 10.5.22), as does Aulus Gellius occasionally. To take one example from Gellius, when a man was afraid to buy property in the city because of the threat of fire, the scholar Antonius Iulianus replied that the man had obviously not read the eleventh book of the *Annals* of Q. Claudius, which describes flame-retardant measures devised by Archelaus, prefect of King Mithridates. This Gellius proffers as an example of Iulianus's "usual happy conversational charm" *(laeta ut mos eius fuit inter fabulandum uenustate,* 15.1.4).[40] The occa-

---

37. Cf. VI.4 below.

38. *sed in primis interrogatio cum debet esse circumspecta, quia multa contra patronos uenuste saepe respondent eique praecipue rei uulgo fauetur;* cf. 5.13.46, 6.3.78, 6.3.84. At 5.13.46, *dantque de se respondentibus uenustissimos lusus* "they give very *uenustus* amusement to those who respond to them" refers to the easy responses made available by pleaders to opposing counsel when they include set pieces appropriate to declamation but lubricious in a real courtroom setting.

39. *Barrus scurra rem uenustissimam dixit* (Sen. *Con.* 1.17.8), *uenustissimus inter rhetoras scurra* (*Suas.* 2.12), *scurram fuisse et uenustum ac dicacem* (Sen. iun. *Dial.* 2.17.3). The elder Seneca's literary critical vocabulary is assembled by Bardon 1940.

40. Cf. *ea cum legisset M. Cato: "ne tu," inquit, "Aule, nimium nugator es, cum maluisti culpam deprecari quam culpa uacare. Nam petere ueniam solemus, aut cum inprudentes errauimus aut cum compulsi peccauimus. Dic," inquit, "oro te, quis perpulit ut id committeres, quod, priusquam faceres, peteres ut ignosceretur?"* "On reading that, M. Cato said, 'Really, Aulus, you are quite the trifler, preferring to ask excuse for a fault instead of avoiding it in the first place. We usually ask for forgiveness when we've made a mistake or been forced to err. Tell me,' he said, 'if you would, who forced you to do something that made you ask for it to be forgiven before you did it?'" (11.8.4). Gellius opines *iuste uenusteque admodum reprehendisse dicitur Aulum Albinum M. Cato* (11.8.1). The same sense is found once in Pliny. The Baetici had the misfortune of

sional use of *uenust(us)* for situations that 'worked out neatly' is plainly related: the contour of a sequence of events displays lovely correspondences.[41]

The humor of reply features an attractive proportionality or correspondence very appropriately described by an adjective that meant 'attractive' and 'well-arranged'; such humor, whether in the form of Iulianus's mannered one-upmanship or of Cicero's pungent rejoinders (cf. VI.4), moves deftly over the conversational terrain. Another use of *uenust(us)* should be noticed in this regard. Arguments about the relationship between the beautiful (καλ[ός]) and the useful (χρήσιμ[ος] inter alia) recur in various forms in the Greek philosophical tradition.[42] In rendering them Cicero generally turns καλ(ός), the 'beautiful,' in two ways: in moral contexts he uses *honest(us)* or *rect(us)*,[43] and in aesthetic contexts he uses *pulch(er)*. *Pulch(er)* can also serve as a bridge between aesthetic and moral.[44] But in certain passages in both the rhetorica and philosophy, *uenust(us)* also appears, as in the following:

> We observe that athletes, and likewise gladiators, execute no motion
> either in cautious parry or aggressive attack that lacks training ("the

---

being ruled by the rapacious Caecilius Classicus—originally one of their own: "Hence— for often grief makes people deft *(uenustus)*—the rather clever *(non inlepidum)* saying of the Baetici that was in circulation: 'I did a bad turn, I was done a bad turn'" (*inde dictum Baeticorum, ut plerumque dolor etiam uenustos facit, non inlepidum ferebatur: 'dedi malum et accepi,' Ep.* 3.9.3).

41. This sort of *uenust(us)* for humorous situations that 'worked out neatly' appears in a letter of Marcus Caelius: *qua in re mihi uidetur illud perquam uenuste cecidisse, quod ab reliquis quoque usque eo est animaduersum ut Curio, qui nihil consilio facit, ratione et insidiis usus uideretur in euitandis iis consiliis qui se intenderant aduersarios in eius tribunatum, †laelios† et Antonios et id genus ualentis dico* "I have to say, I think the whole thing has worked out very neatly *(uenuste)*; everybody else has noticed, too, so much so that Curio, who's never had a plan in his life, looks like he plotted an ambush to dodge the designs of the ones who had set themselves up to be his opponents in his tribunate—†Laelius† and Antonius, bigwigs like that" (*Fam.* 8.4.2; on *Antonios*, cf. K-S 2.1 §20.3). Everyone was so suspicious that even the haphazard Curio seemed a schemer. In his wry appreciation of events, one catches a glimpse of Caelius: astute, detached, amused. On the difficulties of this passage, see SB.

42. Cf., e.g., τοῦτο γὰρ δὴ ἔστω ἡμῖν καλόν, ὃ ἂν χρήσιμον ᾖ. εἶπον δὲ ἐκ τῶνδε ἐννοούμενος· καλοί, φαμέν, οἱ ὀφθαλμοί εἰσιν, οὐχ οἳ ἂν δοκῶσι τοιοῦτοι εἶναι οἷοι μὴ δυνατοὶ ὁρᾶν, ἀλλ' οἳ ἂν δυνατοί τε καὶ χρήσιμοι πρὸς τὸ ἰδεῖν· ἦ γάρ; (Plato *Hippias Major* 295c). Also in use are σύμφερον and ὠφέλιμον, especially in Panaetius; cf. Dyck 1996: 353ff.

43. E.g., *tertium dubitandi genus est cum pugnare uidetur cum honesto id quod uidetur esse utile* (*Off.* 1.9); see further Tsekourakis 1974: 64.

44. E.g., *ergo opifex plus sibi proponet ad formarum quam ciuis excellens ad factorum pulchritudinem?* (*Fin.* 2.115). On καλός see also on *suauis*, p. 146 and n.50.

gymnasium"), with the result that what is useful in battle is also attractive *(uenustus)* to look at. Similarly the orator makes no solid hits, unless the assault was well-aimed *(apta),* nor safely deflects an attack, unless he knows the proprieties of retreat.[45]

(*Or.* 228)

*Venust(us)* is used here, as in other passages, for the graceful form of martial motions.[46] *Venust(us)* was substituted for *pulch(er)* in this passage, I suggest, because the lexeme's element 'well-arranged' (cf. I.6) was appropriate to a graceful kinetic shape.[47] The apt reply also has a kind of kinetic property, negotiating the terrain of a conversation; indeed that kinesis has a distinctly martial quality, like a fencer's parry and riposte.

*Venust(us) (3): The 'Deftness' of Crafted Details. Venust(us)* is also applied to rhetorical effects. The author of *Rhet. Her.,* for example, says that the figure of speech called *repetitio* (cf. III.6) has *cum multum uenustatis . . . tum grauitatis et acrimoniae plurimum* "much *uenustas* and yet considerable weighti-

45. *ut enim athletas nec multo secus gladiatores uidemus nihil nec uitando facere caute nec petendo uehementer, in quo non motus hic habeat palaestram quandam, ut quicquid in his rebus fiat utiliter ad pugnam idem ad aspectum etiam sit uenustum, sic orator nec plagam grauem facit, nisi petitio fuit apta, nec satis tecte declinat impetum, nisi etiam in cedendo quid deceat intelligit.*

46. *et ait . . . [Philippus], cum bracchium concalefecerit, tum se solere pugnare; neque attendit eos ipsos unde hoc simile ducat primas illas hastas ita iactare leniter ut et uenustati uel maxime seruiant et reliquis uiribus suis consulant* (de Orat. 2.316), *tum denique hic nobis orator ita conformandus est et uerbis et sententiis, ut ei, qui in armorum tractatione uersantur, ut, quemadmodum qui utuntur armis aut palaestra, non solum sibi uitandi aut feriendi rationem esse habendam putet, sed etiam, ut cum uenustate moueatur, sic uerbis quidem ad aptam compositionem et decentiam, sententiis uero ad grauitatem orationis utatur* (de Orat. 3.200), *orationis autem ipsius tamquam armorum est uel ad usum comminatio et quasi petitio uel ad uenustatem ipsam tractatio* (de Orat. 3.206). Fronto's use of *uenust(us)* in the phrase *eludendi uenustas* "the ability to escape gracefully" (*Eloq.* 4.6) is comparable. LPW (ad loc. *et uenustati . . .*) suggest that the *lenitas* and *uenustas* of de Orat. 2.316 are appropriate to the 'ethical' aspect of the prologue *(exordium),* which Antonius is there discussing (315–25). Technical language is thus reinvigorated by playing off another sense of the lexeme, as with *uenustus* in *Brut.* 262 (III.4.2) and *lepores* in *Or.* 96 (III.3 n.20).

47. That *uenust(us)* should have such a kinetic quality, beside its appreciation of static shapes, is no paradox. It is frequent for static spatial extension and motion through time to be conflated, if the shapes described are similar: so, for example, "The wolf runs into the woods" and "The road runs into the woods." The road, of course, does not run as a wolf does; the road is static. But its shape, a narrow path aimed in a direction, describes the kind of shape that running would produce, and so, by this trope, "road" can attract the verb "run." Similarly "a river with flowing waters" and "a statue with flowing lines": the lines of the statue do not actually flow, of course, but the shape they describe is like one made by a fluid. Static spatial extension, in short, is conflated with motion through time. This cognitive trope, as it were, is called image-schema transformation by Lakoff 1987: 105–8 et passim.

ness and intensity" (4.19). Apart from the gestural instances discussed above (III.4.1), the author of *Rhet. Her.* always uses *uenustas* to label the effects of single figures of speech. Besides *repetitio,* there is *ratiocinatio* 'putting a question to oneself' (αἰτιολογία or ἐξετασμός), of which this is the author's example:

> Our forefathers observed the sound policy of never executing a king whom they had defeated in battle. Why is that? Because it would have been unjust to take an opportunity that fortune gave to punish those whom the same fortune had shortly before stationed in an honorable position. What of the fact that he led the opposing army? I consider it forgotten (etc.).[48]
>
> (4.23)

This figure can "keep a hearer's attention by virtue of the *uenustas* of the speech as well as the hearer's eagerness to hear answers to the questions" (*et animum auditoris retineat attentum cum uenustate sermonis tum rationum expectatione,* 4.23). The author also assigns *uenustas* to the figure called *effictio* 'character sketch' (χαρακτηρισμός, 4.63), which is a figure "both useful, if you need to depict an individual, and charming *(uenustus),* if it is done briefly and clearly":[49]

---

48. *bene maiores hoc conparauerunt, ut neminem regem, quem armis cepissent, uita priuarent. quid ita? quia, quam nobis fortuna facultatem dedisset, inicum erat in eorum supplicium consumere, quos eadem fortuna paulo ante in amplissimo statu conlocarat. quid quod exercitum contra duxit? desino meminisse, etc.*

49. *habet haec exornatio cum utilitatem, si quem uelis demonstrare, tum uenustatem si breuiter et dilucide facta est.* Cicero once uses *uenustas* in what seems to be a similar way. In *de Oratore* Antonius observes that brevity, in and of itself, is not always ideal in a narrative passage, if it detracts from the pleasure and persuasiveness that narration can provide. By way of example he cites a longish dialogue in Terence (*Andria* 51ff.) in which an old man describes to his slave the character of his son, the death of a *hetaira,* her sister's appearance and emotions, and the course of the funeral. Antonius points out that the dialogue could be reduced to a mere ten lines, if it were only a matter of narrating the essential facts of the funeral. In fact, he observes, the narrative could be told even more briefly: all that was necessary was *effertur, imus, ad sepulcrum uenimus,* | *in ignem imposita est* "He is carried out, we go, we come to the tomb, she was laid on the fire" (= *Andr.* 117 + 128–29; for a restoration of the shortened text, damaged in transmission, see Renting 1992). But such a radical concision, according to Antonius, would be "not so much in service of brevity as of *uenustas*" (*ut non breuitati seruitum sit, sed magis uenustati, de Orat.* 2.327). The *uenustas* of the doubly reduced passage is like that of the *Rhet. Her.*'s *effictio,* a series of short, clean strokes that complete the picture with a few clear words (LPW ad loc. *ita ut . . . venustati* suggest "die zierliche iucunditas"). In effect the sharply reduced passage becomes a figure of speech, rather than a portion of a narrative.

If this helps you recall him to mind, judges, I am talking about a short, stooped, ruddy man, with curly grey hair and grey eyes, and a prominent scar on his chin.[50]

Last, the author assigns *uenustas* to a whole group of ten figures in which "the customary force of a word is abandoned and another meaning substituted with a certain *uenustas*" (. . . *ut ab usitata uerborum potestate recedatur atque in aliam rationem cum quadam uenustate oratio conferatur,* 4.42). His list includes familiar figures such as metonymy (Latin *denominatio*), for example, putting *Liber* for 'wine' (4.43), and hyperbole (Latin *superlatio*), for example, "speech sweeter than honey" (*sermo melle dulcior,* 4.44). I list here some of the other figures, with the putative ordinary speech from which each figure departs:

> PRONOMINATIO (4.42)   *at non Africani nepotes istiusmodi fuerunt*
> (ἀντονομασία)   "But the sons of Africanus were not that sort"
> (instead of "the Gracchi were . . .")
>
> CIRCUMITIO (4.43)   *Scipionis prouidentia Kartaginis opes fregit*
> (περίφρασις)   "Scipio's foresight shattered the resources
> of Carthage" (instead of "Scipio shattered
> Carthage")
>
> TRANSGRESSIO (4.44)   *instabilis in istum plurimum fortuna ualuit*
> (ὑπερβατόν)   (instead of *instabilis fortuna in istum plurimum
> ualuit*)
> "unstable fortune hit him very hard"

In short, the author uses *uenustas* to describe momentary aesthetic pleasure given by discrete acts of artful manipulation. That is the oldest use of *uenust(us)* in connection to rhetorical effects (Ter. *Eu.* 457, IV.5). These instances, I suggest, represent an extension to verbal activity of the senses 'well-arranged' and 'attractive' that were associated with other aesthetic practices. These figures of speech were construed as "gestures" of a sort, artful poses struck from artless raw material. (Cicero interpreted the Greek σχήματα in exactly that way, turning σχήματα as *quasi aliquos gestus orationis* "verbal gestures, so to speak," *Or.* 83.) That is particularly true of the set of ten figures in 4.42–46, which are specifically described as having left ordinary speech behind (*ab usitata uerborum potestate reced[unt]*). *Venust(us)* appreciates the graceful departure of such artful expressions from the predictable norm, which is felt beneath their surface and against which they are judged. Indeed

---

50. *hunc, iudices, dico, rubrum breuem incuruom canum subcrispum caesium, cui sane magna est in mento cicatrix, si quo modo potest uobis in memoriam redire.*

*effictio* 'character sketch' *is* a graceful gesture of a kind, deftly "pointing out" somebody by recalling salient characteristics to mind. Whether or not I am quite right that both *uenust(us)* (2) and *uenust(us)* (3) were construed as gestures of a kind, or indeed that *uenust(us)* denoted 'good arrangement' at all, the consanguinity of the two uses should not be doubted: *festiu(us), lepid(us),* and *facet(us)* are all used both for rhetorical effects and specifically for humor, and in each case the same semantic core generates both uses.

In a handful of passages in his rhetorica, Cicero also uses *uenust(us)* for such 'well-arranged' or 'crafted' details. One kind of Asiatic style is composed of *sententiis non tam grauibus et seueris quam concinnis et uenustis* "sentences not so much weighty and serious as snug and pretty *(uenustus)*" (*Brut.* 325). Hortensius had *Meneclium illud studium crebrarum uenustarumque sententiarum* "Menecles' well-known taste for compact, pretty *(uenustus)* sentences" (*Brut.* 326).[51] Cicero gives the name *quaesitae uenustates* "affected ['sought after'] prettinesses" (*Or.* 84) to those παρονομασίαι, roughly 'puns,' produced by the change of one letter, including them among the "Gorgianic figures."[52] Quintilian also uses *uenust(us)* for punning epigrams.[53] *Venust(us)* is also used in Quintilian of such effects as feigned self-deprecation (*Inst.* 6.3.24), deft connection (9.2.61), irony (9.2.66), and metrical rhythm (10.1.65).

*Venust(us)* and Χάρι(s) *(4)*. Of all the members of the language of social performance, *uenust(us)* has the most consistent relationship with a Greek lexeme, namely χάρι(s) 'charm, grace, beauty.' *Venust(us)* was probably originally equated to χάρι(s) in an erotic capacity; like *uenust(us)*, χάρι(s)

51. Hoc sequuntur *in quibus ut in illo Graeco sic in hoc erant quaedam magis uenustae dulcesque sententiae quam aut necessariae aut interdum utiles,* secl. Friedrich. On the two types of Asiatic style distinguished in *Brut.* 325–26, v. Leeman 1963: 94–95.

52. For some examples of παρονομασία, cf. *Rhet. Her.* 4.29–30. The "Gorgianic figures" among which παρονομασίαι are included are ὁμοιοτέλευτον and ὁμοιόπτωτον *(similiter conclusa = similiter desinens, Rhet. Her.* 4.28; *eodem pacta cadentia = similiter cadens,* ibid.) and ἰσόκωλον *(paria paribus relata = compar, Rhet. Her.* 4.27). Such highly rhythmical and responsive figures go by the name "Gorgianic" after the rhetor Gorgias, in whom they are common; on Gorgias, cf. Kennedy 1963: 61–66.

53. *non agere sed satagere* " . . . that he did not deliver *(agere)* but had his hands full *(satagere),*" of a vehemently gesticulating speaker, a comment made *uenuste* (6.3.54); *quare mihi non inuenuste dici uidetur aliud esse Latine, aliud grammatice loqui* "Accordingly I think it is apt *(non inuenuste)* to say that it's one thing to speak Latin and another to speak grammatically" (1.6.27). Cf. *itaque Iulius Candidus non inuenuste solet dicere, aliud esse eloquentiam aliud loquentiam* "And so Iulius Candidus used to say, attractively enough, that eloquence was one thing, and speaking another," Plin. *Ep.* 5.20.5); *occare et occatorem Verrius putat dictum ab occadendo, quod caedat grandis globos terrae: cum Cicero uenustissime dicat ab occaecando fruges satas,* Paul. Fest. p. 192 Lindsay.

often describes an erotic 'attractiveness' or 'desirability.'[54] Several of the rhetorical uses of *uenust(us)* just detailed may look to χάρι(ς), for example the use for the humor of reply. Not only was χάρι(ς) associated with humor broadly speaking,[55] but χαρίεις is often used, in imperial Greek at any rate, to describe a mannered witticism or pointed aptness not dissimilar to the kind of humor described by *uenust(us)* (2). For example, when Tigranes observed Lucullus's army, wanting "to make a witty jest (χαρίεις εἶναι καὶ σκωπικός)," he said εἰ μὲν ὡς πρεσβευταί, πολλοὶ πάρεισιν· εἰ δ' ὡς στρατιῶται, ὀλίγοι "If they're legates, they're too many; if they're an army, not enough" (Plut. *Luc.* 27.4). Plutarch recalls that when Demades had cried to Phocion, "The Athenians will kill you, if they go mad," Phocion replied wittily (χαριέντως), "Or you, if they stay sane" (*Mor.* 811A = *pr. ger. rei publ.* 14). Similar uses of χαρίεις are common in Athenaeus.[56] Χάρι(ς) might well have been used this way in the second century B.C. and so induced the Romans to seek an equivalent for it, especially if it was a part of the programmatic language of the symposium.[57]

However, the relationship between the Latin and the Greek is by no means one of simple equivalency. The example of *uenust(us)* (3) from the *Rhet. Her.* mentioned above, *multum uenustatis . . . tum grauitatis et acrimoniae plurimum,* looks back to such Greek combinations as πολλὴ δὲ δεινότης

54. On χάρις, cf. MacLachlan 1993: 56–72. Pliny the Elder equates *uenustas* and *uenus* with χάρις: *praecipua eius (sc.* Apellis Coi) *in arte uenustas fuit, cum eadem aetate maximi pictores essent; quorum opera cum admiraretur, omnibus conlaudatis deesse illam suam uenerem dicebat, quam Graeci* χάριτα *uocant; cetera omnia contigisse, sed hac sola sibi neminem parem* "The *uenustas* of Apelles of Cos was outstanding, even in a time when there were other outstanding painters; he admired and praised all their work but said they lacked the quality that distinguished his own work, attractiveness *(uenus),* which the Greeks call χάρις; their work, he said, had every other requisite quality, but regarding χάρις no one was his equal" (Pliny *Nat.* 35.79).

55. Aristotle, for example, uses χαρίεις in the *Nicomachean Ethics* in the discussion of ἀλαζονεία for the aim of ironists: οἱ δ' εἴρωνες ἐπὶ τὸ ἔλαττον λέγοντες χαριέστεροι μὲν τὰ ἤθη φαίνονται· οὐ γὰρ κέρδους ἕνεκα δοκοῦσι λέγειν, ἀλλὰ φεύγοντες τὸ ὀγκηρόν (1127b22–24 = 4.7.14), οἱ δὲ μετρίως χρώμενοι τῇ εἰρωνείᾳ καὶ περὶ τὰ μὴ λίαν ἐμποδὼν καὶ φανερὰ εἰρωνευόμενοι χαρίεντες φαίνονται (1127b30–31 = 4.7.16, cf. 1128a15 = 4.8.4, 1128a36 = 4.8.10). Cf. εὐτραπελίας, ἣν οἱ πολλοὶ καλοῦσι χάριν (Dion. Hal. *Dem.* 54). Χαριεντισμός and χαριεντίζεσθαι mean 'joke' and 'to joke.'

56. Cf. Athen. *Deipn.* 4.162b, 6.233e, 12.535d, 13.592b. In the last one, for example, the first lover of a courtesan named Archippe, who was now keeping company with the aged Sophocles, was asked what she was doing and replied "wittily" (χαριέντως): "What owls do: sitting on a tombstone" (ὥσπερ αἱ γλαῦκες ἐπὶ τάφων κάθηται).

57. For an example of χάρις connected to the wit of the table, cf. ἦν δ' εὔστοχος ὁ Κτησίβιος καὶ χαρίεις περὶ τὸ γελοῖον· διὸ καὶ πάντες αὐτὸν ἐπὶ τὰ συμπόσια παρεκάλουν (Athen. *Deipn.* 4.162f).

τε καὶ χάρις (Demetr. *Eloc.* 37), as Calboli points out. But these two phrases differ importantly in their referents. Demetrius is referring to the overall effect of literary works that combine different styles, with χάρις representing the 'charm' of the plain style and δεινότης the 'force' of the "forceful" style; in situ these two form a counterpoint to the μεγαλοπρέπεια, or 'grandness,' of the "grand" style.[58] The author of the *Rhet. Her.*, by contrast, is referring to the restricted effect of a single figure of speech, as we have seen. *Venust(us)* has no part in the author's discussion of the plain style (which he calls *extenuatus,* 4.11, or *attenuatus,* 4.14) and is not used for an overall 'charm'; nor in assigning *uenustas* to *repetitio* does the author mean that several *repetitiones* make the style "plain."[59] In short, where Demetrius is speaking of an effect, the author is speaking of effects. The use of *uenust(us)* in the Latin rhetorical tradition may have been inspired by the χάρις of Greek rhetorical terminology, but the native semantics of *uenust(us),* and their connection to "attractive gestures," have not been suborned by it. Indeed, in the case of the application of *uenust(us)* to Gorgianic figures, there are much closer parallels in Greek rhetorical terminology than χάρις, namely κομψεία and καλλωπισμός (below, III.7 fin.). In the case of *uenust(us)* (1), which refers to gestures, it is not even possible to determine the underlying Greek, if any.[60] The native semantic features of *uenust(us),* and their connection with certain kinds of performative attractiveness, are the most important influences on the entrance of the lexeme into the terminology of Latin rhetoric.

That said, eventually there does arise a use of *uenust(us)* that simply is a kind of code for χάρι(s), in which the native Latin semantics seem to have been weakened. Quintilian's definition of *uenust(us),* which comes in the context of his discussion of humor, explicitly equates it with *gratia,* which is later a common equivalent for χάρις.[61] In calling Old Comedy *et grandis*

58. The works of Homer, Plato, Xenophon, and Herodotus have πολλὴν μὲν μεγαλοπρέπειαν καταμεμιγμένην . . . , πολλὴν δὲ δεινότητά τε καὶ χάριν.

59. By contrast, when Demetrius speaks of χάριτες (*Eloc.* 128–29), he does mean that the χάριτες in question (not figures of speech, but different sorts of jokes) are instantiations of the overall χάρις of the plain style, which the passage is discussing.

60. "Der Begriff der 'venustas' ist in diesem Zusammenhang neu; in den griechischen Zeugnissen ist davon nicht die Rede," Maier-Eichhorn 1989: 16 n.6. The Augustan poet Crinagoras has τῶν δὲ χερῶν χάριτες (*AP* 9.542.4), in reference to the gestures of the pantomime-dancer Bathyllus. Theophrastus's lost περὶ ὑποκρίσεως probably included a treatment of voice and motion not only for orators but also actors and musicians; cf. Fortenbaugh 1985.

61. *uenustum esse quod cum gratia quadam et uenere dicatur apparet,* "Whatever is said with a certain grace *(gratia)* and charm *(uenus)* appears to be *uenustum*" (6.3.18).

*et elegans et uenusta* (*Inst.* 10.1.65), Quintilian seems to be thinking of its stylistic range, with *uenusta* representing the diffuse χάρις of the "plain" style and *grandis* the grandeur or weight of the "grand" style. In another passage *uenustas* refers to the net effect of certain figures of speech with which narrative passages should be adorned: *caret enim ceteris lenociniis expositio et, nisi commendetur hac uenustate, iaceat necesse est* "For narrative passages do not have recourse to other enticements, and if they are not rendered agreeable by this form of charm *(haec uenustas),* they necessarily fall flat" (4.2.119). Aulus Gellius assigns *uenust(us)* to the "plain" style *(gracili [sc. generi] uenustas et subtilitas,* 6.14.3), the first author to do so directly. When he says *Graecae facundiae copia simul et uenustas* "Greek rhetoric's marriage of abundance and grace" (14.1.32), he is probably thinking of the "grand" style and the "plain" style, respectively.[62] Gellius also associates *uenust(us)* with "pure narration" and with "brevity and elegance."[63] Possibly the younger Seneca's use of *uenustas* to describe Latin translations of Aesop's fables (11.8.3) should be included here.

This use, which must be recognized as a fourth type of *uenust(us),* is as old as Cicero. For example, the only author who merits *uenust(us)* in Cicero is Lysias, the same author who, according to Dionysius of Halicarnassus, is distinguished above all by χάρις.[64] This *uenust(us)* is used particularly in connection with graceful narration, one of the characteristics of the "plain style" (and Lysias's forte). Cicero refers to Caesar's commentaries on the Gallic Wars thus: *nudi enim sunt, recti et uenusti, omni ornatu orationis tamquam ueste detracta* "They are bare, erect and graceful, stripped of all rhetorical artifice as if of their clothing" (*Brut.* 262). *Venustus* as proper to the "plain grace" of simple narration has been enlivened here by alluding to another of the lexeme's senses, 'gracefully shaped,' said of the human body.[65]

62. For *copia* associated with the grand style, cf. Cic. *Opt. Gen.* 2 (*grandis aut grauis aut copiosus,* of the speaker), *Or.* 20 (*grandiloqui . . . uehementes uarii copiosi graues,* of the speaker), 99 (*copiossimus,* of the speaker). On terms for the three styles, cf. Douglas 1966: xliii–xliv.

63. *eaque res perquam pure et uenuste narrata a Pisone* (7.9.1), *breuitas sane et uenustas et mundities orationis est, qualis haberi ferme in comoediarum festiuitatibus solet* (10.3.4), *[uersus] Porcii Licini et Q. Catuli, quibus mundius uenustius limatius tersius Graecum Latinumue nihil quicquam reperiri puto* (19.9.10).

64. *dicat igitur Attice uenustissimus ille scriptor ac politissimus Lysias . . .* (*Or.* 29); ἡ πᾶσιν ἐπανθοῦσα τοῖς ὀνόμασι κἀπ' ἴσης χάρις (Dion. Hal. *Lys.* 10), τῆς δὲ χάριτος καὶ τῆς ἡδονῆς ἀναμφιλόγως ἀπεδίδουν τὰ πρωτεῖα Λυσίᾳ (Dion. Hal. *Isoc.* 11, cf. 3).

65. For *uenustus* used of the form of the human body, cf. *nam et dignitate fuit honesta et uiribus ad laborem ferendum firmis neque tam magno corpore quam figura uenusta* "He was properly handsome, strong enough to work hard, and not so much big in body as attractive in form"

Perhaps *in narrando aliquid uenuste* "in the course of a charming narration" (*Or.* 87) belongs here, too.

It is notable that Cicero does not use *uenust(us)* in this way until the *Orator* and *Brutus*. For that there is more than one possible explanation. In purely linguistic terms, it may be that constant association of *uenust(us)* and χάρι(ς) by a bilingual elite culture led in certain contexts to the collapse of the semantic independence of the former and its suborning by the latter. There might also be a literary cause. The *Orator* and *Brutus* were written after, and in response to, the "Atticist" movement.[66] The "Atticists" valorized the plain style of Lysias and shunned the more elaborate style of Cicero. *Venust(us)* (4), which really is just a calque of the Greek, was, I suggest, the creation of the self-consciously Hellenizing Atticist movement. Cicero, his ear always finely tuned to the contours of contemporary Latin,[67] accepts the new usage beside older ones. It may even be that in the *Orator* and *Brutus* Cicero, in a small way, appropriates the language of those who thought mastery of the plain style alone was sufficient in the course of arguing that great orators must master all, and not only one of the styles.

In short, while *uenust(us)* has a demonstrable relationship to χάρις, it is unequivocal only for the later period, and then only in part. Earlier the distribution of *uenust(us)* is clearly conditioned by its native semantics, in particular the combination of 'attractive' and 'well-arranged.' The influence of the aesthetic practices described above (I.2) is certainly detectable in the *uenust(us)* of gesture, which adapts a theatrical use, and probably in the *uenust(us)* of humor, which is in point of origin or dissemination a convivial use, like other words for "humor." Though the case of *uenust(us)* is more complicated than the others, the guise under which it entered the technical lan-

---

(Nep. *Eum.* 11.5), *forma fuit eximia et per omnes aetatis gradus uenustissima, quamquam et omnis lenocinii neglegens* "His form was excellent and attractive at every stage of life, although also shunning every meretriciousness" (Suet. *Aug.* 79).

66. On Atticism, see below, VI.5.

67. Cf., e.g., Cicero's admission of aspiration into certain words as he got older: *quin ego ipse, cum scirem ita maiores locutos esse, ut nusquam nisi in uocali aspiratione uterentur, loquebar sic, ut pulcros, Cetegos, triumpos, Cartaginem dicerem; aliquando, idque sero, conuicio aurium cum extorta mihi ueritas esset, usum loquendi populo concessi, scientiam mihi reseruaui. Orciuios tamen et Matones, Otones, Caepiones, sepulcra, lacrimas dicimus, quia per aurium iudicium licet* "Since I knew our elders never used aspiration except before vowels, I used to say *pulcri, Cetegi, triumpi, Cartago;* but eventually, and only recently, the truth has been wrenched out of me by the importunate demands of the ear, and I have yielded to the popular pronunciation, keeping the truth to myself. However, we continue to say *Orcivius, Mato, Oto, Caepio, sepulcrum, lacrima,* since the judgment of the ear allows it" (*Or.* 160).

guage of rhetoric may fairly be regarded as that which it acquired to describe the aesthetic practices of the second century.

### III.5. *Bellus:* 'Nice' Moves for Knowledgeable Critics

In the first chapter we saw that *bellus,* which delivers a positive evaluation based on the personal standards of an evaluator, expanded in the period after Plautus from "first person singular" evaluation, which referred to the standards of an individual, to what I called "first person paucal inclusive" evaluation, which referred to the standards of some subgroup (I.7). This sense of "evaluated by the standards of a subgroup" is the ultimate source of *bellus* in the Latin rhetorical tradition. In Cicero, for example, *bellus* several times describes Greek figures or genres:

> παράγραμμα *bellum* (*Fam.* 7.32.2)
> a nice little *jeu de mots*
>
> *bellum* ἀκροτελεύτιον *habet illa tua epistula* (*Att.* 5.21.3)
> a nice little *dénouement*
>
> *misit enim bellum* ὑπόμνημα (*Att.* 16.14.4)
> he sent a nice *mémoire*
>
> *bella ironia, si iocaremur* (*Brut.* 293)
> fine irony, if one were kidding
>
> *bella, ut mihi uidetur,* εἰρωνεία (*Att.* 16.15.3)
> a nice irony, as I think

In the use of technical or quasi-technical rhetorical terms like παράγραμμα and ἀκροτελεύτιον, Cicero is recalling the language of the rhetorical handbooks, showing his command of their categories to fellow learned critics, whose pleasure in seeing those categories instantiated is highlighted by *bellus*.[68] Such uses of *bellus* are common. Sallustius congratulated Cicero on his

---

68. On παράγραμμα, see SB with refs. *Et tu belle* ἠπόρησας (*Att.* 6.1.18) might be included here, too, as meaning "perform a nice ἀπορία." Atticus had reprimanded Cicero on a historical point, whence Cicero casts the exchange in the language of debate, using the technical language of the philosophical schools. Ἀπορία is the "puzzle" of dialectical discussion; ἀπορεῖν is also frequent for 'express [philosophical] doubts about,' e.g., εὐθέως γὰρ τῶν περὶ τῆς ἐπινοίας ζητησάντων Σωκράτης μὲν ἠπόρησε μείνας ἐν τῇ σκέψει (Sex. Empir. *adv. Math.* 7.264), περί τε οὖν τῶν τοιούτων ἠπόρησεν ὁ Χρύσιππος (Posidonius fr. 417.93–94). *Bellus* also occurs in connection to technical language, in this case philosophy, in *Att.* 2.17.2: *di immortales, neque tam me* εὐελπιστία *consolatur ut antea quam* ἀδιαφορία, *qua nulla in re tam utor quam in hac ciuili et publica. quin etiam quod est subinane in nobis et non* ἀφιλόδοξον *(bellum est enim sua uitia nosse) id adficitur quadam delectatione* "No by God, I don't (as I once did) take so much consolation in optimism as I do in indifference, which I never

use of recent historical figures in *de Oratore: oratorum sermonem a me belle remouisse* "It was clever *(belle)* of me, he said, not to have written the orators' dialogue in my own voice" (*Q. fr.* 3.5.1). "Ambiguous statements," observes Caesar Strabo in *de Oratore,* "don't often raise a big laugh but are admired more for having been said cleverly *(belle)* and learnedly *(litterate)."*[69] *Att.* 7.2.1, which introduces a neoteric σπονδειάζων, plays off this idea of *bellus* as recherché (I.7).[70] *Bellus* as describing a good "move" appears a few times in Cicero's philosophy.[71] In *de Oratore* Cicero generally narrows *bellus* to the humor of various conversational games, involving false pretenses of various kinds (VI.2). Once, however, Crassus uses *belle* to represent an exclamation that was common property: *quare 'bene et praeclare' quamuis nobis saepe dicatur, 'belle et festiue' nimium saepe nolo* "I want to hear 'well done!' 'splendid!' as often. as possible, 'nicely done!' 'delightful!' not too often" (*de Orat.* 3.101, cf. VI.6).

This use of *bellus* survives in Latin literary metalanguage well into the Empire. Its status as a stereotypical compliment for 'clever' verbal displays is preserved in Persius:

---

employ except in the current civic and governmental situation. And I even get a certain pleasure out of foolish vanity (nice *[bellum]* to know your own faults, isn't it?)" (my translation owes several phrases to SB). Ἀδιαφορία 'indifference' is a technical Stoic term, so used by Cicero (*huic [= Zenoni] summum bonum est in is rebus neutram in partem moueri, quae* ἀδιαφορία *ab ipso dicitur, Luc.* 130, cf. *Fin.* 3.53) and of broad currency in a variety of philosophers. Two other terms were apparently only popular in the last centuries B.C. Εὐελπιστία 'hopefulness,' first in Aristotle (οὐ προμηθὲς μὲν γὰρ τάχος βλαβερόν, βραβύτης [*sic in disculo* TLG *pro* βραδύτης] δὲ μετ' εὐελπιστίας ὠφέλιμον "Speed without foresight is dangerous but slowness with hopefulness is helpful," Ar. fr. 102 = Philo *de Plant.* Noe 39), appears once in Epicurus (*Sent. Vat.* 39) and seems to flourish, such as it does, only later (2× Polybius, 5× Philo Jud.), which may suggest it was popular philosophical jargon in the period of the late Republic. Ἀφιλόδοξον 'indifferent to fame,' first in Philodemus, appears also in Philo Jud. At any rate, to be able "to know one's own faults" is also to be able to catalog them with pop-psychological jargon, displayed for understanding fellow initiates, much as saying "codependent" or "enabler," however onerous the reality they describe, also invokes the security of a recognized paradigm.

69. *ambigua . . . non saepe magnum risum mouent, magis ut belle ut litterate dicta laudantur* (*de Orat.* 2.253).

70. Cf. Lyne 1978: esp. 167, 169. *Vendito* may also mean 'show off'; see SB.

71. So at *Div.* 2.66 (above, I.7) and *N.D.* 1.84: *quam bellum erat, Vellei, confiteri potius nescire quod nescires quam ista effutientem nauseare atque ipsum sibi displicere* "It would have been a better move, Velleius, to admit you didn't know what you didn't know instead of getting sick and irritating yourself by spouting what you did." The remaining instances from the philosophy are *Fin.* 2.102 (above, I.7) and *est tibi ex eis ipsis, qui adsunt, bella copia, uel ut a te ipso ordiare* (*Rep.* 2.67), where *bella copia* is a "nice supply at one's disposal."

*sed recti finemque extremumque esse recuso*
*'euge' tuum et 'belle.' nam 'belle' hoc excute totum:*
*quid non intus habet? non hic est "Ilias" Atti*
*ebria ueratro? non siquae elegidia crudi*
*dictarunt proceres? non quidquid denique lectis*
*scribitur in citreis?*

The end and the goal of what is right is not, I say,
your "bravo" and "nice." Give "nice" a good going over:
what's *not* in it? You've got Attius's *Iliad,* drunk on gingko
     root,
you've got the darling epigrams written by noblemen
with bad digestion—you've got anything a writer writes
while lying on a couch of citronwood.

(1.48–53)[72]

In Petronius, "do a nice a job of reciting the *deuerbia* (the spoken, not sung, part of a play)" is *belle canturire deuerbia* (64.2).[73] *Bellus* is a common term in the elder Seneca, for example, for any cleverness of declamation. Montanus, for example, had many clever *(bellus)* ideas, but piled too many on.[74] The elder Seneca uses *bellus* to label particularly the clevernesses of *sententiae.* Many listeners "have been taken in by a fine-sounding *(belle sonantis)* epigram."[75] When Labienus's books were burned on the orders of the senate, Cassius Severus made an observation that Seneca calls a *belle dicta res:* "I ought to be burned alive now: I know those books by heart."[76] Since the semantic structure of *bellus* includes a reference to evaluators, it provides a perfect word for highlighting the play to the audience typical of declama-

---

72. Cf. *"fur es" ait Pedio. Pedius quid? crimina rasis | librat in antithetis, doctas posuisse figuras | laudatur: "bellum hoc." hoc bellum? an Romule ceues?* "Somebody charges Pedius with theft, and what does Pedius do? Measures out the charges in buffed-up antitheses. And they praise him for knowing how to use learned figures. 'That's nice *(bellum),*' they say. It's nice? Sure, and Romulus wiggles his ass" (= 'is a pathic homosexual,' advanced as an extreme improbability) (1.85–87).

73. Cf. *dicite aliquid belli* (78.6), said to musicians.

74. *nihil non ex eis bellum est, si solum sit; nihil non rursus ex eis alteri obstat* "Any one of them would be fine in isolation; but they all get in each other's way" (*Con.* 9.5.16). The sense of "acceptable" vs. "unacceptable" is clear from the following contrast: *circa uulnus nouercae quidam bellas res dixerunt, quidam ineptias, immo multi ineptias* (7.5.8), "In regard to the stepmother's wound [part of the premise of the declamation], certain speakers said fine *(bellus)* things, whereas others, or really many, pronounced absurdities *(ineptiae).*"

75. *multis conpositio belle sonantis sententiae imposuit* (7.10.4).

76. *nunc me, inquit, uiuum uri oportet, qui illos edidici* (10.pr.8).

tory practice. In Martial *bellus* is the central characteristic of Atticus, an accomplished declaimer, and writer, and dancer:

> *Declamas belle, causas agis, Attice, belle,*
> *historias bellas, carmina bella facis,*
> *componis belle mimos, epigrammata belle,*
> *bellus grammaticus, bellus es astrologus*
> *et belle cantas et saltas, Attice, belle,*
> *bellus es arte lyrae, bellus es arte pilae.*
> *nil bene cum facis, facias tamen omnia belle,*
> *uis dicam quid sis? magnus es ardalio.*

> You nicely declaim, Atticus, nicely plead cases,
> write nice poems and nice histories,
> compose mimes nicely and epigrams nicely,
> you're a nice grammarian, a nice astrologer,
> you nicely dance, Atticus, and nicely you sing,
> You nicely play lyre and sports in the gym.
> You do everything nicely, nothing the best.
> Shall I tell you what you are? You're a pest.[77]

> (Mart. 2.7)

Of all the members of the language of social performance, *bellus* is the one for which it is hardest to find a Greek equivalent. Κομψός 'refined,'[78] ἡδύς 'pleasant, nice,' and even χαρίεις 'charming' might be seen as equivalents, but the claim that *bellus* is mechanically translating a term or terms from the Greek rhetorical tradition is weak. That the presence of the language of social performance in Latin is a distinctly Roman contribution to the language of rhetorical theory has become steadily clearer in the course of this chapter; we explore the meaning of the adaptation below.

### III.6. *Elegan(s):* The Distinctive Choice of the Social Elite

As we saw above, *elegan(s)* shifted in the second century to describe amelioratively aesthetic choices made in the self-presentations of the social elite, from artwork, to entertainment, to intellectual pursuits. That sense was very naturally and directly imported into the technical language of rhetoric, applied both to speech and to speakers.[79]

---

77. Cf. *bellus homo et magnus uis idem, Cotta, uideri:* | *sed qui bellus homo est, Cotta, pusillus homo est* (1.9); *res pertricosa est, Cotile, bellus homo* (3.36.14, of foppishness); *omnia uis belle, Matho, dicere. Dic aliquando* | *Et bene; dic neutrum; dic aliquando male* "Your goal, Matho, to speak always with charm: Try quality, or nothing, or maybe even harm" (10.46).

78. For the connection of κομψός to figures, cf. ὀλίγου γὰρ ἅπας ὁ λόγος ὑπὸ τῶν τοιούτων αὐτῷ κεκόμψευται σχημάτων (Dion. Hal. *Isoc.* 14 l. 45).

79. Cf. I.5 n. 56.

*Elegan(s)* often refers to 'distinctive choice' on the level of vocabulary. C. Curio developed his own "type of style, as it were" *(suam quandam quasi formam figuramque dicendi)* by way of "grave, abundant, and carefully chosen words" *(uerborum grauitate et elegantia et copia, de Orat.* 2.98). C. Piso's ability to select vocabulary is described as *uerborum dilectus elegans (Brut.* 272). Crassus was "painstaking and careful, though free from pedantry, in his latinity" *(Latine loquendi accurata et sine molestia diligens elegantia, Brut.* 143, tr. Douglas).[80] Julius Caesar's pure speech is described as *haec elegantia uerborum Latinorum (Brut.* 261), and indeed the quality *elegantia* was especially associated with it.[81] The application of *elegan(s)* to style generally refers to 'painstaking' and 'careful' style. Gaius Tuditanus, for example, who was "refined in every aspect of his life and manners" *(omni uita atque uictu excultus atque expolitus),* had a correspondingly "elegant style of speech" *(elegans . . . orationis genus, Brut.* 95).[82] No one had ever heard anything more polished *(politius)* or more elegant *(elegantius)* than Q. Scaevola's speech for M. Coponius.[83]

---

80. For other connections of *elegan(s)* to vocabulary, cf. *abutimur saepe etiam uerbo non tam eleganter quam in transferendo (de Orat.* 3.169); *sermone eleganti (Brut.* 130); *M. Aurelius Scaurus non saepe dicebat, sed polite; Latine uero in primis est eleganter locutus (Brut.* 135); *uerba ipsa non illa quidem elegantissimo sermone (Brut.* 140); *auditus est nobis Laeliae C. f. saepe sermo: ergo illam patris elegantia tinctam uidimus . . . (Brut.* 211); *summa uerborum et grauitas et elegantia (Brut.* 265); *elegantia et iucunditate uerborum sonantium et lenium (Part.* 21); *nam cum omnis pars orationis esse debet laudabilis, sic ut uerbum nullum nisi aut graue aut elegans excidat (Or.* 125); *ut uerbum ex ore nullum nisi aut elegans aut graue exeat (Or.* 134); *uerborum . . . et propriorum et translatorum elegantiam (Opt. Gen.* 4).

81. *sed tamen, Brute, inquit Atticus, de Caesare et ipse ita iudico et de hoc huius generis acerrimo existimatore saepissime audio, illum omnium fere oratorum Latine loqui elegantissime (Brut.* 252); *elegantia horum commentariorum* (Hirt. 8.pr.4, of Caesar's *de Bello Gallico*); *erat autem in Caesare . . . facultas atque elegantia summa scribendi* (ibid. 8); Quint. *Inst.* 10.1.114. For a treatment of Caesar's *elegantia,* see Lomanto 1994–95: esp. 100ff.; Hendrickson 1906: 102–3.

82. *E contrario* Caria, Phrygia, and Mysia adopted a "kind of rich and, so to say, greasy style of speaking" *(opimum quoddam et tamquam adipatae dictionis genus)* precisely because "they completely lack distinction and polish" *(quod minime politae minimeque elegantes sunt, Or.* 25). Caria is mentioned probably as a reference to Alabanda, birthplace of the Asiatic orators Hierocles and Menecles (Sandys 1885: 28n.). The style of speech in Phrygia was attacked by the Atticist rhetorician Caecilius in "Against the Phrygians" (κατὰ τῶν Φρυγῶν).

83. *qua re quis ex populo, cum Q. Scaeuolam pro M. Coponio dicentem audiret in ea causa, de qua ante dixi, quicquam politius aut elegantius aut omnino melius aut exspectaret aut posse fieri putaret? (Brut.* 194). For other examples of *elegan(s)* applied to style of speech, cf. *qui hac dicendi uarietate et elegantia non utuntur (de Orat.* 1.50, in reference to the rhetorical style of Chrysippus as against that of Plato, Aristotle, and others); *historia ipsius non ineleganter scripta (Brut.* 101); *elegans quoddam et eruditum orationis genus (Brut.* 133); *sed adiunxit etiam et litterarum scientiam et loquendi elegantiam, quae ex scriptis eius, quorum similia nulla sunt, facillime perspici potest (Brut.* 153); *nam Scaeuolae dicendi elegantiam satis ex eis orationibus, quas reliquit, habemus*

The 'care' and 'polish' that *elegan(s)* connoted made it especially appropriate to describe the "Attic" or plain styles of oratory.[84]

Careful words may be understood to depend on careful underlying thought; hence 'careful of language' can overlap with 'careful of thought.'[85] *Aut non satis eleganter secuti* is "with an inadequately economical (or 'scientific') treatment" (*Inv.* 2.9). At *Brutus* 130 the consensus of the oldest manuscripts has *atque etiam ingenio et sermone eleganti,* which can be rendered "intellectually discriminating and verbally tasteful"; the phrase need not be emended.[86] This sense of *elegan(s)* is commonest in Cicero's philosophical writings.[87] The use of *elegan(s)* for 'careful of thought' obviously fits hand in glove with its use for systematic knowledge, which we saw above (I.5).

These two strands—'careful of style' and 'careful of thought'—are both sensible in Cicero's use of *elegan(s)* in contrasting the rhetorical styles of C. Laelius Sapiens and Servius Sulpicius Galba (*Brut.* 86–89). Laelius had pled for his clients in a particular case "with his usual accuracy and elegance" (*accurate, ut semper solitus esset, eleganterque,* 86). The presiding consuls called for another set of presentations, and at the next session Laelius made his case "even better and more diligently" (*multo diligentius meliusque,*

---

cognitam (*Brut.* 163); *etiam L. Torquatus elegans in dicendo, in existimando admodum prudens, toto genere perurbanus* (*Brut.* 239); *rationis non inelegans copia* (*Brut.* 282, somewhat paradoxically, in that *copia* is typically associated with grandness); *Terentium cuius fabellae propter elegantiam sermonis putabantur a C. Laelio scribi* (*Att.* 7.3.10); *oratio scripta elegantissime sententiis uerbis ut nihil possit ultra* "The speech is a most elegant composition, the wording and the turn of the sentences could not be bettered" (*Att.* 15.1a.12, tr. SB).

84. *[Lysias] egregie subtilis scriptor atque elegans, Brut.* 35; *[Lysias et Cato] acuti sunt elegantes faceti breues, Brut.* 63, on *facetus* cf. III.2); *[Caluus* sc. *quoddam dicendi genus] quamquam scienter eleganterque tractabat, nimium tamen inquirens in se atque ipse sese obseruans metuensque ne uitiosum colligeret, etiam uerum sanguinem deperdebat* (*Brut.* 283), *sin autem ieiunitatem et siccitatem et inopiam, dum modo sit polita, dum urbana, dum elegans, in Attico genere ponit, hoc recte dumtaxat* (*Brut.* 285), *putant enim qui horride inculteque dicat, modo id eleganter enucleateque faciat, eum solum Attice dicere* (*Or.* 28), *Lysiam . . . non illum quidem amplum atque grandem, subtilem et elegantem tamen* (*Or.* 30), *ergo ille tenuis orator, modo sit elegans,* etc. (*Or.* 81).

85. Cf. "The word *elegans* is not limited in sense to grace of expression, but is also often applied to clearness of thought," Sandys 1885: 33 ad §28.

86. J. Martha in his 1892 edition keeps the reading, citing *Vibius Crispus, uir ingenii iucundi et elegantis* from Quint. *Inst.* 5.13.48. Cf. also *ingenio eleganti* (Gel. 6.3.8), *ingenii elegantia* (11.2.3). Wilkins prints Friedrich's *atque et acri.*

87. *diuisit ineleganter* (*Fin.* 2.26), *sed eos, si possumus, excitemus, qui liberaliter eruditi adhibita etiam disserendi elegantia ratione et uia philosophantur* (*Tusc.* 2.6), *uerae elegantisque philosophiae* (*Tusc.* 4.6). Cf. *Fin.* 2.27 *contemnit enim disserendi elegantiam,* of which Nägelsbach 1905: 41 notes, "So meint er die wissenschaftliche, streng philosophische Erörterung und logische Richtigkeit."

86). The consuls delayed judgment again, at which point Laelius passed the case onto Galba, since he, Laelius, though having performed "diligently and carefully" (*studiose accurateque*, 86), thought Galba would conduct the case "with more gravity and energy" *(grauius uehementiusque)*, for his style of speech was "fiercer and more violent" (*atrocior acriorque*, 86). Galba's energetic speech secured an acquittal. In Cicero's summary of the case, *elegantia* is both 'careful of style' and 'careful of thought,' being to *disputare subtiliter* 'discuss carefully' as *uis* 'force' is to *agere grauiter* 'speak grandly' (*Brut.* 89):[88]

> ex hac Rutili narratione suspicari licet, cum duae summae sint in oratore laudes, una subtiliter disputandi ad docendum, altera grauiter agendi ad animos audientium permouendos, multoque plus proficiat is qui inflammet iudicem quam ille qui doceat, elegantiam in Laelio, uim in Galba fuisse.

Rutilius's account permits the conjecture that Laelius had elegance *(elegantia)* and Galba force *(uis)*—for there are two kinds of oratorical excellence, one that gives careful accounts to prove a point and another that holds forth seriously to rouse the emotions, and the orator who inflames the judge is much more effective than the one who teaches him.

That *elegan(s)* is meant to style such 'clear and correct speech' or 'clear thought' as an elite preserve might easily be surmised, but that very sense comes to the fore in several places. So in an example where *elegan(s)* refers to 'systematic,' virtually 'scientific' thought, contrasted with *popularis*:

> mihi uero, inquit, placet agi subtilius et, ut ipse dixisti, pressius. quae enim adhuc protulisti, popularia sunt, ego autem a te elegantiora desidero.

I would like an examination of the problem that is more nuanced *(subtilius)* and, as you said yourself, closer *(pressius)*. You have so far offered me bromides (*popularia* 'popular, common'), whereas what I'm looking for from you is something more systematic *(elegantiora)*.

(*Fin.* 4.24).

As for word choice, Cicero's theoretical position is that good Latinity should be taken for granted as the common possession of all Roman citizens, and

---

88. Cf. "Here the sense demanded [of *elegantiam*] is clearly 'fastidious restraint,'" Douglas 1966: ad 89.13. For the conjunction of *subtili(s)* (on which cf. VI.4 n. 53) and *elegan(s)*, cf. *de Orat.* 3.187 *(quid disputatione ista adferri potest elegantius aut omnino dici subtilius)*, subtilem et elegantem (*Or.* 30, of Lysias); *de Orat.* 2.28 (III.3 n. 25); *Brut.* 35 (III.6 n. 84); *Fin.* 4.24 (III.6); *tua . . . perelegans et persubtilis oratio* (*Planc.* 58; below, V.6); and *Fam.* 4.4.1, in which Cicero's *diuitiae orationis* are contrasted with the *subtilitas et elegantia* of Servius Sulpicius's writings.

that failures of good Latinity result only from neglect.[89] The "correct speech" of the Athenians, which for Cicero was an analogue to the Roman city dialect, is described as *elegans* and *incorruptum*.[90] But when what is represented as a "given" just so happens to coincide with the patterns of speech that are typical of the social elite, then the "given" is being considered not in a purely descriptive way but in some normative and exclusionary way. When *elegan(s)* is used without illustrative examples, one cannot defend such a claim; but in the two passages in which *elegan(s)* is applied to particular phonetic forms, there are clear connections to elite patterns of speech.

The first passage concerns the phonetic rule of Latin which lengthened vowels that preceded *nf* and *ns*.[91] This meant that transparently parallel forms, for example forms with the same preverb, could end up with different vowel lengths. Cicero discusses this pattern at *Or.* 159, using the following examples:[92]

89. *nam ipsum Latine loqui est illud quidem, ut paulo ante dixi, in magna laude ponendum, sed non tam sua sponte quam quod est a plerisque neglectum: non enim tam praeclarum est scire Latine quam turpe nescire, neque tam id mihi oratoris boni quam ciuis Romani proprium uidetur* "The ability to speak Latin, as I've just said, should be held in high regard, not so much for its own sake as because many neglect it; it is not so much notable to know Latin as it is shameful not to know it, and the ability, it seems to me, belongs not so much to the orator as to the Roman citizen" (*Brut.* 140); *hanc elegantiam uerborum Latinorum, quae etiam si orator non sis et sis ingenuus ciuis Romanus tamen necessaria est* (*Brut.* 261); cf. also *de Orat.* 3.39. Cicero's position that good Latinity is a given in all Roman citizens is polemical, maintained in opposition to those such as Julius Caesar who thought Latinity could be determined and protected more scientifically. Cicero's view is touched upon in *de Oratore* (3.38–39) and defended more closely in the *Orator* and *Brutus,* presumably in response to Julius Caesar's *de Analogia.* On the *de Analogia,* cf. Hendrickson 1906; for an extended treatment of Caesar's views of language, cf. Lomanto 1994–95. Caesar's *de Analogia* has also been treated recently by Papke 1988, not available to me at the time of writing.

90. *quorum [= Atheniensium] semper fuit prudens sincerumque iudicium, nihil ut possent nisi incorruptum audire et elegans. eorum religioni cum seruiret orator, nullum uerbum insolens nullum odiosum ponere audebat* (*Or.* 25). For the linguistic correlation of the Athenian with the Roman city dialect, cf. *sed hanc dico suauitatem, quae exit ex ore; quae quidem ut apud Graecos Atticorum, sic in Latino sermone huius est urbis maxime propria* "But I'm referring to the pleasantness (*suauitas*) that comes from speech, which belongs particularly to this city among those that speak Latin, as it does to Athenians among the Greeks" (*de Orat.* 3.42).

91. Sihler 1995: §81.2, Allen 1978: 65–66, LHS I §89b.

92. *quid uero hoc elegantius, quod non fit natura sed quodam instituto: indoctus dicimus breui prima littera, insanus producta, inhumanus breui, infelix longa et, ne multis, quibus in uerbis eae primae litterae sunt quae in sapiente atque felice, <in> producte dicitur, in ceteris omnibus breuiter; itemque conposuit consueuit concrepuit confecit. consule ueritatem: reprehendet; refer ad auris: probabunt; quaere cur ita sit; dicent iuuare; uoluptati autem aurium morigerari debet oratio* "What is more distinctive (*elegantius*) than a practice that is not natural but a kind of agreed-on practice? We say *indoctus* with a short first vowel, *insanus* with a long one, *inhumanus* with a short one, *in-*

| | With Long Vowel | With Short Vowel |
|---|---|---|
| Compounds with *in-* | *īnfēlix* 'unlucky' | *ĭnhumānus* 'uncivilized' |
| 'un-, not . . .' | *īnsānus* 'mad' | *ĭndoctus* 'untaught' |
| Compounds with *con-* | *cōnsuēuit* 'is accustomed' | *cŏnposuit* 'assembled' |
| 'with; [to completion]' | *cōnfēcit* 'completed' | *cŏncrepuit* 'creaked' |

The variation in epigraphic spellings *(consul cosul, inferus iferos eimferis)* and the Romance outcomes (e.g., Ital. *istruere* < *instruere*) suggest that the nasal was lost early on in vulgar speech, with compensatory lengthening.[93] That is, after the operation of sound laws, but without analogical restoration of the prefixes, there were probably pairs like *īsanus* (or *į̄sanus*) : *ĭndoctus* and *cō-sueuit* (or *cǭsueuit*) : *cŏnposuit*.[94] The pairs that Cicero discusses, with both a long vowel and a nasal stop (viz., *īns-, īnf-*), probably represent a learned reintroduction or "spelling pronunciation" of the etymologically correct *-n-* preserved in other forms.[95] In any case forms were surely still in flux; a grammarian reports that Cicero's own practice was inconsistent.[96] Thus the rule would be difficult to defend even by *consuetudo*, which itself varied, let alone by *ratio*.[97] At this impasse Cicero invokes *elegantia*, which functions here as a defense of last resort. Certain forms just "sound better": "What is more elegant than a practice that is not natural *(quod non fit natura)* but defined by a kind of cultural convention *(quodam instituto)*?" The parties to the agreement, of course, are those who have the right to choose certain speech forms to distinguish themselves, much as they would choose statues for their garden or improve their *cognomina*, as we see in the next example.

The idea of a deliberate self-definition through speech also appears prominently in connection to the other appearance of *elegan(s)* earlier in the same discussion, where "the elegant habits *(consuetudo elegans)* of Latin speech" got rid of the *x* in certain words.

Indeed, words are often contracted not for the sake of utility but of euphony. Why else did your *Axilla* (Little Wing) become *Ala* (Wing)

---

*felix* with a long one, and, in short, in any word that begins with 's' or 'f,' 'in-' is pronounced long, and in all other words short; and likewise *conposuit consueuit concrepuit confecit*. Consult principle ('truth'): it will object; ask your ears: they will approve. Ask them why and they will say it is pleasant; and speech must have due regard for the pleasure of sound ('the ears')" (*Or.* 159).

93. See discussion in Allen 1978: 28–30, 65–66; Sihler 1995: §225.1.

94. *į̄* and *ǭ* represent nasalized long vowels.

95. Cf. Allen 1978: 29.

96. He supposedly said *foresia, Megalesia, hortesia* (Velius Longus in *G.L.* 7.79), where *e* = |e:| or |ę:|.

97. On this distinction (= Gr. ἀνωμαλία vs. ἀναλογία), cf. I.8 above.

except to escape an ungainly sound? That is the sound that the elegant
habits of Latin speech have removed from *maxilla* (jawbone), *taxillus*
(die), *uexillum* (military standard), and *pauxillum* (for a little while) [sc.,
yielding *mala* (jaw, cheek), *talus* (die, knucklebone), *uelum* (sail), and
*paulum* (for a little while)].[98]

(*Or.* 153)

Cicero's opening example, the supposed change of the cognomen *Axilla*
'Little Wing' to *Ala* 'Wing'' (as a cognomen also spelled *Ahala*)[99] is illustrative. Of the pairs he lists, *axilla* is evidently the only form that was completely obsolete.[100] *Pauxill-* was certainly archaic, but the other pairs consist
not of an older and a newer form but of semantically distinct synchronic
variants.[101] Indeed *uexillum* is a word that Cicero himself uses (*Phil.* 5.29,
*Att.* 10.15.2), and if it was un-Latin, it was not un-Latin enough for the verbally fastidious Caesar not to have used it. The supposed change in *axilla*,
in other words, is the strongest example: there it most seems that one form
was gotten rid of for another. Particularly significant is that Cicero cites the
pair *axilla:ala* not in their literal meanings but as cognomina, referring by
"your Axilla" to C. Servilius Ahala, a relative of the mother of Brutus, Cicero's interlocutor in this passage. This section of the discussion begins, in
fact, with the idea of willful change also exemplified by the alteration of a
name, *Bellius* from *Duellius*.[102] Names were a particular focus of aristocratic
pride and might even be taken as predictors of character.[103] They are the

98. *quin etiam uerba saepe contrahuntur non usus causa sed aurium. quo modo enim uester Axilla
Ala factus est nisi fuga litterae uastioris? quam litteram etiam e maxillis et taxillis et uexillo et pauxillo
consuetudo elegans Latini sermonis euellit.* For the origins of the forms, cf. W-H and E-M s.vv.

99. For the history of the proper name, see Sandys 1885 ad loc. *Ahala* is simply an Umbrian spelling of the Latin *āla;* in inscriptions in the Latin alphabet, Umbrian used vowel +
*h* + vowel to indicate a long vowel, e.g., *comohota* = L. *commota; ahauendo* 'turn away' = *\*ā-
wend-etō*, with the *\*wend-* of Gmc., cf. Buck 1928: §26.

100. Only attested in the gloss *axilla:* μικρὰ πτερά, ὡς Βάρρων (Var. fr. 129 GS).

101. In the late Republic *pauxill-* is only in Lucretius (adj. *pauxillus* 1.835, 1.836, 3.229,
adv. *pauxillo* 5.594). As for the other pairs, the diminutives had specialized meanings, so *maxil-
lae* 'jawbones' ~ *malae* 'jaws, cheeks'; *uexillum* 'military standard, banner' ~ *uelum* 'sail, curtain,
awning.' Cicero does not mention the pair *paxillus* 'wooden pin, peg' ~ *palus* (*\*pak-slos*)
'post, stake.' Still possibly a productive diminutive was *taxillus* '(small) die, cube' (Pompon.
*com.* 190, Vitr. 10.8.2), built to *talus* 'ankle-bone, knuckle-bone, die.' The lexicalization or
partial lexicalization of original diminutives is not uncommon, e.g., Polish **łyżka** 'spoon' ~
**łyżeczka** 'teaspoon,' **noga** 'foot, leg' ~ **nóżka** 'stem (of a glass)', **nos** 'nose' ~ **nosek** 'peen
(of a hammer).'

102. *quid uero licentius quam quod hominum etiam nomina contrahebant, quo essent aptiora?*
*Du-* developed into *b-* by rule (Sihler 1995: §185.1), e.g., *bis* 'twice' < *\*dwis,* cogn. with *duo*
'two.'

103. Corbeill 1996: 57–98.

kinds of words Cicero can suppose had been willfully changed to improve social appearances; he had been encouraged to get rid of his cognomen, which means 'Chickpea' (L. *cicer ciceris*, cf. Plut. *Cic.* 1.3–5). In short, Cicero describes by *elegan(s)* certain phonetic changes presented as plainly connected to elite self-presentation and, more importantly, premeditated and even irrational.[104] There is doubtless some irony in that, in that *elegan(s)* is the buzzword associated with Cicero's rationalizing linguistic opponent Caesar and, indeed, with the Atticist movement that, by the time of the writing of the *Brutus* and *Orator*, in which most of the instances of *elegan(s)* in Cicero occur, had risen in opposition to the floridity of Cicero.

As with the other members of the language of social performance, many uses of *elegan(s)* are inspired by the Greek, but the social construction of the native semantics is the most important factor in the application of the lexeme to rhetoric. The uses of *elegan(s)* for socially distinct phonology are reminiscent of ἀττικισμός (cf. Quint. *Inst.* 1.8.8) or ἑλληνισμός, although those terms are typically rendered by *Latinitas* or equivalents like *Latine loqui*. The connection of *elegan(s)* to vocabulary choice recalls Theophrastus's ἐκλογή. The three epithets applied to Hortensius, *in uerborum splendore elegans, compositione aptus, facultate copiosus* (*Brut.* 303), allude respectively to the Theophrastean subdivisions of style into ἐκλογή 'selection,' σύνθεσις 'arrangement,' and perhaps κατασκευή 'device.'[105] The equation to ἐκλογή was abetted by the transparent etymology of *elegan(s)*. Nonetheless the social elitism of the Latin is felt more strongly in *elegan(s)* than in ἐκλογή or

104. The label for the sound *x* is also instructive: it was changed to "avoid a rather ungainly sound" (*fuga litterae uastioris, Or.* 153; cf. *non aspere . . . non uaste non rustice non hiulce sed presse et aequabiliter et leniter, de Orat.* 3.45 and LPW ad loc.). *Vastus*, which includes meanings related to 'huge,' can also mean 'ungainly,' 'awkward' (i.e., 'moving like something too big'). The sense 'clumsy' ('plump, ungelenk' LP) appears in the *de Oratore* as concomitant to 'rustic' *(agrestis)* and 'ugly' *(foedus): uoltu motuque corporis uasti atque agrestes* (1.115), *Q. Varium uastum hominem atque foedum* (1.117). For the relation to χαίνειν, cf. Ernest. The sound *x* is thus presented as a clumsy sound unworthy of the more graceful urban tongue.

105. Douglas 1966 ad loc. and intro. §26. For further examples of *elegan(s)* = ἐκλογή, cf. Stroux 1912: 87–88. Notably the rhetorical form of the Theophrastean trio casts them in the mold of noble accomplishments, as opposed to, say, mere tricks. *Splendor* is a stereotypical aristocratic compliment: *equestris splendor* (*S. Rosc.* 140), *splendor uester* "your prominent social position" (*Ver.* 2.1.22), *splendorem ordinis atque ornamentum curiae* (*Ver.* 2.2.77); *splend(idus)* is associated with "virtue" in *Off.* (1.61, 2.43). On the range of *splendor* as a rhetorical term, see Ernest s.v. *Copiosus* becomes a rhetorical term by way of the literal sense of 'having resources at one's disposal' *(magnifice et ornate, ut erat in primis inter suos copiosus, conuiuium comparat, Ver.* 2.1.65; *urbes iam locupletes et copiosae, Man.* 65), which could also serve as a compliment: *oppidum locuples, honestum, copiosum* (*Ver.* 2.4.50; cf. *Catil.* 2.18). The image of 'resources' is clear in *de Orat.* 3.125: *rerum enim copia uerborum copiam gignit; et si est honestas in rebus ipsis de quibus dicitur exsistit ex rei natura quidam splendor in uerbis.*

even in ἀττικισμός. The description of Crassus as "painstaking and careful, though free from pedantry, in his latinity" (*Latine loquendi accurata et sine molestia diligens elegantia, Brut.* 143, tr. Douglas) shows *elegantia* construed according to the rules of self-presentation: care was expected; fussiness, like that of Horace's Nasidienus, looked down upon. Furthermore *elegan(s)* has a wider range than those words. Unlike ἐκλογή or ἀττικισμός, *elegan(s)* is connected to careful thought, as we have seen, as well as to aristocratic humor.[106]

The importance of the native semantics and social construction of *elegan(s)* in its application to rhetoric appears clearly in the earliest appearance thereof, in the *Rhet. Her.* The author makes the following demands of orators:

> The diction that is proper to an orator must have three characteristics: elegance *(elegantia),* harmonious arrangement *(compositio),* and beauty *(dignitas).*[107]

> (*Rhet. Her.* 4.17)

*Elegantia,* in turn, is itself divisible:

> *Elegantia* is the quality that articulates every element of the speech cleanly and openly. *Elegantia* is divided into Latinity and clarity. Latinity means a clean mode of speech, free of every fault. . . . Clarity means making the speech open and clear.[108]

> (*Rhet. Her.* 4.17)

The *Rhet. Her.* is here defining the ideal "virtues" of style. The "virtues" were first systematized by Aristotle's pupil Theophrastus (on whom more below, IV.2), who grouped them into purity (ἑλληνισμός 'good Greek'), clarity (σαφήνεια), propriety (τὸ πρέπον), and ornament (κατασκευή); ornament was further subdivided into word choice (ἐκλογή), harmonious ar-

---

106. The irony typical of Socrates, whose speech, as we saw above (III.3), Cicero held in high regard, is described as *faceta et elegans (ironiam illam quam in Socrate dicunt fuisse . . . facetam et elegantem puto, Brut.* 292). Irony is elsewhere described as *facetus, elegans,* and *oratorius (perspicitis genus hoc quam sit facetum, quam elegans, quam oratorium (de Orat.* 2.241). In *de Oratore* Caesar Strabo describes irony as *perelegans* "very tasteful" and *cum gratuitate salsum* "witty *(salsum)* without sacrificing weight of character" and appropriate to both oratory and dinner conversation (2.270, cf. VI.3). The forum and the dinner table were, of course, prime venues for elite self-definition. Caesar Strabo's assurance that irony does not sacrifice *grauitas* 'weight of character' speaks to a vision of verbal activity conscious of its social position.

107. *quae maxime admodum oratori adcommodata est, tres res in se debet habere: elegantiam, conpositionem, dignitatem.*

108. *elegantia est, quae facit, ut unum quidque pure et aperte dici uideatur. haec tribuitur in Latinitatem <et> explanationem. Latinitas est, quae sermonem purum conseruat, ab omni uitio remotum. . . . explanatio est, quae reddit apertam et dilucidam orationem.*

rangement (ἁρμονία), and figures of speech (σχήματα). The arrangement of the *Rhet. Her.* does not quite match the Theophrastan scheme. Ἁρμονία, for Theophrastus a subdivision of ornament, has been elevated to the status of a virtue proper. Ἑλληνισμός (which in the *Rhet. Her.* is rendered *Latinitas*) and σαφήνεια (which is rendered *explanatio*) have been subsumed by *elegantia*, which has no correspondent in Theophrastus's scheme.[109] It is possible that this arrangement reflects some other scheme of "virtues" now lost to us, such as the Hermagorean or Rhodian.[110] Be that as it may, I suggest the *Rhet. Her.* or its sources were influenced by the extrarhetorical value of *elegan(s)*. As a word for practices of elite self-definition, it was perfect to describe their linguistic prerogatives: the correct urban accent *(Latinitas)*, the birthright of the upper classes, and a precise expression of the issue at hand *(explanatio)*, the very thing learned in the course of making and interpreting laws, treaties, and the like and valued in floor debates. Put another way, a Roman could not have helped seeing a doctrine of clear and grammatically correct speech except in terms of class structure and might well have turned to a word with class connections to express those ideals. The creation of a superordinate category *elegantia* to subsume *Latinitas* and *explanatio* accords with a social vision that assigns aesthetic control to a certain class, regardless of the Greek it may be translating.[111] In short, *elegan(s)*, which had come to be associated particularly with the careful choices describing elite self-creation, was brought over into the vocabulary of rhetoric in that guise.[112]

### III.7. *Festiu(us)* and the Poetics of the *Convivium*

The debt of Roman rhetorical language to the *convivium* is particularly clear in the case of *festiu(us)*, our last example. *Festiu(us)* may serve to describe 'entertaining,' often of the 'wit' and 'humor' of the raconteur. That use appears already in the *Rhet. Her.*, where "narratives about persons" *(illud genus narrationis, quod in personis positum est* = διήγησις κατὰ πρόσωπα, cf. Cal-

---

109. Cf. Stroux 1912: 64–67. Hendrickson 1906: 105 puts the matter a little differently: "*Latinitas* and *explanatio* . . . form the two constituent elements of the superior heading *elegantia*, a term which, with considerable amplification and widened range, corresponds to the ἐκλογὴ τῶν ὀνομάτων of Theophrastus's analysis of the elements of style." See also LPW 179–82.

110. Cf. Calboli 1969: 298–99 n.55, 300–302 n.57.

111. The *Rhet. Her.*'s choice of *dignitas* for κατασκευή 'ornament' is of a piece, using a word with dense resonances in elite culture; cf. Hellegouarc'h 1963: 388–411.

112. In later Latin there is also a sense of *elegan(s)* virtually absent from Cicero, that of the 'deft' or 'well-contrived' move, which is popular in the literary culture of the empire. The only exception is *elegans* ὑπερβολή (*Fam.* 7.32.2, VI.5), which represents common critical speech and not Cicero's own particular version of it. This use is discussed below (VIII.4).

boli 1969 ad loc.) must have, among other things, *sermonis festiuitas* "an entertaining style" (1.13).[113] Extended narrative humor in Cicero is *perpetua
festiuitas* (*de Orat.* 2.219). A narrative "with clearly drawn characters" *(distincta personis)* and "punctuated with bits of dialogue" *(interpuncta sermonibus)*
has *festiuitas* (*de Orat.* 2.328). Antonius attributes Crassus's success in defending M'. Curius to his "excellent speaking ability" *(dicendi uis egregia),* which
was accompanied by *festiuitas* and *uenustas,* by which Cicero refers to extended and pointed humor, respectively (*de Orat.* 1.243). There was no
speech "more salted with charm and humor" *(neque lepore neque festiuitate conditior)* than the one Crassus gave against his Cn. Domitius (*de Orat.* 2.227).

Another set of uses of *festiu(us)* deserves more attention. The *Rhet. Her.*
applies *festiu(us)* mostly to different figures of speech (4.21, 4.38, 4.67). These
uses of *festiu(us)* bear out in detail the claim that Latin rhetorical language depends on the approbative language of the *convivium.* Let us consider first a
set of *festiuus* figures that involve repetition.

> *in his quattuor generibus exornationum, quae adhuc propositae sunt, non in-
> opia uerborum fit, ut ad idem uerbum redeatur saepius; sed inest festiuitas,
> quae facilius auribus diiudicari quam uerbis demonstrari potest.*

> In these four sorts of figures I have so far described the frequent repe-
> tition of the same word is not a function of the lack of other words but
> of jollity *( festiuitas),* which is easier to hear than describe.

(4.21)

The four figures to which the text refers are as follows:[114]

| | |
|---|---|
| REPETITIO (4.19) | *uobis istuc adtribuendum est, uobis gratia est* |
| (ἐπαναφορά, ἐπιβολή) | *habenda, uobis ista res erit honori.* |
| | That should be credited to you, thanks |
| | should be given to you, that will be an |
| | honor to you. |
| CONVERSIO (4.19) | *Poenos populus Romanus iustitia uicit, armis* |
| (ἀντιστροφή, ἐπιφορά) | *uicit, liberalitate uicit.* |

---

113. Cf. *hoc in genere narrationis multa debet inesse festiuitas, confecta ex rerum uarietate, animorum dissimilitudine, grauitate, lenitate, spe, metu, suspicione, desiderio, dissimulatione, errore, mi-
sericordia, fortunae commutatione, insperato incommodo, subita laetitia, iucundo exitu rerum. uerum
haec ex iis, quae postea de elocutione praecipientur, ornamenta sumentur* (*Inv.* 1.27). The application by Cicero of *festiuus* to his recently deceased *anagnostes* or 'reader' should perhaps be
viewed as a function of this connection; Sositheus knew how to read with panache: *nam puer
festiuus, anagnostes noster Sositheus, decesserat meque plus quam serui mors debere uidebatur com-
mouerat* "A *festiuus* boy, my reader Sositheus, had died and upset me more than it seemed the
death of a slave should" (*Att.* 1.12.4).

114. For the further connections of the figures, cf. Calboli 1969 ad locc.

The Roman people defeated the Carthaginians in justice, defeated them in battle, defeated them in generosity.

CONPLEXIO (4.20)  *quem* senatus *damnarit*, *quem* populus *damnarit*,
(συμπλοκή, κοινότης)  *quem* omnium exeistimatio *damnarit*, eum uos sententiis uestris absoluatis?
Can you by your verdicts acquit a man whom the senate has condemned, whom the people have condemned, whom common opinion has condemned?

TRADUCTIO (4.20)  eum *hominem* appellas, qui si fuisset *homo*,
(ἀντιμετάθεσις,  numquam tam crudeliter *hominis* uitam petisset.
σύγκρισις, ἀντίστασις)  You call him a man, and if he had been a man, he would never have gone after a man's life with such cruelty.

In all the figures repetition plays an important part, as the author himself notes, and as I have indicated by underscores. I suggest that *festiu(us)* was singularly appropriate to describe such figures because such repetition sounded to Roman ears like the sort of verbal games played at the *convivium*. Lucilius preserves an example of such an ἐνθύμημα:

quis hunc *currere* ecum nos atque *equitare* uidemus,
his *equitat curritque*; oculis *equitare* uidemus;
ergo oculis *equitat*.

This horse runs[115] by means of what we see him running by means of. We see him running by means of eyes. So he's running by means of eyes.
(1284–86M, 1250–52W, 1301–3K)[116]

Similar in structure is a captious syllogism at *Div.* 2.107, which Marcus sarcastically describes with *festiue*. Several such *captiones* preserved in Aulus Gellius are worth mentioning:

quod non *perdidisti*, habes; *cornua* non *perdidisti*: habes igitur *cornua*.

What you haven't lost you have; you haven't lost horns; so you have horns.
(18.2.9)

cum *mentior* et *mentiri* me dico, *mentior* an uerum dico?

If I lie and I say I'm lying, am I lying or telling the truth?
(18.2.10)

115. lit. "runs and gallops."
116. As Marx points out, this problem is from Aristotle (ἆρ' ᾧ εἶδες σὺ τοῦτον τυπτόμενον, τούτῳ ἐτύπτετο οὗτος; καὶ ᾧ ἐτύπτετο, τούτῳ σὺ εἶδες;, Sophist. elench. 177a36, cf. b10). Cf. Non. 107.1, Macrob. 6.9.11.

"Milking" a word for a variety of its nuances or meanings (as in *traductio*) is entirely typical of the *Carmina Anacreontea* and must have been a part of the poetic practiced at Hellenized Roman *convivia*:

| | |
|---|---|
| ἡ γῆ μέλαινα πίνει | The black earth drinks, |
| πίνει δένδρεα δ' αὖ γῆν | the tree drinks the earth in turn. |
| πίνει θάλασσ' ἀναύρους, | The sea drinks the rivers, |
| ὁ δ' ἥλιος θάλασσαν, | the sun drinks the sea, |
| τὸν δ' ἥλιον σελήνη· | the moon drinks the sun. |
| τί μοι μάχεσθ', ἑταῖροι, | Why do you resist me, lads, |
| καὐτῶι θέλοντι πίνειν; | when I only want to drink myself? |
| | (*Anacreont.* 21 West) |

The repetition need not be of lexemes but may be of sememes and syntactical structure, as in the example of the *disiunctum* (= *diiunctio*, διεζευγμένον), which is also said to have *festiuitas* (*Rhet. Her.* 4.38):

> *Populus Romanus Numantiam deleuit, Kartaginem sustulit, Corinthum disiecit, Fregellas euertit.*

> The Roman people eradicated Numantia, destroyed Carthage, shattered Corinth, and toppled Fregellae.

Four near-synonyms *(deleuit, sustulit, disiecit, euertit)* here appear in phrases of identical shape and nearly identical size. Cicero labels as *festiuitates* Gorgias's fondness for metrical and conceptual responsions (*paria paribus adiuncta et similiter definita itemque contrariis relata contraria, Or.* 175–76).[117] The author of *Rhet. Her.* also attributes *festiuitas* to various figures of indirect allusion (4.67), namely 'implication' (*consequentia* = ἐπακολούθεσις), 'breaking off' (*abscisio* = *praecisio* [4.41] = ἀποσιώπησις), and 'analogy' (*similitudo* = παραβολή). Figures of indirect allusion require the hearers to complete the thought, and in that they, too, are not unlike another verbal game of the *convivium*, αἰνίγματα, 'riddles.' This is the author's example of *similitudo*:

> *noli, Saturnine, nimium populi frequentia fretus esse: inulti iacent Gracci.*

> Do not rely too much on popular support, Saturninus: the Gracchi lie unavenged.

---

117. Possibly Cicero is thinking of καλλωπίσματα; cf. Dion. Hal. *Thuc.* 46, with the Sandys 1885 note to the *Orator* passage. Cf. *Or.* 84 (III.4.3), where the same figures are labeled *quaesitae uenustates*. Cicero has this sense of *festiu(us)* in mind when he says that an introduction should have *splendoris et festiuitatis et concinnitudinis minimum* (*Inv.* 1.25); cf. IV.4. Likewise when Cicero, in observing that the most intense pleasures quickly become cloying, and that the same applies to an unremittingly pretty speech, labels such a speech *concinna distincta ornata festiua sine intermissione sine reprehensione sine uarietate,* he must by *festiu(us)* be referring to "Gorgianic" figures or similar prettinesses (*de Orat.* 3.100).

In short, the figures of speech labeled by *festiu(us)* have very close structural correspondence with the verbal play probably typical of Hellenized symposia. I hasten to add that I am not claiming that the Romans thought *similitudines* or *conplexiones* were humorous as such, only that their verbal devices were reminiscent of those of the *convivium*. It is from there that the occasional sense of *festiu(us)* as 'artful' must come: Cicero describes Philodemus's poetry as *festiuum, concinnum,* and *elegans* (*Pis.* 70; below, V.2). Cicero also assesses his brother's translation of Sophocles' satyr play Σύνδειπνοι as having been done *festiue* (*Q. fr.* 2.16.3); some element of "jollity" is also not out of place here.

The connection of *festiu(us)* to the wit of the raconteur puts one in mind of εὔχαρις. On the other hand, the *festiuitates* of *Or.* 175 led Sandys 1885 ad loc. to suggest that Cicero was attempting to render the Greek καλλωπίσματα. Criticizing a passage of Thucydides (2.62.3), Dionysius of Halicarnassus takes issue with certain μειρακιώδη καλλωπίσματα "juvenile embellishments," namely wordplay.[118] Dionysius uses the same root to criticize certain responsions in Plato.[119] The most direct equivalent in Latin for καλλωπί(ζω), lit. 'beauty the face; adorn' would of course be something like *ornare* or *exornare*. The recourse of the nascent Latin rhetorical tradition to *festiu(us)*, which has nothing to do with beauty or the face, is the result of the similarity of the verbal patrimony of the *convivium* to the rhetorical figures and devices that Romans were learning. It is therefore that *festiu(us)* takes in both εὔχαρις and καλλωπίσματα.

## III.8. Conclusion

In short, in the extant Latin rhetorical tradition, the language of social performance is by no means an unthinking rendering of Greek rhetorical terminology; the Romans *de suo fecerunt* "produced it from their own resources." Some of the complex relationships may be graphed as follows, with lines linking equivalents (fig. 18):

118. The passage includes a pun: ἰέναι δὲ τοῖς ἐχθροῖς ὁμόσε καὶ ἀμύνεσθαι μὴ φρονήματι μόνον, ἀλλὰ καὶ καταφρονήματι "You must confront your enemies therefore not only with spirit but in a spirit of scorn" (*Thuc.* 46, tr. Usher 1974).

119. Πλάτων δέ, ὃς ἐπαγγέλλεται σοφίαν, τρυφεροῖς καλλωπίζει καὶ περιέργοις σχήμασι τὴν φράσιν (*Dem.* 25, cf. περὶ τὸν περιττὸν καλλωπισμὸν τῆς ἀπαγγελίας, ibid. 26); among the examples Dionysius enumerates are φέροντες μὲν τὰς συμφορὰς ἀνδρείως δόξουσι τῷ ὄντι ἀνδρείων παίδων πατέρες εἶναι "Bearing disasters in a manly way they will truly seem to be the fathers of manly children" (Plato *Menex.* 247a) and καὶ αὐτὸς δέομαι ὑπὲρ ἐκείνων, τῶν μὲν μιμεῖσθαι τοὺς ἑαυτῶν, τῶν δὲ καρτερεῖν ὑπὲρ ἑαυτῶν "On their behalf I appeal personally to the children to imitate the example of their parents, and to the parents to bear their own lot with patience" (Plato *Menex.* 248e, tr. Usher 1974).

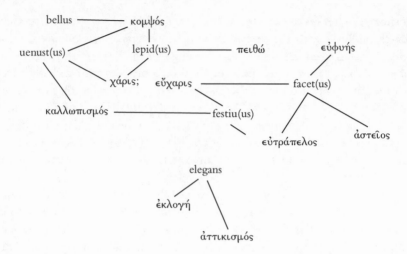

Two cardinal facts emerge: First, despite the difficulties of finding Greek equivalents, in general our terms translate Greek terms that belong in the semantic field of 'playful,' 'funny,' 'witty,' 'jolly,' and the like. Second, the influence of the aesthetic practices of the second century, especially the *convivium,* is clear in virtually every case. From these two facts proceeds the argument of chapter 4. That chapter analyzes the presence of the language of social performance in the Latin rhetorical tradition as an act of cultural translation, arguing that the hint of the *convivium* contained in the extensions described in this chapter is the result of a deliberate attempt to assimilate rhetoric to other semiotic practices that had both a serious and a frivolous aspect, and thereby excuse certain prettinesses of rhetoric as permissible because subordinate to a larger social ideal.

# CHAPTER IV

# *Suauis Grauis*
# The Birth of the Language
# of Rhetoric

κάλλος ἄνευ χαρίτων τέρπει μόνον, οὐ κατέχει δέ,
ὡς ἄτερ ἀγχίστου νηχόμενον δέλεαρ.

Beauty without charms only pleases, does not hold:
Bait floating, without the hook.

*Anth. Pal.* 5.67 (Capito)[1]

## IV.1. Introduction

Chapter 3 surveyed the place of the language of social performance in the extant Latin rhetorical tradition from the late Republic on. Two important results emerged. First, the language of social performance overlaps only partially or inconsistently with Greek rhetorical terminology. Its presence in the theoretical language of rhetoric constitutes a unique Roman contribution to that language. Second, the semantics of the lexemes of the language of social performance in rhetorical theory are identical to, or clearly derived from, the semantics that developed in response to other aestheticizing practices. That is, the language of the *convivium* was adapted to become the language of the *corona*. This chapter analyzes that adaptation, arguing that the presence of the language of social performance in rhetorical theory is an act of "cultural" and not "semantic" lexical extension (IV.3). The language of social performance was applied to rhetorical theory not merely because some rhetorical actions resembled convivial (or comparable) actions, but because aspects of rhetorical action that could be styled frivolous could be defended by claiming that that frivolity supported a more serious semiotic practice, much as in the *convivium* witty banter, light though it might be, supported the serious task of producing social solidarity. The language of social performance was imported into rhetorical language by "aesthetic moderates" (cf. II.2) attempting to define *suauitas* 'aestheticism' by claiming it was complementary to *grauitas* 'respectability,' to translate liberally a jingle that is analyzed below.

---

1. Cf. *non satis est pulchra esse poemata; dulcia sunto | et quocumque uolent animum auditoris agunto* "It is not enough for poems to be beautiful; they must be sweet and take the hearer's mind wherever it please them" (Hor. *Ars* 99–100).

## IV.2. Hellenistic Rhetorical Theory

The application of the language of social performance to rhetorical theory described in chapter 3 cannot be understood without some appreciation of the system it helps to Latinize, namely Greek rhetorical theory in the form it had attained by the Hellenistic period. Although very little of Hellenistic rhetorical theory survives directly, it is nonetheless possible to reconstruct it in broad outline through references and adaptations in Roman and later Greek authors.[2] During the Hellenistic period the Isocratean (or sophistic) and Aristotelean systems of rhetoric had fused to yield a tripartite treatment of persuasive speech, augmented in various degrees by the contributions of later writers.[3] 'Invention' (εὕρεσις, *inventio*) described how to isolate the points at issue (the στάσεις) and marshal proofs appropriate to them.[4] Arrangement (τάξις, *dispositio*) described organizing a speech into parts and assigned functions to those parts.[5] The introduction (προοίμιον), for example, should win an audience's good will; the 'narration' (διήγησις) laid out the elements of the case agreed to by both sides. Style (λέξις, *elocutio* lit. 'diction') described the selection and arrangement of words and clauses. To this system were sometimes added delivery (ὑπόκρισις, *actio*) and memory (μνήμη, *memoria*), which had developed as separate topics after Aristotle.

The old heading of style in particular had developed richly, often beginning from the work of Aristotle's pupil Theophrastus. Building on his

2. The only possible exception is Demetrius's περὶ ἑρμηνείας, formerly dated to the first century A.D., now sometimes dated as early as the third century B.C.; cf. Innes 1995: 312–15. An overview of the history of Greek rhetorical theory can be found in Kennedy 1963: 264ff., a work that may be consulted for further basic bibliography on some of the points briefly stated here. A convenient outline of Greek rhetorical theory as it bears on the terminological and intellectual apparatus of Cicero's rhetorical writing can be found in the introduction to Douglas 1966.

3. The Aristotelean system described three πίστεις, 'proofs' or 'sources of persuasion,' comprising ἦθος, the 'character' of the speaker; πάθος, the 'emotion' effected in the hearer; and λόγος, the speech itself. Aristotle also briefly treated arrangement (τάξις, *Rh.* 1414a31–1416a3 = 3.13–14) and style (λέξις, 1403b6–1414a31 = 3.1–12). On πάθος, cf. Cope 1869: 113–18, on ἦθος and its subdivision by Aristotle, 108–13, on style 279–330. Cf. also Solmsen 1941. The Isocratean system stressed 'invention' (εὕρεσις), that is, isolating the point at issue and the proofs appropriate to proving or refuting it. On the fusion of the two, cf. [Rhetoricians] *ab utrisque ea quae commode dici uidebantur in suas artes transtulerunt,* Cic. *Inv.* 2.8.

4. This was a special interest of Hermagoras; cf. Kennedy 1963: 304.

5. The beginnings can be traced to the fifth-century Syracusan Corax, who had developed a tripartite division of a speech into introduction, ἀγών, and conclusion; cf. Kennedy 1963: 59. Isocrates recognized a division into introduction, narration, proof, and conclusion; ibid. 72.

teacher's remarks, Theophrastus had systematized style into four "virtues," purity (ἑλληνισμός), clarity (σαφήνεια), propriety (τὸ πρέπον), and ornament (perhaps κατασκευή).[6] It may also have been Theophrastus's observations that laid the foundations for a loose canon of 'characters' or 'kinds' of style (ἰδέαι). These are descriptions of the dominant character of passages or authors; in many theorists they number three: the "grand," "middle," and "plain."[7] The figures of speech (σχήματα 'shapes' 'configurations'), such as anaphora, metaphor, and the rest, which Theophrastus was perhaps the first to treat as a separate topic,[8] had come to occupy a prominent place, sometimes absorbing, for example, the kinds of 'proofs' (πίστεις) that Aristotle did not regard as a part of style but as a separate topic.[9] The engagement of Stoic philosophy with linguistic problems led to the theory of tropes (τρόποι), which the Stoics thought of as a way to express ideas that lacked their own names, but which rhetoricians seized upon as means of ornament.[10]

In the late Republic, and in the vast majority of cases even in the Empire, the rhetorical version of the language of social performance which we have just surveyed is used in connection only with certain aspects of the above theory, primarily with λέξις. The figures of speech described by *lep(idus), festiu(us), uenust(us),* and *bellus* belong to λέξις, in particular to κατασκευή. *Lep(idus), uenust(us),* and *facet(us),* especially in the later tradition, are assigned to types of style, another division of λέξις. *Elegan(s)* may describe the clear and correct speech of *Latinitas,* the Roman equivalent of ἑλληνισμός. Ὑπόκρισις is represented by the connection of *uenust(us)* to gesture and of *lep(idus)* to *actio.* The only consistent appearances of the language of social performance outside of λέξις and ὑπόκρισις are those of *uenust(us), facet(us), lep(idus),* and *festiu(us)* to describe humor; humor strictly speaking is a part of ἤθη, or appeals based on character, and is thus ultimately a part of *inventio,* as Aristotle understood it. But in most theorists humor seems not to have been conceived of that way, practically speaking. By *inventio* rhetoricians typically meant arranging the speech into (in many theories) six parts: *exordium, narratio, divisio, confirmatio, confutatio,* and *conclusio.* Humor, by contrast, seems to have been conceptualized in terms of different figures, and fig-

6. Cf. Kennedy 1963: 274–76. On whether this list was canonical, v. Grube 1965: 107ff. Theophrastus's relation to Aristotle is treated by Innes 1985.

7. Cf. Kennedy 1963: 278ff., Russell 1981: ch. 9.

8. Cicero's *de Oratore* 3.199–212 treats figures separately, which suggests Theophrastus did, too, since other details of the arrangement of the third book are paralleled in Quintilian, pointing to a common source in Theophrastus's περὶ λέξεως; cf. Kennedy 1963: 277.

9. Proofs are treated by Aristotle in *Rh.* 1.2ff., whereas style is treated in Book 3.

10. Cf. Kennedy 1963: 297–99.

ures are, of course, a part of λέξις. The long discussion of humor in *de Oratore,* for example, takes the form of a list of "figures of humor."[11] Indeed we have seen the consanguinity of the *uenust(us)* of the humor of reply (III.4.2) with the *uenust(us)* assigned to figures of speech (III.4.3).

By contrast, the language of social performance is virtually never applied to other parts of rhetorical activity, such as arranging parts of the speech or "discovering" arguments (except possibly for the connection to humor just noted). There is no a priori reason why that should be so, as the rare exception proves. As I argue below (IV.5), Terence uses *uenust(us)* to describe the quality of a *principium* or introduction. Quintilian once connects *lepos* to *dispositio:* he says that a father in speaking of the death or grave injury of a child should speak simply; what he should not do is *argumenta diduc(ere) in digitos et propositionum ac partitionum capta(re) leporem (Inst.* 11.1.53) "count off proofs on his fingers and aim for the charm of propositions and divisions." It may be that the occasional *belle* of the legal tradition, used of shrewd questions and interesting conundrums, belongs here, too, inasmuch as a penetrating question that isolates the στάσις could be construed as a part of εὕρεσις; the use is especially common in Ulpian.[12] But the resemblance of these penetrating questions to *sententiae* suggests that the original application of *belle* to them is at least partly stylistic, making applications of the language of social performance to anything other than λέξις or ὑπόκρισις vanishingly rare.[13] This is not to be charged to the inappropriateness of the semantics of the several lexemes. For example, it is easy to imagine a *uenust(us)* describing *dispositio; uenust(us)* is often connected with neatly arranged shapes (cf. I.6). If deft negotiation of the conversational terrain might be *uenust(us),* so might clever πίστεις have been. If *facet(us)* described speech that displayed, and established, social status, it might have been used to distinguish one kind of *inventio* from other, putatively hackneyed kinds.

## IV.3. Semantic Extension, Lexical and Conceptual

The restriction of the language of social performance largely to λέξις, with small bits of ὑπόκρισις and perhaps ἦθος, can be understood by distinguish-

11. Cf. LPR 193–200.

12. E.g., *et belle Sextus Pedius definiit triplicem esse causam operis noui nuntiationis, aut naturalem aut publicam aut imposticiam* "Sextus Pedius nicely *(belle)* defines the reasons for serving notice to prevent new construction as falling in three groups, natural reasons, public reasons, or reasons arising from agreed-upon conditions" *(dig.* 39.1.5.9, cf. 7.8.4.pr., 20.6.4.2, 36.3.1.13, 38.16.2.7, 38.17.2.44, 41.2.10.1, 43.3.1.4, 43.21.3.8, 43.24.7.3, Clem. *dig.* 31.1.53.2, Marcian. *dig.* 20.2.5.2, 48.16.1.10, Pompon. *dig.* 40.5.20.pr.).

13. For the connection of *bellus* to *sententiae,* cf. III.5.

ing between kinds of semantic extension. In one kind of semantic extension, lexemes are pressed into service to describe a new referent because that referent bears many similarities to the standard referents of the lexeme. We might call this sort of semantic extension "lexical," because the extension is made on no other basis than the semantic appropriateness of the lexeme. Vocabulary is simply transferred from the most closely comparable sphere, according to some standard of comparison, for example, similarity of shape or function. Any of us who has ever used "blackboard" to refer to what are now, in fact, often "whiteboards" is using this sort of extension. The same sort of extension is represented in Latin by *acetabulum,* originally 'vinegar cup' (< *acetum* 'vinegar'), then any sort of small cup (cf. Quint. *Inst.* 8.6.35). "Lexical semantic extensions," it may be said, serve to answer the question, "What shall we call this?"

The importation of the language of social performance to rhetorical theory to describe gesture, humor, and verbal elaboration can be seen as simply several instances of that kind of transference, of "lexical semantic extension." The emotive gesturing and posturing of the Greek rhetor, for example, was like that of actors and dancers, whom nobles were not only watching but also imitating, so that *uenust(us)* might simply have been transferred from one realm (I.6) to the other (III.4.1). We saw that *facet(us)*, *lep(idus)*, and *festiu(us)* had narrowed from broader connections to focus on wit and humor (I.8, I.9, I.10, respectively). Thus they were the perfect words for describing the "wit" of figures of speech (III.2, III.3, III.7), particularly since some figures of speech probably closely resembled the verbal "party games" practiced in convivial contexts. *Bellus* as a 'clever move' directed to knowledgeable critics (III.5) describes self-conscious participation in a kind of game, a sense easily transferred from the *convivium* to literary culture (I.7). It is possible to claim, in short, that the language of social performance is applied primarily to λέξις because the sort of referents to which the language was already appropriate simply happened to be severally contained largely within λέξις.

But a transferred vocabulary may also bring with it a frame of reference originating in the ideological or cultural, as opposed to the lexical, function of a lexeme, a kind of semantic extension we might call "conceptual." Conceptual semantic extensions answer the question, "How shall we think of this?" Anyone who says, for example, that "alcoholism is a disease" is not merely labeling alcoholism a bodily defect, like, say, myasthenia gravis or diabetic retinopathy, but is also taking a position on how alcoholics should be understood in the social world—not as persons who have given in to vice but who are done in by illness. When Cicero's opponents labeled him an *inquilinus ciuis urbis Romae* "a citizen-lodger in the city of Rome" (Sal. *Cat.* 31.7), they were not simply finding a convenient analogical expression to describe a *nouus homo;* rather, they were suggesting how Cicero should be thought of in the social world: as worth less than the established nobility. A particularly striking example comes from Marshallese, where **wūliej** means both 'cemetery' and 'head,' because heads and cemeteries are subject to the same sorts of taboos in Marshallese culture.[14] In some cases or in some spheres of cultural activity, as may perhaps be true of the language of social performance, it may be impossible for the extension of a lexical item not to be also conceptual; but that does not mean that lexemes should not be examined for their ideological, above and beyond their lexical, functions.

### IV.4. The Inessentialism of Embellishment and the Defense of Frivolity

I suggest that the language of social performance as applied to rhetoric was not merely the transference of a set of language that described closely analogous referents, a "lexical" semantic extension, but was instead a "conceptual" one, bringing with it a frame of reference. We must review the function of the language of social performance in its application to the aesthetic modes of self-definition adopted by the social elite. To take one example, the *convivium,* the language of social performance there did not describe the central semiotic charges of such parties, such as the establishment of symbolic order, the wealth and status of a host, or the role of *patronus.* Rather it described what we might call "fake" and highly self-conscious actions, such as the polished gesture of acting and dance *(uenustus),* or the convivial spirit *(bellus)* with its deft verbal wit and humor *(lepidus, facetus, festiuus).* In the case of artwork, *uenust(us)* might describe pleasing lines but not important social functions (cf. V.4). The language of social performance could be used to ridicule such aspects, but only by conservative speakers (cf. II.2, IV.5). For many speakers the language of social performance described those aspects of aesthetic practices that augmented or complemented more serious semiotic charges. The language of social performance, in short, characterized a style that was intended to complement substance, and not contradict it: the hook of "charm" in the bait of "beauty."

The language of social performance in its application to rhetoric was intended by the creators of the critical language of Latin rhetoric to serve exactly such a function: to characterize certain "stylish" or "flashy" aspects

14. Abo et al. 1976 s.v.

of Hellenistic rhetorical practice as supportive of, and not antithetical to, substance—a necessary defense. Not everyone thought that the *lepos* of *gradatio* (III.3), the *festiuitas* of *traductio* (III.7), or the *uenustas* of *pronominatio* (III.4.3) were desirable affectations. Into this camp fell Cato the elder, whose view of rhetoric is represented by two famous aphoristic, but telling, scraps. Cato's famous advice for speaking was *rem tene, uerba sequentur* (*Rhet.* fr. 15 = Sen. *Con.* 1.pr.9) "know your subject; the words will follow." He also defined the orator as a *uir bonus, dicendi peritus* (*Rhet.* fr. 14 = Sen. *Con.* 1.pr.9) "a good man who is skilled at speaking," virtually "a good man who happens to be a skilled speaker." These aphorisms of Cato are no "pure" Roman curmudgeonliness. So compelling an intellectual paradigm was Greek rhetoric that it could even provide its own contrarian voice, in the form of Stoic rhetorical theory. Cato's subordination of abilities to moral character has a familiar Stoic ring.[15] His ostensible rejection of rhetorical elaboration is entirely in accord with Stoic rhetorical ideals, which considered rhetoric merely a kind of in extenso version of dialectic.[16] In the formulation of the anonymous prologue to Hermogenes, οἱ Στωϊκοὶ δὲ τὸ εὖ λέγειν ἔλεγον τὸ ἀληθῆ λέγειν "By speaking well the Stoics meant speaking the truth" (*Anon. Prolog. ad Hermog. Rhet. Gr.* 8.8). The Stoics, according to Cicero, were a "sect" (*haeresis*) that "pursues no glory of speech and does not dilate upon an argument."[17] The older Stoics did not "indulge eloquence," as Quintilian put it (*minus indulsere eloquentiae Stoici ueteres, Inst.* 10.1.84).[18]

15. Cf. Diogenes of Babylon (fr. 11 von Arnim from Philodemus *Hypomnematicon* col. viii, i. p. 211 Sudhaus), where the 'good man' (ὁ κάλος) is not only a good dialectician, grammarian, poet, and speaker but uses his abilities for the public good (πρὸς τῶι συ[μφέροντι τῶν π]όλεων). Cicero attributes the view to Mnesarchus: (*[oratores] nihil esse dicebat nisi quosdam operarios lingua celeri et exercitata; oratorem autem, nisi qui sapiens esset, esse neminem, de Orat.* 1.83) and to the Stoics generally (*atque eis [= Stoicis] habeo gratiam, quod soli ex omnibus eloquentiam uirtutem ac sapientiam esse dixerunt,* 3.65). Atherton's 1988: 395 n.10 reading of Cato's line is keen: "This definition of the orator . . . may perhaps suggest Stoic influence: but its totemic rôle may be another, small illustration of the happy coincidence between (some of) the principal tenets of Stoic ethics, and Roman ideology as developed in the face of Greek culture." That Cato compiled some sort of rhetorical precepts is suggested by Quint. *Inst.* 3.1.19; see discussion in Calboli 1981: 39–48.

16. Cf. Atherton 1988.

17. *nullum sequitur florem orationis neque dilatat argumentum; minutis interrogatiunculis quasi punctis quod proposuit efficit* (*Parad.* pr.2), cf. *[Stoici] quorum peracutum et artis plenum orationis genus, sed tamen exile, nec satis populari assensioni accommodatum* (Cic. *Brut.* 114); Cicero observes that the Stoics are concerned only with dialectic and not with "diffuse, flowing, and varied speech" (*uagum illud orationis et fusum et multiplex . . . genus, Brut.* 119); Atherton 1988: 402.

18. Cf. 12.2.25.

Stoic rhetorical theory (which the Stoics themselves conceived of as a part of dialectic) contained many of the elements recognized above.[19] Κατα-σκευή 'ornament,' for example, probably the fourth "virtue" of Theophrastus, was also one of the Stoic rhetorical virtues.[20] However, according to Diogenes the Stoics defined it as λέξις ἐκπεφευγυῖα τὸν ἰδιωτισμόν "style that has avoided vulgarity" (7.59).[21] "Fitting out" the speech is defined, paradoxically, in negative terms; "decoration" is a form of avoidance. The influence of Stoic grammatical theory, which premised that there was one proper word for each thing, is to be seen here: the proper way to "decorate" a speech is, so to speak, to uncover its natural, pre-existing ideal form. Embellishment becomes not only inessential but practically immoral.[22] Of course the idea that "plain speech" is "real speech" had non-Stoic sources, too. Cato's attack on M. Caelius as somebody who talks for the sake of talking—whose speech is, in a word, inessential—uses the folksy image of a *pharmacopola*, something like a traveling "Doc" and his medicine wagon:

> He can't be quiet; he's sick with a disease that makes him talk the way dropsy makes people drink and sleep. If you don't come to assembly when he convenes it, he's so eager to hold forth he'll pay somebody to listen. Just like with a potion-seller, you hear him but don't listen to him: people hear a potion-seller's words but nobody takes his advice, not if they're actually sick.[23]
>
> (Cato *ORF* 8.111)

As we saw above (I.2), M. Caelius participated in such "up-to-date" practices as histrionic gesture and reciting Greek poetry. His oratory likely partook of the latest fashions, which must have been finding their way into elite rhetorical practice. They certainly were firmly established some twenty

---

19. Atherton 1988: 397–98.

20. Cf. Diogenes Laertius 7.59.

21. For this sense of ἰδιωτισμός, cf. Philodemus *Poet.* 271, Long. 31. The sense of the noun is not, however, entirely clear: cf. Atherton 1988: 413.

22. Atherton 1988: 410 productively contrasts the usual rhetorical definition of πρέπον 'appropriateness,' which included topic, audience, speaker, and occasion, to the Stoic definition, which included simply πρᾶγμα.

23. *numquam tacet, quem morbus tenet loquendi tamquam ueternosum bibendi atque dormiendi. quod si non coueniatis, cum conuocari iubet, ita cupidus orationis conducat, qui auscultet. itaque auditis, non auscultatis, tamquam pharmacopolam. nam eius uerba audiuntur; uerum se nemo committit, si aeger est;* cf. *ORF* 8.112, 116. *Pharmacopolae* 'potion sellers' are classed by Horace with *ambubaiae, mendici, mimae,* and *balatrones* 'music girls,' 'beggars,' 'low players,' and 'buffoons' (*Serm.* 1.2.1–2).

years later, when the censors C. Fannius Strabo and M. Valerius Messalla expelled rhetoricians from Rome.[24]

In short, where some Romans were embracing the flourishes and embellishments that Greek rhetorical theory generally encouraged, others, influenced by conservative essentialism, were skeptical, even hostile to them,
and might frame their resistance in terms of Stoic rhetorical theory. Anyone who was fond of theatrical presentation (III.4.1) or of such highly self-
conscious figures as *gradatio* (III.3) or *conplexio* (III.7) therefore opened himself up to attacks of fakery. Faced with such criticism, these more stylish
speakers, I suggest, enlisted the language of social performance to describe
their rhetorical practices, since that language could be used to imply that the
frivolity it described was compatible with higher purposes. That is, more
"artsy" speakers solved the problem of justifying their own practices by
turning, tendentiously, to an idiom which had as one of its functions the
justification of an aestheticism connected to some larger "real" value. In
terms of our diagram (II.2), we may say that these speakers used the language of social performance to describe a phenomenon they wished to be
assigned to category (2). That distinction happened to map very nicely onto
the division of rhetoric, assigning much of λέξις and aspects of ὑπόκρισις
to the aesthetic, and larger structural considerations to the inaesthetic. Here,
then, is the source of the restriction on the language of social performance
that we saw above.

The ideology of those speakers survives through to the late Republic in
passages in which the aestheticism described by the language of social performance is constructed as ancillary to the "real" aspects of oratory. Though
the polarities of these passages are paralleled in the theoretical language of
Greek rhetoric, the polarities, expressed in part by the language of social
performance, were pressed into service to encapsulate a distinctively Roman
cultural debate: what sort of *ethos* an elite speaker should present to his fellows. Here the *Rhet. Her.* describes the effect of various figures of speech:

> But effort *(studia)* of this kind seems better suited to amusement *(delec-*
> *tatio)* than to veracity *(ueritas)*. These literary figures, if they are used
> too often, reduce a speech's trustworthiness, seriousness, and austerity.
> Such a speech not only does away with the speaker's authority, but
> it actually gives offense, since the figures belong to charm *(lepos)* and
> gaiety *(festiuitas)*, not to status *(dignitas)* and beauty *(pulchritudo)*. What
> is rich *(ampla* 'full') and beautiful *(pulchra)* provides lasting pleasure;

24. Cf. p. 143.

what is charming *(lepida)* and neat *(concinna)* quickly sates the ear, which is the most fastidious of the senses.[25]

(4.32)

In counterpoint to *lep(idus)*, *festiu(us)*, and *concinn(us)*, the author sets *dign(us)*, *pulch(er)*, and *ampl(us)*, which are not only aesthetic terms but also keywords of traditional Roman moral identity.[26] *Lepos* is not here antithetical to *grauitas:* rather it is constructed as a kind of lesser complement, admissible, provided care be taken. In much the same fashion, Cicero several times contrasts *lepos* to *grauitas* (VI.6), the latter also a term of traditional moral identity; so, for example, *sic autem grauis, ut in singulari dignitate omnis tamen adsit humanitas et lepos* "weighty, but such that his exquisite bearing did not lack culture and charm *(lepos)*" *(de Orat.* 3.29). In *de Inuentione* Cicero contrasts *festiuitas* and *concinnitudo* to *dignitas* and *grauitas:*

> An introduction should have considerable weightiness *(grauitas)* and should in all respects contain within itself everything that pertains to distinction *(dignitas);* that is the best way to win the hearer's good graces. By contrast the introduction should have very little in the way of luster *(splendor)*, gaiety *(festiuitas)*, and neatnesses *(concinnitudo)*, for these qualities invite the suspicion, as it were, that the speaker has prepared too much and too carefully in advance. That suspicion makes a speech seem unbelievable, and a speaker untrustworthy.[27]

(*Inv.* 1.25)

25. *eiusmodi autem studia ad delectationem quam ad ueritatem uidentur accommodatiora. quare fides et grauitas et seueritas oratoria minuitur his exornationibus frequenter collocatis et non modo tollitur auctoritas dicendi, sed offenditur quoque in eiusmodi oratione, propterea quod est in his lepos et festiuitas, non dignitas neque pulchritudo. quare, quae sunt ampla atque pulchra, diu placere possunt; quae lepida et concinna, cito satietate afficiunt aurium sensum fastidiossimum;* cf. *de Orat.* 3.100, where speech that can be judged "neat, distinctive, decorated, delightful, without pause, without fresh starts, without variety" *(concinnam, distinctam, ornatam, festiuam, sine intermissione, sine reprehensione, sine uarietate)* eventually cloys, just as all intense pleasures do. On this sense of *reprehensio,* see Wilkins ad loc.

26. Cf. Hellegouarc'h 1963, who observes, e.g., that *"Amplitudo* constitue un autre équivalent de *nobilitas"* (229); on *dignitas* cf. 388–411. *Pulcher* may serve for 'morally beautiful, honorable'; cf. *OLD* s.v. 3. Cf. Fyëdorov 1987: 230, who contrasts the "aesthetic fullness" of *pulchritudo* with the beauty "of less value" and "of less significance" expressed by *lepos,* which, with *concinn(us)* and *festiu(us)*, refers to rhetorical devices with "an intentional, artistic character."

27. *exordium sententiarum et grauitatis plurimum debet habere et omnino omnia, quae pertinent ad dignitatem, in se continere, propterea quod id optime faciendum est, quod oratorem auditori maxime commendat; splendoris et festiuitatis et concinnitudinis minimum, propterea quod ex his suspicio quaedem apparationis atque artificiosae diligentiae nascitur, quae maxime orationi fidem, oratori adimit auctoritatem.* On the sense of *festiuitas* here, cf. I.10.

Here, too, "gaiety" and the rest are not antithetical to *dignitas;* they are perfectly admissible, just not in the *exordium.* In the modesty of such formulations is to be felt the pressure of the conservative, essentialist resistance to rhetorical embellishment: the primacy of what I have above called "category (3)" actions (II.2) is carefully asserted. Mutatis mutandis, such assertion is similar to Aemilius Paullus's claim that the same sort of mind was required to set a table as to arrange a battle line. As suggested above (II.3), the language of social performance is a delicate tool for tracking the attitudes of authors and texts toward various forms of aestheticism. The approbative language of Latin rhetoric, unexceptional at first sight, is in fact the cant of partisans in the ideological struggle to assimilate the foreign practice of rhetoric.

## IV.5. Terence, Stoic Rhetoric, and the Language of Social Performance

It is a paradox of the language of social performance, as I have noticed above (II.3), that it can be used with exactly opposite connotations. Speakers who constructed "aestheticism," "individualism," or "Hellenism" as socially worthless used the language of social performance pejoratively. The same is true of the application of the language of social performance to rhetoric. The harsh lines of Lucretius noticed above (II.3) use the language of social performance in exactly this way:

> Dullards delight the more in, have more love for,
> what they see concealed under twisted words;
> and what can touch the ear with pleasure *(belle),* that they
>     take for true,
> or what is rouged with charming *(lepidus)* sound.
>
> (1.641–44)

Lucretius here attacks those who are taken in by Heraclitus, mistaking the allure of form for verities of content. Even Cicero puts a lexeme of language of social performance in Aristotle's mouth in something like the same way: Aristotle was inspired to turn his attention to rhetoric when he noticed that Isocrates "was flush with the very best students" *(florere . . . nobilitate discipulorum)* for having turned his efforts from forensic and civil cases to "vapid oratorical elegance" *(inanem sermonis elegantiam, de Orat.* 3.141).

The first attestations of the language of social performance to describe rhetoric as such are, I suggest, pejorative instances like those just surveyed, to be found in several passages of Terence. We may review the passages first. In the *Adelphoe* the brothers Micio and Demea disagree about child rearing, Micio preferring an indulgent manner and Demea a harsh one. That was a point of contention between the brothers since Micio was raising Aeschinus, one of Demea's two sons, whom he had adopted. *Facetus* appears in one of the brothers' exchanges:

DE. I don't interfere in your business; don't you interfere in mine!
MI. That's not right, what you're saying.
DE. It isn't?
MI. No, for as the old saw goes, "Friends hold all things in common."
DE. How witty *(facetus)!* Finally you start talking that way!

(*Ad.* 803–6)[28]

Micio is quoting a well-known ancient proverb, attested in both Greek and Latin.[29] Demea's ironic response, "Finally you start talking that way!" is a comment on Micio's earlier resistance to Demea's disagreement with the way he was raising Aeschinus. In a comparable passage from the *Eunuchus,* the speakers are Thraso, a *miles gloriosus,* and Gnatho, a parasite:

THR. Gnatho, have I ever told you about the time I nicked a Rhodian at a dinner?
GN. No, you haven't, please, tell me about it. *(aside)* I've heard it, a thousand times!
THR. Well, I was at this party with the Rhodian, that I mentioned, a young fellow. I happened to have a gal *(scortum* 'whore') with me, and he starts to make fun of her and laugh at me. "Watch yourself, punk!" I say. "That's the pot calling the kettle black!"
GN. Ha, ha, ha!
THR. So, what do you think?
GN. Clever *(facetus),* witty *(lepidus),* polished *(lautus),* the best! Did you make that saying up? I thought it was old.
THR. You've heard it before?
GN. Often, people say it all the time.
THR. It's mine all right!

(*Eu.* 419–29)[30]

28. DE. *quando ego tuom non curo, ne cura meum.* | MI. *non aequom dicis.* DE. *non?* MI. *nam uetus uerbum hoc quidemst,* | *communia esse amicorum inter se omnia.* | DE. *facete! nunc demum istaec nata oratiost.*

29. κοινὰ τὰ τῶν φιλῶν, attested in Plato *Lysis* 207c, Aristotle *Eth. Nic.* 1159b31 = 8.9.1, Cicero *Off.* 1.51, Seneca *Benef.* 7.4.2, and Martial 2.43.1 and 56.

30. THR. *quid illud, Gnatho,* | *quo pacto Rhodium tetigerim in conuiuio,* | *numquam tibi dixi?* GN. *numquam; sed narra obsecro.* | *(plus miliens audiui.)* THR. *una in conuiuio* | *erat hic, quem dico, Rhodius adulescentulus.* | *forte habui scortum: coepit ad id adludere* | *et me inridere. 'quid ais' inquam homini 'inpudens?* | *lepu' tute's, pulpamentum quaeris?'* GN. *hahahae.* | THR. *quid est?* GN. *facete lepide laute nil supra.* | *tuomne, obsecro te, hoc dictum erat? uetu' credidi.* | THR. *audieras?* GN. *saepe, et fertur in primis.* THR. *meumst.*

Like Micio, Thraso quotes a proverb. Literally it goes "you're a rabbit, and you're looking for meat," intended to accuse the Rhodian of "having in himself what he was looking for in someone else," to paraphrase Donatus's interpretation.[31] That is, Thraso took the Rhodian to be insulting him for sexual indulgence, when that was a characteristic entirely typical of the Greek East. In fact what the Rhodian was probably insulting him for is not sexual indulgence generally but the particular woman that Thraso brought with him, a *scortum* 'whore' or 'camp follower' and not the elegant and cultured *hetaira* the Rhodian was used to at dinner parties. Not only has Thraso probably misunderstood the Rhodian's insults, but his reply was common property, as Gnatho's comment "I thought it was old" suggests, and as I have suggested by my translation.[32]

The remaining two passages are also from the *Eunuchus*. Gnatho, the parasite attached to Thraso, here addresses Parmeno, the slave of a rival for the affections of Thais, a courtesan:

> GN. Still standing there, Parmeno? I suppose you've been posted on guard duty to intercept clandestine communications to the girl!
> PA. How clever *(facete).* The sort of jokes that please the cap'n are really wonderful stuff.

(Eu. 286–88)[33]

Gnatho now thinks that he and Thraso have the upper hand in the struggle for Thais's affections, and he takes the opportunity to jab at Parmeno, likening him to a border guard whose only function is to hinder other people's designs but who crafts none of his own. It is an obvious metaphor, and that is the point of Parmeno's reply, which suggests that Thraso cannot understand much more than obvious, and perhaps in particular military, metaphors. In another example, when Thraso addresses Thais for this first time after sending her a gift, Parmeno overhears him:

> TH. I think I just heard the soldier's voice. And there he is! Hello, my Thraso.

31. *quod in te habes, hoc quaeris in altero* "What you have in yourself, you look for in somebody else."

32. According to Vopiscus (*Numer.* 13.5) the proverb originated with Livius Andronicus, who may have borrowed it from the Greek attested by Erasmus *inter alios:* δασύπους ὢν κρέως ἐπιθύμεις.

33. GN. *etiamne tu hic stas, Parmeno? eho num nam hic relictu's custos,* | *ne quis forte internuntius clam a milite ad istam curset?* | PA. *facete dictum: mira uero militi quae placeant.*

THR. O my Thais, my darling, how are things? Don't you love me for
    that flute girl I sent you?
PA. *(aside)* Now that's smooth *(uenustus)*. What an *exordium* he starts
    with!

(*Eu.* 454–57)[34]

Parmeno insults Thraso for his awkward rhetoric: not only does he immediately mention the flute girl he had sent to Thais, but he blurts out the result he hopes for.

It is possible to take these several instances simply as ironic instances of
"Plautine" language. Outside of the rhetorical connection we are examining, Terence uses the lexemes of the language of social performance mainly
to parody Plautine language, drawing a contrast between his own characters
and the sort of Plautine characters who might have used similar language.[35]

---

34. TH. *Audire uocem uisa sum modo militis.* | *atque eccum. salue, mi Thraso.* THR. *o Thais
mea,* | *meum sauium, quid agitur? ecquid nos amas* | *de fidicina istac?* PA. *quam uenuste! quod dedit*
| *principium adueniens!*

35. When, for example, Pamphilus exclaims that he is *uenustatis plenus* 'lucky in love'
('full of *uenustas*,' *Hec.* 848), he has not succeeded, as a Plautine character might have, in
hoodwinking a pimp out of a *meretrix;* rather, a *meretrix* who used to be his lover has helped
him recover his estranged wife. In another example, from the *Phormio,* Phaedria finds himself in need of money to keep a soldier from buying a music-girl he is in love with—a typical Plautine situation. When Geta, Phaedria's caretaker, agrees to secure the sum, Phaedria
exclaims *o lepidum!* (*Ph.* 559). But Geta is far from the *senex lepidus* or *servus callidus* of Plautine comedy. When Phaedria and his cousin Antipho were left by their fathers in Geta's care,
Geta had originally tried to keep them on the straight and narrow (*coepi aduorsari primo* "I
started by opposing their wishes" 75). He could be persuaded to help in this situation only
with some difficulty. The context of the exclamation makes this clear; Phaedria is willing to
assume the voice of the *adulescens amans* but Geta rejects labeling as the *senex lepidus:* GE. *age
age inuentas reddam.* PH. *o lepidum!* GE. *aufer te hinc.* "Okay, okay, I'll find the money and give
it to you." "What a splendid fellow!" "Beat it."

This distance is possible because the stock characters and language of Plautine drama, already formulaic, had by Terence's time become completely stereotyped. Terence offers the
fact of this stereotyping as one defense against plagiarism in the prologue to the *Eunuchus*
(35–41), citing the necessity of using figures like the *bona matrona* "good matron," the *meretrix mala* "the wicked courtesan," and the *parasitus edax* "gluttonous parasite" and devices
like *falli per seruom senem* "the old man getting duped by a slave." Among the stock features
of New Comedy enumerated in a passage of Caecilius, a younger contemporary and sur-
vivor of Plautus, the "stingy disagreeable father" is a *parens auarus inlepidus,* with (the negative of) Plautus's standard word for 'agreeable' (*com.* 199–205 Ribbeck). When characters
become stereotyped, it becomes possible to play against the stereotype. In the passages above
this is the response of Terence, in which he was not alone. A satire of Ennius uses *lepide* for
the self-congratulatory cleverness of a trickster, recalling the forte of the *servus callidus;* but

I suggest, however, that in these passages Terence is taking advantage of the nascent application of the language of social performance to rhetoric, using it ironically of rhetorical failures. Parmeno's jibe in *Eu.* 457 uses *principium*, which may serve as a technical term of rhetoric translating the Greek προοίμιον. A knowledge of rhetorical theory certainly seems to underlie Parmeno's remark. The purpose of a *principium*, according to the *Rhet. Her.*, is to "put the hearer in an agreeable frame of mind for listening to the speaker,"[36] and a successful *principium* might well be described by *uenust(us)* meaning 'graceful' or 'deft'—exactly what Thraso's clumsiness is not. (In this case *uenust(us)* no doubt also has its literal flavor, 'suitable for love.') Gnatho's *facete lepide* (*Eu.* 427) and Demea's *facete dictum* (*Ad.* 806) are both occasioned by well-known proverbs. It may be that Micio and Thraso are being insulted for being dull, but I suggest the issue is slightly different: Micio and Thraso are trying to be clever, making use of a *locus communis* at a critical rhetorical juncture; only a proverb is the cheapest kind of *locus communis.* Gnatho's border-guard metaphor is also a rhetorical failure, since it is not truly clever but the kind of stolid and obvious metaphor that would please the coarse taste of Thraso.

These passages permit the cautious suggestion that the language of social performance at the time of Terence was on its way to being used as part of the technical language of rhetoric in the way described in chapter 3. Every instance is sarcastic, and that is exactly what guarantees the status of the words in question as stereotypical compliments for rhetorical excellence. Certainly the dates of the plays (*Eunuchus* 161, *Adelphoe* 160) are consonant with the increasing popularity of Greek-style rhetorical practice. In the same year the *Eunuchus* was presented, C. Fannius Strabo and M. Valerius Messalla issued a censorial edict expelling rhetors, which may suggest their presence in sufficient numbers, or with sufficient influence, to warrant such attention.[37] Cicero asserts that the first Roman to introduce various forms of expansion and decoration was Ser. Sulpicius Galba, who will have been

---

here the trickster is himself tricked (Enn. *Sat.* 59–62). The Plautine version of the language of social performance had become shopworn, and one of Terence's objects is to reinvigorate it by a novel use that at the same time parodies the older idiom. It is for this reason that Terentian language is wholly unreliable as a guide to the lexemes of the language of social performance, *pace,* e.g., Copley 1951: 201; cf. above, Intro. n. 28. The inversion of Plautine stereotypes is a standard strategy of Terence; see Goldberg 1986.

36. *principium est, cum statim auditoris animum nobis idoneum reddimus ad audiendum* (1.6). Cf. *sed quid cessas hominem adire et blande in principio adloqui?* (Ter. *Ph.* 252).

37. Cf. Suet. *Rhet.* 1 with Kaster 1995 ad loc.

in middle manhood by the time of Terence's productions, having been born probably around 200.[38]

Terence's sarcastic use of the language of social performance in these instances ultimately reflects his own perspective on matters rhetorical. His sympathies lay with the "plain" style of rhetoric. Terence describes his own preference for that style with the terms *lenis* 'slight' and *pura oratio* 'clear speech.'[39] Terence, as we have seen, was not alone in his sympathies.[40] And it is important to note that Terence did not scorn rhetoric altogether. He made good use of εὕρεσις and τάξις in the prologue of the *Andria*, which was produced in 166. Terence refutes the rival poet Luscius's charges of *contaminatio*[41] with an elegant synopsis of a judicial speech, as Leeman 1963, whose analysis I reproduce here, has demonstrated:

> When the poet first set his mind to writing     EXORDIUM
> He thought that his only business
> was for the plays he wrote to please the crowd.
> But he realizes it's turning out much differently;
> for he exhausts his effort writing prologues,
> not to explain the plot[42] but to respond
> to the sniping of a malevolent old playwright.
> Here's the fault they impute to him:     NARRATIO
> Menander wrote an *Andria* and a *Perinthia*.
> If you know one play well, you know them both:
> their plots are not dissimilar, although
> the thought and expression are quite different.
> Whatever seemed fitting from the *Perinthia*
> the poet admits he took over into his *Andria,* treating it as his own.
> This is what they assail him for, claiming
> it's not proper for plays to be mixed.
> Is their criticism so sharp they've
>     become uncritical?     ARGUMENTATIO

38. The style of Sulpicius (*RE* Sulpicius 58, *ORF* 19) included digressions, pathetic appeals, and the use of commonplaces (*Brut.* 82 with Douglas's note). Sulpicius served with Aemilius Paullus in Greece in 168, held the praetorship in 151 and the consulship in 144.

39. *Hau.* 45–46. In an epigram preserved in Suetonius's life of Terence Caesar calls Terence a *puri sermonis amator* "lover of pure speech" (*Vit. Ter.* 7 = Caes. fr. 1 Courtney); cf. Cic. fr. 2 Courtney.

40. Cf. Dihle 1957, Fiske 1919, Reitzenstein 1901.

41. Terence's critics evidently used the verb *contaminare,* lit. 'defile' (*Andr.* 16, *Hau.* 17) to attack his procedure of combining pieces of different plays into one. *Contaminatio* has since become the technical term for this procedure.

42. The usual function of a comic prologue.

In making this charge, they charge Naevius,
Plautus, and Ennius, whose lead our author follows,
choosing to follow their carelessness,
and not the obscurantist accuracy of the critics.
I suggest they henceforth be silent, stop               ANTIKATEGORIA[43]
speaking ill, lest they learn their own offenses.[44]
Silence now, be open-minded, learn the facts,     PERORATIO
to see what's left to hope for:
whether the plays he'll next produce
you should watch or censure first.

As a writer who preferred the clean and clear elegances of New Comedy and the minimalist rhetoric of the Stoics, Terence will perhaps not have been inclined to use amelioratively an idiom that aimed to defend frivolities and prettiness.[45] Terence's motivation in using the nascent language of rhetoric only to parody is ultimately the same as those who used it sincerely: a recognition that certain aspects of rhetorical practice were not quite "real." Terence, and others influenced by Stoic rhetoric, happen to have thought what was not "real" ought to be rejected. Many other Romans were not in their camp, and their attempt to defend their brand of aestheticism—an ultimately successful attempt, since the language of social performance did, after all, enter the critical lexicon—is captured in the phrase *suauis grauis*.

## IV.6. *Suauis Grauis*

Notwithstanding the scorn of Cato and his like, in the second century "pleasant inessentiality," in social practice no less than in rhetoric, was important for many Romans.[46] I suggest the pair *suauis grauis,* found mostly in Cicero's rhetorica, was coined in the second century as a kind of slogan to deal with this paradox.

As with so much else of second-century Roman thought, Cato's Stoic response to rhetoric, for example (IV.4), a Greek intellectual paradigm lies behind the slogan. Greek rhetorical theory occasionally contrasted μεγαλο-πρεπ(ής) 'grand' and ἡδ(ύς) 'pleasant.' The distinction was first made by

43. A 'countercharge'; Quintilian (*Inst.* 3.10.3–4) distinguishes two types, one in which an opponent is accused of the same charge he has laid, another in which he is accused of a different charge.

44. Luscius had himself borrowed from Menander's *Phasma* and *Thesauros*.

45. For a fine appreciation of Terence's style, see Goldberg 1986: 170–202. On Terence's evident use of rhetorical theory, see Calboli 1981: 51–71.

46. "But . . . [the] disapproval [of Cato et al.] only highlights how far style had come to occupy central stage in the teaching of oratory," Atherton 1988: 394.

Theodectes, rejected by Aristotle, and accepted by Theophrastus, whose fourth virtue, ornament, seems to have been divided into τὸ ἡδύ and τὸ μεγαλοπρεπές.[47] The pair shows up in that form here and there in Greek rhetorical writing.[48] Another, similar pair, ἡδ(ύς) 'pleasant' and καλ(ός) 'beautiful,' is common in Dionysius of Halicarnassus. Dionysius develops the opposition most fully in ch. 11 of *de Compositione Verborum,* where ἡδονή is said to consist of ὥρη, χάρις, εὐστομία, γλυκύτης, and τὸ πίθανον ("freshness, grace, euphony, sweetness, and persuasiveness"), whereas τὸ καλόν consists of μεγαλοπρέπεια, τὸ βάρος, ἡ σεμνολογία, τὸ ἀξίωμα, and τὸ πίνον ("grandeur, impressiveness, solemnity, dignity, and mellowness").[49] The contrastive principle is clear enough: the lighter, pleasurable elements are classed under ἡδονή, the heavier, serious elements under τὸ καλόν (which has subsumed τὸ μεγαλοπρεπές). Generally the pair appears, not so developed, in complement.[50] No more can be safely said for Theophrastus than that such a division was part of ornament; but in Dionysius the pair has greater valence, being nearly a tag for successful composition.[51]

47. *Theodectes . . . non magnificam modo uult esse, uerum etiam iucundam expositionem* (Quint. *Inst.* 4.2.63); τὸ δὲ προσδιαιρεῖσθαι τὴν λέξιν, ὅτι ἡδεῖαν δεῖ εἶναι καὶ μεγαλοπρεπῆ, περίεργον (Arist. *Rh.* 1414a19–21 = 3.12.6). The inference about Theophrastus depends on passages in Cicero: *unum aberit quod quartum numerat Theophrastus in orationis laudibus: ornatum illud suaue et affluens* (*Or.* 79). Cf. also *dulce igitur orationis genus et solutum et adfluens* (42); Stroux 1912: 86–87.

48. E.g., μιμητέον δὲ ** μάλιστα Ξενοφῶντα καὶ Πλάτωνα τῶν τε ἠθῶν χάριν καὶ τῆς ἡδονῆς καὶ τῆς μεγαλοπρεπείας (Dion. Hal. *Imit.* fr. 31.4.1), οὕτω δὲ ἡδὺς καὶ μεγαλοπρεπὴς ὁ Κατάλογος, ὥστε καὶ πόλεις ἀμφισβητοῦσαι τοῖς Ὁμήρου ἔπεσι χρῶνται (Σ *Il.* 2.494–877).

49. Tr. Roberts 1910.

50. For example, καὶ οὐδ' ὄναρ εἶδον, τί ποτ' ἐστὶ τὸ ποιοῦν ἡ δ ε ῖ α ν καὶ κ α λ ὴ ν τὴν σύνθεσιν "They don't have the slightest idea how to render a composition attractive and beautiful" (*Comp. Verb.* 4) or δοκεῖ δέ μοι δύο ταῦτ' εἶναι <τὰ> γενικώτατα, ὧν ἐφ-ίεσθαι δεῖ τοὺς συντιθέντας μέτρα τε καὶ λόγους, ἥ τε ἡ δ ο ν ὴ καὶ τὸ κ α λ ό ν "The two noblest aims that composers of verse or prose can have, in my opinion, are to be pleasant and beautiful" (10, cf. *de Demosthenis dictione* 47). Note in particular μελῶν καὶ ῥυθμῶν καὶ σχημάτων, καὶ τῶν ἄλλων πάντων, οἷς ἡ δ ε ῖ α καὶ κ α λ ὴ γίνεται σύνθεσις (*de Demosthenis dictione* 51), which resembles *ornamenta elocutionis, in quibus et suauitatis et grauitatis plurimum consistit* (*Inv.* 2.49) "the ornaments of speech in which considerable pleasure as well as substance is found."

51. The importance of the pairing to Dionysius results from his interest in defining a mean between the two extremes, not of the grand and plain, but of the grand and the middle styles, to which τὸ καλόν and τὸ ἡδύ are respectively appropriate. "There is no place here for the unembellished artlessness of a plain style, because Dionysius is searching for an ideal style in which all the devices which he has described are used with balanced skill and propriety," Usher 1985: 11 re *Comp. Verb.* 21.

It is this pair that underlies the *suauis grauis* of the Latin rhetorical tradition. The pair appears here and there in Cicero applied to various phenomena, for example, as a description of an oration (*graui ac suaui commotus oratione, Inv.* 1.3), of the content of ideas (*quamuis enim suaues grauesue sententiae, Or.* 150, cf. 168), of euphony (*compositio . . . seruit grauitati uocum aut suauitati, Or.* 182), and of figures (*ornamenta elocutionis, in quibus et suauitatis et grauitatis plurimum consistit, Inv.* 2.49). But a congener of the pair also appears, noted below, in the *Rhet. Her.,* and the phrase should thus be referred to an older common source. The broad application of the phrase to the overall effect of a speech (*Inv.* 1.3 and *Rhet. Her.* 4.69) suggests an origin in a post-Theophrastan theoretical position, like Dionysius's perhaps, in which the pair was not applied to ornament only.

The pairing is notable both for its lexical choices and for its poetic form. The poetic form of *suauis grauis,* a rhyming jingle, suggests both the date and the intention of the phrase. A jingle is entirely in the spirit of the figures of speech of the earlier language, which features much in the way of rhymes, assonances, and homoioteleuton.[52] These are popular in older Latin poetry and remain available to later poetry as a solemnizing device, for example Cicero's use of *-sti* in a passage *de consulatu suo;* here the Muse Urania is addressing him directly (fr. 6.13–6):[53]

> *tu quoque, cum tumulos Albano in monte niualis*
> *lustrasti et laeto mactasti lacte Latinas,*
> *uidisti et claro tremulos ardore cometas,*
> *multaque misceri nocturna strage putasti . . .*

Such assonance had gone out of fashion by the late Republic. The author of *Rhet. Her.* censures the Ennian-sounding line *flentes, plorantes, lacrimantes, obtestantes* (4.18).[54] In short, the poetic form of the phrase suggests a date ear-

---

52. For a convenient summary of these figures, see Palmer 1954: 104–9. The heavy phonetic play characteristic of the earliest Latin poetry remains available as a solemnizing device through the late Republic. For an analysis of some aspects of the old Italic language of prayer, which is the ultimate source of such figures, cf. Watkins 1995: chs. 17–20.

53. See helpfully Goldberg 1995 for an assessment of the stylistic characteristics of Cicero's epic.

54. The paternity of the line is debated; cf. Calboli 1969: 308 n.67. Lucilius recalls an incident where a chance homoeoteleuton in a letter earned him rebuke as Isocratean: *quo me habeam pacto, tam etsi non quaeris, docebo | quando in eo numero mansi quo in maxima non est | pars hominum . . . | ut periisse uelis, quem uisere nolueris cum | debueris. hoc "nolueris" et "debueris" te | si minus delectat, quod atechnon et Eisocration | lerodesque simul totum ac sit miraciodes, | non operam perdo, si tu hic* "Although you don't ask how I am, I'll tell you, since I still remain among the living, as the greater part of mankind is not. [. . .] that you'd rather the man

lier than the late Republic. That poetic form, resonating by its phonetic play with the old formal language, served to cloak in a mantle of antique legitimacy the concept of a conjoined "pleasantness" and "authority." Poetics makes a unit where there might have been conflict. That certainly seems to have been the poetic intent, since many other Latin words might have been chosen to represent ἡδ(ύς) and μεγαλοπρεπ(ής). For ἡδ(ύς) *iucund(us)* and *dulc(is)* could serve, and for ἡδονή *uoluptas*.[55] In the rhetorical tradition alone μεγαλοπρεπ(ής) seems to underlie instances of *magnificen(s)*, *sublimi(s)*, *grandi(s)*, *ampl(us)*, *illustri(s)*, and *affluen(s)*.[56] *Suaui(s)* and *graui(s)* were chosen first of all to secure the rhyme with its patina of antiquity, as just described.

*Suaui(s)* and *graui(s)* had much to recommend them besides their rhyme. *Graui(s)*, of course, is the word that the Romans used for the "authority" or "weightiness" of their most respected personages. As a rendering of either καλ(ός) or μεγαλοπρεπ(ής), it folds aesthetics or grandeur into social dignity and political estimability.[57] As for *suaui(s)*, if Cicero is any guide, that lexeme had an important function in the language of aristocratic interchange to characterize certain kinds of behavior. In Cicero *suaui(s)* is often connected to the "personable qualities" of a friend, particularly conversational charm. "*Caquetage* (λέσχη) is worth something, after all," Cicero writes to Atticus; "Even if it doesn't help anything, the very conversation affords pleasure *(suauitas)*" (*Att.* 12.1.2).[58] Says Antonius, "We should all love Scaevola, and quite rightly, because of his outstanding *suauitas*."[59] L. Mescinius had often heard from Cicero "how delightful" *(quam suauis)* was his, Cicero's,

---

you didn't want *(nolueris)* to see, though you should have *(debueris)*, had died. And if you don't like the *nolueris* and *debueris*, because it's artless and Isocratean, and so much childish frivolity, well I won't waste my time, if THAT's how you are" (181–88M, 186–93W, 182–89K). *Miraciodes* (= μειρακιώδης) 'juvenile' is also used by Dionysius of Halicarnassus to attack such responsions; cf. III.7. The issue in these lines is probably not distaste for *homoioteleuton* itself as much as its inappropriateness in a personal letter; cf. Puelma Piwonka 1949: 21–23.

55. For ἡδονή turned by *uoluptas* (the unsavory associations of which Cicero exploits), cf. *Fin.* 2.14, *Fin.* 2.75; for ἡδ(ύς) turned by *iucund(us)*, cf. Cic. *de Orat.* 1.57 (*iucunditas et grauitas* = ἡδονή τε καὶ μεγαλοπρέπεια), Quint. *Inst.* 10.1.109 (*iucunditas* of Isocrates' style; Cicero uses *suauitas*, *de Orat.* 3.28, cf. LPW ad loc.; for Isocrates' style as ἡδύς, cf. Dion. Hal. *Isoc.* 3, *Dem.* 4). For ἡδ(ύς) rendered by *dulcis*, cf. Cic. *Off.* 1.3 (*dulcis* of Demetrius of Phaleron, master of the middle style, which par excellence is ἡδύς), Sen. iun. *Ep.* 66.18 (*dulce esse* = ἡδὺ εἶναι, cf. 67.15).

56. Cf. Ernest s.vv.; Stroux 1912: 69.

57. Comparable is the use in *Rhet. Her.*, and elsewhere, of *dignitas* for 'beauty' (4.32, III.3; 4.17, III.6). Cf. Dyck 1996 ad 1.94.

58. *est profecto quiddam* λέσχη, *quae habet, etiam si nihil subest, conlocutione ipsa suauitatem.*

59. *quem omnes amare meritissimo pro eius eximia suauitate debemus* (*de Orat.* 1.234).

friendship with Servius Sulpicius (*Fam.* 13.27.1). T. Pomponius Atticus, Cicero's dear friend, often merits description by *suauis.*[60]

This *suauitas,* much like *festiuitas* and *lepos* in the rhetorical realm, was conceived of as inessential but important. Beside Plancus's courage *(uirtus)* in military affairs, justice *(iustitia)* in administering a province, and good sense *(prudentia)* in all matters, was his *suauitas* in personal relations (*Fam.* 10.3.1). Laelius expatiates on this *suauitas* in *de Amicitia:*

> A friend also needs to have a pleasant way of acting and conversing *(suauitas sermonum atque morum),* which is no small addition ("spice" *condimentum*) to a friendship. Grimness *(tristitia)* and harshness *(seueritas)* in all things does make for weightiness *(grauitas);* but friendship should be more relaxed, freer, sweeter, more ready for everything companionable and easy.
>
> (*Amic.* 66)

There are some earlier instances of *suaui(s)* which suggest its connections to aristocratic intercourse in this way are old.[61] The *suaui(s)* of *suaui(s) graui(s),* I suggest, was in part a socially motivated translation of ἡδ(ύς). The pleasures it described were the inessential, but vital, pleasures of aristocratic intercourse. *Suaui(s)* is especially common as a translation of ἡδ(ύς) when ἡδ(ύς) described the "inessential" member of a contrastive pair.[62] In short the phrase *suaui(s) graui(s)* bridges aristocratic pleasure and traditional social

60. *tuo suauissimo atque amantissimo consilio ac sermone* (*Att.* 1.17.6), *praetermissos fructus tuae suauitatis praeteriti temporis* (*Att.* 4.1.2), *nihil me hercule te mihi nec carius esse nec suauius* (5.1.5).

61. Cf. *doctus, fidelis,* | *suauis homo, iucundus, suo contentus, beatus,* | *scitus, secunda loquens in tempore, commodus* (Enn. *Ann.* 8.279–81 Skutsch). *Comes benigni, faciles, suaues* (Cic. *Balb.* 36) is probably a quote from a comedy, as suggested by Reid 1879 ad loc.

62. *Suauis* appears in two such contrastive pairs in the rhetorica. The first, *suauis et utilis,* appears twice: *suauis autem est et uehementer saepe utilis iocus et facetiae* (*de Orat.* 2.216) and *hoc in omnibus item partibus orationis euenit, ut utilitatem ac prope necessitatem suauitas quaedam et lepos consequatur* (*de Orat.* 3.181). *Suauis* here represents ἡδύς as contrasted with χρήσιμος; Plato divides τὸ καλόν into ἡδονή and χρεία in the *Gorgias* (476d6). On *de Orat.* 3.181, where *suauitas et lepos* represents ἡδονή τε καὶ χάρις, cf. VI.3 n.35. *Suauis* is also contrasted to *necessarius* (ἀναγκαῖος): *inuentam exornari et certas in partes distingui et suauissimum est et summe necessarium et ab artis scriptoribus maxime neglectum* (*Inv.* 1.50) and *nam ut dilucide probabiliterque narremus, necessarium est, sed assumimus etiam suauitatem* (*Part.* 31). Here again *suauis* looks to ἡδύς, cf. ὁ δὲ Λυκούργειός (sc., λόγος) ἐστι διὰ παντὸς αὐξητικὸς καὶ διηρημένος καὶ σεμνός, καὶ ὅλως κατηγορικὸς καὶ φιλαλήθης καὶ παρρησιαστικός· οὐ μὴν ἀστεῖος, οὐδὲ ἡδύς, ἀλλ' ἀναγκαῖος (Dion. Hal. *Imit.* fr. 31.5.3); cf. *Dem.* 3 where τὰ ἀναγκαῖα καὶ χρήσιμα are contrasted to ἡ καλλιλογία and ἐπίθετοι κατασκευαί. For more detail, see Van Wyk Cronjé 1986: 138ff.

worth by an antique poetic figure; the effect of the translation from the Greek is as if "delightful and grand" had been rendered by "fine and firm."

*Suaui(s) graui(s)*, I suggest, was a phrase forged in the second century, inspired by ἡδ(ύς) καὶ μεγαλοπρεπ(ής), but intended to express a social as well as a rhetorical ideal. The connection to social ideals is clearest from the congener of the pair *suaui(s) graui(s)* that appears in *Rhet. Her.* As Sinclair 1993 has shown, the purpose of *Rhet. Her.* is to introduce nonnoble speakers to the ways of noble speech. The author of *Rhet. Her.* is generally more mechanistic than Cicero, in the manner of the rhetorical handbooks, but on occasion he ventures into approbative language. In such cases he is always thoroughly in the spirit of the noble classes whom he wishes to imitate. His peroration to Herennius accordingly employs noble metalanguage:

> *omnes rationes honestandae studiose collegimus elocutionis: in quibus, Herenni,*
> *si te diligentius exercueris, et grauitatem et dignitatem et suauitatem habere in*
> *dicundo poteris, ut oratorie plane loquaris, ne nuda atque inornata inuentio*
> *uulgari sermone efferatur.*

We have carefully surveyed all the means of ennobling *(honestare)* rhetorical presentation: and if you practice them diligently, Herennius, your speech will have weight *(grauitas)*, beauty *(dignitas)*,[63] and attractiveness *(suauitas)*, enabling you to speak as a true orator *(oratorie)*, and keeping you from delivering a bare and undistinguished idea in ordinary *(uulgaris)* speech.

(4.69)

The social weight of *suauitas* is confirmed not only by the context but by the choice of *suauitas* as the abstract, used in this treatise only here. The author's usual choice, the rare alternate form *suauitudo*, is used to describe the quality of a voice that is *suauis* (3.21–22 *tris*), a common metarhetorical usage of the word derived from the original meaning 'sweet' (*\*swadh-wi-* ~ Eng. 'sweet').[64] But the choice of *suauitas* has two effects. First, it is necessary

---

63. *Dignitas* may stand for 'beauty,' but a specifically male beauty; cf. Cic. *Off.* 1.130, VII.2 n. 6.

64. Cf. *uoce pleniorem aut suauiorem* (*de Orat.* 1.132), *uox cum magna tum suauis et splendida* (*Brut.* 203), *uoce suaui et canora* (*Brut.* 234), *uocis et suauitas et magnitudo* (*Brut.* 235), *suauitas uocis et lenis appellatio litterarum* (*Brut.* 259), *canora uox et suauis* (*Brut.* 303), *studium persequendae suauitatis in uocibus* (*Or.* 58), *uocum suauitate* (of the Sirens, *Fin.* 5.49), *[uox] ut clara sit, ut suauis* (*Off.* 1.133). So *suauitas* of Nestor (*Brut.* 40), whom Homer calls ἡδυεπής (*Il.* 1.247). 'Sweetness' of voice is the main way Quintilian uses the word in the *Institutio Oratoria: cum suauitate uocum* (1.5.33), *uocis iucunditas claritasque, oris suauitas, et in utracumque lingua, tamquam ad eam demum natus esset, expressa proprietas omnium litterarum* (6.pr.11), *eloquendi suauitate* (10.1.83), *non oris modo suauitate sed narium quoque, per quas quod superest uocis egeritur*

to secure the rhyme. The archaic-sounding jingle *(et graui̱tatem̱ et digni̱tatem̱ et suaui̱tatem̱)*—a figure, as we just saw, the treatise's author elsewhere warns against—is meant to recall the pair *suaui(s) graui(s)*. Furthermore *suauitas* describes the speech habits of the powerful in their own idiom: *-tas -tatis* was commoner in educated speech.[65] The audience of the *Rhet. Her.* may be outside looking in, but the author assures them that he knows the cant of the insiders.

The places where *suaui(s) graui(s)* appear in Cicero are not so overtly connected to noble metalanguage. Still, aside from the "Theophrastan" instances that refer to ornament, *suaui(s) graui(s)* does seem to suggest the finest combination of qualities a speech can have.[66] At the beginning of *de Inventione,* in a description of the good that oratory can do, Cicero claims that the strong would never have submitted to the rule of law unless persuaded by a speech that was *suaui(s) graui(s): profecto nemo nisi graui ac suaui commotus oratione, cum uiribus plurimum posset, ad ius uoluisset sine ui descendere* "Nobody who was especially strong would have foregone violence and submitted to the rule of law unless a fine and firm speech had convinced him" (1.3). In the *Orator* Cicero argues that the faulty metrical arrangement of words and clausulae spoils sentences no matter how good they are; the way he expresses "no matter how good they are" is *quamuis . . . suaues graues sententiae.* The pair describes the high quality that would guarantee acceptance, if only the delivery system were improved.[67] As he embarks on his discussion of the embellishment of style, Crassus remarks on the qualities that are diffuse in a whole speech:

---

(11.3.16), *suauis appellatio literrarum* (11.3.35), *flexum uocis et flebilem suauitatem* (11.3.170), *[accentus] minus suaues habemus* (12.10.33). There are only a few exceptions: one a quotation of Cicero (4.2.107), once of metaphor *(neque enim uulgaris esse neque humilis nec insuauis haec recte modo adscita potest)* and once of *conciliatio* 'conciliation (of the audience),' which may be accomplished by *orationis suauitas* (11.3.154). Cf. also *suauitas sonitus* 'the agreeability of the sound,' Gel. 13.21.10 and *sonum suauiorem* 'a sweeter sound,' Hyg. *Fab.* 165.3.

65. Cf. Cooper 1895: 44–46. A purely linguistic development may have contributed: for some speakers the abstracts may have undergone semantic differentiation, with *suauitudo* for metaphors derived from the literal use and *suauitas* for other uses.

66. For other examples, not of the same weight, cf. *suauis . . . uideri maluit quam grauis* (*Brut.* 38), *[epistulam] Aristophaneo modo ualde mehercule et suauem et grauem* (*Q. fr.* 3.1.19), *tam suauem oratorem tam grauem tam facetum* (*Brut.* 186). Probably also of Plato: *longe omnium quicumque scripserunt aut locuti sunt exstitit et grauitate <et suauitate> princeps Plato* (*Or.* 62). The better manuscripts lack *et suauitate,* but the form might easily have been lost through its homoioteleuton with *grauitate.* For Plato's *grauitas,* cf. *de Orat.* 1.47; for his *suauitas,* cf. *Div.* 1.78.

67. Cf. similarly *nam et uerba eligebant et sententias grauis et suauis reperiebant sed eas aut uinciebant aut explebant parum* (*Or.* 168).

*nam ut grauis, ut suauis, ut erudita sit, ut liberalis, ut admirabilis, ut polita,*
*ut sensus, ut doloris habeat quantum opus sit, non est singulorum articulorum;*
*in toto spectantur haec corpore.*

The individual joints of a speech cannot make it firm *(grauis)*, fine
*(suauis)*, learned, dignified, wondrous, and polished; nor ensure that it
has the proper proportion of feeling and pathos; these qualities, rather,
are revealed in the disposition of the whole body.

(de Orat. 3.96)

Furthermore in Cicero there is one slight suggestion that *suaui(s) graui(s)*
was read socially as well as literarily: the same pairing provided a jingle to
express social relationships, with roughly the same polarity of appeal vs. so-
briety: *Marcellis, patri et filio, quorum alter apud me parentis grauitatem, alter fili*
*suauitatem obtinebat (Sul.* 19).

*Suaui(s) graui(s)*, in short, may be taken as a phrase that represents the conceptual struggles that brought the language of social performance into rhetorical theory. It is, so to speak, at "full strength" in the *Rhet. Her.*, a little farther from its origins in Cicero, and vanishes from subsequent discourse.[68]
But the kind of forced marriage it expresses, which Cicero calls "the very
difficult alliance between weight of character *(grauitas)* and culture *(humani-*
*tas),*"[69] remains a rocky one in the late Republic, as evidenced below. The
most important passage of those that contain *suauis grauis* is the peroration
of the *Rhetorica ad Herennium*, which suggests that *suauitas, grauitas,* and *dig-*
*nitas* are attainable, and not inherent, qualities. Acquisition of verbal wealth,
as it were, implies social worth. That had long been true in Roman culture,
but the expression of social identity by control of stylish words was an especially contentious issue in the late Republic, an issue that can be tracked
by the language of social performance.

## IV.7. Conclusion

The distribution of the language of social performance in the Latin rhetorical tradition is, I suggest, an artefact of an act of cultural translation. The
language of social performance first arose to describe the pleasant, inessential aspects of certain aesthetic practices, constructed as complements to
more semioticially serious aspects, for example the witty banter of the *con-*
*vivium* as opposed to its function of creating a microcosm of the social or-

---

68. The only exception is *nihil illo uiro grauius, nihil suauius, nihil eloquentia [sua] dignius*
(Sen. *Con.* 1.pr.13).

69. *[tua] et uita et oratio consecuta mihi uidetur difficillimam illam societatem grauitatis cum hu-*
*manitate (Leg.* 3.1, spoken to Atticus).

der. Romans who wished to defend certain "flashy" aspects of Greek rhe-torical practice described them with the language of social performance in order to imply that though they were "merely" pleasant, they supported the serious task of speechmaking, in the same way that witty banter supported the task of reinforcing social order. Such a view was not shared by those sympathetic to Stoic rhetorical theory, such as Terence, who always uses the language of social performance in reference to rhetorical flourish sarcas-tically. We have, then, seen two examples of how the language of social performance tracks the ideological orientation of texts toward aestheticism: the Latin rhetorical tradition, which strove to justify it, and Terence, who scorned aspects of it. Both of these arguments have necessarily been *ex ungue ad leonem*. Much more of the meat and marrow of the beast appear in the richly ideological texts of Cicero and Catullus, which are analyzed begin-ning in chapter 5.

# CHAPTER V

# Non ut Vincula Virorum
# The Language of Social Performance in Cicero's Speeches

*nec tamen mirum est si difficulter adprehenditur uitio tam uicina uirtus.*

Naturally it is difficult to grasp a virtue that is so close to a vice.

Seneca, *Con.* 7.pr.5

## V.1. Introduction

This chapter examines the language of social performance in Cicero's speeches. That language is not common there, as the following table illustrates:

Frequency of the Lexemes of the Language
of Social Performance in Cicero's Speeches[1]

| *bellus* | 4 | *festiu(us)* | 7 |
|---|---|---|---|
| *elegan(s)* | 18 | *lep(idus)* | 6 |
| *facet(us)* | 15 | *uenust(us)* | 9 |

This is hardly a matter of a properly "colloquial" idiom sometimes creeping where it does not belong, like weeds onto manicured lawns. Rather, the few instances where the language of social performance occurs provide a valuable view of the lay of the ideological terrain in which Cicero locates his public voice and the voice he assumes in his rhetorica. The language of social performance in Cicero's speeches is unique vis-à-vis its other appearances in that it is not used of a single gross referent, such as rhetorical practice (cf. ch. 3), humor (cf. ch. 6), or social and poetic style (cf. ch. 7). Instead

---

1. This table includes all the occurrences of the lexemes that may function as part of the language of social performance, whether in that function or not. By the "language of social performance," I mean a certain set of lexemes in connection to a particular cultural model. The presence of the lexeme does not guarantee the presence of the model, and a given lexeme may be connected to more than one cultural model; cf. Intro. p. 10. In particular, *elegan(s)* of 'moral choice' (above, I.5 n.65), which accounts for eight of the eighteen appearances of the lexeme, has little to do with Hellenism, aestheticism, or individualism and on those grounds seems not to be functioning as a manifestation of the cultural model that concerns us.

the language of social performance is widely scattered and infrequent and takes in a number of different referents. Therefore, it is important to recall that, if my analysis is correct, the language of social performance is like political speech, in which a single lexeme can summon a whole set of concepts. In current American politics a politician has only to say "family values" or "protection for workers" to invoke instantly the typical stances of right or left, respectively. The language of social performance in Cicero's speeches is similarly "loaded," I argue, in a way made clearer by combining (in figure 19) the diagrams introduced above (II.2, figs. 15–17):

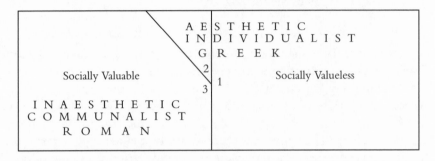

I have argued not only that the language of social performance arose as an attempt to describe category (2), but furthermore that the way the language of social performance is used locates the attitude of a text toward that category (cf. II.3). For example, in chapter 4 I suggested that the entrance of the language of social performance into the Latin rhetorical tradition was the work of "aesthetic moderates" attempting to justify their own aestheticism to skeptical critics. The language of social performance in some passages from rhetorica, notably from the *Rhetorica ad Herennium,* preserves this ideological stance, constructing aestheticism as a modest complement to social worth. In Cicero's speeches there is a congener to this stance to be found in patronizing assessments of various kinds of social inferiors (V.2). But the complications introduced by the creation of category (2) also made other stances available. Cicero also takes what we might call the "Catonian" stance (V.3), a firm assertion of the value of (3) and a rebuke of activities issuing from (1), again a stance reminiscent of one we have already seen. Both these, we may say, inherited ideological stances imply a relative balance of power between categories (3) and (2), viz., that category (3) has greater social importance, and the activities of category (2) need to be justified in terms of (3), just as Aemilius Paullus had likened banquets to generalship (I.2. n. 20).

But a number of other uses of the language of social performance in Cicero's speeches, treated in V.4ff., suggest that a shift in the balance of power between (2) and (3) had occurred; and that (2), far from being a pleasant complement to substance, had become de rigueur. The shift generated a new set of cultural rules in consequence. In particular the aesthetic action required a response in kind. This shift in the balance of power between (2) and (3) has considerable effect on the language of social performance and is vital to the remainder of this analysis. An examination of the language of social performance in Cicero's speeches contributes to an understanding not only of the flexibility of Ciceronian *ethos,* but, more important, also of the contemporary lay of the ideological land.[2]

## V.2. Looking Down from the Inside: The Roman Gaze

As noted above (II.3), the language of social performance was freighted with Roman constructions of aestheticism, Hellenism, and individualism, and therefore the way it is used is a kind of litmus test for the attitude of a text or passage toward those issues. In certain passages in his speeches, Cicero uses the language of social performance to describe the aestheticism of those who are "other." These instances become clearer if understood in terms of the diagram above: they depend on the recognition that aestheticism of various kinds has a certain value, but that admission into quadrant (2) is to be decided by Roman needs or values. This way of using the language of social performance may apply to gesture, poetry, or behavior. In the *pro Archia,* Cicero speaks of the recently dead actor Q. Roscius:

> Who of us was of such hard and crude (*agrestis* "rustic") intellect as not to be moved by the recent death of Roscius? Though he was an old man when he died, still so outstanding was his skill *(ars)* and grace *(uenustas)* that it seemed that he should not have died at all.[3]
>
> (*Arch.* 17)

*Venust(us)* here describes the grace of rhetorical gesture or *actio* (cf. I.6, III.4.1). Several members of the language of social performance cluster around the person and productions of Philodemus, the Greek poet and philosopher and a member of the household of L. Calpurnius Piso, whom Cic-

2. My treatment of Ciceronian *ethos* considers only those passages where the language of social performance is involved—not very common, for reasons cited below. For an extended treatment of the function of *ethos* in Cicero, which traces Cicero's *ethos* from his "struggle for *auctoritas*" through his use of his consular status to his "search for a new persona," closing with the "recovery of [his] independence," see May 1988.

3. *quis nostrum tam animo agresti ac duro fuit ut Rosci morte nuper non commoueretur? qui cum esset senex mortuus, tamen propter excellentem artem ac uenustatem uidebatur omnino mori non debuisse.*

ero attacked after his return from exile.[4] Philodemus produced some very nice poetry:

> The man I am discussing (sc., Philodemus) is very well-versed not only in philosophy, but also in other arts that they say other Epicureans generally neglect; in fact he can make a poem so delightful *(festiuum),*[5] so well-crafted *(concinnum),* so exquisite *(elegans),* that there can be nothing finer *(argutius).*[6] One may reprove him for that if one wishes, but gently: not for being perverse *(improbus),* or impudent *(audax),* or immoral *(impurus),* but for being a typical Greek (*Graeculus* "little Greek"), a flatterer *(adsentator),* and a poet.[7]
>
> *(Pis.* 70)

Once Piso was seduced by Epicureanism's enshrinement of pleasure as the *summum bonum,* Philodemus proved too agreeable to correct his misperception:

> At first the Greek tried to distinguish carefully the senses in which [pleasure was] meant.[8] For his part, Piso hung on to what he'd heard

4. Cicero does not mention Philodemus by name in the speech but the identification, confirmed by Asconius ad *Pis.* 68, is secure. Cf. Nisbet 1961: App. III, IV.

5. On the connection of *festiu(us)* to verbal play, cf. III.7.

6. *Argut(us)* has a wide range, but the basic idea in its application to rhetoric is one of '[excessive] precision.' The proper orator will neither have "a bobbing head" (*mollitia cervicum,* lit. "a softness of neck") nor make "nimble gestures with his fingers" (*argutiae digitorum, de Orat.* 3.220, cf. Gel. *N.A.* 1.5.2, Quint. *Inst.* 11.3.181). *Argutiae* may mean 'tight argument,' ranging from 'cogent' (*si mihi ad haec acute arguteque responderit, tum quaeram denique ex quo iste fonte senator emanet, Cael.* 19) to 'sophistic' (*sed nihil est, quod illi non persequantur argutiis, Amic.* 45). To speak *callide arguteque* is one of the features of the "plain style" (*Or.* 98). "Clearly articulated periods" are *arguti certique et circumscripti uerborum ambitus* (*Or.* 38, cf. *sententiis argutum, Or.* 42), and the *sententiae* of the Asiatic style are 'contrived, (over-) refined' (*unum [genus] sententiosum et argutum, Brut.* 325, cf. *in sententiis argutior* (*Brut.* 65). There can be nothing 'more nicely done up' or 'more finely worked' than Philodemus's poetry. Cf. Ernest s.v., du Mesnil 1879: 22 ad §7.

7. *est autem hic de quo loquor non philosophia solum sed etiam ceteris studiis quae fere ceteros Epicureos neglegere dicunt perpolitus; poema porro facit ita festiuum, ita concinnum, ita elegans, nihil ut fieri possit argutius. in quo reprehendat eum licet si qui uolet, modo leuiter, non ut improbum, non ut audacem, non ut impurum, sed ut Graeculum, ut adsentatorem, ut poetam.*

8. Viz., as "the absence of pain" and not as sensual indulgence: cf. ὅταν οὖν λέγωμεν ἡδονὴν τέλος ὑπάρχειν, οὐ τῶν ἀσώτων ἡδονὰς καὶ τὰς ἐν ἀπολαύσει κειμένας λέγομεν, ὥς τινες ἀγνοοῦντες καὶ οὐχ ὁμολογοῦντες ἢ κακῶς ἐκδεχόμενοι νομίζουσιν, ἀλλὰ τὸ μήτε ἀλγεῖν κατὰ σῶμα μήτε ταράττεσθαι κατὰ ψύχην "In saying that pleasure is the goal of existence, we do not refer to the enjoyable pleasures of the profligate, as some ignorant persons, not speaking the same language as we do or misinterpreting it, think; we refer to the absence of physical pain and spiritual disturbance" (Epic. *Ep. Men.* 131); *ipse enim Epi-*

"like a lame man the ball," as the saying goes,[9] swore his oath, signed
on the dotted line, declared Epicurus a clever man. And after all Epicurus did say, as I understand it, that he could ascertain no good except
those involving bodily pleasures. What else is there to say? A Greek,
agreeable *(facilis)* and the soul of charm *(ualde uenustus)*, did not wish
to be disputatious with a Roman senator.[10]

(*Pis.* 69–70)

In all these passages the language of social performance serves to conde-
scend to "foreign" aestheticism. Though Roscius was personally very popular, he was an actor, a profession that Roman culture did not generally hold
in high esteem.[11] The best Cicero can say about Philodemus, even if he is
not immoral, is that he is a flattering Greek poet. In short neither Roscius
nor Philodemus are advanced as paragons of virtue. It might be said that ceteris paribus their foreign aestheticism would place them in category (1). But
if both men were "mere" aesthetes, why describe them with the language
of social performance, which was potentially a language of social value? The

---

*curus, a quo omnes Catii et Amafinii, mali uerborum interpretes, proficiscuntur, dicit* οὐκ ἔστιν ἡδέως
ἄνευ τοῦ καλῶς καὶ δικαίως ζῆν "Epicurus himself, from whom poor textual interpreters
like Catius and Amafinius derive, says that the pleasant life is impossible without living rightly
and justly" (*Fam.* 15.19.2). Cicero also attacks Piso for a similar misapprehension of Epicureanism at *Red. Sen.* 14: . . . *tum est Epicureus non penitus illi disciplinae, quaecumque est, de-
ditus, sed captus uno uerbo uoluptatis* "Then he became an Epicurean, not devoted to a deep
knowledge of that philosophy, whatever its value, but enthralled by one word: pleasure."

9. Referring to a game in which lameness by preventing a player from handling the ball
gracefully forced him to cling to it with awkward doggedness.

10. *Graecus primo distinguere et diuidere, illa quem ad modum dicerentur; iste, 'claudus' quem ad
modum aiunt 'pilam,' retinere quod acceperat, testificari, tabellas obsignare uelle, Epicurum disertum de-
cernere, et tamen dicit, ut opinor, se nullum bonum intellegere posse demptis corporis uoluptatibus. quid
ultra? Graecus facilis et ualde uenustus nimis pugnax contra senatorem populi Romani esse noluit.* For
*uenustus* as 'charming,' related to 'humorous,' cf. Antonius's grudging appreciation of Crassus: *nam esse quamuis facetum atque salsum non nimis est per se ipsum inuidendem; sed cum omnium
sit uenustissimus et urbanissimus, omnium grauissimum et seuerissimum et esse et uideri, quod isti con-
tigit uni, [id] mihi uix ferendum uidebatur* "That someone should be amusing and witty in whatever measure is itself grounds for some envy, at any rate; but since Crassus is the most charming and urbane of all, it seemed to me intolerable that he should seem to be, and indeed be,
also the weightiest and gravest of all—a fortune that he alone enjoys" (*de Orat.* 2.228). This
use as 'charming' is probably ultimately related to Catullus's application of *uenustus* to Sirmio
and Cicero's to his son (VII.5 n.85), although the latter instances are not fraught with the
kind of ambiguities typical of secure examples of the language of social performance.

11. Cf. [Q. Cic.] *Pet.* 10, I.6 n.102; Wright 1931: 23–30; Richlin 1992: 100; Edwards
1993: ch. 3. As for Roscius himself, " . . . Cicero says . . . that his client Roscius the comic
actor was such a good man that he was worthy never to have gone on the stage at all (*Quinct.*
77–78; *QRosc.* 17)," Richlin 1992: 100, cf. Edwards 1993: 128.

answer is that though their foreign aestheticism may be ultimately valueless, by virtue of category (2) Romans are permitted to appropriate it. The language of social performance in these instances is used to suggest the value of foreign artistic productions to a Roman audience. Ultimately this is the same stance Romans were using to justify artistic interests for a century past. The foreign is, so to speak, rededicated to Roman purposes, just like a captured cult statue.

It is important for Cicero to locate the aestheticism of Roscius and Philodemus in this valuable space—or more precisely, in a space made valuable by the actuating gaze of a Roman—because once there that aestheticism can serve useful functions. Roscius's aestheticism may serve as foil, a pleasant but after all trivial thing compared to the higher literary arts practiced by Archias, which in this section of the speech Cicero defends by an argument a fortiori:

> What then? Roscius managed, by means of bodily movements, to win such great love for himself from all of us, but we shall disregard the wondrous swift movements of talented thought? [12]
>
> (*Arch.* 17)

It would have been inappropriate to disparage Roscius's abilities; they needed to be presented as nice, to be sure, but ultimately less "real" than Archias's— a task for which the language of social performance is perfectly suited. This is the very same use of the language of social performance that, as I have argued, introduced it into the language of Latin rhetorical theory, encoding certain aesthetic practices as inessential but nonetheless attractive.

It is also important for Cicero to be able to present Philodemus and his oeuvre as reasonably worthwhile. The above passages immediately follow Cicero's description of the immoderate life in Piso's household (§63.7–67). In §68 Cicero reveals that his source for information about Piso is the poetry of "a certain Greek who is a member of Piso's household" (*quidam Graecus qui cum isto uiuit*). Cicero has maliciously misinterpreted as literal descriptions of life inside Piso's house epigrams on conventional themes, like love or a modest repast, that Philodemus had dedicated to Piso:

> He wrote many poems to Piso with Piso as their subject, and left a picture in very pretty (*delicatissimus*) verses of all the man's lusts and defile-

---

12. *ergo ille corporis motu tantum amorem sibi conciliarat a nobis omnibus; nos animorum incredibilis motus celeritatemque ingeniorum neglegemus?* More or less the same kind of argument is used at the beginning of the *Brutus,* where Cicero declares that if people grieved at the death of famous poets, how much more the death of Hortensius is worth grieving (*Brut.* 3).

ments, the style of his dinners and parties, and even his affairs *(adulteria)*. The verses are like a window onto (lit. "mirror of") Piso's life for anyone who wants a look.[13]

(Pis. 70)

In short, since Philodemus's verse and behavior is made to have evidentiary value, even if only in jest, Cicero needs Philodemus not to be thought "perverse, or impudent, or immoral," but merely "a typical Greek, a flatterer, and a poet." The language of social performance assists Cicero in saving him for this function: his character, and his literary productions, are, to be sure, not of the highest moral order, but neither are they worthless; like Roscius's dramatic performances, they are pleasant enough, in their proper place. They are the sort of shiny baubles one might like to have around. And in this case their polished surface, it just so happens, reflects the sordid life of Piso. In these instances the language of social performance is used to excuse the Romans in category (2) who gaze on foreign aestheticism, allowing them to devote it to their own higher purposes.

We might say that the Roman gaze dismisses the outsider and excuses the Roman.[14] This double attitude underlies several passages that have to do with onomastic puns, a common form of Roman persiflage.[15] Cicero recalls how the bitterness of the Sicilians at the notoriously abusive governorship of C. Verres found expression in puns on Verres' name, which also means 'boar.'[16] Verres' capricious enforcement of the law earned much annoyance:

> Hence the parties whose suffering makes them humorous. Some, as you have often heard, said it's no surprise if boar soup *(ius uerrinum)* tastes bad. Others, who were less witty (*frigidior* "cooler") but still

13. . . . *ita multa ad istum de isto quoque scripsit ut omnis hominis libidines, omnia stupra, omnia cenarum genera conuiuiorumque, adulteria denique eius delicatissimis uersibus expresserit, in quibus si qui uelit possit istius tamquam in speculo uitam intueri.* Cf. Nisbet 1975: Appendix III "Piso and Philodemus." The poems of Philodemus are now translated with commentary by Sider 1997; for Philodemus's views of poetics, v. the essays in Obbink 1995.

14. For the delight foreigners take in artwork, cf. *Ver.* 2.4.124, 132–34; Vasaly 1993: 109–10. On the Roman attitudes toward Greeks (fairly complex) and other peoples (fairly straightforward), cf. Balsdon 1979.

15. Cf. VI.4 below, on Catulus; Corbeill 1996: 57–58 and ch. 2 passim on the cultural construction of the Roman name.

16. Plutarch passes on a joke that Cicero himself made on Verres' name. A freedman named Caecilius, who practiced Judaism, wanted to bring charges against Verres, against the opposition of the Sicilians themselves; quipped Cicero, "What business does a Jew have with a pig?" (τί Ἰουδαίῳ πρὸς χοῖρον; Plut. *Cic.* 7.6). Plutarch, however, gets the definition of *uerres* wrong, saying it is a castrated male pig (ἐκτετμημένος χοῖρος); in fact it means an uncastrated pig; cf. Var. *R.* 2.4.21, Plin. *Nat.* 18.322.

seemed funny *(ridiculus)* because they were annoyed, cursed [Verres' predecessor] Sacerdos for not having sacrificed so worthless a boar *(uerres)*. These comments are not particularly funny *(perfacetus)* and in any case are inappropriate to these serious proceedings *(haec seueritas)*. I would not have mentioned them at all, were it not that I want you to keep in mind that Verres' wickedness and injustice were at that time on everybody's lips in the form of popular catchphrases.[17]

*(Ver.* 2.1.121)

Since *ius* may mean both 'soup' and 'law' (the former from *\*yūs,* the latter from *\*yowos,* which later merged phonetically), *ius uerrinum* may mean both 'Verres' law,' 'the law as pronounced by Verres' or 'soup made from a boar.' The effect may be grasped by imagining a fraudulent stockbroker named Fish, whose bilked clients remark, "There's nothing worse than Fish stock." As for the other pun, the name of Verres' predecessor *Sacerdos* means 'priest'; the idea is that the 'priest' ought to have sacrificed the 'boar.' The effect is as if Verres' name were Bacon and his predecessor's Cook: the "equivalent" pun would be, "They cursed Cook for not having fried up Bacon."

Another Sicilian pun was occasioned when Verres sent a band of men to make off with a statue of Hercules from his temple at Agrigentum. The firmly mounted statue, foiling the thieves' efforts, gave the townspeople time to amass and drive them off. The Sicilians styled the event as a kind of defeat of Verres by Hercules:

> Things are never so bad for the Sicilians that they can't make an apt *(commodus)* and witty *(facetus)* comment. On this occasion they said that the Labors of Hercules should include not only the Erymanthian Boar *(Erymanthius aper)* but also the Monstrous Hog *(immanissimus uerres).*[18]
>
> *(Ver.* 2.4.95)

Some comparable pun may lay behind a story of L. Aelius, a freedman, who made a joke at Q. Titius Mutto's expense, which Cicero tells in order to mock Triarius's poor research into the charges against Scaurus:

17. *hinc illi homines erant qui etiam ridiculi inueniebantur ex dolore; quorum alii, id quod saepe audistis, negabant mirandum esse ius tam nequam esse uerrinum; alii etiam frigidiores erant, sed quia stomachabantur ridiculi uidebantur esse, cum Sacerdotem exsecrabantur qui uerrem tam nequam reliquisset, quae ego non commemorarem—neque enim perfacete dicta neque porro hac seueritate digna sunt—nisi uos illud uellem recordari, istius nequitiam et iniquitatem tum in ore uulgi atque in communibus prouerbiis esse uersatam.*

18. *numquam tam male est Siculis quin aliquid facete et commode dicant, uelut in hac re aiebant in labores Herculis non minus hunc immanissimum uerrem quam illum aprum Erymanthium referri oportere.*

What kind of accusation are you bringing, which you haven't even in-
vestigated properly? Whence your fierce and certain confidence in at-
tacking the defendant? If I remember rightly, when I was a boy I heard
a story about L. Aelius, a freedman of learning *(litteratus)* and wit *(facetus)*. By way of avenging wrongs done to his patron, he brought charges
against the singularly contemptible Q. Mutto.[19] When the praetor
asked him in what sphere he would be conducting his inquiry and
how many days he would need to gather the evidence, Aelius replied
that he needed until mid-afternoon, just until he could make some en-
quires in the cattle-market. Did you think you only needed to do as
much in dealing with M. Aemilius Scaurus?[20]

*(Scaur. 23)*

Aelius must have been punning on Mutto's *nomen; mutto* (or *mūto*), unfortunately for Mutto, was a rare, evidently low, word for 'penis.'[21] If *mutto*
were also the *vox propria* for the penises of butchered animals sold separately
("Rocky Mountain Sausage," as it were), *muttones* would indeed be for sale
in the *forum boarium,* and that would give Aelius's joke a point. Not only
are penises certainly comestible (the bull's is a not uncommon dish in East
Asia), but a vulgarism in one connection is often a *vox propria* in another (cf.
'bitch,' 'cock').

With slight variations, the language of social performance here reflects
the same dynamic as the previous examples do, appropriating dubious foreign aesthetic productions for higher purposes. In all cases the puns are the
productions of outsiders, thrice those of provincials and once that of a
freedman. Further it is clear that the productions are not quite acceptable
on their own terms. The puns in *Ver.* 2.1.121 *(ius uerrinum, qui uerrem tam
nequam reliquisset)* are expressly contrasted to the seriousness of the proceedings *(haec seueritas).* In both *Ver.* 2.4.95 *(immanissimus uerres)* or in *Scaur.*
23 *(Q. Mutto),* reference to category (3) values (to recall our diagram) is not
made so overtly, but their presence is still felt: attributing the puns respectively to the Sicilians and a freedman excuses Cicero's reporting them in

19. Q. Mutto is also referred to in the lost *pro Fundanio: non modo hoc a Villio Annale, sed
uix mehercule a Q. Muttone factum probari potest (orat.* 5 fr. 1).

20. *quod est igitur hoc accusationis, Triari, genus, primum ut inquisitum non ieris? quae fuit ista
tam ferox, tam explorata huius opprimendi fiducia? pueris nobis audisse uideor L. Aelium, libertinum
hominem litteratum ac facetum, cum ulcisceretur patroni iniurias, nomen Q. Muttonis, hominis sordi-
dissimi, detulisse. a quo cum quaereretur quam prouinciam aut quam diem testium postularet, horam
sibi octauam, dum in foro bouario inquireret, postulauit. hoc tu idem tibi in M. Aemilio Scauro putasti
esse faciendum?* Q. Mutto is probably Q. Titius Mutto (v. *RE* s.v. *Titius*).

21. Cf. Adams 1982: 62–63.

otherwise serious passages.[22] *Ver.* 2.4.95 is preceded by a dramatic and riveting account of the attack of Verres' henchmen and is one of a series of distressing depredations. *Scaur.* 23 is a kind of *rubato* in a passage otherwise *agitato*, with Cicero recalling, in sharp sentences, his own considerable efforts in researching the case against Verres. In *Scaur.* 23 Cicero further distances himself from the pun in two ways: he expresses mild doubt about his memory; and he dates the story to his youth, which subtly excuses him for remembering a schoolboyish joke.

The last element of the dynamic, the assignation of a higher purpose to the aesthetic product, is also present. In the case of Aelius, Cicero legitimates his attack by giving him a respectable purpose, defense of a patron, and by emphasizing the low character of his opponent, Q. Mutto. In *Ver.* 2.1.121 Cicero claims to be reporting the puns not for their own sake but as evidence of the universal knowledge of Verres' criminality. In both *Ver.* 2.1.121 and 2.4.95 it is only the cultural propensities of the Sicilians that enable them to joke at a time like this, which means that a Sicilian joke is as good as a lament and evidence of outrage. It is tempting to think the fictitious bits Quintilian (*Inst.* 6.3.4) says Cicero inserted in the *Verrines* are precisely such as *Ver.* 2.1.121 and *Ver.* 2.4.95, and that by a combination of using the language of social performance and attributing the witticisms to foreigners, Cicero makes the jokes out to be something worth appreciating even as he distances himself from them, a kind of *praeteritio.* The Roman gaze, as I have called it, is important in all these passages. It is that fact that (2) exists as a Roman cultural category that allows Cicero to appropriate "foreign" aesthetic actions of different kinds. The language of social performance, which bridges (1) and (2), locates foreign productions in a space that allows this response.

## V.3. Looking Down from Above: Dangers to *Fides*

The language of social performance can encode a different response: rather than justifying Roman appreciation of trifles, it can reject the trifles altogether. That is, Cicero can use the language of social performance as if it belonged only to category (1) (its point of origin, as I have argued). This is comparable to the stance of Lucretius we saw above (II.3), when "what could touch the ear with pleasure *(belle)*" or "what was rouged with charm-

---

22. In the case of the Sicilian examples, Cicero also means the puns to represent a salty agrarian humor, in accord with his depiction of the Sicilians as honest farmers; cf. Vasaly 1996: 212–17. The Sicilians in any case were notoriously witty: cf. *inueni autem ridicula et salsa multa Graecorum: nam et Siculi in eo genere et Rhodii et Byzantii et praeter ceteros Attici excellunt* (*de Orat.* 2.217); Caelius apud Quint. 6.3.41.

ing *(lepidus)* sound" distracted readers of Heraclitus from the truth. In his speeches Cicero sometimes uses the language of social performance similarly, not to defend philosophical truth, but to assert the primacy of Roman social values threatened by various sorts of impertinence.

All such instances have to do, broadly speaking, with the absence of *fides* 'good faith, faithfulness, trustworthiness,' which is compromised by the irony or mendacity of various parties. In the *Pro Flacco* Cicero ridicules the honors that Decianus received from the Pergamenes by attributing them to their sense of humor *(uenustas et facetiae,* cf. III.4.3, III.2):

> Surely you realized you were being made fun of, when they read to you the phrases, "Most excellent man, outstandingly wise, exceptionally gifted"? Believe me, they were kidding. Couldn't you see their wit and humor *(uenustas et facetiae)* even when they used so little gold in the crown they fitted to the decree that they must have thought you were a jackdaw?[23] These were the same Pergamenes who rejected the titles you were trying to file.[24]

> (*Flac.* 76)

The Pergamenes probably intended merely to ingratiate themselves to a powerful Roman, as they had done to the businessman Castricius, described by Cicero in the immediately preceding passage; his death honors outdid even those of P. Scipio Nasica Serapio (cos. 136), who had died at Pergamum. Decianus had surely made something of the honors he had received, but the language of social performance enables Cicero to drive a wedge between intent and appearance. Decianus becomes, instead of an honorand, a fool who cannot assess the genuineness of social gestures. *Bellus* works in a similar way in another passage. Verres had tried to justify some questionable appropriations of statuary with the claim that they were honorific:

> What then? How many statues will it take to satisfy you? You will have to be satisfied at some point. Think about it, judges. The citizens of Syracuse, to take one example, gave him a statue, the standard honor; and to his father, a fine *(bellus)* show of piety, not to say profitable; and to his son—not unimaginable, they didn't hate the boy; but come

---

23. Lit. "When they were putting a gold crown on the decree and truly were entrusting you with no more gold than they would a jackdaw." The idea is that the Pergamenes were stinting with the gold, just as if they were throwing it away; the jackdaw *(Corvus monedula),* mischievous like most Corvidae, will make off with shiny objects.

24. *quid? tu ludi te non intellegebas, cum tibi haec uerba recitabant: 'clarissimum uirum, praestantissima sapientia, singulari ingenio'? mihi crede, ludebant. cum uero coronam auream litteris imponebant, re uera non plus aurum tibi quam monedulae committebant, ne tum quidem hominum uenustatem et facetias perspicere potuisti? ipsi igitur Pergameni proscriptiones quas tu adferebas repudiauerunt.* The titles are those to the property of a local wealthy man, Amyntas, that Decianus had seized.

now, Verres, how often and under how many guises will you exact statues from the Syracusans?[25]

(Ver. 2.2.145)

Actually the Syracusans probably had dedicated a statue to Verres' father,
who was still alive, but Cicero uses the language of social performance to di-
vorce apparent from real intention: not only was the act a *simulatio*, a 'simu-
lation' or 'imitation,' which I have rendered "show," but it was also *bellus*,
'nice' or 'fine'—a performance aimed at Verres and intended to ingratiate
the Syracusans to him. Verres is presented in a brief stroke, like Decianus,
as unable to appreciate the "moves" of clever foreigners. In fact he was
probably merely conveniently unwilling.

In short, in *Flac.* 76 *(uenustas et facetiae hominum)*, and the closely comparable *Ver.* 2.2.145 *(bella pietatis simulatio)*, the social gestures of the Pergamenes and the Syracusans are depicted as ironic. Irony poses a threat to the
integrity of symbolic actions. Any means of symbolic expression posits a
standard relationship between a symbol and an idea. Ironic intent does not
merely substitute another relationship; it reserves knowledge of the substitution to one party and thus debases communication in much the same way
as mendacity. Another passage, with *bellus*, may therefore be grouped here:

> To come, then, to the testimony of the people of Dorylaeum, who tes-
> tified that they had lost the public records in the caves. Evidently they
> have a problem in those parts: shepherds so interested in literature that
> when they burgle the caves they only steal paperwork. But I think
> there is another reason for this claim: an attempt to avoid looking too
> sly. At Dorylaeum there must be an unusually harsh penalty for falsi-
> fying records; had they produced the original documents, no charges
> would have been filed, but if they produced falsified documents, there
> would have been a punishment. They thought it a very clever little
> stratagem *(bellissimum)* to say the documents were lost. They can stop
> now, score me the point, and let us get on with matters.[26]

(Flac. 39)

25. *quid uero? modum statuarum haberi nullum placet? atqui habeatur necesse est. etenim sic con-*
*siderate. Syracusana ciuitas, ut eam potissimum nominem, dedit ipsi statuam—est honos—et patri—*
*bella haec pietatis et quaestuosa simulatio—et filio—ferri hoc potest, hunc enim puerum non oderant;*
*uerum quotiens et quot nominibus a Syracusanis statuas auferes?*

26. *uenio nunc ad Dorylensium testimonium: qui producti tabulas se publicas ad speluncas per-*
*didisse dixerunt. o pastores nescio quos cupidos litterarum, si quidem nihil istis praeter litteras abstu-*
*lerunt! sed aliud esse causae suspicamur, ne forte isti parum uersuti esse uideantur. poena est, ut opinor,*
*Dorylai grauior quam apud alios falsarum et corruptarum litterarum. si ueras protulissent, criminis nihil*
*erat, si falsas, erat poena. bellissimum putarunt dicere amissas. quiescant igitur et me hoc in lucro ponere*
*atque aliud agere patiantur.* Cf. May 1988: 81.

This instance of *bellus* is importantly different from that of the rhetorical tradition: the "movers" intend not to delight a select, and willing, audience of peers (cf. III.5) but to elude a judicial one of superiors. They are not appealing so much to the audience's taste, in the narrow sense, as to its propensity, as they imagine it, to see certain excuses as probable. False testimony and false honorifics both substitute nonstandard relationships between symbols and ideas, a dishonesty that sets them in opposition to real truth. Bestowing honors and giving testimony, two symbolic actions very important to Roman culture, cannot proceed if abused by ironists or liars.

Indeed legal procedure generally suffers when various sorts of cleverness described by the language of social performance interfere; for *fides* means not only accurate testimony or honest social gestures but also a scrupulous regard for all aspects of procedure. Antony had admitted onto juries persons who constitutionally lacked such regard:

> Now many of us know Lysiades of Athens, the son of the well-known philosopher Phaedrus, and an entirely delightful *(festiuus)* man: he should get along well with M'. Curius, his fellow juryman. And fellow gambler. But my question is this: suppose Lysiades is called to jury duty and does not appear, on the excuse that the Areopagus was in session and that he ought not to have to sit in judgment in Athens and Rome at the same time; will the summoning judge find acceptable the excuse of a little Greek juror, who keeps changing between a toga and a pallium? Or will he ignore the very ancient laws of Athens?[27]
>
> (*Phil.* 5.13–14)

When Verres crafted a law that referred any dispute between a tithe-collector and a farmer to a panel of assessors appointed by Verres himself, Verres, in cahoots with the tithe-collectors, had manipulated formal legal structures to ensure his own gain; Cicero reproves him for this manipulation with *lepidus: quam lepide se furari putat* "How cleverly *(lepide)* he thinks he does his thieving!" (*Ver.* 2.3.25).[28] Another legal example, with *festiu(us)*,

27. *nam Lysiaden Atheniensem plerique nouimus; est enim Phaedri, philosophi nobilis, filius; homo praeterea festiuus, ut ei cum M'. Curio consessore eodemque conlusore facillime possit conuenire. quaero igitur, si Lysiades citatus iudex non responderit excuseturque Areopagites esse nec debere eodem tempore Romae et Athenis res iudicare, accipietne excusationem is qui quaestioni praeerit Graeculi iudicis, modo palliati, modo togati? an Atheniensium antiquissimas leges negleget?*

28. *SI VTER VOLET, RECVPERATORES DABO. quam lepide se furari putat! Vtrique facit potestatem, sed utrum ita scripserit, 'si uter uolet,' an 'si decumanus uolet,' nihil interest; arator enim tuos istos recuperatores numquam uolet* "'If it please either party, I shall appoint assessors.' How cleverly *(lepide)* he thinks he does his thieving! He gives either party the right to sue, but it really makes no difference if he wrote 'if it please either party' or 'if it please the tithe-collectors.' No assessors you appoint are going to be acceptable to any farmer."

is from the *pro Sestio.* In that speech Cicero takes Vatinius to task for flouting a law sponsored by Cicero, the *lex Tullia de ambitu,* which provided that no one host games within two years of standing for office. When challenged on the point, Vatinius split hairs: *do bestiarios, lex scripta de gladiatoribus* "The law forbids gladiatorial games; I'm giving wild animal hunts." Cicero's response to this legalism is *festiue!* "Isn't that clever!" (*Sest.* 135). Legalism is, of course, a perfectly legitimate defense; it is incumbent on legislators to craft laws that cannot be eluded. *Festiue,* however, casts the matter as trifling impertinence—verbal party games played out of context.

*Festiu(us)* is also applied to the tardy, if not outright mendacious, charges laid by the grandson of the king Deiotarus which it is the point of Cicero's *pro Rege Deiotaro* to refute. The king's grandson charged, twenty years after the alleged incident, that the king had plotted to assassinate Caesar, the plan having been to take Caesar, on the pretext of showing him an assemblage of gifts intended for him, to a place where a band of armed assassins waited. The grandson claimed that Caesar was saved only by his ever-attendant good fortune when he decided against reviewing the bounty: *'tua te' inquit 'eadem quae saepe fortuna seruauit: negauisti tum te inspicere uelle.'* At that detail of the story, Cicero exclaims *quam festiue crimen contexitur!* "How delightfully he spins out his tale of the charge!" (*Deiot.* 19).[29] The cogency of the grandson's case—or at least its possibility; Deiotarus had, after all, been a Pompeian—is dismissed by casting it as the work of a clever raconteur, recalling the application of *festiuus* to charming narration (I.10). *Facet(us),* too, in connection with *nebulo* 'rascal,' once serves to mark the absence of *fides* in a legal context:

> Either these sales were never entered in the public record, and this rascal (*nebulo*) is tricking us more cleverly (*facetius*) than we suspect, or if they were entered, the records have been corrupted somehow; for it's obvious they could not have been legally sold.[30]
>
> (*S. Rosc.* 128)

One more example may be grouped here, which involves lying to a parent—perhaps, strictly, a violation of *pietas* rather than *fides,* but mendacity nonetheless. When Falcidius, who was wont to spend his inheritance indulgently at Greek soirées (*patrimonium . . . Graecorum conuiuiis maluit dissipare*), lies to his mother that he had lent a large sum to Flaccus, Cicero calls him

---

29. For *contexere* not as 'weave' but as 'continue,' cf. Gotoff 1993 ad loc. For a similar use of *festiue,* cf. *at quam festiue dissoluitur* (*Div.* 2.35), sarcastically of certain arguments in favor of the possibility of divination.

30. *profecto aut haec bona in tabulas publicas nulla redierunt nosque ab isto nebulone facetius eludimur quam putamus, aut, si redierunt, tabulae publicae corruptae aliqua ratione sunt; nam lege quidam bona uenire non potuisse constat.*

a *festiuus filius* ("jolly lad") lying to his *matercula* ("mother dear"), who is "a nice trusting old lady" (*aniculae minime suspiciosae, Flac.* 91).

In short, various lexemes from the language of social performance are used to expose, or create the impression of, behaviors incompatible with *fides,* whether motivated by irony, legalism, spite, greed, or mendacity.[31] The language of social performance is sharply dismissive, much as Lucretius's rejection of the meretricious devices of Heraclitan poetry. In terms of our diagram, we may say that the solid values of (3) repudiate the impertinent esprit of (1); weighty substance, the possession of communalist Romans, rejects the frivolous flourish of self-absorbed foreigners. This stance is notable, inasmuch as category (2) does not appear at all. *Fides* is simply too important a value to be compromised by any sort of cleverness. A corollary is that no good Roman would even try to compromise it; and indeed for the most part the practitioners of the actions described by the language of social performance are not Romans.[32] The only real exception, beside the minor example of Falcidius, is the maniac Verres, who is perfectly happy to transgress *fides,* or anything else, for his own hedonist purposes. Much more dangerous are spheres of action other than *fides* where category (2) *is* a legitimate possibility for Romans: there they have the option of trying to pass off as belonging to (2) behavior that might also belong to (1). In order to appreciate the dynamics of that "border war," we must look at another stance of Cicero's in which the language of social performance figures: Cicero as outsider.

## V.4. Outside Looking In

But, sires, by cause I am a burel man,
At my bigynnyng first I yow biseche,
Have me excused of my rude speche.
I lerned nevere rethorik, certeyn;
Thyng that I speke, it moot be bare and pleyn.
                The Frankeleyn, *The Canterbury Tales,* V(f) 716–20

31. One more instance has not to do with *fides* proper but may be conveniently grouped here. Cicero reproves Verres for raising not a son who will benefit the state but one who is as much a voluptuary as his father, perhaps even worse: Verres ended up a voluptuary *(homo luxuriosus)* after having been raised by "a thief and bribery agent" *(fur, diuisor),* whereas Verres' son has started out amid decadence from the very beginning: "Can we imagine anything more delightful *(festiuius)* than him, if he is your son by nature, your disciple by habit, and your like by choice?" *(quid isto fore festiuius arbitramur, si est tuus natura filius, consuetudine discipulus, uoluntate similis, Ver.* 2.3.162). *Festiuus,* somewhat like *lepidus* in *Catil.* 2.23 below, contrasts "convivial" to "communal" values.

32. For other examples of the absence of *fides* and *religio* in the testimony of foreign races, cf. *Font.* 27 *(scit Indutiomarus quid sit testimonium dicere?),* Vasaly 1993: 191–200.

Neither of the two uses of the language of social performance just surveyed is especially surprising; both preserve intact the original stances taken, respectively, by Aemilius Paullus and (affectedly) by Cato. More curious, and, as I argue below, more revealing of the contemporary ideological terrain, is a third stance. Cicero occasionally uses the language of social performance in his speeches to depict himself and the audience as outsiders: inexperienced in, or a target of, the aestheticism or aesthetics that the language of social performance describes in each case—honest residents of (3) beyond whose ken lie the sophisticated displays of (2), or (1), or whatever they are. In each case Cicero asserts the primacy of inaesthetic social value, but with false modesty or injured innocence rather than with the haughtiness and disdain of V.3.

One set of examples involves rhetorical style, broadly meant. In the *pro Flacco,* speaking of the reliability of Greek witnesses, Cicero concedes artistic superiority to that nation, who have mastered the art of 'clever speech' *(sermonis lepos). Lepos* is the quality Cicero also ascribes to Stoic dialectic (cf. III.3), and in this passage *lepos* perhaps means something rather like that:

> But this is what I have to say about the Greek people as a whole: I grant them their literary excellence, I allow them their knowledge in many areas of research, I let them have their charming speech *(sermonis lepos),* their clever minds, their ready tongues. In fact I don't refuse them anything else they may claim as their own. But that nation has never cultivated reliability *(religio* 'scrupulousness') and trustworthiness *(fides)* in giving testimony. They simply do not know the weight, force, and influence of such a thing.[33]

(*Flac.* 9)

In this passage the role of the outsider is played by the Roman people as a whole, who are not given to Hellenic glibness. Although in this passage, too, as in those treated above in V.3, the issue is the absence of *fides,* the difference in tone is significant: Cicero does not patronize but rejects with cloying earnestness. The stance of the outsider is handled in another example with greater modesty. The famous actor Roscius had encouraged Cicero to take the case on behalf of P. Quinctius, to whose sister he, Roscius, was married.[34] This Cicero, who was only 26 at the time, was reluctant to do, since the prosecutor was the famous Hortensius:

33. *uerum tamen hoc dico de toto genere Graecorum: tribuo illis litteras, do multarum artium disciplinam, non adimo sermonis leporem, ingeniorum acumen, dicendi copiam, denique etiam, si qua sibi alia sumunt, non repugno; testimoniorum religionem et fidem numquam ista natio coluit, totiusque huiusce rei quae sit uis, quae auctoritas, quod pondus ignorant.*

34. C. Quinctius, the brother of Cicero's defendant, had been a business partner with Sex. Naevius; Gaius on his death left his brother heir. The new partners proved incapable of

When he insisted, I told the man, with the frankness of friendship, that whoever tried to execute a gesture in Hortensius's presence looked to me to have a face made of stone; and that if anyone wanted to contend with him, he lost whatever correctness *(rectum)* or grace *(uenustum)* he previously seemed to have; that I was afraid of the same thing happening to me, since I would be speaking against such an artist *(artifex)*.[35]

(*Quinct.* 77)

*Venust(us)* here describes the grace of rhetorical gesture or *actio* generally (cf. I.6, III.4.1). Cicero depicts himself here as a kind of outsider, an amateur orator compared to the "artiste" Hortensius. But Roscius eventually prevails on Cicero by convincing him that truth will be on his side (§78–80), since the prosecution's case depended on various patent absurdities:

Roscius said, "Now what if you have a case where all you have to do is prove that nobody can walk 700 miles in two or at most three days— would you still be afraid to take this case, if it meant arguing against Hortensius?" "Hardly," I said, "but what does that have to do with it?" "Well," said Roscius, "that's exactly the issue the whole case rests on."[36]

(*Quinct.* 78–79)

The contrast between the "artful" prosecution and the artless defense comes to a head in the impassioned *peroratio*, where Cicero's defendant is contrasted with Naevius:

The point at issue is whether such rustic and uncultured frugality can defend itself against excess and indulgence, or whether, disfigured and stripped of all its honors, it should be handed over unadorned to lust and impudence. Publius Quinctius does not compare himself to you in influence, Sextus Naevius; he does not try to rival you in resources or ability; he concedes you all the arts at which you excel; he admits he cannot speak nicely *(belle)*, that he cannot talk at will, that he does not fly from a friend in trouble to another on stable ground, that

managing the joint enterprise successfully, and a complex series of legal disputes and maneuvers passed between them.

35. *cum cupidius instaret, homini pro amicitia familiarius dixi mihi uideri ore durissimo esse, qui praesente eo gestum agere conaretur; qui uero cum ipso contenderent, eos, etiamsi quid antea recti aut uenusti habere uisi essent, id amittere; ne quid mihi eius modi accideret, cum contra talem artificem dicturus essem, me uereri.* On Cicero's age at the time, cf. Gel. 15.28.3. For a treatment of Cicero's characterizations of himself, his client, and his opponents in this speech, v. May 1988: 14–21. For an introduction to the legal issues and an assessment of the validity of Cicero's case, see Kinsey 1971: 3–6, 219–20, with refs.

36. *'quid? si,' inquit, 'habes eius modi causam ut hoc tibi planum sit faciendum, neminem esse qui possit biduo aut summum triduo dcc milia passuum ambulare, tamenne uereris ut possis hoc contra Hortensium contendere?' 'minime,' inquam, 'sed quid id ad rem?' 'nimirum,' inquit, 'in eo causa consistit.'*

he does not live with extravagant expense, that he does not lay out a party grandly and splendidly, that he does not have a home closed to shame and propriety, and laid wide open to lust and desires; he says that instead he has always preferred duty *(officium)*, faithfulness *(fides)*, diligence *(diligentia)*, and a life entirely dry and rough *(horridus atque aridus)*.[37]

(Quinct. 93)

*Belle dicere* 'speak well' pretty clearly means speaking in the entertaining ways of a trained rhetorician. (There is some irony in that, since, as we will see, Naevius was by profession a *praeco*.) Rhetorical skill is here made the moral equivalent of political opportunism and sexual license, all of which stand in contrast to Quinctius's *officium, fides,* and *diligentia,* bedrock Roman values issuing from his simple country life.[38]

It is instructive to contrast Cicero's treatment of Naevius earlier in the same speech:

Quinctius was the brother of the P. Quinctius you see here, in most respects a *paterfamilias* of care and foresight, but less than well advised on one point, in having entered a partnership with Sex. Naevius. Naevius is a good man *(uir bonus)*, but not educated to know the laws of partnership and the duties of a reliable *paterfamilias*—not for lack of in- telligence *(ingenium);* no one has ever thought Sex. Naevius a wag defi- cient in humor *(parum facetus scurra)* or a herald *(praeco)* without sensi- bility *(inhumanus)*. What explains him then? The best thing nature gave him was his voice, and his father left him with nothing besides his lib- erty; so he hired out his voice, and put his liberty to good use, in or- der to get away with sarcastic comments more easily.[39]

(Quinct. 11)

In this passage Cicero takes the condescending stance he applied to foreign- ers' quips (V.2). The same elements discussed above are present here. Nae-

---

37. *Ea res nunc enim in discrimine uersatur, utrum possitne se contra luxuriem ac licentiam rusti- cana illa atque inculta parsimonia defendere an deformata atque ornamentis omnibus spoliata nuda cu- piditati petulantiaeque addicatur. Non comparat se tecum gratia P. Quinctius, Sex. Naeui, non opibus, non facultate contendit; omnis tuas artis quibus tu magnus es tibi concedit; fatetur se non belle dicere, non ad uoluntatem loqui posse, non ab adflicta amicitia transfugere atque ad florentem aliam deuolare, non profusis sumptibus uiuere, non ornare magnifice splendideque conuiuium, non habere domum clausam pudori et sanctimoniae, patentem atque adeo expositam cupiditati et uoluptatibus; contra sibi ait offi- cium, fidem, diligentiam, uitam omnino semper horridam atque aridam cordi fuisse.*

38. Cf. Vasaly 1993: 171–72.

39. *C. Quinctius fuit P. Quincti huius frater, sane ceterarum rerum pater familias et prudens et attentus, una in re paulo minus consideratus, qui societatem cum Sex. Naeuio fecerit, uiro bono, uerum tamen non ita instituto ut iura societatis et officia certi patris familias nosse posset; non quo ei deesset*

vius is patently made out to be a social lesser: his status as a *praeco* or 'herald' and a *scurra* or 'jester,' positions held in low esteem, is emphasized.[40] The amusing quality of his comments is distinctly attributed to the willingness of his superiors to be amused: it is not that he actually was *facetus* or *humanus*, it is that he was generally thought to be so; *est existimatus* recalls *existimatio*, the word expressing the "social value" or "reputation" imputed to one by others. And whatever Naevius's attractions, he did not understand "real" things, like the business of being a *paterfamilias*. Here, in the milder *narratio* of the speech, Cicero pleasantly condescends, but by the time he comes to the impassioned *peroratio*, he has modulated the hostility between Naevius and P. Quinctius into one of solid simplicity versus elegant decadence and moved from the stance of an insider to the stance of an outsider.

Several other examples where Cicero takes the stance of an outsider have to do with art. Cicero describes with *uenust(us)* the craftsmanship of a piece of artwork (cf. I.6) coveted by Verres, the rapacious proconsul of Sicily:

> I nearly forgot to mention a particular goat, made wonderfully, and with knowledge *(scite)* and charm *(uenuste)*, as even those of us inexperienced *(rudes)* in these matters can tell.[41]
>
> (*Ver.* 2.2.87)

In another passage from the *Verrines*, which also describes statuary with *uenust(us)*, Cicero pretends to have forgotten a name he surely knew perfectly well:

> There were besides two bronze statues, whose charm *(uenustas)* was more than great, it was truly outstanding. The statues depicted young

---

*ingenium; nam neque parum facetus scurra Sex. Naeuius neque inhumanus praeco umquam est existimatus. quid ergo est? cum ei natura nihil melius quam uocem dedisset, pater nihil praeter libertatem reliquisset, uocem in quaestum contulit, libertate usus est quo impunius dicax esset.* This passage involves a pun on the two senses of *libertas* 'freedom' = 'the state of not being servile,' and 'freedom' = 'the absence of restrictions on one's speech.' The label applied to Naevius in this passage, *uir bonus*, is frequent in this speech (16, 38 *[optimus]*, 39, 51, 55, 56, 66, 67, 94) and embodies a social ideal of grace and consideration to which Naevius's hostile and punctilious legalism is usually set in contrast.

40. On the *praeco*, cf. Hinard 1976 ad fin. Naevius's position as a *praeco* is something Cicero elsewhere brings to the foreground: *cum auctionem uenderet* (Quinct. 19), *suos necessarios ab atriis Liciniis et a faucibus macelli corrogat* (Quinct. 25), *ab eo cuius uox in praeconio quaestu prostitit* (Quinct. 95). See Damon 1997: 196–203. The *scurra* was something like a professional buffoon brought in to enliven parties but might also mean a 'man about town' (cf. Cic. *Sest.* 39). Cf. Corbett 1986.

41. *etiam, quod paene praeterii, capella quaedam est, ea quidem mire, ut etiam nos qui rudes harum rerum sumus intellegere possumus, scite facta et uenuste.*

girls in their typical bearing and dress. On their heads they were carrying certain sacral items with uplifted arms, in the manner of young Athenian girls; they were called the *Canephoroe:* and they say the artist was—who again? yes, right—Polyclitus.[42]

(*Ver.* 2.4.5)

Verres by extension is one of the *cognoscenti,* as in another passage where Cicero apologizes for seeming to know too much about art. Verres is represented as insulting less "artsy" Romans in Greek, calling them *idiotae* (ἰδιῶται), something like 'laymen,' 'undistinguished,' 'ignoramuses':[43]

. . . statues that could delight not only a man of Verres' talents and discernment, but indeed any of us rubes (as he calls us); one of them a marble Cupid by Praxiteles—you won't be surprised that I learned the artists' names in the course of my investigations.[44]

(*Ver.* 2.4.4)

In these instances social value is asserted in a different way. Here it is not a matter of two actions, one aestheticizing and the other valuable, but of a single item that has both an aesthetic and a more redeeming social aspect. The pretty goat had been a part of the Carthaginian take from the sack of Himera; Scipio Africanus had permitted Himera's citizens, who had in the meantime moved to nearby Thermae, to have it along with other items, thinking it proper that "upon completion of war allies benefit from [Roman] victory by recovering their own property."[45] Thus Sthenius, a leading citizen of Thermae, declared the goat and the other pieces to be *monumenta P. Africani* "memorials to P. Africanus" (*Ver.* 2.2.85). The same is true for the *Canephoroe:* it was located in a "very ancient *(perantiquum)*" sacrarium in the house of a C. Heius.[46] Of all the praetors and consuls that had been in Sicily, vicious though some of them were, none had ever dared to loot a sacrarium (*Ver.* 2.4.7). We may add another passage here. Verres attention was also attracted by a statue of Sappho:

42. *erant aenea duo praeterea signa, non maxima uerum eximia uenustate, uirginali habitu atque uestitu, quae manibus sublatis sacra quaedam more Atheniensium uirginum reposita in capitibus sustinebant; Canephoroe ipsae uocabantur; sed earum artificem—quem? quemnam? recte admones—Polyclitum esse dicebant.* Cf. also *Ver.* 2.4.94; Vasaly 1993: 109.

43. Cf. *LSJ* s.v. and Lucilius 650M, 675W, 607K *quidni? et tu idem inlitteratum me atque idiotam diceres.*

44. *signa . . . quae non modo istum hominem ingeniosum et intellegentem, uerum etiam quemuis nostrum, quos iste idiotas appellat, delectare possent, unum Cupidinis marmoreum Praxiteli; nimirum didici etiam, dum in istum inquiro, artificum nomina.*

45. *bello confecto socios sua per nostram uictoriam recuperare* (*Ver.* 2.2.86).

46. On the rhetorical effect of the description of Heius's house, cf. Vasaly 1993: 111–14.

The image of Sappho that was taken from the prytanium provides you a just excuse that virtually requires us to forgive you. What private citizen, or indeed what municipality, had more right than the most elegant *(elegantissimus)* and learned *(eruditissimus)* Verres to a work of Silanio that was so well done *(perfectum)*, so elegant *(elegans)*, so highly finished *(elaboratum)?* [47]

(*Ver.* 2.4.126)

The statue was from the πρυτανεῖον, or town hall, of Syracuse, inscribed with what Cicero describes as a "very famous epigram in Greek" (*epigramma Graecum pernobile, Ver.* 2.4.127). The value of artwork in these passages is established by reference to its social or religious functions. "Rubes" might not be able to understand the finer points of art criticism, but they can certainly understand that socially and religiously important artwork ought not to be plundered. [48]

We may conclude our survey with two other examples involving humorous comments; in these Cicero's stance as an outsider is a little different, couched in a tone of injured innocence. Cicero's political enemies styled him a "king" for executing the Catilinarian conspirators without a trial. Torquatus used this uncharitable sobriquet to score a point against Cicero:

But at this point, though it was uncalled for, you tried to be funny *(facetus)*, saying Rome had known three foreign kings—Tarquinius, Numa, and me. I will not deal with the issue of kingship; I want to know why you said I was a foreigner. If I am, one should not wonder at finding me king; after all, there were already two foreign kings in Rome, as you say. Rather one should wonder at finding a foreigner as consul. "What I meant," he says, "was that you're from a *municipium*." Yes, I am: from a *municipium* from whence this city and this government have again found salvation. [49] In any case I would very much like to hear you explain why you think people from the *municipia* are foreigners. No one ever cast that in the teeth of M. Cato the elder, despite his many enemies, or of Ti. Coruncanius, or of M'. Curius, or of our C. Marius himself, though many envied him. For my part I am

47. *Nam Sappho quae sublata de prytanio est dat tibi iustam excusationem, prope ut concedendum atque ignoscendum esse uideatur. Silanionis opus tam perfectum, tam elegans, tam elaboratum quisquam non modo priuatus sed populus potius haberet quam homo elegantissimus atque eruditissimus, Verres?*
48. Cf. *Ver.* 2.4.98, below.
49. The reference is to Arpinum, in whose territory both Cicero and Marius were born. *Municipia* were certain kinds of self-governing Italian towns, some of which were originally recipients of *ciuitas sine suffragio* 'citizenship without voting privileges.' Arpinum was one of these, having received *ciuitas sine suffragio* around 300 and having been raised to full citizenship in 188.

delighted I am the sort of person that, for all your efforts, you can only find room to insult for something for which the better part of the citizenry can also be insulted.[50]

(*Sul.* 22)

*Facet(us)* is used in a similar way—in fact in exactly the same formula, *facetus esse uoluisti*—in an instance concerning M. Antony the (eventual) triumvir. Antony had made fun of Cicero's poetic compositions, in which he described the events of his own political life after the manner of older Latin epic. The infamous line *cedant arma togae* "Let arms give way to the toga" (a verse from *de consulatu suo*) was meant to suggest the predominance of civic over military virtue:

> But on a certain occasion you even tried to be witty (*facetus*). Dear Lord! *That* was beyond *your* abilities. And it's partly your fault. Your wife's a mime: a little of her wit might have rubbed off on you. "Let arms give way to the toga!" Yes, well, didn't they? That is until the toga gave way to arms—your arms. The question is, Was it better for your arms to give way before the liberty of the Roman people, or for our liberty to yield to your arms? I won't have anything else to say about my poetry. Let me just observe that you've never understood that poetry, or literature generally; whereas not only have I have never failed to be of service to the state and to my friends, but I have also managed, in my spare time, to produce every sort of memorial to my accomplishments, so that my lucubrations and my knowledge of literature might prove useful to youth and bring some glory to the name of the Roman people. But now is not the time for this discussion. Let us consider more important topics.[51]

(*Phil.* 2.20)

50. *at hic etiam, id quod tibi necesse minime fuit, facetus esse uoluisti, cum Tarquinium et Numam et me tertium peregrinum regem esse dixisti. mitto iam de rege quaerere; illud quaero peregrinum cur me esse dixeris. nam si ita sum, non tam est admirandum regem esse me, quoniam, ut tu ais, duo iam peregrini reges iam Romae fuerunt, quam consulem Romae fuisse peregrinum. 'hoc dico,' inquit, 'te esse ex municipio.' fateor et addo etiam: ex eo municipio unde iterum iam salus huic urbi imperioque missa est. sed scire ex te peruelim quam ob rem qui ex municipiis ueniant peregrini tibi esse uideantur. nemo istuc M. illi Catoni seni, cum plurimos haberet inimicos, nemo Ti. Coruncanio, nemo M'. Curio, nemo huic ipsi nostro C. Mario, cum ei multi inuiderent, obiecit umquam. equidem uehementer laetor eum esse me in quem tu, cum cuperes, nullam contumeliam iacere potueris quae non ad maximam partem ciuium conueniret.* On *rex* and *regnum* as political terms, including their application to Cicero, v. Berry 1996: 177–78.

51. *at etiam quodam loco facetus esse uoluisti. quam id te, di boni, non decebat! in quo est tua culpa non nulla. aliquid enim salis a mima uxore trahere potuisti. 'cedant arma togae.' quid? tum nonne cesserunt? at postea tuis armis cessit toga. quaeramus igitur utrum melius fuerit libertati populi Romani sceleratorum arma an libertatem nostram armis tuis cedere. nec uero tibi de uersibus plura respondebo:*

In both these last examples, Cicero, injured by haughty scurrility, invokes in extremely sincere, even cloying, terms, the honor attached to his hometown, to high office, to Roman citizenship; and to his own careful subordination of literary studies to true social usefulness. In these, as in the other examples, Cicero takes the stance of an outsider. That stance, of which more interesting examples are presented below, owes its origins to the reconfiguration of Roman cultural conceptions, discussed in the next section.

## V.5. Aestheticism and the Grammar of Social Identity

> *macerat invidia ante oculos illum esse potentem,*
> *illum aspectari claro qui incedit honore,*
> *ipsi se in tenebris uolui caenoque queruntur.*
> *intereunt partim statuarum et nominis ergo.*

> They're drained by envy that someone else wields power
> for all to see, that eyes turn to someone else
> as he enters the scene in conspicuous honor,
> complain that they themselves wallow in obscurity like mire.
> And some exhaust themselves for the sake of fame and statues.

> Lucretius 3.75–78

Although in the passages gathered in section V.4 the language of social performance is applied to different referents—humor, rhetorical grace, and the quality of artwork—all the passages are of a piece ideologically, styling Cicero as an outsider, and setting the aesthetics or aestheticism described by the language of social performance in counterpoise to "real" or "Roman" values. This consistency permits the suggestion that in these instances the language of social performance is still functioning as the lexemic manifestation of a single cultural model. In fact Cicero's stance, I argue, reflects a late Republican development in what we might call the balance of power between the elements of the diagram recalled above (V.1, fig. 19). Let us review the putative first phase of affairs. Aemilius Paullus resorted to the tactic of saying the activities of category (2) could be justified because of structural similarities they bore to activities proper to category (3). Aestheticism was almost a kind of dalliance forgiveable because of its ability to bolster serious actions or because it was practiced by persons who were otherwise "seri-

---

*tantum dicam breuiter, te neque illos neque ullas omnino litteras nosse; me nec rei publicae nec amicis umquam defuisse, et tamen omni genere monumentorum meorum perfecisse operis subsiciuis ut meae uigiliae meaeque litterae et iuuentuti utilitatis et nomini Romano laudis aliquid adferrent. sed haec non huius temporis: maiora uideamus.*

ous." However, the construction of aestheticism as a "side" pursuit was not the only possible response to the intrusion of aestheticism onto the terrain of social worth. With the cultivation of aestheticism by the social elite, the prestige of aestheticism naturally increased, making it desirable to social climbers, for whom it was easier to access than political and military glory, and virtually obligatory for the established elite, who not only could not suffer lessers to outdo them in an idiom they themselves had invented, but also could not permit their peers to add luster to their own names without challenge. In short, category (2), far from remaining a demure handmaiden to (3), could come to be a necessary, even central, component of social identity. One might even hazard that aestheticism was embraced as the only stable and reliable means of displaying class status, as politics became vicious and the amateur generalship a memory.

Just such an increase in the importance of (2) had, I suggest, taken place by the late Republic. That increase explains the behavior of Verres, who is a kind of lens through which the values of the contemporary Roman elite are distorted, but not obscured. Verres, as we have briefly seen, cajoled, coerced, and nakedly stole all manner of artwork. Indeed he inflicted all manner of abuse on his Sicilian charges and managed to combine high-handed arrogance with sensual self-indulgence at every turn. It is almost impossible not to see Verres as a dangerous megalomaniac, even a sociopath. But that conclusion only seems inevitable because our view is colored by Cicero's vigorous prosecution. While Verres' real and appalling brutalities can only be viewed with repugnance, it must also be kept in mind that there is a cultural dimension even to the expression of megalomania; madmen rant in their native tongue (usually). The principle on which Verres' depredations was surely based, that the one with the highest status should have the most status symbols—"whoever dies with the most toys wins," in the covetous slogan of the 1980s—is nothing more than a corollary of the widely accepted idea that the possession and display of art indicated high social status. Confiscating art from his lessers, Verres may have thought, was not all that different from confiscating art from defeated enemies, which was an old practice.[52] Furthermore, a vast collection of objects gave him a ready supply of gifts. Cicero rebukes Verres for having fifty couches and four hundred amphorae of honey (*Ver.* 2.2.183), but he probably intended to lavish them on his favorites, in the role of a grand patron, and the same may well have

---

52. Cf., e.g., Cato *ORF* 8.96 = Fronto p. 212.10; Cato *ORF* 8.173, on the practices of confiscating property from defeated parties; Livy 23.23.6.

been true for some of the *objets* he accumulated. Certainly the expectation of Catullus's interlocutors in c. 10 is that service on a governor's staff ought to bring emolument.[53]

Verres was particularly eager to be himself immortalized by art, but neither was this by any means a new practice with him. There had long been plenty of honorific statues and comparable artifices, in Rome and in many other places. Verres, extending the logic of such dedications, simply wanted his to be the most numerous. Verres' aestheticism may have been particularly acute because he was in a province, with virtually dictatorial powers. That is to say, he was in a place where the possibility for creating an individual personality through symbolic means was greater, absent countervailing pressure from other nobles—and away from a forum already crowded by many statues. But in this, too, Verres was not different from his fellows. The proper locus of Hellenized aestheticism was the country villa.[54] The awesome senate was not in Syracuse, and neither was it in Tusculum. In short, Verres' behavior testifies to the importance of aestheticism in displaying elite social status.

The rising importance of aestheticism took in not only the collection and display of artwork but also performative ability. In the late Republic a taste for performance seems to have veritably overtaken the noble classes. This hunger for the spotlight is a manifestation of the rising individualism, or more precisely the rising need among individuals of the nobler sort for public approval directed to them only, which seems to mark the period, and which is recalled in the epigraph to this section. It is not possible to discuss the causes of that rising individualism here; but the changing population of the city, with its effects on the composition of *contiones* and on public acclamations at *ludi,* the post-Gracchan willingness to exploit popular passions, the weakening of a sense of fair play, the attenuation of patronage ties, the exhaustion and concomitant need to refresh the grammar of self-presentation, all played some part. In any case the legislation that Caesar passed to keep nobles off the stage and out of the ring[55]—paradoxically enough, for a man who so deftly manipulated the semiotics of Roman culture to enhance his own personal status—combated one symptom of a broader trend, a trend very surprising in view of the usual social status of actors and gladiators.[56]

In this climate the social and political stock of wit and rhetorical ability,

53. Cf. 10.6–13.
54. Cf. Zanker 1988: 25–31 "The Villa and the Creation of Private Space"; VI.6.
55. See discussion in Levick 1983.
56. Cf. Barton 1993. Gunderson 1996: 136–42, writing mainly of the imperial period, argues that the distance between *nobilis* and *gladiator* is closer than it appears: *gladiatores* have

already valuable, appreciated, since they not only were established forms of competition but could turn a very bright spotlight on a social performer. Humor was, to be sure, an old Roman means of producing social solidarity, or political advantage, by ostracizing those who violated social norms.[57] But humor also came to be seen as a form of aestheticism: as we saw above, the "humorous" and the "artful" are closely connected concepts in Latin rhetoric. That sort of "artfulness" was virtually obligatory for political competitors in the late Republic.[58] The importance of humor is vouched for by Cicero's special efforts in *de Oratore*, discussed in chapter 6, to build a framework for controlling its volatile power. As for rhetorical ability, its stock had been on the rise since the introduction of the standing jury courts in 149 B.C. and the introduction of the secret ballot at trials before the people in 137 B.C. (Cic. *Brut.* 106). Rhetoric becomes thereafter ever more prominent as a means to create one's political persona. The Gracchi brothers wedded rhetorical skill to populist politics.[59] Both the spectacular oratorical ac-

---

the opportunity of publicly displaying respected martial qualities—an opportunity attractive to a class eager to be thought of as valorous and inured to constructing its own identity by means of public displays.

57. Certain of Catullus's epigrams preserve what is probably an old tradition of abuse poetry. The oral tradition that provided Cicero in the *de Oratore* with his knowledge of the witticisms of earlier ages may be presumed to have been even older than the remotest terminus of his examples. Cf. I.10 n.173.

58. See Corbeill 1996.

59. Cicero's Scaevola put the matter this way: "If I wished, I could cite more instances where eloquent men harmed the state than where they helped it; but one example may suffice. With the exception of you two, Crassus, I think the most eloquent men I have heard were the Sempronii brothers, Tiberius and Gaius. Their father, a shrewd and serious man, despite his complete lack of eloquence, was a great benefit to the state in various functions and particularly as censor: he secured the admission of freedmen to the tribes not with a grand and preened speech but with short comments and a nod of assent; and had he not done so, we would have long ago lost the state to which we now barely cling. But his sons, fluent orators *(diserti)* and fitted for speaking by every device of nature or education, inherited a state that, because of their father's vision and their grandfather's military prowess, was at the peak of its strength. And by means of eloquence, which you style the splendid governess of nations, they destroyed it" *ego uero si uelim et nostrae ciuitatis exemplis uti et aliarum, plura proferre possim detrimenta publicis rebus quam adiumenta, per homines eloquentissimos importata; sed ut reliqua praetermittam, omnium mihi uideor, exceptis, Crasse, uobis duobus, eloquentissimos audisse Ti. et C. Sempronios, quorum pater, homo prudens et grauis, haudquaquam eloquens, et saepe alias et maxime censor saluti rei publicae fuit: atque is non accurata quadam orationis copia, sed nutu atque uerbo libertinos in urbanas tribus transtulit, quod nisi fecisset, rem publicam, quam nunc uix tenemus, iam diu nullam haberemus. at uero eius filii diserti et omnibus uel naturae uel doctrinae praesidiis ad dicendum parati, cum ciuitatem uel paterno consilio uel auitis armis florentissimam accepissent, ista praeclara gubernatrice, ut ais, ciuitatum eloquentia rem publicam dissipauerunt (de Orat. 1.38).*

complishments of M. Crassus and the demagoguery of Saturninus must have encouraged imitation. The professionalizing of jurisprudence meant the law mattered less and presentation mattered more. Judicial legislation at the end of the second century "assured that [factional] rivalries would be more and more settled in the courts,"[60] requiring speech-making—and permitting grandstanding. Prosecutions of prominent figures catapulted prosecutors to prominence. Cicero made his name by crushing Verres.[61] By the late Republic rhetoric really was, more than before, a means to make oneself in Roman society. Caesar's famous funeral orations, in one of which he linked his aunt's maternal lineage to the kings and paternal lineage to the gods,[62] a precursor of his own apotheosis, and in the other praised his young wife, an unprecedented topic for such an oration,[63] were exercises in self-creation that perfectly exemplify what rhetoric had become.

As the center of gravity of our diagram shifted from (3) toward (2), as aestheticism became entrenched and obligatory, the language of social performance gained in weight, associated as it now was with a dominant social paradigm. That language now described values that were not merely acceptable but were expected and even demanded. Aestheticism, in that sense, must have become something like television presence in American politicians—something widely acknowledged as "not real" but something whose lack nonetheless poses a virtually insurmountable problem, as the recent example of Adm. Stockdale illustrated. Here, then, is a claim that will be central for the next three chapters: the new weightiness of aestheticism, and concomitantly of the language of social performance, accounts for the way the language is used in the late Republic. That weightiness explains the uses of the language of social performance to appropriate or repudiate that we saw in sections V.2 and V.3. To be sure, they represent old stances on the issue of aesthetic vs. social worth, but in speeches Cicero takes those stances almost exclusively in opposition to foreigners: the behaviors apt to be described by the language of social performance were now the common possession of the social elite and were rhetorically safe to dismiss or disparage only in the case of outsiders, who had no proper claim on them. How to present as reprehensible the tastes or behavior of fellow members of the elite that fit the rubrics of the language? In a philosophical text, in which the en-

60. Cf. Gruen 1968: 184.
61. Cf. Fantham 1997: 120–21.
62. *amitae meae Iuliae maternum genus ab regibus ortum, paternum cum diis inmortalibus coniunctum est etc.,* Suet. *Jul.* 6 = *ORF* 121.29.
63. Plut. *Caes.* 5.2–6, Suet. *Jul.* 6.

thralling character of aesthetic productions is described by *festiuus* and *uenustus,* Cicero can take a magisterial tone:

> You stand gaping before a painting of Aetion or a statue of Polyclitus. Forget about where you got it from and how you came to have it; when I see you gazing, wondering, exclaiming in admiration, I judge you a slave of every kind of foolishness. Isn't artwork delightful *(festiua)?* As well it should be; we have educated tastes ("eyes"), too. But their charm *(uenusta)* should function as trifles for boys and not shackles for men. What about L. Mummius? He scorned all of Corinth: what would he say if he saw one of you people handling a Corinthian pot with such covetousness? Would he think you an upstanding citizen or an industrious butler?[64]

> *(Parad.* 38).

The term "shackles" is an excellent, if uncharitable, metaphor for a dominant social paradigm.

In other texts, directed to a heterogeneous audience or less agonistic in tone, Cicero's task was more difficult. It is difficult to attack what the prevailing culture permits, even demands. Cicero followed three lines of attack. In one he tried to shorten the reach of such language by introducing powerful countervailing ideals. This is the strategy Cicero pursued in the examples treated in section V.4. Naevius's ability to speak *belle* or Verres' interest in *uenustus* pieces of artwork must have been sufficiently admirable that they could no longer be attacked as such. To try to countermand what was now de rigueur, Cicero had to step outside the circles where it was and to assume some kind of contrarian voice, whether self-righteous or, more typically, modest. The tonality of Cicero's self-exclusion is important to consider: it is often not quite, or not only, the gruff aloofness of the Cato who said *magna cura cibi, magna uirtutis incuria;* it is less "We need not bother with that" than "I'm afraid I don't get it." Cicero does not rebuke Horten-

---

64. *Aetionis tabula te stupidum detinet aut signum aliquod Polycleti. mitto, unde sustuleris, quo modo habeas; intuentem te, admirantem, clamores tollentem cum uideo, seruum esse ineptiarum omnium iudico. 'Nonne igitur sunt illa festiua?' Sunt (nam nos quoque oculos eruditos habemus); sed, obsecro te, ita uenusta habeantur ista, non ut uincla uirorum sint, sed ut oblectamenta puerorum. Quid enim censes? si L. Mummius aliquem istorum uideret matellionem Corinthium cupidissime tractantem, cum ipse totam Corinthum contempsisset, utrum illum ciuem excellentem an atriensem diligentem putaret?* With this passage cf. Hor. *Serm.* 2.7.95–101, where Horace's slave, Davus, lectures him on Stoic virtue, observing that Horace's own mooning over a *Pausiaca tabella* "a painting by Pausias" is no different from his, Davus's, wonderment at posters depicting gladiatorial contests.

sius for his meretricious artfulness; he depicts himself as afraid *(uereri)*. Of artwork he does not say that "it seems nice, not that I care," but that he is one of the *rudes*. He does not scorn Greek intellectuality altogether but allows it its excellences *(Flac. 9)*.

Cicero also responded in two other ways. In *de Oratore* Cicero tried to coopt the language of social performance, retooling it for his own purposes; that co-optation is the subject of chapter 6. Cicero's third response was to embed the language of social performance in contexts that showed off the worst side of the principles it espoused, as we see in the next section (V.6). What I would note here is that when language is handled in these three ways, that suggests that it was connected to a dominant paradigm or master trope in the cultural context that generated it. Consider a loose parallel. In contemporary American social discourse, the most coveted label is that of "victim," which ensures special attention to one's claims and forbearance of one's failings. Attempts to disable the trope of "victimhood" are typically made in exactly the three ways just described: one asserts one's own claim, however, tendentious, to that language ("But the lynch mob were themselves victims of an underprivileged upbringing . . ."); one demonizes it ("'I'm a victim' is another way of saying 'I'm lazy'!"); or one gingerly counterbalances it with other ideals ("It is true that the defendants were victims of racial discrimination, which like all good Americans I deplore, but society simply cannot function unless all citizens are held to equal standards of responsibility."). The handling of the language of social performance thus strongly suggests that it had become attached to a dominant paradigm in late Republican culture.

We may also observe something about the cultural effects of the shift of our diagram's center of gravity from (3) to (2). As the lay of the ideological terrain of aestheticism changed, there developed in consequence new "rules of engagement," so to speak, that that terrain demanded. Let us consider an example from Cicero's speech *de Domo sua* which uses *uenustus* for a 'deft' or 'clever' bit of humor (cf. III.4.2):

> You would have me cease my boasting, and you say my customary declarations about myself are intolerable. And wit that you are *(homo facetus),* you've been making the droll, clever remark *(sermo urbanus ac uenustus)* that I go around saying I am Jupiter and that my sister is Minerva. It would certainly be impudent of me to say I'm Jupiter, but it wouldn't be as stupid as saying Minerva is Jupiter's sister! At least I picked a virgin sister; your sister isn't one, thanks to you. Perhaps you

should use the name Jupiter yourself: you really *can* say your sister is your wife.[65]

(*Dom.* 92)

There are two bases for Clodius's mockery. For having squelched the Catilinarian conspiracy, Cicero may have claimed, or allowed himself to be called by, the epithet *urbis seruator* 'savior of the city,' which resembles cult titles of Jupiter;[66] and he certainly did adopt Minerva as a patroness.[67] Adoption of divine patrons is attested as a means of asserting political identity since King Numa, who consorted with the nymph Egeria. Scipio Africanus had been a more recent example, and the idea became fashionable among the noble classes.[68] Cicero depicted the Muse Urania addressing him in *de Consulatu suo,* substituting a symbol of creative power for the ancient connections to Olympians claimed by powerful clans.[69] Cicero's cultivation of Minerva was surely similar, a way of honoring wisdom personified. But such cultivations, as the case of Caesar shows, were not far from the outright assumption of divine roles.[70] This proximity gave Clodius the chance to style professed clientage as self-apotheosis. One thinks of past Polish president Lech Wałęsa's omnipresent lapel pin of *Matka Boska Częstochowska,* the famous Black Madonna of Częstochowa:[71] was he claiming protection or prerogative? In

---

65. *hic tu me etiam gloriari uetas: negas esse ferenda quae soleam de me praedicare, et homo facetus inducis etiam sermonem urbanum ac uenustum, me dicere solere esse me Iouem, eundemque dictitare Mineruam esse sororem meam. non tam insolens sum, quod Iouem esse me dico, quam ineruditus, quod Mineruam sororem Iouis esse existimo; sed tamen ego mihi sororem uirginem adscisco, tu sororem tuam uirginem esse non sisti. sed uide ne tu te soleas Iouem dicere, quod tu iure eandem sororem et uxorem appellare possis.*

66. The suggestion is Olivetus's; cf. Robert Nisbet 1939 ad loc.

67. Cf. καὶ τὸ μὲν ἄγαλμα τῆς Ἀθηνᾶς, ὃ πολὺν χρόνον ἔχων ἐπὶ τῆς οἰκίας ἱδρυμένον ἐτίμα διαφερόντως, εἰς Καπιτώλιον κομίσας ἀνέθηκεν ἐπιγράψας ''Αθηνᾳ 'Ρώμης φύλακι' κτλ. (Plut. *Cic.* 31.6).

68. Varro's *libri de familiis Troianis* connected the leading families of Rome to the heroes who landed with Aeneas, and thus often to the gods themselves. On Caesar's use of the gods, cf. n. 62.

69. E.g., *tu tamen anxiferas curas requiete relaxans, | quod patriae uacat, id studiis nobisque sacrasti* (*Cons.* 6.77–78).

70. With the acquiescence of the senate, his statue was placed in the temple of Quirinus; his chariot was set up opposite the temple of Jupiter; a temple was erected to his Clemency; the Julian Luperci, a priestly college, were established; and a *flamen* was appointed at least in his honor if not for his worship outright; cf. Suet. *Caes.* 76.

71. This icon, revered as an image of the Queen of Poland, was moved by Prince Władysław to the monastery of Jasna Góra in 1384, where it is still housed.

the case of Cicero, who appeared to many of his contemporaries as vain, the charge of self-apotheosis was likely to stick.[72] Clodius may have made the original joke with the intention of implying incest, a typical insult,[73]— though a risky one for Clodius to make, for obvious reasons.[74] That implication may well have induced Cicero to take the somewhat pedantic defense of pressing the distinction between Zeus and Hera on the one hand and Jupiter and Minerva on the other.

In any case, what is important about Clodius's humor in this passage is that it forces Cicero to reply to it on its own terms. If Clodius waggishly attacked Cicero, a waggish reply was owed. Cicero could not "take the high road"; he obviously felt he had no choice except to rise to Clodius's bait, and he does his best. Scuttlebutt was circulating, Cicero was suffering for it, and something had to be done. Much the same is true for the witticisms of Torquatus and Antony discussed above (V.4). Cicero's tack there is, to be sure, different, sincere, and even cloying, but Cicero had nonetheless to respond. What we have seen about humor, mutatis mutandis, is true about other kinds of aestheticism: aestheticism in the late Republic could force a reply on its own terms. If one person expressed his cultural identity by accumulating artwork, then his competitors had to do so too.[75] Verres' rapacity is no more than the determination to be the best competitor in this way. The explosion of villa building in the 90s, under the dominate of Sulla, suggests that aestheticism had become a means of elite competition when more traditional venues were closed, and it surely retained this function even when those venues opened up again. Neither could rhetorical prowess be ignored. The expectation that such prowess should be matched by equal prowess underlies Cicero's partly apologetic tone in explaining Quinctius's rhetorical ineptitude (*Quinct.* 93) and his own diffidence in competing against Hortensius (*Quinct.* 77). Cicero himself was forced to respond to the "elegant"

72. Cf. πολλοῖς δ' ἐπίφθονον ἑαυτὸν ἐποίησεν ἀπ' οὐδενὸς ἔργου πονηροῦ, τῷ δ' ἐπαινεῖν ἀεὶ καὶ μεγαλύνειν αὐτὸς ἑαυτὸν ὑπὸ πολλῶν δυσχεραινόμενος (Plut. *Cic.* 24.1).

73. Cf. [Sal.] *Cic.* 1.2. *uxor sacrilega ac periuriis delibuta, filia matris paelex, tibi iucundior atque obsequentior quam parenti par est.*

74. In another notable instance an opponent's attack on Cicero backfired: Verres, whose young son was reputed not to have guarded his virtue, reproved Cicero for his μαλακία 'softness,' to which Cicero replied τοῖς υἱοῖς ἐντὸς θυρῶν δεῖ λοιδορεῖσθαι "If you're going to sling mud, sling it on the children in your own house" (Plut. *Cic.* 7.7).

75. In fact sumptuary legislation (above, I.2) may be an early sign of such a development, if it be understood as a kind of "Geneva Convention" of dining practice, prescribing rules and guidelines for what would otherwise be competition à outrance.

presentation of L. Cassius, the *subscriptor* or 'junior counsel' to M. Juventius Laterensis in the prosecution of Cn. Plancius, whom Cicero defended:

> And since your speech was entirely elegant *(perelegans)* and finely calibrated *(persubtilis)*, worthy of a Roman knight's energy and decency alike, and since the jurors listening to you accorded high regard to your talent and culture, I will respond to the points you raised, many of which considered myself; the points you may have scored against me nonetheless brought me a certain pleasure.[76]
>
> (*Planc.* 58)

Cicero here is making a slightly different maneuver from those we have seen: he tries to bend to his own advantage the fact that an *elegans* presentation demanded a countervailing one by seeming to answer Cassius's points not because they were cogent or clever or compelling, as, to judge by the subsequent paragraphs, they evidently were, but because he owes it to the cultured manner of Cassius's presentation, which he affects to regard patronizingly.

One may say that aestheticism, in the broadest sense, is a dominant paradigm of the late Republic: one was *obligated* to conduct oneself publicly with stylishness and grace; one's opponents could not ignore such gestures and were expected to reply in kind. That made aestheticism a very attractive model indeed and made very attractive social labels out of the language of social performance. Hence Catullus's adoption of the language of social performance to describe his poetic ideals, explored below (VII.4); and hence the evident use of the language by the wickedly, or even criminally, stylish, treated in the next section.

### V.6. Inside or Outside? The Struggle for the Control of the Approbative Vocabulary

In section V.5 I suggested that the three ways the language of social performance is disabled by Cicero—by appropriating it, by counterbalancing it gingerly, and by trying to bring out its bad side—make clear the connection of the language to a dominant social paradigm or master trope. The first strategy, as I have mentioned, is not one Cicero pursues in his speeches, taking it up only in normative portions of his rhetorica (ch. 6 below). The

---

76. *et quoniam tua fuit perelegans et persubtilis oratio, digna equitis Romani uel studio uel pudore, quoniamque sic ab his es auditus ut magnus honos et ingenio et humanitati tuae tribueretur, respondebo ad ea quae dixisti, quae pleraque de ipso me fuerunt; in quibus ipsi aculei, si quos habuisti in me reprehendendo, tamen mihi non ingrati acciderunt.* For the pairing of *elegan(s)* and *subtil(is)*, cf. III.6 n.88.

other two strategies Cicero does pursue in his speeches; one we have already examined, wherein Cicero counterbalances the values of the language of social performance by presenting himself as an outsider (V.5). This section considers examples of the third strategy. In them the programmatic value of the newly weighty language of social performance can be felt keenly: the attacked parties seem to have been using the language for themselves.

Two passages use *lepid(us)* for 'attractive performances.' In one Cicero ridicules the young nobles attracted to the revolutionary designs of Catiline:

> In that crowd you'll find every gambler, everyone who cheats on his wife, everyone shameless and unchaste. These fine *(lepidus)* pretty *(delicatus)* boys have learned much: not only how to love—and be loved—and how to dance and sing, but also how to brandish a knife and spike things with poison. Know this: if they do not go away, if they are not done away with, even if Catiline is, this state will be nothing but a breeding ground for more Catilines.[77]
>
> (*Catil.* 2.23)

A second passage applies *lepid(us)*, along with *uenust(us)*, to Verres. Verres summoned a certain Servilius to Lilybaeum to answer a charge, lodged by a slave, that he had stolen something from a temple of Venus. On his arrival Servilius found no prosecutor but was challenged by a lictor of Verres to stipulate, by way of *sponsio*, a kind of legal wager, that Verres was not a thief. Servilius made the *sponsio*, but under protest, since if he lost the *sponsio*, he would probably be convicted on the capital charge of *maiestas*, or "treason," for having charged Verres falsely; thus in being forced to make the *sponsio* Servilius was in effect being tried on a capital charge without an accuser.[78] That protest earned him a fatal beating at the hands of Verres' lictors. Verres confiscated Servilius's property, and "with the profits from Servilius's goods, that man of Venus, awash with every grace *(lepos)* and charm *(uenustas)*, placed a silver Cupid in the temple of Venus" (*Ver.* 2.5.142).[79]

In both instances *lep(idus)* refers to 'attractive performances' (I.9). The "fine pretty boys" are expert in singing and dancing; one is reminded of Scipio Aemilianus's dancing youths (*ORF* 21.30, II.2) and of Horace's

---

77. *in his gregibus omnes aleatores, omnes adulteri, omnes impuri impudicique uersantur. hi pueri tam lepidi ac delicati non solum amare et amari neque saltare et cantare sed etiam sicas uibrare et spargere uenena didicerunt. qui nisi exeunt, nisi pereunt, etiam si Catilina perierit, scitote hoc in re publica seminarium Catilinarum futurum.*

78. Cf. Greenwood 1953: 622.

79. *iste . . . homo Venerius, adfluens omni lepore ac uenustate, de bonis illius in aede Veneris argenteum Cupidinem posuit.*

dancer *Lepos* (*Serm.* 2.6.72, I.9). As for Verres, doubtless he could claim the statue was recompense to the goddess whose temple was supposedly violated; but by naming Verres *homo Venerius,* Cicero depicts him as someone ostentatiously dedicating a statue to his patroness, a self-conscious and pregnant gesture. The erotic sense of *uenustas,* as demonstrated below, is probably primary here, but many of its other overtones, from 'charming' (like Philodemus) to 'clever,' are consonant with the behavior of someone putting himself on display.

In both cases Cicero tries to bring out the bad side of the taste for performance that *lep(idus)* certainly, and *uenust(us)* probably, describes. In the first *Catilinarian* Cicero is suggesting that the young nobles' fondness for the display of social identity by artful skills (cf. *didicerunt* "they have learned") has dulled their moral sense and encouraged them to apply the standards of convivial performance to spheres where it does not belong. They cannot distinguish between playing at being a dancing slave, or even a pathic Alcibiades—decadent, but pedigreed, roles—and playing the bodkinned hooligans or venomous stepmothers of farce. All is play to them. Verres exhibits a comparable sort of impropriety. Having come into Servilius's property by way of chicanery, bullying, and murder, he does not even have the decency to keep the money quietly but makes an evidently prominent public dedication. The performance was perhaps even more sinister than Cicero seems to acknowledge. The slave who brought the original charge, and who evidently never materialized at the trial, was a temple slave—at the temple of Venus.[80] Surely there never was such a slave. The "slave of Venus," I suggest, was Verres himself; his ruse, and his dedication, display the oddly humorous cruelty of Batman's nemesis the Joker.[81]

To his demonstration of the danger of the taste for performance Cicero adds an erotic element. In the presence of *Venerius,* and with reference to a dedication to a goddess of sensuality of an image of her son, a god of sensuality, *uenustas* recovers its erotic resonances, which still survived (cf. VII.2). The erotic resonances of *lep(idus),* so common in Plautus, also survived (cf. VII.8 n. 126), and they, too, may be brought to the fore in reference to Verres. *Lep(idus)* certainly has erotic overtones in its application to the *lepidi pueri* of *Catil.* 2.23: not only are they engaged in the erotic behavior in which *convivia* might issue—"loving and being loved"—but they are also described as *delicatus* 'delicate, pampered, luxurious,' a sensual word.

---

80. *hominem iubet Lilybaeum uadimonium Venerio seruo promittere, Ver.* 2.5.141.

81. By which I mean the Joker not of Cesar Romero but of Jack Nicholson, and more particularly of the graphic novels, as in, e.g., Moore and Bolland 1989.

Indeed we have seen the eroticizing of the language of social performance in some other passages already. *Delicatus* is also applied to Philodemus's epigrams (*Pis.* 70). To produce delicate verses could be taken as a sign of pathic homosexuality, as evident in Catull. c. 16 (VII.7). As a purveyor of an aestheticism that is *elegans, uenustus,* and the rest, Philodemus, as we saw, opened himself up to charges of being *impurus,* which is a sexually charged term.[82] Sex. Naevius, who had the ability *belle dicere,* also had "a home closed to shame and propriety, and laid wide open to lust and desires" (*Quinct.* 93, V.4). The coterie of slave boys that surrounded the wicked Chrysogonus, expert in "every pleasure *(deliciae)* and every art *(ars),*" is described as having been "gathered from the most elegant *(elegantissimus)* households" (*S. Rosc.* 120).[83] The description of the slave boys with the diminutive *pueruli* and their expertise in *deliciae* 'pleasures, delights' gives them an erotic charge, intended in this passage to discredit the claim that two missing slave workmen are with Chrysogonus; his tastes are more delicate.

Cicero obviously means the eroticism of our passages to be taken negatively. The Romans on the whole saw sex in terms of power relationships, with the active masculine role as the dominant one.[84] Catullus's insult of C. Memmius as *irrumator,* 'oral rapist,' casts power in terms of sex, like AmE "fuck" or "prick."[85] But both Verres and the *lepidi pueri* seem to valorize any openly erotic persona, whether a dominant, masculine one or not. Verres is a *homo Venerius,* a man wholly given over to Venus and, indeed, a sexual libertine. The Catilinarian youth are so taken with conviviality that they take both active and passive sexual roles. From Cicero's point of view, eroticism and aestheticism are of a piece: both involve being controlled by, and not controlling, a symbolic means of articulating power. To delight in love, like delighting in a bronze statuette, is, from one point of view, to confuse the end with the means. The introduction of a pejorative element of eroticism in these examples thus fits perfectly with Cicero's ideological stance.

The paradox of Cicero's attack is that the very qualities he is trying to suggest were dangerous—a taste for performance and eroticism—were doubtless cultivated by the parties in question, qualities willingly assumed

82. Cf. *coniugem infidamque, pathicam familiam, inpuram domum* "and a . . . and faithless wife, a lustful family, a tainted house" (Lucil. 680M, 639W, 633K).

83. *ita credo; litteris eorum et urbanitate Chrysogonus ducitur ut inter suos omnium deliciarum atque omnium artium puerulos ex tot elegantissimis familiis lectos uelit hos uersari, homines paene operarios, ex Amerina disciplina patris familiae rusticani.*

84. The Roman construction of sexuality, of which the aggressive male role is the ideal, is treated by Richlin 1992. For Cicero's use of sexual insinuations as invective, cf. ibid.: 96–104.

85. On *irrumare* cf. VII.7 nn. 109, 113.

and paraded gladly, neither compulsive nor furtive. An anecdote about Hortensius is telling:

> When L. Torquatus, a man with a rather uncultured and sour *(infesti-uus)* cast of mind, was being interrogated in a case involving Sulla, he asserted with grim bitterness in front of the jury that Hortensius was not an actor but a mime dancer, and he called him "Dionysia" after the name of a well-known dancer. Hortensius, in a low soft voice, replied, "Dionysia! For my part I had rather be Dionysia than what you are, Torquatus—*étranger à les Muses, à Aphrodite, à Dionysos* (ἄμουσος, ἀναφρόδιτος, ἀπροσδιόνυσος)."[86]

(*ORF* 92.39 = Gel. 1.5.3)

Attacked for his stylish self-presentation and likened to a dancer—his gestures were indeed notable[87]—not only does Hortensius respond that eroticized artfulness is preferable to artlessness, but he responds in Greek, a language rare in the Roman Forum, but the primary vehicle of the idea of artfulness into Roman culture. Julius Caesar also actively cultivated a dashing androgynous persona. Even Pompey scratched his head with one finger, a gesture considered effeminate, to avoid disturbing his elegant coiffure.[88] Verres and the *pueri lepidi* were no aberrancies.[89] Doubtless *lep(idus)* and *uenust(us)* are exactly the words such parties used for themselves. Indeed *elegans* was exactly the word evidently cultivated by lovers of beaux arts: Cic-

86. *sed cum L. Torquatus, subagresti homo ingenio et infestiuo, grauius acerbiusque apud consilium iudicum, cum de causa Sullae quaereretur, non iam histrionem eum esse diceret, sed gesticulariam Dionysiamque eum notissimae saltatriculae nomine appellaret, tum uoce molli atque demissa Hortensius 'Dionysia,' inquit 'Dionysia malo equidem esse quam quod tu, Torquate,* ἄμουσος, ἀναφρόδιτος, ἀπροσδιόνυσος.' Edwards 1993: 97 remarks: "A soft voice, a rare one, that spoke for sophistication, philhellenism and even the feminine. This may be as close as a Roman text ever comes to suggesting virility need not be the ultimate virtue."

87. In a lost book of *de Republica*, Cicero had slighted the gesture of some actor, whom Atticus took to be Hortensius: οὐκ ἔλαθέ σε *illud de gestu histrionis? tu sceleste suspicaris, ego* ἀφελῶς *scripsi (Att.* 6.1.8), "You say you got the point about the actor's gesture I mentioned? You have a wickedly suspicious mind, I wrote that innocently." Cicero did find Hortensius's gestures too histrionic: *uox canora et suauis, motus et gestus etiam plus artis habebat quam erat oratori satis (Brut.* 303); for more on Hortensius's gestures, see Gel. 1.5.2–3.

88. Cf. VIII.2. To a certain extent charges of effeminacy are stereotyped, but see V.6 n.89. On the gesture of scratching one's head with a single finger, cf. Edwards 1993: 63–64 with refs. The charge is levied against Pompey by Clodius (Plut. *Pomp.* 48.7) and in an epigram of L. Licinius Calvus (*Magnus, quem metuunt omnes, digito caput uno | scalpit. quid credas hunc sibi uelle? uirum,* Baehrens, *Poetae Latini Minores* vol. 6.18).

89. "I have argued that the effeminate banqueter is not simply a literary fiction, a composite figure patched together from the groundless anxieties of the orator's audience. Instead I presume that invective's efficacy requires at least some degree of correlation between the charges raised publicly and the realities of contemporary society," Corbeill 1996: 154.

ero lumps Verres, angrily, with "those who like to be called elegant" *(istos qui elegantis dici uolunt).*[90] Not only had such words long since described the attractive quality of the kinds of social actions or characters they embraced, but with the increase in weight, as I have described it, of category (2), such language created prerogative: if *lepos* was so important now, and a particular act was *lepidus,* how could it be wrong? Cicero's pejorative use of *lep(idus)* and *uenust(us)* in these passages is an attempt to bring out the negative side of a self-imposed label. In that his use reflects a common feature of political speech: how often a conservative venomously spits out "liberal," the very word his opponent proudly uses for himself.

It is worth adding here another example of a "sympathetic" use of an adjective, in which opponents agree on what it denotes and disagree on its larger social construction. *Suauis* has a certain kinship to the language of social performance, describing a pleasurable quality that is ancillary to real character in much the same way as the language of social performance originally described a style that supported substance (cf. IV.6). In an attack of Cicero against L. Calpurnius Piso, *suauis* works in the same way as the instances of *lep(idus)* and *uenust(us)* we just saw. Piso, while proconsul of Macedonia, had slipped out of town without paying a contingent of soldiers at Dyrrachium what they were owed. The soldiers surrounded with bonfires the house they thought he was still in. At that point,

> roused by this threat, the Dyrrachini declared that the generalissimo had fled by night, wearing sandals.[91] The soldiers then went to the

90. *tu uidelicet solus uasis Corinthiis delectaris, tu illius aeris temperationem, tu operum liniamenta sollertissime perspicis! haec Scipio ille non intellegebat, homo doctissimus atque humanissimus: tu sine ulla bona arte, sine humanitate, sine ingenio, sine litteris, intellegis et iudicas! uide ne ille non solum temperantia sed etiam intellegentia te atque istos qui se elegantis dici uolunt uicerit. nam quia quam pulchra essent intellegebat, idcirco existimabat ea non ad hominum luxuriem, sed ad ornatum fanorum atque oppidorum esse facta,* †*ut posteris nostris monumenta religiosa esse uideantur* † "Yes, you're the only one who enjoys Corinthian ware, you're the only one who has a keen eye for the composition of the bronze and the lines of the work! Scipio had no sense for these matters, despite his learning and culture; but you do, and you judge them well, despite your lack of respectable pursuits (cf. *Cael.* 77), of culture, of talent, and of literature! You may be sure that he surpassed you, and those who style themselves 'elegant,' not only in moderation but also in perceptiveness: it was precisely because he perceived those items were beautiful that he thought they were designed not for human extravagance but for the adornment of shrines and cities, †so that they may seem† to be religious monuments for our descendants†" (*Ver.* 2.4.98).

91. "Wearing Greek sandals (κρηπῖδες), suitable for a phil-Hellene, unseemly for a proconsul" (Nisbet 1975 ad 92, where see note); cf. *consularis homo soccos habuit et pallium* (*Rab. Post.* 10). Philhellenism could be constructed differently: L. Scipio Asiagenus had a statue of himself in these sandals, and also a Greek cloak *(chlamys),* erected on the Capitol (Cic. *Rab. Perd.* 27). On Asiagemus, cf. I.2 n. 3, II.2.

statue in his image, which he had wanted to be erected in a frequented place to keep alive the memory of so fine *(suauissimus)* a man, and they cast the statue down, struck at it, broke it into small pieces, and scattered them.[92]

(*Pis.* 93)

*Suauissimus* here represents Piso's, probably Epicurean, vision of himself. *Suauis* could render the Epicurean keyword ἡδύς.[93] Cicero had made much of Piso's Epicureanism earlier in the speech (§§63–67) and begins the tale of these closing events with a comparison of Piso to another Epicurean, T. Albucius (§92). Cicero represents Piso as having used it to describe his own indulgent, Hellenized life. The same may be true of the inscriptional phrases *quoat uixit uixit suauiter* (*CIL* 6.6548.1) and *uix(it) a(nnis) l suauissume* (35722.5), which are perhaps tombstones of Epicureans; the combination *uiuere suauiter* suggests ἡδέως ζῆν, an Epicurean phrase.[94] Piso might have legitimately taken pride in such aestheticism as he may have cultivated— legitimately, that is, by the standards of sympathetic peers. Political opponents created higher (or different) standards. Furthermore, *suauis,* as discussed above, was also an important word for describing the pleasures of aristocratic intercourse and could have been used by Piso of himself in all sincerity. As in the examples of this section that feature the language of social performance proper, Cicero here tries to set aestheticism, or rather, in this case, Hellenism, in a light that shows it poorly.

All these elements—eroticism, aestheticism, and a struggle over language—come together in two passages of spirited invective. In one Cicero attacks his nemesis Clodius:

> It's no surprise that he thinks we're rubes *(rusticus),* since we can't wear a sleeved tunic and a headband and purple sashes. No, you alone are genial *(festiuus)* and discriminating *(elegans)* and urbane *(urbanus)!* Yes, since you're the one who looks good in women's clothes, or when you walk like a lute girl *(psaltria).* After all you can womanize your face, heighten your voice, and smooth your body.[95]

(*in P. Clodium et Curionem,* fr. 22)

92. *quo metu commoti Dyrrachini profugisse noctu crepidatum imperatorem indicauerunt. illi autem statuam istius persimilem, quam stare celeberrimo in loco uoluerat ne suauissimi hominis memoria moreretur, deturbant, adfligunt, comminuunt, dissipant.*

93. Cf. Cic. *Fin.* 1.37, 2.13, and signally Lucr. 2.1, 2.4, 2.5.

94. Plutarch composed an essay οὐδ' ἡδέως ζῆν ἐστιν κατ' Ἐπίκουρον (1086C ff.).

95. *nam rusticos ei nos uideri minus est mirandum, qui manicatam tunicam et mitram et purpureas fascias habere non possumus. tu uero festiuus, tu elegans, tu solus urbanus, quem decet muliebris ornatus, quem incessus psaltriae, qui effeminare uultum, attenuare uocem, leuare corpus potes.* Cf. also frr. 23–24. On the reading *leuare* for the transmitted *laeuare* see Puccioni 1960: 120–21.

Plainly Clodius cultivated a personal style that he is likely to have described as *festiuus, elegans,* and *urbanus,* as well he might have. Cicero inflates the agonistic aspect of such aestheticism into insult, as if Clodius's style were meant to criticize everyone as uncultured. (The same polarizing of aestheticism we saw above, *Ver.* 2.4.4.) Furthermore, this fashion sense is undercut by an allusion to Clodius's disguise as a woman in the *Bona Dea* affair,[96] which gives Cicero the opportunity to impute sexual passivity to Clodius. Clodius was representing his own actions to himself and others as *festiuitas* and *urbanitas,* precisely because those were acceptable, indeed very powerful, social ideals.

An even more striking passage is the peroration of the *pro Caelio,* with its description of Clodia's retinue:

> They can be as witty *(facetus)* and clever *(dicax)* as they wish at parties, and even fluent from time to time in their cups; but the forum is one thing and the couch quite another. The courtroom and the bedroom don't work the same way. An audience of judges is not an audience of revelers. The light of the sun is much different from the light of lamps. We will accordingly cast aside all their prettinesses *(deliciae)* and trivialities *(ineptiae)* if they come forward. But let them hear what I say: let them expend their energies another way, seek favor somewhere else; let them vaunt themselves in other arenas, let their delicacy *(uenustas)* flourish in that woman's house, let indulgence rule them, let them cling and grovel and fawn: but the life and fortunes of an innocent man they must spare.[97]
>
> *(Cael.* 67)

The behavior of Clodia's retinue is described by the language of social performance *(facetus, uenustas)* and similar terms *(dicax, deliciae, ineptiae).* This remarkable, almost poetic passage has many of the ideological characteristics with which we are familiar. Cicero presents himself as the outsider, a stranger to Clodian parties and the ways of "revelers." He counterposes their behavior to real social worth, contrasting the natural light of the sun, under which justice is resplendent, to the false light of lamps, whereby flourishes vacuous refinement. For Clodia's retinue their aestheticism is not a trifle but a shackle: they are "ruled by their indulgences" *(sumptibus domi-*

---

96. Cf. Crawford 1994: 233–39.

97. *quam uolent in conuiuiis faceti, dicaces, non numquam etiam ad uinum diserti sint, alia fori uis est, alia triclini, alia subselliorum ratio, alia lectorum; non idem iudicium comissatorumque conspectus; lux denique longe alia est solis, alia lychnorum. quam ob rem excutiemus omnis istorum delicias, omnis ineptias, si prodierint. sed me audiant, nauent aliam operam, aliam ineant gratiam, in aliis rebus se ostentent, uigeant apud istam mulierem uenustate, dominentur sumptibus, haereant, iaceant, deseruiant: capiti uero innocentis fortunisque parcant.*

*nari).* These men disregard their sexual passivity, serving *(deseruire)* and grov-
eling *(iacere)* before a woman, an image which recalls that of the *imperatrix*
'dame commander' or 'generalissima' *(Cael.* 67).

Nonetheless this passage contains the clear implication that their aesthetic behavior represents a threat. "We will cast aside their prettinesses"
etc. is a preemptive strike against what were, or would be, entirely elegant
attacks against Caelius, delivered in the latest fashion and with great style.
*Facetus, dicax,* and *uenustas* are the labels these men use to justify their behavior, but Cicero tries to bring out the negative side of that coin by assigning it to parties *(conuiuia),* couches *(lecti),* and Clodia's house *(apud istam
mulierem),* previously depicted as a den of iniquity. These labels must indeed
have described something almost irresistably attractive to many contemporary Romans, or else Cicero would not have tried to push back against it.
Rhetorical posturing though this may be, it indicates, to be sure, the contours of contemporary expectations; and in Cicero's stance there is an indication of the dominance of the paradigm of aestheticism in the late Roman
republic, and of the linguistic strategies of self-representation by which that
paradigm was expressed.

## V.7. The Fragile Power of the Language of Social Performance

The passages examined so far dispose of the bulk of the instances of the language of social performance in Cicero's speeches. Those instances can be
characterized as "negative": in them the language of social performance is
associated with values that Cicero repudiates or struggles against. We may
close with an examination of those few passages where Cicero uses the language of social performance positively.

The positive uses, like the negative, fall into two types: those involving
foreigners, and those involving Romans. Cicero's *de Prouinciis consularibus*
contains the one example of the former type. As a part of his praise of Caesar Cicero constructs an *expeditio (Rhet. Her.* 4.40) to show that Caesar must
be remaining in Gaul out of a sense of duty to the state; for Rome would
welcome him gladly and Gaul can hold no attractions for him. *Lepos* appears as part of the last argument:

> What other reason keeps Caesar in the province except wanting to
> hand over to the state fully completed the tasks he has largely finished
> already? What else could keep him there? The loveliness of the place?
> The beauty of its cities? The culture *(humanitas)* and charm *(lepos)* of
> those people and nations? The desire for victory and furthering the
> bounds of empire? The terrain of Gaul is very harsh; its towns are very

coarse; its peoples are very brutish; it is already the scene of many important victories; and one can hardly get farther from the Ocean than
there.[98]

(*Prov.* 29)

Skirting the real reasons Caesar was staying in Gaul—a desire to maintain
his *imperium* as defense against prosecution—Cicero holds up as foil for
Caesar's purported dutifulness the other possible motives a Roman noble
might have, glory and pleasure. *Lepos* (paired, as often, with *humanitas;* see
VI.3 n.31) describes the pleasures of sophisticated interaction and performs
the same task as in *Flac.* 9 (V.4), to exclude "us" from "them": only now the
sophisticated Romans are inside the circle and the brutish *(immanis)* Gauls
outside. Even in this relatively straightforward, humorous passage the exclusionary force of the language of social performance is plainly present.
On the other hand, since this passage enumerates discarded possibilities, the
ideological volatility of *lepos* is not something Cicero needs to control: he
can leave undefined the relative proportions Caesar might assign to duty and
pleasure if there *were* pleasure to be had. Just as when the language of social
performance describes qualities imputed to foreigners with condescension
(V.2) or hostility (V.3), so here when it is used of a quality possessed by Romans and not by foreigners, there is little ideological complexity.

As do the negative uses of the language of social performance, the positive uses have more complex ideological resonances when the parties are all
Romans struggling over the hierarchy of values. In the *pro Murena* Cicero
ridicules the juristic expertise of Sulpicius Rufus, one of the prosecutors,
suggesting that heavily periphrastic "legalese" had its origins in the revenge
of patricians for the publication of the calendar:

> And so, since they were worried that common knowledge of the cal-
> endar would permit lawsuits without their control, in a fit of pique
> they composed certain formulae in order to stay involved in every
> case. It would have been perfectly fine *(bellissime)* to say, "The Sabine
> farm is mine," "No it's mine," then have a verdict. That they didn't
> want. Now it's "The farm that is located in the field known as the
> Sabine." Enough words there! And how does the rest go? "I state that

98. *nam ipse Caesar quid est cur in prouincia commorari uelit, nisi ut ea quae per eum adfecta sunt
perfecta rei publicae tradat? amoenitas eum credo locorum, urbium pulcritudo, hominum nationumque
illarum humanitas et lepos, uictoriae cupiditas, finium imperi propagatio retinet. quid illis terris asperius, quid incultius oppidis, quid nationibus immanius, quid porro tot uictoriis praestabilius, quid
Oceano longius inueniri potest?*

that field is mine by the right of the Quirites." And then? "Thus I thee
summon from the courtroom to the property to contest the issue."[99]

(*Mur.* 26)

*Bellissime* is more than a mere colloquial outburst.[100] Rather, attractiveness
of expression, which *bellus* often labels (III.5), is being advanced as the correct standard for judging speech. So obscure and tortured are lawyerly *legis
actiones*—Gaius, a jurist of the first century A.D., attributes to their framers
"excessive subtlety" (*nimia subtilitas, Inst.* 4.30)—that Cicero represents even
ordinary speech counting as *bellus*. The subgroup which *bellus* commonly
circumscribes expands to include everyone in the world except lawyers.
The jest is possible because jurisprudence had become increasingly profes-
sionalized and separated from forensic patronage. But the small verbal stroke
jibes well with the strategy of this section of the speech, which is to depict
legal expertise as "paltry" (*res . . . paruae,* 25) and without "status" or "influence" (*dignitas, gratia,* 28). Indeed one overall strategy of the speech is to
illustrate the inadequacy of the narrow legalism embodied in Sulpicius and
the other chief prosecutor, Cato.[101] Their rectitude, like the rectitude of
Herennius (*Cael.* 25, below), may be literally accurate, but it falls short of
exactly that kind of shared sensibility that *bellus* commonly expresses.

*Elegans* is used to represent the shared taste of the social elite in Cicero's
mendacious attack on the crude taste of Piso:

> At Piso's there's nothing fine *(lautum),* nothing elegant *(elegans),* noth-
> ing choice *(exquisitum);* I must complement my opponent: he limits his
> extravagance to sexual indulgences. Embossed work? None. The cups?
> Enormous—and from Placentia, at that (he doesn't want it to look like
> he's slighting his countrymen). His table is arranged not with mussels
> or fish, but with meat—a lot of it, and that a bit high. The service is
> provided by slaves in dirty clothes, some of them old men; the cook
> is also the steward; he doesn't have his own baker or wine cellar: he
> buys bread from the street-seller and wine from the cask. There are

99. *itaque irati illi, quod sunt ueriti ne dierum ratione peruolgata et cognita sine sua opera lege agi
posset, uerba quaedam composuerunt ut omnibus in rebus ipsi interessent. cum hoc fieri bellissime posset:* "Fundus Sabinus meus est." "Immo meus," *deinde iudicium, noluerunt.* "FVNDVS" *inquit* "QVI
EST IN AGRO QVI SABINVS VOCATVR." *satis uerbose; cedo quid postea?* "EVM EGO EX IVRE QVIRI-
TIVM MEVM ESSE AIO." *quid tum?* "INDE IBI EGO TE EX IVRE MANVM CONSERTVM VOCO."

100. "Conversational," Hietland 1936: 53; "umgangsprachlich[ . . . ]," Adamietz 1989:
138.

101. On the prosecutors, see Adamietz 1989: 4–12; on Cicero's rhetorical strategies, see
Craig 1986 and Leff 1998.

five Greeks to a couch, and he reclines by himself; they drink until
they have to go straight to the barrel.

(*Pis.* 67)

In fact Piso's crudities have a pedigree: having failed to keep up with the
times, he preserves the old table manners of the ancients.[102] Cicero's short
travesty of antique parsimony begins with a remarkable caveat:

> Don't think for a moment that that is the sort of luxury that he prac-
> tices: although every kind of luxury is repugnant and shameful, there
> is, after all, a sort more worthy of a person of free and noble station.[103]

(*Pis.* 67)

The slipperiness of the cultural category that the language of social performance standardly represented could not be more poignantly expressed. To
refer again to our diagram (V.1), the crudity of Piso's table inhabits the stable
ground of (3), and to attack it requires acknowledging, even in a short, humorous set-piece, the solid moral principles that also belong there. A comparable passage with *suauitas,* a word that, as we have seen, has certain re-
semblances to the language of social performance proper, should be included
here. M. Caelius had been attacked for his dissolute behavior by L. Herennius before the *quaestio de ui,* the standing jury court that prosecuted cases
of political violence.[104] Cicero, in his defense speech, *pro Caelio,* was put in
the difficult position of having to speak against a doubtless impeccably in-
dicted character. His defense involves *suauitas:*

> Herennius spoke at length about extravagance *(luxuries),* about lust *(li-*
> *bido),* about the sins of youth *(uitia iuuentutis),* about character *(mores).*
> A man who usually is mild *(mitis)* and partakes with great delight in the
> pleasant and civilized culture *(in hac suauitate humanitatis)* in which vir-

---

102. According to Horace, *rancidum aprum antiqui laudabant* "the ancients thought highly
of rancid boar" (*Serm.* 2.2.89). For pretty boys and cooks as signs of corruption, cf. I.2 nn. 11
through 13. See also the discussion in Edwards 1993: 200–202.

103. *luxuriem autem nolite in isto hanc cogitare: est enim quaedam, quamquam omnis est uitiosa
atque turpis, tamen ingenuo ac libero dignior. nihil apud hunc lautum, nihil elegans, nihil exquisitum;
laudabo inimicum, ne magno opere quidem quicquam praeter libidines sumptuosum. toreuma nullum,
maximi calices, et ei, ne contemnere suos uideatur, Placentini; exstructa mensa non conchyliis aut pis-
cibus, sed multa carne subrancida. serui sordidati ministrant, non nulli etiam senes; idem coquus, idem
atriensis; pistor domi nullus, nulla cella; panis et uinum a propola et de cupa; Graeci stipati quini in
lectulis, saepe plures; ipse solus; bibitur usque eo dum de dolio ministretur.*

104. For the circumstances of the case, see the commentary of Austin 1960, Wiseman
1985: 54–91, Craig 1989: 314–16; for bibliography, see Classen 1973, Stroh 1975, Craig
1989. The aspects of the speech of interest to my argument are handled by Gotoff 1986.

tually all of us find enjoyment became, for this case, a sort of Dutch uncle,[105] a censor, a schoolmaster;[106] he upbraided M. Caelius as no father ever did his son; he held forth about "lack of restraint" *(incontentia)* and "lack of discipline" *(intemperantia).* What more can I say, judges? I am prepared to forgive the rapt attention you paid to his speech; so sour *(tristis)* and harsh *(asper)* it was that I shuddered to hear it myself![107]

(*Cael.* 25)

To wriggle out of the inexorable logic of the public language of virtue which had pinned down his client, who must actually have been something of a rake,[108] Cicero alludes with the phrase *in hac suauitate humanitatis* to the aestheticizing practices of aristocratic self-definition.[109] This use of metalanguage has a very particular effect: the creation of a position outside of the public language of virtue by gesturing to an alternate, civilized worldview. Of the same stripe is the use of literary critical language to label, and therefore control, Herennius's attack *(triste, asperum genus orationis).*[110]

*Lepos* and *facetiae,* in their narrower application to 'humor,' have a simi-

105. Lit. *patruus* 'father's brother,' a familial role associated with stern advice.

106. "These three roles are mentioned, not for the sake of the tricolon, but to make clear the point that, as far as Cicero is concerned, Herennius was adopting a dramatic persona," Gotoff 1986: 128. Cf. May 1988: 115: "The *Pro Caelio* is unique among the speeches in the Ciceronian corpus for its widespread and very carefully wrought use of dramatic ethos."

107. *dixit enim multa de luxurie, multa de libidine, multa de uitiis iuuentutis, multa de moribus et, qui in reliqua uita mitis esset et in hac suauitate humanitatis qua prope iam delectantur omnes uersari periucunde soleret, fuit in hac causa pertristis quidam patruus, censor, magister; obiurgauit M. Caelium, sicut neminem umquam parens; multa de incontinentia intemperantiaque disseruit. quid quaeritis, iudices? ignoscebam uobis attente audientibus, proptera quod egomet tam triste illud, tam asperum genus orationis horrebam.*

108. On Caelius's habits, cf. *si licet, si fas est defendi a me eum qui nullum conuiuium renuerit, qui in hortis fuerit, qui unguenta sumpserit, qui Baias uiderit (Cael.* 27) *et passim.*

109. *Humanitas* and *suauitas* are often connected, though never in this precise phrase. E.g., *suauiter diligenter officiose humaniter (Att.* 1.20.1), *suauissimum hominem et summi offici summaeque humanitatis (Fam.* 16.4.2); cf. Mamoojee 1981: 232–36. On the power of the invocation of *suauitas* and *humanitas* as core aristocratic values, cf. Hall 1996: 102–3. Gotoff 1986 argues that Cicero has to some extent invented the harshness of Herennius's position as foil for his own sophistication. Thus one should perhaps say not "to wriggle out of the inexorable logic of the public language of virtue," but "in order to seem to need to wriggle out" etc.

110. V. Ernest s.vv. *triste, asperum. Asperitas* renders the τραχύτης and σφοδρότης of the Greek rhetorical tradition. The opening anaphora in effect reads Herennius's speeches merely as a stringing together of predictable loci and is thus also literary critical language, *pace* Heinze p. 225 n.2. Gotoff 1986 demonstrates that Cicero aims to separate the form of Herennius's speech from its content; literary critical labels are one such means of separation.

lar spectatorial function in the most remarkable of the oratorical passages
where Cicero uses the language of social performance positively. In the *pro
Cluentio* Cicero was in an unusual position. At the behest of a patron, Cicero had pled the opposite side in an earlier case; in arguing, as he now was,
on behalf of A. Cluentius he was arguing, in effect, against himself.[111] Had
there not been some feeling that the switch was at the least odd, Cicero
would not have felt he had to defend himself, but he does: "People are quite
wrong if they think judicial speeches are the authorized version of my opinions. They are relative to the cases and the situation, not to the individuals
or patrons in question."[112]

*Lepos* and *facetiae* appear in a striking element of this defense. Cicero tells
a story (140–42) about Crassus, who had once found himself in a similar
position (and with whom Cicero especially associates *lepos* in the rhetorica,
as evidenced below [VI.3]). Brutus, his opponent in a case, called two readers to recite passages from two speeches of Crassus which disagreed over the
scope of the senate's authority. Crassus, addled *(aliquantum . . . commotus),*
replied that the cases were each argued on their merits *(ex re et ex causa)* and
that such absolute claims as were made served the individual cases. But he
capped his defense with a comic stroke "so that Brutus could know he had
attacked a man, and one equipped not only with eloquence but with charm
*(lepos)* and wit *(facetiae)*."[113] He had readers pronounce three passages taken
from works by Brutus's father, each set in a different rural property. Crassus, asking where these properties were now, suggested the elder Brutus must
have used them as settings to prove that he once owned what he knew a dissolute son would liquidate.

On the simplest level this is just an amusing story to distract the judges
from Cicero's self-contradiction. But there is much more here. Cicero had
been pressed into an ideological corner. Character, inferred by culturally
acceptable εἰκός arguments about service, class, and clan, was a standard line
of defense in criminal cases. But having once derided Cluentius and corrupt
judicial procedures, presumably in part by precisely such argument, how
could Cicero now be defending their probity? The Roman construction of
the self did not easily admit of conversion, deathbed or otherwise; Cicero's
contortions to the contrary in the *pro Caelio* (§§28–30) are instructive.

111. For the background to the case, cf. the references in Kirby 1990.

112. *sed errat uehementer, si quis in orationibus nostris quas in iudiciis habuimus auctoritates nos-
tras consignatas se habere arbitratur. omnes enim illae causarum ac temporum sunt, non hominum ipsorum aut patronorum (Clu. 139).*

113. *deinde ut intellegere posset Brutus quem hominem et non solum qua eloquentia uerum etiam
quo lepore et quibus facetiis praeditum lacessisset.* The same story is told in *de Oratore* 2.223–24.

Claims made about character, based on deeds recorded in *elogiae* and on breeding displayed in a parade of *imagines,* were implicitly absolute; hence their manipulation.[114] A change of position about character was therefore a tall order. Cicero solved the problem not by proposing a theoretical dynamic of such change but by telling a story about someone who was also forced to change course. To assume the role of storyteller (or actor, as Cicero does in the *pro Caelio,* §§33–38) is to step back from one's role as agonist in the current situation. From that position one can label moves, which is exactly what Cicero does, giving Crassus a kind of report card.[115] *Lepos* and *facetiae* are the kinds of things scorers looked for: agonists who were not merely "real men," nor merely "eloquent," but also able to compete aesthetically, by the rules of the *convivium,* as it were. That was what made a social victor, and his sincere but witless opponent found himself on the outside of the circle drawn by *lepos.*

Nevertheless, despite the obviously considerable power of the language of social performance to exclude and excuse, only in these few instances does Cicero use it so. Furthermore he is sometimes under compunction and he always handles the act of exclusion humorously. That apparent reluctance to use the language of social performance positively is of a piece with its infrequency even in negative applications: that very rarity, I suggest, is itself a mark of Cicero's sensitivity to its double edge. Cicero uses the language of social performance only once to express diffidence about himself before an opponent's rhetorical skill: when he was young, and when he was facing the notoriously artful Hortensius.[116] There are no other examples of such uses of the language of social performance in Cicero's speeches because, I suggest, it was he who came to be the master of that sort of aestheticism: the sorts of things he says about Hortensius are probably what his opponents, their words now lost to us, used to say about him. The language of social performance could have been used against Cicero in virtually every

114. Cf. Cic. *Brut.* 62, who observes that *mortuorum laudationes* contained false triumphs, extra consulships, and confusions about families.

115. Cicero uses exactly the same strategy in *pro Plancio* 33–34, where he combats Juventius's charge that Plancius spoke "too harshly" *(asperius)* by recalling several barbs of Granius (on whom cf. VI.3) who, among other things, had jabbed at L. Crassus and M. Antonius "with his rather harsh witticisms" *(asperioribus facetiis),* and by then suggesting *a fortiori* that what was permitted to a *praeco* should be permitted to an *eques Romanus.* Cicero then adds that in any case all the witticisms attributed to Plancius were not actually made by him, a position with which he, Cicero, could sympathize; see below. In both these uses of *facet(us),* Cicero almost becomes a kind of reporter, observing politics, and deploying critical language, from the outside.

116. On Hortensius and his Asiatic style, cf. Leeman 1963: 92–95.

way he uses it against others. The young Cicero, according to Plutarch, was so given to literary studies that he earned the nicknames Γραικός "the Greek" and σχολαστικός "scholar, academic." [117] His own ability as an *actor* was considerable; he had learned much from the comic actor Roscius and the tragic actor Aesop (Plut. *Cic.* 5.4–6). He was himself interested in philosophy, not, to be sure, in Epicureanism like Hortensius or Piso, but interested nonetheless. Cicero's sense of humor was notorious (cf. VI.5). He was a keen appreciator of art.[118] His oratorical style might seem excessively artful.[119] In short, Cicero possessed in great degree most of the qualities that could be described by the language of social performance. If it was not conventional invective, these qualities are doubtless what Verres had in mind when (surprisingly, in view of what we have seen of him) he accused Cicero of "effeminate living" (μαλακία, Plut. *Cic.* 7.3).[120] It is difficult to damn a vice that is so close to a virtue; or laud a virtue that is so close to a vice. Notably, when Cicero confronts his reputation for comedy, he stops short of assigning a member of the language of social performance to himself, not out of modesty only, but because the safest course is always to steer clear of such treacherous shoals:

> From time to time I say things, not out of any hostility, but in the course of argument or after having been attacked myself. And from time to time—as happens with many people—a comment comes out that, if it is not truly witty *(perfacetus)*, at least is, one might say, not boorish *(non rusticum)*. And as a result whatever anyone says, they say I said.[121]
>
> *(Planc.* 35)

117. καὶ τόν γε πρῶτον ἐν Ῥώμῃ χρόνον εὐλαβῶς διῆγε καὶ ταῖς ἀρχαῖς ὀκνηρῶς προσῄει καὶ παρημελεῖτο, ταῦτα δὴ τὰ Ῥωμαίων τοῖς βαναυσοτάτοις πρόχειρα καὶ συνήθη ῥήματα, Γραικὸς καὶ σχολαστικὸς ἀκούων (Plut. *Cic.* 5.2).

118. Cf. Bartman 1994, Leen 1991.

119. Quintilian records that certain of Cicero's contemporaries thought him "rather bombastic, Asiatic, redundant; too fond of repetitions, occasionally wooden in his jests, weak, extravagant, and, incredibly, virtually unmanly in his composition" *(tumidiorem et Asianum et redundantem et in repetitionibus nimium et in salibus aliquando frigidum et in compositione fractum, exultantem ac paene, quod procul absit, uiro molliorem, Inst.* 12.10.12). Though Quintilian has in mind the Atticists, the much different rhetorical ideal of Caesar shows that opposition to Cicero's floridity need not be tied to the Atticist movement as such.

120. λοιδορηθεὶς οὖν ὁ Κικέρων εἰς μαλακίαν ὑπὸ τοῦ Βέρρου, τοῖς υἱοῖς, εἶπεν, ἐντὸς θυρῶν δεῖ λοιδορεῖσθαι (Plut. *Cic.* 7.7).

121. *Ego quia dico aliquid aliquando non studio adductus, sed aut contentione dicendi aut lacessitus, et quia, ut fit in multis, exit aliquando aliquid si non perfacetum, at tamen fortasse non rusticum, quod quisque dixit, me id dixisse dicunt.* See also n. 115 above, and cf. pp. 302–3.

## V.8. Conclusion

Cicero's use of the language of social performance in speeches reveals five distinct ideological stances. The language may be used to patronize (V.2), or pillory (V.3), foreigners or social lessers. In other uses Cicero figures himself an outsider (V.4) and seeks to diminish the force of the language of social performance by extravagant reference to traditional Roman social values (V.6). Last, Cicero may himself use the language to exclude or excuse (V.7). I suggest that the last three ideological patterns are the sign of a shift in the "balance of power" between style and substance, so that they were now taken to be coextensive, rather than complementary. Aestheticism had become a dominant paradigm for social interaction in the late Republic. Cicero's hostile or deprecatory treatment is an atavistic attempt to decouple aestheticism from social worth. But its ability to draw circles that embrace, and exclude, also made the language of social performance attractive to the like of Verres and Clodius, and to Cicero. These are not circles drawn by inherited status or money but by performative ability. Roman culture as a whole obviously assigned considerable value to such performances. That is a value to which Cicero rarely, and then only delicately, appeals in his speeches (V.7), but which he attempts to coopt for his own purposes in *de Oratore,* the topic of chapter 6.

# CHAPTER VI

# *Sermo Facetus et Nulla in Re Rudis*
# The Language of Social Performance
# in Cicero's *de Oratore*

If you do not know goodness, how can you be a skillful speaker?

Confucian Analects 5.4.2

... λόγος γὰρ ἔκ τ' ἀδοξούντων ἰὼν
κἀκ τῶν δοκούντων αὐτὸς οὐ ταὐτὸν σθένει.

The same opinion, coming from the inglorious
and the glorious, has not the same force.

Euripides *Hecuba* 294–95

## VI.1. Introduction

The language of social performance is common in Cicero's three major rhetorical writings, the *de Oratore,* the *Brutus,* and the *Orator.*[1] Its use there poses a difficult question. While, as I have argued, the entrance of the language of social performance into the critical language of rhetoric was ideologically motivated, and traces of the motivating ideology remain (IV.4), nonetheless, ensconced in a largely technical discourse, the language of social performance in its application to rhetoric must have become something of a technical idiom (its eventual fate by the time of Gellius, as discussed below). The rising stock of the language of social performance described in chapter 5 might very well have left such technical applications unaffected. As a loose parallel, the valorizing or demonizing of "liberal" in its political applications would doubtless leave unaffected such phrases as a "liberal helping," which would not, ceteris paribus, suddenly become admirable or suspect political speech. Since words function as a manifestation of cultural models, and a given word may function in more than one, it is the history of models that decides the history of words.

That said, several of the examples from chapter 5 (*Quinct.* 93 [V.4], *Dom.* 92 [V.5]) show that the language of social performance in its application to rhetoric, or to public or publicized speech generally, could indeed be af-

---

1. Out of some two hundred occurrences, the language of social performance appears only a few times in the early *de Inventione* and in the later *Partitiones Oratoriae, de Optimo genere oratoris,* and *Topica.* Cf. the Index Locorum.

fected by the ascendancy of aestheticism. After all, since rhetoric is obviously a form of a social performance, the difference between (say) Verres' *lepos* (*Ver.* 2.5.142, V.6) and the *lepos* that Antonius says an orator must have (*de Orat.* 1.213) is rather less than that between "liberal policies" and a "liberal helping" (though opponents of the Welfare State might disagree). I suggest in this chapter that the rise of aestheticism did have a distinct effect on some aspects of Cicero's use of the language of social performance in *de Oratore*.[2] In certain respects his handling of the language is a kind of opposite to the strategy discussed above, where he embeds the language of social performance in ideological contexts that attempt to deny it its dominance (V.5). In the *de Oratore* Cicero pursues a comparable strategy, positive rather than negative, and synthetic rather than polarizing, embedding the language of social performance in ideological contexts that conjoin its power to higher purposes. *Sermo facetus et nulla in re rudis* "witty speech in no way rude" (*de Orat.* 1.32) is made into a symbol for elite social cohesion. A shared ideology of attractiveness is trajected into an ideology of shared political identity.

## VI.2. The Uniqueness of the Language of Social Performance in Cicero's *de Oratore*

Cicero's use of the language of social performance as rhetorical metalanguage is unique vis-à-vis the rest of the rhetorical tradition. To be sure, all of Cicero's rhetorica feature the uses described in chapter 3, which, to judge by the presence of most of them in the *Rhetorica ad Herennium*, Cicero inherited. But Cicero exhibits peculiarities, concentrated in *de Oratore*, which fall into two, sometimes complementary, types. First, Cicero apparently avoids senses otherwise well attested and presumably common. *Bellus*, for example, was typically used for good "moves" in the Latin rhetorical tradition (III.5). This sense was plainly known to Cicero, as we have seen above, for example παράγραμμα *bellum* "a nice *jeu de mots*" (*Fam.* 7.32.2, III.5, VI.5), but he does not use *bellus* as a technical term in this sense in the rhetorica. *Venust(us)* is used for the humor of reply (III.4.2), but only for a very particular type, as we see below. *Elegan(s)* of a 'deft move' (III.6 n. 112) never appears in any of Cicero's rhetorica.[3] The second, and more important, peculiarity, is that Cicero seems to have added his own meanings. *Bellus*, for example, is used, but in connection to certain types of humorous affectations. *Lep(idus)*, which was connected to verbal performance broadly meant (I.9), does appear a few times in the rhetorica in this broader sense, for example in connection to *actio* (III.3), but the majority of instances of *lep(idus)* in Cicero's rhetorica

---

2. The *Brutus* and the *Orator* are treated below, for reasons made apparent there.
3. The use was known to Cicero: cf. *elegans* ὑπερβολή (*Fam.* 7.32.2, VI.6).

are connected to humor. For example, when Caesar Strabo describes Crassus as *in utroque genere leporis excellens* (*de Orat.* 2.220) "outstanding in both
kinds of *lepos*," he is referring to the just-made distinction between *cauillatio*, extended or narrative humor, and *dicacitas*, the humor of biting one-
liners;[4] *lepos* is clearly serving as a superordinate term for 'humor.'

It is noteworthy that whereas the inherited uses occur in both descriptive and, occasionally, normative passages, the unique uses virtually always
occur in normative passages. By descriptive passages I mean those that describe an effect incidentally or in passing, or are not of central theoretical
import. Normative passages, by contrast, are of central theoretical import,
in which the production or assessment of the qualities the language of social performance describes is the main issue. The use of *lepos* in connection
to *actio*, for example, occurs twice in one-line descriptions of orators in the
*Brutus*; its only appearance in *de Oratore* is in a formulation spoken by M. Antonius, who, significantly, believes oratory is primarily a matter of performative excellence, a 'knack' (τριβή) rather than an 'science' (τέχνη).[5] Caesar Strabo's division of *lepos* into' *cauillatio* and *dicacitas*, by contrast, occurs
in the beginning paragraphs of his discussion of humor. The distinction between normative and descriptive that I am suggesting may be compared to
that in a philosopher who uses "good" in a fairly narrow intended sense, but
also to describe, incidentally, a "good time" or a "good point," without reference to the *summum bonum* of his argument. In the case of the language
of social performance in Cicero's rhetorica, the distinction is not so sharp,
but the essential point can be isolated by casting the issue in reader-response
terms: a reader familiar with the standard senses of the language of social
performance in its application to rhetoric would have noticed the occasional
peculiarity, even tendentiousness, in Cicero's usage. This peculiarity is most

4. Some have seen in these the Peripatetic distinction between χάρις and γέλως; cf.
Grant 1924: 103–6, LPR 188–89. The same distinction is made with different terminology at *Or.* 40, where *sales* is divided into *facetiae* and *dicacitas*.

5. *hunc ego appello oratorem eumque esse praeterea instructum uoce et actione et lepore quodam
uolo* (*de Orat.* 1.213). M. Antonius is here contrasting his own view of the orator with that
of Crassus. Whereas Crassus would require of the orator mastery of moral philosophy and
law, Antonius considers an orator someone who knows how to use "words pleasant to hear
and opinions designed to support one's point in law courts and public debates" (*qui et uerbis
ad audiendum iucundis et sententiis ad probandum adcommodatis uti possit in causis forensibus atque
communibus*); "That is what I mean," says Antonius, "by an orator, and I think he should be
equipped with a good voice, the ability to gesture, and certain grace *(lepos)*." It is appropriate that the one time *lepos* is used in connection to *actio* in *de Oratore*, it comes from Antonius, for whom oratory is primarily a matter of the performative excellence of which he
himself possessed a great measure (cf. *Brut.* 139ff.), including gestural excellence (cf. III.4.1
n.36). The positions of Crassus and Antonius are represented as those of Cicero and Quintus, respectively; v. *de Orat.* 1.5.

pronounced in *de Oratore,* in particular in the *excursus de ridiculis* (2.216 – 90), in which Caesar Strabo treats the place of humor in the orator's repertoire, mainly by way of example.[6] That *excursus,* where more than a fifth of all of Cicero's uses of the language of social performance appear, occupies most of my attention in this chapter.

## VI.3. Useful Scurrility and Learned Wit

In the *excursus de ridiculis* Caesar Strabo applies *bellus* to acts of the able wit, as in this example:

> It's also nice *(bellus)* when someone is made fun of according to the very pretext he established, as in an exchange between Q. Opimius, the consular, who had had a bad reputation as a young man, and Egilius, a jolly *(festiuus)* fellow who seemed effeminate *(mollis)* but wasn't. Opimius said to Egilius: "So Egilia! When are you coming by with your loom and wool?" "Oh heavens me," Egilius replied, "I dare not, Mother won't let me visit girls of ill repute."[7]
>
> (*de Orat.* 2.277)

It is worth quoting a longer passage entire:

> Incongruous comments are also funny *(ridentur),* such as "He has everything. Except property. And character." It is also nice *(bellus)* to scold gently like a friend; as, for example, when Albucius seemed to have proved a certain point in a trial against Scaevola by reference to Albius's account books. After Scaevola was acquitted, Albius was delighted, but Granius upbraided him: "You don't understand: there *was* a conviction — of the way you keep your books."[8] Similar to this is a friendly warn-

6. The excursus on humor has been treated separately by Monaco 1968. Strabo begins with a kind of *recusatio,* positing the difficulty of defining or teaching humor on the one hand but on the other giving examples of its effectiveness (217–27); only after intermediate remarks by Crassus and Antonius (228–30) is Strabo finally prevailed upon by Sulpicius (231) and Crassus (232) to embark on a more systematic discussion, which commences at 235. Strabo begins with a *divisio* of his discussion: what the laughable is, what its source is, whether it is proper to the orator, to what extent, and what the types of humor are. He dispenses fairly quickly with the first four questions and spends the bulk of his discussion (240ff.) classifying and exampling types of humorous comments.

7. *est bellum illud quoque, ex quo is, qui dixit inridetur in eo ipso genere, quo dixit; ut, cum* Q. *Opimius consularis, qui adulescentulus male audisset, festiuo homini Egilio, qui uideretur mollior nec esset, dixisset 'quid tu, Egilia mea? quando ad me uenis cum tua colu et lana?' 'non pol' inquit 'audeo, nam me ad famosas uetuit mater accedere.'* Q. Opimius was consul in 154. How well Egilius crafted his own persona is perhaps suggested by the oath *non pol* 'no by Pollux!' According to Varro, who complains that by his time the stricture had loosened, anciently only women swore by Castor or Pollux (Gel. 11.6).

8. "Albucius (cf. *de Orat.* 3.171) accused Scaevola *de repetundis* (*Brut.* 102), and to establish his case called for the account-books of a certain Albius, a friend of Scaevola's, which,

ing in the course of giving advice. An ineffective lawyer had lost his voice from speaking too much, and Granius encouraged him to drink cold mead as soon as he got home. "But I'll lose my voice if I do that," protested the lawyer. Said Granius, "Better that than your defendant." It's also nice *(bellus)* when a comment particularly apt to the recipient is made. For example, there was a time when Scaurus's reputation was suffering somewhat for having taken possession of the property of the wealthy Phrygio Pompey without testamentary right. While Scaurus was sitting as a part of the defense at Bestia's trial, a funeral happened to pass by; C. Memmius, one of the prosecutors, said, "Look, Scaurus, there goes a corpse—maybe you can take over his things, too."[9]

*(de Orat.* 2.281–83)

The *bellus* that describes this sort of humor should be counted the normative one.[10] The use for 'good moves' (III.5) is rarer and incidental.[11] Still the

---

as he thought, proved his guilt. In spite of the evidence thus supplied, Scaevola was acquitted. Granius taunted Albius with having been delighted at the acquittal, and at the same time not having seen that a severe condemnation had been passed upon the accuracy of his own accounts" (Wilkins ad loc.).

9. *ridentur etiam discrepantia: 'quid huic abest nisi res et uirtus?' bella etiam est familiaris reprehensio quasi errantis; ut cum obiurgauit Albium Granius quod, cum eius tabulis quiddam ab Albucio probatum uideretur, et ualde absoluto Scaeuola gauderet neque intellegeret contra suas tabulas iudicatum. huic similis est admonitio in consilio dando familiaris, ut, cum patrono malo, cum uocem in dicendo obtudisset, suadebat Granius, ut mulsum frigidum biberet, simul ac domum redisset, 'perdam' inquit 'uocem, si id fecero': 'melius est' inquit 'quam reum.' bellum etiam est, cum quid cuique sit consentaneum dicitur; ut, cum Scaurus non nullam haberet inuidiam ex eo, quod Phrygionis Pompei, locupletis hominis, bona sine testamento possederat, sederetque aduocatus reo Bestiae, cum funus quoddam duceretur, accusator C. Memmius 'uide' inquit 'Scaure, mortuus rapitur, si potes esse possessor.'* I have translated loosely and interpolated freely to preserve comic effects.

10. Cf. also *de Orat.* 2.238: discussing the extent to which humor is to be employed, Strabo observes that the orator must not make light of matters that properly deserve hatred or pity, and hence that "the proper sphere of humor" *(materies omnis ridiculorum)* is to be found in human foibles, which "are funny if they are treated *belle*" *(eaque belle agitata ridentur)*—exactly the sort of topic, and the sort of treatment, apparent in the anecdotes about Granius and Memmius. Immediately after making this point, Strabo uses *bellus* again in a way that, it seems to me, is somewhat different: he adds that "there is also a nice *(bellus)* supply of comic material in deformity and bodily faults" *(est etiam deformitatis et corporis uitiorum satis bella materies ad iocandum, de Orat.* 2.239). *Bellus* here has its occasional meaning of 'nice,' as at Cic. *Rep.* 2.67 *(est tibi ex eis ipsis, qui adsunt, bella copia [sc., uirorum prudentium], uel ut a te ipso ordiare* "You have a nice supply of them ready to hand—you yourself, for starters"). Strabo's point in using this perhaps mildly colloquial version of *bellus* here is surely to secure an amusing oxymoron by playing off another sense of *bellus*: there is a 'pretty' supply of jokes to be found in the realm of 'ugliness.' (The point is Corbeill's 1996: 22; for *bellus* as 'pretty,' cf. VII.5 n.75.) Strabo's word order makes the pun work: *deformitas* and *corporis uitia* set the reader's mind thinking about 'ugliness,' when along comes a word that might mean 'pretty.'

11. *Brut.* 293 (III.5), *de Orat.* 3.101 (III.5; cf. VI.6), and in the *excursus de ridiculis* itself, possibly 2.253 (III.5, cf. the nearby *litterate*).

kind of wit that *bellus* describes in each case is consonant with the semantic characteristics discussed above (I.7). To stay pointedly within the confines of a premise known to be false (that one is a woman) or unlikely to be true (that one approves of illegal seizure), or to establish such a premise (pretending to scold), is to play a conversational game. Game-playing, of course, is highly conscious behavior, which the element of 'reference to evaluator' well fits. The player who makes a good move knows he has made a good move and knows that the audience, if they know the game, also know.

The range of *lepos* in *de Oratore* is also notable. In normative passages Cicero uses it, often in connection with *facetiae*, only to mean something like 'humor,' 'the charm of humor,' or 'genteel wit' as opposed to 'performative attraction' more generally, as in 2.220 above. Among Crassus's requirements for a good orator is "a certain charming wit *(lepos)* and sense of humor *(facetiae)*" (*de Orat.* 1.17, below). In another example Antonius describes Crassus's success in a fractious assembly against Cn. Domitius, his colleague in the censorship (cf. *Brut.* 94):

> . . . in that assembly to which I've referred, every humorous *(facetus)* remark that Crassus made came by way of his response to an attack; and furthermore such was Domitius's weight and influence that it seemed better for his attacks to be deflected (*leuandum* "made light") with humor *(lepos)* than broken in direct attack *(contentio).*[12]
>
> (*de Orat.* 2.230)

*Lepos* here does not refer, like *uenustas* or *sal,* to a specific kind of humor but is serving as a general term.[13] In vitro a meaning like 'charm' gives equally good sense, but this passage does, after all, come from the *excursus de ridiculis.*

　　12. . . . *in ipsa ista contione nihil fere dictum est ab hoc, quod quidem facetius dictum uideretur, quod non prouocatus responderit; erat autem tanta in Domitio grauitas, tanta auctoritas, ut, quod esset ab eo obiectum, lepore magis leuandum quam contentione frangendum uideretur.* Contentio recalls the Greek ἀγών in the sense of an adversarial forensic speech and is thus contrasted on the one hand with epideictic oratory (cf. Quint. *Inst.* 10.5.16ff.) and on the other with *sermo* 'conversation[al style]' (cf. *sale uero et facetiis Caesar, Catuli patris frater, uicit omnes, ut in ipso illo forensi genere dicendi contentiones aliorum sermone uinceret, Off.* 1.133). Caesar Strabo accepted half, at any rate, of Gorgias's injunction: καὶ δεῖν ἔφη Γοργίας τὴν μὲν σπουδὴν διαφθείρειν τῶν ἐναντίων γέλωτι τὸν δὲ γέλωτα σπουδῇ, ὀρθῶς λέγων (Arist. *Rh.* 1419b4–6 = 3.18.7).

　　13. Cf. also *de Orat.* 1.243 *(tuo lepore et sale et politissimis facetiis),* 2.219 *(lepore et facetiis),* 2.225 *(hoc lepore et his facetiis),* 2.340 *(facetiae . . . et celeritas et breue aliquod dictum nec sine dignitate et cum lepore).* Cicero sometimes uses *lepos* in this way outside the rhetorica. He laments to Paetus that the city's population has so changed that no trace of the old "sense of humor" *(lepos)* is left *(ut nullum ueteris uestigium leporis appareat, Fam.* 9.15.2). In describing the principles of oratory that apply to conversation, Cicero advises "that one bring gravity to serious matters and charm to humorous matters" *(si seriis, seueritatem adhibeat, si iocosis, leporem, Off.* 1.134).

Much as Cicero in his speeches embeds the language of social performance in ideologically particular contexts as a way of (re)defining it (cf. esp.
V.6), so has he done here with these uses of *lepos* and *bellus*. They are, in a
word, tailored specifically to Cicero's vision of the elite. As in the examples
treated in chapter 5, *bellus* seems to describe a certain sauciness, even impudence. Several of the *bellus* comments belong to Granius. Granius was a
*praeco* 'crier, herald,' a less than ideal social position, and furthermore he had
a reputation for acerbic comments.[14] When in a letter Cicero compares his
friend Paetus to the wits of the past, Granius and the satirist Lucilius seem
to form a harsher pair, in contrast to the more charming Laelius and Crassus: "And so when I see you, I seem to see every Granius and Lucilius; really, every Crassus and Laelius, too" (*Fam.* 9.15.2).[15] As for C. Memmius
(tr. 111), he was notoriously hostile to the senatorial elite, and something
of an attack dog, a less morally defensible position (cf. VI.5 n.79).[16] Even
Egilius was evidently a kind of outsider if the label *mollis* 'soft, effeminate'
routinely attached to him.

Nonetheless the comments of Granius and the others occur in contexts
that redeem them. Most of them appear in the interstices of legal action, in
other words, in the contexts of political power. The witticisms are, so to
speak, "public" rather than "private." The political capital of the principals
was surely affected by the bon mots Cicero records, which is what preserved
them to society scuttlebutt in the wake of the trials or other proceedings.
Cicero, after all, had heard of them somehow, sometimes generations later.[17]
Furthermore, most of the *bellus* jokes touch on matters that are all relatively
serious—illegal seizure of property, the failure to keep proper records, los-

14. On the *praeco,* cf. Hinard 1976 ad fin.; on Granius, cf. *Granio quidem nemo dicacior* (*de
Orat.* 2.244) and *Planc.* 33–34, where Granius is described as using *asperiores facetiae* "fairly
harsh witticisms." In *Planc.* 34 two of Granius's bon mots against P. Nasica and M. Drusus
are related, by way of defending Plancius's habit of speaking "too freely" (*liberius* 33).

15. *itaque te cum uideo, omnis mihi Granios, omnis Lucilios, uere ut dicam, Crassos quoque et
Laelios uidere uideor.*

16. On Memmius's hostility to the nobility, *uir acer et infensus potentiae nobilitatis* (Sal. *Jug.*
27); on his aggressiveness, cf. *orator mediocris, accusator acer atque acerbus* (*Brut.* 136). There is
also a stylistic issue here: a certain vigor or violence was typical of the *eloquentia popularis*, the
oratorical style associated with speakers from outside the Roman city elite; cf. David 1983:
312–13. When Crassus observes that beginning from one's "normal tone of voice" (*quiddam
medium*) and increasing one's volume from there gradually (*hinc gradatim ascendere*) is "pleasant and useful" (*suaue et utile*), he adds *nam a principio clamare agreste quiddam est* "There's
something rustic about shouting from the very beginning" (*de Orat.* 3.227). On the pair
*suauis et utilis,* cf. IV.6 n.62.

17. For the sources of the jokes, v. LPN ad loc. Some of Cicero's own jokes, for example
about Verres, were preserved this way (ὅμως δὲ πολλὰ χαρίεντα διαμνημονεύεται καὶ
περὶ ἐκείνην αὐτοῦ τὴν δίκην, Plut. *Cic.* 7.6).

ing a lawsuit, being bankrupt or immoral—and so have the effect of enforcing community standards. That is true even of Egilius's riposte to Q. Opimius (not the stern opponent of the Gracchi, but his father): Opimius, as Cicero notes, had a bad reputation, an account corroborated by Lucilius.[18] In fact Cicero is careful to point out that Egilius's reputation did not fit the true facts, which further redeems his character. In short, we may say that in the *excursus de ridiculis* the smallish circle of evaluators that post-Plautine *bellus* standardly implies (I.7) is the senatorial elite, which approved of humor if it enforced their own social standards, even if the jab came from a *praeco,* attack dog, or reputed sybarite. There is indeed something saucy about *bellus,* but the way Cicero uses it suggests distinctly that in the right contexts, before the right audience, and doing the right job, the *bellus* remark is not without value. This use of *bellus* is between that in *belli homines* and *belle negare,* where it circumscribes shared standards, and the use of the language of social performance to appropriate foreign aestheticism by way of the "Roman gaze" (V.2).

The ideology of Cicero's normative *lepos* is subtler. Were it not clear from the above treatment (III.3) that *lep(idus),* though it could include humor, was not properly a word for the 'humorous' or 'funny,' Cicero's handling of the word might alone have suggested the same conclusion.[19] Cicero's use of *lepos* for 'humor' often exhibits one or both of two peculiarities. *Lepos* may be paired with another word for 'humor(ous),' as if to secure the sense 'humor' by hendiadys. (This is not quite true for the frequent pair *lepos et facetiae,* which had an independent existence; cf. I.9 n. 162, III.3). The extension of *lepos* may also be made with a certain tentativeness indicated by the use of *quidam* 'a certain; something like, sort of, kind of.'

### *Lepos* of 'Humor' with *Quidam* or Collocates in *de Oratore*[20]

> *accedat eodem oportet lepos quidam facetiae*que . . . *celeritasque et breuitas et respondendi et lacessendi subtili uenustate atque urbanitate coniuncta* (*de Orat.* 1.17)

18. *Quintus Opimius ille, Iugurtini pater huius | et formosus homo fuit et famosus, utrumque | primo adulescens; posterius dat rectius sese* "The well-known Q. Opimius, father of this Jugurthine [Opimius], was a man of fine form (*formosus*) and ill fame (*famosus*), both, when he was younger; afterwards he conducted himself better" (418–20M, 450–52W, 422–24K). "The Jugurthine" is L. Opimius, opponent of the Gracchi, and recipient of Jugurtha's bribes in 116. Stressing the phrase *nec esset,* Corbeill 1996: 151–52 takes the import of the joke to be that Opimius "lacks a proper regard for how to use visible evidence."

19. Cf. Quint. *Inst.* 6.3.102; below, n. 31.

20. Cf. *erat cum grauitate iunctus facetiarum et urbanitatis oratorius, non scurrilis lepos* (*Brut.* 143), *nemo umquam urbanitate nemo lepore nemo suauitate conditior* (*Brut.* 177). Fyëdorov notices the frequent use of *lepos* with *quidam* (1987: 223) and its frequent pairing with other nouns

*libandus est ex omni genere urbanitatis facetiarum quidam lepos, quo*
*tamquam sale perspergatur omnis oratio* (de Orat. 1.158)
*[Caesar] inusitatum nostris quidem oratoribus leporem quendam et salem*
*. . . est consecutus* (de Orat. 2.98)
*multum in causis persaepe lepore et facetiis profici uidi* (de Orat. 2.219)
*hoc lepore et his facetiis non minus refutatum esse Brutum quam illis*
*tragoediis* (de Orat. 2.225)
*sale tuo et lepore et politissimis facetiis* (de Orat. 1.243)
*oratio . . . lepore et festiuitate conditior* (de Orat. 2.227)
*quod mutatis uerbis salem amittit, in uerbis habet leporem omnem* (de Orat.
2.252)

Cicero's importation of *lepos* to humor, where it did not quite belong, is
inspired by the concepts and theoretical language of Greek rhetoric. In discussions of humor, theoreticians did not enshrine the laughable, τὸ γελοῖον,
as an end in itself but instead subordinated it to other concerns, ethical or
stylistic.[21] The discussion of humor in *de Officiis* (1.103–4), for example,
which presumably follows Panaetius, comes under the head of propriety,
*decorum* (= τὸ πρέπον).[22] The discussion of humor in *de Oratore* continues
the immediately preceding discussion of ἦθος and πάθος, a task of which
humor, in view of its conciliatory power, is but one part.[23] In treatments of
style χάρις 'charm, pleasure' was the word often used to encapsulate this

---

(ibid.: 224ff.) and for the latter phenomenon adduces a reason somewhat different from the
one I have offered, suggesting that the frequent connection of *lepos* with other words for 'humorous' indicates "the presence in the lexeme of that semantic component, which in certain
cases becomes so dominant, that it may lead to an understanding of the lexeme as a general
noun for 'humor'" (ibid.: 225).

21. See Grant 1924: 76–87, "The Ethics of the Laughable"; LPR 206–10. An interesting discussion of the social propriety of humor is to be found in Plutarch *Quaest. Conviv.*
631C–634F.

22. Cf. Dyck 1996 ad 104.

23. ἦθος, a speaker's 'character,' and πάθος, the audience's 'emotions,' are two divisions
of Aristotelian rhetoric (*Rh.* 1388b31–1391b6 = 2.12–17, *Rh.* 1377b1–1388b30 = 2.1–11),
referring, respectively, to the measures a speaker may take to enhance his own credibility and
the feelings that may be aroused in the hearers to accept a speaker's claims. The definitions
of [ps.-] Dionysius of Halicarnassus and Longinus, respectively, are useful: τὸ ῥητορικόν[. . .
πάθος ἐστὶ] τὸ πρέποντας καὶ προσήκοντας τοὺς λόγους ποιεῖσθαι περὶ τῶν ὑποκει-
μένων πραγμάτων τῷ λέγοντι αὐτῷ, καὶ τῷ ἀκούοντι (*Ars. Rhet.* 11.2); φορὰ ψυχῆς καὶ
συγκίνησις (Long. 20.2). The polarity ἦθος ~ πάθος is rendered into Latin by various
means, typically loosely by casting the issue as two different sorts of action by the speaker,
e.g., *commenda(tio)* vs. *concita(tio)* (de Orat. 2.201) or *fidem faciendi* vs. *commouendi* (*Part.* 9),
sometimes directly by *mores* vs. *affectus* (Quint. *Inst.* 6.2.8, who suggests for the former *morum quaedam proprietas*). See Wisse 1989, LPR 1989: 118–33.

sensibility; it could stand for 'humor'[24] but was superordinate to mere humor.[25] In the realm of style the 'humorous' could be subordinated to the 'charming' (τὸ εὔχαρι), as probably in the lost Theophrastean περὶ χάριτος α' (v. LPR 190). Such subordination is implicit in Demetrius's division of χάριτες into two kinds, one nobler (μείζων 'greater,' σεμνότερος 'more solemn') and one lighter (εὐτελής 'slight,' κωμικώτερος 'more suitable to comedy'), the latter of which are like jests (σκώμμασιν ἐοικυῖαι, *Eloc.* 128).

Cicero's use of *lepos* as a term for humor reflects his desire to have an equivalent for χάρις. *Lepos* is a word well-suited to serve for χάρις.[26] As a word for 'attractive performance,' *lepos* emphasizes the relationship between a performer and a spectator, mirroring the element of attention to audience that is often a part of χάρις—an element that was also singularly important to Cicero in his conception of elite humor. This aspect of the ideology of Ciceronian *lepos* becomes clear in examining the persons to whom it is attributed. When Cicero connects *lepos* to a person, it is very likely to be Crassus: six of the eight instances of *lepos* in the discussion of humor in *de Oratore* apply to Crassus; of the six instances in the *Brutus* (only three of which apply to humor), two are applied to Crassus, and *lepos* is also connected to Crassus outside the rhetorica in several places.[27] Not only was Crassus a particularly witty and elegant speaker, but he was, of course, one of the men at whose feet Cicero learned of political and social life at Rome. In his portrait in *de Oratore,* there is an element of admiring personal reminiscence. *Lepos* is the word that Cicero uses to capture the engaging quality of the man whom he took as his model (and whom he depicts as pointing forward to

24. Since 'humor' was a part of 'charm,' 'charm' was used for 'humor' outright by synecdoche: Dionysius of Halicarnassus notes that 'lively wit' (εὐτραπελία) is commonly known as 'charm' (χάρις, *Dem.* 54). Demetrius's effort to distinguish between τὸ εὔχαρι and τὸ γελοῖον (163ff.) suggests their partial identification. Indeed one word for 'joking' was χαριεντίζεσθαι.

25. *Venustas* could be sometimes used for χάρις (cf. III.4 ad fin.), but Cicero felt it was suitable only to a particular kind of humor (VI.5). W. Rhys Roberts 1910 in his appended glossary recognized the equivalence of χάρις and *lepos,* but it has been largely ignored since.

26. The way was perhaps paved by the phrase *lepos et facetiae,* which may be a translation of χάρι(ς) καὶ εὐτράπελ(ος) (III.3).

27. *Brut.* 143, 203; *Clu.* 140 (V.8); *Off.* 1.108 *(erat in L. Crasso, in L. Philippo multus lepos, maior etiam magisque de industria in C. Caesare L. filio), Fam.* 9.15.2 *(above). Cf. also et Crassus, ut praesens ingenio semper, ut faceto lepore sollers* (Plin. *Nat.* 17.4). The investiture in Crassus of *lepos* makes its application to C. Claudius Ap. f. Pulcher, a brother of Cicero's nemesis, all the more sarcastic: *sed uereor ne <te> lepore suo detineat diutius praetor Clodius* "I hope the praetor Clodius doesn't keep you longer with all his charm" (*Att.* 4.15.2).

him).[28] Notably all of the Romans to whom Cicero applies *lepos* in the rhetorica, in any sense, are ones he actually observed.[29] That 'charm' or 'engaging quality' is the sort of thing one might expect he could judge only by
personal observation.

This engaging quality meant two things to Cicero. First, it meant a sense
of propriety. Crassus is distinguished from 'wags' *(dicaces)* like Granius and
Vargula because of his restraint *(de Orat. 2.224)*. Crassus had "real" *lepos*, not
the kind that belonged to *scurrae* *(non scurrilis lepos, Brut.* 143), 'clowns' or
'jesters' who do anything to raise a laugh.[30] The formulation *scurrilis lepos* is
noteworthy, since it implies that by some *lepos* might indeed be attributed
to *scurrae*. The phrase is offered not to pose an oxymoron (like, say, "clumsy
grace"), but to refine the sense of *lepos* by narrowing it (on the order of "genuine, not superficial, charm"). Notably Crassus's primary contribution to
Caesar Strabo's *excursus* is to stress the importance of propriety and restraint
(*praetermittendarum . . . facetiarum,* cf. *de Orat.* 2.229–30). Second, Ciceronian *lepos* is often concomitant to, and implicitly produced by, education
and culture. Inside the rhetorica and out, Cicero connects *lepos* to *suauitas,*
*urbanitas,* and *humanitas,* all of which in one way or another have to do with
the cultural standards of the urban elite.[31] Caesar Strabo, to whom the dis-

28. Cf., e.g., *de Orat.* 3.95.

29. The remaining instances in the *Brutus* are to Antonius (140); C. Iulius L. f. (177); C.
Macer, tr. pl. 73 (238); and Q. Pomponius A. f. Bithynicus, who was legate for creating
Bithynia upon Nicomedes' bequest of 74 (240, cf. III.3 n. 15 above). *Lepos* is also applied to
Pericles (= πειθώ, *de Orat.* 3.138 [III.3 n. 23]) and is lacking in Epicurus (*hominem sine arte,*
*sine litteris, insultantem in omnes, sine acumine ullo, sine auctoritate, sine lepore, N.D.* 2.74).

30. Cf. *ergo haec, quae cadere possunt in quos nolis, quamuis sint bella, sunt tamen ipso genere*
*scurrilia* "The sort of jokes that may apply to targets you don't intend, however clever *(bellus)*
they may be, are nonetheless inherently scurrilous" *(de Orat.* 2.245); LPR 184. On the *scurra,*
see Grant 1924: 91–96, Corbett 1986, Rudd 1987.

31. *ex omni genere urbanitatis facetiarum quidam lepos (de Orat.* 1.158); *nemo umquam urbani-*
*tate, nemo lepore, nemo suauitate conditior (Brut.* 177), . . . *sic profecto se res habet, nullum ut sit uitae*
*tempus, in quo non deceat leporem humanitatemque uersari (de Orat.* 2.271), *[oratio] sic autem grauis,*
*ut in singulari dignitate omnis tamen adsit humanitas et lepos (de Orat.* 3.29), *hominum nationumque*
*illarum humanitas et lepos (Prov.* 29), *omnia me tua delectant, sed maxime maxima cum fides in ami-*
*citia, consilium grauitas constantia, tum lepos humanitas litterae (Fam.* 11.27.6). On the ideological resonances of *suauis,* cf. IV.6. The Augustan poet Domitius Marsus, quoted by Quintilian (*Inst.* 6.3.102), also connects *lepos* and *urbanitas: his adicit Domitius Marsus, qui de urbanitate*
*diligentissime scripsit, quaedam non ridicula, sed cuilibet seuerissimae orationi conuenientia eleganter*
*dicta et proprio quodam lepore iucunda: quae sunt quidem urbana, sed risum tamen non habent* "Domitius Marsus, who wrote very thoroughly about *urbanitas,* adds that there are certain elegant phrasings that delight with a kind of charm *(lepos)* of their own, not funny per se, but
proper to a speech, however stern it may be."

cussion of humor in *de Oratore* is assigned, is elsewhere described as "paragon of culture, wit, pleasantness, and charm" (*specimen fuisse humanitatis salis suauitatis leporis, Tusc.* 5.55).[32] *Lepos* may also find itself in the company of words describing education and learning.[33] Cicero's assignation of *lepos* to Stoic dialectic (III.3) accords with this use. When Cicero attacks Epicurus for lacking *lepos* (*N.D.* 2.74, III.3 n.29), Cicero means that he lacks the wit, grace, and humor of Socratic dialectic.

In short, *lepos,* like *bellus,* is used by Cicero in programmatic passages in *de Oratore* to reflect an ideal vision of the urban elite. Cicero was inspired to press *lepos* into an equivalent for χάρις because, as a word that could be applied to humor but really went humor to include a broader sensitivity to audience, χάρις jibed with that vision. The influence of χάρις may account for a morphological peculiarity in Cicero's handling of *lep(idus).* In rhetorical contexts he uses only *lepos* and never *lepidus. Lepos* and *lepidus* do not seem to have undergone sufficient semantic differentiation to warrant such a restriction independently.[34] Cicero, perhaps, uses only *lepos* in the rhetorica because he has in mind χάρις, which can mean not only 'charm' and 'humor' but also 'goodwill,' whereas χαρίεις, though it can mean 'charming' and 'humorous,' does not mean 'exhibiting goodwill, benevolent.' In any case it is notable in this regard that Cicero, uniquely in the history of Latin, uses *lepos* in another place where χάρις is very likely to have been underlying in the Greek.[35] Where *bellus* is made to reflect the sort

32. For the probable sense of *sal* here, 'dry' or 'ironic' humor, cf. 220n.

33. *Fam.* 11.27.6 (n. 31).

34. The *Rhet. Her.* knows no such restriction, using both *lepos* and *lepidus* for the effects of charming figures (*lepos* 4.35, III.3, *lepidus* and *lepos* 4.32, IV.4). As for Cicero, Verres in his wicked *lepos* does not seem to me to be appreciably different from the *lepidi pueri* of *Catil.* 2. Gellius uses only the adjective, Pliny the Younger usually only the noun (*Ep.* 1.16.5, 6.8.7, 6.21.5, 7.4.6), the adjective once (3.9.4). For examples of the semantic specialization of one morphological expression of a lexemic set, cf. on *uenus/uenustus/uenustas, honor/honestus/honestas;* above, I.6.

35. In *de Orat.* 3.181 Cicero observes that utility often results in attractiveness: *hoc in omnibus item partibus orationis euenit, ut utilitatem ac prope necessitatem suauitas quaedam et lepos consequatur* "It also happens in all aspects of a speech that a sort of pleasure and charm follow upon utility or even necessity." The pair *suauitas et lepos* represents ἡδονή τε καὶ χάρις, an occasional pairing in Greek for the effect of rhetoric (and other pleasures): according to Socrates, rhetoric is "[the knack] of producing a certain gratification and pleasure" (χάριτός τινος καὶ ἡδονῆς ἀπεργασίας, *Gorg.* 462c). The pair shows up in various forms in Dionysius of Halicarnassus (*Isoc.* 11, *Is.* 3, 11, *Comp. Verb.* 3) and is a favorite pairing of Plutarch in a variety of applications (cf., e.g., *Luc.* 23.1, *Gracch.* 30.1, *Anton.* 29.1, *Mor.* 16A *[Quomodo adolescens poetas . . .],* 514F *[de Garrulitate]*). 'Pleasure' was of course contrasted

of humor the senatorial elite can approve of, from a certain distance, *lepos* is made to reflect the engaging quality they themselves possess.

## VI.4. Natural Superiority and Distinctive Humor

Cicero's idealizing vision of the elite also effects his use of *uenust(us)* in *de Oratore* in a still subtler but perhaps more ideologically interesting way. *Venust(us)* for the 'charm of crafted details' or 'of narrative' is not common and has been treated above (III.4.3). Commoner, and more curious, is the normative application of *uenust(us)* to humor. As we saw above (III.4.2), *uenust(us)* refers especially to the humor of reply. These replies may be on the spur of the moment (e.g., Quint. *Inst.* 5.7.31 [III.4.2], Gel. 15.1.4 [ibid.]) or at a remove (e.g., Gel. 11.8 [ibid.]). *Venust(us)* was used the latter way in its application to 'humor' in chapter 5: there is something "staged" or "premeditated" about the witty gestures of the Pergamenes (*Flac.* 76, V.3) and the clever remark of Clodius (*Dom.* 92, V.5), and perhaps (if *uenustas* there has any overtones of 'humor') in the dedication of Verres (*Ver.* 2.5.142, V.6). Whenever *uenust(us)* refers to humor in *de Oratore*, however, it refers to spur-of-the-moment humor. In the catalogue of the orator's attributes at the beginning of *de Oratore*, *uenustas* characterizes the quick short response:

> The orator also needs to have a certain charming wit *(lepos)* and sense of humor *( facetiae),* learning that befits a free man, as well as the ability to reply and attack quickly and curtly, with measured deftness *(subtilis uenustas)* and wittiness *(urbantias).*[36]
>
> (*de Orat.* 1.17)

---

with 'utility' or 'necessity'; ἡδονή τε καὶ χάρις, or variants, could serve for the former, so in rhetorical contexts in Demosthenes (τῆς ἐπὶ ταῖς λοιδορίαις ἡδονῆς καὶ χάριτος τὸ τῆς πόλεως συμφέρον ἀνταλλαττόμενοι "turning from the pleasures of insult to public utility," *de Cor.* 138) and Plutarch (εἰ δὲ μήτε τῷ λέγοντι χρήσιμον μήτ' ἀναγκαῖον τοῖς ἀκούουσι τὸ λεγόμενον ἡδονὴ δὲ καὶ χάρις οὐ πρόσεστι, διὰ τί λέγεται; "But if what is being said is neither useful for the speaker nor compelling to the hearers and pleasure and charm are missing, why is it being said?" *de Garrulitate* 514F). The peculiarity of *Off.* 1.98 (*ut enim pulchritudo corporis apta compositione membrorum mouet oculos et delectat ipso, quod inter se omnes partes cum quodam lepore consentiunt,* cf. 95n.15), in which *lepos* refers to proportionality, an idea usually expressed by *uenust(us)* (p. 47), is perhaps to be explained in part by the influence of χάρις, if it, with συμμετρία or the like, was in the original passage of Panaetius Cicero had in mind. At any rate, the contrast between 'useful' and 'pleasant' (as opposed to 'useful' and 'beautiful,' for which see p. 102) is more typically made by pairing *utilis* to *iucundus: neque inutili et nobis etiam iucundo genere* (Quint. *Inst.* 2.4.26), cf. 2.7.4, 4.5.8, *neque inutilem neque iniucundam* (Apul. *Apol.* 8).

36. *accedat eodem oportet lepos quidam facetiaeque et eruditio libero digna celeritasque et breuitas et respondendi et lacessendi subtili uenustate atque urbanitate coniuncta.*

There are several examples of just this use in Caesar Strabo's *excursus*. The παρὰ προσδοκίαν becomes "particularly deft *(uenustissimus)* when one can snatch something from an opponent and turn it against him, as Catulus did against Philip."[37] In that incident Catulus's name, which means 'pup, whelp,' had provided Philip with a handle to attack him.[38] "Why all the yapping?" said Philip; replied Catulus, "I see a thief" *(de Orat.* 2.220). Another example involves Lamia, who was physically unattractive. As Lamia was interrupting, Crassus said, "Let's listen to the pretty boy" *(pulchellus,* the diminutive of *pulcher* 'beautiful'). After general laughter, Lamia replied, "I could not fashion my body but I did fashion my mind"; to which Crassus replied, "Ah: Let's listen to a good speaker" *(disertus).*[39]

*Venust(us)* does not appear in the typology of humor in *de Oratore* until this particular type of joke, the echoing retort or quick riposte, is discussed.[40] These all occur in and depend on the flow of conversation, which is why they are classed by Caesar Strabo as being *in uerbo* rather than *in re.*[41] The identical sense is sometimes found in the letters—for example, of an attack on Clodius:

> I crushed Clodius to his face in the senate both in a monologue full of seriousness and in give-and-take *(altercatio)* as follows—of which I can only give you a small sample; the rest wouldn't have the same force or

37. *hoc tum est uenustissimum, cum in altercatione arripitur ab aduersario et ex eo, ut a Catulo in Philippum, in eum ipsum aliquid, qui lacessiuit, infligitur (de Orat.* 2.255).

38. Cf. Wilkins ad loc.

39. *inuertuntur autem uerba, ut, Crassus apud M. Perpernam iudicem pro Aculeone cum diceret, aderat contra Aculeonem Gratidiano L. Aelius Lamia, deformis, ut nostis; qui cum interpellaret odiose, 'audiamus' inquit 'pulchellum puerum' Crassus; cum esset adrisum, 'non potui mihi' inquit Lamia 'formam ipse fingere, ingenium potui'; tum hic 'audiamus' inquit 'disertum': multo etiam adrisum est uehementius. Sunt etiam illa uenusta ut in grauibus sententiis, sic in facetiis etc. (de Orat.* 2.262).

40. Cf. also *uenustas* in this description of Socrates: *quorum princeps Socrates fuit, is qui omnium eruditorum testimonio totiusque iudicio Graeciae cum prudentia et acumine et uenustate et subtilitate tum uero eloquentia, uarietate, copia, quam se cumque in partem dedisset omnium fuit facile princeps (de Orat.* 3.60). *Venustas,* which appears associated with qualities comprising intelligence *(prudentia)* and precision *(subtilitas* [cf. below, n. 53], *acumen),* probably means 'deft reply' (not "Verfeinerung" LPW), part of Socrates' ability to handle himself in pointed exchanges. In his case that ability was matched by a gift for lyrical profusion, here described partly in terms connected to the grand style *(eloquentia, uarietas, copia;* cf. *uehementes uarii copiosi graues* of orators in the grand style, *Or.* 20).

41. *quare ea quoque, quoniam mutatis uerbis non possunt retinere eandem uenustatem, non in re, sed in uerbis posita ducantur (de Orat.* 2.258). Humor *in uerbo* is discussed in 253–64, that *in re* in 265–88; cf. Quint. *Inst.* 3.5.1 *omnis autem oratio constat aut ex iis quae significantur aut ex iis quae significant, id est rebus et uerbis.* The distinction ultimately reflects that between ὀνόματα and πράγματα in the Greek philosophical tradition, a distinction tied to problems of presentation and knowledge; cf. Hellwig 1973: 64–110.

charm *(uenustas)* in the absence of that gamesmanship *(studium contentionis* "zeal for struggle") that you Greeks call the *agon.*[42]

(*Att.* 1.16.8)

The letter goes on to quote a sample of the exchange, which took place in
the wake of Clodius's acquittal in the *Bona Dea* affair. In one volley Cicero
bested Clodius by way of a pun on *credere,* 'believe' and 'give on credit, loan':

> "So you've bought a house," said he.
> I rejoined, "One might think he was saying that I had bought a jury."
> "They didn't credit you on oath."
> "On the contrary 25 jurymen gave *me* credit and 31 gave *you* none—
> they got their money in advance." [43]

Cicero may have failed to use *uenust(us)* in *de Oratore* of the more mannered rejoinder from afar simply because spur-of-the-moment witticism is
funnier: Caesar Strabo advises that "jokes that seem to have been prepared
aren't as funny." [44] But Cicero's ideal vision of elite interaction also played
a role. The effect of humor was to create political capital.[45] That effect is
illustrated well by Cicero's exchange with Clodius. When Cicero volleyed
every one of Clodius's shots, Clodius was defeated and the senate roused to
support Cicero: *magnis clamoribus adflictus conticuit et concidit* "Beset by great
shouting, he fell silent and collapsed" (*Att.* 1.16.10). *Clamor* 'shout' can mean
'applause,' [46] but its patina is significant: *clamor* is also the word for the vocal
remonstration that had recognized status in the legal system.[47] Clean shots

42. *Clodium praesentem fregi in senatu cum oratione perpetua plenissima grauitatis tum altercatione eius modi—ex qua licet pauca degustes; nam cetera non possunt habere eandem neque uim neque
uenustatem remoto illo studio contentionis quem* ἀγῶνα *uos appellatis.*

43. Tr. SB. Cf. *Fam.* 8.11.2, from the hand of Caelius: *quibus hac re ad intercessionem euo-
candam interpellantibus uenustissime Curio respondit se eo libentius non intercedere quod quosdam qui
decernerent uideret confici nolle* "When they were interrupting to provoke Curio into exercis-
ing his veto, he replied very deftly *(uenustissime)* that he was that much gladder not to do so
because he saw that certain parties who were voting for the issue didn't actually want it car-
ried." On the political situation, see SB.

44. *ea, quia meditata putantur esse, minus ridentur (de Orat.* 2.246), cf. *uitabit etiam quaesita
nec ex tempore ficta sed domo allata quae plerumque sunt frigida* "[The orator] will also avoid contrived jokes brought from home, and not made up on the spur of the moment, since such
jokes generally fall flat" (*Or.* 89).

45. See Corbeill 1996: ch. 5, "A Political History of Wit."

46. Cf. Wilkins ad 1.152.

47. *Lex duodecim tabularum furem noctu deprehensum occidere permittit, ut tamen id ipsum cum
clamore testificetur: interdiu autem deprehensum ita permittit occidere, si is se telo defendat, ut tamen
aeque cum clamore testificetur* (Gaius *dig.* 9.2.4.1), "A law of the Twelve Tables permits the
killing of a thief caught by night, with the stipulation that witness be made to the act by out-

could rouse a Roman audience not simply to pleasure, as "applause" implies, but to a kind of sanctioned disapproval of a victim, something, perhaps, like the huzzahs of the British House of Commons during the Prime Minister's Question Time.[48] Waggish comments from afar, however, like Clodius's likening of Cicero to Jupiter (*Dom.* 92, V.5), also reaped political capital; in that case, at least, Cicero felt the pressure to counterattack. And indeed Caesar Strabo does include a little of the more mannered sort of humor in his taxonomy.[49] Cicero practiced it himself, according to Quintilian.[50]

Restricting *uenust(us)* to spur-of-the-moment replies also restricts the sort of person who can produce political capital, and in what context. For one thing the person who only made *uenust(us)* comments in direct reply had societal sanction to do so. It was generally held that defensive thrusts were morally justifiable.[51] In *de Oratore* Antonius makes the point:

> As a whole, what we say when we've been injured is more acceptable than what we say on the attack ("first"): a greater swiftness of intellect is required in making a response, and furthermore a response is understandable *(humanitatis est)*; it seems as if we would have said nothing, had we not been accosted.[52]
>
> (*de Orat.* 2.230)

---

cry *(clamore)*; and it permits the killing of a thief caught by day if the thief defends himself with a weapon, with the same stipulation." An instance of this sort of *clamor* is related in the story from *Rhet. Her.* cited above (III.2). The sense of 'outcry of public indignation' is more frequent in Cicero than 'applause'; perhaps we should imagine Clodius being shouted down rather than Cicero lauded.

48. Cf. *OLD* 1b s.v.; the usual word is *adclamatio*, cf. *OLD* 2b s.v.

49. To depict the character of the savage Memmius, who, in a fight over a mistress in the town of Tarracina, had bitten his rival, Crassus concocted a story: he claimed that in Tarracina he had seen the graffiti LLLMM (close to the common inscriptional LLM = *lubens laetus merito*) and that when he asked after the meaning, an old townsman told him it meant *lacerat lacertum Largi mordax Memmius* (an iambic trimeter) "Nippy Memmius wounds the arm of Largus" (*de Orat.* 2.240; cf. LPR). Cicero then adds, *perspicitis genus hoc quam sit facetum, quam elegans, quam oratorium, siue habeas uere quod narrare possis, quod tamen est mendaciunculis aspergendum, siue fingas* "You see how witty, elegant, and befitting the orator this type of humor is, whether you have an actual tale to tell—not that it can't be spiced with little lies—or whether you make one up" (2.241).

50. Quintilian says that Cicero put made-up anecdotes about Verres in the mouths of witnesses (*Inst.* 6.3.4), cf. V.2 ad fin.

51. Cf. *de Off.* 1.20: *sed iustitiae primum munus est, ut ne cui quis noceat nisi lacessitus iniuria.* . . . Cf. Plut. *Mor.* 634A–F = *Quaest. Conviv.* 2.1.13.

52. *omnino probabiliora sunt, quae lacessiti dicimus quam quae priores, nam et ingenii celeritas maior est, quae apparet in respondendo, et humanitatis est responsio; uidemur enim quieturi fuisse, nisi essemus lacessiti.*

In the *Pro Plancio,* Cicero justifies his own humor, and by extension that of
Plancius, who had an acid tongue, by saying he uses it "not out of some passion for wit, but in verbal struggles, or when I'm attacked" (*non studio adductus sed aut contentione dicendi aut lacessitus,* 35). The addition of the element of
accuracy to *uenustas* in *de Orat.* 1.17 speaks to the same point: *subtilis,* reminiscent of the acuity and precision of dialectic and the "plain" style, connotes an accuracy that distinguishes acceptable humor from the broad brush
of *scurrae* (cf. above, p. 212 and below, p. 226).[53]

In preferring not the clean stroke but the clean stroke in the heat of battle,
Cicero also has a particular audience in mind: the elite on the senate floor
or in court, where such exchanges could, and did, take place. *Venustas* is denied to those with a more mannered taste in humor, who brought set pieces
from home or circulated their own witty concoctions socially. To prefer the
spontaneous over the mannered is, in effect, to take a position on the ideal
structure of the elite person: meant to be, rather than made to be.[54] What
is at issue in such distinctions is ideology, not fact: one can of course make
a very good case that Cicero "made" himself, that he was a "created" personality in an era when self-creation was eminently possible. That is not the
point: the point is that, possibly without being entirely aware of it, Cicero

53. For a good sketch of the word's range and possible path of development, cf. Wilkins
ad loc., with the longer note of Ernest 1983 s.v. *Subtilis* always contains the notion of 'fine-
ness,' which yields a variety of metaphorical outcomes, such as 'careful' (e.g., *a quo haec quae
ego nunc percurro subtilissime sunt omnia perpolita, Balb.* 50), 'discriminating' (e.g., *qui haec subtiliter iudicat, Ver.* 2.4.12; *homo doctus et a suis Graecis subtilius eruditus, Prov.* 14; *palatum,* Hor.
*Serm.* 2.8.38), 'precise' (*interfecta inde quattuor milia et, exsequendo subtiliter numerum, ducentos
ait et triginta* Livy 3.5.13, ἄπαξ), 'cogent' (*quoniam philosophia in tris partis est tributa, in naturae obscuritatem, in disserendi subtilitatem, in uitam atque mores, de Orat.* 1.68, where *in disserendi
subtilitatem* is put for ἡ λογική, cf. *subtilitate quadam disputandi, Brut.* 31; *in docendo edisseren-
doque subtilior, Brut.* 65, cf. *Fin.* 1.7, *Tusc.* 4.14), and 'in detail' (*sed haec ad te scribam alias subtilius, Att.* 1.13.4; *de re publica quid ego tibi subtiliter? Att.* 2.21.1). It is also associated with the
"plain style"; cf. *tenuis aut subtilis aut breuis* (*Opt. Gen.* 2), *subtilis* (*de Orat.* 3.177), *subtili quadam
et pressa oratione et limita* (*Or.* 20), *subtilis oratio* (78), *subtilis* (96), *subtilis et acutus* (98), *egregie
subtilis scriptor atque elegans* (*Brut.* 35, of Lysias, master of the plain style). The sense of a "clean
shot" that I see in *de Orat.* 1.17 is found in Sen. *Con.* 7.pr.1: *argumentabatur moleste magis quam
subtiliter: argumenta enim argumentis colligebat, et, quasi nihil esset satis firmum, omnes probationes
probationibus aliis confirmat.*

54. Cicero typically treats a sense of humor as natural, impossible to acquire: *[iocus et face-
tiae] etiam si alia omnia arte tradi possunt, naturae sunt propria certe neque ullam artem desiderant* (*de
Orat.* 2.216), *sed cum illo in genere perpetuae festiuitatis ars non desideretur (natura enim fingit
homines et creat imitatores et narratores facetos adiuuante et uultu et uoce et ipso genere sermonis) tum
uero in hoc altero dicacitatis quid habet ars loci, cum ante illud facete dictum emissum haerere debeat,
quam cogitari potuisse uideatur?* (*de Orat.* 2.219).

has used words in a way that reflects an ideological bias. The gracious aristocrats who bemusedly sanctioned the *bellus* and exhibited educated *lepos* might well be expected to make *uenust(us)* comments only when provoked, and to valorize them only in those contexts where such comments reinforced their own privileges. We might even account for this use of *uenust(us)* by saying that Cicero construed the element of 'arrangement' that was a part of lexeme (I.6) as referring to a natural shape, or a shape that cleanly imitated natural forms, the "lovely" defensive strokes of verbal gladiators, not the mannered gesticulations of dancers.[55] Note that, in this regard, whereas an element of 'choice' is often apparent in Cicero's use of *elegan(s)*, ultimately he seems to think that *elegantia* is a kind of natural correctness independent of the props of the grammatical study: it, too, is meant to be, rather than made to be (III.6; contrast VIII.4).

In the light of Cicero's tendentious handling of *lep(idus)*, *bellus*, and *uenust(us)*, it is significant that the commonest word for humor in *de Oratore* is *facet(us)*.[56] That is the word that most commonly serves a generic term.[57] As we saw above (III.2), *facet(us)* referred to verbal performance that established or displayed social status. It is used by Cicero as a term for 'humor' in view of this feature;[58] the truly neutral terms are *ridiculus* and *iocus*.[59] Fa-

---

55. Cf. III.4.2 ad fin.     56. Cf. Index Locorum.

57. *suauis autem est et uehementer saepe utilis iocus et facetiae* (*de Orat.* 2.216); *de ipsis facetiis* (*de Orat.* 2.217); *duo genera facetiarum* (*de Orat.* 2.218); *imitatores et narratores facetos* (*de Orat.* 2.219); *multum facetias in dicendo prodesse* (*de Orat.* 2.227); *artem facetiarum* (*de Orat.* 2.229); *praeceptum praetermittendarum . . . facetiarum* (*de Orat.* 2.229); *primum loquar de facetiis* (*de Orat.* 2.233); *duo sunt enim genera facetiarum* (*de Orat.* 2.239); *sic in facetiis* (*de Orat.* 2.262); *uerborum quidem genera, quae essent faceta* (*de Orat.* 2.264); *omnia quae a me de facetiis disputantur* (*de Orat.* 2.271).

58. Cf. Grant 1924: 113 ". . . the proper province of the *facetus* was the humor depending on the substance of the thought . . . ," as opposed to buffoonery.

59. *Ridiculum*, related to *ridere*, serves as the closest rendering of γελοῖον 'laughable, causing laughter'; the technical sections of the discussion in which it is embedded are thoroughly in the spirit of Greek philosophy and rhetoric. Cf. Grant 1924: 101, LPR 186. Aristotle uses γελοῖον as the generic term in the *Rhetoric* (1419b3 = 3.18.7); the corresponding section of the *Poetics* to which he there refers is lost. Theophrastus wrote a περὶ γελοίου (fr. 130), and humor was a special interest of the Peripatetics. For possible sources of Cicero's discussion, cf. LPR "Der Ursprung der ciceronischen Witzlehre" 190–206.

*Iocus* simply describes the thing said, without specification of its character, as indeed its etymology suggests (\*yek- > OHG **jëhan, gehan** 'say, speak,' Bret. **iez** 'speech'; other derivatives all of speech acts: Skt. **yaçāti** 'entreats', **yaççñā** 'request'; Umbr. **iuka** 'religious formula, request made at a solemnity,' Osc. **iúkleí** 'formula of consecration' (loc. sg.) (Pok. 1.204). So for a famous joke of Novius (2.285) or the joke of a *scurra* or *mimus* (*iocus scurrilis aut mimicus,* 2.239). *Iocus* is often used collectively in this sense (216, 229, 236, 250). Since

*cet(us)* expressly distinguishes socially acceptable wit from mere humor in *de Oratore* in a passage we have seen (*non esse omnia ridicula faceta*, 2.251, I.8) and has the same function in the *de Officiis:*

> We do not permit children to play at any game they choose, but only at those which are consonant with proper behavior. In the same way, the light of a proper character, so to speak, should show through in humor. Jests fall into one or the other of two types: one is undignified *(illiberalis)*, impudent *(petulans)*, disgraceful *(flagitiosus)*, and crude *(obscenus)*; the other is elegant *(elegans)*, sophisticated *(urbanus)*, intelligent *(ingeniosus)*, and witty *(facetus)*. This latter sort of humor is common not only in Plautus and Attic Old Comedy,[60] but also in the books of the Socratic philosophers and in the collections of ἀποφθέγματα, or

---

*iocus* is also the only term with a usable verbal derivative, *iocari* also serves when a verb is called for, e.g., *totum hoc genus iocandi* (2.231). *Hoc genus ridendi* would, of course, refer to audience response.

I may add here that *sal* and *salsus*, which are also common terms in *de Oratore*, refer to a particular kind of humor, one that has an ironic, dissimulating, or deadpan quality. So, for example, of irony proper, a kind of humor "very elegant, and witty *(salsum)* without sacrificing weightiness, appropriate to oratorical speech and sophisticated conversation both" (*genus est perelegans et cum grauitate salsum cumque oratoriis dictionibus tum urbanis sermonibus accommodatum*, 2.270) and of "irritated and rather annoyed" comments *(stomachosa and submorosa)*, but not made by someone who is, in fact, annoyed; for then the humor is in their character, not their wittiness *(tum enim non sal sed natura ridetur).*' Almost all of the other instances of *salsus* or its relatives refer to such disparities: so for a made-up story (240), taking words literally (259), oblique suggestion (277), feigned irritation (270 bis), feigned foolishness (274), comic ἀδύνατα (287), and gentle refusal (287). In *de Orat.* 2.289 Crassus is deadpanning. The only exception is 280, referring to attacks on foolishness. *Insulsitas* is used in 216 for the witlessness of those who attempt to define humor precisely.

The application of the terms for humor as described in this note and chapter 6 is clear in its outlines, even if it cannot be insisted on dogmatically. The approach taken here is different from LPR, who divide the terminology for humor by practico-grammatical categories (those pertaining to the joker, those to the joke, and those to the effect on the hearer); but their interest in translation, and not core semantics, leads them to ἀπορία: "jedes der hier untersuchten Wörter hat also seinen eigenen Bedeutungskreis und wird auch manchmal in spezifischer Bedeutung benutzt. Dennoch überwiegen die Fälle, wo man nicht leicht einen Unterschied in der Bedeutung feststellen kann. Letzteres gilt besonders bei den frequenten Synonymenhäufungen" (187). In fact the perception of synonymy is precisely Cicero's object. By combining elements of the native vocabulary, he manages to describe an idea that had not been described before; Latin lacked an adaptable superordinate term for the kind of "humor" that Cicero is attempting to define.

60. For Cicero's acquiescence in Panaetius's judgment of Old Comedy, cf. Dyck 1996 ad loc.

witty sayings *(facete dicta);* for example, the collection of sayings made
by Cato.[61]

(*Off.* 1.104)

The broad application of *facet(us)* in Cicero might seem to belie the claim
that *facet(us)* implies humor that is 'socially distinctive' as opposed to merely
'funny.' We have seen *facet(us)* used of the likes of Torquatus (*Sul.* 22, V.4),
Marc Antony (*Phil.* 2.20, V.4), and Clodia's retinue (*Cael.* 67, V.6). Cicero
applies *facet(us)* to *scurrae* (*Quinct.* 11, V.4) and to "cut-ups" (beside *dicax, de
Orat.* 2.221).[62] But this broader use of the word still has the feature 'to establish social status' underlying. In an age when performance, as I have argued in chapter 5, was valued highly, even excessively, the range of application of the lexeme must naturally have extended widely, since many
persons will have wanted to explain their behavior in those terms; as we
have seen, in the case of Clodia's coterie, *facet(us)* probably sarcastically re-
peats labels they were using for themselves (*Cael.* 67, V.6). In short, the fact
that *facet(us)* implied social distinction was precisely what made it attractive,
and precisely what inspires Cicero's efforts in his speeches to countermand
the values it described. In the rhetorica Cicero faces no such difficulties and
could rather let the lexeme resonate with the character of the speakers who
use it: in the mouth of Caesar Strabo or Crassus—speakers who (to recall
the epigraph to this chapter) are δοκοῦντες—*facet(us)* connoted a respectable social performance. In any case the potentially hostile edge of *facet(us)*
is actively muted by modifiers or collocational partners. Crassus's *facetiae*
were *politissimae* "very polished" (*de Orat.* 1.243). *Dignitas,* beside *lepos,* is
an essential accompaniment in this passage:

> Humor *(facetiae),* quickness, and bon mots that are charming *(cum le-
> pore)* and not at odds with one's social standing *(nec sine dignitate)* are no-
> where more useful than in this case; for there is nothing so easy as lead-

61. *ut enim pueris non omnem ludendi licentiam damus, sed eam, quae ab honestatis actionibus
non sit aliena, sic in ipso ioco aliquod probi ingenii lumen eluceat. Duplex omnino est iocandi genus,
unum inliberale, petulans, flagitiosum, obscenum, alterum elegans, urbanum, ingeniosum, facetum, quo
genere non modo Plautus noster et Atticorum antiqua comoedia, sed etiam philosophorum Socraticorum
libri referti sunt, multaque multorum facete dicta, ut ea, quae a sene Catone collecta sunt, quae uocan-
tur* ἀποφθέγματα. Chs. 8–9 of Plutarch's life of Cato are a collection of his own *dicta.*

62. *quod [= parcere aduersari dignitati] est hominibus facetis et dicacibus difficillimum, habere hominum rationem et temporum et ea, quae occurrunt, cum salsissime dici possunt, tenere* (*de Orat.* 2.221).
This is not a strong case of *facetus* as a neutral term, since its sense is affected by that of
*dicax.*

ing the audience out of sourness and even bitterness with an apt, quick,
keen, and amusing phrase.[63]

(*de Orat.* 2.340)

Crassus's comments from a particular *contio* are called *faceta . . . et urbana* (*de
Orat.* 2.227).[64] In *de Oratore, facet(us)* is once connected with *elegan(s),* the
value of which in elite self-definition we saw above (III.6).[65]

It is also significant that, just as *facet(us)* is the commonest, so *festiu(us)* has
the smallest place.[66] There is a practical semantic reason for that: *festiu(us)*
refers to a more diffuse, narrative humor (III.7), which is more difficult to
exemplify except in extenso, whereas the *excursus de ridiculis* for the most
part compiles short bon mots. But there is also an ideological reason for the
restricted appearance of *festiu(us).* It is the least appropriate lexeme for the
ideal of humor Cicero is representing, being bodily reminiscent of festivity,
rather than the cooler urbanity that Cicero valorizes. *Festiu(us),* as we saw,
is one of the words Crassus does not want to hear too often (*de Orat.* 3.101,

63. *nullo autem loco plus facetiae prosunt et celeritas et breue aliquod dictum nec sine dignitate et
cum lepore; nihil enim tam facile quam multitudo a tristitia et saepe ab acerbitate commode et breuiter
et acute et hilare dicto deducitur.* Cf. *de Orat.* 3.30, *Brut.* 143 *(non scurrilis lepos),* 158 *(multae et cum
grauitate facetiae).* Nec sine dignitate probably renders something like κατὰ τὸ ἀξίωμα or κατὰ
τὸ πρέπον; my translation, "not at odds with one's social standing," attempts to suggest
the extra-rhetorical flavor of *dignitas* which I believe is appropriate here. A more conservative translation would be simply "not without propriety." On *dignitas* = πρέπον vel sim., cf.
Stroux 1912: 49 re Cic. *Top.* 97, with Quint. *Inst.* 4.2.64.

64. Cf. *et splendida et grandis et eadem in primis faceta et perurbana . . . oratio* (*Brut.* 273).

65. *perspicitis genus hoc quam sit facetum, quam elegans, quam oratorium* (*de Orat.* 2.241), of
anecdotes. For the union of *facet(us)* and *elegan(s),* cf. *ironiam illam quam in Socrate dicunt fuisse
. . . facetam et elegantem puto* (*Brut.* 292), *sed mehercules extra iocum ualde mihi tuae litterae facetae
elegantesque uisae sunt* (*Fam.* 7.32.3). Irony is also described by *elegan(s)* in the company of *salsus* and *urbanus*: *genus [hoc ridiculi = ironia] est perelegans et cum grauitate salsum cumque oratoriis
dictionibus tum urbanis sermonibus accommodatum* "Irony is very tasteful (*perelegans),* witty *(salsum)* without sacrificing weight of character *(grauitas),* and just as appropriate to oratory as
to dinner conversation" (*de Orat.* 2.270).

This is a convenient place to record a few instances of *facetus* in Cicero's letter to describe
the 'intelligent wit' of his correspondents—or himself. In addition to *Fam.* 7.32.3 (just
cited), cf. *de uilla Seliciana et curasti diligenter et scripsisti facetissime* (*Fam.* 9.16.10), *ioca tua plena
facetiarum* (*Att.* 14.14.1), *. . . si apud te plus auctoritatis mea quam tua siue natura paulo acrior siue
quaedam dulcedo iracundiae siue dicendi sal facetiaeque ualuissent* (*Q. fr.* 1.2.7).

66. *summa festiuitate et uenustate coniuncta* (*de Orat.* 1.243, III.7); *illo in genere perpetuae festiuitatis* (*de Orat.* 2.219), *neque lepore et festiuitate conditior* (*de Orat.* 2.227), *festiuitatem habet narratio . . . etc.* (*de Orat.* 2.328, III.7, of entertaining narrative), *concinnam distinctam ornatam festiuam* (*de Orat.* 3.100, IV.4 n. 25, of decorated speech), *belle et festiue* (*de Orat.* 3.101, probably
not of humor).

III.5); and though in that passage he means precious figures, the word bespoke a kind of 'jollity' that Cicero felt incompatible with the purpose of his *excursus de ridiculis*.

## VI.5. *Apologia pro Facetiis Suis*

In short the normative, as opposed to descriptive, uses of the language of social performance in Cicero's *de Oratore* have largely to do with a kind of humor that is plainly envisioned as the common possession of an idealized social elite. We must now consider why that is so. I would suggest that this tendentiousness on Cicero's part is a response to pressures from various quarters. Cicero himself was very much given to humor. He confesses to Paetus, a correspondent with whom his tone is often jocular, that he is enthralled with humor *(facetiae),* particularly Roman humor.[67] In another letter he reveals that he enjoys the reputation of a wit, glad to have all keen and clever witticisms attributed to him—regardless of whether they are genuine:

> I had hoped the sorts of sayings I left behind me were sufficiently well marked that they could be immediately recognized. But the dregs of the city are such that there is nothing so tasteless (ἀκύθηρον) that it doesn't seem charming *(uenustus)*[68] to somebody. So please, weigh in and swear on oath that they aren't mine—unless the joke is a keen double entendre, an elegant overstatement, a nice little jeu de mots, a funny inversion of expectation, or anything else that looks keen *(argutus)* and artful (ἔντεχνος), the things I discussed on the topic of humor in the second book of *de Oratore* through the character of Antonius.[69]
>
> (*Fam.* 7.32.2)

Quintilian records that Cicero "made many humorous *(facetus)* comments in everyday conversation and more than anyone in exchanges and in inter-

---

67. *ego autem (existimes licet quidlibet) mirifice capior facetiis, maxime nostratibus* (*Fam.* 9.15.2).

68. There is a cross-linguistic pun between ἀκύθηρον 'without Cytherea,' i.e., 'without Venus,' and *uenustum*.

69. *equidem sperabam ita notata me reliquisse genera dictorum meorum ut cognosci sua sponte possent. sed quoniam tanta faex est in urbe ut nihil tam sit* ἀκύθηρον *quod non alicui uenustum esse uideatur, pugna, si me amas, nisi acuta* ἀμφιβολία, *nisi elegans* ὑπερβολή, *nisi* παράγραμμα *bellum, nisi ridiculum* παρὰ προσδοκίαν, *nisi cetera quae sunt a me in secundo libro de oratore per Antoni personam disputata de ridiculis* ἔντεχνα *et arguta apparebunt, ut sacramento contendas mea non esse* (*Fam.* 7.32.2). The character, as we have seen, is actually C. Iulius Caesar Strabo, not Antonius. As mentioned above, Cicero did have the problem of jokes being wrongly attributed to him, cf. *Planc.* 35. Antony apparently tried to turn against Cicero some of the jokes he had made before Pharsalus (*Phil.* 2.39, cf. Plut. *Cic.* 38).

rogating witnesses."[70] As discussed in chapter 6, and above in considering *uenust(us)*, humor had considerable power, putting the less artful party on the defensive. Like any powerful social instrument, humor therefore had to be used with care and restraint. That is something that some felt Cicero lacked. His comic tactics as defense counsel in the *pro Murena* led Cato, the prosecutor, to remark, "Our consul is quite the comedian, gentlemen!"[71] Quintilian reports that Cicero's comedic streak was not always welcome to his peers,[72] and Plutarch avers that Cicero sometimes transgressed propriety (τὸ πρέπον) in his jesting, falling into "scurrility" (τὸ βωμολόχον) and treating serious matters lightly[73]—the very sin Cicero himself advises against in *Or.* 98–99 (see below). Plutarch attributes the origin of "much enmity" (πολὺ . . . μῖσος) against Cicero to his penchant for raising a laugh (*Cic.* 27.1). His enemies called him a *scurra consularis* (Macrob. *Sat.* 2.1.12) and even his friend Paetus a *scurra ueles* 'light-armed jester' (*Fam.* 9.20.1, where see SB).

Cicero's treatment of humor in *de Oratore* is designed, perhaps first and foremost, to justify humor to such critics. No doubt Cicero's opponents used the language of social performance against him in exactly the same way he used it against Hortensius, Clodius, or Sex. Naevius. It is not hard to imagine the part the language of social performance must have played in the petulance of Cicero's opponents. "I'm not as *facetus* as M. Tullius," someone doubtless said, "but I know that a jury must judge by the facts of the case and not the *lepos* of the patrons. If cases were to be decided by *lepos* alone, juries would need only to ask Roscius what he thought." "If I do not make *uenustus* replies," some thwarted duelist must have snapped, "the reason is that I always prefer to think first, and then act, rather than seek immediate applause, like a rope-dancer." Indeed Cato's remark about Cicero's conduct of the *pro Murena,* which Plutarch records as ὡς γελοῖον, ὦ ἄνδρες, ἔχομεν ὕπατον, was probably exactly such an instance: Cato's

---

70. *nam et in sermone cotidiano multa et in altercationibus et interrogandis testibus plura quam quisquam dixit facete* (6.3.4).

71. ὡς γελοῖον, ὦ ἄνδρες, ἔχομεν ὕπατον (Plut. *Cat. Min.* 21).

72. Cf. Quint. *Inst.* 12.10.12; above, V.7 n.119.

73. Κικέρων δὲ πολλαχοῦ τῷ σκωπτικῷ πρὸς τὸ βωμολόχον ἐκφερόμενος καὶ πράγματα σπουδῆς ἄξια γέλωτι παιδιᾷ κατειρωνευόμενος ἐν ταῖς δίκαις εἰς τὸ χρειῶδες ἠφείδει τοῦ πρέποντος "The frequent approach of Cicero's humor to scurrility and his comic, playful ironizing of serious matters in the course of trials exceeded the requirements of propriety" (*Comp. Dem. cum Cic.* 1.4). Cf. ἡ δὲ περὶ τὰ σκώμματα καὶ τὴν παιδιὰν ταύτην εὐτραπελία δικανικὸν μὲν ἐδόκει καὶ γλαφυρὸν εἶναι, χρώμενος δ' αὐτῇ κατακόρως πολλοὺς ἐλύπει καὶ κακοηθείας ἐλάμβανε δόξαν (Plut. *Cic.* 5.6).

comment would be more pungent—indeed more *facetus*—if it was not the purely dismissive *quam ridiculum habemus consulem* but rather *quam facetum* or *quam lepidum habemus consulem,* with *facetus* or *lepidus* acknowledging the attractions, and suggesting the dangers, of aestheticism.[74] In his treatment of humor in *de Oratore,* Cicero reconfigures a volatile language doubtless applied to him, and not entirely by way of compliment, until it seems to describe a dignified humor that suits, indeed is virtually required of, aristocrats—nor merely contemporary aristocrats, but aristocrats just beyond the horizon of recent history and untainted by current roils. Cicero might construct *lepos* and *facetiae* as an addendum,[75] but that construction, far from simple modesty, asserts that those qualities really can exist in harmony with *grauitas.* Indeed that harmony is something of a minor theme in Cicero's use of the language of social performance. Speaking of Crassus, for example, Cicero says that his "presence was such that his exquisite bearing nevertheless did not lack culture and charm *(lepos)*" *(sic autem grauis, ut in singulari dignitate omnis tamen adsit humanitas et lepos, de Orat.* 3.29).[76] In such formulations there is perhaps something of a challenge, if, in order to be an aristocrat, one has to have a firm control of wit, for then one has to become not like the august Cato but like Cicero himself. Apology, as often, shades into didaxis.

There may have been a second party before whom Cicero had to defend wit, really a sensibility rather than a party: the "Atticists" who favored a plainer, more Stoic style of speech. "Attic" was a buzzword for the literary movement that opposed Cicero's grandiloquence and floridity, a movement centered on the orator L. Licinius Calvus. Calvus is likely to have died shortly after 54,[77] and the beginning of the "Atticist movement" may be as

74. The suggestion is Leeman's 1963: 61; 398 n.100, who submits that *facetus consul* would have been "an oxymoron in Roman ears."

75. Thus "the orator *also* needs to have a certain wit *(lepos)* and sense of humor *(facetiae)*" *(de Orat.* 1.17), and "The orator should *also* take a kind of humorous charm *(facetiarum lepos)* from every kind of urbanity, as a kind of salt to season the whole speech with" *(de Orat.* 1.158, Latin above). For the image of *lepos* as an added 'spice' or 'condiment,' cf. also *nemo umquam urbanitate nemo lepore nemo suauitate conditior (Brut.* 177), *nec apud populum grauior oratio . . . neque lepore et festiuitate conditior (de Orat.* 2.227).

76. For other instances of the juxtaposition of *lepos* and *grauitas,* cf. *erat summa grauitas, erat cum grauitate iunctus facetiarum et urbanitatis oratorius, non scurrilis lepos (Brut.* 143); *itaque cum Socratem unice dilexisset eique omnia tribuere uoluisset, leporem Socraticum subtilitatemque sermonis cum obscuritate Pythagorae et cum illa plurimarum artium grauitate contexuit (Rep.* 1.16); *et modus in dicendo et grauitate mixtus lepos et summum uel discendi studium uel docendi et orationi uita admodum congruens (Rep.* 2.1).

77. Bowersock 1979: 61.

early as 60,[78] which means it was already afoot when Cicero was composing *de Oratore*. "Atticists" took a dim view of humor, as Cicero observes ten
years after *de Oratore* in a passage of the *Orator* describing the ideal version
of the plain style. I quote the passage at length also to illustrate Cicero's continued devotion to the ideal expressed in the *excursus de ridiculis*:

> The [plain-style] orator ought to use humor *(ridiculum)* in such a way
> that it not be clownish *(scurrilis)* for being too frequent, nor like a mime's
> humor for being off-color, nor reprehensible for being impudent, nor
> unfeeling for making light of disasters, nor substitute laughter for out-
> rage by making light of misdeeds; nor should the humor be inappro-
> priate *(alienum)* to the orator's persona, or that of the judges, or to the
> occasion. These are examples of impropriety *(indecorum)*. The orator
> will also avoid contrived jokes, ones not made up on the spot but
> brought from home; such jokes generally fall flat. He will treat friend-
> ships *(amicitiae)* and social status *(dignitas)* carefully, he will avoid irre-
> mediable abuse, he will attack only his adversaries and then not always,
> nor every one of them, nor in all ways possible. With these exceptions,
> ` he will make use of wit *(sal)* and humor *(facetiae)* in a way that I have
> seen none of the latter-day Atticists do, despite the fact that doing so
> is quite in accord with the Attic character.[79]
>
> (*Or.* 98–99)

Possibly, then, there is something polemical about Cicero's use of the language of social performance for humor in *de Oratore*, suggesting a performative attractiveness implicitly denied to plainer, "Attic" speakers. In defending the importance of humor, Caesar Strabo notably assigns cardinal
significance to that fact that the sour moods of an audience call for humor,
for they cannot be altered by argument—the forte of the plain style and the
ideal of the "latter-day Atticists."

> It is clearly in accord with the orator's duties to raise a laugh, for many
> reasons: merriment wins goodwill for the person who has raised it; lis-
> teners are impressed particularly by keen, short replies and at times even

---

78. Cf. the plausible arguments of Wisse 1995. On Atticism generally, see Gelzer 1979.

79. *illud admonemus tamen ridiculo sic usurum oratorem, ut nec nimis frequenti ne scurrile sit, nec
subobsceno ne mimicum, nec petulanti ne improbum, nec in calamitatem ne inhumanum, nec in facinus ne odii locum risus occupet, neque aut sua persona aut iudicum aut tempore alienum. haec enim ad
illud indecorum referuntur. uitabit etiam quaesita nec ex tempore ficta sed domo allata quae plerumque
sunt frigida, parcet et amicitiis et dignitatibus, uitabit insanabilis contumelias, tantummodo aduersarios
figet nec eos tamen semper nec omnis nec omni modo. quibus exceptis sic utetur sale et facetiis, ut ego
ex istis nouis Atticis talem cognouerim neminem, cum id certe sit uel maxume Atticum.*

attacks; humor breaks an opponent's attack, slows him down, makes him look foolish, keeps him back, refutes him; humor shows that the orator is a polished *(politus),* educated *(eruditus),* urbane *(urbanus)* man; and above all, humor mitigates grimness and severity and, with a laugh and a joke *(ioco risuque),* often does away with noisome matters that cannot be easily resolved with argumentation.[80]

*(de Orat.* 2.236)

In sum, the distinctive uses of the language of social performance in *de Oratore* cluster around humor, where they serve two purposes: to justify Cicero's own comic propensities, and perhaps to justify the use of humor generally against a new, plainer oratorical sensibility. Thus the ostensibly technical use of the language of social performance in the *excursus de ridiculis* was indeed influenced by the contemporary cultural developments affecting the language elsewhere: the allure that the language had come to possess is something that Cicero both soft-pedals, with an eye to sterner critics, and espouses, with an eye to plainer speakers, on the one hand subduing, and on the other defending, a set of characteristics imputed to him. The simultaneous appropriation and deminution of the language of social performance includes, but limits, "stylish attractiveness" in the structure of the elite persona.

The peculiarity of the language of social performance in *de Oratore* is set into relief by the *Brutus* and *Orator,* which postdate it by ten years. The former gives an account of oratory from its origins to Cicero's time,[81] and the latter attempts to define the Platonic form of the public speaker, in a leaner and less leisurely way than *de Oratore.*[82] The lexemes of the language of social performance are common in these works as rhetorical technical terms, and less distinctive vis-à-vis the evidently received uses. The *bellus* of appreciable waggery is gone; indeed *bellus* is gone almost altogether.[83] *Lepos* appears proportionally more rarely and much more rarely in absolute terms; and of its eight appearances (compared to some twenty in *de Oratore),* only

---

80. *est autem . . . plane oratoris mouere risum; uel quod ipsa hilaritas beneuolentiam conciliat ei, per quem excitata est; uel quod admirantur omnes acumen uno saepe in uerbo positum maxime respondentis, non numquam etiam lacessentis; uel quod frangit aduersarium, quod impedit, quod eleuat, quod deterret, quod refutat; uel quod ipsum oratorem politum esse hominem significat, quod eruditum, quod urbanum, maximeque quod tristitiam ac seueritatem mitigat et relaxat odiosasque res saepe, quas argumentis dilui non facile est, ioco risuque dissoluit.*

81. V. the introduction to the commentary of Douglas 1966.

82. V. the introduction to the commentary of Sandys 1885.

83. *bella ironia si iocaremur (Brut.* 293), on which see III.5 above.

three apply to the ideal sort of humor described in the *excursus de ridiculis,* and only in passing.[84] The *uenust(us)* of the quick rejoinder is gone; the lexeme is used of *actio* and of graceful shapes, as also in *de Oratore;* of mannered rhetorical effects, a use doubtful in the earlier work; and as an apparent equivalent for χαρίεις, unexampled in *de Oratore.*[85] *Facet(us)* is common in the sense 'humor' but has lost its old partner *lepos.* The application of the adjective to the "plain style," nowhere in *de Oratore,* is found a few times.[86] The most notable feature of the *Brutus* and *Orator* is the explosion in the use of *elegan(s):* whereas in *de Oratore* the lexeme appears only about five times for every one hundred *OCT* pages, in the *Orator* the number jumps to nearly seventeen, and in the *Brutus* to almost thirty, just about every third page.

This later configuration of the language of social performance as rhetorical language has one principal cause. The Atticist movement, which may have had certain effects even on *de Oratore,* certainly had considerable effects on the later major rhetorica. The presence of the new school is felt strongly in the *Brutus,* the addressee of which, M. Iunius Brutus, was an adherent of Atticism.[87] In the *Orator,* which is also addressed to Brutus, the rhetorical ideal espoused, that a speaker should have at his disposal each of three styles and their functions,[88] is also a response to the Atticists, who by Atticism meant, not the virtuoso variety of Demosthenes, but the tepid elegance of Lysias.[89] The resistance of Atticists to humor, which is explicitly defended in the *Orator* and implicitly approved in the *Brutus,* we have seen above. The by-now significant Atticist movement may have affected the range of some of our lexemes. *Venust(us)* as a simple equivalent for χάρι(s), which appears first in the *Orator* may, as I have suggested above (III.4 ad fin.), be an innovation of the Atticists, by way of describing the signal quality of Lysias. *Elegan(s),* which also had connections to the plain style (III.6),[90] and certainly well expressed the economy so favored by Atticists, must also have been an important item in their lexicon. They may well have avoided *lepos* and *bellus* as expressive of a "showiness" or "sauciness" that did not suit their lean restraint. That Cicero should have adopted the newer uses of the language is not surprising; not only was his ear keen (*Or.* 160, cf. III.4 n. 67),

84. *Brut.* 143, 177, 203.

85. ACTIO: *Brut.* 203, 235, 237, 272; MANNERED EFFECTS: *Brut.* 325, 326, *Or.* 84; ΧΑΡΙΕΙΣ: *Or.* 29.

86. *Brut.* 63, 186, *Or.* 20.                    87. Cf. Leeman 1963: 136ff.

88. Ibid., *Or.* 69–74.                    89. Cf. *Or.* 29, 75, 110–11.

90. For other terms appropriate to the "plain" and "grand" styles in the *Brutus,* cf. Douglas 1966: xliii–iv, Leeman 1963: 146–47.

but he manifests a subtle *decorum,* using language in a way suitable to his audience.

A second, and complementary cause, for the configuration of the language of social performance in the later major rhetorica is that the kind of innovation Cicero put forth in *de Oratore* was simply no longer possible. At the time of *de Oratore,* the language of social performance described a stylishness that was plainly cultivated in elite competition. Julius Caesar, himself a notoriously stylish and dashingly androgynous man, mastered that kind of performance. By the time of *Brutus* and *Orator,* which were written during the days of Caesar's control—the *Brutus* just before his departure for Africa and the *Orator* after his victory at Thapsus—the language of social performance, as I suggest in greater detail below (VIII.2), may have come to be sufficiently associated with a kind of political persona that Cicero no longer wished—or rather was no longer able—to appropriate. The gap between "liberal policies" and "liberal helping," as it were, may now have been too difficult to bridge. Cicero's sensitivities to the expressive possibilities of the moment were highly refined.

## VI.6. *Incursus in Delicatos?*

To this point we have answered a positive question, why Cicero's innovative handling of the language of social performance describes primarily wit and humor. The remaining uses of the language of social performance in *de Oratore,* which are largely incidental descriptions of rhetorical effects, and most of which have been noticed above in chapter 3, raise a corresponding negative question: why, in view of the rising place of aestheticism in contemporary Roman culture, did Cicero not introduce comparable innovations for those other sorts of rhetorical attractiveness? Put another way, the conservative use of an idiom, beside an innovative one, might be just a preservation (especially if the idiom had stereotyped applications); but since innovations, perforce, demonstrate that innovations are possible, one may ask whether accompanying instances of conservation, and the absence of other kinds of innovation, were also purposeful. The question is more easily asked than answered, inasmuch as it risks, on the one hand, overreading what are surely in the main stereotyped applications of an established idiom, and on the other, fabricating tenuous *argumenta ex silentio.* Cicero's scattered uses of the language of social performance for other rhetorical effects outside of the *excursus de ridiculis* would seem to be primarily the deployment of an already-established technical vocabulary. The absence of other kinds of innovation, however—which is to say a thoroughgoing rhetoric of the attractive—is perhaps more significant. That absence can be understood in terms of the ideology of the dialogue, which is very particularly established at the outset (1.24ff.). Cicero carefully establishes a "Greekish" scene: the characters are out in the country, in a villa (*in Tusculanum*, 24), which was certain to have been decorated in a Greek manner. Scaevola recalls the setting of Plato's *Phaedrus* by remarking on a plane tree on Crassus's property (28). The main characters recall their encounters with Greek theoreticians.[91] But the characters are not in thrall to Hellenism. They are unwilling to embark on theoretical discussions. All of them only just happened to hear the theoreticians' disquisitions incidentally, or because they were in the course of other important duties.[92] Their discussion at the villa begins with topics of pressing political concern (24–26) and makes a transition to rhetoric only after passing through a *convivium* marked by Crassus's "charming conversation" (*in loquendo lepos* 27). Even their theoretical disquisitions constantly turn for examples to real-life forensic experiences or incidents. In short, the characters of the dialogue are anchored firmly in the Roman political world and avail themselves of the Greek world only to the extent that it supports their "real" political identities. In terms of our diagram, the details of the setting establish a complementarity between (2) and (3) weighted in favor of (3).

The language of social performance in *de Oratore* reflects this position intimately. An innovative use to describe only humor, beside otherwise largely incidental conservations and the absence of other kinds of innovation, and coming from solid and sensible characters, is a kind of refusal to valorize aestheticism more generally. The feverish competition for status in the late Republic made it possible for a subversive, or amoral, mind to write a rhetoric in which charm and charm alone was the τέλος of the spoken word; indeed I argue in chapter 7 that Catullus, mutatis mutandis, did exactly that. But Cicero was not of that mind. For all his floridity, and for all the success that his rhetorical skills brought him, he was ultimately a traditionalist. Indeed one of the ultimate aims of *de Oratore* is to restrict performative power by claiming it belongs only to a sort of Stoic σοφός;[93] and that not only transcends the mechanical view of rhetoric in ordinary handbooks, it also rejects the view that attractiveness is all that matters. The point is well illustrated by Crassus's use of the received senses of *bellus* and *festiuus*: *qua re 'bene et praeclare' quamuis nobis saepe dicatur: 'belle et festiue' nimium saepe nolo* "I want

---

91. Crassus 1.45–47, Scaevola 1.74–75.

92. Crassus: *cum quaestor ex Macedonia uenissem Athenas* (1.45), Scaevola: *cum ego praetor Rhodum uenissem* (1.75).

93. Cf. LP 42–43.

to hear 'well done! splendid!' as often as possible, 'nicely done! delightful!' not too often" (*de Orat.* 3.101, III.6). *Bene* could serve as the opposite of *belle* for 'real' quality throughout the history of Latin.[94] *Praeclarus* was a key word for the clans, property, and achievements of the highest levels of Roman society and is frequent in these senses in Cicero.[95] In assimilating his own speech-making efforts to such states or achievements, Crassus in effect wishes for nobility, even immortality; *praeclarum,* at least, is a common word for "famous quotes" in Cicero.[96] Crassus is here judging speeches by the terms of the traditional reward structure. Neither he, nor any of the other characters in the dialogue, is in the thrall of aestheticism. Thus the narrow scope of the realignment of the language of social performance is not only an *apologia* but may also be a by-product of the text's agonistic stance *in delicatos,* against the "pretty boys" who abused, or embodied, the dominance of the aesthetic paradigm, and who, like Verres or the young Catilinarians, confused the aesthetic and the political in dangerous ways.

Of course Cicero's careful equilibriums did not fit the facts of Roman culture at all, as Cicero himself seems to have realized. The *de Oratore* is a dialogue located in the near past, near enough so that the dialogue did not seem out of place but old enough to lend *auctoritas* to the assertions of the main characters. To be sure Cicero selects Crassus and Antonius as protagonists of *de Oratore* because of their great reputation as orators and his personal knowledge of them. But he has also selected men who met unhappy ends because of political circumstances. The strain of Crassus's vigorous opposition to Philippus would make him so ill that it cost him his life (*de Orat.* 3.6). Antonius would later meet his death at the hands of the Marians (Plut. *Mar.* 44), as did Caesar Strabo (*de Orat.* 3.8). Issued in an atmosphere of heated social competition, the *de Oratore* almost becomes a dialogue of men under whom things would have been different, if they had been in charge. An elite that followed Strabo's strictures about humor, that tolerated but did

94. So in Plautus: *fui ego bellus lepidus: bonu' uir numquam, neque frugi bonae,* | *neque ero umquam: ne spem ponas me bonae frugi fore* (*Capt.* 956–57), "I've been nice (*bellus*), agreeable (*lepidus,* on this sense see above, p. 66), but never a good (*bonus*) man, never useful (*bonae frugi* 'yielding good fruit'), nor will I ever be! Harbor no hope that I'll be useful (*bonae frugi*)." The same contrast, in regard to rhetorical style, survives in Martial (10.46, 110 n. 77).

95. Well before Cicero *praeclarus* was already ensconced in this sense, e.g., *Famae iam nobilitas late ex stirpe praeclara euagat* (Acc. *Trag.* 643), *praeclarorum hominum ac primorum signiferumque* (Lucil. 90M, 89W, 91K); Plautus's sole use of *praeclarus* depends on this sense: *ecastor haud mirum, si te habes carum,* | *hominem tam pulchrum et praeclarum uirtute et forma <et> factis* (*Mil.* 1041–42). Also compare *et ita rebus praeclariter gestis Romam reuerterunt* (Q. Claud. Quadrig. *hist.* 48.1), *re praeclarissime gesta* (*B. Afr.* 30.1, 47.5).

96. E.g., *Off.* 1.63, 1.87.

not practice jibes, that was uniformly gracious, elegant, and well-educated, whose *facetiae* were the modest handmaidens of their *grauitas,* was certainly not the order of the day anymore. The year in which Cicero published the high-minded *de Oratore* was the same year that he himself delivered an invective against L. Calpurnius Piso *(in Pisonem)* remarkable for its distortive scurrility.[97] Cicero was well educated, to be sure, and especially well trained in the intellectual attainments of the Greeks; but not all the potentates of the latter days of the Republic were so learned, and none would have considered himself as anything but elite. Pompey comes to mind. That Cicero chose eventually to locate such a dialogue as *de Oratore* in the past is significant, for he originally intended to populate the dialogue with contemporary characters, including himself. His friend Sallustius approved the change (*oratorum sermonem a me belle remouisse, Q. fr.* 3.5.1; above, III.5); Cicero had known Crassus and Antonius, and that would give the dialogue an air of authenticity. But one wonders whether Sallustius, and indeed Cicero himself, might not have felt that in the contemporary atmosphere of overcharged one-upmanship the sort of gracious and high-minded characters of *de Oratore* simply did not ring true, any more than does James Stewart in *Mr. Smith Goes to Washington* today. The language of social performance, carefully tailored to an ideal elite, or used by them sparingly and judiciously, plays a smallish, but suggestive, part in Cicero's retrojection into the past of an ideal vision driven by contemporary concerns—that most Roman manner of treating history. Cicero's solution to the problem of aestheticism was to push it in a different form into the past, as if to make the present turn out differently. The gleefully *delicatissimus* Catullus, by contrast, embraces the madness of the present. He is the topic of chapter 7.

---

97. Cf. Nisbet 1975: 192–97 "Appendix VI: the *in Pisonem* as an Invective." The comment of May 1988: 127 is apt: "The tone of [the *post reditum*] speeches is at times strident, grating, and unappealing. We actually seem to feel the feelings of a man who appears to be grasping almost desperately in his attempt to regain his self-confidence and his public persona."

# CHAPTER VII

# *Leporum Disertus Puer*
# The Language of Social Performance
# in Catullus

Did [Catullus] have, like Heraclitus, and like the Western Greek, Gorgias, a quite different—polyphonic, polysemous, musical—theory of truth, in which the transrational use of language enlarged the scope of ordinary discourse, but in so doing abandoned its claim to make any definitive statement?

J. K. Newman, Roman Catullus

> *i nikt mnie nie uprzedził, że cały mój glob*
> *to ten odstęp, dzielący przeciwne bieguny,*
> *między którymi nie ma właściwie odstępu*

And no one has warned me that my entire globe
is the space separating the opposing poles
between which there really is no space

Stanisław Barańczak, 8.2.80: I Nikt Mnie Nie Uprzedził[1]

καὶ ἐν ταῖς δρυπεπέσιν ἐλαίαις αὐτὸ τὸ ἐγγὺς τῇ σήψει
ἴδιόν τι κάλλος τῷ καρπῷ προστίθησιν.

When the olive is about to fall, the very propinquity of decay gives the fruit a certain peculiar beauty.

Marcus Aurelius

## VII.1. Introduction

The language of social performance, as I have argued, arose as the lexemic manifestation of a new cultural model that survived in Roman culture to the late Republic. A shift in the balance of power between its categories produced Cicero's use of the language in his oratory and rhetorica, each of which deploys the language of social performance in ways that are for the most part ideologically consistent. The thesis of this chapter is that Catullus's use of the language of the performance, which is prominent in his

---

1. In S. Barańczak, ed., *Poeta Pamięta: Antologia poezji świadectwa i sprzeciwu 1944–1984* (London: Puls, 1984): 345; English translation from Baranczak, *The Weight of the Body* (Chicago: Another Chicago Press, 1989): 37.

poetry, especially in the form of programmatic keywords in the polymetrics,[2] is meant to recall the same cultural model. Put another way, Catullus needs to be read against the background provided by Cicero, which permits one to explain, and not merely observe, Catullus's use of the language of social performance. Where Cicero tried to restrain the language of social performance and the dominance of the paradigm of aestheticism it represented, Catullus embraces that dominance, but not without bending the language of social performance to his own purposes. *Lepores* and *facetiae* become not the handmaidens of *grauitas* but the province of apolitical, and supremely self-controlled, *pueri*. But when apoliticism is expressed in the vocabulary describing the aesthetic aspects of political power, there is something to be said both about politics and aestheticism. "The lyric voice," as Batstone 1993: 149 puts it, "may appear as the location of discourses of power which the poet may expose only by falling under their spell." Our investigations of the social construction of the semantic features of the language of social performance will permit us to complement and augment "post-biographical" and "post-New Critical" readings of Catullus.[3] Incidentally the danger of adducing parallels from the language of comedy, to which commentators commonly refer to explicate Catullus's use of our lexemes, but which issues from a different social world, will become apparent. We may begin by examining three poems, one about love, one about social style, and one about poetry, which can provide a paradigm for our reading of the use of the language of social performance in Catullus.

## VII.2. *Callida Iunctura* and a New Erotics

*Arte regendus Amor.*

Love, too, needs the rule of art.

Ovid, *Ars Amatoria* 1.4

2. The collection of Catullus's poetry falls into three parts. The polymetrics, cc. 1–60, written in a variety of metres, are short occasional poems. The long poems or *carmina maiora*, cc. 61–68, also in a variety of metres, are poems of greater length. The elegiac fragments, cc. 69–116, are written in elegiac distich. See Quinn 1972: 9–20. Ross 1969 passim argues, largely on technical grounds, that the last third of the book exhibits the language and style of a pre-existing tradition of Roman epigram. For the difference in rhetorical stance between the two kinds of short poems, cf. Solodow 1989. In this chapter I regard the genres of polymetrics and elegiacs as epiphenomena of "voices," by which I mean culturally conditioned patterns of expression not unlike the "styles" of traditional rhetorical theory (cf. IV.2). As with "styles," one or the other of these "voices" usually dominates a single work, but not so as to block the occurrence of the other; cf. below on cc. 22 (VII.6), 24 (VII.6), 86 (VII.2). Indeed Ross 1969: 130–31, 132 n.42, 135, 137 distinguishes between "traditional" and "experimental" or "neoteric" elegiacs.

3. Indispensable are Selden 1992, Batstone 1993, and Fitzgerald 1995.

*Venustas* appears in the well-known epigram in praise of Lesbia's beauty (c. 86):

> *Quintia formosa est multis. mihi candida, longa,*
>> Quintia is beautiful,
>> so they say:
>> I would say, tall and fair-complected,
>
> *recta est: haec ego sic singula confiteor,*
>> perfect posture,
>> would grant
>> the single points, deny
>
> *totum illud formosa nego. nam nulla uenustas,*
>> they all add up to beauty.
>> So grand a body!
>
> *nulla in tam magno est corpore mica salis.*
>> But without attraction *(uenustas),*
>> without a single grain of salt.
>
> *Lesbia formosast, quae cum pulcherrima totast,*
>> Now Lesbia is beautiful:
>> not only the fairest in every way,
>
> *tum omnibus una omnes surripuit Veneres.*
>> but also the one woman
>> who's pinched from all the others
>> every gift that Venus gave them.[4]

It is possible to take *uenustas* as here referring simply to 'attractiveness,' in particular an 'erotic attractiveness.' Aside from its particular connection to the language of social performance, where the eroticism of the lexeme generally faded out (I.6), *uenust(us)* did retain such functions. That is, it remained connected to cultural models other than the one that produced the language of social performance. For example, a small group of attestations has to do with the attractiveness of the face. Cicero speaks of *uenusti oculi* "attractive eyes" (*Tusc.* 5.46),[5] Pliny of Parrhasius's ability to render *uenustas*

---

4. Lit. "all Venuses, every instance of Venus," or possibly "charms" (i.e., *ueneres* and not *Veneres;* see Syndikus 1987: 63 n.11). As Wiltshire 1977: 326 suggests, Catullus may have in mind a story about the painter Zeuxis told by Cicero in *Inv.* 2.1–3. Commissioned by the people of Croton to make a painting for the temple of Juno, Zeuxis held a contest for the ideal model and ended up picking five winners, since he "did not think the ideal of beauty could be found in one body, since in a state of nature nothing is refined to perfection in all respects" *(neque enim putauit omnia, quae quaereret ad uenustatem, uno se in corpore reperire posse ideo, quod nihil simplici in genere omnibus ex partibus perfectum natura expoliuit).* Braunlich 1943 sees *AP* 5.67 (the epigraph to chapter 4 above) as a possible source for the idea.

5. Cf. *quidam uenustatis non fuco inlitus sed sanguine diffusus debet color* (Cic. *de Orat.* 3.199),

*oris* "the beauty of the face" (*Nat.* 35.67), Apuleius of the *uenustas* of a visage (*frons, Met.* 3.11) and of flashing eyes (*micantes oculi, Met.* 5.31). *Venustus* appears in connection with pretty girls and boys. Catullus describes the sister of a Gellius as *uenusta* (89.2, cf. VII.8). A graffito from Pompeii encourages a muleteer to make haste: *diligo iuuenem uenustum, rogo, punge, iamus [sic]* "I love a pretty young man: I ask you, give spur, let's go!" (*CIL* 4.5092.3 = *CLE* 44.3). Apuleius speaks of *tam uenustus tamque pulchellus puellus* "so pretty and so lovely a boy" (*Met.* 9.27). These lovely young men notwithstanding, Cicero says that *uenustas* is the kind of beauty that belongs to women, as *dignitas* to men.[6]

But taking *uenustas* as merely meaning such physical attractiveness is obviously inadequate. The poem describes the insufficiency of mere physical beauty, symbolized by Quintia, whose shapeliness (*formosa ~ forma* 'shape, beauty') is all she has. Lesbia, by contrast, is not only beautiful in that way, she also possesses *uenustas,* which Catullus is obviously using to mean something beyond mere physical beauty. I would suggest that *uenustas* in the context of this poem draws on two senses of the lexeme familiar to us. By making *uenustas* parallel to *sal* 'salt, wit,' Catullus recalls the connections of *uenustas* to humor, in particular the humor of reply (III.4.2). Lesbia is not only stunning, she is engaging, well able to handle herself in conversation. *Sal* reinforces the emphasis on the cleverness of Lesbia as a performer. *Sal* refers particularly to humor that has an ironic, dissimulating, or deadpan quality (cf. VI.4 n.59). That sort of humor involves anticipating what is expected and controverting it. In that act of anticipation lies the cleverness.

*Venust(us)* serves the same function in Catullus's first impression of Varus's girlfriend. She is a *scortillum . . . non sane illepidum neque inuenustum* "a nice piece, no witless *(inuenustus)* or charmless *(illepidus)* one here" (10.3–4). As Quinn 1973 ad loc. puts it, "It is clear from what follows that the approval expressed is not of the girl's appearance but of the impression she gave (to begin with) of knowing how to conduct herself in the presence of sophisticated young men." The same idea is also expressed by other members of the language of social performance. C. 43 enumerates the flaws against Ameana, a provincial beauty wrongly compared to Lesbia; one of the flaws is that she "lacks a tongue too refined" (*nec sane nimis elegante lingua,* 43.4; see further below). She evidently has not the gift of saying the right thing that is part

---

*salsum . . . et uenustum* (Cic. N.D. 1.80, ironically of a facial deformity), *uoltus uero qui secundum uocem plurimum potest quantam affert tum dignitatem tum uenustatem* (Cic. Or. 60).

6. *cum autem pulchritudinis duo genera sint, quorum in altero uenustas sit, in altero dignitas, uenustatem muliebrem ducere debemus, dignitatem uirilem* (Off. 1.130).

and parcel of attractiveness.[7] Much the same is true of Flavius's girlfriend, whom Catullus teases in c. 6 because he will not reveal her to him:[8]

> *Flaui delicias tuas Catullo,*
> *ni sint illepidae atque inelegantes,*
> *uelles dicere nec tacere posses.*

> You should be glad to tell Catullus
> who your sweetheart is, Flavius—
> How can you keep it quiet?
> Must be she lacks wit *(illepidus)*,
> must be she lacks taste *(inelegans)!*

> (6.1–3)

As we see below, Flavius is having a purely sexual affair with a lover who is not up to the "performative" standards that Catullus espouses.

In c. 86 *uenustas* also serves to represent that element of Lesbia's beauty which is not the chance gift of nature but the result of cultivation. This sense of *uenustas* plays against the connection of the adjective with 'well-arranged' shapes; here 'arrangement' means the result of concerted human effort. It may be that *surripuit* 'stole, pinched' is merely a clever way of saying "outstripped." But when the phrase is set against the conventional language of amatory verse, an element of cultivation does seem to come to the fore. *Veneres* 'Venuses, goddesses of love' probably recalls the Χάριτες 'Graces' of Greek love poetry.[9] It was conventional to style an attractive woman as "the fourth Grace"[10] or to assign to her the several virtues of different erotic deities.[11] In the light of such conventions, it seems Catullus has made Lesbia's erotic attraction more active: it is predicated not upon his equation of

---

7. Cf. Quinn 1973 ad loc.: "C. puts it the way he does to preserve an element of continuity [viz. in a list of body parts]. Ameana's looks were bad enough, but when she opened her mouth. . . ." Ellis 1889, by contrast, suggests that *lingua* "refers not so much to what she was in the habit of saying, as to some unfeminine movement, perhaps an immodest protrusion of the tongue," comparing inter alia Strabo Caesar's witty likening of Helvius Mancius to a painting of a Gaul which was *distortum, eiecta lingua, buccis fluentibus* (Cic. *de Orat.* 2.266).

8. On this poem, see further below, VII.4.

9. Ellis 1889 compares *AP* 5.95 (Anon.), Musaeus *Her. et Leand.* 63. Cf. also Fordyce ad 3.1. The most important comparanda are perhaps the *Carmina Anacreontea*, in which the Χάριτες frequently appear. Cf. below, n. 74.

10. Cf. Callimachus 51 (Pfeiffer), *AP* 5.70 (Rufinus), 5.148 (Meleager), 5.95 (Anon.), 9.515 (Anon.).

11. Cf. *AP* 5.70 (Rufinus), where the beloved has the beauty of Cypris, the mouth of Peitho, the voice of Calliope, etc.; *Anacreont.* 16.18–28, instructions to a painter to use the beauty of several goddesses, cf. above, n. 4 on Zeuxis.

her to deities, but upon her own astuteness. Lesbia is represented as having "stolen," or "pinched," the bits of attractiveness that other women may have —such things, perhaps, as "bon mots, witty comments, dalliances, charming speech, laughter."[12] That is, she is presented as actively recognizing what is worth adopting from the conduct of others into her own repertoire, and stealing it away. Indeed *uenustas* as a term for "conversational skill" implies a similarly "active" attractiveness: the graceful thrust or volley requires skillful action. Likewise the *elegans lingua* of 43.4 on its own might suggest deliberately careful and correct speech.[13]

But while these aspects of *uenust(us)*, viz., its connection to the humor of reply and to attractive arrangements, are more appropriate to the poem than a diffuse erotic "attractiveness," neither are these senses of the lexeme alone adequate to the poem, for the obvious reason that they are not typically eroticized, whereas Lesbia's erotic attractiveness is clearly at issue. When Cicero says an orator requires "the ability to reply and attack quickly and curtly, with measured deftness *(subtilis uenustas)* and wittiness *(urbanitas)*" or Vitruvius that "proportion implies a graceful *(uenusta)* semblance and the suitable display of details in their context," there is no good reason for believing an erotic element was present to their minds.[14] We can say that both *uenust(us)* applied to humor or attractive arrangements, and *uenust(us)* applied to (erotic) attractiveness, are "partial" lexemes, using only one subset of the significative elements of the "full" lexeme. The conclusion seems inescapable: in this poem Catullus has conflated two branches of the word that normally moved independently. "Attractive (erotically)" and "artful" are made to overlap. As a rough parallel, one may imagine a poet writing in English discussing a woman's "charm" in a way that suggests it is like a "magic charm," conflating two usually independent branches of the word, "captivating personal manner" (*OED* 'charm' 3a–b) and "magical totem" (*OED* 'charm' 1b). To put the matter more abstractly, if we imagine the structure of *uenust(us)* comprising three features (v. I.6 fig. 5), we may say that by the late Republic the lexeme was usually used for 'erotic and attractive' (III + I) or for 'well-arranged and attractive' (II + I), but that Catullus brings them together (I + II + III). We may illustrate Catullus's use of *uenust(us)* here, with several other instances for contrast, as follows (fig. 20):

---

12. *dicta sales lusus sermonis gratia risus | uincunt naturae candidioris opus*, Petronius, *Anth. Lat.* 479.3–4 Reise, a poem quoted by Ellis 1889 the sentiments of which resemble those of c. 86.

13. Cf. III.6.

14. *de Orat.* 1.17 (VI.3); 1.2.3 (I.6 n.88), tr. F. Granger (Loeb).

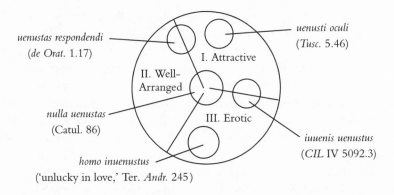

I suggest there is even more to c. 86 than just the conflation of two branches of a word's meaning (which is itself a deft poetic act). We saw above (IV.3) that semantic extensions could be grouped into two kinds, lexical and conceptual. In the latter kind the occurrence of a lexeme or set of lexemes indicates the presence not only of its semantic core, but also of its ideological or cultural construction. That is, a conceptual semantic extension invites a reader or listener to think of a referent in a particular, culturally constructed way. In connecting *uenustas* in c. 86 to conversational wit and studied self-presentation, Catullus is using semantic aspects of *uenustas* that were normally associated with the language of social performance. I suggest that this use is a kind of conceptual semantic extension on Catullus's part, intended to summon to mind, by its characteristic lexemes, the cultural model I have been treating.

The late Republican history of that model is especially relevant to c. 86. As we saw in considering the language of social performance in Cicero's speeches (V.1, V.6), by the late Republic the balance of power between quadrants (2) and (3) in our diagram had shifted, with (2) having become de rigueur. Aestheticism had become a dominant paradigm, increasing the value of our lexemes accordingly. By using *uenustas* in a way that recalls its use in the language of social performance, I suggest that Catullus means to have the reader think about Lesbia's attractiveness in terms of the dominance of aestheticism. If Lesbia's beauty is the kind of thing the language of social performance normally describes, it is not mere beauty, but the erotic congener of Crassus's *lepos:* a compelling, irresistable artfulness, and the possession of a special elite. That resonance obviously fits the poem well. And if Lesbia's beauty is the kind of thing the language of social performance normally describes, Lesbia is implicitly a competitor, vying against other women in artfulness. That resonance fits the ending of the poem, which pictures

Lesbia's superiority in terms of "pinching," exceedingly well. In effect Catullus has taken a political idiom and applied it to erotic artfulness. More
precisely, the language of social performance takes a position on three topics that usually figured in the creation of *political* identity: aestheticism, Hellenism, and individualism; Catullus has used that language to insert those
topics into the creation of *erotic* identity. The Hellenic character of Lesbia's
attractiveness is clear: not only is she lauded by the reinvigorated tropes of
Greek lyric, but her possession, and Catullus's appreciation, of an exclusive
beauty has Callimachean overtones, and her very name alludes to Sappho.
The aestheticism that is appropriate to erotics, on Catullus's view, is not in
the sole control of the male viewer who makes the woman an object but is
like the "active," vaunting aestheticism so important in political life. Lesbia
is also a woman who "makes herself," not merely a statuesque beneficiary of
nature's bounty. The use of *uenustas* in this poem therefore resembles Catullus's well-known use of the formal language of treaties and *amicitia* 'friendship; political alliance' to describe a permanent relationship with Lesbia.[15]

As Fitzgerald 1995: 115–20 has suggested, the language of political alliance presupposes a web of social contacts that embodies and enforces the
ideals that language describes; and in the absence of such a network surrounding Catullus and Lesbia the language of political alliance fails. The
adoption of the language of social performance is more successful. By fus-
ing two branches of the meaning of *uenustas,* and by allowing the larger cultural resonances of the language of social performance to come to the fore,
Catullus has created a new erotic idiom. Eroticism was commonly constructed, for men, as boyish dalliance (in one's friends) or (in one's enemies)
as a contemptible or even dangerous carnality (V.6). In an example of the
former, Cicero downplays Caelius's affair with Clodia because, as the Scots
say, "Royet lads may make sober men" (*Cael.* 28). The self-absorption of the
*adulescens amans* of comedy was a well-known stereotype. The construction
of eroticism as contemptible, even dangerous, is one with which we are familiar from Cicero's use of eroticism to attack opponents (V.6). Catullus in
c. 86 has eluded these Roman constructions of eroticism by casting it in

15. So c. 87, which refers to *fides* and *foedus* and c. 109.6 *aeternum . . . sanctae foedus amicitiae* "a pact of holy friendship forever"; cf. Ross 1969: 80–95. For another appreciation of
the uniqueness in Roman society and Latin literature of the vision presented of Lesbia in
c. 86, see Quinn 1963: 69. For the Callimachean overtones of Lesbia's exclusive beauty, cf.
Syndikus 1987: 60: "Aber schon diese Anerkennung der vielen [of Quintia's beauty] mußte
einen Kallimacheer wie Catull mißtrauisch machen. Man denkt unwillkürlich an Kallimachos' 28. Epigramm, in dem der gleiche Widerwille gegenüber einer Allerweltsschönheit wie
gegenüber abgedroschener Dichtung zum Ausdruck kommt."

terms of what late Republican society held dearest, aesthetic performance. Put another way, Catullus appropriated a piquant contemporary idiom important in public life and exhausted it by making it coextensive with eroticism. This claim about lexemes is the equivalent of the claim of Selden 1992: 498 about rhetorical structures:

> While [Catullus's] compositions are regularly organized around a commonplace schema or trope—metaphor, metonymy, amphibolia, prosopopeia, metalepsis, chiasmus—all of which feature prominently in [rhetorical] treatises of the period, they invariably push this figuration to the point where it compromises the standards of perspicuity or decorum which it is the purpose of the handbooks to ensure.

Lesbia's attractiveness is something more compelling than the then-current constructions of eroticism allowed for. By verbal dexterity Catullus creates a new space in which to locate Lesbia, and, as discussed below, not only eroticism as a whole, but social life and poetics as well.

### VII.3. A New View of the Social World

*de minimis non curat lex*

The law does not concern itself with trifles.

Latin proverb

*mauolt uersiculos foro relicto*

He has left the forum behind,
preferring little verses.

Q. Gellius Sentius Augurinus (apud Plin. *Ep.* 27.3)

The lexemes of the language of social performance figure prominently in c. 12, directed to an Asinius Marrucinus who is represented as having stolen from Catullus a napkin with sentimental value. I would argue that *mutatis mutandis* what was true of *uenustas* in c. 86 is true of *non belle* and the rest here: they are the characteristic language of a cultural model that Catullus employs so he can make his own use of the expectations the model raises.

> *Marrucine Asini, manu sinistra*
> Marrucinus Asinius, as we jest in our cups,
> *non belle uteris in ioco atque uino*
> *très gauche (non bellus)* your left-handed trick,[16]

16. Marrucinus pinches the napkin, slyly, with the hand of the elbow on which he is reclining ("Hier ist es doch wichtig, daß er *in vino* die rechte Hand braucht, um das Trinkgefäß zu halten," Eduard Fraenkel, 1962: 258); furthermore the left hand was associated with thieving, e.g., Pl. *Per.* 226 *ubi illa altera est furtifica laeua,* cf. other refs. in Ellis 1889. Napkin

*tollis lintea neglentiorum.*
   stealing the napkins of hosts
   whose attention lapses a little.
*hoc salsum esse putas? fugit te, inepte:*
   You think it's funny *(salsus)*? Your mistake:
5     *quamuis sordida res et inuenusta est.*
   it's the cheapest *(sordidus* 'dirty'),
   clumsiest *(inuenustus)* thing you can do.
*non credis mihi? crede Pollioni*
   Don't believe me? Ask your brother, Pollio,
*fratri, qui tua furta uel talento*
   who'd gladly pay to undo your thefts,
   if it cost him twenty grand;
*mutari uelit—est enim leporum*
   that boy can tell you what is what
*disertus puer ac facetiarum.*[17]
   when it comes to charms *(lepores)*
   and wittiness *( facetiae).*
10    *quare aut hendecasyllabos trecentos*
   Expect a hundred epigrams, then,
*exspecta, aut mihi linteum remitte,*
   unless you give me the napkin back.
*quod me non mouet aestimatione,*
   And it's not the cost I care about:
*uerum est mnemosynum mei sodalis.*
   it's a *mémento* of my companion.
*nam sudaria Saetaba ex Hiberis*
   When they were in Spain,[18] Fabullus and
15    *miserunt mihi muneri Fabullus*
   Veranius sent me a gift:
   flaxen kerchiefs from Saetabis.
*et Veranius; haec amem necesse est*
   That makes me love the kerchiefs
*ut Veraniolum meum et Fabullum.*
   just like I love Fabullus,
   and Veranius, my dear one.

---

theft was apparently something of a problem at dinners, or at least it is apparently also mentioned in Lucilius (*et uelli mappas,* 1164M, 1238W, 1184K). The motif also appears in Martial (8.59, 12.29). On Hellenistic precedents for "theft" poetry, cf. Coppola 1929.

17. For a discussion of this reading, see n. 39 below.

18. Perhaps in the retinue of L. Calpurnius Piso Caesoninus, with whom they were later in Macedonia, and who may earlier have been governor of Hispania Citerior; so the qualified speculation of Syme 1956.

The members of the language of social performance have here the semantic values with which we are now familiar. Because of the connection of *uenus-t(us)* to studied gesture (I.6, III.4.1), *inuenusta* is especially appropriate to register disapproval of Marrucinus's use of his left hand. *Lepores* and *facetiae* are not simply 'wit' in some diffuse sense. Their nuances as, respectively, 'charming performances' (I.9) and *facetiae* 'clever strokes, witty actions' (I.8), the former of which, at least, was still current, would be appropriate to the poem; but even more appropriate, as I argue below (VII.4), is the use of *lepores* and *facetiae* as a pair to refer to performed verbal wit (I.9 ad fin.)—an appropriate quality to assign to Marrucinus's brother Pollio, who is almost certainly the orator C. Asinius Pollio. *Bellus,* as we have seen, often implies the standards of a particular small subgroup (I.7). The presence of just such a group, against whom Marrucinus's offense was committed, is felt in several places. The phrase *in ioco atque uino,* lit. "amid jesting and wine" suggests the intimate setting of the *convivium.* Catullus and Calvus exchanged poetry in a similar setting (*per iocum atque uinum,* 50.6).[19] Further, the matter is referred to an etiquette master described as a *puer* 'boy, lad,' which is to say, not only literally a boy, which Asinius Pollio, who was born in 76, virtually was at the time, but a select member of the suave young generation, and not one of the *senes seueriores* "strict old men" of c. 5:

> *Viuamus mea Lesbia atque amemus*
> *rumoresque senum seueriorum*
> *omnes unius aestimemus assis.*

> Let us live, my Lesbia,
> let us love,
> and know that the mutterings
> of old men who like to be harsh
> aren't the lot of them worth one dime.

> (5.1–3)

Third, Marrucinus, perhaps the addressee's cognomen, recalls the Marrucini, a tribe from the Adriatic coast, thereby suggesting the rusticity and ineptitude of the addressee, which excludes him from an implicitly more urbane circle.[20] Above all, the poem depicts a small subgroup by specifying Catullus and Pollio as a credentialed audience issuing critical reviews.

19. On this phrase see further below, VII.4 n. 58.

20. For the connections of the *gens Asinia* with this geographical area, cf. Fordyce 1961 ad loc. "Gauche behavior was perhaps to be expected of a man connected with such a remote part of Italy," Quinn 1973: 130 ad loc. Asinius's grandfather had led the Marrucini during the Social War; cf. Neudling 1955: 12–13.

One does not need to have known the history of the language of social performance to sense that its several members here describe social performance. That is, after all, what this poem is obviously about. Nonetheless, knowing that history has two useful results. It makes several nuances entirely clear. *Inuenustus, bellus, lepores,* and *facetiae* are not loose equivalents for 'wit' or 'style' but recall respectively gesture, the evaluation of small subgroups, and performances, all of which are plainly appropriate to the poem. More importantly, if the lexemes of the language of social performance are present in their standard senses, so very likely is the cultural model with which they are associated, and I would argue that that is so. The cultural rules associated with that model are, as in c. 86, very appropriate here. As I have been claiming, the language of social performance was associated with the aestheticism that was a dominant social paradigm of late Republican culture. In chapter 6 we saw how Cicero attempts to define that language, and the aestheticism it represents, as the proper possession of the social elite as he envisioned it. In other words Cicero converts the aestheticism expressed by the language of social performance into a mark of social solidarity—or really, uses it in a way that preserves its original function. Catullus uses the language of social performance for the very same purpose here. In the context of this poem, possession of the common aesthetic standards described by the language of social performance is also a mark of social solidarity between a kind of elite, comprising Catullus, Pollio, and like-minded persons. Like Cicero's elite, Catullus's circle distinguishes between kinds of wittiness. In Cicero, Caesar Strabo observes, "Not everything funny *(ridiculus)* is witty *(facetus)*."[21] Catullus makes the same point: Marrucinus is attempting to be clever *(salsus)* but that does not make him stylish *(bellus* etc.). There will be no more place for him in his brother's discussion of *lepores* and *facetiae* than there is for *scurrae* in Caesar Strabo's.

Like Cicero in his rhetorica, Catullus defines the language of social performance as the possession of a social group that conforms to his own ideal. Where Cicero defined it as the possession of Romans with an acute sense of social propriety (VI.4), Catullus puts judgment of what is *lepidus* and *bellus* and *uenustus* in the hands of those who understand the assignation of private, emotional value. Line 12 *(non me mouet aestimatione)* reads as a *refutatio* to a possible objection by Marrucinus that the napkin was not worth much, referring to its value with the technical legal term *aestimatio* 'assessed value.'[22] The claim that one napkin was as good as another had Roman law on its

21. *non esse omnia ridicula faceta (de Orat.* 2.251), VI.4.
22. For the range of the word, cf. Gradenwitz 1897 s.v.

side, which in fact did not reckon sentimental value in calculating loss.[23] In asserting the value of the napkin on precisely such grounds, Catullus is rejecting the legal and official in favor of the private and personal.[24] Pollio, the master of *lepores* and *facetiae*, is also presented as embracing that private world: he would gladly pay a talent to undo his brother's thefts. Paying a talent to make up for a pilfered napkin, and perhaps similar thefts, is not a sensible business deal. It may even be that the very choice of the Greek word *mnemosynum* (only here in Latin) is also meant to suggest the private world of sentimental value by recalling the language of Greek epigram[25] and excluding the Latin equivalent, *monimentum*, which usually described reminders of grand achievements (though in Greek itself μνημόσυνον can have the same function). Greek words often served for small, personal or household items.[26] The napkin itself is wrested from the grand impersonality of a sys-

23. *Paulus libro secundo ad Plautium: si seruum meum occidisti, non affectiones aestimandas esse puto, ueluti si filium tuum naturalem quis occiderit quem tu magno emptum uelles, sed quanti omnibus ualeret. Sextus quoque Pedius ait pretia rerum non ex affectione nec utilitate singulorum, sed communiter fungi: itaque eum, qui filium naturalem possidet, non eo locupletiorem esse, quod eum plurimo, si alius possideret, redempturus fuit, nec illum, qui filium alienum possideat, tantum habere, quanti eum patri uendere posset. in lege enim Aquilia damnum consequimur: et amisisse dicemur, quod aut consequi potuimus aut erogare cogimur.* "(Paul in the second book on Plautius) If you have slain my slave, I think that evaluation should not be of personal feelings—e.g., if someone slays your natural son whom you would buy for a high price—but rather of the worth to everybody. Sextus Pedius also says that the prices of property stem not from personal feelings or individual needs, but from general usage; thus, he who possesses a natural son is not wealthier because he would repurchase him for a very large amount if another possessed him, nor does someone who possesses another's son have as much as he could sell him for to the father. For under the Lex Aquilia we recover loss *(damnum);* and we shall be held to have lost what we either could gain or were forced to pay out" *dig.* 9.2.33.pr., tr. Frier 1989: 57.

24. *Sordida* in l. 5 may also have been meant to anticipate and confute this legalistic derogation of the napkin's value. By suggesting the theft was 'cheap,' 'venal,' or 'low,' which are also meanings of the word, *sordida* implies Marrucinus should not have stolen the napkin in the first place. *Sordidus* is associated with cheapness (e.g., *de Orat.* 2.352) and poverty (*homine egenti sordido sine honore sine existumatione sine censu, Flac.* 52) and thus ignobility (*Pis.* 62, *Phil.* 1.33). In *Off.* 1.150ff. *sordidus* describes the 'low' professions; when Dionysius's daughters had to cut the hair of their father, the king, it was *sordidum ancillareque artificium* "a lowly art fit for a servant" *(Tusc.* 5.58).

25. *AP* 12.68.7 (Meleager) has μναμόσυνον στόργης for the tears of the poet, which will serve a boy taken to heaven like Ganymede as a reminder of the poet's love.

26. Cf. Palmer 1954: 81ff. For a collection and analysis of Catullus's use of Greek loan-words, see Oksala 1982. For a quite similar case to that of *mnemosynum,* where a small personal item, named in Greek, is of sentimental value, cf. *hanc scripsi ante <lucem> ad lychnuchum* (= λυχνοῦχον) *ligneolum, qui mihi erat periucundus quod eum te aiebant, cum esses Sami, curasse faciendum* "I wrote this letter before sunrise by the light of a wooden lampstand, which pleased me very much, since they said you had it made when you were on Samos" *(Q. fr.* 3.5.9).

tem whose law *de minimis non curat* and made into a symbol for a circle bound by affections and tastes.

The clash of the fiscal and fashion worlds is instructive. Cicero's use of the language of social performance, indeed, the whole history of the language of social performance, is very much a part of competitive elite Republican society, marking political inclusion or exclusion; in that respect, the language of social performance could be said to work hand in glove with the legal, public world of *aestimatio*. Catullus has converted the resonances of a public idiom to define a view of the social world at odds with the world where the language of social performance usually did its work. As in c. 86, in c. 12 Catullus has used the language of social performance to take a position on exactly those ideological issues with which it was implicated. He and his like belong to a "Greek" world (cf. *mnemosynum*), value aestheticism, and accept the "created" aspect of personalities. But for them the Greek world is not a complement to, but a negation of, the Roman world; aestheticism replaces, and does not augment, politics; and the "created" personality has not learned to make a name for itself by prosecution but rather to judge the stylish. Catullus's use of the language of social performance thus constitutes a kind of critique of political discourse. As Fitzgerald 1995: 96 puts it, the issue of c. 12 "is not what the napkin signifies but who makes it signify and how." Politicians scored points with *lepos* and *facetiae;* Catullus's art is in applying the rhetoric of performance to a place it did not "belong."

## VII.4. A New Poetics

As he did with erotics and the social world, Catullus also converts the resonances of the language of social performance to define a new view of poetics, as we may illustrate by examining c. 36, certainly addressed to Lesbia. Lesbia has sworn to burn "the choicest works of a most wretched *(pessimus)* poet," with *pessimus* meant in the original vow (if there was one) as "behaving wretchedly," applied to Catullus.[27] Catullus deliberately misunderstands her to have meant by *pessimus* "writing wretchedly" and presses another poet's poem into service to fulfill the vow:[28]

> *Annales Volusi, cacata charta,*
> > Hey "Annals" by Volusius,
> > sheet after sheet of shit!
> *uotum soluite pro mea puella.*
> > Help out my girlfriend
> > and answer her prayer.

27. So most commentators since Ellis; for a different view, see Comfort 1929.
28. Cf. Østerud 1978: 141–42.

*nam sanctae Veneri Cupidinique*
  She vowed to holy Venus
  and Cupid, you see,
*uouit, si sibi restitutus essem*
  that if I were restored
  to her, if I stopped
5 *desissemque truces uibrare iambos,*
  brandishing my brutal pen,
*electissima pessimi poetae*
  she'd make thank-offering
  to the Slowfoot God,
*scripta tardipedi deo daturam*
  roasting on ill-omened logs[29]
*infelicibus ustulanda lignis.*
  the finest works
  of the most wretched poet.
*et hoc pessima se puella uidit*
  A clever joke *(iocose lepide)* of a vow to the gods
10 *iocose lepide uouere diuis.*
  she thinks she's made—
  most wretched girl that she is.
*nunc o caerulea creata ponto*
  Well then *(ahem):*
  "O goddess born of cerulean deep,
*quae sanctum Idalium Vriosque apertos*
  who dwellest on holy Idalium, and on Urii exposed,
*quaeque Ancona Cnidumque harundinosam*
  and in Ancona, and on the sandy shores of Cnidos,
*colis quaeque Amathunta quaeque Golgos*
  and who also in Amatheus, and likewise Golgi,
15 *quaeque Durrachium Hadriae tabernam*
  and in Dyrrachium, victualler to the Adriatic,
*acceptum face redditumque uotum,*
  stamp the vow REMITTED, PAID IN FULL.
*si non illepidum neque inuenustum est.*
  Unless it's unlovely *(inuenustum)*
  or witless *(illepidum),* then don't."
*at uos interea uenite in ignem,*
  In the meantime, you there—into the fire!

---

29. Macrobius 3.20.2ff. lists *ligna infelicia* that were used for destroying evil omens and portents. For the background of burning, cf. with refs. Clarke 1968, who identifies a Greek proverb (*Corp. Paroemiograph. Graec.* II, ed. Leutsch, *Mant. proverb.* 1.57): Ἐπίτρεπε ὧδε τὸν Ἥφαιστον προμολεῖν· λέγεται ἐπὶ τῶν ἀξίων πυρὸς εἴτε προσώπων εἴτε πραγμάτων.

*pleni ruris et inficetiarum*
Full of boorish ineptitudes,
20      *Annales Volusi, cacata charta,*
"Annals" by Volusius,
sheet after sheet of shit.

The *lepide, illepidum, inuenustum,* and *inficetiarum* of this poem are certainly instances of the language of social performance. That is, the lexemes recall the meanings produced in them by the development of the cultural model described above.[30] *Neque inuenustum* (corresponding to *iocose*) describes the humor of reply (III.4.2, VI.5). It is singularly appropriate to describe Catullus's "hymn," which is a poetic counterattack to Lesbia's wickedly humorous vow.[31] The narrower resonances of *lep(idus)* as 'humorous' (cf. VI.2) or 'verbally deft' (III.3) are obviously entirely appropriate. The broader sense of *lep(idus)* as describing the effect of a performance generally also very much befits the miniature drama this poem describes, with move and countermove staged not only for the principals but for readers. *Inficetiarum,* which notably appears in a rhythmically unusual line (see Townend 1980), marks Volusius's failure to achieve distinction by verbal acts (cf. I.8).

As with the other two poems, the language of social performance here indicates the subcutaneous presence of the rules associated with the cultural model of which the language is the standard lexemic manifestation. Acts of aestheticism in the late Republic, as we have seen, demanded a response in kind (V.5), and the language of social performance in this poem is associated with precisely such an idea. *Lep(idus)* and *uenust(us)* are associated not just with poetry, but with the poetic response of Catullus to a *lepidus* and *iocosus* vow, which was itself a response to earlier attacks of Catullus.[32] *Lepos* and *facetiae* are connected to a comparable "aesthetic response in kind" in

30. For another appreciation of the value of this vocabulary in this poem, see Buchheit 1959: 316–22.

31. The long list of a god's cult sites, styled as dwelling places, is typical of the language of prayer; Syndikus 1984: 208–9. For hymnic elements in poetry, cf. Norden 1913: 143ff., Williams 1985: 222. Østerud 1978 trajects the obvious element of competition between Catullus and Lesbia into a polarity of tone: if Lesbia's original vow was flippant—it is certainly couched in a parody of high-style poetry (cf. Syndikus 1984: 206–7)—then Catullus's hymn must be meant seriously. One need not go that far to accept Østerud's suggestion that Catullus's hymn itself is a counteroffer to Venus, and that *non illepidum neque inuenustum* are meant to describe that hymn and, indeed, the quality of c. 36 as a whole.

32. Thomson 1997: 296–97, on the basis of the adjective *trux* 'savage, fierce' and of the evidently complementary distribution of *hendecasyllabi* and *iambi,* suggests that *truces . . . iambos* (36.5) refers to the immediately subsequent poem, c. 37, a harsh attack in limping iambics on the denizens of a particular tavern with whom Lesbia shares her favors.

c. 50. The premise of the poem is that Catullus and Licinius Calvus had spent a day poetizing together, writing reciprocal compositions, in the tradition of Greek responsive poetry:[33]

> *scribens uersiculos uterque nostrum*
> > Both of us wrote little verses
> *ludebat numero modo hoc modo illoc,*
> > playing in one meter, then in another,
> *reddens mutua per iocum atque uinum.*
> > giving and taking[34] in jest over wine.
> *atque illinc abii tuo lepore*
> > And I left there, Licinius, aflame
> *incensus, Licini, facetiisque . . .*
> > with your charm *(lepos)* and your wit *(facetiae)* . . .
> > (50.4–8)

Calvus's *lepos* and *facetiae* induce Catullus to respond; the response is c. 50 itself: *hoc, iucunde, tibi poema feci | ex quo perspiceres meum dolorem* "and this, my friend, is the poem I composed so you could see my grief" (50.16).

The expectations raised by the language of social performance are also put to use in c. 36 other ways. I argued above that by the late Republic aestheticism had moved from complementing social worth to being in large degree coextensive with it. Dominant political personalities were distinguished by their control of *lepos* and *facetiae*. Catullus uses the language of social performance to describe a similarly compelling poetic personality. *Lep(idus)* and *uenust(us)* in c. 36 describe the quality of the superior competitor or more compelling writer, as, indeed, do the *lepos* and *facetiae* of c. 50. The superiority of such qualities is brought to the fore in a special way in c. 36 by recasting a common form of political vaunt. In c. 36 Venus will only mark the vow "paid in full" if it is not *illepidum* and *inuenustum* to do so; that is as much as to say that Catullus is representing *lepos* and *uenustas* as Venus's province. That assignation parallels the standard use of divinities in political self-representation. The gods of Rome were in large measure, even primarily, political symbols. One might ascribe to a god as such qualities that one valued in oneself, as a way of magnifying—and justifying—one's own possession of them. When Marc Antony embraced Dionysius and Octavian Apollo, they were vindicating, respectively, a benevolent but dangerous po-

---

33. Cf. Burgess 1986, who describes the tradition of Greek responsive poetry as background to this poem and shows that Calvus must reply because "he is bound by the requirements of *amicitia,* by the rules of reciprocal composition, and, at the level of this poem's central metaphor, by the beloved's obligation to show favor to the lover" (586).

34. The phrase is Fordyce's.

tency, and a propensity for imposing order (with violence, as against Niobe or the Lapiths?). In c. 36 Catullus assigns to Venus the same quality he himself eminently possesses: the ability to create realities verbally. Catullus can secure Venus's presence by using traditional hymnal language; Venus can acquit an obligation by using traditional chancellary language.[35]

In short, the qualities of the language of social performance, associated in the culture at large with political vaunt, are associated by Catullus with a poetic vaunt made in the image of its political sibling. That is also true for other poems where the language of social performance is applied to poetics. In c. 6, the beginning of which we have seen, Catullus gaily reproves Flavius for refusing to reveal the identity of his lover. Encouraging Flavius to tell him all the details, Catullus excuses his prying by claiming that he "want[s] to bring [him] and [his] darling to the sky in *lepidus* verse" (*uolo te ac tuos amores | ad caelum lepido uocare uersu,* 6.16–17). Praising something or someone *ad caelum* 'to the sky,' a common hyperbole, implied particularly ebullient praise and evidently had some currency in elegant colloquial language.[36] The hyperbole was not, however, excluded from more serious contexts and subjects; it might, and usually did, refer to praise for military or civic tasks.[37] The use of *uocare* (lit. 'call') here is also usually more "serious." This uncommon use, 'bring to' (*OLD* 8), not well attested before the Late Republic, typically refers to being 'brought to' extreme states like salvation or ruin, or into legal conditions like 'infamy' or 'suspicion.'[38] In this con-

---

35. "Stamp the vow REMITTED, PAID IN FULL" *(acceptum face redditumque uotum)* is chancellary language, complete with an archaic form of the imperative *(face* for *fac)*. Other idioms are *in acceptum referre* (*Ver.* 2.1.149), *acceptum referre* (*Phil.* 2.40), *acceptum ferre* (Pap. *dig.* 2.14.41.pr, Gaius *dig.* 4.4.27.2), but *acceptum facere* is also found (Ulp. *dig.* 4.2.14.9, Paul. *dig.* 46.3.10.pr, Plin. *Ep.* 2.4.3, 6.34.3). The usual verb with *uotum* is *soluere,* but *reddere* is common in the sense 'pay back.'

36. Cf. *de Orat.* 3.146.

37. It is the phrase used by Cicero to describe Caesar's reception by future generations (*alii laudibus ad caelum res tuas gestas efferent, Marc.* 29); cf. *Fam.* 9.14.1, *Fam.* 12.25a.2, *Fam.* 15.4.11, *Fam.* 15.9.1, Livy 2.49.1, 9.10.3, 22.30.8, cf. Sal. *Cat.* 53.1, Verg. *Aen.* 10.548 *caeloque animum fortasse ferebat* "Perhaps he was hoping for glory (lit. 'the sky')."

38. Extreme states: *ad salutem* (Cic. *Red. Sen.* 24), *ad perniciem . . . ad salutem* (*de Orat.* 2.35), *in exitium* (*Catil.* 1.12), *in periculum ac discrimen* (*Man.* 12), *in locum mortui* (*Att.* 2.19.4), *ad uitam* (*Att.* 3.7.2); legal or quasi-legal states: *in inuidiam* and *in crimen* (*Fam.* 5.17.2), *in suspicionem* (*Ver.* 2.5.10). That *uocare* can only be used of that 'calling' which implies that the calling party occupies the space to which the called party is summoned is, *pace* Nisbet 1978: 93, not true: this is clearly demonstrated by such examples as *de Orat.* 3.25, where *fraus hominum ad perniciem et integritas ad salutem uocatur* is "criminal activity is brought to destruction and innocence to safety"; the orator sorts, and does not summon, the sheep and the goats.

text *uocare* also stresses Catullus's verbal power: he can 'voice' (*uocare* ~ *uox* 'voice') Flavius and his paramour to the heavens the way an orator offers *laus*. In short *lepidus uersus* finds itself in a line that recalls political speech, in particular exaggerating political speech.

There is also a subtle "politicizing" element in c. 12, which we considered in section VII.3 above. I suggested there that *lepores* and *facetiae* (12.8 – 9) had their typical late Republican meanings, referring to verbal dexterity and wit. That suggestion is reinforced by their connection to *disertus*, a "speaking" word (eloquent, expressive).[39] If that is so, there is something of

39. For *disertus*, read by Ellis 1889 and Merrill 1893, some editors and commentators (Baehrens 1885, Mynors 1967, Fordyce 1961, Quinn 1970, Syndikus 1984, Thomson 1997) have preferred *differtus*, after Passerat. The MSS have *disertus* or *dissertus*, which can easily have come from *differtus;* cf. Goold 1958: 93 – 94. But there are arguments to be made in favor of *disertus*. Part of the humor is that *disertus*, though a notch below *eloquens* (cf. Cic. *de Orat.* 1.94, *Cael.* 67, Quint. 8.pr.13), and sometimes more like 'glib' than 'fluent,' nonetheless could have elevated associations (*homo disertissimus et omni doctrina et uirtute ornatissimus, Ver.* 2.3.204; *equitibus Romanis, honestis hominibus et disertis, Clu.* 100; *huiusce aetatis homines disertissimos, fortissimos, florentissimos nostrae ciuitatis,* Quinct. 7). 'To speak clearly' usually meant, by default, 'to speak clearly about serious topics' (hence the hierarchy at *Cael.* 67 [V.6], *quam uolent in conuiuiis faceti, dicaces, non numquam etiam ad uinum diserti sint*); and if Pollio was C. Licinius Pollio, as is virtually certain, he was an orator, to whom *disertus* is therefore appropriate. *Disertus* is the word Catullus uses for Cicero in c. 49.1. But Catullus here connects Pollio's ability to make clear presentations to lighter topics instead. Pollio becomes a kind of etiquette master, able to expound on the topics of charm and grace. The same juxtaposition between 'speaking clearly [about serious topics]' and a 'lighter' element is certainly the point of 53.5 *salaputium disertum*, whether the 'lightness' be in the form of vulgarity (see Adams 1982: 65 and cf. Augustus's *purissimus penis* of Horace apud Suet. *Poet.* fr. 40) or of regionalism (*salaputium* may be an Oscanism, \**salpūtim* 'the purification of salt,' referring to Calvus's "Attic" style; cf. Weiss 1996). *Differtus* spoils this complex solely to repair the difficulty of genitives, which are to be sure unparalleled with *disertus* but not impossible, particularly if *disertus leporum ac facetiarum* looks to a phrase like δεινὸς λέγειν τοὺς χαριεντισμούς. It may be added that *differtus* 'stuffed,' a sausage-making word, is a "bloated" word (*non satiatus modo . . . sed differtus quoque,* Sen. *Suas.* 6.19), inappropriate, as it seems to me, for mastery over something as light and ephemeral as Catullan *lepos*, which can also serve as a programmatic term for polymetric or neoteric poetry (VII.4, below). As Fordyce notes, "If Catullus used *[differtus]* here, it is a colloquial pleasantry . . . but one may wonder whether he would have thought that pleasantry appropriate here." *Lepores* are to be sown with the hand and not the whole sack. Thomson 1997: 241 solves the difficulty of the genitives in a different way, preferring *pater* for *puer*, an exchange palaeographically easy if *pater* was abbreviated. The phrase so produced is syntactically easier and in some ways very attractive: *pater*, applied to a young man like Pollio, recalls his precocious achievement (cf. Tac. *Dial.* 34.7) even as it emphasizes his *youth*, ironically where *puer* does so directly; and *pater* also preserves the juxtaposition between "heavy" and "light" elements that I consider important to the poem (with *pater* doing for "heavy" and *lepores et facetiae* doing for "light").

a disjuncture in c. 12: Marrucinus's *gestural* action is referred to the judgment of Pollio, an expert in *verbal* expression. The poem implies that judgments of *actions* should be referred to one who controls *words*.[40] That is a
proposition to which Cicero would have assented in some measure. But here
the one who controls words—*disertus*—exercises control *over* the dominant
ideology, *over* its legal discriminations and disregard of affection. He can
*uocare ad caelum* much as a political partisan can *tollere laudibus ad caelum*. Although *lepores* and *facetiae* here do not describe poetry as such, they may be
classed with the metapoetic instances we have been considering because
they also acknowledge the dominating quality of the verbal aestheticism described by the language of social performance.

However, Catullus's metapoetic cooption of the dominance of *lepos, uenustas,* and *facetiae* is not straightforward. Rather, it is consistently accompanied by what at first sight is paradoxical: modesty, dismissiveness, or contradiction. When Catullus attributes *uenustas* and *lepos* to Venus in c. 36, he
does so by means of a modest litotes: *si non illepidum neque inuenustum est.*
Asinius Pollio, the *disertus leporum,* is not an accomplished orator like, say,
Gorgias, whom such a phrase might describe, but a *puer.* The love affair that
Catullus will "sing to the heavens" is depicted in the earlier part of the poem
in sordid terms. Flavius has not told Catullus who his lover is, and he
concludes that she must be "some kind of fevered whore" (*nescioquid febricu-
losi | scorti,* 4–5) who would embarass him.[41] Catullus has inferred the ex-
istence of the affair from the incontrovertible evidence of Flavius's room,[42]
which he describes somewhat tactlessly, enumerating the perfumed boudoir,
two dents in the bedding, the creaking of the bed, and, the pièce de résis-
tance, Flavius's bowlegged gait.[43] Catullus's ability to "voice someone to the
stars" is to be used to—what? conceal? redeem? rarefy?—a distinctly car-

40. Cf. Fitzgerald 1995: 96 (cited above, VII.3 ad fin.).

41. Morgan 1977 suggests that *febriculosus* recalls a malarial prostitute (cf. Pl. *Cis.* 405–
8), a shocking and perhaps deliberately untrue assertion, since Flavius is represented as having spent the night with his lover, rather than taking her back to, or meeting her in, the bordello, as might be expected if his lover was a prostitute.

42. Morgan 1977 stresses Kroll's observations that a room in disarray revealing the signs
of lovemaking is a "new variation on [the] old theme" of a lover betraying his love by his
discomportment. Passages cited by Kroll or Morgan are *AP* 5.87 (Rufinus), 5.175 (Meleager), 12.71 (Callimachus), 12.135 (Asclepiades).

43. Tracy 1969 stresses the onomatopoeic value of *arguati(o)inambulatioque* (l. 11), two
probable Catullan neologisms that describe the creaking bed; the line sounds like a bed
clunking rhythmically across the floor, a blunt image that contrasts with the ending.

nal affair with a woman who is *illepida* and *inelegans*.[44] The paradox of c. 6 is even sharper in c. 16 (treated below, VII.7), where verses have 'charm and wit' *(lepos* and *sal)* if, and only if, they are 'delicate and not quite decent' *(molliculus* and *parum pudicus)*.

The contrast between political vaunt and modesty or contradiction is a deliberate device of Catullus. One could say that his modesty is agonistic. As Buchheit 1976a: 169 puts it:

> Catull versteht die Kenntlichmachung seiner Dichtung mit *nugae, ineptiae, versiculos facere, ludere* als Auszeichnung. Er gibt also Dinge, die im Urteil der öffentlichen Meinung allenfalls den Wert einer Nebensächlichkeit hatten und an ungemäßen Ort oder zu ungehöriger Zeit für verwerflich gehalten wurden, als das eigentlich Wichtige, als Lebensinhalt und Lebensaufgabe aus.[45]

Catullus's use of the language of social performance is comparable, but not identical, to this use of *ludere* etc. The language of social performance was, as I have argued, associated with a dominant social paradigm of aestheticized behavior. However, that behavior could still be construed as ancillary. That is, to recall our diagram, there were still Romans who thought that (2) should be a territory permissible only to those who were firmly anchored in (3). The paradox of the language of social performance was that even as it described a dominant paradigm it was, or could be, styled as marginal in the prevailing ideology (cf. IV.4, VI.6). A claim by a late-night talk-show host to be "just an entertainer" is entirely comparable: even as such hosts influence the shape of political discourse by whom and how they attack, they can also claim—the culture *permits* them to claim—that they are not "serious." One dominant paradigm of contemporary American culture is entertainment, but the prevailing ideology still constructs entertainment as "insubstantial." Catullus's deftness lies in making the language of social per-

---

44. To say with Quinn 1973 ad loc., "Catullus coaxes Flavius, tongue in cheek," is to confuse the tone of the beginning with the deliberately different tone of the ending; so in Quinn 1972: 226: "The closing lines come nearer to the truth of the matter. If the affair were as sordid as lines 4–5 make it sound, there'd hardly be any question of 'celebrating the affair to the skies in polished verse.'" On the contrary, polished verse *makes,* and does not *obey,* "reality." Catullan poetry is, in a sense, metastasized Roman oratory. Cf. Fitzgerald 1995: 52: "The nature of Flavius' love is immaterial to the poet, who can produce elegance even out of the silence that betrays the inelegance of his friend. Just as the silence of Flavius has not protected him from being pilloried by his sophisticated friend, so his speech would have no control over the poet even if he were to reveal his love."

45. On modesty cf. also Copley 1951: 204–5.

formance do two jobs at once: he appropriates for his own poetry its cachet as describing dominating aesthetic behavior, even as he acknowledges its possible construction as ancillary. In this way he takes a position that is both above and below standard political discourse. The complexities of the cultural model underlying the language of social performance were critical for providing Catullus with an idiom to express a new view of poetics: one in which nonce pleasure is elevated to paradigm, in which moments of effective performance are created for themselves and preserved by themselves.[46] Unlike Crassus, Catullus wants to hear *belle et festiue* often, to the exclusion of *bene et praeclare* (cf. VI.3).

All the same tensions appear in the introductory ode, in which Catullus dedicates his *lepidus nouus libellus* (c. 1.1) to Cornelius Nepos. Though this phrase has long been recognized as programmatic,[47] it is more striking than has sometimes been seen: to be sure *lepidus* has here, as not in the other metapoetic instances, a palpably literal function, describing, perhaps as 'bright' or 'shiny,'[48] a scroll whose ends have been smoothed with pumice (*arido modo pumice expolitum* "just now buffed with a dry pumice stone," 1.2). But not only does the literal description serve as a metaphor for the *labor limae* that characterizes Catullus's poetry, which like the papyrus has been buffed to perfection, it also appropriates a highly charged contemporary critical language that sustains the overtones of both dominance and modesty we have just seen in other poems. As with the *lepos* and *uenustas* of c. 36, the *lepidus libellus* of c. 1 is in the care of a goddess, Catullus's *patrona uirgo*. But— unlike Horace, who is confident that his collection of poetry is a monument "more lasting than bronze" (*aere perennius,* Hor. *Carm.* 3.30.1)—Catullus asks his patroness to let "his little book, such as it is" (*quidquid hoc libelli* |

46. Cf. Newman 1990 on the value of *lepos* in Catullus's poetry.

47. The programmatic nature of the poem has been clear since Copley 1951, with Elder 1966.

48. For the connection of *lep(idus)* to sources of light in late Republican Latin, cf. I.9 n. 154. It is possible that *lepidus* in c. 16 had some quality of 'brightness' lingering on the edges, inasmuch as *lepidus* there is associated with, and immediately next to, *caelum*. Catullus's use of metapoetic *lepidus,* if it plays against still-surviving literal uses of the lexeme, would thus be comparable to Cicero's occasional reinvigoration of rhetorical technical language by the same device: cf. *uenustus* in *Brut.* 262 (III.4.4), *lepores* in *Or.* 96 (III.3). For Zicàri 1965: 233–34 *lepidus* has to be literal, since "noi ci stupiremmo d'un Catullo che, subito nel primo verso, vantasse la sua opera come faceta, gentile, piena di novità, e al v. 9 parlasse di un libretto 'checchesia, qualunque'"; I would argue that such a contrast is exactly the point, and entirely typical of the rest of Catullus's use of the language of social performance. The tension between what is 'performatively brilliant' and ostensibly modest, colloquial, and minor is exactly the stuff of Catullan *poesis*.

*qualecumque,* 8–9) survive "more than one generation" (*plus uno . . . saeculo,*
1.10). Indeed the phrase *patrona uirgo* itself encapsulates the same tension of
political vaunt *(patrona)* and marginal social status *(uirgo)* as *leporum disertus
puer.*[49] Similarly *habe tibi* is both a formula for legal transfer of property ('receive') and a colloquial, somewhat indifferent phrase ('go ahead, take it').[50]
The element of responsion, if not agonistics outright, reminiscent of c. 36
and c. 50, is perhaps to be seen here, too, inasmuch as Catullus's *lepidus* verse
is dedicated to a writer whose own work was, like Catullus's, "learned and
painstaking" *(doctus* and *laboriosus,* 7). Indeed the poem, and therefore the
collection of polymetrics, opens with the question of whom to dedicate the
poem to *(cui dono?* 1.1): the collection inaugurates, and instantiates, a cycle
of giving.[51]

As has been recognized, *lep(idus), facet(us),* and *uenust(us)* serve Catullus
specifically as terms for Callimachean poetry.[52] It is clear that the poetry of
c. 50 was neoteric: the opening verses are full of programmatic vocabulary
like *ludere* 'play' *(lusimus* 2, *ludebat* 5), *uersiculi* 'verselets' (4), *delicatus* 'dainty'
(3).[53] Catullus's antipode in c. 36, Volusius, is also attacked in terms of Callimachean poetic: the *Annales* were *cacata charta* "shitty sheets" or even "shat
sheets," perhaps smeared with shit (= *concacata*), perhaps produced en masse
without polish, like so many turds.[54] In another poem Catullus sentences the
*Annales* to serve as fish-wrappers (95.7–8), an ignominious fate something
like being relegated to lining the bottom of a birdcage. The hymn Catullus
offers to Venus in c. 36 is a miniature neoteric tour de force, with Greciz-
ing forms (*Ancona* for *Anconam, Hadriae* after ʽΑδρίας), learned epithets *(cae-
ruleo creata ponto, Cnidum . . . harundinosam),* and an etymological gloss *(Vriosque apertos).*[55] The theme of Volusius's work, presumably great events of

49. One may thus add ideological propriety to the arguments adduced by Mayer 1982
and Arkins 1983 in favor of the transmitted text against the emendation of Goold 1981; cf.
also Cairns 1969.

50. Cf. Fordyce 1961 ad loc., Fitzgerald 1995: 38–41.

51. For the ambiguous status of this gift, in which "we acquiesce in our frustrated possession of these trifles in order to participate in the eternal freshness of the work," cf. Fitzgerald 1995: 38–42.

52. Buchheit 1959: 319–21, 1976a: 171 n. 48 with refs.

53. Cf. Buchheit 1976a: esp. 165–69.

54. For the idea that the "Callimachean" polemic of Catullus's attack on Volusius bore
only on technique, not on subject matter or genre, see Cameron 1995: 460–62.

55. A site *Vrii* connected with Venus has eluded commentators (but cf. Thomson 1997:
299); Ross 1973 offers the convincing suggestion that *Vrios . . . apertos* is an etymological
gloss in the manner of Alexandrian poetry, where *apertos* 'open, exposed to the wind' glosses
*Vrios,* phonetically similar to οὔριος 'windy.' For some examples of such glosses in Vergil,

Roman history, certainly lent itself to the old-fashioned style against which neoteric poets were reacting;[56] it remained for Vergil to find a way to bring neotericism to grand historical vision. The "polished" verse of Catullus and the "learning" and "painstaking work" of Nepos we saw in the opening polymetric.

Catullus, in short, turned to the language of social performance to provide himself with programmatic terms for Callimachean poetry. In part, as Buchheit 1976a, b, c has demonstrated, that choice is influenced by the values the lexemes had in the rhetorical tradition. This is to take Catullus's use of *lep(idus)*, *uenust(us)*, etc. as a lexical semantic extension. I suggest that it should also be taken as a conceptual semantic extension (IV.3). Catullus means to characterize his poetry as performances with the same overwhelming attractiveness as the social performances dear to contemporary society. It is appropriate that *lep(idus)* should function as the central word: its complex resonances in Catullus (and in Cicero as well) are no more than the embodiment of the contemporary cultural definitions of "performances" with which *lep(idus)* had long been associated (I.9). The phonetic similarity of *lepidus* to Callimachus's own programmatic term λεπτός 'fine' recalls the Greek[57] and overtops it with a politically much more resonant term. Catullus's use of the language of social performance, in short, encodes his own reading of Callimachean and other Greek poetry. The independence of Catullus's vision is to be seen in his emphasis on *uinum*, which strictly speak-

---

from McCartney 1927, cf. *Aen.* 1.744 *pluuiae Hyades* 'rainy Hyades' (cf. ὕειν 'rain'), 3.693 *Plemyrium undosum* 'Plemyrium abounding in waves' (cf. πλημυρίς 'flood tide'; Plemyrium is a headland), 3.703 *arduus Acragas* 'steep Acragas' (cf. ἄκρος 'height').

56. The strictly literary reading of this poem by Buchheit 1959 was countered by Wiseman 1969: 429ff., who, emphasizing that there are no famous shrines to Venus at Ancona, Urii, or Dyracchium, suggested Catullus had stopped at these very places on a sailing trip from Greece. Williams 1985: 223 also accepts the idea of an Adriatic trip, suggesting that *restitutus* refers not to emotional "reconciliation" but to actual "restoration" after a voyage; and that that is why Catullus is paying Lesbia's vow for her, since he himself wishes to thank a Venus who saw him safely home. Morgan 1980 proposes an ingenious solution that accounts for the sites, while retaining the literary critical thrust of the poem: suggesting the unusual phrase *Hadriae tabernam* parodies the content of the *Annales,* and that Urii and Dyracchium were also places that figured in that epic, Morgan argues that the *Annales* described the pirate campaigns in 67 B.C. of Pompey the Great—Volusius's townsman from Picenum. Morgan adduces the further evidence of c. 95, where Cinna's swift clear Satrachus is counterposed, by way of Callimachean polemic, to Volusius's slow muddy Po, which feeds into the Adriatic—the sea that was Pompey's theater of operation.

57. For the etymological connections between λεπτός and *lepidus,* see above, I.9 n.146. When Catullus has to translate *lepidus* literally, he uses *tenuis: tenuis . . . flamma* (51.9–10) renders Sappho's λεπτόν . . . πῦρ (fr. 31.9–10 Lobel-Page).

ing is anti-Callimachean and in contrast with Lucretius, who also uses *lep(i-dus)* as a programmatic term.[58] The Augustan poets, for whom Callimachean poetics were also important, also provide an important contrast: they do not use the language of social performance programmatically at all (VIII.3).[59] By then, as I argue, the place and the language of aestheticism had suffered the excesses of Antony, and the language of social performance was no longer suitable. Indeed, their reading of Callimachus was different: whereas Augustan poets would turn to Callimachean poetics as a means of withdrawal from political life, Catullus turns to them as a means of engagement with, antagonism toward, and ultimately abnegation of, such life (VII.9).

## VII.5. Fusions

In short, we have seen that Catullus uses the language of social performance to summon to mind the cultural rules with which it was standardly associated, so as to use them for his own purposes. Effectively Catullus has used the language of social performance as a kind of metaphor, affecting perceptions of erotics, poetics, and a symposiastic social life, in somewhat the same way as Vergil would use military language in the *Georgics* to affect perceptions of agricultural practice and human culture generally. The application of the language of social performance to those three distinct spheres would in itself suggest that they have something in common in Catullus's ideology. Indeed the language of social performance works to elide differences between erotics, poetics, and a symposiastic social life, and we have seen many examples already. I have treated the instances of *lep(idus)* and *uenust(us)* in c. 36 as largely metapoetic in sense. The *lepos* and *uenustas* on which Venus

58. For Catullus and wine, cf. *in ioco atque uino* (12.2, VII.3), *per iocum atque uinum* (50.6, VII.3). Buchheit 1976a: 169–70 sees in the phrase more than a definition of a symposiastic context: "Es kommt aber als wesentlich hinzu, daß Catull *vinum* nicht nur als Kennzeichen seiner dichterischen Lebensform, gerade in Verbindung mit *iocus* bzw. *sal,* versteht, sondern daß er damit hier—er spricht ja vom Dichten—auf den Enthusiasmus des Dichters durch Dionysos anspielt, diesen also für Calvus und sich beansprucht und sich damit keineswegs als lupenreiner Anhänger des Kallimachos erweist" (169). Callimachus's self-representation as a "drinker from pure springs" (cf. *Aet.* 5.33) may have led to his derogation as a "water-drinker," in distinction to the "wine drinking" symbolic especially of the dithyramb (cf., e.g., Call. fr. 544 Pfeiffer τοῦ <˘> μεθυπλῆγος φροίμιον Ἀρχιλόχου, Epicharmus fr. 132 οὐκ ἔστι διθύραμβος ὅκχ' ὕδωρ πίῃς); cf. Wimmel 1960: 225–38, Crowther 1979, Knox 1985, Cameron 1995: 363–66. On Lucretian *lepos,* see below, n. 69.

59. Given the state of the evidence, not too much should be made of the fact that the language of social performance does not appear in the surviving scraps of other *poetae novi.* The scraps are collected by Granarolo 1973 and Courtney 1993: 189ff. The only possible exception is Laevius fr. 20 *nunc, Laertie belle, para ire Ithacam,* but this surely is the *bellus* of 'familial affection'; cf. I.7 n. 113.

passes judgment include not merely the wittiness of Catullus's substitution but the literary quality of Volusius's poem and indeed of Catullus's own offering, c. 36 itself. To that extent *lepos* and *uenustas* are metapoetic. But the issue of the poem is the effecting of a reconciliation between lovers. Erotic deities figure prominently in the poem: Lesbia made her original vow to Venus and Cupid, and Catullus offers a hymn to Venus, a neoteric flourish that can win Lesbia's heart the way Caecilius's neoteric production *Magna Mater* won over his *candida puella* (c. 35, cf. below). In such a context, *lep(i-dus)* and *uenust(us)* acquire erotic overtones as well.[60] These are particularly strong in the case of *uenust(us)*, in which it is impossible not to feel eroticism when the lexeme occurs in the presence of *Venus*.[61] Fitzgerald 1995: 40 suggests that even the *pumex* and *expolitus* of c. 1 are subtly erotic, suggesting depilatories.

Furthermore, metapoetics shades into social performance, and social performance into eroticism. In c. 36 both Lesbia and Catullus perform their actions on a kind of stage, judged not only by the gods to whom the performances are veritably dedicated, but by the readers of the poem, who by the act of writing are made privy to the drama. The erotic energy between Catullus and Lesbia is not quite public but exposed, its moves and countermoves on display for savvy audiences to enjoy, a taut and witty version of the *lepos* and *uenustas* of Verres' showy dedication (*Ver.* 2.5.142, V.6). Flavius of c. 6 would have admitted who his girlfriend was if he could be confident her witty moves would delight not only him but Catullus and the other "beautiful people." As it is, their relationship seems to be purely sexual, without a stylishness Flavius might have liked to show off. In c. 86 I concentrated on Lesbia's erotic attractiveness, but there is obviously much that her attractiveness, as defined in that poem, has to do with artful presentation and social performance. The *lepores* and *facetiae* of c. 50, which, as I have suggested above, stand for the performative grace of Callimachean poetry, inspire in Catullus a consuming, eroticized passion.[62] Catullus suffers from *furor* (11), "the technical term for mental derangement" (Fordyce),[63] and the condition into which Ariadne falls.[64] *Incensus* 'set aflame' (8) and *dolorem*

60. Cf. Buchheit 1976: 55–57; Wiltshire 1977; Fitzgerald 1995: 35–36.

61. Cicero does the same thing in *Ver.* 2.5.142 (V.6); cf. ἀκύθηρον (~ Κυθέρεια = *Venus*) and *uenustus* in *Fam.* 7.32.2 (VI.5).

62. Cf. Segal 1970: 27: "The amatory language [of c. 50] reveals a man who feels his literary experience as something sensual. For Catullus (or for the Catullus presented in the poem) the life of art has an intensity which approaches the life of passion. Art and sensual passion become, in this case, virtually inextricable."

63. On the erotic applications of *furor*, cf. Grassmann 1966: 94–100.

64. *indomitos in corde gerens Ariadna furores* (64.53–54).

'grief' (17) belong to the same register.[65] Charm and wit are overwhelmingly important, so important that Catullus emphasizes his grief with the language of the exaggerating victims of comedy in *me miserum* (9).[66] This association of *lepos* with sexual power has its precedent in the Plautine connection of *lepidus* with eroticism (cf. I.9) and probably continued into the late Republic, as suggested by Lucretius (below n. 69) and Catullus himself (78.1–2, VII.8). But as with *uenustas* (VII.2), Catullus has allowed a lexeme to resonate with all of its possible meanings.

We may turn, then, to other poems in which there are similar fusions. *Venust(us)* appears signally in c. 35 in a way that fuses metapoetics with erotics. In c. 35 Catullus summons his friend Caecilius the "tender poet" (*poeta tener,* cf. 35.1) to come to him at Verona.[67] His lover (*candida . . . puella,* 7) will resist his departure, for she has been madly in love with him (*illum deperit impotente amore,* 12) ever since she read *Magna Mater,* his poem on Cybele. That is, the excellence of Caecilius's poem is what makes him erotically attractive.[68] Thus when Catullus ends the poem by forgiving her because "the *Magna Mater* has been attractively *(uenuste)* begun," *uenuste* means compelling both artistically and erotically.[69] Caecilius's lover is evi-

65. On the eroticism of this part of the poem, v. Scott 1969.

66. Instances of *miser* connected to pronouns (often as grammatical constituents, as here, rather than independent exclamations) are gathered by Lodge 1926, s.v. *miser.* And yet the disaster is not being able to eat, rather than, as typically in the comic instances, being set upon (e.g., *quasi incudem me miserum homines octo ualidi caedant,* Pl. *Am.* 159) or hearing terrible news (e.g., *mihi horror membra misero percipit dictis tuis,* Pl. *Am.* 1118).

67. For *tener* not as 'love poet' (on which see Syndikus 1984: 201) but 'neoteric poet,' cf. Buchheit 1976b: 48–50, Fredricksmeyer 1985: 215–16. Buchheit establishes the literary character of the poem and strongly rejects a real autobiographical intent.

68. Cf. Buchheit 1976b.

69. Cf. Solodow 1989: "Catullus, punning, unites two meanings in the word *uenuste,* one reflecting the girl's feelings toward the poem, the other her feelings toward Caecilius: Caecilius's poem is 'charming,' and it also inspires erotic passion *(Venus)*." Catullus is not alone in his use of *lepos* for erotic energy and poetic attractiveness, and the contrast is instructive. *Lepos* appears twice in the proem to book I of Lucretius. It is the attractiveness by which Venus encourages procreation (*ita capta lepore | te sequitur cupide quo quamque inducere pergis* "Each beast enthralled by charm follows you eagerly where you persuade it to go," 1.14) as well as the "charm" she is asked to bestow on Lucretius's poetry (*quo magis aeternum da dictis, diua, leporem* "All the more, then, goddess, give my words undying charm," 1.28). The two uses of *lepos* are plainly meant to be related, not only because they are in close proximity, but because both refer to a pleasure that has a higher purpose: the attractiveness of Venus leads to the propagation of species, and the attractiveness of Lucretius's poetry leads to enlightenment. The ideological construction of these uses of *lepos* is thus reminiscent of such passages as *Rhet. Her.* 4.32 (IV.4), where the attractive is ancillary to the real (cf. Giancotti 1989: 433, "[l']aspetto armonico-edonistico nella poetica lucreziana è subordinato a quello che possiamo chiamare l'aspetto comunicativo-didascalio"). That same sense of *lepos*

dently stylish (cf. *candida puella*, the same as Fabullus's dinner companion, 13.4 below) and herself capable of appreciating what is attractive, in this case poetry; for she is "more learned than Sappho the Muse" (*Sapphica puella | musa doctior*, 16–17).[70] *Sapphica musa* also recalls the epithet *Lesbia*, a name chosen to represent someone both attractive and a good judge of attractiveness. It is no accident that this poem is followed by c. 36, which has many of the same themes, as Buchheit 1976b: 60–64 is right to insist.

In two poems Catullus infuses eroticism into the connection of *uenustus* to metapoetics in a different way. The "beautiful people" (*homines uenustiores*) are invited to mourn Lesbia's sparrow, beside the very gods of love and beauty:

> *Lugete, o Veneres Cupidinesque,*
> > Weep, ye gods of love and beauty,
> *et quantum est hominum uenustiorum:*
> > and all the beautiful people there are:
> *passer mortuus est meae puellae,*
> > my darling's sparrow has died,
> *passer, deliciae meae puellae*
> > my darling's precious sparrow.

> > > > > > > > > > > > (3.1–4)

In a bantering dinner invitation, Fabullus is addressed as *uenuste noster:*

> *Cenabis bene, mi Fabulle, apud me*
> > In a few days, a fine dinner *chez moi*, my Fabullus,
> *paucis, si tibi di fauent, diebus—*
> > if the gods smile on you!
> *si tecum attuleris bonam atque magnam*
> > And if you bring the dinner.
> > Good food, then, and plenty of it!

---

comes out clearly in the other passage where L. uses it programmatically, in which *lepos* is the charming delivery of a difficult substance: *deinde quod obscura de re tam lucida pango | carmina, musaeo contingens cuncta lepore* "and also because I craft poems clear and bright about obscure matters, touching them all with the charm (*lepore*) of the Muses" (1.933–34 = 4.8–9; on the repetition, cf. Bailey 1947: 756–58). We miss in these passages the overtones of pure aestheticism, competition, and suave social action so prominent in Catullus's use of *lep(idus)* and the other lexemes, overtones that, as I have argued, represent Catullus's appropriation and reconfiguration of a piquant contemporary idiom. The dominance of the paradigm of aestheticism nonetheless makes itself felt in Lucretius, too. In the proem Lucretius turns Venus into a symbol for ἡδονή, the central concept of Epicureanism (for the idea that her procreative activity corresponds to the Epicurean ἡδονή κινητική and her subdual of war to ἡδονή καταστηματική or ἀταραξία, and on the allegory of Venus generally, see Bignone 1945: 427–43, Bailey 1947: 1749–50; also Schilling 1954: 346–50). In order to capture the overwhelmingly attractive quality of such ἡδονή, Lucretius turned to a contemporary idiom that expressed exactly that sort of attraction: the language of social performance.

70. For this translation see Fordyce 1961 and Quinn 1973 ad loc.

*cenam, non sine candida puella*
    And don't forget the perfect girl
*et uino et sale et omnibus cachinnis;*
    and the wine
    and the salt
    and a laugh of every kind!
*haec si, inquam, attuleris, uenuste noster,*
    If you bring them along, my lovely lad,
*cenabis bene; nam tui Catulli*
    you'll have a fine dinner;
*plenus sacculus est aranearum.*
    your Catullus's wallet is chock-full:
    of spiderwebs and moths!

                              (13.1–8)

It is notable that in both these poems *uenustus* is connected to hortatory statements. The *homines uenustiores* are asked to mourn *(lugete)*. Fabullus is addressed as *uenuste noster* when the premise of the poem, that he bring dinner with him, is repeated.[71] I suggest that *uenustus* has a similar performative function in each of these cases: it is a kind of hortatory vocative that asks the addressees to participate in the fiction of the poem. In other words to be called *uenustus* in these poems is to be asked to appreciate the conventions of polymetric poetry. For both poems are versions of motifs or genre types familiar from the *Anthologia Graeca:* c. 3 of reflections on the death of a pet,[72] c. 13 on the dinner invitation by a host with slim resources.[73] Both poems invoke the "gods of love and beauty" (Χάριτες and Ἔρωτες) familiar from

71. On the value of postposed *noster*, cf. Clausen 1990, who describes the *o funde noster* of 44.1 as "an elegant colloquialism" after the evidence of Varro's *Res Rustica,* where the gentlemen address each other in this way (2.3.1, 3.14.1 bis, 3.17.10).

72. The poems are collected at *AP* 7.189–213.

73. Edmonds 1982 demonstrates that the motifs of the Latin invitation poem (invitation, menu, and entertainment) are known to Hellenistic epigram, but not the genre proper, which he suggests reflects Roman social conventions. At any rate that a poor host can provide good company even if he cannot provide good food seems a natural rhetorical turn for the invitation-poem, and was actually used by Philodemus in a roughly contemporary example: εἰ δ' ἀπολείψῃς | οὔθατα καὶ Βρομίου χιογενῆ πρόποσιν, | ἀλλ' ἑτάρους ὄψει παναληθέας "If you leave behind fertile lands and toasts of Chios-grown Bromius, in return you will see absolutely genuine companions" (*AP* 11.44.3–6). Dettmer 1986 aims to demonstrate on structural and stylistic grounds that Catullus's poem is modeled directly on Philodemus's poem; Catullus would thereby be overtopping Philodemus, who succeeded as a member of Piso's staff where Fabullus had failed. As Marcovich 1982 points out, every familiar motif of invitation is exaggerated, for example, the request for a guest to bring something is here inflated to a request to bring everything. Cf. Vessey 1971: 46: "Fabullus will be in an even worse position than the *parasitus* of comedy: not only has he to keep his host amused—but he is to provide the food and drink as well."

Greek lyric, in particular the *Carmina Anacreontea*.[74] Both poems share a particular structural similarity, ending with precious inversions. The epitaphion of Lesbia's sparrow, c. 3, banks at the end to the real reason for Catullus's maudlin grief: the death of the bird has upset Lesbia.

> *at uobis male sit, malae tenebrae*
>> Damn you, wicked shades
> *Orci, quae omnia bella deuoratis:*
>> of Hell, who gobble everything pretty!
> *tam bellum mihi passerem abstulistis.*
>> A pretty sparrow it was
>> you took away from me.[75]
> *o factum male! o miselle passer!*
>> Dastardly deed! Poor little sparrow!
> *tua nunc opera meae puellae*
>> It's your doing that my darling's sweet little eyes
> *flendo turgiduli rubent ocelli*
>> are all swollen up from crying.

> (3.13–18)

---

74. For the plu. of Ἀφροδίτη, cf. Call. fr. 200a.1–3 P. τὰς Ἀφροδίτας—ἡ θεὸς γὰρ οὐ μία—| ἡ Καστνιῆτις τῷ φρονεῖν ὑπερφέρει | πάσας; as Quinn 1973: 97 notes ad 3.1, "The idea that there was more than one Aphrodite seems to have become a commonplace of Alexandrian mythology." Ἔρωτες is attested more anciently, e.g., ὃς Χαρίτων πνείοντα μέλη, πνείοντα δ' Ἐρώτων | τὸν γλυκὺν ἐς παίδων ἵμερον ἡρμόσατο (*AP* 7.25.3–4 Simonides) and not uncommon later (πάντῃ με περιστείχουσιν Ἔρωτες *AP* 5.139.3 Meleager, ναί, ναί, βάλλετ' Ἔρωτες *AP* 12.166.5 Asclepiades, cf. 5.194.1–2). *Veneres* could also be put for Χάριτες, common figures in Greek erotic poetry appearing in the Simonides epigram above, cf. also ἦν γὰρ Ἐρώτων | καὶ Χαρίτων ἡ παῖς ἀμβρόσιόν τι θάλος (*AP* 6.292.3–4 Hedylus). In the *Carmina Anacreontea* Ἔρωτες and Χάριτες appear commonly (4.18, 25.19, 28.3, 38.5, 44.1, 55.7; 16.28, 44.11, 46.2, 55.6), sometimes together (5.15–16, cf. 55.6–7). On her raft Cleopatra was attended by both Ἔρωτες and Χάριτες, as well as Νηρηίδες (Plut. *Ant.* 27.1).

75. *Bellus* is not here functioning as a member of the language of social performance but is imitating, appropriately in an epitaphium, the use of *bellus* for family members held in affection (cf. I.7 n.113) and its use for things that are 'pretty' or 'dainty.' For *bellus* as 'pretty' or 'dainty,' cf. *bello pede* (Catul. 43.2), *sociis es <hostis>, hostibus socius, bellum ita geris ut bella* | *omnia domum auferas* "You're an enemy to allies and an ally to the foe, you conduct war *[bellum]* so as to make off with everything pretty *[bella]*" (Var. *Men.* 64).

It should be noted that this light and affectionate use of *bellus* is at variance with the mock-solemn tone of the lines in which it occurs. As Quinn 1973 ad loc. notes, the words *uobis . . . malae tenebrae* "mark more plainly the assumption of a mock serious style." *Orcus* is "an old and solemn word" (Quinn, "feierlich" Kroll). *Male . . . malae*, not merely a "jingle for emphasis" (Quinn), recalls the Greek expression κακὸς κακῶς (Ellis, cf. Kroll) and imitates a stylistic tick of the oldest poetry, polyptoton (cf. Palmer 1954: 104–9).

In c. 13, Fabullus's recompense for bringing dinner will be the receipt of a perfume:

> *sed contra accipies meros amores,*
> > But in return you'll get nothing but love [76]
> *seu quid suauius elegantiusue est:*
> > or whatever is sweeter and finer still:
> *nam unguentum dabo, quod meae puellae*
> > for I can give you some scented oil. [77]
> > yes, some scented oil—
> *donarunt Veneres Cupidinesque:*
> > which the gods of love and beauty
> > gave to my girl,
> *quod tu cum olfacies, deos rogabis*
> > which when you smell it
> > will make you wish to the gods
> *totum ut te faciant, Fabulle, nasum.*
> > that you, Fabullus, were nothing but nose.
> > > (13.9–14)

The close of 13, which Quinn calls a "final extravagance," is not merely rhetorical flair but meant to recall in spirit such verses as *PMG* 900 and 901,

76. Marcovich 1982 with lit. summarizes the arguments for the meaning of the phrase: (1) *meri amores* = *mera suauitas,* a reference to the upcoming perfume; (2) *meri amores* = φιλία 'pure love'; and (3), Marcovich's own suggestion, supported by Dettmer 1986 via structural parallels between cc. 12 and 13, *meri amores* = Ἔρωτες 'love stories, love poetry,' but intended to be ambiguous with (1), since *suauis* and *elegans* are epithets appropriate both to poetry and to the perfume. Some measure of ambiguity between the various possibilities is doubtless the poet's intention. I favor an ambiguity between (2) and (1), since, *contra* Marcovich, *suauis* and *elegans* are also appropriate to aristocratic interchange: *suauis* describes acts of attentive service (cf. IV.6) and *elegans* a 'neat' and 'proper' solution to a problem (I.5 n.65), but this 'attentive and proper' solution turns out to be something that is literally *suauis* and *elegans* (for *elegans* of a scent, cf. *uestes tuetur odore non ineleganti* Plin. *Nat.* 21.169, of the effects of *oenanthe*).

77. Voss suggested that Catullus was thinking of *Od.* 18.192–94, κάλλεϊ μέν οἱ πρῶτα προσώπατα καλὰ κάθηρεν | ἀμβροσίῳ, οἵῳ περ ἐϋστέφανος Κυθέρεια | χρίεται, εὖτ' ἂν ἴῃ Χαρίτων χορὸν ἱμερόεντα, to which Ellis 1889: 47 ad 1.12 added that Catullus may also have known "the interpretation which seems early to have been put upon the passage that the ointment [of Aphrodite] was itself called κάλλος"; see also Vessey 1971, who argues that Catullus, by transferring the conventional element of perfume "entirely to the world of make-believe," is using it "as a symbol for something else, a symbol that gains its meaning (aptly for a *doctus poeta*) from a passage of Greek literature" (p. 48). Closer to a model for Catullus are the lines of Rhianus: Ὡραί σοι Χάριτές τε κατὰ γλυκὺ χεῦαν ἔλαιον | ὦ πυγά (*AP* 12.38.1–2).

*AP* 5.83, 5.84, 5.174 (Meleager) and *Anacreontea* 22, in which the reciter asks to be transformed into something that brings him into closer contact with the beloved.[78] In short, the poetic persona and rhetoric of these poems are thoroughly in the spirit of Greek light lyric. I suggest that *uenustus,* which in both poems is connected to hortatory statements concerning the fiction of the poem, therefore has a metapoetic function, with 'wittiness' meaning the "ability to appreciate polymetric poetry."

This metapoesis, however, is also distinctly erotic. The "gods of love and beauty" that appear in both poems are, to state the obvious, divinities of erotic experience. The *uenustiores* can appreciate maudlin excess out of sympathy with the posture of a sympathetic lover. Fabullus's recompense is distinctly erotic. *Vnguenta,* to be sure, were often associated with sexual activity,[79] and so were dinner parties.[80] In Greek poetry the trope of bodily conversion is invoked to bring the metamorphosed closer to a lover or object of erotic interest.[81] The *uenustus* parties in both poems may also be expected to recognize in the ointment and the sparrow erotic double entendres.[82] In this complex of metapoesis and eroticism, it seems to me there is

78. E.g., *AP* 5.83 εἴθ' ἄνεμος γενόμην, σὺ δ' ἐπιστείχουσα παρ' ἀγὰς | στήθεα γυμνώσαις, καὶ με πνέοντα λάβοις "Would I were the wind, and you walking the beach bared your breasts, and took me in as I blew."

79. Cf. Holmes 1992.

80. Cf. *ibi pro scorto fuit, in cubiculum subrectitauit e conuiuio, cum partim illorum iam saepe ad eundum modum erat* (Cato *ORF* 8.213 = Gel. 10.13.1); *in conuiuiis, dediti uentri et turpissumae parti corporis* (Sal. *Jug.* 85.41).

81. V., e.g., ὕδωρ θέλω γενέσθαι, | ὅπως σε χρῶτα λούσω· | μύρον, γύναι, γενοίμην, | ὅπως ἐγώ σ' ἀλείψω "I want to become water, that I may bathe your skin; may I become oil, woman, that I may rub you" (*Anacreont.* 22.9–12), *AP* 5.83 above, n. 78.

82. Fabullus's conversion to a nose may imply an ithyphallic response to Lesbia's beauty. See Dettmer 1986: 83–85. The argument of Littman 1977, with Hallett 1978, that the *unguentum* is formed by Lesbia's vaginal secretions, is met by Witke 1980. Fitzgerald's (1995: 99) subtle formulation of the meaning of the offering of the perfume is well worth repeating: "The perfume is generously overdetermined: a commodity that has a real, though nonculinary function for the dinner, it also suggests a substitute food—the gods, after all, consume the *aroma* of our sacrifices—as well as the essence of sex appeal. . . . I am not suggesting that Catullus is offering Lesbia sexually to his guest; rather, I would put it like this: smelling the perfume is to enjoying Lesbia as smelling the aroma of food is to eating—if you are human you are tantalized, but if you are a god you are satisfied. Fabullus will be both tantalized and apotheosized by his experience." As for the sparrow, Thomas 1993 summarizes the arguments for taking *passer* as code for the penis by reference to similar images in Meleager. See the bibliography cited by Thomson 1997: 203. The only use of *uenustus* that is not an instance of the language of social performance applies to Sirmio, which is *uenusta* (31.12); but even here Catullus has combined two senses in the word. *Venusta,* as previous commentators, reviewing the adjective only in Catullus, have not stressed, is entirely appropriate to places: cf. Cicero's ῥωπογραφία (I.6 n.89). Commentators since Havelock 1929: 120

also an element of social performance: it is not only that Fabullus and the *uenustiores* are to be familiar with Greek poetry and comfortable with eroticism, they are also in effect challenged by Catullus to make a show of their familiarity by understanding the stance he has taken. Paradoxically that show of familiarity probably means *not* doing what they are asked to do (mourn or bring dinner), out of knowledge that the poems are Greek conventions reworked into Latin.

Poem 43, directed to Mamurra's lover Ameana,[83] uses three lexemes of the language of social performance, *bellus, facet(us),* and *elegan(s),* to express a fusion of erotics and an exclusive social world:

> *Salue nec minimo puella naso*
>> Hail, girl who lacks a small nose,
> *nec bello pede nec nigris ocellis*
>> lacks dainty feet, lacks dark eyes,
> *nec longis digitis nec ore sicco*
>> lacks slender fingers, lacks dry lips,
> *nec sane nimis elegante lingua,*
>> and lacks, indeed, a tongue too refined!
> *decoctoris amica Formiani,*
>> Lover of the Bankrupt of Formiae,
> *ten prouincia narrat esse bellam?*
>> they say in the province that *you* are pretty?
> *tecum Lesbia nostra comparatur?*
>> They compare our Lesbia to *you*?
> *o saeclum insapiens et infacetum!*
>> A senseless and witless age!

---

have, by contrast, stressed what is surely right, that *uenusta* plays a part in the personification of Sirmio; see also Putnam 1962 and Baker 1970. But this part is not played, as most have it, because in Catullus *uenustus* "is normally applied to persons" (Quinn 1969: 35). Rather it is probable that Catullus also has in mind another rare use of *uenustus* here. Cicero once applies *uenustissimus,* with *dulcissimus,* to his son, whom he misses from exile: *[quid] quod [desidero] filium uenustissimum mihique dulcissimum?* (*Q. fr.* 1.3.3). This way of describing a child is found only here and nowhere else in Cicero, but it may represent a tender familiar use that Catullus has in mind: his tone toward Sirmio is as an affectionate superior; cf. *ero gaude* "rejoice in your master," and the remarks of Quinn 1973 ad loc.: "In the valediction [which includes a reference to nearby lakes], the personification becomes sharper: Sirmio is the faithful retainer, attended by a chorus of lesser slaves—all smiles and happy chatter as they welcome their master home." Sirmio is both a "lovely place," like the villa at Astura, and a "dear child," held in affection by a social superior.

83. Ameana is insulted as the "lover of the Bankrupt of Formiae" (l. 5), an insult that also occurs in 41.4, a poem in which she is named (41.1). The "Bankrupt of Formiae" must be Mamurra, who was from Formiae (cf. *urbs Mamurrarum,* Hor. *Sat.* 1.5.37 and Catullus's *[macula] Formiana,* 57.4), and whose profligacy is attacked by Catullus in c. 29.

The kind of attractiveness attributed to Lesbia in c. 86, which comprised both physical and intellectual qualities, is probably also at issue here. Ameana, who lacks standardly admired physical attributes,[84] has no spry intellect either—hers is not a "tongue too refined" (cf. above, p. 236). Here, then, is an overlap between eroticism and social performance. The main force of the poem, however, is to demarcate groups of the social world according to their tastes—their erotic tastes. The "province" reveals its lack of *lepos* and *facetiae* because of its inability to distinguish real attractiveness. Indeed a premise of the poem is that erotic attractiveness is a field of public interest something like theatrical or even oratorical ability.

In short not only does Catullus use the language of social performance, an idiom of considerable contemporary piquancy, to define a new view of erotics, poetics, and the social world (which becomes largely coextensive with the symposium), but he also uses the language of social performance in such a way as to blur the distinctions between them.[85] In joining those

84. There are various parallels for the ideal woman as small of foot (Hor. *Sat.* 1.2.93, Ov. *Am.* 3.3.7), long of finger (Prop. 2.2.5), and slight of nose (Hor. *Sat.* 1.2.93). Cf. other parallels in Ellis 1889, Thomson 1997.

85. The remarkable *lepores* of c. 32, I suggest, is informed by the same fusion—or rather, in this poem, tension—between eroticism, social performance, and poetics. C. 32 is Catullus's attempt to arrange for an afternoon assignation with a certain Ipsitilla (or Ipsicilla; on the name see Gratwick 1991: 547 and refs. in Heath 1986: 28 n. 2). Catullus begins the poem by addressing her *amabo, mea dulcis Ipsitilla | meae deliciae, mei lepores* (32.1–2). *Deliciae,* a common word for 'darling' or 'sweetheart,' suggests that *lepores,* too, unparalleled as the description of a person, be taken as a term of erotic endearment. Such strings of "Schmeichelworte" are reminiscent of the language of amatory scenes in comedy (Syndikus 1984: 190, who compares Pl. *Poen.* 365–67, *Cas.* 134–38). However, if *lep(idus)* here has its usual postsecond-century meaning, the vocative *lepores* would mean, translated expansively, something like 'a person who repeatedly performs attractively'; plural abstracts indicate that the referent is the focus of repeated instantiations of the abstract (cf. K-S 2.1 §22.1). The elevation of a word describing 'performative attractiveness' into a word virtually equivalent to 'darling' suggests that such compelling charm or wit was paradigmatic in Catullus's conception of erotic attractiveness. Here, as in other polymetrics, eroticism and social performance fuse. The effect of the juxtaposition of *lepores* to the common *deliciae* might be captured thus: "If you would, my sweet Ipsitilla, my darling, my flash. . . ."

But *lepores,* I suggest, also has a metapoetic function. As the poem concludes, we discover that Catullus's interest in Ipsitilla apparently has nothing to do with her wit or charm. He is interested only in sex, asking her to prepare him *nouem continuas fututiones* "nine 'fuckages' in a row" (32.8), and now so aroused that *pertund[it] tunicamque palliumque* "[He] pounds through tunic and cloak" (32.11). Has the element of "social performance" vanished, giving way to simple carnality? Perhaps—unless the performance in question is literary interpretation. The two sexual lines, 8 and 11, which break the atmosphere of politeness with which the poem begins, are not only patent exaggerations (e.g., nine times? "Four," "five," and "seven" also would have fit, metrically) but are also the most self-consciously poetic of

three spheres, and in using the language of performance to describe them, Catullus is not unique. In Roman culture as a whole, those three spheres of activity were closely connected and occasionally described by our lexemes. Poetry and eroticism fuse in Cicero's characterization of the *uenustus* Philodemus: because he wrote delicate epigrams, he might be *impurus* (*Pis.* 70; above, V.2), which has connotations of sexual impropriety. Catullus's c. 16, discussed below (VII.7), depends on the presence in the culture at large of a hermeneutic that fused poetry and erotics. Eroticism also had commonalities with the symposium, which, as we have seen, might end with sexual

---

the whole poem. Both have only three words (if we discount bound enclitics). One has an urbane polymetric neologism (*fututiones,* on which see Ross 1969: 111–12; Quinn 1973 ad loc.); the other has *-que -que,* a mock-epic, or as Ross 1969: 63–65 argues, more probably a neoteric feature. (With 32.11 compare *percurrent raphanique mugilesque* 15.19, also the last line of the poem.) In short the lines about sex are the very lines that point to themselves as poetry. Much as the *uenustus* of c. 13 is a hortatory vocative, so here *lepores,* I suggest, challenges Ipsitilla to *deliver* a social performance, in this case the act of interpreting Catullus's lines: is he serious or not? His joke, rather like that of c. 49 (VII.6 n.92) and c. 16 (VII.7), is that the puzzle is impossible to solve: if Ipsitilla takes the sex lines literally, she betrays her ignorance as a reader and forfeits any claim to (as it were) *lepos interpretatiuus;* but if she takes the lines poetically, and refuses sex, she forfeits her claim to *lepos amatorius.* The discourse situation of the poem fits very nicely with a reading that puts such an onus on Ipsitilla. She is asked to take control, issuing orders (*iube* 3, *iubeto* 9, and possibly *adiubeto* 4; on the last see Gratwick 1991: 550–51), whereas Catullus, supine in bed (lines 10–11), awaits them: *she* must decide how to act and so declare her analytical abilities. Perhaps the rare plural of *lepos* is no accident here: charmed at first by an apparent endearment, Ipsitilla will shortly discover that in this poem different kinds of *lepos* are at loggerheads—with her in the middle.

At any rate, the Plautine expression *respice o mi lepos* (*Cas.* 235–6), sometimes cited as a precedent for *lepores,* is not a real precedent. Despite his frequent use of *lepid(us),* only twice does Plautus use *lepos* as a vocative. (Heath 1986: 31 n.15 cites *Cas.* 1.50, but *mi lepus* there is from *lepus lepŏris* "hare.") In the *Curculio* the old tippler Leaena has been drawn out of doors by the bouquet of wine, to which she sings a *canticum* (95–109), comparing the scent to myrrh, cinnamon, roses, saffron oil, casia, and fenugreek. In the midst of this rapturous praise, she declares *salue anime mi Liberi lepos* "Hail, my darling, *lepos* of Bacchus" (*Cur.* 98). In the other instance Lysidamus, perfumed and drunk on thoughts of his love for the slave-girl Casina, addresses his suspicious wife Cleostrata: LY. *respice o mi lepos.* | CL. *nempe ita ut tu mihi es.* | *unde hic amabo unguenta olent?* "Look back, my *lepos.*" "Yes (I am your *lepos*) just as you are mine. Tell me, where is this smell of perfume from?" I suggest that in both instances *lepos* is motivated by qualities of scent, probably as a version of its old meaning 'soft' (cf. I.9). In that case the *lepos* of *Cas.* 235–36 is a kind of "straight line," preparing for a comment about perfumes; we might render thus: "Look back, my precious"—"Yes I'm precious to you; and as far as I'm concerned, you're also precious. How about telling me why you smell of perfume?" In any case the difference between Plautine *lepos* and Catullan *lepores* is a difference between the cultural models of their times: for Plautus *lep(idus)* belongs to the bordello, but for Catullus *lep(idus)* bore the weight of two centuries of the interpenetration of aestheticism with political self-expression.

activity—and which were the province of *lepidi pueri* (V.6). In his use of the
language of social performance, Catullus is only taking over an idea and an
idiom that already existed. His use of that language is nonetheless striking,
even shocking. Among foreigners the complex of aestheticism, Hellenism,
and individualism marked their inability or unworthiness to participate in
political life (V.3), whereas among Romans the same complex signified social status and a means of competition, which is precisely what attracts Cicero's efforts to coopt (ch. 6) or reject (V.4, V.6) it. Catullus has welded the
competitive element of the latter use of the language of social performance
to the apoliticism of the former use and altered those elements accordingly:
style becomes not a means, but the end, of competition, and apoliticism becomes not a fault, but a choice. The ease with which the political could be
converted to the apolitical will be cause for comment presently (VII.9). We
will see, as Selden 1992: 498 puts it, that "[b]y redirecting critical attention
from questions of personal circumstance to the logic of self-presentation,
the poet gets to the very heart of the politico-discursive system."

## VII.6. The Difficulty of Trumping Polymetric Values

We have observed some remarkable points of correspondence between Cicero's and Catullus's use of the language of social performance, suggesting
that they both had in mind the cultural rules associated with the cultural
model of which the language of social performance was a lexemic manifestation. In both, the language of social performance is associated with agonistic performances that required responses in kind. In both, the language
of social performance is embedded in contexts that make clear the sort of
person each author thinks is worthy to judge by means of that language, and
in both, agreement about who or what should be labeled by the language
of social performance is a mark of social solidarity. Another point of correspondence is even more remarkable. Much as Cicero countermanded the
alluring values expressed by the language of social performance with strident reference to traditional social values (V.6), so does Catullus resort to
traditional modes of discourse when he faces the same task.

C. 22 describes the contradictions of a certain Suffenus, who is described
as *uenustus et dicax et urbanus* (22.2), and as *bellus . . . et urbanus* (22.9). He is
a fine social performer: Catullus also calls him a *scurra* 'clown,' or in the
world of the polymetrics perhaps something more like 'wag,' a person not
merely witty but constantly angling to purvey his wit (the opposite of Cicero's ideal of humor). Unfortunately Suffenus's poetic abilities do not match
up to his drolleries:

*Suffenus iste, Vare, quem probe nosti,*
    The Suffenus whom you know so well, Varus,
*homo est uenustus et dicax et urbanus,*
    Is a lovely and witty and civilized man,
*idemque longos plurimos facit uersus.*
    and unfortunately also writes poems without end.

. . . . . . . . . . . . . . . . . . . .

*haec cum legas tu, bellus ille et urbanus*
    When you read them, that civilized stylish
*Suffenus unus caprimulgus aut fossor*
    Suffenus, *violà,* seems like a
    goatherd or ditchdigger instead,
*rursus uidetur: tantum abhorret ac mutat.*
    mutated to somebody totally different!
*quid hoc putemus esse? qui modo scurra*
    It doesn't make sense. A minute ago he was
*aut si quid hac re scitius uidebatur,*
    a perfect wag, or whatever is smarter than that,
*idem infaceto est infacetior rure,*
    but as soon as he touches a poem,
*simul poemata attigit.*
    there goes his wit, he's left with less
    than a hick who has no wit at all.
                                        (22.1–3, 9–15)

Suffenus's poetic productions do not match his social style. His poetry, which is characterized in terms of Callimachean polemic,[86] absorbs him completely, so that he becomes wrapped up in himself, losing the sense of being "on stage" that was critical to the "polymetric ethos": "He's never happier than when he's writing a poem, so pleased with himself, so proud of himself."[87]

Suffenus thus represents a contradiction to the totality of the "polymetric ethos," which demands social, poetic, and erotic graces in equal measure. Catullus's solution to this problem is to turn to a proverb:

*nimirum idem omnes fallimur, neque est quisquam*
    But that's how it is, though.

86. He writes excessively and voluminously (*plurimos . . . uersus* 3; cf. *milia aut decem aut plura* | *perscripta* 4–5; Syndikus 1984: 156); he is concerned with grandness (*chartae regiae* etc. 6ff.); he becomes inurbane (*bellus ille et urbanus* | *. . . caprimulgus aut fossor* | *rursus uidetur* 9–11).

87. *neque idem umquam* | *aeque est beatus ac poema cum scribit:* | *tam gaudet in se tamque se ipse miratur,* 15–17. For *beatus* as 'self-satisfied,' cf. Fordyce 1961.

> We're all deceived in just that way,
>> there's no one
>
> *quem non in aliqua re uidere Suffenum*
>> you can't see Suffenus in,
>> in some respect.
>
> *possis. suus cuique attributus est error:*
>> Everyone's got their own failing assigned them;
>
> *sed non uidemus manticae quod in tergo est.*
>> we just can't see the part of the bag
>> that's hanging on our backs.

(22.18–21)

Catullus is alluding to the old fable that mortal faults hang in two bags, our own on our backs, other people's on our chests, so that we can see everyone else's vices but not our own.[88] The turn to a proverb (an old rhetorical trick, the *sententia* or γνώμη, cf. *Rhet. Her.* 4.24) is significant. The "polymetric" world is a world of passionate emotion: judgments, harsh or mild, are delivered quickly and confidently. On the basis of Suffenus's poetry, Catullus might be expected to condemn him as harshly as he does Volusius. But Suffenus is so delightful in other respects that Catullus wishes to spare him. The only solution to the difficulty is to invoke a frame of reference that is not so passionate or judgmental—here, the objective, traditional world of the proverb.[89] The turn to proverb thus suggests the attraction of the kind of performer that could earn the label *bellus:* Catullus wants to "save" him, even at the risk of switching value systems. The turn to proverb also suggests the character of the self-absorbed, judgmental world in which those labels were applied: a kind of conceptual deus ex machina is needed to keep delicts from bringing condemnation. If, with Selden 1992: 477, we take Suffenus not as a personality whose life Catullus is actually recording, but "principally as a figure for the rift between the poet and the persona projected by his work," the implication of the deus ex machina becomes even starker: the proverb represents a kind of retreat to a world of shared folk life from the ultimately inaccessible world of stylistic perfection. A corollary of that inaccessibility is that the ideals of political performance, which were described in the same language, are also alluring and also ultimately inaccessible.

    *Bellus* occupies a similar place in c. 24, addressed to Juventius. Juventius was an attractive young man, and the occasional object of Catullus's affections:

---

88. Babrius 66, Phaedrus 4.10.

89. Catullus also turns to proverbial expressions in cc. 51 and 70, with the comparable intent of creating perspective on an all-absorbing emotion; cf. Williams 1985[2]: 584.

*O qui flosculus es Iuuentiorum,*
> O precious flower of the Juventii,

*non horum modo, sed quot aut fuerunt*
> not only of this generation,
> but of generations past,

*aut posthac aliis erunt in annis,*
> or of those in time yet to come,

*mallem diuitias Midae dedisses*
> I'd rather you'd given Midas's money

*isti, cui neque seruus est neque arca,*
> to that friend of yours,
> who hasn't a slave or money in the bank,

*quam sic te sineres ab illo amari.*
> than let yourself be loved by him.

*'quid? non est homo bellus?' inquies. est:*
> "How's that?" you'll say,
> "Surely he's au courant?"
> That he is:

*sed bello huic neque seruus est neque arca.*
> au courant, without a slave or money in the bank.

*hoc tu quam libet abice eleuaque:*
> Make light of it, downplay it
> as much as you wish:

*nec seruum tamen ille habet neque arcam.*
> He hasn't a slave, or money in the bank.[90]

Juventius was surely a part of the bright life of Catullus's circle: not only is attraction, particularly in the polymetrics, bound up with a multifarious sense of style, but the rhetoric of addressing Juventius in other poems is similar to the rhetoric of addressing Lesbia, a prominent member of that circle.[91] In the value system of the polymetrics, Juventius's point that his lover is *bel-*

---

90. The phrase *cui neque seruus est neque arca* (24.5) suggests the lover is Furius, who is so identified in the previous poem (*Furi, cui neque seruus est neque arca,* 23.1) and whose insolvency is mocked in c. 26. Furius, with Aurelius, was a rival of Catullus for Juventius's affection. The unnamed boy linked to Aurelius in cc. 15 and 21 is assumed to be Juventius; Juventius is linked to unnamed lovers in c. 81.

91. In c. 48, a poem reminiscent of the Lesbia kissing poems (cc. 5 and 7), Catullus would kiss Juventius's eyes with kisses as thick as stalks of wheat. C. 99 is especially important in establishing Juventius's status as a demi-Lesbia: the long elegy, which laments Juventius's sullen reaction to a stolen kiss, is, as Quinn 1973: 436–37 points out, "one of the few elegiac poems apart from those addressed to Lesbia to take the form of a personal statement to an addressee." The poems typically included in the Juventius cycle are cc. 15, 21, 23, 24, 26, 48, 81, 99, and possibly 16 and 40.

*lus* is unassailable. Indeed thus was described the charm that made Catullus defend even the turgid Suffenus. Much as Catullus needed to find an alternative voice to defend Suffenus, so here he has to find other means of attack against Juventius's lover. He therefore turns to means not otherwise prominent in the polymetric world and more typical of traditional Roman panegyric: family and wealth. Attention is drawn to Juventius's family from the beginning of the poem: he is addressed as the flower of his *gens*, not only now but in past and future too. The long view of a family's history, a perusal of its *imagines*, so to speak, is wholly untypical of the polymetrics. Even of his patron Muse Catullus makes only the modest request that she make his poetry last "longer than a generation" (*plus uno maneat perenne saeclo*, 1.10). The long view, rather, belongs to traditional panegyric; the description of the generations in the teasingly proper compliment to Cicero (c. 49) is very similar to that here.[92] The Juventii were certainly a distinguished family with *imagines* to peruse.[93]

Catullus's second line of attack is also traditional, viz. the abuse of poverty,[94] which probably implies bankruptcy and thus a lack of the fiscal virtues the Romans so valued.[95] At any rate *bellus*, as in 22, is connected to the powerful attraction of stylishness which Catullus cannot trump except in non-polymetric voices. Of course Catullus's implicit claim, that the scion of a distinguished family deserves a wealthier lover, is absurd: scions of distinguished families ought not to have been trafficking in stylish, homoerotic affairs in the first place. The diminutive *flosculus* may be read as en-

92. *Disertissime Romuli nepotum | quot sunt quotque fuere, Marce Tulli, | quotque post aliis erunt in annis* (49.1–3) "Marcus Tullius, most fluent of all the sons of Romulus that are, have been, or will be in years to come." Some critics have taken the poem as serious, others as flippant. See with notes Selden 1992: 464–67 and Batstone 1993: 155–63, who themselves take the poem as deliberately undecidable, doubtless the right view. The use of a similar phrase in c. 21, *pater esuritionum | non harum modo, sed quot aut fuerunt | aut sunt aut aliis erunt in annis* (1–3), is of course ironic.

93. Cf. Cic. *Planc.* 19, addressed to T. Iuventius Laterensis, the opposing counsel: *tu es e municipio antiquissimo Tusculano, ex quo sunt plurimae familiae consulares in quibus est etiam Iuuentia*.

94. Furius's poverty is attacked in the immediately preceding poem, c. 23, Aurelius's in c. 21. For absence of property as insult, cf. *quid huic abest nisi res et uirtus?* (*de Orat.* 2.281). The stereotypical value of *locuples* as a compliment can be appreciated by considering the pairings of *honestus* 'honorable' in Cicero's orations and letters: the most frequent mates of *honestus* are *bonus* (11 times), *ornatus* (6 times), *nobilis* (6 times), and *locuples* (6 times). 'Wealthy' is not far from 'good' and 'noble.' When Ennius translates the ἀδοξοῦντες and δοξοῦντες of Euripides (the epigraph to ch. 6 above), he turns them by *ignobiles* and *opulenti* respectively (*scen.* 199 Vahlen[2], cf. Gel. 11.4).

95. Hence the insult of Mamurra as *decoctor* 'one who boils food over' 41.4; for gluttony as a symbol of financial profligacy, cf. Corbeill 1996: 131–34.

capsulating the absurdity. Juventius is not just the "flower" of his family, but the "dear little flower": glory, viewed tenderly. That Catullus must resort to this absurdity only shows the power of Juventius's defense: to be the lover of someone who is *bellus* is, in the polymetric world, self-justifying and impossible to discourage. The clash of the worlds is felt in Catullus's stubborn repetition of "neither a slave *(seruus)* nor a moneybox *(arca)."* This is not the typical rhetoric of the polymetrics, graceful inversion, or παρὰ προσδοκίαν. It is a drumbeat without nuance, like Cato's *delendam esse Cartaginem.* It is, in fact, something like the figure that the *Rhet. Her.* calls *commoratio* (= ἐπι-μονή): *"Commoratio* is when one lingers over a secure point that encapsulates the whole case and returns to that point frequently." [96]

Juventius also appears as the object of Catullus's affection in c. 81, which is a poem in elegiac distich rather than one of the polymetric meters.

> *Nemone in tanto potuit populo esse, Iuuenti,*
>> The city is so large, Juventius,
> *bellus homo, quem tu diligere inciperes,*
>> and you could not find even one stylish man
>> to whom to take a liking
> *praeterquam iste tuus moribunda ab sede Pisauri*
>> exclusive of that man you're with
>> from Pisaurum's dying seat,[97]
> *hospes inaurata pallidior statua,*
>> a foreigner yellower than a gold–gilt statue,[98]
> *qui tibi nunc cordist; quem tu praeponere nobis*
>> who's now your dear,
>> whom now you dare prefer to us,
> *audes, et nescis quod facinus facias?*
>> ignorant what deed you do?

Where c. 24 juxtaposed two perspectives, the 'polymetric' and the 'proverbial,' c. 81 juxtaposes several tones of voice. Parts of the poem are distinctly neoteric, displaying the stylistic idiosyncrasies of the 'New Poets' of Catullus's generation. In the fourth line an adjective comes before the cae-

---

96. *commoratio est cum in loco firmissimo a quo tota causa continetur manetur diutius et eodem saepius reditur* (4.58). For a discussion of the difference in rhetorical stance between polymetrics and elegiacs, cf. Solodow 1989, who compares the "indirect" and "narrative" literary criticism of cc. 35 and 36 to the "direct statement" of c. 95.

97. Juventius's lover comes from Pisaurum in Umbria. For its poor climate, the probable motivation for the adjective *moribunda,* cf. Ellis's note. For *pallidior* not 'paler' but simply 'yellow,' cf. Fordyce 1961.

98. On gilt statuary, cf. Ellis.

sura and modifies a substantive at the end of the line. The remaining two elements interlock, thus:

hospes$_a$ inaurata$_b$ ‖ pallidior$_A$ statua$_B$

The word order *abAB* is a word-order pattern typical of neoteric hexameters and shared also by pentameters,[99] as in the following examples from Catullus:

Graia$_a$ Canopiis$_b$ ‖ incola$_A$ litoribus$_B$ (66.58)
"A Greek inhabitant on Egyptian shores"

lymphaque$_a$ in Oetaeis$_b$ ‖ Malia$_A$ Thermopylis$_B$ (68.54)
"And the Malian spring in Oetaean Thermopylae"

cum grauis$_a$ exustos$_b$ ‖ aestus$_A$ hiulcat agros$_B$ (68.62)
"When the heavy heat makes the burnt fields gape"

The same word-order pattern appears in two of the three pentameters of Cornelius Gallus:

maxima$_a$ Romanae$_b$ ‖ pars$_A$ eri\<s> historiae$_B$ (Gal. 4)
"You will be a great part of Roman history"

fixa$_a$ legam spolieis$_b$ ‖ deiuitiora$_A$ tueis$_B$ (Gal. 6)
"I shall read \<sc. temples> the richer, fitted with your spoils"

The epicisms of the poem may also be considered neoteric, inasmuch as neoteric hexameter poetry imposes "Alexandrian artifices . . . on the traditional style of the Latin hexameter as it had come down from Ennius" (Fordyce 1961: 275). The periphrasis and word order of the phrase *moribunda ab sede Pisauri* is mock-epic;[100] Quinn 1973 compares *angusta ab sede Pelori* "from Pelorus' narrow seat" (*Aen.* 3.687). *Praeterquam* 'other than,' only here in Catullus, is especially common in the legal tradition and seems to have something of a technical flavor, recalling what Fordyce calls the "prosaic connexions" of the Ennian tradition that are also common in Lucretius, viz., *utpote qui, qui quoniam, quandoquidem.*

The poem closes, by contrast, in a different register. Juventius is pictured as "daring" *(audes)* to prefer somebody else and committing a *facinus* 'deed,

---

99. Cf. Ross 1969: 132–37 with bibliography.

100. On the possible epic ring of *ab* before *s-*, v. Ross 1969: 49 n.98. Compare *Aen.* 1.270 *ab sede Lauini*, 7.255 *externa ab sede;* 7.324, 7.454; Zicàri 1955: 66. The original phrase was doubtless based on a translation of a Greek expression with ἕδος and a genitive; cf. Zicàri 1955: 65–66. On the form *moribunda*, which adds to the epic effect, cf. ibid.: 62–64.

notable deed, misdeed.' The enjambement of *audes* into the last pentameter connects it more closely with *facinus facis* and thus suggests the nexus of *audacia* and *facinus (facere)*, common for "outrageous" acts in comedy, as illustrated in the following examples:

> facinus audax incipit (Pl. *Aul.* 460)
> istuc facinus facere tam malum? (Pl. *Bac.* 682)
> ne tale quisquam facinus incipere audeat (Pl. *Capt.* 753)
> quis me audacior | sit, si istuc facinus audeam? (Pl. *Ps.* 541–42)
> o facinus audax! (Ter. *An.* 401)
> hoccin tam audax facinu' facere esse ausum! (Ter. *Eu.* 644)
> qua audacia tantum facinus audet? (Ter. *Eu.* 958–59)

The dramatic, even larger-than-life quality of the nexus is suggested by Cicero's avoidance of it, although *facinus* appears often in the orations.[101] There are still other speech registers in the poem. The poem begins with three pleonasms or periphrases: *nemo . . . homo* 'no one . . . man,' *diligere inciperes* 'undertake to love, go ahead and love' (instead of just 'love') and *iste tuus* 'that one of yours.' The poem closes with a repetition: *cordist* 'is dear to' and *praeponere | audes* 'dare to prefer' express Juventius's affection for the *hospes* in two ways. These redundancies suggest an intense and emphatic speaker. But the speech register of the whole is not easy to determine. Whereas *esse cordi* is distinctly familiar in tone, *praeponere* is not.[102] *Nemo . . .*

101. In nearly two hundred occurrences of *facinus*, Cicero only once uses it with *facere*, as a part of the conversation in a philosophical dialogue: *si enim ita est, uide ne facinus facias, cum mori suadeas* (*Fin.* 2.95). Cicero prefers other verbs, for example *committere* (*Quinct.* 79, *S. Rosc.* 65, *Ver.* 2.1.40, *Cael.* 56, *Leg.* 1.40, *Fam.* 3.10.2) and *admittere* (*Mil.* 103, *Sul.* 16, *Deiot.* 4, *Off.* 3.95), which are also preferred by Caesar (*BG* 3.9.3, 7.38; *BC* 3.60.4). By contrast the overtones of 'dastardliness' or 'derring-do' in the phrase *facinus facere* made it appealing to Sallust (*Cat.* 7.6, 11.4, 19.5, 51.6, 53.2, *Jug.* 5.4). Cicero connects *auda(x)* and *facin(us)* occasionally (*nullum facinus, nullam audaciam, nullam ium, Cael.* 1; *cum facinerosis audaciter, Cael.* 13; *paulo ad facinus audacior, Catil.* 2.9; *perniciosum ciuem, sceleratum, libidinosum, impium, audacem, facinerosum, Phil.* 8.16; *ad omne facinus immanis audacia, Phil.* 13.10), but these connections are neither as proportionately frequent nor as pointed as they are in the historians (*multa saepe uirilis audaciae facinora conmiserat,* Sal. *Cat.* 25.2; *magno audacique aliquo facinore,* Liv. 2.12.3; *audaci facinori,* Liv. 2.54.7; *ipse egregium facinus ausus,* Liv. 8.24.9; *id facinus ausus,* Liv. 8.35.6; *plebem . . . magnum ausuram facinus,* Liv. 23.2.3; *tantum ausi facinus sunt,* Liv. 28.27.16; *fraude auso facinus,* Liv. 30.25.6; *ut pessimum facinus auderent pauci,* Tac. *Hist.* 1.28).

102. Cicero at any rate uses *cordi esse* rarely, and when some particular affectionate or pathetic effect is required (*uitam omnino semper horridam atque aridam cordi fuisse,* Quinct. 93, above, V.4; *ut mihi, cui mea filia maxime cordi est, Ver.* 2.1.112; cf. *Or.* 53, *Amic.* 15, *Att.* 5.3), whereas *praeponere* is his regular word for 'prefer (one person to another)' without such limitations (e.g., *me omnibus patronis esse praepositum,* Q. *Caec.* 16; *ita factum ut nobilissimis hominibus longe praeponerer, Leg. Agr.* 2.7).

*homo* and *iste tuus* belong both to comedy and to Cicero's oratory and high-style prose.[103] Periphrases with inceptive verbs and infinitive, instead of the simple verb, are typically colloquial but not so colloquial that they were off limits to Cicero in a speech or Ennius in a tragedy.[104]

Even if some of these phrases or constructions, appearing as they do in both comedy and refined speech, are simply part of the *sermo cotidianus,* the everyday speech of the educated class, the poem is still a tonal farrago.[105] This mixed and at times even deliberately ambiguous register is, I think, precisely Catullus's intention: the speaker is, by turns, a contemporary orator, a neoteric poet, and an exaggerating *adulescens amans* of comedy. The exaggeration of the comic actor and the intensity of the orator provide a counterpoint to the infinite regression of irony into which Catullus's poly-metric voice so easily slips. But if the poem were pitched only in that tone, it would be easy for the (evidently) stylish and urbane Juventius to reject it as the cloying sincerities of a dullard. To assert his claim on Juventius's world, Catullus presents himself also as a mocking neoteric poet; the neoteric touches, in effect, form the speaker's credentials and obligate Juventius to listen. C. 81 is an attempt to puncture, by way of the comic and the oratorical, the impenetrable and solipsistic world of polymetric approbation, encapsulated in the refrain *bellus homo* which Juventius, here as in c. 24, trills in his defense. Unlike Cicero, who attacks the 'trumping' use of the language of social performance petulantly, from the outside (V.4, V.6), Catullus attacks from the outside *and* from the inside. The resulting poem barely holds together, an icon for the erotically tortured Catullus and a testimony *e contrario* to the potency of 'polymetric values.'

---

103. NEMO HOMO: *id dicere audes, quod nemo umquam homo antehac | uidit nec potest fieri* (Pl. *Am.* 566–67), *alienum hominem intro mittat neminem* (Pl. *As.* 756), *hominem ego iracundiorem quam te noui neminem* (Pl. *Merc.* 142), *ego hominem callidiorem uidi neminem | quam Phormionem* (Ter. *Ph.* 591–92); *hominem esse arbitror neminem, qui nomen istius audierit* (Cic. *Ver.* 1.1.15), *neminem umquam hominem homini cariorem fuisse quam te sibi* (Cic. *Mil.* 68), *ea te re publica carere in qua neminem prudentem hominem res ulla delectet* (Cic. *Fam.* 5.17.3). ISTE TUUS: *istis tuis pro dictis* (Pl. *Am.* 285), *istaec tua dicta* (Pl. *Cis.* 510), *istaec flagitia tua* (Pl. *Men.* 719), *ex istac tua sorore* (Pl. *St.* 111), *iste tuos ipse sentiet | posteriu'* (Ter. *Ad.* 139–40); *iste tuus cliens* (Cic. *S. Rosc.* 96), *ista tua intolerabilis potentia* (Cic. *Ver.* 1.1.35), *istis tuis defensoribus* (Cic. *Ver.* 2.2.149), *digito denique isto tuo* (Cic. *de Orat.* 2.188), *ista tua* (Cic. *Luc.* 126), *per istum tuum sodalem Publium* (Cic. *Att.* 2.9.3).

104. Cf. *quod iter incipiam ingredi?* "On what journey shall I embark?" lit. "begin to embark" (Enn. *scen.* 217 Jocelyn) and *cogere incipit eos* (Cic. *Ver.* 2.2.41), *retinere incipit tabulas* (Cic. *Ver.* 2.4.148), cited by K-S 2.2 §242.3. For a comic example, cf. *o Daue, itan contemnor abs te? aut itane tandem idoneus | tibi uideor esse quem tam aperte fallere incipias dolis?* (Ter. *Andr.* 493).

105. Cf. Zicàri 1955: 66.

## VII.7. The Difficulties of Fusion (1):
## Contemporary Ways of Reading

We have seen, then, that Catullus takes advantage of the resonances of the language of social performance to define a new view of erotics, poetics, and the social world, in which each blends into the others, and that, as in Cicero's speeches (V.4–6), the language of social performance created a kind of compelling, self-enclosed world that could be countermanded, somewhat feebly, only from the outside. The language of social performance seems very much at home in the Catullan corpus in these functions, which is what has induced most commentators to see it, along with other words, as proper to Catullus's circle.[106] But that does not mean the language of social performance in these functions would not have seemed striking to contemporary readers, even if Catullus's use owes something to other contemporary patterns of self-expression. Catullus's hostile defense of himself and his poetry to Furius and Aurelius in c. 16 encapsulates the hazards he encountered in formulating a new view of erotics, poetics, and the social world in Roman society.

> *pedicabo ego uos et irrumabo,*
> > Fuck you, Aurelius, you faggot.
> *Aureli pathice et cinaede Furi,*
> > Suck my dick,[107] Furius, you queer.
> *qui me ex uersiculis meis putastis,*
> > You read my little poems and think that
> *quod sunt molliculi, parum pudicum.*
> > I must be indecent if they are nice and soft?
> 5     *nam castum esse decet pium poetam*
> > The dutiful poet has to be clean
> *ipsum, uersiculos nihil necesse est;*
> > himself, his verses don't at all;
> *qui tum denique habent salem ac leporem,*
> > and it's then, and only then,
> > that they have charm *(lepos)* and wit *(sal)*
> *si sunt molliculi ac parum pudici,*
> > if they're nice and soft,
> > a little indecent,

106. Cf. the Introduction, pp. 10–12.

107. Lit. "I will fuck you in the mouth." "Suck my dick" on the surface seems to reverse the power relations that are important to the poem's meaning, but in AmE the phrase is very often metaphorical, implying contempt, whereas the literal words or phrases are "blowjob," "knobbie," "give head," etc.

> *et quod pruriat incitare possunt,*
> and if they're able
> to excite the part that itches—
> 10 *non dico pueris, sed his pilosis*
> not in schoolboys, but in these hairy men
> *qui duros nequeunt mouere lumbos.*
> who can barely move their stiff old loins.
> *uos, quod milia multa basiorum*
> So you read my poem of a thousand kisses,
> *legistis, male me marem putatis?*
> and think that I'm no man? I'll
> *pedicabo ego uos et irrumabo.*
> fuck you, make you
> suck
> my
> dick.

The poem concerns the distortions Catullus's poetry suffers because of contemporary ways of reading.[108] The poem posits the reaction of Furius and Aurelius to Catullus's poetry. The poetry they have read includes poems "of many thousands of kisses" *(milia multa basiorum)*, with reference to the Lesbia and Juventius cycles.[109] From such verse Furius and Aurelius have

---

108. Cf. Buchheit 1976c for a defense of the literary character of the poem, with a review of previous literature; Selden 1992, Batstone 1993, Fitzgerald 1995.

109. There has been some disagreement about which poems of Catullus Furius and Aurelius misread. Line 12, *multa milia basiorum* "many thousands of kisses," has suggested to some critics, e.g., Ellis 1889, Kroll 1929, Rankin 1970, the "kissing poems" addressed to Lesbia (cc. 5 and 7); to others, e.g., Baehrens 1885, Merrill 1893, Sandy 1971, Quinn 1973, c. 48, a homoerotic poem addressed to Juventius. Both poems contain the image of "thousands of kisses" *(da mi basia mille, deinde centum* etc. "give me a thousand kisses, then a hundred," 5.7; *usque ad milia basiem trecenta* "I would kiss you up to three hundred thousand [kisses]," 48.3). To defend their positions, both camps generally turn to the meanings of *molliculus* and *parum pudicus*. These are usually referred by scholars of the Juventius camp to pathic homosexual behavior, and by scholars of the Lesbia camp to a general *mollitia* or 'delicacy,' or more specifically to penile flaccidity or cunnilingus. The arguments of neither side are decisive. *Mollis* may refer either to pathic homosexuality or a more diffuse 'delicacy.' *Parum pudicus* may take in both the *irrumatus* (cf. *impudice* at *Catalepton* 13.9, which the context shows = *irrumate*) and the performer of cunnilingus; cf. Adams 1982: 81: "*Cunnum lingere* at Mart. 1.77.6, 2.84.3 was a formula of graffiti (e.g., *CIL* 4.2400, 4304), and no doubt of the coarsest form of sexual abuse." Catullus's defense of himself as *castus* may suggest either someone not pathic or someone who has not performed cunnilingus; v. Winter 1973: 261. The crucial point is that Furius and Aurelius have styled Catullus as passive and even impotent. Cf. Selden 1992: 508 n.139: "Critics have often argued that the reference is to one set of poems or the other; the necessity to stake the claim is evidence enough that any knowledgeable reader is inevitably reminded of both."

deduced that Catullus is a sissy. To be sure, polymetric verse is delicate (*mol-liculus,* dim. of *mollis* 'soft') and less than decent *(parum pudicus).* The infer-ences Furius and Aurelius make about Catullus derive from one contempo-rary hermeneutic, viz., that light speech means a light character.[110] Cicero's deliberate misinterpretation of Philodemus's conventional Hellenistic epi-grams as representing the actual life lived in Piso's house *(tamquam in speculo* 'as in a mirror') depends on exactly the same mode of interpretation (*Pis.* 70–71, V.2). The origins of that hermeneutic are clear: it is simply the re-verse of the typical hermeneutic of public discourse, where serious speech means a serious character. The whole *Rhetorica ad Herennium,* indeed the whole Roman tradition of rhetorical instruction, is founded on this very principle.[111] The application of *durus* to those who interpret c. 16 this way suggests pelvic immobility, whether induced by time or stipulated by social role, which in turn suggests the group to whom the hermeneutic belongs, viz., the older generation, the *seueriores* of c. 5 (above, VII.3).[112]

Catullus has constructed a poem designed to foil readers who use this hermeneutic. The same line, *pedicabo ego uos et irrumabo,* begins and ends the poem. The first time the line sounds simply like an idiomatic curse ("fuck you"). But by the final line, once the poem has developed the image of poet as virile, the identical words are literalized ("I'll *fuck* you"). Much the same is true of the insults *pathicus* and *cinaedus,* the literal meanings of which are not realized until the poem's end, when the repeated *pedicabo* and *irrumabo* retrospectively reinvigorate them. When Furius and Aurelius reach the final line of the poem and realize the first line meant something different from what it seemed to mean, they discover they have been forced to misread, much as they misread Catullus's kissing poems. Where they forced him, by their act of reading, into being *parum pudicus,* now he forces them, by his act of writing, into being *pathicus* and a *cinaedus.* Their inability to under-stand the poetry of nonce pleasure means they will have to suffer enduring shame: for the *pedicatus* 'butt-fucked' and *irrumatus* 'mouth-fucked' were acutely stigmatized in the very ideology that generated the hermeneutic

---

110. "But no one, so far as I know, has remarked that, in poem 16, Catullus makes the claim with the serious intention of debunking what had been and was to a large extent to remain a principal tenet of literary criticism in antiquity: *non potest alius esse ingenio, alius animo color* (Sen. iun. *Ep.* 114.3)," with cits., Sandy 1971: 54. Cf. Fitzgerald 1995: 48–50. Selden 1992 offers a powerful reading of c. 16 in which he demonstrates that Catullus's poem forces the three canonical functions of a speech, "to teach, to delight, and to move" (*docere, delectare, mouere,* cf. *Or.* 69) not to complement but to contradict each other.

111. Cf. Selden 1992, Sinclair 1993, and above (IV.6) on the tendentious creation of the phrase *suauis grauis.*

112. Cf. Skinner 1981: 53–54.

that led to Furius and Aurelius's misreading.[113] They are smitten by the same hermeneutic that encouraged them to smite. What is more, the punishment Catullus threatens to inflict, which casts him in effect as a defender of the traditional ideology, could not be inflicted by *pilosi* who are, presumably, most invested in the ideology: they cannot thrust their hips anymore.[114] Catullus, younger and more limber, can defend their stodgy ways even better than they can, if he wants to.[115] C. 16 thus captures some of the difficulty of what one might call the Catullan project: elevating nonce pleasure to a paradigm, for its own sake, is not easy in a culture whose ideals of performance have to do with outstripping political rivals. Catullus writes c. 16 as a corrective on misinterpretations of his project: to have a "soft" poetic voice is, in Catullus's case, a deliberate construction of someone fully in control of himself, who at will can dally like Adonis or rise up like Priapus. That, indeed, was probably the intended message behind the softnesses of the young Catilinarians (V.6) and Julius Caesar (VIII.2).

113. Sexual subservience was a charge leveled against Catiline's coterie by Cicero (v. *Catil.* 2.23, V.6) and against Catiline himself in Sallust, who suggests Catiline bought alliances at any price: *postremo neque sumptui neque modestiae suae parcere, dum illos obnoxios fidosque faceret* "in short, he spared neither chastity nor expense if he could make them obliged and loyal to him" (*Cat.* 14.6). Ps.-Sallust makes the same charge against Cicero: *an non ita a pueritia uixisti ut nihil flagitiosum corpori tuo putares quod alicui collibuisset?* (*in Cic.* 2), *homo . . . cuius nulla pars corporis a turpitudine uacat* (5); if the attacks are not purely conventional here, they may have been motivated by Cicero's personal delicacy, if such there was (cf. Verres' attack in Plut. *Cic.* 7.3, V.7). At any rate *irrumare* in particular could imply subservience forced on one in recompense for a wrong, so several times in the *Priapea* as a punishment for thieves (35, 44, 56, 70; likewise *pedicatio* 'butt-fucking' 28, 35, 38). Catullus sometimes uses *irrumare* in this way (21.8, 21.13, 37.8; otherwise 10.12, 28.10, 74.5), and so here: it is not only that these sexual acts establish his dominance, as of course they do. But more than that, in the vocabulary of Priapus they are the recourse of someone who has been wronged, just as Catullus was when Furius and Aurelius misread his poetry; that act, one might say, was a "theft" of the poem. V. Wiseman 1985: 11–12. On the threats conventionally assigned to Priapus, cf. Richlin 1992: 121–23, *passim* for Priapus as the persona of purveyors of sexual humor.

114. This takes *mouere lumbos* as meaning 'thrust the hips' as a penetrator, but the phrase is ambiguous. I follow the reading of Richlin 1992: 248 n. 9. Selden 1992 and Fitzgerald 1995 take it to mean 'wiggle the hips (like a pathic),' which, to be sure, is the usual sense of *mouere lumbos*, cf. Adams 1982: 48, 194; "Catullus claims that his performance turns his audience into excitable pathics," Fitzgerald 1995: 50. My interpretation of the poem does not necessarily require taking *mouere lumbos* as I have. The old men's stiffness can serve as a term in an a fortiori argument: they cannot even wiggle pathically, much less mount a Priapic defense.

115. Cf. Rankin 1970: "What Catullus is refuting here is not the whole notion that he would have anything to do with homosexual practices, but that he was *mollis*, unmanly, given excessively to sensual pleasures, incapable of action. For it is clear that he jokingly refutes their conclusions about him by means of a sexual threat of a homosexual kind—but one in which he is the active and aggressive agent, not passive and '*mollis*'."

There is an additional layer of complication, which brings us to the meaning of *lepos* and *sal*. Furius and Aurelius's error was taking Catullus's request for kisses literally. But then Catullus's threat to fuck them might *also* not be literal. As Batstone 1993: 152 puts it:

> Since the misreading of Furius and Aurelius was precisely the error of taking the request in the *basia* poems literally, and since poem 16 denies any necessary connection between a poem's request and the poet's own desires, one is forced to ask: what is the status of *this* poem's explicit threat, *pedicabo ego vos et irrumabo?* Can we let Catullus assert that only his *molliculi versuli* are poetic creations and that his manly threats of buggery are true expressions of self? Surely, if a poem can be *parum pudicum* while its poet is *pius,* a poem can be fierce and threatening while its poet means no literal threat at all.

The poem, we might say, is designed to dupe on the first reading and entrap on the second. The surprise of discovering an epigrammatic inversion gives way to a cognitive aporia. When readers return to the beginning of an epigram, they recognize the red herrings set up by the poet; to return to the beginning of c. 16 brings no such pleasure of recognition, but only mutually exclusive and equally plausible possibilities. *Lepos* and *sal* are meant here to encapsulate this aporia. That *lepos* and *sal* should share terrain with *mollitia* and *impudicitia* is not paradoxical: as we have seen, the *Rhet. Her.* recommends avoiding too much *lepos* (4.32, IV.4), and Cicero carefully constructs it as an ancillary quality (VI.6). On the other hand the *lepos* and *sal* of the Lesbia and Juventius cycles puts Catullus in a position of control over the "hairy men," the very ones who relegate *lepos* and *sal* to secondary status.[116] If *lepos* and *sal* are really ancillary, then they should not have control over old men; but if they have control over old men, they must not be ancillary.[117] The difficulties Catullus's readers have are, in short, induced by

116. Although in the context of the poem *lepos* and *sal* refer to the Lesbia and Juventius cycles, they are singularly appropriate to this poem. *Sal* describes a particular kind of humor, one that has an ironic, dissimulating, or deadpan quality (VI.4 n. 59): that is, humor which assesses, then controverts expectations—exactly what this poem does. *Lepos,* of course, refers to attractive verbal performance, but its special connection to repetition (III.3) is particularly relevant in this poem, which depends signally on repetition.

117. Cf. Pedrick 1993: 184: "The abrupt shift from the oddly solemn use of *castus* and *pius* to describe a poet in line 5 to the playful, neoteric elegance of *sal* and *lepos* in line 6 is supposed to confuse [Furius and Aurelius]. How can a poet be *castus* or, for that matter, *pius?* How can a term they thought so pejorative—*molliculus*—be turned so quickly on its head? And even as Furius and Aurelius are aware that they have missed an important truth about art amidst the *arcana* of lines 5–7, Catullus introduces a further twist that deflates his own rhetoric: the pure, dedicated poet and his elegant verses are actually about provoking erections in old men."

the contemporary construction of performance; the same cultural developments that provided Catullus with a piquant metapoetic idiom also abetted his misreaders.

## VII.8. The Difficulties of Fusion (2): Old Words Die Hard

The Catullan project faced a more profound difficulty, on the level of the lexeme at any rate, than the existence of a hermeneutic that caused his poetry to be misread. That difficulty was perhaps unavoidable since the new aesthetic, as we have seen, seems to have been generational. A greater difficulty is that novel semantic usages meant as the extension of a given sense may be reinterpreted according to the culturally standard construction of the new referent, and the generative sense forgotten. As a loosely parallel example, consider the formula "shucks" ("aw, shucks") in American English. "Shucks" are properly the husks of ears of maize, or the shells of nuts or oysters. Thus "shucks" was used to mean "nothing." The use of "shucks" as a modest dismissal ("That's good" "Shucks, I just threw it together") is of course derived from the metaphorical use of "shucks" as "nothing." But, I hazard, many speakers of AmE only know that "shucks" is a modesty formula and haven't the slightest idea where it comes from. These speakers have generated a meaning for the expression based on their perception of the contexts in which it occurs without reference to the original metaphor.[118]

Catullus's use of the language of social performance, however deft or subtle in his hands, probably owes something to the real speech habits of his circle.[119] Inasmuch as the nuances of the language of social performance in connection to erotics, poetics, and the symposiastic life were the possession of Catullus's circle, they created for speakers outside the circle the opportunity for precisely the kind of reinterpretation I have just described. The metaphorical extensions of Catullus and his circle may have been misunderstood by some speakers. Speakers who saw the stylish people describing themselves as *bellus* and *uenustus* could easily impute into those terms their own construction of stylishness. The possibilities for misunderstanding were increased because the lexemes of the language of social performance survived in other uses, attached to other cultural models. I suggest that in several poems Catullus, hearing the argot of his own circle as if from the outside, uses the language of social performance as it was misinterpreted by such speakers.

118. Cf. the evident loss of 'eroticism' in certain applications of *uenustus* (I.6).
119. Cf. V.6 above, where Cicero seems to be casting fashionable slang in the teeth of its users.

Two instances of *uenustus* in Catullus appear in lampoons in elegiac meter. C. 97 crudely lambasts a certain Aemilius who styled himself *uenustus* (*se facit esse uenustum* "he makes himself out to be *uenustus,*" 9). Catullus's objection is partly to Aemilius's hygiene. The preceding lines compare his fetid mouth to an asshole and his gum-bearing grin to the cunt of a pissing mule.[120] To understand the poem correctly requires understanding the pitch of Catullus's voice. Certain metrical effects in the opening lines serve to characterize the speaker. The expression *ita me di ament* is found only in Plautus and Terence and never after, except here: not only was the expression colloquial, as has often been observed, but, to the urban ear, it was probably already old-fashioned, perhaps something like "Goodness me" in contemporary English. The comic provenance of the phrase is underscored by the maintenance of the prosody it usually has in comic verse, with correption, and not elision, of *di.*[121] The first line of the poem (*utrum os an culum olfacerem Aemilio* "whether I'm smelling Aemilius's mouth or his asshole") is often emended to read *utrumne,* in order to prevent hiatus between *culum* and *olfacerem.* This emendation probably spoils another reminiscence of comic verse, hiatus at the end of a metron. Catullus knows both correption and hiatus, but not in consecutive lines. Our expectations are set for a comic voice.

The voice of the poem is further characterized when it attributes to Aemilius *gingiuas ploxeni ueteris,* evidently "the gums of an old wagon-box" (Paul. Fest. 260 Lindsay). Aemilius's gums are likened to a wagon-box with a split or damaged covering (cf. Ellis 1889 ad loc.). Quintilian (*Inst.* 1.5.8) says that *ploxenum* is a Paduan regionalism, probably familiar to Catullus from his youth. The region of Gallia Cisalpina was long under Celtic influence, and from the Celts came many words for wheeled vehicles, such as *carpentum, petorritum,* and *essedum,* that found broad circulation in Latin (v. Palmer 1954: 53). *Ploxenum* may be such a Celticism (cf. W-H) that did not make it as far south. But it should not be inferred that in this poem Catullus has merely lapsed into a native dialect. There is nothing else particularly Umbrian about his speech—not that we can tell, at any rate. The regionalism, rather, has a calculated effect: it characterizes the speaker as an inhabitant of a rustic district—the very sort of person to preserve in his speech an old formula like *ita me di ament.* "Saints preserve, his gums look like a dried-up wainhap!" gives something of the effect.

---

120. On the idea of the impure mouth in Roman culture in connection to this poem, cf. Fitzgerald 1995: 79–80; on the social construction of mouths generally, Corbeill 1996: 99–127.

121. That is, the scansion is *ĭtă mē dĭ ămēnt,* not *ĭtă mē d[ī] ămēnt.*

The character of the voice of the poem, suggested by these slight touches, is important to understanding the appearance of *uenustus* here. The speaker does not belong to an urban elite, whether Ciceronian or Catullan. This *uenustus* comes from outside that circle. It may therefore simply continue, without the complex shadings of the polymetrics, a use of *uenustus* attested in comedy, 'lucky in love' or a 'lover boy.'[122] But it seems to me that this instance of *uenustus* is intended as, so to speak, deliberately anti-Catullan. Aemilius's offense, in addition to being physically repulsive, is not merely promiscuity but a kind of erotic vaunt. It is not only that he sleeps around, but that "he fancies himself a lover" *(se facit esse uenustum)*. The force of *se facere* is very much that of 'fancy oneself,' self-congratulation for a studied pose. That is, one detects here a version of the element of carefully manipulated self-presentation that is typical of Catullus's polymetric *uenustas;* only here it is reduced, in the mind of the "Paduan," to promiscuity. That, Catullus knew, is how his *uenustus* could sound to the outsider: a bit of the poseur and a lot of the morally loose. To Aemilius this "outsider's voice" suggests a punishment from the repertoire of comic dreads in accord with his character: the millstone ass.[123] This is not the deft skewering one associates with the polymetrics.

The same posture of the gruff lampoonist is the perspective of c. 89, another poem in elegiac couplets which attacks a certain Gellius:

> *Gellius est tenuis: quid ni? cui tam bona mater*
> Gellius is thin, and that's no surprise.
> After all his good mother,
> *tamque ualens uiuat tamque uenusta soror*
> who's in excellent health, is alive,
> and so's his lovely *(uenustus)* sister
> *tamque bonus patruus tamque omnia plena puellis*
> and his good uncle
> and a whole bevy of female family—
> *cognatis, quare is desinat esse macer?*
> why shouldn't Gellius be skinny?
> *qui ut nihil attingat, nisi quod fas tangere non est,*
> He specializes in touching things
> he shouldn't be touching.

---

122. The sense 'lucky in love' occurs once in Terence, *adeon hominem esse inuenustum aut infelicem quemquam ut ego sum!* (*Andr.* 245) "Can there possibly be a man as loveless and luckless as I?" V. fig. 20 and VII.2.

123. *te in pistrinum scis actutum tradier* (Pl. *Mos.* 17), *iuberes hunc praecipitem in pistrinum trahi* (*Ps.* 494), *uerberibu' caesum te in pistrinum, Daue, dedam usque ad necem* (Ter. *Andr.* 199), *hominem pistrino dignum!* (*Hau.* 530), cf. Cic. *Q. fr.* 1.2.14.

*quantumuis quare sit macer inuenies.*
>    That right there is plenty of reason
>    why he should be so skinny.

Catullus turns abuse of appearance, an old form of persiflage, into evidence of Gellius's incest. Much as *bonus,* otherwise a complement, is applied ironically to his mother and uncle, *uenusta* is applied to his sister (89.2), appropriately to a member of the younger, stylish generation—and one who evidently welcomes her brother's affections. Thus in both c. 97 and c. 89, *uenustus* is associated with sexual excess or impropriety and is invoked scornfully. In cc. 78 and 106 Catullus uses *bellus* in a similar way.[124] The outsider's stance in these epigrams, however, is not disdainful but mordant and devilish. The target of c. 78 is Gallus:

> *Gallus habet fratres, quorum est lepidissima coniunx*
>> Gallus has brothers, one of whom
>> has a very saucy *(lepidissima)* wife,
> *alterius, lepidus filius alterius.*
>> and the other a saucy *(lepidus)* son.
> *Gallus homo est bellus: nam dulces iungit amores*
>> Gallus is a suave *(bellus)* man:
>> he arranges for a sweet love-match,
> *cum puero ut bello bella puella cubet.*
>> so a suave *(bellus)* girl
>> can sleep with a suave *(bellus)* boy.
> *Gallus homo est stultus, nec se uidet esse maritum,*
>> Gallus is a stupid man, forgets he has a wife,
> *qui patruus patrui monstret adulterium.*
>> an uncle teaching how to cuckold uncles.

Gallus prides himself on his participation in the new morality by arranging for a liaison, perhaps by providing a trysting place, for lovers with an equal enthusiasm for unconventionality. All three parties are described as *bellus:* but the liaison, as the first distich describes, is between Gallus's sister-in-law and nephew, and patronage of cuckoldry puts Gallus himself in danger. The object of the poem is not to decry Gallus's morals, on which the poem is wryly neutral, but to point out that he is nursing a serpent that could bite him. The triple use of *bellus* makes this point sharper. Evaluative language not only describes, it also asserts: an agent may describe his own behavior with an evaluative term as a kind of suggestion to take it that way; re-

---

124. Cf. Ross 1969: 110–11, who suggests that *bellus* belongs properly to the polymetrics and that the elegiacs in which it appears are experimental.

call Cicero's *haec ipsa fero equidem etiam fronte, ut puto et uolo, belle* (*Att.* 5.10.3, I.7). *Bellus* is used in both ways in this poem. In regard to the "boy" and the "girl" *bellus*, to my ear, is simply descriptive: they are members of the suave new "liberated" generation, as is clear from their willingness to commit adultery.[125] On the other hand, Gallus is probably older: if he is near in age to his brothers, he is certainly at least ten and perhaps as many as forty years older than the couple. The new *mores* are not really his, but he tries to appear up-to-date by fulfilling an auxiliary role, roughly that of the *senex lepidus* of Plautine comedy. *Gallus homo est bellus* is not a description authorized by the poet's observation, but a report of Gallus's hopeful explanation of his own actions. That he should describe himself as *bellus* is entirely apt: it indicates membership in an "in" crowd, which Gallus want to be a part of.[126] Catullus's stance in c. 106 is also that of a wry observer:

> *cum puero bello praeconem qui uidet esse,*
>     *quid credat, nisi se uendere discupere?*

A pretty boy and a salesman [127]
spotted together
can only mean one thing:
The boy is *very* eager
to put himself on the market.

In the polymetrics proper we do not have any sense that *bellus* is associated with sexual license. But in this couplet, as in 78, *bellus* seems to have precisely those associations. The joke of c. 108 is not made for other *urbani* but for those who share a dim view of *belli homines*, to say nothing of *praecones*.

---

125. *Bellus* with overtones of 'sexually active' was evidently a common use, if the Pompeian graffiti are any witness: *Euplia hic cum hominibus bellis MM* "Euplia [did it] here with 2000 *bellus* men" (*CIL* 4.2310b), *nemo est bellus nisi qui amauit mulierem adulescentulus* "Nobody's *bellus* unless he's loved a woman while he's young" (*CIL* 4.1883 = *CLE* 233).

126. *Lepidus* here probably recalls not the language of social performance, which is a set of lexemes in connection to a particular cultural model, but the older language of comedy, standing simply for 'attractive' (cf. I.9 and Syndikus 1987: 34 n. 1). Especially telling here is that *lepidus* applied to the wife appears in the superlative: Catullus's programmatic language is always in the positive or comparative degree; to the superlative belong, for example, ironic or cloying complements (*iucundissime*, 14.2; *disertissime*, 49.1), the confident claims of a garrulous yacht (*cognitissima*, 4.14, imitated *App. Verg. Cat.* 10.13), ironic or comic exaggerations (*urbis o piissimi*, 29.23; *electissima . . . scripta*, 36.6–7), and emphatic descriptions surrounding a *municeps* of Catullus he would like to see ducked in a swamp during a rural festival (*liuidissima . . . uorago*, 20.9; *insulsissimus est homo*, 20.12; *uiridissimo . . . flore*, 20.14).

127. Lit. *praeco* 'barker, herald'; on the *praeco* cf. above, V.4 n. 40. For the interpretation that the *praeco*, not the *puer bellus*, wants to sell himself (a syntactically easier reading), see Bushala 1981.

The association of *bellus* with sexual liberty is also to be seen in Catullus's jibes against Rufus: his unclean habits make his armpits smell like a goat, which "is really a nasty beast, not the kind a chic girl will sleep with" (*nam mala ualdest | bestia, nec quicum bella puella cubet,* 69.7–8).

It is easy to see how *bellus* and *uenust(as)* could have become pejorative terms for "sexually liberated" for speakers outside Catullus's circle. Because of its stylish habits, outsiders no doubt associated the circle with sexual license, which to some extent was certainly true. At any rate foppishness readily attracted such accusations in Roman culture. It is a small step for outsiders to impute to the prominent elements of a circle's vocabulary their own view of that circle. Catullus makes use of the outsider's view of his circle's language when it suits his rhetorical purpose.[128] That devilishly clever and gaily indifferent command of *ethos,* outdoing the orators at their own game, has far-reaching implications.

## VII.9. From Fusion to Cancellation

We have seen that Catullus's use of the language of social performance depends intimately on the use of that language in Roman society more broadly. This is quite a different claim from saying that the language of social performance is simply the slang of Catullus's circle, like "jive talk," when "flappers" and "sheiks" borrowed the language of the jazz clubs to show how smart they were. The case of "jive talk" is a case of an idiom of originally restricted circulation, namely the slang of black musicians, being borrowed by members outside that cultural circle (cf. Intro n. 25).

Catullus works in the opposite direction: he takes language in circulation in the society at large and heats it to piquancy. We have seen already how Catullus fuses the sense of lexemes in the language of social performance with senses of those lexemes outside that application. For example, we have seen how *uenustus* as 'conversationally deft' was mapped over the older, still surviving meaning of *uenustus* as 'erotically attractive.' It is attractive to think such verbal dexterity is evidence of the *urbanitas* of Catullus's circle. For one thing, puns and double entendres, other versions of doubleness, were certainly a part of the culture of speech practiced by elite Romans. But in Catullus's hands this doubleness is supremely subtle: it makes the language itself glimmer just at the edge of comprehensibility, evanescent and unstable— exactly like the performances it aimed to describe. The medium becomes the message. The words themselves oscillate in a kind of "drama of position," to borrow Fitzgerald's (1995) phrase for the shifting positions taken

128. Catullus also adopts the speech of the "old men" he otherwise mocks when it suits his purpose, signally in c. 39, which I hope to treat in future.

by Catullus vis-à-vis the reader or hearer. The relationship of Catullus's language to his Greek models, which I have for the most part not explored, makes the equation even more complicated. To read Catullus's *uenustas* against the χάρις of the Greek Anthology, as some Romans surely must have, sets Catullus into sharp relief: in the Anthology the χάρις of erotic attractiveness and the χάρις of metapoetics for the most part do not meet; a Roman reader knowledgeable of Greek lyric and the metarhetorical equation of *uenustas* with χάρις could not help being pulled in two directions by Catullus's poetry.

This doubleness destabilizes language, and therefore it has political implications. The legalistic cast of the Roman mind often strove to make words draw lines as clear as centuriation, in clauses like *quod bonum, faustum felixque sit,* an old prayer formula in Livy (1.17.10, 1.28.7, etc.), covering all possible kinds of goodness, or, from the *senatus consultum de Bacchanalibus* (*CIL* I² 581), a veritable thesaurus entry for "conspire," *inter sed coniourasse neue comuouise neue conspondise neue compromesise.* The doubleness of Catullus's language does the opposite: it kicks over the boundary stones, makes words rich and resonant and polyvalent. The doubleness, like Pollio's willingness to spend a talent to undo his brother's gaucherie, is a rejection of the ethic of permanence and stability that underlay political ideology. In *de Oratore* Cicero is gingerly with all the words in the language of social performance precisely because of this unsuitability.

Even more, Catullus rejects political ideology in the very language used to support political maneuvering. It is not a counterargument to say Catullus had no other choice than to express "bright performance" except in the current idiom. That choice only seems inevitable after the fact, because Catullus has done so deft a job. The Augustan poets make no use of the language of social performance as programmatic language for Callimachean poetry (VIII.3). The close correspondence of the ideological contexts of the language of social performance in both Cicero and Catullus suggests that Catullus has made a conceptual, and not a lexical, semantic extension (IV.3); and here that constitutes an act of creative will. If the paradigms of public life can be extended so readily to cover private life, what does that say about public life? It says that the ideals of permanence and stability are lies, and that public life is nothing else but vyings for position, reciprocal compositions and symposiastic posturings writ in rustic capitals. Public life is eclipsed in favor of a private world where its characteristic idiom is more piquant and resonant than in its "proper" context. Not only can Catullus defend the stodgy ideas of the old men better than they can, he can use their politically charged language more deftly. Nothing could be more suggestive than Catullus's phrase *e foro otiosum* (10.2). Varus took Catullus away to see his girl-friend while Catullus was "passing time in the forum." There potentates vie, and there Catullus idles.[129] His friend Calvus delivers an important speech that is reported in c. 53 only for the clever remark it occasioned (above n. 39); the view of Calvus is from the *corona,* the "circle of spectators" who surrounded the Rostra—and were not *on* the Rostra.

The public world is erased. But perhaps there is not even a world at all. For the private world is fictional. As we saw of c. 13 and c. 2, the educated hearer is meant *not* to do what the poem asks, and to appreciate the verses only for the stance they depict. The polymetrics as a whole present vividly depicted events that need never have happened. They are occasional verse without an occasion.[130] For his poems to make their point, Catullus need not really be inviting Caecilius (c. 35), or Fabullus (c. 13); Marrucinus (c. 12) need not have actually stolen a napkin, Lesbia need not even have made her vow (c. 36). In the political world, situations and crises could become only backdrop for the stances of the antagonists. If the stance is all that mattered, why should the situation even be real?

But then that alluring fictive world, which has eclipsed the political, is also erased. Catullus can also stand outside his own circle and see how it looks to the outsiders. He can see how his own language (which he has himself stolen!) could be misunderstood thoroughly. That Suffenus was *bellus* and *uenustus* made Catullus want to save him; and he knows that on lips outside of his circle *bellus* and *uenustus,* absorbed by contemporary constructions of sexuality, just mean "immoral." One reading of Catullus's poetry is that a society predicated on moments of attractive performance can only collapse.[131] Its primary categories constantly enthrall, anchor never. Marc

129. As Buchheit 1976a: 165 puts it, "[*Otium* ist] für Catull nicht der Bereich, der nach fester Norm dem Römer allenfalls nach dem *negotium* erlaubt ist und dann in Dienst des *negotium* zu stehen hat, sondern *otium* tritt bei ihm an die Stelle des *negotium,* zu *otium* bekennt er sich in c. 51 als Ursache der ihn verzehrenden Liebesleidenschaft mit letzter Konsequenz ebenso, wie er in c. 50 *otium* bejaht also Lebensraum für seine leidenschaftliche Ergebenheit an die Dichtung."

130. See the essay of Selden 1992: 480ff. for a formulation of this idea in the terms of J. L. Austin, which "shift[s] critical attention from what [Catullus's] work reveals to what it does."

131. Cf. Selden 1992: 497–98: "Catullus' poetry is provocative, then, not because it severs the connection to its originary context by generating mutually exclusive understandings of the same piece of language, but, in fact, just the reverse: that a set of propositions, however self-critical or self-undermining, is part and parcel of a historical reality that it does not cease to modify in decisive ways. . . . In Catullus' hands, poetry becomes the place where social, political, and historical issues are submitted to the most exacting kinds of questions, and this stakes out for literature a role that is authentically progressive."

Antony would prove exactly that, turning his political life into a grand Hellenized performance, assuming the mantle of Dionysus until it destroyed him. Catullus's poetry, from that perspective, can be read as reformist, even radical, poetry. By stealing away a language of political competition and centering it on stylish parties, small poems, and personal passions, Catullus leaves political competitors with no language at all. But Catullus's ability to appropriate is matched by an ability to discard. The bright world of the polymetrics and the gruff world of the elegiacs are opposing poles, between which there really is no space.

# CHAPTER VIII

# O Omnia!
# Remarks on the Subsequent History of the Language of Social Performance

Presume not that I am the thing I was.

*Henry VI, Part II* 5.5.57

## VIII.1. Introduction

Cicero and Catullus both handle the language of social performance in a way that suggests the values it described were wonderful and dangerous in late Republican society. The allure of *lepos* and *uenustas* and *facetiae* was something that Cicero wished to deny his opponents (V.6) and to reserve, suitably modulated, as the sole possession of an idealized social elite (VI.4). For Catullus the language of social performance served to encapsulate the core values of his interconnected view of erotics, poetics, and the social world (ch. 7); and although Catullus stripped away from "allure" any practical value it might have and, what is more, forced it to undo itself (VII.9), it is plain the language was suggestive and powerful, worth appropriating, however subversively. It would therefore not have been surprising to find the language of social performance ensconced in the idiom of the increasingly grandiose self-presentations of Pompey and Caesar and the subsequent vyings of the likes of Octavian, Sextus Pompeius, and Antony. But in fact the language of social performance is almost entirely absent in any writing from, or about, those tumultuous times. However, that very absence, viewed together with the flowering of the language of social performance in the days of the *elocutio novella,* is suggestive. This brief and speculative coda outlines some of the story of the political death and literary rebirth of the language of social performance.[1]

---

1. Martial, in whom the language of social performance is frequent, is not treated here, since his use of the language is driven not only by contemporary developments but also by his reading and imitation of Catullus and so poses a problem more difficult than what I propose to solve in this short sketch. Quintilian's use of the lexemes we are considering also poses problems I do not propose to treat here, inasmuch as his usage seems to stand midway between those of Cicero and Gellius.

## VIII.2. Politics and Performance

We have seen several members of the late Republican social elite who practiced the "Hellenized social performance of identity": the young Catilinarians (*Catil.* 2.23, V.6), Clodius (*in Clod.* 22, V.6), Q. Naevius (*Quinct.* 93, V.4), Hortensius (V.6), M. Caelius, and L. Calpurnius Piso (*Pis.* 93, V.6). This manner of self-representation obviously held considerable attraction. The subsequent history of the language of social performance is, I suggest, affected crucially by the political fate of such self-representation. Julius Caesar and Marc Antony were Q. Naevius or M. Caelius writ large—very large.

Julius Caesar was a master of the Hellenized social performance. According to Plutarch, he owed the gradual growth of his political influence to his practice of hosting dinners.[2] Caesar was also notable for the grooming habits. He paid careful attention to his clothing,[3] which earned him Sulla's hatred (Dio 43.43.4). The senatorial tunic he wore had fringe at the hands.[4] His habit of cinching his tunic loosely—what Suetonius calls *fluxior cinctura* "a rather loose manner of belting"[5]— drew a remark of Cicero's. Cicero is also supposed to have said that a man as punctilious in these respects as Caesar could not overthrow the state.[6]

We saw above that Cicero accused the young Catilinarians of pathic homosexuality (*amare et amari, Catil.* 2.23, V.6). Under this political invective probably lies a grain of truth; those noble youth may well have cultivated dashing, androgynous personae. Caesar certainly did. He was not only carefully barbered and shaved but also had superfluous body hair plucked, an effeminate practice that met with some reproach.[7] Curio accused Caesar of being every man's woman and every woman's man.[8] At Caesar's Gallic triumph, his soldiers sang in jest, "Caesar subdued the Gauls, and Nicomedes subdued Caesar."[9] When Caesar secured Gallia Cisalpina and Comata as his proconsular provinces over the resistance of his opponents, flush with delight

---

2. ἦν δέ τις καὶ ἀπὸ δείπνων καὶ τραπέζης καὶ ὅλως τῆς περὶ τὴν δίαιταν λαμπρότητος αὐξανομένη κατὰ μικρὸν αὐτῷ δύναμις εἰς τὴν πολιτείαν (Plut. *Caes.* 4.5).

3. Cf. Corbeill 1996: 194–95.

4. *usum enim lato clauo ad manus fimbriato* (Suet. *Jul.* 45.3), cf. Macr. 2.3.9.

5. *Jul.* 45.3.

6. ἀλλ' ὅταν, ἔφη, τὴν κόμην οὕτω διακειμένην περιττῶς ἴδω, κἀκεῖνον ἑνὶ δακτύλῳ κνώμενον, οὔ μοι δοκεῖ πάλιν οὗτος ἄνθρωπος εἰς νοῦν ἂν ἐμβαλέσθαι τηλικοῦτον κακόν, ἀναίρεσιν τῆς Ῥωμαίων πολιτείας (Plut. *Caes.* 4.9).

7. Suet. *Jul.* 45.2, Scipio (*ORF* 21.17) refers to *femina* (< *femur*) *subuolsa* 'plucked thighs' as a sign of effeminacy.

8. Suet. *Jul.* 52.3.

9. *Gallias Caesar subegit, Nicomedes Caesarem* (Suet. *Jul.* 49.4).

he boasted that he would "jump on all their heads" *(insultaturum omnium capitibus)*, referring to *irrumatio*.[10] "How could a woman do that?" a fellow senator retorted, alluding to his effeminacy. Caesar, far from becoming outraged, accepted the comparison to women, adverting to Semiramis and the Amazons, "who once ruled a great part of Asia."[11] Once victory was won, he permitted his soldiers to indulge in all manner of license[12] and boasted that his soldiers were good fighters even when they were wearing perfume.

Caesar was also a master of the spoken word. He had a deft and powerful wit that he used to great advantage, deflecting opponents' attacks and reinforcing his own prerogative.[13] His oratorical skill was considerable. Cicero has words of high praise for Caesar's diction, his command of figures of speech, and his delivery.[14] In a letter to Cornelius Nepos (which survives only in Suetonius), Cicero writes:

> Confine your choice to orators who devoted themselves to oratory alone: who do you think is better than Caesar? Whose epigrams *(sententiae)* are sharper or more frequent? Whose diction *(uerba)* is more carefully chosen *(elegantior)* or better fitted with figures *(ornatior)?*[15]
>
> (Suet. *Jul.* 52)

Marc Antony, Caesar's former lieutenant, crafted his public persona along similar lines, though without Caesar's discipline. Where Caesar sanctioned his soldiers' indulgences, Antonius was himself given over to them. When Antony was young, he immersed himself "in drinking bouts, whoring, and expensive, excessive feasting."[16] He continued these habits as an adult, and according to Plutarch earned the hatred of οἱ χρηστοὶ καὶ σώφρονες "the

10. Suet. *Jul.* 22.2; Adams 1982: 200; on *irrumare*, cf. VII.7 n.13. Cf. Corbeill 1996: 195–96, Richlin 1992: 149–50.

11. Corbeill 1996: 196–97.

12. *remisso officiorum munere licentiam omnem passim lasciuiendi permittebat* (Suet. *Jul.* 67.1), *milites suos etiam unguentatos bene pugnare posse* (ibid.).

13. Corbeill 1996: 193–209.

14. DICTION: *illum omnium fere oratorum Latine loqui elegantissime* (*Brut.* 252), where *Latine loqui* recalls ἑλληνισμός, cf. *Brut.* 261; FIGURES OF SPEECH: *adiungit illa oratoria ornamenta dicendi, tum uidetur tamquam tabulas bene pictas conlocare in bono lumine* (*Brut.* 261; for *ornamentum* and *lumen* in this sense, cf. Ernest s.v. *lumen, ornare*); DELIVERY: *splendidam quandam minimeque ueteratoriam rationem dicendi tenet, uoce motu fora etiam magnificam et generosam quodam modo* (*Brut.* 261), cf. Suet. *Jul.* 55.1. Quintilian draws attention to the force *(uis, acumen, concitatio)* of Caesar's style (10.1.114).

15. *quid? oratorem quem huic antepones eorum qui nihil aliud egerunt? quis sententiis aut acutior aut crebrior? quis uerbis aut ornatior aut elegantior?* For other ancient judgments of Caesar's oratorical abilities, cf. Quint. *Inst.* 10.1.114, Tacitus *Ann.* 13.3.4.

16. εἰς πότους καὶ γύναια καὶ δαπάνας πολυτελεῖς καὶ ἀκολάστους, Plut. *Ant.* 2.4. Cf. Cic. *Phil.* 2.44–45.

good and temperate" because of them.[17] But such carnality, which the historical tradition seems to imply was unthinking, was not without symbolic import, as Antony, like Cicero's *pueri lepidi ac delicati,* was surely aware: to indulge oneself was a form of self-display. Certainly once Antony took up with Cleopatra, he enjoyed extravagant banquets daily (Plut. *Ant.* 28.2), hardly out of extravagance only, but also to send a political message: a daily banquet demonstrates the status of the banqueter, godlike, enacting an Olympian life. Antony had been going in that direction before he knew Cleopatra: he linked lions to chariots, a Dionysian or Herculean affect (Plut. *Ant.* 9.8, Plin. *Nat.* 8.55); eventually he would turn himself completely into Dionysus, a god who can comfort kindly—or savagely destroy.[18] Pleasure could complement, not contradict, power.

According to Plutarch, Antony also adopted a remarkable mode of dress, fittingly splashy where Caesar was precious. Whenever he was to appear in public, Plutarch says he hitched his tunic up to the thigh, donned a heavy cloak, and belted himself with a large sword, the more to resemble Hercules from whom the Antonii were supposedly derived (Plut. *Ant.* 4.1).[19] There was an erotic element to his public persona, as there was to Caesar's: Antonius had "something of a not unattractive erotic quality" (ἦν δέ που καὶ τὸ ἐρωτικὸν οὐκ ἀναφρόδιτον) that permitted him to acquire political influence (τούτῳ πολλοὺς ἐδημαγώγει, Plut. *Ant.* 4.5). Like Caesar, Antony

17. τοῖς μὲν οὖν πολλοῖς ἐκ τούτων ἀπηχθάνετο, τοῖς δὲ χρηστοῖς καὶ σώφροσι διὰ τὸν ἄλλον βίον οὐκ ἦν ἀρεστός, ὡς Κικέρων φησίν, ἀλλ' ἐμισεῖτο, βδελυττομένων αὐτοῦ μέθας ἀώρους καὶ δαπάνας ἐπαχθεῖς καὶ κυλινδήσεις ἐν γυναίοις, καὶ μεθ' ἡμέραν μὲν ὕπνους καὶ περιπάτους ἀλύοντος καὶ κραιπαλῶντος, νύκτωρ δὲ κώμους καὶ θέατρα καὶ διατριβὰς ἐν γάμοις μίμων καὶ γελωτοποιῶν (Plut. *Ant.* 9.5). Cf. Macr. 3.17.15.

18. Lions attached to a wagon of Antony's also appear in Cicero (*Phil.* 2.85), but for *raeda cum leonibus, comites nequissimi* Shackleton Bailey reads *lenonibus,* after the *codex Harleianus* 2682. At Ephesus Antonius was greeted not merely as Dionysus but under the epithets Χαριδότης and Μειλίχιος 'Giver of Joy' and "The Gracious One'; Plutarch suggests other labels were sometimes more appropriate: Διόνυσος Ὠμηστής 'The Destroyer' and Ἀγριώνιος 'The Savage One.' Antony surely selected the role of Dionysus for this political bivalence: as Pelling 1988: 180 puts it, Dionysus is a "complex character" who is "gracious and liberating to those who welcome him as a vital force, yet devastating to those who resist."

19. Pelling 1988 ad loc. doubts that this is true, on the grounds that Cicero can hardly have failed to mention such a splashy, and dangerously suggestive, habit; a sword, however, is also mentioned by Dio (τῷ δὲ δὴ ξίφει ὃ παρέζωστο, 42.27.2) as one of the signs that Antony was running a monarchy despite the semblance of democracy. At any rate, Antony may well have permitted himself some other Herculean affect, and in restricted contexts perhaps even this very one, rather like Octavian's reputed assumption of the costume of Apollo at a "Dinner of the Twelve Gods" (*cena* δωδεκάθεος, Suet. *Aug.* 70). For Antony's connection to Hercules, see Zanker 1988: 45–46.

also had a powerful wit, boisterous and ebullient where Caesar was cool and devilish. Antony delighted in raillery:

> His excess in the way of humor and jesting was its own remedy, inasmuch as he tolerated being jested at and abused in return, and he was as happy to be laughed at as he was to laugh.[20]
>
> (Plut. *Ant.* 24.11)

Plutarch assumes those who made fun of Antony to his face must have been disingenuous when they praised him. But Antony's tolerance was a performance of political identity: openness to a certain equality or a genuine love for his retinue (unlike, say, the martinet Lucullus). At any rate Antony was also a powerful and versatile orator (τὴν ἐν τοῖς λόγοις δεινότητα καὶ πανουργίαν, 25.2). He preferred the "Asiatic style," which Plutarch considered a perfect match for his character:

> He favored the so-called Asiatic style of speech that was in particular favor at that time and which closely resembled his manner of life, which was vainglorious, hot-tempered, and full of empty exultation and inconstant desire for fame.[21]
>
> (Plut. *Ant.* 2.8)

Augustus also spoke accusingly of Antony's use of that style, calling it "the voluble speech of the Asiatic orators, with its empty epigrams" *(Asiaticorum oratorum inani[bu]s sententiis uerborum uolubilitas)*[22] and, worse yet, mixed in Antony's case with archaisms plucked from Cato (Suet. *Jul.* 86.3). Augustus accused Antony of composing "to give delight and not understanding."[23] Even though the judgments of Augustus and Plutarch are obviously affected, respectively, by hostility and moralism, there is perhaps a sign, *e contrario,* of

20. ἡ δὲ περὶ τὰς παιδιὰς καὶ τὰς ἐπισκώψεις ὕβρις ἐν αὐτῇ τὸ φάρμακον εἶχεν· ἀντισκῶψαι γὰρ ἐξῆν καὶ ἀνθυβρίσαι, καὶ γελώμενος οὐχ ἧττον ἢ γελῶν ἔχαιρε.

21. ἐχρῆτο δὲ τῷ καλουμένῳ μὲν Ἀσιανῷ ζήλῳ τῶν λόγων ἀνθοῦντι μάλιστα κατ' ἐκεῖνον τὸν χρόνον, ἔχοντι δὲ πολλὴν ὁμοιότητα πρὸς τὸν βίον αὐτοῦ κομπώδη καὶ φρυαγματίαν ὄντα καὶ κενοῦ γαυριάματος καὶ φιλοτιμίας ἀνωμάλου μεστόν.

22. Antony was therefore an Asiatic orator in the manner of Hierocles and Menecles, rather than Aeschylus of Cnidus or Aeschines of Miletus; cf. *Brut.* 325–26, Leeman 1963: 94–95.

23. *M. quidem Antonium ut insanum increpat* [sc. Augustus], *quasi ea scribentem quae mirentur potius homines quam intellegant* (Suet. *Aug.* 86.2), cf. *ORF* 159.4. M. Antony studied with Sex. Clodius (Suet. *Rhet.* 29.1), cf. Kaster 1995: 307–13; and with M. Epidius (Suet. *Rhet.* 25.3), about whom little is known, cf. Kaster 1995: 301–3. Nothing is known about their styles, but it may be relevant that they were Sicilian and Campanian, respectively.

Antonius's affect in his letters: these sound rather Ciceronian in tone.[24] In public he girt himself with a speaking style no less flamboyant than his sword. What Corbeill observes of Caesar is equally true of Antonius: "In dress and in speech, Caesar promotes an untraditional individuality" (1996: 197).

## VIII.3. The Rise of Octavian and the Death of the Language of Social Performance

The political personae of Caesar and Antony can hardly have escaped being described by the language of social performance. They hosted, or were, *bellus* and *festiuus* convives (I.7, I.10). Their *facetiae* (I.8), which will have been *lepidus* and *bellus* and *uenustus,* were famous (I.9, I.7, III.4.2). Their panache must have earned them description by *bellus.* With reference to the erotic elements of their personae, they must have been called *bellus, uenustus,* and *lepidus.*[25] Caesar's figures of speech, if they were "sharp" and "frequent," were very likely described as *lepidus* or *bellus* or *uenustus,* and the same can scarcely have failed to be true of Antony's Asiatic style. Indeed, it is possible that the language of social performance even provided Antony with political catchwords. If he wished to be called Μειλίχιος, he might have liked being called *lepidus,* too.

Although I think it very probable, there is no evidence that the language of social performance was specifically associated with Caesar. But two arguments, *ex silentio* to be sure but nonetheless very suggestive, may be advanced in support of the claim that the language of social performance had become associated with Antony. If Clodius was worth repudiating as *festiuus,* and Quinctius as an immoral master of speaking *belle,* and the Catilinarian noble youth as *lepidi ac delicati,* how much the more so Antony, whose indulgences, and whose political threats, were greater? But in the sustained assault of the *Philippics,* Cicero uses the language of social performance against Antony only once, styling a witticism of his a failure by way of what was perhaps something of a set formula.[26] If by the time of the *Philippics* Antonians, or Antony himself, were using the language of social performance as a sort of normative idiom to describe political style, and if, more important, that attempt were meeting with some success, Cicero might have shunned the language because it could no longer evoke the response it obviously once

---

24. Cf. *Att.* 10.8a, 10.10.2, 14.13a.

25. On the eroticism of *bellus* and *lepidus,* v., e.g., Catul. 78 (VII.8).

26. *facetus esse uoluisti* (V.4). The instances of *elegans* belong to the *elegan(s)* of "moral choice," which does not seem to be a real member of the language of social performance; cf. I.5 n.65. On *festiuus,* see p. 166.

could. In that regard it is worth noting that the very carefully crafted normative version of the language of social performance that is at the heart of Caesar Strabo's discussion of humor in *de Oratore* (VI.4) is absent from the later rhetorica, which return for the most part to a purely descriptive, and largely incidental, use of the language (VI.5 ad fin., and see further below).

The speculation that the language of social performance had come to have Antonian associations, or even provide Antonian propaganda, would be very tenuous indeed, if it depended only on the silence of Cicero's speeches, in which the language is already so rare (albeit ideologically consistent). But another pattern of silence is more suggestive. The Augustan poets avoid using the language of social performance as a programmatic poetic language. As we saw above (VII.4), Catullus expressed his poetic ideals with the language of social performance. Many of the poetic ideals important to Catullus — careful craftsmanship, allegiance to Alexandria, a concern with internal, psychological space — were also important to the Augustan poets. But Augustan poets do not use the language of social performance to express those ideals. If the language of social performance had become tainted by its associations with Antony, it is easy to see why the Augustan poets would have avoided it. Octavian, Antony's rival, had been forced in a different direction from him: Antony's extravagances and adversions to Dionysus had for the time being veritably exhausted the imagery of self-indulgence *qua* powerful. Octavian's response was to turn gradually, and in the end completely, to symbols of peace, stability, and harmony.[27] In short, Octavian's eventual consolidation of power and the success of his symbolic program might well have driven the language used for his enemy's political style into disfavor.

But the language of social performance need not have been specifically or only Antonian in character for the Augustans to have avoided it. The language in and of itself might easily have been construed as expressing a contentious and aggressive individualism or that sort of paradoxically flaccid potency which under Augustus had fallen out of fashion. The language of social performance always dealt in the precarious: to perform was to move across a web partly of one's own design, which therefore risked entanglement. It was a language that approved successful risk-taking. In the wake of the civil wars, different attitudes toward risk-taking came to the fore. Anxieties about hazardous competition were displaced onto war, wealth, and travel, which are distasteful, even anathema, to the poet and form the prov-

27. See Zanker 1988.

ince of the great men just beyond the poet's world. In the *Eclogues* Vergil's
Tityrus had never visited Rome until he went to plead for his property with
a benefactor whom he calls a god (v. *Ecl.* 1). *Serm.* 1.5 tells the story of Horace's trip to Brundisium in 37 B.C. with Maecenas, who was going on the
mission that ended with treaty of Tarentum—mending, temporarily, the
rift between Antony and Octavian. When Maecenas leaves to take some exercise with other emissaries, Horace excuses himself and Vergil, who was also
there, pleading physical ailments: "For playing catch does not suit the sore-
eyed and dyspeptic" (*namque pila lippis inimicum et ludere crudis, Serm.* 1.5.49).
At the very moment when shared athletic activity, symbolic of shared status and active political roles, begins, the poets take their leave.

The inability of a poet to accompany his patrons or friends on a military
expedition is something of a minor theme. In the case of Horace, he was
forbidden to accompany Maecenas when the latter, with other influential
senatorials and equestrians, went to Brundisium to meet with Octavian before he sailed to Epirus against Antony. Horace laments that he cannot accompany Maecenas, not because he would be able to do any good, but
because he would be less worried:

> *roges, tuum labore quid iuuem meo,*
> *imbellis ac firmus parum?*
> *comes minore sum futurus in metu,*
> *qui maior absentis habet.*

> You may ask how I could work to aid you,
> since I am unwarlike and not strong enough?
> My fear will be less if I accompany you,
> is greater now that you're away.

> (*Epod.* 1.15–8)

As in *Serm.* 1.5, Horace leaves aside the political and configures the situation in strictly personal terms, almost those of a lover. Tibullus, for his part,
evidently was accompanying Messalla to Cilicia and Syria (that, at any rate,
is the premise of the poem) but fell ill and had to be left behind on Cor-
cyra. *Eleg.* 1.3, in which Tibullus gloomily dwells on the prospect of lonely
death, begins with a send-off comparable to Horace's:

> *Ibitis Aegaeas sine me, Messalla, per undas*
> *o utinam memores ipse cohorsque mei:*

> You sail the Aegean waves without me, Messalla,
> and I hope that you and the company remember me!

> (1.3.1–2)

Tibullus and Propertius configure the polarity between their powerful friends and themselves as one between a man of action and a man in the service of, or in servitude to, love:

> *te bellare decet terra, Messalla, marique*
>    *ut domus hostiles praeferat exuuias:*
> *me retinent uinctum formosae uincla puellae,*
>    *et sedeo duras ianitor ante foras.*

> It befits you to war on land and sea, Messalla,
>    in order that your house may display enemy trophies:
> me the shackles of a beautiful girl hold bound,
>    and I sit, a gatekeeper before harsh doors.
>
> (Tib. 1.1.53–56)

Propertius could not go East with a Tullus, probably a nephew of L. Volcatius Tullus who was assuming the proconsulship of Asia:

> *Non ego nunc Hadriae uereor mare noscere tecum,*
>    *Tulle, neque Aegaeo ducere uela salo,*
> *cum quo Rhipaeos possim conscendere montes*
>    *ulteriusque domos uadere Memnonias;*
> *sed me complexae remorantur uerba puellae,*
>    *mutatoque graues saepe colore preces.*

> I do not fear, Tullus, to learn the Adriatic with you,
>    nor to set sail for the Aegean Sea;
> with you I could climb the Rhipaean mountains,
>    and wander beyond Memnon's abodes;
> but I'm slowed by the words and embrace of a girl,
>    and frequent earnest entreaties with pale cheek.
>
> (Prop. 1.6.1–6)

Even in the grand Roman Odes, Horace modulates his authority. One example has already been noted. A subtler but more telling example, and one in keeping with the *recusationes* of Tibullus and Propertius, is to be found in *Odes* 3.2. Beginning from a description of the hardiness of rural stock for military service, Horace regresses to the principles that underlie military achievement: the honorable death for the fatherland is one instantiation of a "Virtue" upon which Horace then meditates, asserting that it disregards popular whims and opens the path to heaven and immortality. Horace then adds a coda: there is also a reward for faithful silence (*est et fideli tuta silentio, Carm.* 3.2.25). That more modest version of virtue Horace himself can claim: he will not stand under the same roof or in the same boat with "the one who has exposed the secret rite of Ceres" (*qui Cereris sacrum | uulgarit arcanae, Carm.* 3.2.26–27). Moving from war to the virtue that informs it, Horace finds for himself a species of that virtue that is unwarlike, not to say passive.[28] Some kinds of virtue are not for the poet. In short, whether the language of social performance had specifically Antonian associations or not, its associations with performance and competition must certainly have made it inappropriate to a new, modest, and anxious poetic sensibility.

The poetic creed of the Augustans valorized not the enthralling "performance" but the "slight" or "small" ditty. Tityrus beneath the spreading beech plays a "slender reed" (*siluestrem tenui Musam meditaris auena,* Verg. *Ecl.* 1.2); Mopsus blows "light pipes" (*tu calamos inflare leuis,* Verg. *Ecl.* 5.2). These expressions are plainly meant metapoetically: in a *recusatio* of epic poetry, Vergil says there will be others who will sing of "bitter wars"; he will prefer to "practice a rural poetic on a slender reed" (*agrestem tenui meditabor harundine Musam, Ecl.* 6.8).[29] The shepherd's flock should be fat but his tune dainty (*deductum . . . carmen,* Verg. *Ecl.* 6.5). Horace cannot take on the task of praising Agrippa's military prowess, "a grand theme for a slight poet" (*tenues grandia, Carm.* 1.6.9). The strident voice of *Carm.* 2.1 gives way at the end to a plea to the Muse to "find measures in a lighter lyric key" (*quaere modos leuiore plectro,* 2.1.40). Even the mantic tone of the Roman Odes is broken, in a similar way: the end of the third ode also calls the Muse down from her high flight back to a "light-hearted lyre" (*non hoc iocosae conuenient lyrae: | quo, Musa, tendis? Carm.* 3.3.69–70). Propertius tries to raise himself to the level of epic from his "modest song" (*ex humili iam carmine,* 2.10.11) but in the end is better suited to the small stream Permessus and not the fountains of Aganippe and Hippocrene (*Ascraeos . . . fontes,* 2.10.25; cf. 3.3). Propertius asks the great Alexandrian elegists Callimachus and Philetas where they have "spun their song to fineness" (*carmen tenuastis,* 3.1.5). "Mighty sails" will not do on Propertius's "little boat" (*non sunt apta meae grandia uela rati,* 3.9.4). The agonistic character of Catullus's images of "triviality" appears here by contrast, since in his hands such images are conjoined to an idiom of considerable political piquancy and form an agonistic vaunt (VII.4, cf. p. 253).

As we have seen, the language of social performance had a special connection with the *convivium*. The language arose or was disseminated, as I have argued, largely in convivial contexts and continued to be associated with them in the late Republic. Catullus's inversions of the political charge of

28. See the analysis in Williams 1969.
29. V. Clausen 1994 ad *Ecl.* 6.

language of social performance, for example, are typically set in convivial contexts (cf. VII.3). But in the Augustan poets the *convivium* is typically derogated or reconfigured. Horace caricatures the "modern" *convivium* as antithetical to traditional Roman values:

> *motus doceri gaudet Ionicos*
> *matura uirgo et fingitur artibus*
>     *iam nunc et incestos amores*
>       *de tenero meditatur ungui.*
> *mox iuniores quaerit adulteros*
> *inter mariti uina*

> The young girl ready to marry delights
> to learn Ionian dance, is schooled in the arts,
> with every tender fiber of her being[30]
> thinks of unchaste loves.
> Soon she looks for younger lovers
> among her husband's winecups. . . .

> (Hor. *Carm.* 3.6.21–26)

In a less vatic mode, Horace rejects Eastern luxury in favor of simpler fare: *Persicos odi, puer, apparatus . . .* "Persian finery I despise" (*Carm.* 3.37.1). To be sure such attacks on the *convivium* have old precedents, and perhaps not too much should be made of them. More important is the reconfiguration of the *convivium*. For Catullus the *convivium* was not unpolitical but quasi-political: it appropriated the values associated with political life and wickedly deconstructed them. For Horace, by contrast, the *convivium* may be figured not as the locus of political intrigue or display, but as a symbol of retreat: *nos conuiuia, nos proelia uirginum | . . . | cantamus* "We sing of parties, sing of the battles of young girls" (*Carm.* 1.6.17, 19).[31] Propertius's vaunt of his poetry is comparable:

> *aspice me, cui parua domi fortuna relictast*
>     *nullus et antiquo Marte triumphus aui,*
> *ut regnem mixtas inter conuiua puellas*
>     *hoc ego, quo tibi nunc eleuor, ingenio!*

> Look at me! I've no great fortune left to me,
> no ancestor who triumphed of a long-ago war;

---

30. On this phrase, cf. Williams 1969 ad loc.

31. Murray 1993 suggests that in his use of sympotic motifs Horace was experimenting with the creation of a Roman sympotic poetry to rival that of the Greek poetic tradition; in this new poetry wine and song serve to foster *amicitia* between social unequals.

at parties I reign, with girls among the guests,
by means of the very talent that you run down in me!
(Prop. 2.34.55–58)

The *convivium* is here figured as the opposite of, not a complement to, traditional paths to reward, wealth, and breeding. With the assignation of different ideological qualities to the *convivium* might well have come the avoidance of a language associated with the kinds of display and competition practiced therein.

The only uses of the language of social performance in connection with poetic ideals in Augustan poetry are to be found in Horace's hexameters. There are only four occurrences all together, two in the *Satires* and two in the *Epistles*. These texts, separated by twenty years and different in tone and purpose, need to be treated separately. In the *Satires* both instances of the language of social performance mark what Horace is *not,* or not quite. We have already met Horace's use of *molle atque facetum* (*Serm.* 1.10.43–44) as a description of Vergil's *Eclogues* (III.2 n. 12), with *facetus* serving in the sense "polished," and referring to Vergil's technique. That assessment figures as part of an enumeration of genres that are already spoken for, leaving Horace with satire: Beside Vergil and his command of "the soft and the polished," there is Fundanius, who writes comedy (40–42); Pollio, a writer of tragedy (42–43); and Varius, unrivaled as an epic poet (43–44). And even in the genre of satire Horace is *inuentore minor* "poorer than the founder" (48), namely Ennius.

In the second passage Horace recounts the debt of Lucilius to Old Comedy:

> *hinc omnis pendet Lucilius, hosce secutus,*
> *mutatis tantum pedibus numerisque, facetus,*
> *emunctae naris, durus conponere uersus*

> Lucilius depends on all of them and modeled himself on
>     them,
> changing only their meter; witty *( facetus),*
> keen-scented—and bad at writing verse.
> (Hor. *Serm.* 1.4.6–8)

*Facetus* here plainly refers to Lucilius's sense of humor, and not to any overall poetic sensibility, as the passage, which derogates his technique, makes clear. Even in that meaning the status of *facetus* here is delicately ambiguous. If Horace is improving on Lucilius's poetical technique, is he also substituting a new, refined sense of humor to which *facetus* is *not* appropriate? To be sure, Horace certainly asserts no direct claim to be *facetus* himself.

The most he will say about himself directly is more modest: *liberius si |
dixero quid, si forte iocosius, hoc mihi iuris | cum uenia dabis* "If I say anything a
little on the free side, or the joking side, let's say, you'll indulge my exercise
of this right" (103–5). This failure to claim *facetiae* is occasioned not merely
by the delicacy appropriate to an approbative idiom, which it is tactless to
apply to oneself, but also, and more specifically, by the anxieties associated
with the social performances that our language typically described. Cicero,
too, predicated of himself more modest terms in place of the language of
social performance (*Planc.* 35, V.7 ad fin.). Indeed, much as Cicero defended
the use of humor by invoking higher principles, such as self-defense (*Planc.*
35, de Orat. 2.230, VI.4), support of a patron (*Scaur.* 23, V.2), or the need
for evidence (*Ver.* 2.1.121, V.2), Horace defends his own satirical propensity by invoking the moral authority of his father, who ingrained in him the
habit of gleaning lessons from others' foibles (*insueuit pater optimus hoc me |
ut fugerem exemplis uitiorum quaeque notando*, 105–6); and where Cicero constructed an ideal of humor styled as the proper possession of a graceful social elite (ch. 6), Horace, comparably but rather more modestly, claims his
own lampoons are not intended for public circulation (*nec recito cuiquam nisi
amicis*, 73). *Facetus* for Horace, as for Cicero, is rather too hot to handle; not
only does Horace mean it in this satire in a restricted sense, applying it, unlike Catullus, to humor only, but he handles it with delicacy and even anx-
iety. It is perhaps less to be wondered that Horace, whose social position
was, after all, modest, matches Cicero than that Cicero matches Horace.

In short, both this and the preceding *facetus* are qualities that Horace ascribes to others; and even if we say that that is only the modesty appropriate to Horace's stance, still neither *facetus* is central to Horace's discussion of
poetics as is the *facetus* that appears in Catullus's assessment of Suffenus as *infaceto . . . infacetior rure* (22.14, VII.6) or in Calvus's *lepos* and *facetiae* (50.7–8,
VII.4). The language of social performance in connection to poetics appears
nowhere else in the *Satires,* despite the prominence in them of stylistic concerns.[32] Its only other appearances grade social performances, and that sarcastically: in the realm of social performance, too, Horace applies the language not to himself but to somebody else.[33] Even there the language is
not brought to bear where it might have been, for example, in connection
to the ostentatious dinner of Nasidienus (2.8) or Horace's obsession with art
(2.7.95–101).

32. See Freudenburg 1993.
33. Cf. *Serm.* 1.2.25–26 (I.8 n.135), *Ep.* 1.6.55 (I.8); *deprensi non bella est fama Treboni*
(*Serm.* 1.4.114) and *hoc quidam non belle* (*Serm.* 1.4.136) are examples of "*bellus* of the first
person plural" and so only at best marginal members of the language of social performance.

In a poetic sensibility like the Augustan that was so anxious, decorous, and
earnest, it is not surprising that a volatile idiom like the language of social
performance, to whose volatility even the handful of appearances in the *Satires* is adequate testimony, could find only a very restricted place. This restriction can, to be sure, be explained on purely generic grounds, by arguing that that language, prominent in Cicero's *de Oratore* and Catullus's
polymetrics, was a part of *sermo cotidianus* and therefore inappropriate to the
lofty or mannered tone of Vergilian hexameter, Horatian lyric, and love elegy.[34] This is not the place to discuss whether the speech registers of classical Latin are analytical or descriptive categories, still less the place to discuss
genre theory; I would suggest only that one choice among the many made
by Augustan poets in bounding their characteristic idiom, the choice to reject the language of social performance, can be explained precisely, by referring to the cultural model that that language commonly brought to
mind, and perhaps to a particular set of political associations. Another
influence may also have played a part. The constant association of the language of social performance with particular rhetorical effects eventually reduced it to a kind of technical language (cf. VI.1). Since this process was already well under way by the Augustan period, it may be that the language
of social performance was disagreeable to Augustan poets not only because
it was redolent of flash and vaunt but also because it recalled *grammatici*. I
suggest that the passages in Horace's second book of *Epistles* in which, after
more than twenty years, the language of social performance reappears, exhibit this faintly technical, though by no means ideologically bland, character, and are harbingers of the form that the language of social performance
would take for the rest of its life in classical Latin.

## VIII.4. The *Triclinium* Yields to the *Stibadium*

In the first letter of the second book of *Epistles*, the *Epistula ad Augustum*,
Horace complains to Augustus about the excessive respect still paid to any
poetry that happens to be old:

> *indignor quicquam reprehendi, non quia crasse*
> *compositum inlepideque putetur, sed quia nuper,*
> *nec ueniam antiquis, sed honorem et praemia posci.*

> I find it outrageous that it's not the crude
> or unattractive *(inlepidus)* writing that people blame,
> but simply recent writing—when people read old poets,

---

34. So Copley 1951: 201–2, though ignoring the evidence of the rhetorica.

they don't ask for forgiveness for them:
they ask for rewards and honor.

          (Hor. *Ep.* 2.1.76–78)

The issue is specifically the metrical character of the verse, its *compositio*. In the *Ars Poetica*, *lepidus* is connected to humor:

> at uestri proaui Plautinos et numeros et
> laudauere sales, nimium patienter utrumque,
> ne dicam stulte, mirati, si modo ego et uos
> scimus inurbanum lepido seponere dicto
> legitimumque sonum digitis callemus et aure.

> But your great-grandfathers praised Plautus's wit
> and praised Plautus's meter, too tolerant in both respects,
> not to say stupid: amazed, if you and I know how
> to tell the witty *(lepidus)* word from the inurbane,
> if you and I have learned to hear and count the meter.

          (Hor. *Ars* 270–74)

*Lepidum dictum* is counterposed to *inurbanum* and refers to Plautus's deficiencies in the way of *sales* 'saltiness, wit.'[35]

 These appearances of the language of social performance, slight to be sure, are nonetheless notable. In both instances *lepidus* marks off a self-consciously new literary sensibility that Horace possesses, unlike the *facetus* that marked what Horace was not.[36] That is significant when viewed in the light of the subsequent history of the language. Cicero aside, the author in whom the language is attested in greatest numbers is Aulus Gellius. In Gellius the language of social performance, often in unprecedented applications or configurations, has plainly become the technical language of literary criticism. Gellius observes that Vergil "attractively [deftly?] substituted two words" (*duobus uocabulis uenuste inmutatis,* 13.27.2) in translating Parthenius's line Γλαύκῳ καὶ Νηρεῖ καὶ εἰναλίῳ Μελικέρτῃ; Vergil's version runs *Glauco et Panopeae et Inoo Melicertae* (G. 1.437). One of Cato's speeches was done

---

 35. For a different ancient judgment of Plautus's humor, cf. Cic. *Off.* 1.104 (above, VI.4).

 36. Horace's accession to the inner circle is, as it happens, marked by a member of the language of social performance: Augustus himself "among other jokes" *(inter alios iocos)* called Horace "a most *lepidus* little man" *(homuncionem lepidissimum),* as well as "a very clean dick" *(purissimum penem, Poet.* fr. 40 = Aug. *ep.* fr. 41)— epithets that, as Rostagni 1944 ad loc. points out, "non poterono essere adoperati se non dopo che le relazioni fra i due cominciarono a diventare più intime, cioè suppergiù nell'ultimo decennio o quindicennio della vita del poeta, 23-8 a. C."

*cum multa quidem uenustate atque luce atque munditia uerborum* "with considerable grace *(uenustas)*, distinction, and elegance of diction" (1.23.1).[37] Varro's
definitions of a rare word feature *lepida atque iucunda breuitas* "a charming
and pleasant brevity" (1.25.3). Certain verses of Varro were composed *lepide et scite* "with charm and knowledge" (6.16.1). Aesop's fables are *festiui
delectabilesque apologi* (2.29.1). A translation of Theocritus by Vergil was done
*non infestiuiter* (9.9.9). Compared to Greek comedy, Latin comedy comes
up short *facetiis et luminibus* "with respect to its witticism and excellences"
(2.23.3). A line of Plautus's *(scrattae, scrupedae, strittiuillae sordidae* fr. 97) delighted Favorinus *faceta uerborum antiquitate* "with witty vintage words"
(3.3.6). Sallust's "tendency to coin or alter words" *(uerborum fingendi et
nouandi studium)* is a sign of his *elegantia orationis* (4.15.1). Judging by the
Latin of his own day, Gellius reads certain grammatical peculiarities of the
older language as affectations in service of *elegantia*. In using nonstandard
plurals, such as *uitae* for *uita* or *otia* for *otium*, Q. Claudius's "intended effect
was elegance" *(elegantia . . . quaesita est*, 17.2.22–23). Changing the voice of
a verb is a "type of elegance" *(elegantiae genus*, 18.12.1); Varro's use of *mu-
tant* for *mutantur* was done so "very elegantly" *(elegantissime*, 18.12.8).[38] In
this literary critical guise, the language of social performance is frequent in
subsequent commentaries, such as Porphyrio and Servius.

   This development in the language of social performance is precipitated
by the changing function of literary activity under the Empire. Political oratory had lost its teeth and was survived by declamation, which in turn came
to interpenetrate poetry thoroughly. Belles lettres now had a firmly established existence as an affect of the upper classes. The practice could provide
a caricature already in Horace's time:

> *Romae dulce diu fuit et sollemne reclusa*
> *mane domo uigilare, clienti promere iura,*
> *cautos nominibus rectis expendere nummos,*
> *maiores audire, minori dicere per quae*
> *crescere res posset, minui damnosa libido.*
> *mutauit mentem populus leuis et calet uno*
> *scribendi studio: pueri patresque seueri*
> *fronde comas uincti cenant et carmina dictant.*

---

   37. Gellius may have in mind the characteristic virtues of the plain style. For *uenust(us)*
of the plain style in Gellius, cf. *gracili [sc., generi] uenustas et subtilitas* (6.14.3, III.4 ad fin.); for
Cato read as a proponent of that style, cf. *Brut.* 63 (III.6 n.84).

   38. In the older language certain deponents could still be used actively (e.g., *contemplo*
for *contemplor*) and certain transitive verbs could be used intransitively in the active (e.g., *auxit*
for *auctum est*).

At Rome it was long pleasant and customary
to remain home mornings with the house open;
to offer clients legal advice; to offer secure loans
to honest debtors; to hear from the older,
and tell the younger, how to multiply wealth
and how to reduce destructive desire.
The capricious people changed its mind,
and burns with one zeal: to write.
Boys and grim fathers both, their locks girt in leaf,
dine and dictate poems.

(Hor. *Ep.* 2.1.103–10)

Persius's remarks on the same practice we have seen above (III.5). In short, as "verbal skill" came to mean not the oratorical or jocular ability that marked one's temporary advantage at the top of the social hierarchy, but the literary ability that marked off the social upper crust as a whole, the language of social performance, associated both with oratory and poetry, came to be less of a "political" and more of a purely "literary" idiom.[39]

Horace's use of *lep(idus)* in the *Epistulae* may be the vanguard of this later usage. The tone of the *Epistles* has a cool dignity, what Fraenkel 1957: 395 called a "dignified freedom," that reflects the established status of their author. The position of Horace is now something of a poet laureate. Indeed the *Epistula ad Augustum* was written in response to a request of Augustus himself, though the final product may not be quite what he wished.[40] If the language of social performance had already begun to be converted to describe the belletristic activity ever more popular among the upper crust, it makes sense that it should appear in Horace at the very point when he had become part of a self-conscious inner circle now in firm possession of new modes of expression. For Horace, the new literary sensibility still had considerable political charge: to prefer an older, freer poetic was not without political point in what was, for all practical purposes, a monarchy. But with the institutionalizing of the principate and of belletristic pursuits, that particular charge diminished, and the language of social performance—which by this point is a misnomer—became the technical language of literary crit-

39. The association of *lepos* with literary culture, counterposed to political life, is to be found in the *Laus Pisonis: mira subest grauitas inter fora, mirus omissa | paulisper grauitate lepos* "Wondrous his *grauitas* in civic duties, wondrous his *lepos*, when he sets his *grauitas* briefly aside" (162–63); the poem goes on to describe Piso's skill at poetry (163–65) and at playing the lyre (166–77).

40. Augustus apparently asked Horace to include him as an interlocutor in a *sermo* (Suet. *Poet.* fr. 40); the *Epistula ad Augustum* is rather a disquisition on the place of poetry in the political order.

icism. The origins of this use of the language of social performance may even extend back to Cicero's *Brutus*.[41]

In any case, by the second century A.D. the conversion of the language of social performance into a technical critical language for a new and different literary culture, now firmly belletristic, affects the range and application of its constituent lexical items. Several of the lexemes seem to move in the direction of "precious, refined, clever," which is not surprising in a critical language for a literature that is often described as "precious" or "artificial." The use of *bell(us)* for 'precious' or 'refined' effects has been noticed above (III.5). The case of *uenust(us)* is not entirely clear because of the apparent influence on the lexeme of χάρις (III.4). However, two of the types used by Cicero, one describing the quality of the humor of reply (III.4.2), the other the quality of precious or mannered effects (III.4.3), are still discernible.[42] The cardinal fact is that the latter type blossomed in the new literary culture. The elder Seneca uses it for the deftness of declamatory effects. A certain Hispanus handled a particular *color* "more deftly" (*uenustius, Con.* 1.1.20); a certain Silo used "a deft type of *sententia*" (*uenusto genere sententiae, Suas.* 5.7). The younger Seneca and Gellius, especially the latter, use *uenustas* as a general term for skillful literary composition, both generally and on the level of specific details.[43] That this use of *uenust(us)* had to do with 'careful arrangement' or 'nice craftsmanship' is suggested by its complementary pairings in Gellius; such pairings can reveal something of a word's character.[44] Gellius often pairs literary critical *uenust(us)* with *mund(us)* 'clean, neat, elegant':[45]

41. The idea that the language of social performance in the later *rhetorica* may mark the inauguration of a culture of literary exchange comes from S. C. Stroup.

42. For examples of *uenust(us)* describing the humor of reply, cf. *nihil erat illo uenustius, nihil paratius* (Sen. *Con.* 10.pr.2), *non tantum disertissimus homo sed uenustissimus, qui nullius umquam inpunitam stultitiam transire passus est* (*Con.* 1.2.22), cf. 1.7.18, 7.4.8 (?), 9.3.14, *sunt enim longe uenustiora omnia in respondendo quam in prouocando,* "Everything is more charming (*uenustiora*) in a comeback than on the attack," Quint. *Inst.* 6.3.13.

43. *non audeo te usque <eo> producere ut fabellas quoque et Aesopeos logos, intemptatum Romanis ingeniis opus, solita tibi uenustate conectas* (Sen. iun. *Dial.* 11.8.3); *tria . . . epigrammata . . . nobilitatis eorum gratia et uenustatis scribenda in his commentariis esse duxi* (Gel. 1.24.1), *quin lepide quoque et uenustae scriptae uideantur* (Gel. 2.23.2), *nam quae reliquit perfecta expolitaque quibusque inposuit census atque dilectus sui supremam manum, omni poeticae uenustatis laude florent* (Gel. 17.10.5), cf. also, e.g., 7.9.1, 7.16.2, 10.17.pr.

44. Cf. Buchheit 1976b: 57.

45. Other pairings include *scite admodum et uenuste* (2.29.20), *perquam pure et uenuste narrata* (7.9.1), *utque est Graecae facundiae copia simul et uenustas* (14.1.32), *uenustius gratiusque* (18.12.2), *erotica dulcia ac uenusta* (19.9.4). For the influence of χάρις on Gellius's *uenust(us)*, see above, III.4 ad fin.

*cum multa quidem <u>uenustate</u> atque luce atque <u>munditia</u> uerborum* (1.23.1)
<u>munditiae</u> *et <u>uenustatis</u> et prudentiae* (9.3.3)
*breuitas sane et <u>uenustas</u> et <u>mundities</u> orationis est, qualis haberi ferme in*
  *comoedearum festiuitatibus solet* (10.3.4)
<u>mundius, uenustius</u>, *limatius, tersius* (19.9.10)

Where Cicero's *uenust(us)* seemed to describe natural shapes (VI.4), Gellius's *uenust(us)* seems, with *mund(us)* 'clean, well-scrubbed' (a term that appears in Cicero's rhetorica only once),[46] to emphasize rather the process of refinement itself.

This emphasis on "making" or "polishing" becomes the dominant characteristic of *elegan(s)*, too. The later tradition, to be sure, continues some of Cicero's uses, such as that for 'careful word choice.'[47] But a sense wholly absent from Cicero, that of the 'deft' or 'well-contrived' move, now comes to the fore. "He made a smooth transition to the narrative section" *(ad partem narrationis eleganter transit),* says Seneca of an Artemo (*Con.* 7.1.26, cf. 1.1.25). *Elegans* in Seneca is frequently connected to the deft *sententia,* as when Miltiades said of orators who affected a harsh antiquarian style that they were "mad, but on the right track" (ἐπὶ τὸ δεξιὸν μαίνονται, *Con.* 9.2.26, cf. 2.5.20, 7.5.12). Augustus's σπεῦδε βραδέως "make haste slowly," which Gellius praises with *elegantissime* (10.11.5), resembles a *sententia.* Gellius connects Sallust's *elegantis orationis* to his "tendency to coin or alter words" *(uerborum fingendi et nouandi studium,* 4.15.1)—the exact opposite of Cicero's equivalence of *elegans* and *incorruptum* (*Or.* 25, III.6 n. 90).

In the later period the use of *lep(idus)* to describe diffuse qualities, such as the 'charm' or 'humor' of a literary work, remains. It is the standard word to Apuleius for the 'charm' of the Milesian tales he tells.[48] But the lexeme more often has the sense of 'clever, keen, concise' (an old usage, cf. III.3).

---

46. *tum remouebitur omnis insignis ornatus quasi margaritarum, ne calamistri quidem adhibebuntur. fucati uero medicamenta candoris et ruboris omnia repellentur: elegantia modo et munditia remanebit* (*Or.* 78).

47. Quintilian has that sense in mind when he recommends that someone with a "strong and untamed" *(forte, indomitum)* character not try to speak in a subtle style, since it is not true to his nature: he would "fail of the elegance he desires" *(elegantiam quam cupit non persequatur, Inst.* 10.2.19). Like Cicero (*Brut.* 86), Quintilian ascribes *elegantia* to Laelius's careful diction (*Inst.* 1.1.6). Gellius has the same sense in mind when he says that if one changes a single word in a passage of Plato, the elegance is destroyed (2.5.1).

48. *uarias fabulae conseram auresque tuas beniuolas lepido susurro permulceam* (1.1), *fabularum lepida iucunditas* (1.2), *lepidae fabulae festiuitate* (1.20), *narrationibus lepidis anilibusque fabulis* (4.27), *lepidam de adulterio cuiusdam pauperis fabulam* (9.4). Gellius has *lepide . . . et uenustae scriptae,* of Roman comedies (2.23.2) and *lepide atque iucunde promonet,* of a fable of Aesop (2.29). Fronto has *lepide* of Claudius's writing of history (*Eloq.* 1.2).

In Gellius *lep(idus)* is several times connected to 'clever' etymologies. For example, a contribution of P. Nigidius to the debate whether language is natural or arbitrary (φύσει τὰ ὀνόματα *sint* ἢ θέσει) is *lepidum et festiuum:* Nigidius argued in favor of natural language by observing that the lip-rounding of *uos* /wo:s/ 'you (pl.)' seems to point at the addressee, whereas in pronouncing *ego* 'I' and *nos* 'we' a speaker's lips curl in toward himself (10.4.4).[49] *Lep(idus)* describes various sorts of verbal cleverness, such as 'neat' philosophical arguments, entertaining declamatory topics or epigrams, puzzling questions posed as dinner entertainment, and once an 'apt' double entendre.[50] To take one example, a *declamatiuncula* about Scipio and Alexander "is fun to argue about" (*lepide . . . agitari potest,* 7.8.3). *Lep(idus)* is also used for the 'keen' or 'concise' quality of pungent or incisive remarks or formulations, as when Demosthenes, astounded that the services of the famous courtesan Lais cost 1000 drachmas, remarked, "Regret isn't worth that much." Gellius, who gives Demosthenes' remarks in Latin *(ego paenitere tanti non emo),* observes that the original Greek words, οὐκ ὠνοῦμαι μυρίων δραχμῶν μεταμέλειαν, are *lepidiora* (1.8.6).[51]

49. Cf. 5.7.1 (Gavius Bassius's etymology of *persona* from *personare*); 11.11.4 (the difference between *mentiri* and *mendacium dicere* postulated by Nigidius), 12.14.7 (*saltem* 'at least' derived from *salutem* 'safety, salvation' by way of the sense 'last resort'), 13.10.3 (*soror* 'sister' derived by Labeo Antistius from *seorsum* 'separate, apart' because a sister "is separated from her birth home and joins another family").

50. NEAT PHILOSOPHICAL ARGUMENTS: *dum id mendacium argumento aliquo lepido iuuetur,* Front. *Laud.* 3; *exemplo non hercle nimis alieno neque inlepido [Chrysippus] utitur,* Gel. 7.2.11, cf. 18.1.12, 19.4.2; *[sententia] lepidus et uenustis uocum modis uincta* of an argument of Demosthenes, Gel. 10.19.2; ENTERTAINING DECLAMATORY TOPICS OR EPIGRAMS: *sententias quas in declamandis controuersiis lepide arguteque dictas putat,* Gel. 9.16.5, cf. 17.12.2; PUZZLING QUESTIONS AS DINNER ENTERTAINMENT: ἐνθυμήματα *quaedam lepida et minuta et florentem uino animum lacessentia* (7.13.4); *per hercle anticum perquam lepidum . . . aenigma* (12.6.1, cf. 17.12.2, of ἀδόξοι ὑπόθεσεις); *sententia poetae ueteris lepide obscura* (18.2.6); *non satis scite ac paene etiam inlepide* (18.13.5) refers to *captiones* (= σοφίσματα) that are awkward in Latin. DOUBLE ENTENDRE: when Aristotle, on his deathbed, tasted two wines, a Rhodian and a Lesbian, he proclaimed ἡδίων ὁ Λέσβιος "The Lesbian is sweeter"; this was taken to mean he had designated the Lesbian Theophrastus, and not the Rhodian Menedemus, as his successor, a designation done, as Gellius says, *lepide simul et uerecunde* (13.5.10).

51. Cf. 1.25.3 (Varro's two definitions of *indutiae* are dismissed as *lepidae magis atque iucundae breuitatis . . . quam plana aut proba; cf. lepidissimi et uenustissimae breuitatis,* of Greek epigrams), 5.5.6 (Hannibal replies *lepide* and *acerbe* to Antiochus, who was fishing for compliments about his well-arrayed army, observing, "Yes, they should be enough for the Romans—despite their considerable greed"). Pliny has *non inlepidum* for a clever saying of the Baetici (*Ep.* 3.9.4). For another instance of *lep(idus)* in Gellius describing the original Greek as against the Latin, cf. 18.13.5 *tametsi Latina oratione non satis scite ac paene etiam inlepide exponuntur,* of *captiones.*

The movement of several of our lexemes in the direction of 'cleverness' or 'deftness' may have blunted their semantic particularity. Whereas in Cicero, as I have argued, the force of *uenustus* as against that of *facetus* or *lepidus* was specifiable, it is less easy to tell (for me at any rate) what distinguishes a *sententia* that is *elegans* from one that is *bellus, lepidus,* or *uenustus.* Doubtless there are subtleties that this brief treatment has not uncovered. But one measure of the blunting is perhaps to be seen in the fact that the language of social performance—or better said, the former language of social performance—is applied to authors of widely, even wildly, different styles. In Gellius *elegan(s)* describes the Attic orators (5.20.3), Catullus (6.20.6), and Plautus (6.17.4). *Lepid(us)* is applied to a book of Varro (*lepidissimus liber est M. Varronis ex satiris Menippeis . . . ,* 13.11.1), one of the *carmina Anacreontea* (*uersiculis lepidissimis Anacreontis senis,* 19.9.5, referring to *Anacreont.* 4), proverbs from Publilius Syrus (*Publilii sententiae . . . lepidae et ad communem sermonum usum commendatissimae,* 17.14.3), and perhaps even Plato (there is a sort of person who reads Plato "not to adorn his life, but to dress up his habits of speech; not to become chaster, but more clever" *non uitae ornandae, sed linguae orationisque comendae gratia, nec ut modestior fiat sed ut lepidior,* 1.9.11). *Venust(us)* takes in Cato (his speech *ad milites contra Galbam* was written *cum multa quidem uenustate atque luce atque munditia uerborum,* 1.23.1), Latin comedy (*lepide . . . et uenuste scriptae,* 2.23.2), verses from Ennius's satires (*scite admodum et uenuste uersibus quadratis composuit,* 2.29.20) and Laberius's mimes (10.17.pr.), and an episode from Piso's *Annals* (*perquam pure et uenusta narrata a Pisone,* 7.9.1), as well as verses from Catullus (7.16.2), the letters of Philip of Macedon (9.3.3), a passage of Demosthenes (10.19.2), and a line of Vergil (13.27.2).

This promiscuity of the former language of social performance has a reasonably clear explanation. By the second century A.D., the former language of social performance no longer marked off the life and language of the superior competitor in a shifting hierarchy; it simply marked off the language of the *honestiores* from the *humiliores,* the two social classes into which society was becoming polarized. The social elite saw their own patterns of speech, literary and extraliterary, as critical to displaying, and maintaining, their social position; and to the extent that they derived models for that speech from the ancients, whose writings were the standard grist of the educational system, they imputed the same set of laudable qualities to *any* sort of speech or writing that was socially distinctive and sanctioned by the educational system. The labels provided by the former language of social performance simply served to mark off literary texts that were on "our side" of the line. Indeed control over Latin itself had for some time been develop-

ing into a form of social legitimation.[52] Much as the fine distinctions of the
*triclinium* gave way to the semicircular *stibadium* at about this period, so the
finer distinctions of the language of social performance seem to lose their
edge. Aurelius's effusion to Fronto, where *elegantia, lepos,* and *uenustas* are
little more than stereotyped praise, represents the limit of this tendency:

> Whether the ancient Greeks managed to write anything like that I
> leave it to experts to judge. For my part, if I am permitted to say so, I
> have never seen even M. Porcius delivering blame as well as you de-
> livered praise. For you my teacher to receive adequate praise would
> require your very own services! "They don't make things that way
> anymore." It would have been easier to imitate Phidias, Apelles, De-
> mosthenes himself, or Cato than to produce this work, so well-made
> and well-wrought. I have never read anything that was more refined,
> more well-structured, in finer Latin idiom, or more in the style of the
> ancients. Fortunate are you to be blessed with such eloquence, fortu-
> nate I to be entrusted to such a master! The figures (ἐπιχειρήματα)!
> The arrangement (τάξις)! The elegance *(elegantia)!* The attractiveness
> *(lepos)!* The grace *(uenustas)!* The word choice *(uerba)!* The sheen *(nitor)!*
> The subtleties *(argutiae)!* The charms *(charites)!* The skill (ἄσκησις)! All
> of it! Damn me but you shouldn't someday have had a sceptre put in
> your hand, a diadem on your head, a tribunal at your feet: then the
> herald would summon us all—what am I saying, 'us'?—would sum-
> mon every philologist and fluent speaker and you would direct them
> with your sceptre, instruct them with your words.[53]

> *(Aur.* 2.3.1)

As now there are, more and more, only *honestiores* and *humiliores,* so formerly
discrete honors—a *uirga, diadema, tribunal*—are now of a piece, the province of the former group; and the articulations of their aesthetic are also less
distinct, serving not to discriminate among those scrambling near the pin-
nacle but as marks to distinguish what is above from what is below.

52. See Bloomer 1997.

53. *sane si quid Graeci ueteres tale scripserunt, uiderint qui sciunt; ego, si fas est dicere, nec M. Por-
cium tam bene uituperantem quam tu laudasti usquam aduorti. O si dominus meus satis laudari posset, profecto a te satis laudatus esset!* τοῦτο τὸ ἔργον οὐ γίνεται νῦν. *Facilius quid Phidian, facilius Apellen, facilius denique ipsum Demosthenen imitatus fuerit aut ipsum Catonem, quam hoc tam
effectum et elaboratum opus. nihil ego umquam cultius, nihil antiquius, nihil conditius, nihil Latinius
legi. O te hominem beatum hac eloquentia praeditum! O me hominem beatum huic magistro traditum!
O* ἐπιχειρήματα! *o* τάξις! *o elegantia! o lepos! o uenustas! o uerba! o nitor! o argutiae! o kharites!
o* ἄσκησις! *o omnia! ne ualeam, nisi aliqua die uirga in manus tibi tradenda erat, diadema circumpo-
nendum, tribunal ponendum; tum praeco omnis nos citaret, quid 'nos' dico? omnis, inquam, philolo-
gos et disertos istos; eos tu singulos uirga perduceres, uerbis moneres.*

The history of the language of social performance in the empire, even as thinly sketched here, therefore presents an acute paradox. A language that developed originally to describe various aspects of social performance and was, as I have argued, only latterly imported to rhetoric, ends its life in Latin by losing its application to other spheres and becoming associated primarily with rhetoric. But throughout the language of social performance never ceased to perform the one function that it acquired sometime in the second century B.C.: the assessment of aesthetic qualities important in the conduct of the life of the social elite. How different were L. Aemilius Paullus and M. Tullius Cicero, C. Valerius Catullus and Aulus Gellius, nobody needs to be reminded; but the lexemes of the language of social performance, stationed, like all approbative language, at the borders of cultural categories, give a highly suggestive glimpse of the shifting ideological terrain upon which, in pursuit of "that very difficult alliance between weight of character and culture" *(difficillima illa societas grauitatis cum humanitate),* they, and other Romans, positioned the images of their opponents and themselves.

# WORKS CITED

Abbenes, J. G. J., S. R. Slings, and I. Sluiter, eds. 1995. *Greek Literary Theory after Aristotle: A Collection of Papers in Honour of D. M. Schenkeveld.* Amsterdam: VU University Press.

Abo, Takaji, Byron Bender, Alfred Capelle, and Tony DeBrum, eds. 1976. *Marshallese-English Dictionary.* Honolulu: University Press of Hawaii.

Adams, James Noel. 1982. *The Latin Sexual Vocabulary.* Baltimore, Md.: Johns Hopkins University Press.

Allen, William Sidney. 1978. *Vox Latina.* 2d ed. Cambridge, New York: Cambridge University Press.

Arkins, Brian. 1983. "Further Thoughts on Catullus I." *Liverpool Classical Monthly* 8.2: 18–20.

Arlotto, Anthony. 1972. *Introduction to Historical Linguistics.* New York: Houghton Mifflin.

Astbury, R. 1983. "Notes on Varro's Menippeans." *Classica et Mediaevalia* 34: 141–60.

Atherton, Catherine. 1988. "Hand over Fist: The Failure of Stoic Rhetoric." *Classical Quarterly* 38 (iii): 392–427.

Austin, Roland Gregory. 1960. *"Pro M. Caelio" Oratio.* 3d ed. Oxford: Clarendon Press.

Ax, Wolfram. 1991. "Sprache als Gegenstand der alexandrinischen und pergamenischen Philologie." In Schnitter 1991: 275–301.

Badian, Ernst. 1958. *Foreign Clientelae 264–70 B.C.* Oxford: Clarendon Press.

Baehrens, Aemilius [Emil]. 1879–86. *Poetae Latini Minores.* 6 vols. Leipzig: Teubner.

———. 1885. *Catulli Veronensis Liber.* Vol. 2 (commentary). Leipzig: Teubner.

Bailey, Cyril, ed. and tr. 1986 [1947]. *Titi Lucreti Cari "De rerum natura" libri sex.* 3 vols. Oxford: Clarendon Press.

Baker, Robert John. 1970. "Catullus and Friend in Carm. XXXI." *Mnemosyne* 23: 33–41.

———. 1983. "Catullus and Sirmio." *Mnemosyne* 36: 316–23.

Balsdon, John Percy Vyvian Dacre. 1979. *Romans and Aliens.* London: Duckworth.

Bardon, H. 1940. *Le vocabulaire de la critique littéraire chez Sénèque le Rhéteur.* Paris: Les Belles Lettres.

Bartman, Elizabeth. 1994. "Sculptural Collecting and Display in the Private Realm." In Gazda 1994: 49–70.

Barton, Carlin. 1993. *The Sorrows of the Ancient Romans.* Princeton, N.J.: Princeton University Press.

Batstone, William W. 1993. "Logic, Rhetoric, and Poesis." *Helios* 20 no. 2: 143–72.

Berry, D. H. 1996. *Cicero "pro Sulla" oratio.* Cambridge: Cambridge University Press.

Bignone, Ettore. 1945. *Storia della letteratura Latina.* Vol. 2. Florence: G. C. Sansoni.

Bloomer, W. Martin. 1997. *Latinity and Literary Society at Rome.* Philadelphia: University of Pennsylvania Press.

Bonner, Stanley Frederick. 1938. "The Peripatetic Mean of Style." *Classical Philology* 33: 257–66.

Bowersock, Glen Warren. 1979. "Historical Problems in Late Republican and Augustan Classicism." In Gelzer 1979: 57–78.

Braunlich, Alice Freda. 1943. "Comment and Conjecture on Catullus: Catullus and Capito." *Classical Weekly* 36: 249.

Brink, C. O. 1963. *Horace on Poetry: Prolegomena to the Literary Epistles.* Cambridge: Cambridge University Press.

———. 1971. *Horace on Poetry: The "Ars Poetica."* Cambridge: Cambridge University Press.

———. 1982. *Horace on Poetry: "Epistles" Book II.* Cambridge: Cambridge University Press.

Briscoe, John. 1991. *Titi Livi "Ab urbe condita": Libri xxxi–xl.* Stuttgart: Teubner.

Brown, P. Michael. 1988. *Lucretius "de Rerum Natura" I.* Bristol, Eng.: Bristol Classical Press.

Browning, Robert. 1983. *Medieval and Modern Greek.* Cambridge, New York: Cambridge University Press.

Buchheit, Vinzenz. 1959. "Catulls Dichterkritik in C. 36." Hermes 87: 309–27.

———. 1976a. "Catull c. 50 als Programm und Bekenntnis." *Rheinisches Museum* 119: 162–80.

———. 1976b. "Dichtertum und Lebenform in Catull c. 35/36." In *Lebendige Romania: Festschrift für Hans-Wilhelm Klein,* ed. A. Barrera-Vidal, E. Ruhe, and P. Schunck: 47–64. Göppingen: A. Kümmerle.

———. 1976c. "Sal et Lepos Versiculorum (Catull c. 16)." *Hermes* 104, no. 3: 331–47.

Buck, Carl Darling. 1949. *A Dictionary of Selected Synonyms in the Principal Indo-European Languages.* Chicago: University of Chicago Press.

———. 1974 [1928]. *A Grammar of Oscan and Umbrian.* 2d ed. Boston: Ginn. Rpt. Hildesheim, New York: Olms.

Burgess, D. L. 1986. "Catullus c. 50: The Exchange of Poetry." *Classical Philology* 64: 169–73.

Bushala, E. W. 1981. "A Note on Catullus 106." *Harvard Studies in Classical Philology* 85: 131–32.

Cairns, Francis. 1969. "Catullus I." *Mnemosyne* 22: 153–58.

Calboli, Gualtiero. 1969. *Cornifici "Rhetorica ad Herennium."* Bologna: R. Pàtron.

———. 1981. "La retorica preciceroniana e la politica a Roma." In Stroh et al. 1981: 41–108.

Cameron, Alan. 1995. *Callimachus and His Critics.* Princeton, N.J.: Princeton University Press.

Cèbe, Jean-Pierre. 1972–. *Varron, "Satires ménippées." Edition, traduction et commentaire.* 12 vols. Cited herein are vol. 3 (1975, fr. 71–108), vol. 8 (1987, fr. 288–332), and vol. 12 (1998, fr. 485–543). Rome: Ecole française de Rome.

Cébeillac-Gervasoni, Mireille, ed. 1983. *Les 'bourgeoisies' municipales italiennes aux II$^e$ et I$^r$ siècles av. J.-C.: Centre Jean Bérard, Institute Française de Naples, 7–10 décembre 1981.* Paris: Editions du Centre national de la recherche scientifique; Naples: Bibliothèque de l'Institut français de Naples.

Cichorius, Conrad. 1908. *Untersuchungen zu Lucilius.* Berlin: Weidmannsche Buchhandlung.

Clarke, G. W. 1968. "The Burning of Books and Catullus 36." *Latomus* 27: 575–80.

Clarke, John Robert. 1991. *The Houses of Roman Italy 100 B.C.–A.D. 250: Ritual, Space, and Decoration.* Berkeley: University of California Press.

Classen, Carl Joachim. 1973. "Ciceros Rede für Caelius." *Aufstieg und Niedergang der römischen Welt* 1.3: 60–93.

Clausen, Wendell. 1964. "Callimachus and Latin Poetry." *Greek, Roman and Byzantine Studies* 5: 181–96.

———. 1990. "Philology (the Problem of Definition)." *Comparative Literature Studies* 27.1: 13–15.

———. 1994. *A Commentary on Virgil, "Eclogues."* Oxford: Clarendon Press.

Colin, Jean. 1952–53. "Juvénal, les baladins et les rétiares d'après le MS d'Oxford." *Atti dell'Accademia delle Scienze di Torino* 87–88: 315–86.

Comfort, Harold. 1929. "An Interpretation of Catullus XXXVI." *Classical Philology* 24: 176–82.

Cooper, Frederic Taber. 1975 [1895]. *Word Formation in the Roman Sermo Plebeius.* Rpt. Hildesheim, New York: Olms.

Cope, Edward Meredith. 1966? [1867]. *An Introduction to Aristotle's "Rhetoric."* Rpt. Dubuque, Iowa: W. C. Brown Reprint Library.

Copley, Frank Olin. 1951. "Catullus C.1." *Transactions of the American Philological Society* 82: 200-206.

Coppola, Goffredo. 1929. "Archiloco o imitazione ellenistica?' *Studi italiani di filologia classica* 7: 155–68.

Corbeill, Anthony. 1996. *Controlling Laughter.* Princeton, N.J.: Princeton University Press.

Corbett, Philip B. 1986. *The Scurra.* Edinburgh: Scottish Academic Press.

Costa, Charles Desmond Nuttall. 1984. *"De Rerum Natura" V, Lucretius.* Oxford: Clarendon Press; New York: Oxford University Press.

Courtney, Edward. 1993. *The Fragmentary Latin Poets.* Oxford: Clarendon Press; New York: Oxford University Press.

Craig, Christopher P. 1989. "Reason, Resonance, and Dilemma in Cicero's Speech for Caelius." *Rhetorica* 7: 313–28.

Crawford, Jane W. 1994. *M. Tullius Cicero: The Fragmentary Speeches.* Atlanta, Ga.: Scholars Press.

Crowther, N. B. 1979. "Water and Wine as Symbols of Inspiration." *Mnemosyne* 32: 1–11.

Damon, Cynthia. 1997. *The Mask of the Parasite.* Ann Arbor: University of Michigan Press.

David, Jean-Michel. 1983. "Les orateurs des municipes à Rome: intégration, réticences et snobismes." In Cébeillac-Gervasoni 1983: 309–31.

Degrassi, Attilio. [1963–65]. *Inscriptiones latinae liberae rei publicae.* Firenze: La Nuova Italia.

Dettmer, Helena. 1986. *"Meros Amores:* A Note on Catullus 13.9." *Quaderni urbinati di cultura classica* 23: 87–91.

Dihle, Albrecht. 1957. "Analogie und Attizismus." *Hermes* 85: 170–205. Rpt. with additional notes in Stark 1968: 402–37.

Dominik, William J., ed. 1997. *Roman Eloquence: Rhetoric in Society and Literature.* London and New York: Routledge.

Doroszewski, Witold, ed. 1958–68. *Słownik Języka Polskiego.* Warsaw: Wiedza Powszechna.

Douglas, Alan Edward. 1955. "M. Calidius and the Atticists." *Classical Quarterly* 49: 241–47.

———. 1966. *M. Tulli Ciceronis "Brutus."* Oxford: Clarendon Press.

———. 1973. "The Intellectual Background of Cicero's rhetorica: A Study in Method." *Aufstieg und Niedergang der römischen Welt* 1.3: 95–138.

Dover, Kenneth James. 1968. *Aristophanes: "Clouds."* Oxford: Clarendon Press.

Drummond, Andrew. 1989. "Early Roman *clientes*." In Wallace-Hadrill 1989: 89–115.

Du Mesnil, Adolf. 1879. *"De legibus" libri tres*. Leipzig: Teubner.

Dyck, Andrew R. 1996. *A Commentary on Cicero, "de Officiis."* Ann Arbor: University of Michigan Press.

Edmonds, L. 1982. "The Latin Invitation Poem: What Is it?" *American Journal of Philology* 103: 184–88.

Edwards, Catherine. 1993. *The Politics of Immorality in Ancient Rome*. Cambridge: Cambridge University Press.

Elder, John Petersen. 1966. "Catullus 1, His Poetic Creed, and Nepos." *Harvard Studies in Classical Philology* 52: 143–49.

Ellis, Robinson. 1889. *A Commentary on Catullus*. Oxford: Clarendon Press.

Ernout, Alfred. 1957. *"Venus, Venia, Cupido."* In *Philologica II*: 87–11 = *Revue de Philologie* 3. ser. 30 (1956): 7–27.

Fantham, Elaine. 1997. "The Contexts and Occasions of Roman Public Rhetoric." In Dominik 1997: 111–28.

Fiske, George Converse. 1919. "The Plain Style in the Scipionic Circle." University of Wisconsin Studies in Language and Literature 3. Madison: University of Wisconsin Press.

Fitzgerald, William. 1995. *Catullan Provocations: Lyric Poetry and the Drama of Position*. Berkeley and Los Angeles: University of California Press.

Fordyce, Christian James. 1961. *Catullus*. Oxford: Clarendon Press.

Fortenbaugh, William. 1985. "Theophrastus on Delivery." In Fortenbaugh et al. 1985: 269–88.

Fortenbaugh, William, P. M. Huby, and A. A. Long, eds. 1985. *Theophrastus of Eresus: On His Life and Works*. Rutgers University Studies in Classical Humanities 2. New Brunswick, N.J.: Transaction Books.

Fraenkel, Eduard. 1957. *Horace*. Oxford: Clarendon Press.

———. 1962. Review of Fordyce 1961. *Gnomon* 34: 253–63.

Fraenkel, Ernst. 1962. *Litauisches Etymologisches Wörterbuch*. Vol. I. Heidelberg: Carl Winter.

———. 1965. *Litauisches Etymologisches Wörterbuch*. Vol. II. Heidelberg: Carl Winter.

Fredricksmeyer, E. A. 1985. "Catullus to Caecilius on Good Poetry (C. 35)." *American Journal of Philology* 106: 213–21.

Freudenburg, Kirk. 1993. *The Walking Muse: Horace on the Theory of Satire*. Princeton, N.J.: Princeton University Press.

Frier, Bruce. 1989. *A Casebook on the Roman Law of Delict*. Atlanta: Scholars Press.

Fyëderov, N. A. 1987. "Leksicheskaya gruppa *lepos-lepidus* w systeme esteticheskoy leksiki Tsiterona" ("The lexical group *lepos-lepidus* in the system of the aesthetic lexicon of Cicero"). *Voprosy klassicheskoy filologii* 9: 213–30.

———. 1990. "Semanticheskaya spetsifika termina *venustas* w tekstach Tsitserona" ("The semantic specificity of the term *uenustas* in the texts of Cicero"). *Voprosy klassicheskoy filologii* 10: 113–27.

Gamberale, Leopoldo. 1979. *"Venuste Noster*: Caratterizzazione e ironia in Catullo 13." In *Studi di poesia latina in onore di Antonio Traglia*, vol. 1: 127–48. Rome: Edizioni di storia e letteratura.

Gazda, Elaine K., ed. 1994. *Roman Art in the Private Sphere*. Ann Arbor: University of Michigan Press.

Gelzer, Thomas. 1979. "Klassizismus, Attizismus und Asianismus." In Gelzer et al., eds., 1979: 1–55.

Gelzer, Thomas, et al., eds. 1979. *Le classicisme à Rome aux I^{ers} siècles avant et après J.C. Fondation Hardt, Entretiens sur l'anquité classique* no. 25. Geneva: Vandœuvres.

Giancotti, Francesco. 1989. *Religio, Natura, Voluptas: Studi su Lucrezio.* Edizioni e saggi universitari di filiologia classica no. 37. Bologna: Pàtron.

Goldberg, Sander. 1986. *Understanding Terence.* Princeton, N.J.: Princeton University Press.

————. 1995. *Epic in Republican Rome.* New York: Oxford University Press.

Goold, G. P. 1958. "A New Text of Catullus." *Phoenix* 12: 93–116.

————. 1981. "Two Notes on Catullus I." *Liverpool Classical Monthly* 6.9: 233–38.

Gotoff, Harold Charles. 1986. "Cicero's Analysis of the Prosecution Speeches in the *pro Caelio:* An Exercise in Practical Criticism." *Classical Philology* 1981: 122–32.

————. 1993. *Cicero's Caesarian Speeches: A Stylistic Commentary.* Chapel Hill and London: University of North Carolina Press.

Gradenwitz, O., et al. 1897. *Vocabularium Iurisprudentiae Romanae.* Vol. 1. Berlin: G. Reimer.

Granarolo, Jean. 1973. "L'époque néotérique ou la poésie romaine d'avant-garde au dernier siècle de la République (Catulle excepté)." *Aufstieg und Niedergang der römischen Welt* 1.3: 278–360.

Granger, Frank. 1931–34. *Vitruvius "On Architecture."* 2 vol. Loeb Classical Library. Cambridge, Mass.: Harvard University Press.

Grant, Mary. 1924. *The Ancient Rhetorical Theories of the Laughable: The Greek Rhetoricians and Cicero.* Madison, Wis.: University of Wisconsin Press.

Grassmann, Victor. 1966. *Die erotischen Epoden des Horaz.* Munich: Beck.

Gratwick, A. S. 1991. "Catullus XXXII." *Classical Quarterly* 41: 547–51.

Greenwood, Leonard Hugh Graham. 1953 [1928]. *The Verrine Orations, Cicero.* Vol. II. Loeb Classical Library. Cambridge, Mass.: Harvard University Press; London: Heinemann.

Grube, George Maximilian Anthony. 1965. *The Greek and Roman Critics.* Toronto: University of Toronto Press.

Gruen, Erich Stephen. 1968. *Roman Politics and the Criminal Courts, 149–78 B.C.* Cambridge, Mass.: Harvard University Press.

————. 1990. *Studies in Greek Culture and Roman Policy.* Berkeley: University of California Press.

————. 1992. *Culture and National Identity in Republican Rome.* Ithaca: Cornell University Press.

Gunderson, Erik. 1996. "The Ideology of the Arena." *Classical Antiquity* 15.1: 113–51.

Hall, J. 1996. "Social Evasion and Aristocratic Manners." *American Journal of Philology* 117: 95–120.

Hallett, Judith P. 1978. "Divine Unction: Some Further Thoughts on Catullus 13." *Latomus* 37: 747–48.

Hamel, Bernard H. 1996. *Hamel's Bilingual Dictionary of Mexican Spanish.* Los Angeles, Ca.: Bilingual Book Press.

Hanssen, Jens S. Th. 1951. *Latin Diminutives: A Semantic Study.* Bergen: John Griegs Boktrykkeri.

Havelock, Eric Alfred. 1929. *The Lyric Genius of Catullus.* Oxford: Clarendon Press.

Heath, J. R. 1986. "The Supine Hero in Catullus 32." *Classical Journal* 82: 28–36.

Heinze, R. 1925. "Ciceros Rede 'Pro Caelio.'" *Hermes* 60: 193–258.

Hellegouarc'h, Joseph. 1963. *Le vocabulaire latin des relations et des partis politiques sous la république.* Paris: Les Belles Lettres.

Hellwig, Antje. 1973. "Untersuchungen zur Theorie der Rhetorik bei Platon und Aristoteles." *Hypomnemata* 37. Göttingen: Vandenhoeck and Ruprecht.

Hendrickson, George Lincoln. 1906. "The *De Analogia* of Julius Caesar; Its Occasion, Nature, and Date, with Additional Fragments." *Classical Philology* 1: 97–120.

———. 1917. "Horace and Valerius Cato." *Classical Philology* 12: 77-92.

Heskel, Julia. 1994. "Cicero as Evidence for Attitudes to Dress in the Late Republic." In Sebesta and Bonfante 1994: 133–45.

Hexter, Ralph, and Daniel Selden. 1992. *Innovations of Antiquity*. New York, London: Routledge.

Hezel, Oskar. 1932. *Catull und das griechische Epigramm*. Stuttgart: W. Kohlhammer.

Hinard, François. 1976. "Remarque sur les *praecones* et le *praeconium* dans la Roma de la fin de la République." *Latomus* 35: 1976.

Hock, Hans Henrich. 1986. *Principles of Historical Linguistics*. Berlin, New York: Mouton de Gruyter.

Holden, Hubert A. 1881. *M. Tulli Ciceronis "Pro Gnaeo Plancio" Oratio ad Iudices*. Cambridge: Cambridge University Press.

Holland, Dorothy, and Naomi Quinn. 1987. *Cultural Models in Language and Thought*. Cambridge, New York: Cambridge University Press.

Holmes, Lorna. 1992. "Myrrh and Unguents in the *Coma Berenices*." *Classical Philology* 87: 47–50.

Hughes, Geoffrey. 1988. *Words in Time: A Social History of the English Vocabulary*. Oxford, New York: Blackwell.

Hughes, J. J. 1992. "Piso's Eyebrows." *Mnemosyne* IV 45.2: 234–37.

Innes, Doreen. 1985. "Theophrastus and the Theory of Style." In Fortenbaugh et al. 1985: 251–67.

———. 1995. *Demetrius "On Style."* Loeb Classical Library. Cambridge, Mass.: Harvard University Press.

Jahn, Otto, and Wilhelm Kroll. 1962. *Cicero "Brutus."* 6th ed. Germany: Weidmann.

Johnson, Mark. 1987. *The Body in the Mind: The Bodily Basis of Meaning, Imagination, and Reason*. Chicago: University of Chicago Press.

Jones, F. 1984. "A Note on Catullus 12.1–3." *Classical Quarterly* ns 34 no. 2: 486–87.

Kajanto, Iiro. 1965. *The Latin Cognomina*. Societas Scientiarum Fennica, *Commentationes humanarum litterarum* 36.2. Helsinki: Helsingfors.

Kaster, Robert A. 1995. *"De grammaticis et rhetoribus," Gaius Suetonius Tranquillus*. Oxford: Clarendon Press; New York: Oxford University Press.

Kennedy, George Alexander. 1957. "Theophrastus and Stylistic Distinctions." *Harvard Studies in Classical Philology* 62: 93–104.

———. 1963. *The Art of Persuasion in Classical Greece*. Princeton, N.J.: Princeton University Press.

Keyser, Paul T. 1993. "Cicero on Optics (*Att.* 2.3.3)." *Phoenix* 47: 67–69.

Kinsey, T. E. 1966. "Catullus 16." *Latomus* 25: 101–6.

———. 1971. *M. Tulli Ciceronis "Pro P. Quinctio Oratio."* Adelaide, Australia: Sydney University Press.

Kirby, John T. 1990. *The Rhetoric of Cicero's "Pro Cluentio."* Amsterdam: J. C. Gieben.

Knox, Peter E. 1985. "Wine, Water, and Callimachean Polemics." *Harvard Studies in Classical Philology* 89: 107–19.

Köpke, E. 1873. *Ciceros Rede für Cn. Plancius*. Leipzig: Teubner.

Krenkel, Werner. 1970. *Lucilius Satiren.* 2 vol. Leiden: E. J. Brill.

Lakoff, George. 1987. *Women, Fire, and Dangerous things: What Categories Reveal about the Mind.* Chicago: University of Chicago Press.

Lakoff, George, and Mark Johnson. 1980. *Metaphors We Live by.* Chicago: University of Chicago Press.

Landolfi, Luciano. 1990. *Banchetto e Società Romana dalle origini al I sec. a.C.* Rome: Edizioni dell'Ateneo.

Lebreton, Jules. 1901. *Caesariana Syntaxis quatenus a Ciceroniana differat.* Paris: Hachette.

Leeman, Anton Daniel. 1963. *Orationis Ratio.* 2 vols. Amsterdam: A. M. Hakkert.

Leen, A. 1991. "Cicero and the Rhetoric of Art." *American Journal of Philology* 112: 229–45.

Lejay, Paul. 1966 [1911]. *Œuvres d'Horace: "Satires."* Hildesheim: Georg Olms; Paris: Hachette.

Leonard, William Ellery, and Stanley Barney Smith. 1942. *T. Lucreti Cari "de Rerum Natura" Libri Sex.* Madison: University of Wisconsin Press.

Leumann, Manu. 1977. *Lateinische Grammatik I: Lateinische Laut- und Formenlehre.* Munich: Beck.

Levick, Barbara. 1983. "The *Senatus Consultum* from Larinum." *Journal of Roman Studies* 73: 97–115.

Lisçu, Marin. 1930. *Etude sur la Langue de la Philosophie Morale chez Cicéron.* Paris: Les Belles Lettres.

Littman, Robert J. 1977. "The Unguent of Venus: Catullus 13." *Latomus* 36: 123–28.

Lodge, Gonzalez. 1926. *Lexicon Plautinum.* Vol. II. Leipzig: Teubner.

Lomanto, Valeria. 1994–95. "Cesare e la teoria dell'eloquenza." *Memorie della Accademia delle scienze di Torino, Classe di scienze, morali, storiche e filologiche,* ser. 5, no. 18–19.

Lyne, R. O. A. M. 1978. "The Neoteric Poets." *Classical Quarterly* 28: 167–87.

MacLachlan, Bonnie. 1993. *The Age of Grace: "Charis" in Early Greek Poetry.* Princeton, N.J.: Princeton University Press.

Maier-Eichorn, Ursula. ca. 1989. *Die Gestikulation in Quintilians Rhetorik.* Frankfurt am Main, New York: P. Lang.

Mamoojee, A. H. 1981. "*Suauis* and *Dulcis:* A Study of Ciceronian Usage." *Phoenix* 35: 220–36.

Marcovich, M. 1982. "Catullus 13 and Philodemus 23." *Quaderni urbinati di cultura classica* 11: 131–38.

Marouzeau, Jules. 1946. *Traité de stylistique latine.* 2d ed. Paris: Les Belles Lettres.

Marx, Fredericus (Friedrich). 1904. *C. Lucili Carminum Reliquiae.* Vol. 1 *(prolegomena, testimonia, fasti Luciliani, carminum reliquiae, indices).* Leipzig: Teubner.

———. 1905. *C. Lucili Carminum Reliquiae.* Vol. 2 *(commentarius).* Leipzig: Teubner.

May, James. 1988. *Trials of Character: The Eloquence of Ciceronian Ethos.* Chapel Hill and London: University of North Carolina Press.

Mayer, R. 1982. "On Catullus 1.9, Again." *Liverpool Classical Monthly* 7.5: 73–74.

McCartney, E. S. 1927. "Modifiers That Reflect the Etymology of Words Modified." *Classical Philology* 22: 184–200.

Meillet, Antoine. 1977. *Esquisse d'une histoire de la langue latine.* Paris: Klincksieck.

Meillet, Antoine, and J. Vendreyes. 1948. *Traité de grammaire comparée des langues classiques.* 2d ed. Paris: Honoré Champion.

Merrill, Elmer T. 1893. *Catulli Veronensis Liber.* Leipzig, Berlin: Teubner.

Michaels, L., and C. Ricks. 1980. *The State of the Language*. Berkeley: University of California Press.

Mielsch, Harald. 1987. *Die römische Villa*. Munich: C. H. Beck.

Momigliano, A. 1960. *Secondo contributo alla storia degli studi classici*. Rome: Edizioni di Storia e letteratura.

Monaco, Giusto. 1968. *Cicerone: L'excursus "de ridiculis."* Palermo: Palumbo.

Monteil, Pierre. 1964. *Beau et laid en latin*. Paris: Klincksieck.

Moore, Alan, and Brian Bolland. 1989. *Batman: The Killing Joke*. DC Comics.

Morgan, M. G. 1977. "A Note on Catullus 6." *Classical Quarterly* ns 27: 338–41.

———. 1980. "Catullus and the *Annales Volusi*." *Quaderni urbinati di cultura classica* ns 4: 59–67.

Murray, Oswyn. 1993. "Symposium and Genre in the Poetry of Horace." In Rudd 1994: 89–105.

Murray, Oswyn, ed. 1990. *Sympotica: a Symposium on the "Symposium."* Oxford: Clarendon Press.

Nägelsbach, Karl Friedrich. 1905. *Lateinische Stilistik*. 9th ed., ed. Iwan Müller. Nuremberg: K. Geiger.

Neudling, Chester Louis. 1955. *A Prosopography to Catullus*. Iowa Studies in Classical Philology No. 12. [London]: Oxford.

Newman, John Kevin. 1990. *Roman Catullus and the Modification of the Alexandrian Sensibility*. Hildesheim: Weidmann.

Nisbet, Robert M. 1979 [1939]. *M. Tulli Ciceronis "De domo sua" ad pontifices oratio*. Oxford: Clarendon Press; Rpt. New York: Arno Press.

Nisbet, Robin George Murdoch. 1961. *M. Tulli Ciceronis "In L. Calpurnium Pisonem" Oratio*. Oxford: Clarendon Press.

———. 1973. "Notes on the Text of Catullus." *Proceedings of the Cambridge Philological Society* n.s. 24: 92–115.

Nisbet, Robin George Murdoch, and Margaret Hubbard. 1985. *A Commentary on Horace "Odes," Book I*. 4th ed. Oxford: Clarendon Press.

Nixon, Paul. 1916–38. *Plautus*. 5 vols. Loeb Classical Library. Cambridge: Harvard University Press; London: W. Heinemann.

Norden, Eduard. 1913. *Agnostos Theos: Untersuchungen zur Formengeschichte religioser Rede*. Leipzig: Teubner.

Nussbaum, A. J. 1976. "Umbrian *pisher*." *Glotta* 54: 241–53.

Obbink, Dirk, ed. 1995. *Philodemus and Poetry*. New York: Oxford University Press.

Oksala, Teivas. 1982. "Zum Gebrauch der griechischen Lehnwörter bei Catull." *Arctos* 16: 99–119.

Olson, S. Douglas, and Alexander Sens. 2000. *Archestratos of Gela*. Oxford: Oxford University Press.

Østerud, S. 1978. "Sacrifice and Bookburning in Catullus' Poem 36." *Hermes* 106: 138–55.

Palmer, Leonard Robert. 1954. *The Latin Language*. London: Faber and Faber.

Papke, Roland. 1988. *Caesars "De analogia."* Phil. Diss. Eichstätt.

Pease, Arthur Stanley. 1963 [1920, 1923]. *M. Tulli Ciceronis "de divinatione" libri duo*. *University of Illinois Studies in Language and Literature* 6: 161–500 and 8: 153–474. Rpt., 2 vols. in 1, Darmstadt: Wissenschaftliche Buchgesellschaft.

Pedrick, Victoria. 1993. "The Abusive Address and the Audience in Catullan Poems." *Helios* 20 no. 2: 173–95.

Pelling, Christopher Brendan Reginald. 1988. *"Life of Antony," Plutarch.* Cambridge, New York: Cambridge University Press.

Puccioni, Giulio. 1960. "Prolegomeni ad un'edizione dei frammenti oratorii di Cicerone." *Ciceroniana* 2: 97–124.

Puelma Piwonka, Mario. 1949. *Lucilius und Kallimachos.* Frankfurt am Main: V. Klostermann.

Putnam, Michael C. J. 1962. "Catullus' Journey (Carm. 4)." *Classical Philology* 57: 10–19.

———. 1968. "Catullus 22,13." *Hermes* 98: 552–58.

———. 1969. "Catullus 36.19." *Classical Philology* 64: 235–36.

Quinn, Kenneth. 1959. *The Catullan Revolution.* London and New York.

———. 1963. *Latin Explorations: Critical Studies in Roman Literature.* Routledge and Paul: London.

———. 1969. *The Catullan Revolution.* 1st ed. revised. Cambridge: Heffer.

———. 1972. *Catullus: An Interpretation.* London: Batsford.

———. 1973. *Catullus: The Poems.* 2nd ed. London: Macmillan; New York: St. Martin's Press.

Ramage, Edwin S. 1960. "Early Roman Urbanity." *American Journal of Philology* 81: 65–72.

———. 1961. "Cicero on Extra-Roman Speech." *Transactions of the American Philological Society* 92: 481–94.

Ramos i Duarte, Feliz. 1895. *Diccionario de Mejicanismos.* Mexico: Eduardo Dublan.

Rankin, H. D. 1970. "A Note on Some Implications of Catullus 16, 11–13." *Latomus* 29: 119–21.

Rawson, Elizabeth. 1985. *Intellectual life in the late Roman Republic.* Baltimore: Johns Hopkins University Press.

Reid, James Smith. 1879. *Ciceronis "pro L. Cornelio Balbo" Oratio.* Cambridge: Cambridge University Press.

———. 1925. *M. Tulli Ciceronis "de Finibus Bonorum et Malorum" Libri I, II.* Cambridge: Cambridge University Press.

Reiley, Katharine Campbell. 1909. *Studies in the Philosophical Terminology of Lucretius and Cicero.* New York: Columbia University Press.

Reitzenstein, R. 1901. "Scipio Aemilianus und die Stoische Rhetorik." In *Strassburger Festschrift zur XLVI. Versammlung deutscher Philologen und Schulmänner:* 143–62. Strassburg: K. J. Trübner.

Renting, D. S. A. 1992. "Three Textcritical Notes on Cicero de Oratore (II 321; 327; 364)." *Mnemosyne* IV 45.2: 228–34.

Ribbeck, Otto. 1897–98. *Scaenicae Romanorum poesis fragmenta.* 3d ed., 2 vols. (vol. 1, *Tragicorum fragmenta;* vol. 2, *Comicorum fragmenta*). Leipzig: Teubner.

Rich, John. 1989. "Patronage and Interstate Relations in the Roman Republic." In Wallace-Hadrill 1989: 117–35.

Richlin, A. 1992. *The Garden of Priapus.* 2d ed. New York: Oxford University Press.

Roberts, William Rhys. 1910. *Dionysius of Halicarnassus "On Literary Composition."* London: Macmillan.

Ross, David O. 1969. *Style and Tradition in Catullus.* Cambridge, Mass.: Harvard University Press.

————. 1973. "*Vriosque Apertos:* A Catullan Gloss." *Mnemosyne* 26, ser. 4: 60–62.

Rostagni, Augusto. 1944. *Suetonio "de Poetis" e Biografi Minori.* Torino: Loescher.

Rudd, Niall. 1987. Review of Corbett 1986. *Classical Review* 37: 319–20.

————. 1994. *Horace 2000: A Celebration; Essays for the Bimillennium.* London: Duckworth.

Russell, Donald Andrew. 1981. *Criticism in Antiquity.* Berkeley: University of California Press.

Saint-Denis, Eugene. 1939. "Evolution sémantique de 'urbanus-urbanitas.'" *Latomus* 3: 5–25.

Saller, Richard P. 1982. *Personal Patronage under the Early Empire.* Cambridge, New York: Cambridge University Press.

Sandy, Gerald N. 1971. "Catullus 16." *Phoenix* 25: 51–57.

Sandys, John Edwin. 1885. *M. Tulli Ciceronis ad M. Brutum "Orator."* Cambridge: Cambridge University Press.

Santamaria, Francisco J. 1959. *Diccionario de Mejicanismos.* Rorrua: Mexico.

Sauerwein, I. 1970. *Die Leges Sumptuariae als römische Massnahme gegen den Sittenverfall.* Diss. Hamburg.

Schilling, Robert. 1954. *La religion romaine de Venus.* Paris: E. de Boccard.

Schnitter, Peter, ed. 1991. *Sprachtheorien der abendländischen Antike.* Vol. 2. Tübingen: Gunter Narr.

Scott, W. C. 1969. "Catullus and Calvus (Cat. 50)." *Classical Philology* 64: 169–73.

Seager, Robin. 1969. "*Venustus, lepidus, bellus, salsus:* Notes on the Language of Catullus." *Latomus* 33: 891–94.

Sebesta, Judith L., and Larissa Bonfante. 1994. *The World of Roman Costume.* Madison: University of Wisconsin Press.

Segal, Charles. 1970. "Catullan *Otiosi:* The Lover and the Poet." *Greece & Rome* 17: 25–31.

Segal, Erich. 1987. *Roman Laughter: The Comedy of Plautus.* 2nd ed. New York: Oxford University Press.

Selden, Daniel. 1992. "*Ceveat Lector:* Catullus and the Rhetoric of Performance." In Hexter and Selden 1992: 461–512.

Sider, David. 1997. *The Epigrams of Philodemus.* New York: Oxford University Press.

Siebenborn, Elmar. 1976. *Die Lehre von der Sprachrichtigkeit und ihren Kriterien. Studien zur antiken normativen Grammatik.* Amsterdam: B. R. Grüner.

Sihler, Andrew. 1995. *New Comparative Grammar of Greek and Latin.* New York: Oxford University Press.

Sinclair, Patrick. 1993. "A Study in the Sociology of Rhetoric: The *Sententia* in *Rhetorica ad Herennium.*" *American Journal of Philology* 114: 561–80.

Singleton, D. 1972. "A Note on Catullus' First Poem." *Classical Philology* 67: 192–96.

Širvydas, Konstantinas. 1979 [1620]. *Pirmasis Lietúvių Kalbos Žodynas [= Dictionarium trium linguarum].* Vilnius: Leidykla "Mokslas."

Skinner, Marilyn. 1981. *Catullus' Passer: The Arrangement of the Book of Polymetric Poems.* New York: Arno Press.

Skinner, Quentin. 1980. "Language and Social Change." In Michaels and Ricks 1980: 562–78.

Solmsen, Friedrich. 1941. "The Aristotelean Tradition in Ancient Rhetoric." *American Journal of Philology* 52: 35–50, 169–90.

Solodow, Joseph B. 1989. "Forms of Literary Criticism in Catullus: Polymetric vs. Epigram." *Classical Philology* 84: 312–19.

Stark, Rudolf, ed. 1968. *Rhetorika: Schriften zur aristotelischen und hellenistischen Rhetorik.* Hildesheim: Georg Olms.

Stroh, Wilfried. 1975. *Taxis und Taktik.* Stuttgart: Teubner.

Stroh, Wilfried, et al. 1981. *Eloquence et rhétorique chez Cicéron.* Fondation Hardt, Entretiens sur l'anquité classique no. 28. Geneva: Vandœuvres.

Stroux, Joannes. 1912. *De Theophrasti virtutibus dicendi.* Leipzig: Teubner.

Syme, Ronald. 1956. "Piso and Veranius in Catullus." *Classica et Medievalia* 17: 129–34.

Syndikus, Hans Peter. 1984. *Catull: Eine Interpretation; Erster Teil: die kleinen Gedichte (1–60).* Darmstadt: Wissenschaftliche Buchgesellschaft.

———. 1987. *Catull: Eine Interpretation; Dritter Teil: die Epigramme (69–116).* Darmstadt: Wissenschaftliche Buchgesellschaft.

Taylor, Daniel J. 1974. *Declinatio: A Study of the Linguistic Theory of Marcus Terentius Varro.* Amsterdam: John Benjamins.

Terzaghi, Nicolà. 1934. *Lucilio.* Turin: L'Erma.

Thomas, Richard F. 1988. *Virgil "Georgics."* Cambridge: Cambridge University Press.

———. 1993. "Sparrows, Hares, and Doves: A Catullan Metaphor and Its Tradition." *Helios* 20: 131–43.

Thomson, Douglas Ferguson Scott. 1967. "Catullus and Cicero: Poetry and the Criticism of Poetry." *Classical World* 60: 225–30.

———. 1997. *Catullus.* Toronto: University of Toronto Press.

Till, Rudolf. 1953. "Zu Plutarchs Biographie des älteren Cato." *Hermes* 81: 440ff.

Townend, Gavin B. 1980. "A Further Point in Catullus' Attack on Volusius." *Greece & Rome* 27: 134–36.

Tracy, Stephen V. 1969. *Argutatiinambulatioque* (Catull. 6.11). *Classical Philology* 64: 234–35.

Treggiari, Susan. 1969. *Roman Freedmen during the Late Republic.* Oxford: Clarendon Press.

Tsekourakis, Damianos. 1974. *Studies in the Terminology of Early Stoic Ethics.* Hermes Einzelschrift 32. Wiesbaden: Steiner.

Usher, Stephen. 1974. *Dionysius of Halicarnassus: The Critical Essays.* Vol. 1. Loeb Classical Library. Cambridge, Mass.: Harvard University Press.

———. 1985. *Dionysius of Halicarnassus: The Critical Essays.* Vol. 2. Loeb Classical Library. Cambridge, Mass.: Harvard University Press.

Van Wyk Cronjé, Jacobus. 1986. *Dionysius of Halicarnassus "de Demosthene": A Critical Appraisal of the Status Quaestionis.* Hildesheim, New York: Olms.

Vasaly, Ann. 1993. *Representations: Images of the World in Ciceronian Oratory.* Berkeley: University of California Press.

Vessey, D. W. T. C. 1971. "Thoughts on Two Poems of Catullus: 13 and 30." *Latomus* 30: 45–55.

Wackernagel, Jacob. 1928. *Vorlesungen über Syntax mit besonderer Berücksichtigung von griechisch, lateinisch und deutsch.* Basel: E. Birkhäuser.

Wallace-Hadrill, Andrew. 1988. "The Social Structure of the Roman House." *Papers of the British School at Rome* 56 ns 43: 43–97.

———. 1989. "Patronage in Roman Society: From Republic to Empire." In Wallace-Hadrill ed. 1989: 63–87.

Wallace-Hadrill, Andrew, ed. 1989. *Patronage in Ancient Society.* New York: Routledge.

Walsh, Peter Gerard. 1993. *Livy Book XXXVIII.* Warminster, England: Aris & Phillips.

———. 1994. *Livy Book XXXIX.* Warminster, England: Aris & Phillips.

———. 1999. *"Ab Urbe Condita" Vol. VI: Books XXXVI–XL.* Oxford: Clarendon Press.

Warmington, Eric Herbert. 1937. *Remains of Old Latin*. Vol. III. Loeb Classical Library. Cambridge, Mass.: Harvard University Press.

Watkins, Calvert. 1995. *How to Kill a Dragon: Aspects of Indo-European Poetics*. New York: Oxford University Press.

Weiss, Michael. 1996. "An Oscanism in Catullus 53." *Classical Philology* 91: 353–59.

Weissenborn, Wilhelm, and Hermann Johannes Müller. 1962. *Titi Livi "ab urbe condita" libri*. Vol. 9, Books 39–40. Berlin: Weidmann.

Williams, Gordon. 1969. *The Third Book of Horace's "Odes."* Oxford: Clarendon Press.

———. 1985. *Tradition and Originality in Roman Poetry*. 2nd ed. Oxford: Clarendon Press.

Wills, Jeffrey. 1996. *Repetition in Latin Poetry*. Oxford: Clarendon Press; New York: Oxford University Press.

Wiltshire, Susan Ford. 1977. *Catullus Venustus*. *Classical World* 70: 319–26.

Wimmel, Walter. 1960. *Kallimachos in Rom*. Hermes Einzelschrift 16. Wiesbaden: F. Steiner.

Winter, T. N. 1973. "Catullus Purified: A Brief History of Carmen 16." *Arethusa* 6: 257–63.

Wiseman, Timothy Peter. 1969. *Catullan Questions*. Leicester: Leicester University Press.

———. 1985. *Catullus and His World: A Reappraisal*. Cambridge, New York: Cambridge University Press.

Wisse, Jakob. 1989. *Ethos and Pathos from Aristotle to Cicero*. Amsterdam: Hakkert.

———. 1995. "Greeks, Romans, and the Rise of Atticism." In Abbenes et al: 65ff.

Witke, Charles. 1980. "Catullus 13: A Reexamination." *Classical Journal* 75: 325–31.

Wooten, Cecil W. 1987. *Hermogenes' "On Types of Style."* Chapel Hill, N.C.: University of North Carolina Press.

Woytek, Erich. 1970. *Sprachliche Studien zur "Satura Menippea" Varros*. Wiener Studien. Supplement 2. Vienna, Cologne, Graz: Böhlaus.

Wright, Frederick Warren. 1931. *Cicero and the Theatre*. Smith College Classical Studies 11. Northampton, Mass.

Zanker, Paul. 1988. *The Power of Images in the Age of Augustus*. Ann Arbor: University of Michigan Press.

Zicàri, Marcello. 1955. "*Moribunda ab sede Pisauri* (Nota a Catull. 81)." *St. Oliv.* 3: 57–69 = *Scritti Catulliani* 187–99.

———. 1965. "Sul primo carme di Catullo." *Maia* 17: 232–40 = *Scritti Catulliani* 143–52.

———. 1976. *Scritti Catulliani*. Ed. Piergiorgio Parroni. Urbino: Argalìa.

Zorzetti, Nevio. 1990. "The *Carmina Convivalia*." In Murray 1990: 289–307.

# INDEX RERUM ET NOMINUM

Names mentioned incidentally and names of literary characters are generally omitted.

aestheticism in Roman culture: cultural model of, 78; diagrams depicting, 32, 78, 155; function of, in elite self-representation, 26–27; and Hellenism, 80–82; humor as a form of, 179; and individualism, 82–84; and social worth, complementary, 15–16, 77, 155; —, difficult to reconcile, 79–80; —, incompatible, 78–79; —, union represented by *suauis grauis*, 145–52; —, shift in relationship of, in late Republic, 177–82. *See also* elite, Roman social; language of social performance

Albucius, Titus, 81–82, 95, 205–6

Antonius, Marcus, 223 n.69; as character in *de Oratore*, 30, 97 n.25, 104 n.49, 124, 148, 203, 205 n.6, 207, 217, 223 n.69, 231–32; rhetorical technique of, 95, 100; view of rhetoric, 204

Antony, Marc, 18, 166, 175–76, 221; effect on language of social performance of, 296–97; public image of, 249, 289–90, 293–95; rhetorical style of, 295–96

artwork, symbolic value of: in private life, 23–25, 177–78, 184; in public life, 23

Atticism, 110, 115 n.82, 120–21, 200 n.119, 225–26, 228

Atticus, Titus Pomponius, 37 n.59, 97

Batman, 187; and the Joker, 187

*bell(us)*

etymology of, 51

applications: affective bonds, 53 n.113, 257 n.59, 262 n.75; conundrums, in the legal tradition, 132; *convivium*, 56–57; etiquette, 55; intellectual culture, 56; literary culture, 58; rhetorical effects, 111–14, 131, 132, 171, 195, 203, 206–7; rhetorical effects, in Empire, 308; weather, 53; wit, in *de Oratore*, 205–7, 227

idioms: *belle facere*, 52; *belle habere*, 7 n.16, 51–52; *belle negare*, 55

semantics: *bene* or *bonus*, contrasted with, 51–52, 54, 231 n.94; evaluating parties implied by, 54–55, 58; "first person paucal inclusive," 54, 59, 111, *cf.* 207, 209, 243; "first person plural," 54, 303 n.33; "first person singular," 54, 59, 111; Greek equivalents, in rhetorical theory, 114; highlights subjectivity of evaluator, ≈ 'nice,' 52, 165–66, 206 n.10; 'pretty, dainty,' 206 n.10, 262 n.75; semantic development, 56, 59; semantic structure, 54; 'sexually active,' 286 n.125

Bunker, Archie, 10

Caelius, Marcus (1), 26, 30, 64, 70, 83, 136

Caelius, Marcus (2), 102 n.41, 193, 196, 197, 240

Caesar, Gaius Iulius, 18, 144 n.39, 167, 183, 193, 194, 229; oratory of, 100, 180, 293; public image, 183 n.70, 189, 292–93; style of, 109, 115, 120; view of language, 118 n.89

Cato, Marcus Porcius, the elder, 23–24, 25, 30, 78, 79, 80 and n.5, 101 n.40, 155, 169, 224, 295; as plain style author, 91; view of rhetoric, 2, 134–36

Cato, Marcus Porcius, the junior, 17 n.32, 224

Catullus, Gaius Valerius. *See* language of social performance, in Catullus; *and under individual lexemes*

Cicero, Marcus Tullius: contemporaries' view of, 200, 224–25; sensitivity to linguistic change, 110 n.67, 228; use of humor, 227; view of humor in *de Ora-*

# INDEX VERBORUM

This index excludes the lexemes of the language of social performance, the names of *figurae dicendi,* and χάρις, all of which appear in the *Index Rerum.* In Latin or Greek forms, R indicates a form cited for its connection to rhetoric. The Latin alphabet is used for alphabetization, except in Greek.

# INDEX LOCORUM

The *index locorum* has two kinds of page references for passages that contain a member of the language of social performance: a boldface reference marks a locus that is discussed, interpreted, or cited in the main argument as exemplary of a semantic nuance of one of the lexemes; a perusal of these references should permit a reader to find the primary treatments of a particular passage and the chief examples of the nuances of a particular lexeme in a given author. When a passage contains a member of the language of social performance, the particular lexeme is indicated (e.g. 140–41 *fac, lep*). Passages are listed twice if two separate portions of the same passage are treated. Cicero's speeches, rhetorica, and philosophical works are listed in probable chronological order.

## Works in Greek